Legal Guide to GATS

Global Trade Law Series

VOLUME 31

Kluwer Law International

Legal Guide to GATS

Nellie Munin

Wolters Kluwer
Law & Business

AUSTIN BOSTON CHICAGO NEW YORK THE NETHERLANDS

Published by:
Kluwer Law International
PO Box 316
2400 AH Alphen aan den Rijn
The Netherlands
Website: www.kluwerlaw.com

Sold and distributed in North, Central and South America by:
Aspen Publishers, Inc.
7201 McKinney Circle
Frederick, MD 21704
United States of America
Email: customer.service@aspenpublishers.com

Sold and distributed in all other countries by:
Turpin Distribution Services Ltd.
Stratton Business Park
Pegasus Drive, Biggleswade
Bedfordshire SG18 8TQ
United Kingdom
Email: kluwerlaw@turpin-distribution.com

Printed on acid-free paper.

ISBN 978-90-411-2824-9

Printed in Great Britain.

To my mother, Bilha Rechler, with all my love

The Author

Dr Nellie Munin (LLD, Adv.) is a senior lecturer at the law school, Zefat Academic College, Israel and a private legal consultant experting on EU law and International Trade Law.

She formerly served as Minister of Economic Affairs in the Israeli Mission to the EU, and as Chief Legal Advisor of State Revenue Administration in the Israeli Ministry of Finance. In 1997 she was an intern at the Legal Affairs Division of the WTO. Dr Munin published four books and many articles in her fields of expertise.

More information about the author and her publications may be found on her Internet site: <www.nelmun.com>.

Table of Contents

List of Abbreviations

BOT	Built-Operate-Transfer
CRTA	Committee on Regional Trade Agreements
CTS	Council for Trade in Services
DSB	Dispute Settlement Body
DSU	Understanding on the Rules Governing the Settlement of Disputes
EEC	European Economic Community
EU	The European Union
FDI	Foreign Direct Investments
FTA	Free Trade Agreement
GATS	General Agreement on Trade in Services
GATT	General Agreement on Tariffs and Trade
HS	Harmonized System
ILO	International Labour Organization
IMF	International Monetary Fund
ITC	International Trade Center
ITO	International Trade Organization
LDCs	Least Developed Countries
MRA	Mutual Recognition Agreement
NGOs	Non-governmental Organizations
OECD	Organization for Economic Cooperation and Development
OEEC	Organization for European Economic Cooperation
PPP	Public-private-partnership
SCM	Agreement on Subsidies and Countervailing Measures
SPS	Agreement on Sanitary and Phytosanitary Measures
TBT	Agreement on Technical Barriers to Trade
TNC	Trade Negotiations Committee

TRIMs	Agreement on Trade Related Investment Measures
TRIPs	Agreement on Trade Related Intellectual Property Rights
UNCTAD	United Nations Committee on Trade and Development
UNDAP	UN Development Programme
US	United States
WCO	World Customs Organization
WPDR	Working Party on Domestic Regulation
WPPS	Working Party on Professional Services
WTO	World Trade Organization

Acknowledgements

I would like to express my gratitude to the WTO staff: Abdel-Hamid Mamdouh, Head of Trade in Services Division, Markus Jelitto, Peter Morison, Aik Hoh Lim, Mireille Cossy, Sheila Coyle, all from Trade in Services Division, and to Carlo Gamberale from the Appellate Body Secretariat, for sharing with me their precious time and great knowledge.

I would like to thank my academic home, Zefat Academic College, Israel, for providing financial support to this research, and for motivating and encouraging me to conclude it.

Special thanks to the editor of this book, Lou Rolla, for his support and professional guidance through the publishing process, to Mithra Vinudha, the Project Manager, for professionally and efficiently coordinating this project, to Rudra Krishna, for the lingual editing that contributed to the quality and clarity of the text and to the professional staff of Kluwer International Law, for turning my manuscript into a book.

Finally, thanks to my supportive family: my husband and best friend Gilad, and my children: Roy, Shany, Ofir and Adva, who experienced with me the peeks and valleys of the long process of writing, making this adventure possible.

Introduction

The General Agreement on Trade in Services (GATS) is a multilateral trade agreement, aimed at enhancing trade liberalization in services through the elimination of barriers to such trade and the development and application of legal disciplines supporting the achievement of this end.

More than 150 states already joined GATS, which was concluded in 1994 and came into force in 1 January 1995. The large number of participants reflects its importance, as well as its scope of influence.

GATS is one of the World Trade Organization (WTO) agreements, a group of agreements that were developed under the auspices of GATT-WTO, all aimed at eliminating barriers to international trade, thereby encouraging its development. The WTO agreements refer to different aspects of international trade, including trade in goods, agriculture, subsidies, investments, intellectual property rights and government procurement. To a certain extent, they all share the same ends, a similar legal language and a similar intrinsic logic. However, each of the WTO agreements has its different and unique characteristics, stemming first and foremost from the unique characteristics of the trade aspect regulated by them. These two poles are also reflected by GATS, and are essential for its interpretation and understanding.

The importance of GATS cannot be overestimated: the term 'international trade in services' covers all international trade except for trade in goods. It includes independent services, services embodied in goods and services facilitating trade in goods. International trade in services, that was considered to be of negligible importance in the past, grew considerably in terms of scale and importance in recent decades, and is now estimated to amount for more than 20% of total world trade. International trade in services is shared by developed and developing countries, and its future development seems to hold the key for the future growth and prosperity of the world economy.

Although most of the countries realize the importance of international services trade liberalization, the road to achieve this goal is still long. There are many reasons for it. Conflicting interests, political considerations, and above all lack of knowledge and experience, fears from the unknown and from the loss of control, together with mutual suspicions, are the major forces shaping the arena of international trade in services, and are accordingly reflected by the legal framework that forms the basis to it.

This book concentrates on the legal text of GATS, as formed and concluded in 1994. The GATS provisions reflect, to a large extent, the conflict between the forces and interests mentioned above. The result often boils down to ambiguous wording, which makes the application and the interpretation of GATS difficult to handle. The fifteen years of GATS existence produced extensive literature, but only five dispute settlement cases. This small number of cases may be surprising at first glance. However, it may either reflect the relatively narrow scope of commitments under the agreement, due to which its potential is not yet exhausted, or rather a fear of WTO Members to initiate disputes under GATS, which is still a relatively new legal instrument. This book reflects an attempt to navigate through the ocean of literature and interpretative possibilities embodied in GATS. It is aimed at equipping the readers with a road map of interpretative possibilities and dilemmas imposed by GATS. The book suggests a legal analysis of GATS provisions, based on their historical and institutional roots, while at the same time taking into account their future ends and prospects and the due balance of interests involved.

Following GATS since its conclusion in 1995, it is assessed that a long time will pass before it will be thoroughly and comprehensively understood, and before its potential as a decisive legal instrument in the process of future development of international trade in services will be exhausted. It is hoped that this book will contribute to this global effort.

Part 1

The General Agreement on Trade in Services: History, Structure and Basic Principles

Chapter 1
The General Agreement on Trade in Services

1.1 INTERNATIONAL TRADE IN SERVICES

1.1.1 THE INTERNATIONAL TRADE ARENA

International trade is believed to be one of the world growth engines.[1] It existed through the history of mankind, but has gained its momentum in recent decades. The development of transportation, telecommunication, and technology in the twentieth century facilitated the development of new fields of international trade, particularly trade in services.[2] Newly developed devices allow the supply of professional advice through e-mail,[3] or the exercise of professional control over medical processes like operations by video conference; online information from all over the world, as well as improved telecommunication networks, allow the engagement of investors in financial instruments' trade, regardless of their distant location. The improvement in means of transportation facilitates faster travel for business people around the globe, thereby turning the world into 'one small village'. The global media further encourages this feeling. In addition, trade in certain

1. A. Mattoo, R. Rathindran & A. Subramanian, 'Measuring Services Trade Liberalization and its Impact on Economic Growth: an Illustration', *21 Journal of Economic Integration* (2006), 64–98; B. Hoeckman & A. Mattoo, 'Services Trade and Growth', *Policy Research Working Paper 4461, The World Bank* (2008).
2. B. Hoeckman & C.A. Primo Braga, 'Protection and Trade in Services: A Survey', *World Bank Policy Research Working Paper No. 1747* (2004), 2–4, <http://papers.ssrn.com>.
3. For the effect of the internet on the expansion of trade in services see: C. Freund & D. Weinhold, 'The Internet and International Trade in Services', *92 The American Economic review* (2002), 236–240.

services, such as transportation and communication, facilitates international trade in goods.[4] All these developments enhance the process of globalization.

The process of globalization creates many new and exciting opportunities for global trade expansion. Foreign services suppliers and domestic consumers might enjoy the benefits accrued by this global competition.[5] Thus, the global scope of trade in services seems to grow fast,[6] motivating more growth in itself and supporting other industries. At the same time, objections to this process grow. Opponents to liberalization of world trade may be divided into two major groups: one group consists of domestic producers, wishing to avoid competition by imported goods and services. Such competition would imply the adaptation of their industries in terms of price, quality and efficiency of production process. These domestic producers sometimes recruit domestic politicians to guard their interests. The second group consists of global sustainability supporters who claim, that world trade liberalization should not be promoted disregarding vast public interests such as the environment and labour conditions. They insist that any progress in international trade liberalization should not be allowed without regulating these fields first. The political pressure exercised by these two groups sometimes encourages domestic politicians to lead a protectionist policy, namely: a policy that applies barriers to imported goods and services, in order to protect domestic production from external competition. Naturally, this trend gains particular momentum in periods of economic slow-down and recession.

Protection of domestic production from external competition is achieved, *inter alia*, by the application of trade barriers to import.

1.1.2 Barriers to Trade

Barriers to import may be of divided into two major groups:

(1) *Direct Barriers* block import, completely or partially, making it either impossible or too expensive to be worthwhile. Direct barriers to import include import bans, import quotas and customs duties. The advantage of these barriers, though, lies in their transparency and quantifiability.

(2) *Indirect Barriers* have the same effect as direct barriers, but they are non-transparent and non-quantifiable. They are usually applied when a country

4. J. Blyde & N. Sinyavskaya, 'The Impact of Liberalizing Trade in Services on Trade in Goods: An Empirical Investigation', *11 Review of Development Economics* (2007), 566–583; A.V. Deardorff, 'International Provision of Trade Services, Trade, and Fragmentation', *9 Review of International Economics* (2002), 233–248.

5. See research on pro-liberalization lobbying: C. Woll, *The Politics of Trade Preferences: Business Lobbying on Services Trade in the US and in the EU*, Institut d'Etudes Politiques de Paris, und Wirtschafts- und Sozialwissenschaftliche Fakultät der Universität zu Köln (2004), <http://kups.ub.uni-koeln.de>.

6. P. Nicolaides, *Liberalizing Services Trade: Strategies for Success*, Taylor and Francis e-Library (2005), 20–23. This is true despite the explanation there, that some of this alleged growth is a result of statistical measurement development.

makes commitments to abolish direct barriers to trade in international trade agreements, but nevertheless wants to protect domestic production in a non-transparent manner. Therefore, they are often concealed in domestic regulation, allegedly aimed at achieving a justified domestic policy goal.

Trade barriers are applied by most of the countries facing the conflict of interests of supporting trade liberalization on the one hand, while on the other hand wanting to protect domestic industries, mainly for domestic political considerations. International trade agreements aim at eliminating such barriers, in order to enhance world trade liberalization.

1.1.3 International Trade in Services

Services amount for more than 20% of the global GDP.[7] There are many attempts to define 'services'. They mainly reflect the difficulty to do so.[8] The term 'services' covers a variety of sectors and modes of supply.[9] It seems that the safer and simpler way to define trade in services is as any trade which is not trade in goods. For these reasons, even the General Agreement on Trade in Services (GATS) does not include a comprehensive and accurate definition of 'services'. Article I:3(b) and (c) of GATS provides:

> (b) 'services' includes any service in any sector except services supplied in the exercise of governmental authority;
> (c) 'a service supplied in the exercise of governmental authority' means any service which is supplied neither on a commercial basis, nor in competition with one or more service suppliers.

7. See also: 'Structure and Trends in International Trade in Services', *OECD* (2007), <www.oecd.org>.
   Interestingly, trade in services proved to be more resistant to the recent global economic crisis than trade in goods: I. Borchert & A. Mattoo, 'The Crisis-Resilience of Services Trade', *The World Bank Policy Research Working Paper* (2009), <www-wds.worldbank.org>.
   This fact may reflect the importance of services to economies.
8. See, for example, B. Ghosh, *Gains from Global Linkages* (in association with IMO), Geneva (1997), 6; J.D. Aaronson & P.F. Cowhey, *Trade in Services – A Case for Open Markets*, American Enterprise Institute for Public Policy Research, USA (1984), 3; A. Sapir, 'North-South Issues in Trade in Services', *8 The World Economy* (1985), 27, 31; R.M. Stern & B.M. Hoekman, 'Issues and Data Needs for GATT Negotiations on Services', *10 The World Economy* (1987), 39; S. Hirsch, 'A Service or not A Service', *11 The World Economy* (1988), 565; P. Nicolaides, n. 6, 7–16.
9. For information on services' trade and its development in OECD countries see: 'The Service Economy', *OECD, STI Business and Industry Policy Forum Series* (2000), <www.oecd.org>.
   See also: A. Maurer & P. Chauvet, 'The Magnitude of Flows of Global Trade in Services', in B. Hoeckman, A. Mattoo & P. English (eds), *Development, Trade and the WTO: a Handbook, The World Bank* (2002), 235–246, <www-wds.worldbank.org>.

The difficulty to define services and follow their international flows stems from their unique characteristics:

- Unlike goods, *services are intangible*. It is therefore sometimes difficult to follow international transactions in services. This difficulty affects the scope and quality of statistics that may be gathered about trade in services,[10] as well as the attempts to explain international trade flows of services according to existing economic theories,[11] and the possible economical assessment of the effect these barriers have on trade.[12] Despite these difficulties, it seems that economic analysis already reflects some differences in the behaviour of international trade in services compared to international trade in goods.[13] However, intangibility makes it difficult to tax services and to apply to them barriers to trade, which are common for trade in goods, such as customs duties and import quotas.

---

10. P. Dee, 'Modeling the Policy Issues in Services Trade', *94–95 Economie Internationale* (2003), 283–300, <www.cairn.info/article.php?>; See also G. Karsenty, 'Assessing Trade in Services by Mode of Supply', 33 and T. Warren, C. Findlay, 'Measuring impediments to trade in Services', 57 both in P. Sauvé & R. Mitchell (eds), *GATS 2000: New Direction in Services Trade Liberalization*, The Brookings Institution, Washington USA (2000), <http://books.google.com>.

    These difficulties were addressed by the WTO Secretariat, starting a short time after GATS was concluded. See, for example, S/C/W/5 GATS and Statistics on Trade in Services, 17.7.1995; S/C/W/75 Presence of Natural Persons (Mode 4) – Background Note by the Secretariat, 8.12.1998. In order to facilitate statistics concerning international trade in services, in recent years an effort is made by six international organizations, including the WTO, the UN, UNCTAD, the IMF, the EU and the OECD to develop a manual on statistics of international trade in services, to meet the need for more comparable and comprehensive statistics on services trade. General information concerning trade statistics of commercial services in each WTO Member is published by the Secretariat in the Statistic Database in the WTO internet site: <http://unstats.un.org>. See also the OECD statistical databases for international trade in services: <www.oecd.org>.

    For a new method suggested for measuring the services content characterizing a firm's output based on new statistical vehicles see: P. Cloninger & B. Oviatt, 'Measuring services Content: A Scale development', *48 Thunderbird International Business Review* (2006), 643–665. See also: A. Harrison & T. Britton, 'Providing Services to Foreign Nationals', *Report of the OECD Round Table on Sustainable Development* (2003), <www.oecd.org> and 'Measuring Bilateral Trade in Services: A Note on the Data Collected and Estimated for the Service Trade Restrictiveness Index' (presentation), OECD (2008), <www.oecd.org>.
11. For a summery of most significant economic surveys on services in recent years: B. Hoeckman, 'Liberalizing Trade in Services: a Survey', *World Bank Policy Research Working Paper No. 4030* (2006), 1–32, <http://papers.ssrn.com>.

    See also C.Y.P. Wong & J. Wu, A. Zhang, 'A Model in Trade Liberalization of Services', *14 Review of International Economics* (2006), 148–168. It is recently realized that common economic theories, developed to explain trade in goods, might not suffice: R. Banga, 'Trade in services: A Review', *5 Global Economy Journal* (2005), Art. 3, 16, <www.bepress.com>.
12. R.M. Stern, 'Quantifying Barriers to Trade in Service', *Discussion Paper No. 470, University of Michigan* (2000), <www.fordschool.umich.edu>.
13. International trade in services seems to be less sensitive to variables related to physical geography (distance, contiguity and landlocked status) but more sensitive to language variables, either for cultural or for information gap reasons: C. Lennon, 'Trade in Services and Trade in

- There is *a great variety of services*. The World Trade Organization (WTO) divides them into 12 sectors and 155 sub-sectors.[14] In general, they may be divided into *personal services*, supplied personally, for example, by lawyers, accountants, architects, physicians, and *public services*, such as aviation, communication, health, education, financial services. The latter are publicly supplied and often hold strategic importance for governments. Each sector of services has its own unique characteristics and unique manner of operation. As a result, specific barriers to trade may apply to different services' sectors.
- Sometimes it is difficult to distinguish the production of a service from the service itself, *because the production and consumption of the service coincide.*
- *Services may be embodied in goods.* For instance: discs containing music or information and drawings. In such cases, it is even more complicated to follow their international movement, since many times their trade is reflected only in the records referring to trade in goods. This situation may somewhat 'immunize' these services from bearing barriers usually applied to trade in services. However, such services may indirectly suffer from barriers applied to the goods in which they are embodied.
- Unlike goods, which are internationally traded in one mode of supply: cross-border, *services are internationally traded in four modes of supply*, defined in Article I:2(a)–(d) of GATS.[15]

  Cross-border (Mode 1): 'from the territory of one Member into the territory of any other Member' – according to this mode, the service may cross a border, not necessarily being accompanied by the service supplier,[16] for example, by telephone, fax or Internet.[17] In this mode, the location of the service supplier in a Member is the crucial factor, except for the special case

---

Goods: Differences and Complementarities', *Working Paper No. 52 Paris School of Economics* (2008), <www.pse.ens.fr>.

14. In fact, eleven sectors are recognized, and the twelfth option is 'others'. For classification instructions see: MTN.GNS/W/120, Services Sectoral Classification List, 10.7.1991, <http://docsonline.wto.org> and S/L/92 Guidelines for the Scheduling of Specific Commitments Under the General Agreement on Trade in Services (GATS), published 28.3.2001, 35–40, adopted by the Council for Trade in services on 23.3.2001, S/C/M/52, para. 11. See the text of the guidelines in <http://docsonline.wto.org>.
15. This definition is broader than the balance of payment (BOP) concept of services trade. The latter focuses on residency: a service is being exported if traded between a resident and a non-resident. In GATS, certain transactions, particularly under Mode 3, take place between residents of the same country (while the commercial presence is foreign or the nationality of one of them is foreign).
16. See the analysis of Art. I:2(a) by the WTO Panel in WT/DS204/R Mexico – Measures Affecting Telecommunications Services, adopted on 1.6.2004, paras 7.30–7.31, 7.45. A requirement by a host Member that supply under this Mode in a specific case would be subject to local incorporation of the supplying firms is not necessarily hampering this mode of supply: it may be necessary to ensure the responsibility of the supplier to the service rendered.
17. See more information about the unique characteristics of this mode and its dynamic global growth: A. Mattoo & S. Wunsch, 'Securing Openness of Cross-Border Trade in Services:

of maritime transport services[18] (see Chapter 5). This question is particularly relevant to services based on new technologies. Thus, in *Mexico – Telecoms* it was established that although telecommunication services, which are considered an example to cross-border supply,[19] are supplied 'between two or more points', the transmission between these 'points' does *not* have to be undertaken by a *single* service supplier:

> [i]t would be unreasonable to assume that the definition of telecommunication services applies only where the telecommunication supplier itself owns or controls a complete global infrastructure allowing it to reach every potential 'point' requested by its consumers.[20]

It was therefore found that although the United States' suppliers link their networks at the border with those of the Mexican suppliers and are thus not operating or being present in Mexico, the service is nevertheless supplied under Mode 1 (cross-border). In *US – Gambling*,[21] with respect to electronically supplied gambling services, a question arose whether these were Mode 1 services, electronically sent by the supplier to the home country of the consumer, or rather Mode 2 services, as the consumer 'visited' the site of the supplier to receive them, thus electronically 'travelling' abroad. The practical implications of this classification difference may be the different scope of commitments by the relevant Member for each mode.[22] In that case the Panel stressed that 'cross border' is different than 'remote' supply: 'cross border is necessarily remote, but remote supply amounts to "cross border" supply only when the service supplier and the consumer are located in territories of different Members'.[23]

Consumption abroad (Mode 2): 'in the territory of one Member to the service consumer of any other Member' – according to this mode, usually

---

A Possible Approach', *Center for International Development at Harvard University* (2004), 3–10, <www.cid.harvard.edu>.

See information on the development of trade in this mode in recent years: A. Mattoo, 'Services in a Development Round', *The World Bank Policy Research Paper No. 3718* (2005), 5–6, <http://papers.ssrn.com>.

18. W. Zdouc, 'WTO Dispute Settlement Practice Relating to the GATS', *Journal of International Economic Law* (1999), 295, 328.
19. WT/DS204/R *Mexico – Telecoms*, n. 16, para. 7.43, based on MTN.GNS/W/164, Scheduling of Initial Commitments in Trade in Services: Explanatory Note, 3.9.1993.
20. WT/DS204/R *Mexico-Telecoms*, n. 16, para. 7.34.
21. WT/DS285/R, AB/R United States – Measures Affecting the Cross-Border Supply of Gambling and Betting Services, adopted on 22.5.2007.
22. Thus, in WT/DS285/AB/R *US-Gambling*, n. 21, the United States preferred that the gambling services at stake would be defined as Mode 2 services, to avoid the application of Mode 1 commitments undertaken by it to these services. Neither GATS nor the WTO Work Program on E-Commerce solved this difficulty: S. Wunch-Vincent, 'The Internet, Cross-Border Trade in Services, and the GATS: Lessons from *US-Gambling*', *5 World Trade Review* (2006), 319, 324–327.
23. WT/DS285/R *US-Gambling*, n. 21, Panel report, para. 6.31.

the consumer crosses a border to receive the service in the supplier's country. For example, tourism services, medical services. But sometimes, it is only the consumer's property that crosses a border to receive a service, for example, a ship or a car to be repaired.[24]

Commercial presence (Mode 3): 'by a service supplier of one Member, through commercial presence in the territory of any other Member' – according to this mode, the service supplier establishes a commercial presence, such as a branch, an affiliate or a service centre, in the country of destination, in order to supply the service from it. This concept includes the constitution, acquisition or maintenance of a juridical person, but avoids the requirement as to full incorporation or establishment in the host state.[25] In *Mexico – Telecoms* it was explained:

> The definition of a service supplied through a commercial presence makes explicit the location of the service supplier . . . The definition is silent with respect to any other territorial requirement . . . Supply of a service through commercial presence would therefore not exclude a service that originates in the territory in which a commercial presence is established . . . , but is delivered into the territory of any other Member. . . .[26]

A permanent establishment will not be protected by GATS if and to the extent that it deals with a non-service sector (and as far as specific commitments are concerned – if it engages in a service sector uncovered by the specific commitments of a certain Member)[27] (see Chapter 7). This mode is partly covered, in many countries, by investment treaties.[28]

Movement of natural persons (Mode 4): 'by a service supplier of one Member, through presence of natural persons of a Member in the territory of any other Member' – according to this mode, the service supplier, which is a natural person, either working independently or as an employee of a service supplier, crosses a border in order to supply a service, for example, legal or architectural consultation. This mode of supply may facilitate the exercise of Modes 1 and 3.[29] In fact, by now many Members refer to it mainly as such, thus neglecting its potential importance for independent service

24. The Members did not reach a satisfactory decision whether electronic delivery of services would always be treated under Mode 1 (cross-border) or rather would sometimes be treated under Mode 2 (consumption abroad): A. Mattoo & S. Wunsch, n. 17, 11.
25. W. Zdouc, n. 18, 325.
26. WT/DS204/R *Mexico-Telecoms*, n. 16, para. 7.375.
27. 'The General Agreement on Trade in Services (GATS): an Analysis', *OECD* (1994), 7, <www.olis.oecd.org>.
28. R. Adlung, 'Services Liberalization from a GATS/WTO Perspective: in Search for Volunteers', *WTO Staff Working Paper ERSD-2009-05* (2009), 12, <www.wto.org>.
29. M. Jansen & R. Piermartini, 'The Impact of Mode 4 on Trade in Goods and Services', *WTO Staff Working Paper No. ERSD-2004-07* (2004).

suppliers.[30] This mode is considered to be sensitive[31] because it interferes with countries' sovereign right to control entry of individuals into their territory.[32] It could be strongly affected by wage-parity.[33] However, it should be stressed that this mode concerns temporary stay and not immigration of workers.

Each mode of supply has particular characteristics. A different approach is required in order to follow international transactions that take place according to each mode. Different methods are required in order to apply barriers to trade, to each mode.[34] Thus, for example, if a service is traded under Mode 1 (cross-border), for example, a professional advice given by e-mail, it is clear that no customs duty or quantitative restriction would be an efficient barrier to its trade. On the other hand, if a service is supplied by commercial presence (Mode 3), such a commercial presence may employ domestic labour that might be adversely affected by trade barriers applied to it. Thus, the domestic government may face a conflict of interests concerning the decision on whether to apply such barriers in this case.

It should be noted that the supplier's choice of mode of supply implies the choice of whether to stay subject to home country law (Mode 1) or to become subject to the host country law (Modes 3, 4). On the other hand, by liberalizing only certain modes of supply, a government may use trade liberalization as an instrument for the implementation of domestic policies.[35]

To further complicate things:

> Commercial linkages may exist among all four modes of supply. For example, a foreign company established under mode 3 in country A may employ nationals from country B (mode 4) to export services cross-border into countries B, C etc. Similarly, business visits into A (mode 4) may prove necessary to complement cross-border supplies

30. P. Bhatnagar & C. Manning, 'Regional Arrangements for Mode 4 in the Services Trade: Lessons from the ASEAN Experience', *4 World Trade Review* (2005), 171, 176.
31. This may be a reason for the ambiguity of many of the Members' commitments according to this mode. For detailed description of these ambiguities see: R. Chanda, 'Movement of Natural Persons and the GATS', *24 The World Economy*, Blackwell Publishers Ltd (2001), 631, 643.
32. The inclusion of this mode in GATS is considered to be of particular importance to developing countries: GATS analysis (OECD), n. 27, 8, although effective market access depends on specific commitments.
33. Several Members have explicitly preserved their right, in their current GATS commitments, to operate wage-parity and/or minimum-wage requirements. Others might have thought that this fact should not be part of their commitments under Arts XVI and XVII, being covered by Art. VI (domestic regulation): R. Adlung, n. 28, 11.
34. For the different modes of supply, their different characteristics and trade barriers see: T. Clark, 'International Services: Perspective at Century's End', *13 Journal of Services Marketing* (1999), 298–310.
35. W. Zdouc, *Legal Problems Arising Under the General Agreement on Trade in Services – Comparative Analysis of GATS and GATT*, dissertation der Universität St. Gallen (2002), 103.

into that country (mode 1) or to upgrade the capacity of a locally established office (mode 3).[36]

As a result of the differences mentioned, the relatively simple methods used to block imports of goods, like customs duties, quotas and measures equivalent thereto, will not do in order to block trade in services. *Barriers to trade in services are, thus, more elaborated than barriers to trade in goods. They are usually embodied in domestic regulation, non-transparent and non-quantifiable.*[37] In addition to intended regulatory barriers to trade in services, certain barriers result from outdated regulatory regime, which are unable to follow the quick rhythm of technological change.[38]

Due to all these differences between trade in goods and trade in services, *the legal disciplines* historically developed in the General Agreement on Tariffs and Trade (GATT) context to overcome relatively simple barriers to trade in goods, *had to be adapted* to efficiently prevent barriers to trade in services.

However, it is commonly agreed that 'no country is completely self-sufficient in services, which suggests that there is scope for beneficial specialization through liberalization'.[39]

1.2 THE LEGAL FRAMEWORK AND ITS HISTORIC EVOLUTION

1.2.1 From GATT (1947) to WTO (1994)

GATS was formed in 1994 as one of the WTO agreements. The conclusion of these agreements in 1994 marked the peak of a process that started after World War II, back in 1947. After that war ended, the states that participated in it felt that it was necessary to establish certain international economic organizations that would facilitate the rehabilitation of Europe after the war and at the same time create an economic alliance that might prevent future world wars of the same kind. Following this logic, three international economic organizations were planned, known as the 'Bretton Woods organizations'. Two of them were established within a relatively short time afterwards: the World Bank, aimed at the monetary policy (1944), and the International Monetary Fund (IMF) (1945), aimed at collecting and allocating funds for rehabilitation. At that time (1947), another important economic organization was established: the forerunner of the Organization for

36. WTO explanatory paper, WTO Secretariat, 29.3.2006 (3776.4), 3.
37. One implication of this difference is that the cost of protectionist policy, usually born by consumers, is not partly offset by revenues from trade barriers such as customs revenues and quota rents: A. Mattoo, 'Shaping Future GATS Rules for Trade in Services', *The World Bank* (2001), 7, <www-wds.worldbank.org>.
38. T. Ito & A.O. Kruegger (eds), *Trade in Services in the Asia-Pacific Region*, University of Chicago Press, Chicago USA (2003), 4.
39. P. Nicolaides, n. 6, 19.

Economic Cooperation and Development (OECD), the Organization of European Economic Cooperation (OEEC), which consisted of the developed countries, aimed at administering the Marshal Plan for the reconstruction of Europe after the war.

The third 'Bretton Woods' organization that was planned to be established was the International Trade Organization (ITO). It was meant to set a platform for the elimination of international barriers to trade; first and foremost, customs duties and import quotas. Discussions took place among some fifty-three interested countries, some of which summed up their mutual agreements for lowering rates of customs duties in GATT. GATT was viewed as a technical protocol that would be part of a more comprehensive move: the establishment of the ITO. However, this move was finally backed-off by the United States' Congress, who refused to create a mechanism that could diminish its sovereign power to decide United States' external trade policy. Other countries that participated in the discussions followed, and the ITO was never founded. GATT remained a technical protocol for lowering customs duties' rates, without any formal organization to support and administer the process. Twenty-three countries joined GATT in the beginning. A temporary small secretariat was founded to administer it. During the coming years, GATT mechanism was proved to be a success: until 1994, GATT already had 124 signatories, and it succeeded to considerably lower globally the rate of average customs duties.

GATT notion and mechanism was developed gradually, based on three pillars serving all the WTO agreements since 1994, including GATS: schedules of specific commitments, rounds of negotiations and a dispute settlement mechanism:

- *Schedules of specific commitments* – each Member files such a schedule, which specifies its detailed agreement to adhere to the Agreement's principles. Once submitted, the schedules form an integral part of the agreement. The Schedules are dominated by two principles: *standstill*, according to which a country is not allowed, as a rule, to back off its commitments specified in the schedule; and *rollback*, according to which at each round of negotiations a Member is expected to improve its commitments, thereby enhancing trade liberalization.
- *Rounds of negotiations* – every few years a new round of negotiations is initiated among WTO Members. It is aimed at improving the parties' commitments, namely, the terms of trade liberalization. Out of the first eight rounds (that took place when only GATT existed), the first six concentrated on trade in goods and the barriers thereto: customs duties and import quotas. The seventh round, known as the 'Tokyo Round' (1973–1979) expanded the scope of subjects discussed to additional trade aspects, such as subsidies, government procurement etc., but the rules and disciplines agreed in these fields were included in voluntary codes.[40] A substantial break-through took place in the eighth round, known as the Uruguay Round (1986–1994).

40. See the comprehensive list of codes in <www.wto.org>.

In this round, the Members finally accomplished the establishment of the World Trade Organization: a formal organization that governs the multilateral framework of world trade rules and disciplines. They further succeeded to agree on a set of mandatory agreements, some of which replaced the Tokyo Round voluntary codes. These agreements extended the rules and disciplines developed in GATT context to many other fields of international trade, such as agriculture, subsidies, intellectual property rights, treatment of foreign investments, technical barriers to trade, sanitary and phytosanitary measures, customs valuation and of course – trade in services. GATS is one of the resulting agreements of this round. Being the first round to include services, it is commonly assessed, that most of the schedules of specific commitments submitted by the Members do not reflect a substantial break-through in terms of benefits accorded to international trade, but rather reflect, to a large extent, the legal situation that was in force for the submitting Members, at the time of Schedules' submission.[41] However, these schedules of specific commitments contribute to enhanced transparency concerning the legal situation reflected by them. In 2001 a new round of negotiations started and is still in the process. This is the ninth round, known as the Doha Round. This round is expected to deepen the Members' commitments in different fields of international trade, including trade in services.[42] Improvement of market access terms in this round shall be based on the information embodied in the Uruguay Round schedules of specific commitments, and this is another aspect of their importance.

- *Dispute settlement mechanism* – GATT 1947 included a dispute settlement mechanism. According to it, when a dispute concerning the application or the legal interpretation of the agreement took place, and could not be solved by mutual consultations among the parties involved, a panel of three trade experts, not necessarily jurists, from Members that were not involved in the dispute, was established by GATT Secretariat. The panelists acted as arbitrators, hearing the parties involved and finally coming to conclusions. Their decision had to be approved by the representatives of all the Members (at that time, referred to as 'Contracting Parties'), in full consensus. Consensus was difficult to achieve, and therefore many of the panel's decisions were not approved. The whole process was more politically than legally oriented, therefore being relatively flexible and less deterring for the countries involved.[43] This practice was modified in Uruguay Round, with the conclusion of the Understanding on the Rules and Procedures

41. B. Hoeckman, 'Tentative First Steps: An Assessment of the Uruguay Round Agreement on Services', *The World Bank Policy Research Working Papers* (1995), 16–25, <www-wds.worldbank.org>; P. Sorsa, *The GATS Agreement on Financial Services – A Modest Start to Multilateral Liberalization*, IMF, Geneva (1997); L. Altinger & E. Enders, 'The Scope and Depth of GATS Commitments', *19 The World Economy* (1996), 307.
42. For information on this round see <www.wto.org>.
43. The GATT dispute settlement mechanism was first introduced in 1951, and its procedures developed over the years. For details see: E. Remirez Robles, 'Working Paper No. 9: Political &

> Governing the Settlement of Disputes (DSU).[44] It added to the dispute settlement process another phase, where the panel decision[45] may be appealed before an Appellate Body that consists of persons who must be 'persons of recognized authority, with demonstrated expertise in law, international trade and the subject matter of the covered agreements generally'. They are nominated for a period of four years, and may be reappointed once.[46] The Appellate Body's contribution to the process turned it into a more legal and less politically oriented process. The representatives of the Members, now referred to as the Dispute Settlement Body (DSB), still have the last word, but their approval depends now on a 'reversed consensus': *consensus not to adopt* the panel and Appellate Body decisions.[47] Since such a consensus is hard to achieve, most of the dispute settlement authorities' decisions are approved.

Being one of the WTO Agreements, disputes concerning GATS application and legal interpretation are subject to the dispute settlement mechanism described. The 'juridization' process that takes place since 1994 in the WTO dispute settlement process affects these disputes and is well reflected in their results, to be presented in the next chapters.[48]

1.2.2 GATS History: The Uruguay Round (1986–1994)

GATT 1947 covered mainly trade in goods. Nevertheless, it addressed trade in services in some, limited respects, particularly where services were embodied in goods or complementary thereto.[49]

As the importance of trade in services to the development of the world economy grew, its regulation within GATT-WTO framework was considered. The United States led this move. By the end of Tokyo Round, the United States started to persuade its trade partners to include international trade in services within GATT-WTO framework.[50] Most of the developing countries, GATT

Quasi-Adjudicative Dispute Settlement Models in European Union Free Trade Agreements', WTO (2006), 6–10, <www.wto.org>.

44. For the full text of this agreement see <www.wto.org>.
45. Article 12 of the DSU.
46. Article 17 of the DSU.
47. Articles 16 and 17:4 of the DSU.
48. J.H.H. Weiler, 'The Rule of Lawyers and Ethos of Diplomats – Reflections on the Internal and External Legitimacy of WTO Dispute Settlement', *35 Journal of World Trade* (2001), 191.
49. M.L. Sims & R.R. Rivers, *The International Trade* in S*ervices Agenda: Origins, Revolution and Agenda*, Canada (1987), 32.
50. Three phases in the transformation of attitude towards a multilateral services agreement are identified: (1) a period of issue identification, which began with the meeting organized by the OECD in 1972 on trade in services; (2) a period of issue consolidation from 1982 to 1986, when services were discussed in GATT meetings as a new issue and (3) the multilateral negotiations in Uruguay Round (1986–1994), which arguably continues since then: C. Woll, n. 5, 141.

Members, strongly objected this idea, relying on two formal excuses. They claimed, that GATT framework contained no competence to discuss liberalization of international trade in services, and moreover: GATT rules were formed to apply to trade in goods and were not suitable for trade in services. In essence, these countries were concerned that such a move would impede some very important interests they had: the protection of infant industries; the world allocation of trade profits; the balance of payments and their sovereign power to regulate domestic policy goals.[51] They were concerned about the effect of international services trade liberalization on employment and prices,[52] and that concentration on trade in services would draw attention from customary GATT subjects. They did not anticipate any expected profit from trade liberalization in services, assuming that the developed countries have the comparative advantage in this field, particularly for the supply of 'modern' services. They were afraid of being forced to open their markets to imported services, without any compensating balance of payment (BOP) improvement. They thought that such a move might undermine their efforts to develop domestic service industries. They further worried, that the subject of trade in services would stimulate discussion on another, very sensitive subject for their domestic markets: treatment of foreign direct investments. They alleged that since developed countries often infringe GATT rules on trade in goods, thereby causing damage to developing countries, there is no reason to extend their scope of application to trade in services.

In view of this conflict of interests, a vague decision was accepted in the meeting of GATT Members' ministers at the end of 1982. It was contrarily interpreted by the two groups of interests, and therefore no action was taken concerning this subject until the end of 1984. In 1984 a compromise was achieved that paved the way for the beginning of discussions on trade in services. Only in 1986, in Punta del Este, was it agreed that a multilateral initiative on this subject is necessary. The Punta del Este Declaration reflects the compromise achieved. It provides:

> Negotiations in this area shall aim to establish a multilateral framework of principles and rules for trade in services, including elaboration of possible disciplines for individual sectors, with a view of expansion of such trade under conditions of transparency and progressive liberalization and as means of promoting economic growth of all trading partners and the development of the developing countries. Such a framework shall respect the policy objectives of national laws and regulations applying to services and shall take into account the work of relevant international organizations.[53]

The developing countries finally surrendered to the pressure of the developed countries and agreed to include liberalization of trade in services as a subject of

---

51. D. Nayyar, 'Some Reflections on the Uruguay Round and Trade in Services', *22 Journal of World Trade* (1988), 35.
52. A. Lehmann, N.T. Tamirisa & J. Wieczorek, 'International Trade in services: Implications for the IMF', *IMF Policy Discussion Paper* (2003), 12.
53. <http://sul-derivatives.stanford.edu>, 19.

discussion in the Uruguay Round. However, the Punta del Este Declaration reflects their fears. Thus, no special and differential treatment to the developing countries was mentioned; the right to promote domestic policy objectives was recognized; although the declaration aimed at creating a multinational framework for liberalization of trade in services, no GATT principles were mentioned in this context.

Unable to prevent discussions on international trade liberalization, the developing countries concentrated their efforts in separating discussions on trade in services from other subjects, in order to prevent the creation of links between customary GATT subjects and trade in services. As a result, two different negotiating groups were formed: one for trade in goods and the other for trade in services. However, the two groups reported to the Committee on Trade in Services, so practically, a space for trade-offs between services and other subjects discussed was reserved.[54]

1.2.3 Why Services Were Not Included in GATT?

Before GATS was phrased, the possibility of including trade in services in GATT was considered. This option raised many difficulties, the major problem stemming from the fact that GATT was designed to regulate trade in goods. Therefore, the measures provided for by it are not suitable for trade in services. The intangibility of services as well as their four modes of supply, dictate a different nature of barriers to their international trade. These are administered mainly by domestic regulation that may limit the number of foreign services suppliers given access to a country, ignore professional diplomas of service suppliers, dictate the incorporation manner of service suppliers etc. GATT does not cover these kinds of barriers to trade. The difference in essence, combined with the political requirement of the developing countries to separate the field of services from the other subjects matters, finally led to the initiation of a separate agreement to regulate liberalization of international trade in services: GATS.

1.2.4 GATS Drafts

The first major draft of GATS is the *July 1990 Draft of the Chairman* of the Group of Negotiations on Services.[55] This draft did not cover all the issues (e.g., provisions on dispute settlement and enforcement) and embodied some disagreements between Members. Intensive negotiations lead to another draft, known as the *Dunkel draft*, named after the Director General of GATT at the time. It was

54. See more details on the history of negotiations in B. Hoeckman & P. Sauvé, 'Liberalizing Trade in Services', *The World Bank Discussion Papers* (1994), 40–43 <www-wds.worldbank.org>.
55. MTN.GNS/35 Group of Negotiations on Services, Uruguay Round, Draft, Multilateral Framework for Trade in Services, Introductory Note by the Chairman on the GNS Negotiations on a Framework Agreement, 23.7.1990.

published in December 1991.[56] This draft was followed by additional negotiations and in December 1993, the Trade Negotiations Committee (TNC) adopted the final Act of the Uruguay Round Multilateral Trade negotiations. In April 1994, the schedules of the Members were added to the agreement.[57]

1.2.5 The 'GATS 2000'

The concept of 'GATS 2000 talks' is part of the recent Round of negotiations: the Doha Round. These talks were launched on 1 January 2000 in Geneva. These talks faced two major challenges: the completion of the legal framework of GATS rules and the achievement of deeper services trade liberalization. It was scheduled to be completed by 2005, but was not yet completed. Before these talks were launched, the developing countries and civil society groups called for assessment of current liberalization according to GATS prior to further advancement, but the developed countries and the WTO Secretariat succeeded in launching the talks on further liberalization of services trade without conducting this assessment. The talks were already taking place for almost two years when they were incorporated into the Doha Development Agenda.[58] Based on their dynamics so far it is generally assessed, that these talks will not achieve far-reaching results concerning both challenges mentioned.

1.2.6 Conclusion

GATS is a multilateral agreement aimed at eliminating barriers to international trade in services. It was concluded in 1994 and came into force in 1995. However, it is one of the WTO agreements, and should be regarded as part of this general framework, historically rooted in GATT 1947. This fact affects its structure, general concept, approach and formation and legal norms, as will be presented in the next chapters.

---

56. MTN.TNC/W/FA General Agreement on Trade in Services, in Draft Final Act Embodying the Results of the Uruguay Round of Multilateral Trade Negotiations, 20.12.1991, Annex I.
57. For detailed overview of the course of negotiations see: R. Worfrum, P.T. Stoll & C. Feinäugle (eds), *WTO – Trade in Services*, Max Planck Commentaries on World Trade Law, Martinus Mijnhoff Publishers, Leiden, Boston (2008), 1–16.
58. R. Leal-Arcas, 'The GATS in the Doha Round: A European Perspective', in K. Alexander, M. Andenas (eds), *The World Trade Organization and Trade in Services*, Brill/Nijhoff (2008), 46–47. For further details on the dynamics of these talks see *ibid.*, 54–83, <http://papers.ssrn.com>.

Chapter 2
The Framework of GATS

2.1 THE FRAMEWORK OF GATS

2.1.1 A Structure Typical to International Trade Agreements

International – multilateral as well as regional – trade agreements usually have a typical common structure. They start with a *preamble*, presenting the intentions of their drafters and therefore serving as interpretative instruments to their operative provision. The preamble is followed by a *corpus* of disciplines and operative rules, as well as their exceptions. Some of these rules and disciplines are applied unconditionally immediately after a state joins the agreement. Others are subject to specific commitments by the Member States, included in *schedules of specific commitments*, submitted by each Member State. These schedules are annexed to the agreement, and are considered as an integral part of it. Sometimes, such agreements also declare some general principles that should be developed into additional, operative provisions, in the future. Finally, international trade agreements include *institutional* provisions, specifying the nature and authorities of the institutions responsible for their conduct and future development, and provisions concerning their entry into force and termination. By and large, the structure of GATS follows this formula.

2.1.2 The Structure of GATS

GATS consists of seven parts:

Preamble – describes the basic principles of GATS, the philosophy behind it and its goals.

Part I – includes one article, defining ‘trade in services’ and the agreement’s scope of application.
Part II – includes the legal *corpus* of the agreement, the major legal obligations and disciplines, and their exceptions.
Part III – describes the structure of the schedules of specific commitments.
Part IV – provides for enhancement of trade liberalization and gradual improvement of the specific commitments.
Parts V and VI – address the institutional and procedural aspects of the agreement.

The disciplines included in the *corpus* of the agreement include conditional and unconditional obligations. While the latter apply to all the services sectors immediately and unconditionally after a country joins the agreement, the former apply to services and service suppliers of a Member subject to their inclusion in its schedule of specific commitments, and to the terms and conditions set forth by it (see Chapters 1 and 7). Thus, theoretically, a Member that joins GATS may take minimal specific commitments, and as a result only a very narrow portion of foreign-originated services and service suppliers would practically enjoy market access in this country.

This formula is inspired by GATT formula, successfully operating over more than sixty years now. It is based on the principle of establishing a gradual liberalization process.

2.2 THE PREAMBLE

GATS preamble presents the motives behind it, the measures to be taken in order to achieve its goals and the relevant interests that are involved in the creation and application of GATS. Moreover, it reflects the balance of interests achieved between developed and developing countries, based on their positions before concluding the agreement, as described in Chapter 1. Thus, it sets the ‘stage’ for the play to begin. This preamble is an important legal instrument for the interpretation of GATS operative provisions, because it reflects the intentions, motives and expectations of the parties to it. This aspect will be discussed in detail in Chapter 3.

2.3 RULES OF ORIGIN

Like most of international trade agreements, GATS includes rules of origin. These rules are meant to ensure, that only services and service suppliers from Members will enjoy its benefits, thus depriving ‘free riders’ of them. GATS rules of origin define what a country of origin is and differentiate an individual or a legal entity from a Member, entitled to GATS benefits. This subject is discussed in Chapter 5.

2.4 PART I

2.4.1 The Definition of 'Services'

The term 'services' enfolds a variety of service sectors and sub-sectors. The WTO Secretariat recognized twelve service sectors: business services (including professional and computer services); telecommunication; construction and engineering; distribution; education; environmental services; financial services (including banking and insurance); health; tourism and travel; culture and sport; transportation; other services. These twelve service sectors were divided by the Secretariat into 155 sub-sectors.[1]

In order to ensure, that GATS will apply to all services and even to services that could be developed in the future, as well as to every measure that might affect trade in services, the term 'services' is defined in Article I in a very broad manner, including 'any service in any sector except services supplied in the exercise of governmental authority'.[2] This subject will be addressed in Chapter 4.

2.4.2 GATS Scope of Application

The desire to potentially subject every possible barrier to international trade in services, be it direct or indirect, current or future, to GATS disciplines resulted in the very broad provision, determining GATS shall apply to 'measures by Members affecting trade in services'. This drafting deliberately avoids any further specification in order to allow full flexibility of its interpretation.

Two more elements ensure GATS broad scope of application: its application to service suppliers and to all government levels.

2.4.2.1 Application to Service Suppliers

Unlike GATT that applies only to goods and not to their suppliers, the disciplines of GATS apply to measures affecting services *and* service *suppliers*, thus recognizing that many of the barriers to trade in services are directed at their suppliers. This personal aspect raises some particular difficulties, to be discussed in Chapter 4.

2.4.2.2 Application to All Government Levels

Article I ensures that the disciplines of GATS will apply to all government levels: national, regional and local, subject to exceptions. Furthermore, it provides for their application even to non-governmental bodies in the exercise of powers

1. See instructions concerning services' classification in S/L/92 Guidelines for the Scheduling of Specific Commitments under GATS, published 28.3.2001, 35–40, adopted by the Council for Trade in services on 23.3.2001, S/C/M/52. See the text of the guidelines in <http://docsonline.wto.org>.
2. Government procurements are excluded from the scope of GATS in Art. XIII of GATS.

delegated by central, regional or local governments or authorities. This practice reflects the intention to prevent, as much as possible, claims of irresponsibility by national governments who are parties to the agreement, to acts and omissions by lower levels of government. It is clear, that allowing such practices would have potentially circumvented the purpose of the agreement. This aspect will be discussed in detail in Chapter 4.

2.5 PART II

2.5.1 General Framework

Part II of GATS includes the general, conditional and unconditional, obligations:

Unconditional Obligations
Most favoured nation
Transparency
Recognition
Business practices
Conditional Obligations
Regulations
Monopolies
Payments and transfers
Increased participation of developing countries.

2.5.2 Unconditional Obligations

This group includes legal obligations that apply immediately and unconditionally once a Member joins GATS.

2.5.2.1 Most Favoured Nation

According to Article II of GATS, services and service suppliers from Members are entitled to the most favoured treatment accorded by the importing Member to like imported services and service suppliers from any source, even from a country which is not a WTO Member. The application of this discipline is unconditional, and therefore is not subject to negotiations, but it may be derogated. Each Member is entitled to submit a list of exemptions to this principle only once, when it first becomes a party to GATS.[3] The list is reviewed after five years and should be eliminated after a maximum period of ten years. The most favoured nation (MFN) principle thus represents a 'top down' approach applied by the agreement. This subject will be addressed in Chapter 6.

3. See Annex on Art. II Exemptions, Art. XXIX of GATS.

The agreement includes some exceptions to this principle, to be addressed below.

2.5.2.2 Transparency

Foreign service suppliers sometimes find it difficult to do business in other countries, due to lack of information concerning the relevant regulations in these countries. Non-transparency of rules and regulations may be decisive for trade in services, where regulation is a major instrument to protect domestic production. GATS provides[4] that the Members should report and inform the other parties of their laws, regulations or administrative guidelines affecting trade in services.

However, GATS excludes from this obligation confidential information that 'would prejudice legitimate commercial interests of particular enterprises, public or private'.[5] This provision will be further analysed in Chapter 13.

2.5.2.3 Recognition

Trade in services depend, to a large extent, on recognition of service suppliers' professional diplomas, qualifications, vocational training and experience obtained. Each country recognizes professional training and experience from certain other countries. GATS does not subject this practice to the MFN principle. Therefore, mutual recognition of professional education and experience may take place as a unilateral act of a country, or be achieved by bilateral or multilateral agreements. GATS allows each Member to choose its preferred techniques to achieve this end, but provides that a Member, who has a preference agreement with another country, should 'afford adequate opportunity for other interested Members to negotiate their accession to such an agreement or arrangement or to negotiate comparable ones with it'.[6]

GATS does not allow the use of professional recognition processes as means of discrimination or disguised barriers to trade, and urges the Members to inform the Secretariat of the status of these practices in their territories.

The agreement further calls the Members to 'work in cooperation with relevant intergovernmental and non-governmental organizations towards the establishment and adoption of common international standards and criteria for recognition and common international standards and criteria for recognition and common international standard for the practice of relevant services trades and professions'.[7] However, it is assumed that this process will be relatively slow, since mutual recognition of professional diplomas usually takes place in a bilateral framework, recognized as an exception to the MFN principle.

4. Article III of GATS.
5. Article III*bis* of GATS.
6. Article VII:2 of GATS.
7. Article VII:5 of GATS.

These rules apply to all professional services of the Members, whether or not these countries took specific commitments concerning specific services.[8] This subject will be further discussed in Chapter 12.

2.5.2.4 Business Practices

GATS expresses its Members' recognition that certain business practices by service suppliers, other than monopolies or exclusive suppliers (separately dealt with), may restrain competition, and thereby restrict free trade in services. It therefore provides that Members shall consult with other requesting Members, in order to eliminate such practices. It does not oblige Members, though, to act against such practices.

This provision sets the basis for further discussions on the wishful relationship between trade and competition policy.[9] It will be discussed in details in Chapter 11.

2.5.3 Conditional Obligations

This group of obligations does not apply automatically to the Members, but is subject to certain conditions.

2.5.3.1 Domestic Regulation

GATS provides that the Members should ensure, in sectors where specific commitments are undertaken, that all measures of general application affecting trade in services are administered in a reasonable, objective, impartial and non-discriminating manner. This provision concentrates the administrative aspect, and not on the substance of treatment.

The agreement provides that the Members should establish a judicial, arbitral or administrative tribunal or procedure, to address complaints by service suppliers concerning administrative decisions affecting trade in services.[10] This provision will be addressed in Chapter 12.

2.5.3.2 Monopolies and Exclusive Service Suppliers

GATS does not prohibit the existence of monopolies and exclusive service suppliers. But it provides that a Member undertaking specific commitments in a certain service sector should ensure that such monopolies and exclusive service suppliers will not act in a manner inconsistent with its MFN obligation, as well as with its national treatment and market access commitments (subject to certain conditions specified in the agreement).

---

8. Article VII of GATS.
9. Article IX of GATS.
10. Article VI of GATS.

The agreement further determines a few obligations concerning disclosure of relevant information in this context.[11] This subject will be discussed in Chapter 11.

2.5.3.3 Payments and Transfers

GATS recognizes that efficient trade liberalization depends, to a large extent, on the liberalization of capital flows which facilitate trade in services. It therefore prohibits Members from applying restrictions to international transfers and payments for current transactions relating to their specific commitments.[12] This subject will be addressed in Chapter 9.

2.5.3.4 Increased Participation of Developing Countries

GATS provides, that 'the increasing participation of developing and least developed country Members in world trade shall be facilitated through negotiated specific commitments . . . '. It also provides for the developed Members to establish contact points, in order to improve access of developing and least developed Members to information about their respective markets,[13] and entitles these countries to time-delays in the fulfilment of their legal obligations according to the agreement, as well as to technical assistance by the Secretariat. This subject will be further specified in Chapter 14.

2.6 EXCEPTIONS TO THE AGREEMENT'S OBLIGATIONS

GATS includes some groups of exceptions to its obligations. They function as safety valves, to guard some core interests of the Members from being hampered for the sake of international free trade. Three major groups of exceptions may be identified:

- Economic integration agreements.
- Balance of payment difficulties.
- General and security exceptions.

2.6.1 Economic Integration Agreements

GATS recognizes the framework of economic integration agreements, between or among a relatively small number of Members, as a faster track to achieve a more advanced degree of trade liberalization. It is basically assumed, that the trade-creating effects of such agreements are larger than their trade-distorting effects.

11. Article VIII of GATS.
12. Article XI of GATS.
13. Article IV of GATS.

GATS therefore recognizes such agreements as an exception to the MFN principle, subject to some conditions, that are basically aimed at ensuring *comprehensive* trade liberalization in services between or among the partners to such an economic integration agreement. GATS drafters chose the broad term 'economic integration agreements', thereby abstaining from specifying the degree of liberalization provided for by such agreements, thus deviating from GATT practice that explicitly referred to free trade area agreements and customs union agreements.[14]

When an economic integration agreement is concluded, it has to be reported to the WTO Secretariat, and the terms set by GATS for its recognition as an exception to the MFN principle are examined by the Committee on Regional Trade Agreements (CRTA), composed of representatives from all Members.[15] This subject will be addressed in Chapter 10.

2.6.1.1 Labour Markets' Integration

According to the same logic, GATS recognizes agreements between or among Members, providing for full integration of their labour markets, as an exception to the MFN principle, subject to conditions set forth by it, also aimed at ensuring the comprehensiveness of such arrangements.[16] This subject will be addressed in Chapter 10.

2.6.2 Restrictions to Safeguard the Balance of Payments

GATS allows Members to adopt temporary restrictions to international trade flows of services for which they made specific commitments, in case of 'serious balance of payments and external financial difficulties or threat thereof'. Such measures are subject to a necessity proof and to conditions specified in the agreement. Furthermore, they should be temporary.[17] This subject will be discussed in Chapter 15.

2.6.3 General and Security Exceptions

GATS includes a list of general interests, recognized by the Members as allowing the application, to external services' trade flows, of measures:

- Necessary to protect public morals or maintain public order.
- Necessary to protect human, animal or plant life or health.
- Necessary to secure compliance with laws and regulations which are not inconsistent with GATS provisions.

---

14. Article XXIV of GATT.
15. Article V of GATS.
16. Article V*bis* of GATS.
17. Article XII of GATS.

- Inconsistent with the national treatment obligation, provided that the difference in treatment is aimed at ensuring the equitable or effective imposition or collection of direct taxes in respect of services or service suppliers of other Members.
- Inconsistent with the MFN obligation provided that the difference in treatment results from an agreement on the avoidance of double taxation or provisions for that purpose included in another international agreement or arrangement by a Member.

The measures taken to protect the interests included in this list may not be applied 'in a manner which would constitute a means of arbitrary or unjustifiable discrimination between countries where like conditions prevail, or a disguised restriction on trade in services'.[18]

In addition, GATS includes a security exception, allowing the application to external services' trade flows of restricting measures for state security reasons, subject to the conditions specified.[19] All these subjects will be addressed in details in Chapter 15.

2.7 PART III: SPECIFIC COMMITMENTS

This part includes the sectors where the existence and scope of a legal obligation depends on specific commitments made by the Members. The schedules of specific commitment thus reflect a 'bottom up' approach by which these disciplines apply according to the agreement, unlike the MFN discipline which is subject to a 'top down' approach (see above). The specific commitments further reflect a combination of a positive list approach, by which a Member is entitled to choose the *services* to which it wished to accord preferred treatment, and a negative list approach, allowing this Member to subject these benefits to restrictions, qualifications and conditions.[20]

2.7.1 MARKET ACCESS

Market access is the basic instrument to ensure international trade. GATS does not impose on the Members a general obligation to allow the access of foreign services or service suppliers into their domestic markets. This right is negotiable for each sector and mode of supply. The results of such negotiations are reflected by the schedules of specific commitments.[21] This subject will be further discussed in Chapter 9.

18. Article XIV of GATS.
19. Article XIV*bis* of GATS.
20. P. Delimatsis, *International Trade in Services and Domestic Regulations – Necessity, Transparency and Regulatory Diversity*, Oxford University Press (2007), 31.
21. The relevant provisions concerning the contents and administration of the schedules of specific commitments are included in Part IV (Arts XIX–XXI) of GATS.

2.7.2 QUANTITATIVE RESTRICTIONS

Quantitative restrictions affect the quantity of foreign services or the number of service suppliers that gain market access. GATS excludes the use of six kinds of such restrictions, in manners specified by it, unless such measures were explicitly included in a Member's schedule of specific commitments:

- Limitations on the number of service suppliers.
- Limitation on the total value of service transactions or assets.
- Limitation on the total number of service operations or on the total quantity of service output.
- Limitations on the total number of natural persons that may be employed in a particular service sector or that a service supplier may employ, and who are necessary for, and directly related to, the supply of a specific service.
- Measures which restrict or require specific types of legal entity or joint venture through which a service supplier may supply a service.
- Limitations on the participation of foreign capital.[22]

This subject will be further elaborated in Chapter 9.

2.7.3 QUALITATIVE RESTRICTIONS

Qualitative restrictions are addressing the quality of treatment accorded to imported services or to foreign services suppliers, compared to like domestic services or services suppliers.

2.7.3.1 National Treatment

According to this discipline, foreign services and service suppliers are entitled, in the country of import, to no less favourable treatment than that accorded to like domestic services or service suppliers. In fact, this provision calls for non-discrimination between imported and like domestic services and service suppliers. This principle is not applied immediately and unconditionally in GATS, but is subject to the results of mutual negotiations, reflected by the schedules of specific commitments. This subject will be addressed in Chapter 8.

2.7.3.2 Non-discrimination: Additional Commitments

GATS foresees future negotiations between the Members concerning commitments on measures affecting trade in services, which are not subject to the national treatment or market access principles, including those regarding qualifications, standards and licensing matters. Such commitments, if they exist, are inscribed

22. Article XVI of GATS.

in the Members' schedules, under 'additional commitments'.[23] This subject will be discussed as part of the general structure of the schedules of specific commitments, in Chapter 7.

2.8 INSTITUTIONAL PROVISIONS

2.8.1 Part V

The institutional provisions of GATS include a consultation mechanism between or among the Members.[24]

They subject the agreement to the WTO dispute settlement and enforcement mechanism.[25] This subject will be discussed in Chapter 17.

Part V of GATS also includes provisions concerning the competences of the Council for Trade in Services,[26] technical cooperation and assistance to developing countries through the national contact points and by the Secretariat,[27] and relationship with other international organizations.[28]

It also provides that acts of retaliation due to GATS infringement may involve trade in goods, and vice versa.

2.8.2 Part VI

This part includes the final provisions of GATS, including definitions,[29] denial of benefits and the annexes on specific service sectors.

2.8.2.1 Denial of Benefits

GATS allows the denial of benefits accorded by a Member through the agreement, in one of two cases:

- Where the service supplied, or the service supplier is from a territory of a non-Member.

  In this case, the reason for denial of benefits is the lack of mutuality, which is a basic principle in international trade agreements. In other words, this provision is meant to prevent 'free riders' from enjoying the benefits of the agreement without consideration.

23. Article XVIII of GATS.
24. Article XXII of GATS.
25. Article XXIII of GATS.
26. Article XXIV of GATS.
27. Article XXV of GATS.
28. Article XXVI of GATS.
29. Article XXVIII of GATS.

- Where the service supplied, or the service supplier is from a Member to which the denying Member does not apply the WTO agreement.[30]

  In this case, the denial of benefits emanates from the framework of political relationships between the involved Members.[31]

This subject will be mentioned in Chapter 15.

2.8.2.2 GATS Sector-Specific Instruments

By the end of the Uruguay Round (1994) it became clear, that some specific service sectors need more detailed reference, while in certain service sectors, trade liberalization could not be accomplished among all GATS Members. It was therefore decided to initiate some annexes and other sector-specific instruments to GATS. These instruments include specific disciplines concerning specific service sectors: financial services, telecommunication and negotiations on basic telecommunications, negotiations on maritime transport services, air transport services and movement of natural persons supplying services.[32] The annexes form an integral part of GATS, while participation in some of the other sector-specific instruments was voluntary. These instruments will be reviewed in detail in Chapter 16.

2.9 SUBJECTS STILL UNDER NEGOTIATION

GATS conclusion did not complete negotiations on some elaborated and sensitive matters. It was decided not to delay its conclusion but to continue negotiations on these subjects after GATS conclusion. These subjects are: safeguard measures for trade in services; government procurement of services; and subsidies that distort international trade in services. GATS does not contain provisions regarding the first two subjects.

Concerning subsidies, GATS expresses its Members' recognition, that 'in certain circumstances, subsidies may have distortive effects on trade in services', although no mandatory disciplines were yet developed in GATS to confront this difficulty. For the time being, it only provides for the Members to negotiate in order to develop such disciplines, and to exchange information necessary for such negotiations. In addition, it opens the way for each Member, believing it is adversely affected by such subsidies by another Member, to ask for consultations with that other state. The requested Member is expected to accord this request sympathetic consideration.[33]

---

30. Article XXVII of GATS.
31. See Art. XIII of the Marrakech Agreement Establishing the World Trade Organization, <www.wto.org>.
32. Article XXIX of GATS.
33. Article XV of GATS.

It was thought, that agreement on these three subjects could be achieved within three years after the end of the Uruguay Round, but in fact it has not been achieved by now.[34]

2.10 CONCLUSION

The general overview of GATS presents an elaborated agreement including legal norms in different phases of development. Some are already developed disciplines that require compliance. Others are still in early developmental stages, under negotiations. Some legal norms are unconditionally obliging, while others are conditional, their scope of application depending on Members' schedules of specific commitments. Some legal norms are included in GATS, while others are still included in its voluntary legal instruments. The second part of the book will address specific legal norms in detail, analyzing their meaning and scope of application.

---

34. See further reference to these subjects in: A. Jara & M.D.C. Domingez, 'Liberalization of Trade in Services and Trade Negotiations', *40 Journal of World Trade* (2006): 113, 125–126; R. Adlung, 'The GATS Turns Ten: A Preliminary Stocktaking', *WTO* (2004), 19–21, <www.wto.org>.

    P. Sauvé, 'Completing the GATS Framework', in B. Hoeckman, A. Mattoo & P. English (eds), *Development, Trade and the WTO: A Handbook, The World Bank* (2002), 259, 326–335, <www-wds.worldbank.org>.

Chapter 3
GATS Interpretation

3.1 INTRODUCTION

GATS is an international agreement, governed by the rules of public international law. This principle is recognized, *inter alia*, by Article 3.2 of the DSU, providing that:

> The dispute settlement system of the WTO is a central element in providing security and predictability to the multilateral trading system. The Members recognize that it serves to preserve the rights and obligations of Members under the covered agreements, and to clarify the existing provisions of those agreements *in accordance with customary rules of interpretation of public international law.* Recommendations and rulings of the DSB cannot add to or diminish the rights and obligations provided in the covered agreements. [Emphasis added].

This provision includes some guidelines concerning the interpretation of the WTO agreements, including GATS:

- *Interpretation should ensure security and predictability of the system* – this principle implies systematic interpretation, based on the wording of the agreements as well as on former decisions.
- *Preservation of the rights and obligations of Members under the agreement* – this principle is subject to an interpretative case-by-case decision about what the 'rights' and 'obligations' under the agreement are. However, once defined, an interpretation preserving them should be adopted. This principle is complemented by another instruction included in this provision: 'recommendations and rulings of the DSB *cannot add to or diminish* the rights and obligations . . . ' [Emphasis added]. In principle this is clear, since it is obvious that the DSB does not have an authority overriding the

authority of the agreement's drafters. However, in practice the WTO adjudicating bodies define, by interpretation, what the 'rights' and 'obligations' are under the agreement, and through this interpretative process they may effectively broaden or narrow their scope. Thus, it seems that despite this provision, treaty interpreters have the last word. Therefore, they are expected to exercise a cautious and balanced approach.

3.2 THE VIENNA CONVENTION ON THE LAW OF TREATIES, 1969

The Vienna Convention on the Law of Treaties, 1969[1] (Hereby: 'the Vienna Convention') incorporates the public international customary rules concerning the interpretation of treaties between or among states.[2] As such, its rules are often addressed by the WTO adjudicating bodies in the course of interpretation of different WTO agreements, including GATS.

Articles 31–32 of that treaty are two major provisions relevant to GATS interpretation. They provide:

Article 31
General Rule of Interpretation

1. A treaty shall be interpreted in good faith in accordance with the ordinary meaning to be given to the terms of the treaty in their context and in the light of its object and purpose.
2. The context for the purpose of the interpretation of a treaty shall comprise, in addition to the text, including its preamble and the annexes:
   (a) Any agreement relating to the treaty which was made between all the parties in connection with the conclusion of the treaty.
   (b) Any instrument which was made by one or more parties in connection with the conclusion of the treaty and accepted by the other parties as an instrument related to the treaty.
3. There shall be taken into account, together with the context:
   (a) Any subsequent agreement between the parties regarding the interpretation of the treaty or the application of its provisions;
   (b) Any subsequent practice in the application of the treaty which establishes the agreement of the parties regarding its interpretation;
   (c) Any relevant rules of international law applicable in the relations between the parties.
4. A special meaning shall be given to a term if it is established that the parties so intended.

1. <http://untreaty.un.org>.
2. In WT/DS2/AB/R United States – Standards for Reformulated and Conventional Gasoline, adopted on 20.5.1996, 17 DSR 1996:I, 3 at 16, the status of Art. 31(1) of the Vienna Convention as a rule of customary law was explicitly recognized by the Appellate Body.

Article 32
Supplementary Means of Interpretation
Recourse may be had to supplementary means of interpretation, including the preparatory work of the treaty and the circumstances of its conclusion, in order to confirm the meaning resulting from the application of article 31, or to determine the meaning when the interpretation according to article 31:

(a) leaves the meaning ambiguous or obscure; or
(b) leads to a result which is manifestly absurd or unreasonable.

Theoretically, these provisions provide for a certain order, or rather hierarchy, of examination:

(1) *Ordinary meaning* of the text.
(2) *Context* (agreements and instruments related to the treaty) and subsequent agreements and practices and relevant rules of international law applicable to the parties.
(3) *Object and purpose.*
(4) *Supplementary means*, to be addressed only in one of two cases:
   (a) in order to confirm the Article 31 interpretation; or
   (b) where Article 31 leads to an ambiguous or absurd result.

All these elements seem to be governed by the *good faith* standard.

However, the Panel in *US – Sections 301–310 Trade Act of 1974*[3] provided that 'the elements referred to in Article 31 – text, context and object-and-purpose as well as good faith – are to be viewed as *one holistic rule of interpretation* rather than a sequence of separate tests to be applied in a hierarchical order'. [Emphasis added].

The same approach was adopted by the Panel in *Canada-Autos*, based on the explanation provided for these provisions in the Yearbook of the International Law Commission (1966).[4]

The holistic approach allows for some flexibility, since discretion may be exercised by the adjudicating bodies in terms of the *weight* accorded to each element.[5]

Even according to this approach, it is clear that the sources mentioned in Article 32 are *secondary* to those included in Article 31, and may be used only under the circumstances mentioned in this provision.

---

3. WT/DS152/R United States – Sections 301–310 Trade Act of 1974, adopted on 22.12.1999, para. 7.22.
4. WT/DS139,142/R, AB/R Canada – Certain Measures Affecting the Automotive Industry, adopted on 19.6.2000, Panel report para. 10.12 and n. 806 thereof, referring to the 1966 yearbook, vol. II, A/CN.4/SER.A/1966/Add.1,219 and 220.
5. F. Ortino, 'Treaty Interpretation and the WTO Appellate Body Report in *US – Gambling*: a Critique', 9 *Journal of International Economic Law* (2006), 117, 130–131, criticizes the *US – Gambling* decision for not practicing this holistic approach. See also 148.

Two additional interpretative principles used in the context of the WTO agreements should be mentioned: *the principle of full effectiveness of the text*, providing that 'interpretation must give meaning and effect to all terms of the treaty',[6] and the legitimacy given to Panels to *rely on previous cases* because '[t]hey create legitimate expectations among WTO Members, and, therefore, should be taken into account where they are relevant to any dispute'. Nevertheless it is stressed that a single, isolated act is not sufficient to establish subsequent practice in the sense of Article 31:3(b) of the Vienna Convention, and only a *sequence* of such decisions establishes the agreement of the parties to the principle or to the interpretation at issue.[7]

In *China – Publications and Audiovisual Products* the Appellate Body noted:

> The purpose of the interpretative exercise is to narrow down the range of possible meanings of the treaty term interpreted, not to generate multiple meanings or to confirm the ambiguity and inconclusiveness of treaty obligations. Rather, the treaty interpreter is required to have recourse to context and purpose to elucidate the relevant meaning of the word or term . . . treaty interpretation is an integrated operation, where interpretative rules and principles must be understood and applied as connected and mutually reinforced components of a holistic exercise.[8]

The Appellate Body further reiterated that 'the purpose of treaty interpretation . . . is to ascertain the "common intention" of the parties . . . the circumstances of the conclusion of the treaty may thus be relevant to this "common intention"'.[9]

3.3 INTERPRETATION IN GOOD FAITH

According to Article 31:1 of the Vienna Convention, interpretation of an international agreement should be conducted in good faith. The essence of this rule is the *pacta sunt servanda* rule, meaning that agreements should be respected, thus precluding a state from exploiting an ambiguity in the text or advancing an interpretation contrary to the expectations of the parties.[10]

6. WT/DS8/AB/R Japan – Taxes on Alcoholic Beverages, adopted on 1.11.1996, para. 12.
7. *Ibid.*, para. 14.
8. WT/DS363/R, AB/R China – Measures Affecting Trading Rights and Distribution Services for Certain Publications and Audiovisual Entertainment Products, adopted on 19.1.2010, Appellate Body report, para. 399.
9. *Ibid.*, Appellate Body report, para. 405.
10. F. Ortino, n. 5, 129. See implementation of this rule, for example, in WT/DS285/R, AB/R United States – Measures Affecting the Cross-Border Supply of Gambling and Betting Services, adopted on 22.5.2007, Appellate Body report paras 269, 272. For implementation of this rule in GATT cases see *WTO Appellate Body Repertory of Reports and Awards 1995–2006* (3rd edn), WTO, Cambridge University Press (2007), 436–440.

3.4 'OBJECT AND PURPOSE'

The major object of GATS is to abolish direct and indirect barriers to international trade in services, thereby enhancing its world-wide development. This object could be drawn from GATS Preamble.[11] Thus, its provisions should be, allegedly, interpreted in a manner facilitating this purpose. Accordingly, provisions for the abolition of such barriers should be broadly interpreted, while exceptions to this principle should be narrowly interpreted.

However, a thorough reading of GATS Preamble as well as of some of its provisions, and an understanding of its history and current international context, reveals a more elaborated picture of mixed objectives, expressing a compromise, or rather an agreed balance, between different governments and interests' groups. Thus, for example, in *US – Shrimp*, the Appellate Body recognized that the sustainable development objective, specified in the preamble of the WTO agreement, 'must add colour, texture and shading' to its interpretation of GATT provisions since it reflects the intentions of negotiators.[12]

GATS reflects, on the one hand, encouragement of its Members to adopt, in certain cases, international standardization and harmonization. On the other hand, it is understood that such steps are reducing the regulatory autonomy of its parties, thus deviating from the sheer purpose of non-discrimination and reduction of trade barriers. Thus, it may be concluded that 'a reference to its object and purpose can be used to support different interpretative results'.[13] This duality is reflected in *China – Publications and Audiovisual Product* where the Panel, in the course of interpretation of the measures before it, referred to the general purpose of GATS: international enhancement of trade liberalization, while the Appellate Body noted that the Preamble to GATS reflects more than one purpose.[14] It should be recognized that:

> [l]egal principles of normative integration are not merely technical . . . They have political meaning for the entire international system's structure of authority and governance. Their result (even if not their goal) is not only normative consistency, coherence and regularity, but also a trend towards

---

11. See, for example, the Panel report in WT/DS363/R *China – Publications and Audiovisual Products*, n. 8, paras 7.1219, 7.1348 where the Panel referred to the aim of establishing 'a multilateral framework of principles and rules for trade in services with view to the expansion of such trade under conditions of transparency and progressive liberalization', as well as to 'securing the overall balance of rights and obligations' between the Members. It is interesting to note, though, that GATS Preamble seems to describe this aim of trade liberalization and expansion of trade in a narrower manner than it is described in GATT and in the WTO agreement, referring only to economic growth and development: M. Krajewski, *National Regulation and Trade Liberalization in Services*, Kluwer Law International (2003), 56.
12. WT/DS58/AB/R United States – Import Prohibition of certain Shrimp and Shrimp Products, adopted on 6.11.1998, para. 153.
13. Krajewski, n. 11, 59.
14. WT/DS363/AB/R *China – Publications and Audiovisual Products*, n. 8, Appellate Body report, paras 392–393.

> greater centralization and rationalization of governance and/or harmonization of authority.
>
> Moreover: the integration of norms is generally associated with a correlative . . . integration of authority.[15]

Since the WTO system does not represent a relatively high degree of economic integration, the Appellate Body's approach in *China – Publications and Audio-visual Product* seems to better reflect the desired caution that should underline any interpretation of the WTO agreements, including GATS.

3.5 THE TEXT

The starting point for the interpretation of GATS is, naturally, its text. It should be interpreted 'in good faith in accordance with the ordinary meaning'. The language of Article 31:2 of the Vienna Convention implies that the 'text' includes the *Preamble and Annexes* to the agreement.

The first step in determining the 'ordinary meaning' is, in many cases, the examination of dictionary definitions.[16] However, dictionaries do not always contain an interpretation which is suitable for a trade context. Sometimes, their definition is neutral and does not serve to support the claims of any of the parties. In other cases, the dictionary suggests some options from which one has to be chosen. Consequently, the Appellate Body realizes that dictionary interpretation alone is not enough, since dictionary meanings 'leave many interpretative questions open'.[17] This point will be further addressed below.

The major difficulty encountered by GATS interpreters stems from the fact that, being a multilateral agreement with more than 150 participants, one of its characteristics, which is typical to the general framework of the WTO agreements, is vague drafting, using many unclear expressions. This manner of drafting is very efficient in the conclusion stage, since every party believes that it reflects its position. However, its disadvantages are revealed in the implementation stage, as each party sticks to its own interpretation of the ambiguous expressions. Interpretation of such expressions is alleged to be conducted on a case-by-case basis, in order to solve a pending dispute, while, at the same time, leaving maximal maneuvering space in future cases. This flexibility is somewhat narrowed by the tendency of WTO adjudicating bodies, strengthened since 1995, to refer to interpretations developed in former cases as a precedent, that would be further discussed below.

---

15. T. Broude, 'Principles of Normative Integration and the Allocation of International Authority: The WTO, the Vienna Convention on the Law of Treaties, and the Rio Declaration', the Hebrew University of Jerusalem, Faculty of Law, International Law Forum Research Paper no. 07-08 (2008), 8, 16–17, <http://papers.ssrn.com>.
16. See, for example, WT/DS285/R *US – Gambling*, n. 10, Panel report para. 6.21, WT/DS285/AB/R Appellate Body report para. 164.
17. WT/DS70/AB/R Canada – Measures Affecting the Export of Civilian Aircraft, adopted on 20.8.2000, para. 153; WT/DS285/AB/R *US – Gambling*, n. 10, para. 164.

3.5.1 The Preamble

GATS text begins with a Preamble.[18] The Preamble presents the object and purpose of the agreement, as well as different considerations and intentions of the parties that formed GATS. It is therefore considered an important interpretative instrument to GATS operative provisions,[19] and recognized as part of the agreement's context according to Article 31:2 of the Vienna Convention.

GATS Preamble expresses the *motives* behind its conclusion:

- The growing importance of trade in services to the growth and development of global economy.
- The intention to create a legal framework that would enhance transparency and progressive liberalization.

It further presents the *mechanism* to be used to achieve these ends: successive rounds of negotiations, and their *aims*. The Preamble expresses a clear indication that such rounds should be mutually advantageous to all participants, knowing that otherwise, this mechanism will not be effective.

The Preamble then addresses some of *interests* of the Members, which might potentially collide with the general interest of global trade liberalization, enhanced by GATS:

- The right of Members to domestically regulate trade in services, subject to the enhancement of domestic policy goals.[20]
- Recognition of the particular difficulties of developing and least developed countries, as well as the desire to encourage and improve their participation in the general framework of world trade.[21]

---

18. For the drafting history of the Preamble see: R. Worfrum, P.T. Stoll & C. Feinäugle (eds), *WTO – Trade in Services*, Max Planck Commentaries on World Trade Law, Martinus Mijnhoff Publishers, Leiden, Boston (2008) (hereby: GATS commentary), 20–21.
19. WT/DS58/AB/R *US – Shrimp*, n. 12, para. 153; WT/DS246/AB/R EC – Conditions for the granting of tariff preferences to developing countries, adopted on 20.4.2004, para. 107; WT/DS176/AB/R US – Section 211 Omnibus Appropriations Act of 1998, adopted on 2.1.2002, para. 216.
20. This notion, cautiously phrased in the non-obligatory part of the agreement, stands in the centre of an ongoing public debate about the due balance of interests between trade liberalization and domestic regulation. It should be stressed, that GATS aims at progressive liberalization, not at deregulation of trade in services, and the wrong understanding of liberalization as necessarily implying for deregulation is one of the motives behind this debate. However, many countries view the liberalization process as implying, at least to a certain extent, a loss of sovereignty to regulate its service sectors in a manner it deems appropriate: A. Mattoo & P. Sauvé, in A. Mattoo & P. Sauvé (eds) *Domestic Regulation and Service Trade Liberalization*, the World Bank and Oxford University Press (2003), 1–2.
21. This recognition may have practical implications beyond trade issues if, for instance, it would be broadly interpreted to allow governments to regulate domestic policies enhancing basic human rights, such as the right for development and cross-subsidization of basic services. See: Krajewski, n. 11, 60–61.

Due to the potential conflict between these interests and the major goal of GATS, always threatening to create a legitimacy crisis of the WTO, a cautious approach was taken by GATS drafters, explicitly providing in the Preamble that these interests should be observed and balanced with the major goal of the agreement: liberalization of trade in services. However, the result of such balance may differ, depending on the treaty interpreters' approach. Two alternative approaches may be considered:[22]

- *A market integration approach* – favouring trade liberalization over national regulatory autonomy, believing that the major goal of a multilateral trading system is the integration of markets. According to it, any national policy deviating from this integration purpose by enhancing an independent policy goal needs specific legitimization that could only be obtained in exceptional circumstances. At this stage of WTO development, this option seems far-reaching.
- *Restricting the function of the WTO law to the prevention of protectionism, calling for deference to national autonomy* – theoretically, this seems the prevailing approach in the WTO reasoning. However, a closer look at dispute settlement decisions in recent years seems to reflect a tendency, at least in certain cases (see discussion below in 3.5.5) to give priority to international trade liberalization over domestic policy goals, by interpreting the notion of 'protectionism' broadly, thus rejecting domestic policy goals as being 'protectionist'.[23]

Since at least some of GATS provisions are vaguely drafted, the window opened by the Preamble to the intentions of its parties and to the goals they wished to promote by the agreement, may be a very helpful instrument for its interpretation. Moreover, once clearly expressed in writing, the motives, goals, mechanism and balance of interests reflected in the Preamble may not be overlooked by GATS interpreters due to the requirement for interpretation 'in good faith', based on the ordinary meaning of the text, set forth by Article 31 of the Vienna Convention. The problem is that the Preamble reveals the same duality in the balance of interests as is reflected in the ambiguous drafting of the operative provisions and consequently – in the WTO jurisprudence.

The practical difficulty to using the Preamble as an interpretative instrument to outline the object and purpose of GATS, in order to interpret China's measures at stake in their light, was reflected in the case of *China – Publications and Audiovisual Products.* In that case, the Panel drew certain interpretative conclusions based on the principle of progressive liberalization embodied in the Preamble.

---

22. *Ibid.*, 57–58.
23. This seems to be the case in WT/DS161,169/R, AB/R Korea – Measures Affecting the Imports of Fresh, Chilled and Frozen Beef, adopted on 10.1.2001; WT/DS332/R, AB/R Brazil – Measures Affecting Imports of Retreaded Tyres, adopted on 17.12.2007; WT/DS291,292,293/R EC – Measures Affecting the Approval and Marketing of Biotech Products, adopted on 21.11.2006.

However, the Appellate Body noted that 'the GATS preamble lists various objectives . . . none of the objectives . . . provides specific guidance as to the correct interpretation to be given to China's GATS Schedule entry . . . '.[24] This case raises two interpretative questions:

(1) in a specific case, which purpose mentioned in the Preamble prevails?
(2) choosing a purpose, what meaning should be attributed to it, out of all possible meanings?

In this case, despite its allegedly cautious approach, the Appellate Body finally used the principle of progressive liberalization, mentioned in the Preamble, for the interpretation of specific commitments at issue:

> We do not consider, however, that the principle of progressive liberalization lends support to an interpretation that would constrain the scope and coverage of specific commitments that have already been undertaken by Members and by which they are bound.[25]

According to this interpretation, explicit commitments should be given as broad a scope as possible. Such an approach, in its extreme version, implies a clear preference of the purpose of international trade liberalization over the freedom for domestic regulation, once a Member took a relevant specific commitment. In *China – Publications and Audiovisual Products* this approach led to the interpretation of China's commitments to include the transfer of voice recordings over the internet, despite China's position that this was not its intention while drafting these commitments.

3.5.2 Annexes and Additional Instruments

GATS annexes were accepted by all GATS Members and are considered as an integral part of the agreement,[26] and should be interpreted accordingly.

Other sector-specific instruments (specified in Chapter 16) are voluntary, and do not necessarily reflect the agreement of all GATS Members. Thus, despite the explicit provision of Article 31:2 of the Vienna Convention, it seems that such instruments, which do not reflect the intention of *all* GATS Members, should not be automatically used for the interpretation of GATS provisions.

However, comparative analysis of their provisions with similar provisions in GATS may prevent a too broad interpretation of the latter, based on a negative implication claim.

---

24. WT/DS363/AB/R *China – Publications and Audiovisual Products*, n. 8, paras 392–393.
25. *Ibid.*, 8, para. 394.
26. WT/DS204/R Mexico – Measures Affecting Telecommunications Services, adopted on 1.6.2004, para. 7.14.

3.5.3 Schedules of Specific Commitments

All GATS Members submitted schedules of specific commitments once they joined the agreement. These schedules, formed and submitted according to Part III of the agreement, and considered to be an integral part of GATS,[27] reflect their market access, national treatment and additional commitments (see Chapter 7). GATS disciplines concerning market access and national treatment apply, subject to these specific commitments. Therefore, a legal analysis of the conditional obligations according to GATS should combine, where relevant, the analysis of the general discipline with the relevant specific commitments included in a Member's schedule. However, while the general disciplines were drafted after obtaining a consensus among the Members, the schedules of specific commitments are *unilaterally* drafted. In addition, unlike GATT negotiations, which usually proceed on the basis of mechanical formulas, negotiations in GATS proceed in a manner allowing the Members a broader scope of manoeuvring, in selecting their levels of commitment.[28] This flexibility stems from the broad scope of services and modes of supply, as well as from the separate reference to services and to service suppliers. In *US – Gambling* this scope of manoeuvring was reflected even in a simpler aspect, as it turned out that the Unites States' schedule explicitly states that it 'is authentic in English only', disregarding the two other official languages of the WTO.

While the relevant part of a Member's schedule, which is the subject of dispute, would be considered as part of the *text*, other parts of the same schedule, as well as schedules of other Members, may be considered as *context* for its interpretation.[29] Nevertheless, such interpretative use of other Members' schedules should be cautious, taking into account their unilateral drafting. This point will be further addressed below. (See additional discussion on the interpretation of schedules in Chapter 7 – 7.12.)

3.5.4 Footnotes

GATS includes many footnotes. Theoretically, one would expect a footnote to have a different and lesser interpretative weight than the text, based on the assumption that its content was not considered important enough by the drafters of the agreement to be included it in the text. Thus, it may be assumed to have an interpretative value as a remark clarifying the drafters' intentions concerning the relevant text. Surprisingly, this is not the case with GATS footnotes, which seem to be

27. Article XX:3 of GATS provides: 'Schedules of specific commitments shall be annexed to this Agreement and shall form an integral part thereof.'
28. F. Ortino, n. 5, 124.
29. WT/DS285/R *US – Gambling*, n. 10, Panel report, paras 6.54–6.134. In GATT context, the concessions at issue in a dispute, as reflected in the relevant schedule, are also considered an integral part of the text. See, for example, WT/DS375,376,377/R *EC and its Member States – Tariff Treatment of Certain IT Products*, published 19.8.2010 (not adopted yet at the time of writing), para. 7.16, citing former GATT jurisprudence.

attributed with the same weight as the text of the agreement. The reason for this interpretation stems from their drafting history: in the course of the negotiations, the footnotes were excluded from the text of the agreement with the hope to remove them by the end of the negotiations. However, at the end of the negotiations the Members refused to remove the footnotes, thus indicating their importance to the achievement of mutual agreement. Therefore, GATS footnotes are considered an integral part of its text and are interpreted accordingly.

3.5.5 Interpretation of the Text by the WTO Adjudicating Bodies

Despite the long period that has passed since GATS conclusion, there are relatively not many dispute settlement cases involving this agreement. However, some cases were already decided by the dispute settlement tribunals, and the interpretation of GATS provisions included in them should be taken into account. Since GATS is an international agreement its interpretation does not establish a precedent. However, as already mentioned, in recent years there is a growing tendency to rely on interpretation and reasoning developed in former cases in order to solve a pending dispute. This attitude is encouraged particularly by the Appellate Body who modified, to some extent, the spirit of flexibility and diplomacy-driven solutions that characterized the interpretation of GATT 1947, opting for a more comprehensive legal approach, attempting to create a systematic, well established reasoning for WTO agreements' interpretation in general, to promote their transparency, predictability and certainty.[30] This change of approach affects GATS interpretation, as much as it affects the interpretation of all other WTO agreements.

The WTO adjudicating bodies, in particular the Appellate Body, were criticized, on the one hand, for sticking to dictionary definitions as decisive instruments to achieve a decision.[31] On the other hand, the same adjudicating bodies, in particular the Appellate Body, were criticized that despite the positive implications of its trend to 'minimize the hermeneutic relevance of dictionary definitions', the outcome in *US – Gambling* undermines the predictability, certainty, stability and security of GATS provisions.[32]

---

30. J.H.H. Weiler, 'The Rule of Lawyers and the Ethos of Diplomats: Reflections on the Internal and External Legitimacy of the WTO Dispute Settlement', *35 Journal of World Trade* (2001), 191.
31. H. Horn & J.H.H. Weiler, '*European Communities – Trade Description of Sardines*: Textualism and its Discontent', in H. Horn & P.C. Mavroidis (eds), *The WTO Case Law of 2002*, Cambridge, CUP (2005), 252.
    W. Davey, 'The WTO Dispute Settlement System: The First Ten Years', *8 Journal of Economic International Law* (2005), 17. <http://papers.ssrn.com>.
32. F. Ortino, n. 5, 123, 147; P. Delimatsis, 'Don't Gamble With the GATS – The Interaction between Arts VI, XVI, XVII and XVIII GATS in the Light of the *US – Gambling* Case', *40 Journal of World Trade* (2006), 1059, 1076.

In *China – Publications and Audiovisual Products* the Appellate Body noted that the establishment of the 'ordinary meaning' according to Article 31 of the Vienna Convention should *not* rely *only* on dictionary interpretation:

> Dictionaries alone are not necessarily capable of resolving complex questions of interpretation because they typically catalogue all meanings of words. Dictionaries are important guides to, but not dispositive of, the meaning of words appearing in treaties... 'ordinary meaning' of treaty terms may be ascertained only in their context and in light of the object and purpose of the treaty.[33]

This interpretation, which is justified both by the language of Articles 31–32 of the Vienna Convention and in light of the difficulties embodied in dictionary definitions, mentioned above, makes it necessary to refer to the context, as a complementary aspect to the text.

3.6 THE CONTEXT

It is thus, common understanding that:

> [f]or the purpose of arriving at the *ordinary meaning* of the terms of the treaty in accordance with the customary rules of interpretation, the 'raw text' is only *one* piece of the puzzle. Contextual and teleological elements constitute other relevant pieces.[34]

The Vienna Convention describes some layers of 'context', according to their proximity to the text:

The *first layer* is provided for by Article 31:2, and is comprised of:

(a) Any agreement relating to the treaty which was made between all the parties in connection with the conclusion of the treaty.
(b) Any instrument which was made by one or more parties in connection with the conclusion of the treaty and accepted by the other parties as an instrument related to the treaty.

'Translating' this provision to GATS context, the Appellate Body in *US – Gambling*, followed by the Panel in *China – Publications and Audiovisual Products*, noted that it includes:[35]

> (i) the reminder of the Member's Schedule, (ii) the substantive provisions of the GATS, (iii) the provisions of covered agreements other than the GATS,[36] and (iv) the GATS Schedules of other Members.

---

33. WT/DS363/AB/R *China – Publications and Audiovisual Products*, n. 8, Appellate Body report, para. 348.
34. F. Ortino, n. 5, 123.
35. WT/DS285/AB/R *US – Gambling*, n. 10, Appellate Body report para. 178; WT/DS363/R *China – Publications and Audiovisual Products*, n. 8, Panel report, para. 7.1182.
36. Referring, probably, to other WTO agreements.

Thus, for example, in *US – Gambling*, contextual elements examined were, *inter alia*, the reminder of the United States' schedule, and GATS schedules of other Members.[37]

With reference to the use of GATS schedules as context, in *China – Publications and Audiovisual Products* the Appellate Body noted that this practice is 'a logical consequence of Article XX:3 of GATS'.[38] However, the Appellate Body cautioned that 'the use of other Members' schedules as context must be tempered by the recognition that "each Schedule has its own intrinsic logic", which will be different from the Schedule being interpreted'.[39] The Appellate Body added:

> The provisions of the GATS itself, insofar as they concern the scheduling of specific commitments, also provide relevant context for the interpretation of specific commitments.[40]

The *second layer* is included in Article 31:3, providing:

> There shall be taken into account, *together with the context*:
>
> (a) Any subsequent agreement between the parties regarding the interpretation of the treaty or the application of its provisions;
> (b) Any subsequent practice in the application of the treaty which establishes the agreement of the parties regarding its interpretation;
> (c) Any relevant rules of international law applicable in the relations between the parties. [Emphasis added].

3.6.1 Any Subsequent Practice

In GATT case *Japan – Alcoholic Beverages II* the Appellate Body, referring to Article 31:3(b) provided:

> Generally, in international law, the essence of subsequent practice in interpreting a treaty has been recognized as a 'concordant, common and consistent' sequence of acts or pronouncements which is sufficient to establish a discernable pattern implying the agreement of the parties regarding its interpretation. An isolated act is generally not sufficient to establish subsequent act; it is a sequence of acts establishing the agreement of the parties that is relevant.[41]

In *Mexico – Telecoms* Mexico tried, without success, to use this provision to support its suggested interpretation by the alleged behaviour of all Members that inscribed a similar commitment to the relevant Mexican commitment. The Panel

37. WT/DS285/R *US – Gambling*, n. 10, paras 6.83–6.109.
38. WT/DS363/AB/R, n. 8, para. 382.
39. *Ibid.*, (the sentence in brackets is a citation from the Appellate Body report in WT/DS285/AB/R *US – Gambling*, n. 10, para. 182).
40. WT/DS363/AB/R, n. 8, para. 376.
41. WT/DS8,10,11/R *Japan – Alcoholic Beverages II*, n. 6, para.106.

rejected the Mexican interpretation, contending that it did not necessarily lead to the conclusion suggested by Mexico.[42]

The words 'together with the context' may imply that these elements are *not* considered as part of the context. However, they could be differently interpreted to imply a layer of context which is comparably more remote from the text than the 31:2 items.

3.6.2 WTO Agreements

3.6.2.1 Alternative Legal Basis

The WTO agreements form the natural surroundings of GATS. This group of agreements is a combination of GATT, first concluded in 1947, and another group of agreements, concluded at the end of the Uruguay Round (1994), including, in addition to GATS, the Agreement on TBT, the Agreement on Sanitary and Phytosanitary Measures (SPS), the Agreement on Customs Valuation, the Agreement on Trade Related Investment Measures (TRIMs), the Agreement on Trade Related Intellectual Property Rights (TRIPs), the Agreement on Agriculture, the Agreement on Subsidies and Countervailing Measures (SCM), the Agreement on Anti Dumping, etc.

Some of these agreements are relevant only to trade in goods. However, it is not rare that some of the Uruguay Round agreements may apply to the same situation involving aspects of trade in goods as well as aspects of trade in services. In such cases, the relevant provisions in some of the agreements could turn out to be alternative, or complementary. Where the agreements' disciplines plus specific commitments, where necessary, cover both trade in goods and trade in services involved in the situation, they could by treated as complementary. This strategy was applied, for example, in the *EC – Bananas III* case.[43] In this case, Members exporting of bananas to the EU complained that the EU discriminated their exports by a priori designating a certain percentage of bananas' import licenses to certain countries. The case involved goods: the bananas; and services: the marketing and distribution of the bananas. Therefore, both GATT and GATS were addressed, thereby functioning as complementary agreements.

Nevertheless, where a thorough examination of the relevant disciplines and specific commitments according to a certain WTO agreement reveals that they do not cover a situation examined, another set of rules, from another WTO agreement, could be used alternatively, to offer a satisfactory solution. This strategy was used, for example, in the case of *Canada – Periodicals*,[44] where Canada was blamed for

42. WT/DS204/R *Mexico-Telecoms*, n. 26, para. 7.120.
43. WT/DS27/R, AB/R European Communities – Regime for the Importation, Sale and Distribution of Bananas, adopted on 25.9.1997.
44. WT/DS31/R, AB/R Canada – Certain Measures Concerning Periodicals, adopted on 30.7.1997. A similar decision was taken in WT/DS308/R, AB/R Mexico – Tax Measures on Soft Drinks

taxing periodicals printed in the United States but distributed in Canada in access, compared to similar periodicals printed in Canada, thereby discriminating the former to the benefit of the latter. Although the circumstances in this case involved goods (the periodicals) and services (advertising), it seems that an examination revealed lack of relevant commitments concerning trade in services (GATS),[45] and therefore the case concentrated on GATT (trade in goods) commitments. Thus, in this case the existence of GATT supplied an alternative solution to ensure trade liberalization, since GATS did not cover the situation. The Panel explained:

> According to Article 31(1) of the 1969 Vienna Convention on the Law of Treaties ('Vienna Convention'), a treaty must be interpreted in good faith in accordance with the ordinary meaning to be given to the terms of the treaty in their context and in the light of its object and purpose. Furthermore, as the Appellate Body has repeatedly pointed out, 'one of the corollaries of the "general rule of interpretation" in the Vienna Convention is that interpretation must give meaning and effect to all the terms of the treaty. An interpreter is not free to adopt a reading that would result in reducing whole clauses or paragraphs of a treaty to redundancy or inutility.' [Original footnote] The ordinary meaning of the texts of GATT 1994 and GATS as well as Article II:2 of the WTO Agreement, taken together, indicates that obligations under GATT 1994 and GATS can co-exist and that one does not override the other. If the consequences suggested by Canada were intended, there would have been provisions similar to Article XVI:3 of the WTO Agreement or the General Interpretative Note to Annex 1A in order to establish hierarchical order between GATT 1994 and GATS. The absence of such provisions between the two instruments implies that GATT 1994 and GATS are standing on the same plane in the WTO Agreement, without any hierarchical order between the two...
>
> In any event, since Canada admits that in the present case there is no conflict between its obligations under GATS and under GATT 1994..., there is no reason why both GATT and GATS obligations should not apply...[46]

---

and other Beverages, adopted on 24.6.2006, where the tax being the subject of dispute was levied on the commissioning, mediation, agency representation, brokerage, consignment and distribution (namely: services) of soft drinks and other beverages using any sweetener than cane sugar, but the claims concentrated solely on GATT; In WT/DS332/R, AB/R *Brazil – Retreaded Tyres*, n. 23, where a fine-per-unit was imposed by Brazil on the importation, as well as the marketing, transportation, or storage (namely: services) of retreaded tyres. Nevertheless, here, too, the case concentrated on GATT. Another complaint, finally withdrawn, following the same line of reasoning was WT/DS371/R Thailand – Customs and Fiscal Measures on Cigarettes from the Philippines, where the Philippines complained against Thailand's dual license requirement, that tobacco and/or cigarettes retailers hold separate licenses to sell domestic and imported cigarettes. In this case, the claims also concentrated on GATT, despite the involvement of services suppliers: the retailers, suffering from this practice.

45. Indeed, one of Canada's defence arguments was that it did not include any GATS commitments on advertising services (WT/DS31/R, n. 44, Panel report, para. 5.14). In Canada's view, restrictions on advertising could not have been considered as violating Art. III:4 of GATT.

46. WT/DS31/R n. 44, paras 5.17–5.19.

This approach was supported by the Appellate Body in *EC – Bananas III*, where the EC made an attempt to bring up the same claim.[47]

3.6.2.2 Means of Interpretation

Since the disciplines in the different WTO agreements draw from the same source, sometimes agreements such as the TBT and SPS, as well as the specific voluntary Annexes to GATS and the sector-specific disciplines developed for the accountancy sector are turned to in the process of interpretation of similar GATS provisions. However, the different context of each such agreement should be always taken into account in doing so, to prevent an automatic analogy between the compared agreements.

3.6.2.3 GATS-GATT Relationship

GATT-GATS link is a private case of the former analysis. However, it is addressed separately due to the decisive importance of GATT as the basic agreement of the WTO system and due to the close link between the two agreements. This link is relevant in two possible contexts: one – where there is an *overlapping scope of application* of the two agreements on the same situation, involving trade in goods as well as trade in services.[48] The second context is the use of GATT as an *ancillary* interpretative instrument for the understanding of ambiguous GATS provisions or expressions. 'Negotiators did not pay particular attention to the relationship between GATT and GATS, since the two agreements were not negotiated and concluded at the same time.'[49] Thus, while the WTO agreements which are included in Annex 1A to the WTO agreement are explicitly considered *lex specialis* with respect to GATT, and thus, in case of a conflict between them and GATT, will be examined by the WTO adjudicating bodies first, there is no such hierarchy with regard to GATS, which is included in Annex 1B of the WTO Agreement.[50]

47. WT/DS27/AB/R n. 43, para. 221.
48. This scenario had already occurred in some GATS cases. In WT/DS363/AB/R *China – Publications and Audiovisual Products*, n. 8, the Appellate Body, citing two former cases where this situation occurred: WT/DS27/AB/R *EC-Bananas III*, n. 43, and WT/DS31/AB/R *Canada-Periodicals*, n. 44, noted 'that a measure could be simultaneously subject to the obligations relating to trade in goods under GATT 1994 and to obligations relating to trade in services under the GATS'. It was further noted that such measures include those involving 'a service relating to a particular good or a service supplied in conjunction with a particular good'. Note 6, Appellate Body report, para. 193. Such a situation may further occur in respect of future disciplines concerning foreign direct investment policy and to movement of natural persons, both referring to trade in goods and in services. See: G. Feketekuty, 'Setting the Agenda for the Next Round of Negotiations on Trade in Services', in J.S. Schott (ed.), *Launching New Global Trade Talks: an Action Agenda*, Institute for International Economics (US) (1998), 91, 101–103.
49. P. Delimatsis, *International Trade in Services and Domestic Regulations – Necessity, Transparency and Regulatory Diversity*, Oxford University Press (2007), 13.
50. P. Delimatsis, n. 49, 15. See detailed analysis of the case law, leading to this conclusion, *ibid.*, 15–19.

Historically, GATS stems from GATT tradition that was developed through almost fifty years of its existence, until 1994. GATS phrasing and legal norms are inspired by the phrasing and legal norms of GATT. GATS phrasing uses many expressions that developed in GATT. It may be assumed, that this is a result of a deliberate policy, driven by three considerations: Firstly, the creation of a 'codified' system of agreements, reflecting a similar perception and a similar language. Secondly, GATS drafters preferred to rely on an almost fifty years of interpretative experience of GATT provisions and expressions, than to create a totally new terminology. Thirdly, the Uruguay Round agreements, including GATS, were designed to reflect continuity, that contributes to their certainty and predictability.

This may be the reason behind the Appellate Body's approach that the jurisprudence interpreting a concept in one WTO agreement may be relevant for the interpretation of the same concept in another WTO agreement, at least where the relevant provision uses a similar language.[51] In *EC – Bananas III* the Appellate Body stressed that reference to GATT while addressing GATS claims should be made only where the obligations are of the same type.[52]

However, it should not be forgotten, that GATS created a *new* legal context. This fact should be taken into account in its legal interpretation. It means that an interpretation of an expression used in GATT and in GATS, developed in GATT context, *cannot* be adopted *automatically* to GATS context. It should be thoroughly examined first, to see whether the different context created by GATS conclusion, dictates a different meaning from the same expression in GATT. Moreover, it should be remembered that the conclusion of the Uruguay Round agreements, in 1994, created a *new context* for the interpretation of *GATT 1994*, compared to that of the former GATT 1947. This consideration should be taken into account while relying on GATT 1947 provisions and jurisprudence as *interpretative* instruments. In effect, GATT jurisprudence reflects changes in the interpretation of certain provisions since 1995. Some of these changes would be addressed in this book.

Another error may occur regarding the necessity to analyse the facts of a given case according to the relevant agreement. In *Canada – Autos* an example to such an error occurred, as the Panel, examining the application of the MFN principle in GATS Article II (non-discrimination among services and service suppliers from different origins – see Chapter 6), concentrated on the affect of the measures involved on goods, determining that discrimination occurred in terms of the services and service suppliers involved as well, without thoroughly examining the elements of GATS provision. The Appellate Body said:

> Clearly, here the Panel is confusing the application of the import duty exemption to manufacturers with its possible effect on wholesalers. In our view, *the Panel has conducted a 'goods' analysis* of this measure, and has simply

51. This determination referred to the concept of 'no less favourable treatment' (see Ch. 8): Appellate Body report WT/DS176/AB/R US – Section 211, n. 19, para. 242, cited with approval in Panel report WT/DS291,292,293/R *EC – GMOs*, n. 23, para. 7.2392.
52. WT/DS27/AB/R, n. 43, para. 231.

> extrapolated its analysis of how the import duty exemption affects manufacturers to wholesale trade service suppliers of motor vehicles. The Panel surmised, *without analyzing the effect of the measure on wholesalers as service suppliers*, that the import duty exemption, granted to a limited number of manufacturers, ipso facto affects conditions of competition among wholesalers in their capacity as service suppliers. As we stated earlier in respect of whether the measure at issue 'affects trade in services', the Panel failed to demonstrate how the import duty exemption granted to certain manufacturers, but not to other manufacturers, affects the supply of wholesale trade services and the suppliers of wholesale trade services of motor vehicles. In reaching its conclusions under Article II:1 of the GATS, the Panel has neither assessed the relevant facts – we see no analysis of any evidence relating to the supply of wholesale trade services of motor vehicles – nor has it interpreted Article II of the GATS and applied that interpretation to the facts it found.[53] [Emphasis added].

3.6.3 'Any Relevant Rules of International Law'

The interpretation of this expression is disputed by commentators,[54] since it is not quite clear whether it should be understood as referring only to those rules of international law which are legally binding on *all* WTO Members (which would effectively preclude most of these rules from being taken into account), or only to rules of international law which are legally binding on the parties to the dispute, or rather to international law rules which only reflect the 'common intentions' of the parties to the agreement.

3.7 SUPPLEMENTARY MEANS

Yet a *third layer* of context, although not defined as such by the Vienna Convention, is to be found in Article 32, referring to 'supplementary means of interpretation', which are even more remote from the text than the items included in Article 31:3 of the Convention. The difference between 'context' and 'supplementary means' is explained in the ILC Commentary on the Draft Vienna Convention[55] as meant to focus treaty interpretation on

> the elucidation of the meaning of the text rather than an investigation *ab initio* of the supposed intentions of the parties . . . The word supplementary emphasizes that article [32] does not provide for alternative, autonomous, means of

53. WT/DS139,142/AB/R *Canada – Autos*, n. 4, Appellate Body report, para, 181.
54. J. Pauwelyn, 'The Role of Public International Law in the WTO: How Far Can We Go?', *95 American Journal of International Law* (2001), 535; J. Meltzer, 'Comment: Interpreting the WTO Agreements – A Commentary on Professor Pauwelyn's Approach', *25 Michigan Journal of International Law* (2004), 917, 919; J. Pauwelyn, a reply to J. Meltzer, *ibid.*, 924.
55. *Yearbook of the International law Commission (1966)*, vol. II, 223, <http://untreaty.un.org>.

> interpretation but only for means to aid the interpretation governed by the principles contained in article [31].

The *US – Gambling* case reflects a disagreement between the Panel and Appellate Body about the classification, according to these distinctions, of two Secretariat documents that were used by the Members to shape their schedules of specific commitments: W/120 entitled 'services classification list' and the 1993 Scheduling Guidelines (see details in Chapter 7). While the Panel thought that these documents were part of GATS *'context'*, according to Article 31:2(a) of the Vienna Convention, the Appellate body reiterated that they are *supplementary means of interpretation* under Article 32(a) of the Vienna Convention.[56] While in this case this dispute did not bear any practical implications, this might not be the case in future disputes. The Appellate Body's approach was criticized by one commentator to be 'excessively formalistic', reiterating that it should have gone beyond the formal features of these documents to see whether they 'constitute evidence of an underlying, albeit more limited in scope, consensus among parties that had emerged during negotiations', to follow the lines of these documents to achieve more clarity and uniformity in the drafting of specific commitments.[57]

In *Mexico – Telecoms* the Panel used three supplementary means to support the 'ordinary meaning' interpretation of the introductory heading to Mexico's schedule: the Draft Model schedule, the related Note by the Chairman and the Scheduling Guidelines.[58]

In *China – Publications and Audiovisual Products* the Appellate Body noted:

> The elements to be examined under Article 32 are distinct from those to be analyzed under Article 31, but it is the same elements that are examined under Article 32 irrespective of the outcome of the Article 31 analysis. Instead, what may differ, depending on the results of the application of Article 31, is the *weight* that will be attributed to the elements analyzed under Article 32.[59] [Emphasis added].

3.7.1 Preparatory Work

Article 32 of the Vienna Convention provides for the use of supplementary means, such as the preparatory work, when the interpretation according to Article 31

56. This approach seems to be supported by the practical analysis of the Panel in WT/DS204/R *Mexico – Telecoms*, n. 26, paras 7.43–7.44.
57. F. Ortino, n. 5, 128.
58. WT/DS204/R *Mexico-Telecoms*, n. 26, paras 7.53–7.72, referring to the following supplementary documents: Draft Model Schedule of Commitments on Basic Telecommunications, Informal Note by the Secretariat, Job No. 1131, 12.4.1995; S/GBT/W/2/Rev.1 Note for Scheduling Basic Telecommunications Services Commitments, Note by the Chairman, 16.1.1997; S/L/92 Guidelines for the Scheduling of specific Commitments under the General Agreement on Trade in Services (GATS) adopted on 23.3.2001, 28.3.2001.
59. WT/DS363/AB/R, n. 8, para. 403.

leaves the meaning ambiguous or obscure, or leads to a result which is manifestly absurd or unreasonable.

There are many records reflecting the preparatory work that has been done before GATS conclusion that may help to understand the intentions and motives behind it. In addition, much work is done in committees and working groups functioning under the WTO auspices since GATS conclusion. This work, which is also documented, should not be overlooked, because in many cases it reveals the shortcomings of the existing agreements, as well as the different options weighed and/or rejected by the representatives of the Members.

Yet another source of preparatory work is the discussions and the Members' suggestions in the framework of the Doha Round, also reflecting the shortcomings of the existing agreement and the thoughts and ideas regarding its future improvement.

3.8 BROADER POLICY CONSIDERATIONS

3.8.1 The International Arena: The Hidden Layer of Interpretative Context

A *fourth layer*, which is not explicitly mentioned in the Vienna Convention or explicitly admitted to affect interpreters' positions, but which is always in the background of interpretation of international agreements, consists of broader policy considerations referring to the general international arena.

GATS is an international agreement among countries. This fact affects its interpretation. Agreements among countries are different from agreements among private parties. Their goals are different: affecting the general international terms, rather than promoting a certain transaction between private parties. GATS was concluded to affect the terms of trade in services in the international arena. It reflects a long-term arrangement, not an ad hoc deal. It is constructed as a framework agreement, the contents of which develop in a dynamic process, reflecting progress of thinking, as well as of the reality. The interpretation of GATS provisions has to reflect considerations stemming from its essence and unique characteristics. Any interpretation of GATS provisions cannot concentrate only on the pragmatic solution of a current dispute. It has to consider, *inter alia*, the possible implications of a chosen interpretation on the international trade arena, and on the purposes that the WTO agreements intend to promote, including:

- Other global aspects of life, for example, the environment, labour conditions.
- The domestic sovereign power of the Members, and as a result – their willingness to follow and deepen their commitments according to the agreement.
- The interests of developing and least developed GATS Members, who may find it more difficult than other Members to follow high standards of

liberalization, and the indirect interest of developed Members to encourage them, nevertheless, to participate in this global process. It should be noted, that this group already encompasses more than two thirds of the WTO Members.[60]

In the careful weigh of such considerations and sensitivities lies the key for GATS long life and success. The WTO adjudicating bodies, which are in charge of GATS interpretation, should be careful not to surrender to a short-term temptation to overlook one or more of these considerations in exercising their power, because such an imbalanced approach could undermine the enhancement of GATS purposes or may even threaten its very existence, in the long run.

3.8.2 Other International Organizations

The WTO is one of many existing international organizations. The clear-cut division of authorities and power that existed among the economic organizations established after World War II, described in the first chapter, was blurred with time. Thus, the OECD offers, nowadays, legal instruments to regulate investments, financial services and other economic fields related to trade in goods and services. The World Bank and the IMF produce reports on world trade statistics and are involved in the shaping of macro-economic policies. Other international organizations may also have overlapping or interfacing powers and responsibilities: the International Labour Organization (ILO) is in charge of labour conditions. The WIPO is in charge of intellectual property rights. The UN engages in certain economic and trade affairs. Accordingly, the WTO has to find its way, pronouncing its unique voice, in this multi-organizational labyrinth.

3.8.2.1 Inter-organizational Cooperation for the Achievement of Common Goals

In GATS context, there are many overlapping subjects, or at least subjects linked to the authority of another organization. Thus, for example, recognition of professional diplomas could be of interest to the ILO, the treatment of developing countries could be of interest to United Nations Conference on Trade and Development (UNCTAD), the encouragement of Members to adopt international standards developed by other international organizations, embodied in some GATS provisions, may be of interest to these respective organizations. In many cases, cooperation between or among international organizations could promote the achievement of a mutual goal better than an act solely in GATS framework. One successful example is the collaboration between international organizations to collect and analyse statistical data on trade in services (see Chapter 2). Indeed, some of GATS

60. <www.wto.org>.

provisions explicitly provide for such collaboration. Beyond this cooperation, GATS jurisprudence should take into consideration, the activities of other international organizations in its jurisprudence, whether directly, in cases where the Members are guided by the agreement itself to take consideration of international standards, or indirectly, as a background and policy consideration, taking into account the general global treatment of the matter at issue, and the specific role of GATS in the general picture.

3.8.2.2 Other International Organizations as Alternative Frameworks

In current reality, each international organization has to fight for its place, demonstrating a unique contribution to the global economy. Furthermore, each organization depends on the willingness of its Members to continue to support its activity by obeying its rules, participating in its activities and contributing financially to keep it functioning. Any interpretation of the rules and authorities set forth by the WTO agreements, including GATS, has to take this consideration into account. A too extreme, unacceptable approach by its adjudicating bodies could create an antagonistic reaction by the Members, thereby endangering the very existence of this framework. The Members may opt for possible alternative frameworks, suggesting other, less constraining types of solutions, like the soft law, promoted by the OECD, for instance.

In addition to other organizations GATS also suffers, to a certain extent, competition from the alternative framework of economic integration agreements (see Chapter 10).

3.8.2.3 Other International Organizations as Complementary Frameworks

On the other hand, GATS development and interpretation may be approached as a complementary instrument for the activities of other international organizations for the promotion of a common goal. Besides inter-organizational cooperation, addressed above, such a complementary effect may be achieved through conscious interpretation of GATS provisions, aware of the contents and scope of application of other international agreements or arrangements, covering the same field.

3.8.3 GATS: A WTO Agreement

GATS is part of the WTO framework, therefore being subject to its institutions and administration: any decision concerning the modification of its wording is subject to a decision by the Council of Ministers; the WTO Secretariat is responsible for its administration; and the WTO adjudicating bodies are responsible for its legal interpretation and analysis. The DSB (Dispute Settlement Body) is responsible for the approval and enforcement of any dispute settlement decision concerning GATS.

Besides the institutional aspect, GATS interpretation draws from the general spirit, purpose and policy of the WTO. The unique character of this organization, which is combined of, and lead, by Members and reflects their different, as well as common, interests, should be taken into account in its interpretation.

3.8.3.1 The WTO: A Politically Motivated Organization

The WTO is a politically motivated organization. Its decision-making organs are political organs, combined of political representatives of the Members. Its political character dictates the flexibility of its provisions, gained *inter alia* by their vagueness. This flexibility leaves some room for manoeuvring, in order to balance between or among the different interests involved.

Since its establishment in 1995 (or rather since the conclusion of GATT 1947), the WTO is torn between two major groups of interests: protectionism and liberalism. This conflict was reflected in GATS negotiations and drafting, as explained in Chapter 1. These two conflicting tendencies are influenced, to some extent, by global economic fluctuations between periods of prosperity and slow down. Liberalization of international trade in services raises many policy considerations that are relevant to the gap between these two conflicting views, referring, *inter alia*, to short- and long-term service suppliers' immigration, having social and economic implications; to the control over strategic services industries; to the balance between domestic and international policies; to financial implications of policies applied.

Any interpretation of GATS provisions should therefore take a cautious attitude, striving to understand the delicate balance of such political interests reflected by its chosen wording.

3.9 A DYNAMIC AGREEMENT IN A CHANGING REALITY

Finally, it should be remembered that GATS is a dynamic agreement in a changing world, driven by rapid technological changes. This fact may impose on GATS drafters and interpreters huge challenges in the future. They may have to deal with a rapidly changing reality that would force them to adapt GATS disciplines to this reality. To a certain extent, the flexibility of GATS provisions may prove an advantage, allowing for flexible interpretation suggesting some adaptation of the provisions to the changes occurring. In this sense, GATS interpreters should not fear deviating from former interpretation to achieve this goal, since the power of an agreement like GATS would be measured, *inter alia*, in its relevance in a changing world. However, this flexibility should be limited by GATS wording (that should not be overlooked, according to the Vienna Convention) and there may be cases where GATS drafters might be forced to interfere, reacting to the changing reality by modifying the provisions of the agreement.

3.10 CONCLUSION

This chapter presented some of the considerations that should be taken into account for GATS interpretation. The general customary interpretation rules stem from the Vienna Convention on the Law of Treaties, 1969, that provides taking into consideration, the text and context of the interpreted treaty, and exercise interpretation in good faith. GATS text includes many vague expressions, stemming from the unique character typical to the WTO agreements in general, and from their political context. Therefore, cautious reference to the object and purpose, as well as to the context, is decisive for GATS interpretation.

Part 2
GATS in Details

Chapter 4
GATS Scope of Application

4.1 GATS PROVISION

GATS aims at imposing market-based disciplines on the distribution of services. 'Under the GATS, almost everything is conceived of as a commodity that can be bough and sold on the market . . . The commodifying logic of the market-based discipline is operationalized by the legally enforceable terms of the agreement.'[1]

This perception is supported by the broad scope of application of GATS, determined by Article I thereof.[2] Article I:1 Provides:

This Agreement applies to measures by Members affecting trade in services.

4.1.1 The Considerations behind Drafting

GATS drafters chose a very broad and flexible definition in order to achieve the Agreement's maximal scope of application, thus potentially facilitating the broadest possible liberalization of international trade in services.

The wide diversity and complexity stemming from the unique characteristics of trade in services, reflected in GATS (see Chapter 1) make the scene of international trade in services much more elaborated compared to the scene of

---

1. T. Lawson-Remer, 'Values Under Siege: NAFTA, GATS, and the Propertization of Resources', *NYU 14 Environmental Law Journal* (2006), 481, 488–490. According to the author, GATS, as other international trade agreements, reflects the idea of 'propertization' of resources, which is a process of increasing the legally protected ownership rights of private economic actors, although it is admitted that in effect this notion is highly contested at present, and therefore 'GATS has a loud bark but a limited legal bite'. *Ibid.*, 494, <http://papers.ssrn.com>.
2. For the historic evolution of this Article see: R. Worfrum, P.T. Stoll & C. Feinäugle (eds), *WTO – Trade in Services*, Max Planck Commentaries on World Trade Law, Martinus Mijnhoff Publishers, Leiden, Boston (2008), 35–36. (Hereby: 'GATS commentary').

international trade in goods. This is another reason why GATS drafters could not do with a relatively simpler definition for its scope of application, compared to GATT.[3]

However, a distinction should be drawn between the *potential scope* of GATS, provided for by Article I:1 thereof, and the *actual coverage* thereof, which is subject to different exceptions and exemptions, as well as to the specific commitments undertaken by Members, therefore being much narrower.[4]

4.2 GATS ARTICLE I:1 COVERAGE: BEFORE ANY SUBSTANTIVE ASSESSMENT

In *Canada – Autos* the Panel noted that the fulfilment of GATS Article I:1 requirements shall be determined subject to an assessment of whether a substantive breach of the agreement by the complainant occurred.

This approach was rejected by the Appellate Body, providing:

> The fundamental structure and logic of Article I:1, in relation to the rest of the GATS, require that determination of whether a measure is, in fact, covered by the GATS must be made *before the consistency of that measure with any substantive obligation of the GATS can be assessed.*[5] [Emphasis added].

Therefore, a threshold question that must be addressed in determining whether or not GATS is applicable to the measures identified in each dispute as the subject of that dispute is whether this measure 'affects trade in services' within the meaning of Article I:1 of GATS. This threshold question must be addressed regardless of the specific Article of GATS that is being invoked in support of a claim concerning a GATS violation.[6]

4.3 LEGAL ANALYSIS

Article I:1 of GATS includes three elements that should be analysed:

(1) Measures
(2) By Members
(3) Affecting trade in services.

3. GATT Arts I (MFN) and III (National Treatment) apply to import duties, taxes, charges and quantitative restrictions on the import of goods.
4. W. Zdouc, *Legal Problems Arising Under the General Agreement on Trade in Services – Comparative Analysis of GATS and GATT*, dissertation der Universität St. Gallen (2002), 95, 97; A. Jara & M.D.C. Domingez, 'Liberalization of Trade in Services and Trade Negotiations', *40 Journal of World Trade* (2006), 113, 120.
5. WT/DS139,142/R, AB/R Canada – Certain Measures Affecting the Automotive Industry, adopted on 19.1.2000, Appellate Body report, para. 181.
6. See, for example, WT/DS285/R, AB/R United States – Measures Affecting the Cross-Border Supply of Gambling and Betting Services, adopted on 22.5.2007, Panel report, para. 6.250.

4.3.1 MEASURES

The term 'Measure' is defined in Article XXVII(a) of GATS:

> 'Measure' means any measure by a Member, whether in the form of law, regulation, rule, procedure, decision, administrative action or any other form.

This is an open, indicative definition that could include legislative or administrative measures, fiscal activities, promotional or informational activities by governments and the implementation of international agreements, standards or decisions of international bodies through national measures, as well as a signature on an international agreement, for example, bilateral investment agreement.[7] It should be noted, that such measures need not be in a written form.[8]

Despite the general wording 'or any other form', it seems from the context that measures taken by private parties, which where not taken in the course of delegation of governmental powers, or at least encouraged or supported by a government, would be excluded from the scope of GATS, even if they affect international trade in services.[9]

In addition, it seems that a 'measure' 'must be obligatory, in the sense that it is not only authorizing, but requiring a government to act or that it is not only recommending private behaviour but giving an incentive or disincentive to act in a certain way'.[10]

It should be further noted that aside from the general, potential application, of GATS to a broad scope of 'measures', for the purpose of examination of application of *specific* GATS provisions to a 'measure', the adjudicating bodies must determine, first, 'the applicability of the provisions invoked by the complaining party as the basis for its claims with respect to the measures at issue'.[11]

4.3.2 'WHETHER IN THE FORM OF LAW, REGULATION, RULE, PROCEDURE, DECISION, ADMINISTRATIVE ACTION OR ANY OTHER FORM'

The wording of GATS Article XXVII(a) explicitly refers not only to substantive measures, but also to measures of administrative character. This is to stress that even such measures could cause barriers to international trade in services. The words 'any other form' may imply that not only active, but also passive

7. F. Ortino, 'The Principle on Non-Discrimination and its Exceptions in the GATS: Selected Legal Issues', *King's College London* (2006), 21, <http://papers.ssrn.com>.
8. WT/DS363/R, AB/R China – Measures Affecting Trading Rights and Distribution Services for Certain Publications and Audiovisual Entertainment Products, adopted on 19.1.2010, Panel report para. 7.1689.
9. M. Krajewski, *National Regulation and Trade Liberalization in Services*, Kluwer Law International (2003), 64–65.
10. GATS commentary, n. 2, 544.
11. WT/DS363/R *China – Publications and Audiovisual Products*, n. 8, Panel report para. 7.1619.

behaviour or deliberate omission may be considered as a 'measure'.[12] Nevertheless, a measure must be defined and specified. In *US – Gambling* it was determined that a general reference to a 'total prohibition', without specifying the measures causing to it, will not do.[13]

It seems that this explicit reference to such measures in GATS is the result of the interpretative experience gained concerning GATT provisions.

4.3.3 The Interpretation of 'Measure' in Article 3.3 DSU

In *China – Publications and Audiovisual Products*, the term 'measures' in the context of Article 3.3 DSU was examined. This provision subjects to review under the DSU, only 'measures taken by another Member'. In that case, China argued that certain administrative instruments challenged by the United States as violating GATT and GATS could not serve as legal basis for any administrative act and thus were not subject to a DSU review. Although China did not explicitly argue that these instruments are not 'measures' under Article 3.3 DSU, the Panel examined this question, coming to a conclusion that some of these instruments were 'measures' and some were not. Doing so, the Panel determined some rules that seem applicable in GATS context as well:

(a) The Panel noted, first, that '[a] determination of whether something is a "measure" must be based on the content and substance of the instrument, and not merely on its form and nomenclature'.[14]
(b) The Panel set forth a double test to determine whether an administrative instrument is a 'measure':
   (i) Is the instrument an act taken by the organs of the state, and thus attributable to that state?
   (ii) If the answer to (i) is affirmative, it should be determined whether this instrument sets forth rules and norms that are intended to have general and prospective application.[15]
(c) Based on the *US – Oil Country Tubular Goods Sunset Reviews*[16] jurisprudence, the Panel in *China – Publications and Audiovisual Products* determined that a *non-binding* internal government document that served as guideline for the formulation of implementation procedures by the competent authorities ('several opinions'), is a 'measure'.[17]

12. Where the omission is not deliberate, for example, backed by a government decision, but merely stems from slow work of the administration, it might be difficult to detect a 'measure': GATS commentary, n. 2, 55.
13. WT/DS285/R *US – Gambling*, n. 6, Panel report, paras 6.152–6.185; WT/DS285/AB/R Appellate Body report 116–126.
14. WT/DS363/R *China – Publications and Audiovisual Products*, n. 8, Panel report para. 7.172.
15. *Ibid.*, Panel report paras 7.189–7.190, 7.210–7.211, 7.222–7.225.
16. WT/DS286/R, AB/R United States – Sunset review of Anti Dumping Measures on Oil Country Tubular Goods from Argentina, adopted on 17.12.2004.
17. WT/DS363/R *China – Publications and Audiovisual Products*, n. 8, Panel report para. 7.198.

Applying these tests to the instruments subject to its review, the Panel in *China – Publications and Audiovisual Products* came to the conclusion that all these instruments fulfil the first test, that is, attributable to China.[18] Turning to the second test, the Panel distinguished between instruments that *have a functional life of their own, that 'do something concrete, independently of any other instruments'* and therefore constitute 'measures'[19] (since they 'set forth rules and norms that are intended to have general and prospective application'), and instruments that do not fulfil this requirement, since they merely summarize legal requirements which are sourced in other instruments, thus not fulfilling this latter requirement and not constituting 'measures'.[20]

4.3.4 GATT Experience

GATT Article III:4 (national treatment), provides that imported goods shall be entitled to treatment no less favourable compared to like domestic goods, 'in respect of all laws, regulations and requirements affecting their internal sale, offering for sale, purchase, transportation, distribution or use'. In this context, the terms 'laws, regulations and requirements' were broadly interpreted by GATT 1947 dispute settlement Panels. 'Regulations' were interpreted to include 'mandatory rules applying across-the-board'. 'Requirements' were interpreted to 'encompass commitments entered into on a voluntary basis by individual firms as a condition to obtaining an advantage or a government action involving a demand, request or imposition of a condition'.[21] This category was also interpreted to include requirements having a procedural nature. It was explained that enforcement procedures should not be detached from substantial law; otherwise, Members could have avoided the enforcement of substantial law that fulfills the non-discrimination standard, by using less favourable procedural treatment to imported, compared to like domestic products, thus undermining the purpose of this provision. It was further determined, that the laws, regulations or requirements subject to the non-discrimination standard may include such measures that are not directly determined by the government, as well as non-mandatory, voluntary requirements undertaken by an enterprise.[22] The national treatment non-discrimination standard is one of GATT disciplines that were developed in order to ensure the abolition of barriers to trade in goods. Therefore, generally speaking, the interpretation

18. *Ibid.*, Panel report paras 7.189, 7.210, 7.222.
19. *Ibid.*, Panel report paras 7.198, 7.214–7.215.
20. *Ibid.*, Panel report paras 7.211–7.215.
21. *Ibid.*, Panel report para. 7.1448.
22. See L/6439, US – Section 337 of the Tariff Act of 1930, adopted on 7.11.1989, 36S/345, 385-6, para. 5.10; Japan – Trade in Semi Conductors, adopted on 4.5.1988, BIDS 35S/116, para. 109; L/6657 EEC – Regulation on Imports of Parts and Components, adopted on 16.5.1990, 37S/132, para. 5.20; WT/DS31/R Canada – Certain Measures Concerning Periodicals, adopted on 30.7.1997, paras 5.35–5.37.

attributing to it a broad scope of application serves a similar purpose to the attribution of a broad scope of application to GATS disciplines. It should be noted that unlike the national treatment discipline in GATS, the scope of application of which is limited by the Members' schedules of specific commitments, in GATT, the national treatment discipline is unconditional, thus having the broadest possible scope of application. Therefore, the same interpretation for these terms could be adopted, in principle, in the context of GATS, but the different scope of application of each GATS provision in which the word 'measure' is included will be affected not only by the broad scope of this word, but also by other elements. Thus, for example, the scope of the national treatment provision in GATS will be affected not only by the broad perception of 'measures' but also by the narrowing effect of specific commitments to which it is subject.

4.3.5 Specific Groups of Measures

4.3.5.1 Five Categories Examined by the Sub-Committee for Trade in Services

During the Uruguay Round, five categories of measures were examined by the sub-committee for trade in services in 1994 to determine whether they fall within the scope of GATS:

- *Measures relating to judicial and administrative assistance* between government authorities, including those pursuant to international agreements on such matters – it was agreed that GATS provisions/Article II would not apply to such measures.[23]
- *Measures relating to the entry and stay of natural persons*, including those pursuant to international agreements on labour mobility – the sub-committee discussed on what basis a distinction between 'temporary' and 'permanent' residency and employment should be made. It ultimately decided that the commitments set out in the individual countries' schedules were sufficiently clear, so that there was no need for further multilateral work on this issue.[24]

The other three categories of measures, for which *a-priori* no agreement was achieved, were: *measures relating to social security*, including those pursuant to bilateral agreements on the avoidance of double contributions to, and/or double benefits from social security systems; *measures relating to the settlement of disputes* pursuant to bilateral investment protection agreements dispute; and *measures*

23. MTN.GNS/W/177/Rev.1/Add.1 Uruguay Round – Group of Negotiations on Services – Issues Relating to the Scope of the General Agreement on Trade in Services – Note by the Secretariat – Addendum, 6.12.1993, <http://docsonline.wto.org>.
24. S/C/M/1, Council for Trade in Services – Report of the Meeting Held on 1 Mar. 1995 – Note by the Secretariat, 22.3.1995, para. 14.

relating to the entry and temporary stay of natural persons pursuant to certain bilateral agreements.[25]

4.3.5.2 Electronic Commerce

The intangible nature of electronic commerce makes it difficult to follow the transactions made. Such transactions could involve trade in personal services, for example, the delivery of a reasoned professional opinion, or rather, trade in public services, for example, telecommunication services. It could also involve a sale of goods by electronic means, where such electronic delivery could be considered a service facilitating the sale of goods. It is possible, and even relatively easy, to apply barriers to such trade. The treatment of electronic commerce in GATS legal framework was examined according to a work program adopted by the Council for Trade in Services in 1998.[26] Agreement was achieved as to the following basic principles:

> It was the general view that the electronic delivery of services falls within the scope of the GATS, and that electronic delivery can take place under any of the four modes of supply. Measures affecting the electronic delivery of services are measures affecting trade in services in the sense of Article I of the GATS and are therefore covered by GATS obligations. It was also the general view that the GATS is technologically neutral in the sense that it does not contain any provisions that distinguish between the different technological means through which a service may be supplied.

Beyond these basic principles, many interesting questions were raised concerning the application of GATS rules to this specific manner of commerce, but no practical conclusions followed.[27]

4.3.5.3 Can a Practice Be Considered 'A Measure'?

This question may arise due to the words 'any other form'. In *US – Gambling* the Panel expressed its opinion 'that 'practice' can be considered as an autonomous measure that can be challenged in and of itself or it can be used to support an interpretation of a specific law that is challenged "as such"'. This determination was criticized by the Appellate Body in that case, which noted that since no such practice was at issue, this was an *obiter dictum.* Accordingly, the Appellate Body abstained from ruling on this point, but nevertheless stressed its disagreement with the Panel's understanding of its previous decisions, contending: '[t]he Appellate

---

25. MTN.GNS/W/177/Rev.1, n. 23; S/C/W/1 First Meeting of the Council for Trade in Services – Note by the Secretariat, 15.2.1995, 2–3.
26. WT/L/274 Work Program on Electronic Commerce Adopted by the Council for Trade in Services in 25.9.1998, paras 1–2.
27. WT/L/274, n. 26; S/C/M/34 Report of the Meeting Held in 22 and 23 Mar. 1999 – Note by the Secretariat, 16.4.1999, para. A; S/L/74 Work Program on Electronic Commerce – progress report to the general council, 27.7.1999.

Body has not, to date, pronounced upon the issue of whether "practice" may be challenged, as such, as a "measure" in WTO dispute settlement'.[28]

4.3.6 'Measures by Members'

4.3.6.1 GATS Provision

Article I:3(a) of GATS provides:

> 'Measures by members' means measures taken by:
> (i) Central, regional or local governments and authorities;
> (ii) Non-governmental bodies in the exercise of powers delegated by central, regional or local governments and authorities.

The parties to GATS are its Members. GATS applies to measures undertaken by them, including measures taken by organs of the state and executive branches thereof.[29] Thus, the subject of *US – Gambling* was federal and state measures that discriminated foreign service suppliers of internet gambling services, compared to like domestic services suppliers. The Appellate Body in this case stressed that 'a nexus must exist between the responding Member and the "measure", such that the "measure" – whether an act or omission – must be "attributable" to that Member'.[30]

GATS cannot apply to measures taken by states which are not WTO Members, neither to trade barriers applied by private parties; for example, a refusal by a private firm to hire individual service suppliers from a certain Member.

According to this provision, the government of a Member shall be held responsible for barriers to international trade in services infringing the agreement, applied by lower levels of government. The government of a Member shall also be held responsible for measures infringing GATS provisions, taken by non-governmental bodies, exercising governmental authorities delegated to them. Such bodies could be associations, institutions or other entities, regardless of their legal constitution, if governmental powers were delegated to them,[31] for example, private service suppliers collecting taxes for a governmental authority or conducting an administrative process for it. Such delegation of powers may indirectly restrict the number of service suppliers who may act in the market. Thus, in *China – Publications and Audiovisual Products*, the Chinese government delegated the powers to conduct 'content review' of cultural goods to a wholly owned governmental entity, refusing to allow other entities to perform this function.[32]

---

28. WT/DS285/AB/R *US – Gambling*, n. 6, Panel report, para. 6.197, Appellate Body report, paras 131–132.
29. See, for example, *China – Publications and Audiovisual Products*, n. 8, Panel report paras 7.166, 7.198, 7.222.
30. WT/DS285/AB/R *US – Gambling*, n. 6, Appellate Body report, para. 121.
31. Krajewski, n. 9, 63.
32. WT/DS363/R, n. 8, Panel report, paras 7.850–7.911. See also Ch. 9.

The delegation of powers would normally be a formal act. Therefore, measures of self-regulatory bodies, without expressed delegated regulatory powers, should not be considered within the scope of GATS.[33]

This provision, principally based on general international practice,[34] considerably deepens the level of responsibility expected from a Member according to the agreement. However, the government responsibility is not ultimate, but relative. It is subject to two major conditions that diminish the actual burden put on the governments by the same Article, further providing:

> In fulfilling its obligations and commitments under the Agreement, each Member shall take such *reasonable measures as may be available to it* to ensure their observance by regional and local governments and authorities and non-governmental bodies *within its territory*. [Emphasis added].

First, the governments are only responsible to acts by lower levels of government or non-governmental bodies within their territory, namely: acts that are not conducted abroad, outside their territory. In other words, the agreement's disciplines cannot be enforced extra-territorially to lower levels of government.[35]

Second, the governments at stake are not expected to take every possible step to prevent lower government levels or non-governmental bodies from infringing GATS disciplines. They are only expected to take *reasonable* measures available to them. It means that they are not expected to take measures involving an exaggerated extra-administrative effort, or exceptional costs, to achieve this end.

These narrowing standards balance between the interest in deepening the level of GATS disciplines scope of application, on the one hand; while, on the other hand, not subjecting the governments of the Members to an unreasonably high standard of behaviour. It should be noted, though, that reasonability is an objective legal test, usually applied *ex post* by the adjudicating bodies. Thus, a Member will not always be sure how to act *ex ante*.

Closely observed, this provision seems to somewhat deviate from the general international law-rule concerning governments' responsibility to the activity of all branches of power within their jurisdiction. However, it is somewhat balanced read in conjunction with Article 22.9 DSU, providing for the application of compensation and the suspension of obligation, where a Member concerned has not been able to secure the observance of the agreement in its territory.[36]

---

33. M. Krajewski, n. 9, 63. It is further noted there: '[i]f, however, the non-governmental body is merely formally non-governmental, but in fact controlled by the government, it could be argued that the activities of such an organization are in fact measures taken by the government according to the meaning of Art. I:3(a)(i) of the GATS'. According to this logic, one of the elements for which China was held responsible in *China-Publications and Audiovisual Products*, n. 6, was the delegation of the authority to conduct 'content review' of cultural goods only to state-owned enterprises, thus creating an effective monopoly.
34. M. Krajewski, n. 9, 64.
35. This provision was implemented in WT/DS285/R *US – Gambling*, n. 6, Panel report para. 6.252.
36. F. Ortino, 'Regional Trade Agreements and Trade in Services', in *S.* Lester & B. Mercurino (eds), *Bilateral and Regional Trade Agreements: Commentary, Analysis and Case Studies*, Cambridge CPU (2007), 3, n. 11, <http://papers.ssrn.com>.

A practical difficulty underlying this provision stems from the great differences in treatment of different public services in different Members, as the same public service may be supplied in one Member by a government monopoly, while in another Member it is supplied in a free market. The result in terms of this provision would be that GATS disciplines would apply where the government, or governmental bodies, are supplying the service, but would not apply to the same service in another Member, where it is supplied by private market forces.[37]

4.3.6.2 Comparison to GATT Provisions

GATT Article XXIV, dealing *inter alia* with the territorial application of the agreement, provides:

> Each Member shall take such reasonable measures as may be available to it to ensure observance of the provisions of this Agreement by the regional and local governments and authorities within its territories.

This provision, which probably formed a source of inspiration for GATS drafters, provides for the responsibility of the central government to acts of lower government levels, subject to the reasonability and availability standards, and to the limitation of its scope of application to these Members' territories.

4.3.6.2.1 Application to Non-governmental Bodies

GATT Article XXIV:12 does not explicitly attribute to governments, any responsibility to the acts of non-governmental bodies, but rather uses the more general word 'authorities'. It is not clear whether this word covers only official authorities or also non-governmental bodies to which governmental authorities were delegated. In GATS, a clearer phrasing was chosen, relating explicitly to non-governmental authorities, to prevent doubts.

4.3.6.2.2 The Reasonability Standard

Both in GATT and in GATS, the central government's responsibility is subject to the reasonability standard. According to the experience gained in GATT, the Members chose this standard realizing, that they do not always have enforcement power over lower government levels, nevertheless being ready to make their best effort to secure compliance with the agreement's disciplines in these levels.[38]

In GATT 1947 case *Canada – Gold Coins*, Canada suggested that each Member would be entitled to decide for itself what is 'reasonable' according to GATT

37. GATS commentary, n. 2, 59.
38. In this spirit, Austria declared in the preparatory committee meeting in London: 'Where the matter is one solely of action by the State, and our "external powers" laws do not give the Commonwealth authority to act, we would agree to use our best efforts to secure modification or elimination of any practice regarded as discriminatory'. ECPT/C.II/5, 1.

Article XXIV:12. This approach was rejected by the Panel, explaining that such an interpretation may deprive this standard of any substance. The Panel stressed that the only indication to the possible substance of this standard may be drawn from the Interpretative Note to GATT Article III:1, providing:

> The term 'reasonable measures' in the last mentioned paragraph [Article XXIV:12-N.M.] would not require, for example, the repeal of existing national legislation authorizing local governments to impose internal taxes which, although technically inconsistent with the letter of Article III, are not in fact inconsistent with its spirit, if such repeal would result in a serious financial hardship for the local governments or authorities concerned. With regard to taxation by local governments or authorities which is inconsistent with both the letter and spirit of Article III, the term 'reasonable measures' would permit a contracting party to eliminate the inconsistent taxation gradually over a transition period, if abrupt action would create serious administrative and financial difficulties.[39]

The Canadian position was rejected again in GATT 1947 case *Canada – Alcoholic Drinks*,[40] where the Panel determined that the reasonability of a central government shall be finally determined by the Contracting Parties (GATT 1947 equivalent to the current DSB).

In that case, the Panel determined that Canada took reasonable measures to secure compliance of lower-government levels to GATT provisions, as interpreted by it. Unfortunately, the Panel found that Canada's interpretation of GATT obligations was wrong, and the measures taken by the lower government levels to secure their compliance with GATT were unreasonable. This ruling reflects one of the difficulties folded in this provision, in GATT as well as in GATS: the measures taken by a Member to secure compliance of lower government levels with GATT or with GATS, respectively, are derived, in each case, from its interpretation and understanding of its obligations according to the agreement. If it turns out, retrospectively, that such interpretation and understanding were wrong, the sincere efforts taken by the Member involved will not prevent the ruling against it. Motives will not be taken into account.

In the context of GATT 1947, this authority of the central government was viewed as referring mainly to federations.[41] However, the language of GATT as well as of GATS provision does not imply its application only to federal governments. It may also apply to any state having regional and/or local government, as well as to a system of super-national government like that of the EU. In each structure of government, the scope and essence of the central government's

39. L/5863 Canada – Measures Affecting the Sale of Gold Coins, unadopted, dated 17.9.1985, para. 12.30. This Interpretative Note assumes that the central government has the competence to eliminate local taxation which is inconsistent with GATT provisions. Such competence may not always exist.
40. DS17/R Canada – Import, Distribution and Sale of Alcoholic Drinks by Provincial Marketing Agencies, adopted on 18.2.1992, 39S/27.
41. See, for example, L/5863 *Canada – Gold Coins*, n. 39, para. 53.

competence to interfere in the acts of lower levels of government may be different, raising different difficulties of application concerning these provisions, in GATT as well as in GATS.

In GATS, the reasonability standard in this context was not yet addressed by the WTO adjudicating bodies, but it seems that the interpretative approach and difficulties raised in GATT context would be relevant to GATS as well.

4.3.6.2.3 The Conditions for Assuming Central Government Responsibility over Acts of Lower Government Levels

According to the Understanding on the interpretation of GATT Article XXIV:12 from 1994, the acts covered by this Article could be subject to dispute settlement procedures in the WTO. It is clear that such acts cannot be taken directly against lower-government levels or authorities, and therefore they will be taken against the government of the relevant Member. The Understanding does not address the question of whether the central government of the relevant Member acted according to the reasonability and availability requirements or not. Its language allows the invocation the dispute settlement procedures 'in respect of measures affecting its [GATT] observance taken by regional or local governments or authorities within the territory of a Member'.[42] Thus, according to this Understanding, a Member may allegedly be exposed to dispute settlement procedures even if it acted according to the standards required by the provision of GATT Article XXIV. However, since the Understanding interprets GATT provision, it seems that it should be interpreted and applied *subject* to that provision, and not in a manner overriding it.

This difficulty is solved, at least partly, since the Understanding further provides that the relevant Member shall be responsible to 'take such reasonable measures as may be available to it' to ensure observance of the lower-governmental levels and authorities to the DSB decision. 'In cases where it has not been possible to secure such observance', the Understanding allows the application of GATT provisions concerning compensation and suspension of concessions. The Understanding thus suggests a similar arrangement as that provided for by the equivalent GATS provision, balancing between the same interests: on the one hand, subjecting the responsibility of the central government to standards of reasonability and possibility, while, on the other hand, allowing the affected Member to require compensation, where the central government was not able to prevent the adverse effect of acts taken by lower government levels.

4.3.6.2.4 The Same Standard of Behaviour for All Government Levels

In the preparatory discussions for GATT 1947 that took place in Geneva, the United States' representative suggested the application of a relatively

42. Paragraph 14.

lower standard of observance of GATT provisions to lower government levels, stressing:

> It is necessary to distinguish between central or federal governments, which undertake these obligations in *a firm way*, and local authorities, which are *not strictly bound, so to speak*, by the provisions of the Agreement.[43] [Emphasis added].

This double standard notion seems to have been generally rejected both by the language of GATT[44] and by the Understanding, as well as by the WTO adjudicating bodies.[45]

4.3.6.2.5 The Nature of Measures Taken by the Lower Government Levels

In the case of federal government, it was established in GATT 1947 case *Canada – Gold Coins*[46] that according to its drafting history, Article XXIV:12 applies only to such measures by the regional or local government 'which the federal government cannot control because they fall outside its jurisdiction under the constitutional distribution of competence'. The Panel was of the opinion that it should also apply 'in those cases in which the exact distribution of competence still remains to be determined by the competent judicial or political bodies'.

Again, having the opportunity, this GATT 1947 Panel chose a broad interpretation, thus broadening the scope of the application of this provision.

Having said that, it should be noted that in GATS context, there are two possible ways to narrow the scope of lower governmental levels' responsibility according to Article I:3(a)(ii): first, the exemption contained in Article I:3(b) could apply to these authorities, implying that if such an authority supplies a service 'in the exercise of governmental authority' it should be 'carved out' from the relevant specific commitment. In addition, the commitments themselves may be drafted in a manner excluding this service.[47]

43. ECPT/TACPV/19, 32.
44. See, for example, the Interpretative Note to Art. III:1 of GATT; Art. III:4 of GATT.
45. See, for example, in GATT 1947 case DS17/R *Canada – Alcoholic Drinks*, n. 40, the Panel held the central government of Canada responsible for acts conducted by the provincial liquor boards. In GATT 1947 case DS23/R United States – Measures Affecting Alcoholic and Malt Beverages, adopted 19.6.1992, 39S/206 the Panel held the US federal government responsible for measures taken by some States. In both cases, the Panel applied to lower government levels standards similar to those applied to central governments.
46. L/5863, n. 39, paras 53–54.
47. Based on Art. XVI, providing that a government can schedule specific commitments 'on the basis of a regional subdivision or on the basis of its entire territory' and the Scheduling Guidelines indicating that '[w]here commitments do not cover the entire national territory, the entry should describe the geographical scope of measures taken according to Article I:3(a)(i)': M. Cossy, 'Water Services at the WTO', in E. Brown Weiss, L. Boisson de Chazournes & N. Bernasconi-Osterwalder (eds), *Fresh Water and International Economic Law*, Oxford University Press (2005), 117, 138.

4.3.6.2.6 *The Legal Consequences of Central Government Responsibility*

In *Canada – Gold Coins*[48] the Panel determined, that GATT Article XXIV:12 does not limit the *applicability* of the other GATT provisions to local governments, but rather limits the *obligation of federal governments to secure their observance* by local governments. The Panel explained that this provision in fact gives a special right to federal states, without giving an offsetting privilege to unitary states, since it is an exception to the general principle that a party to a treaty may not invoke its internal law as a justification for not performing its treaty obligations. The Panel thus recommended to interpret this provision 'in a way that meets the constitutional difficulties which federal States may have... while minimizing the danger that such difficulties lead to imbalance in the rights and obligations of contracting parties'.

It seems that the same interpretation, due to the same reasoning, could be adopted in GATS context.

4.3.7 Measures by Members, Affecting Trade in Services

4.3.7.1 Distinguishing the Source from the Effect of a Measure

In *US – Gambling*[49] Antigua claimed that different federal and state laws, together with policy statements and other governmental actions, constituted together a 'total prohibition' of the cross-border supply of gambling and betting services. Antigua addressed this 'total prohibition' as 'a measure in and of itself', thus raising the question whether such a 'total prohibition' could constitute a measure to be challenged under WTO law. The Appellate Body rejected this notion, stressing:

> To the extent that a Member's complaint centres [sic] on the effects of an action taken by another Member, the complaint must nevertheless be brought as a challenge to the measure that is the source of the alleged effects.[50]

In other words, the *legal source* for the measure at stake should be specified, and a mere *description* of its effect will not do to initiate a complaint.

The Appellate Body in this case further explained:

> [i]f the 'total prohibition' were a measure, the complaining party could fulfill its obligation to identify the 'specific measure at issue', pursuant to Article 6.2 of the DSU, merely by explicitly mentioning the 'prohibition'. Yet, without knowing the precise source of the 'prohibition', a responding party would not be in a position to prepare adequately its defence, particularly where, as here, it

48. L/5863, n. 39, para. 59.
49. WT/DS285/AB/R, n. 6, paras 116–117.
50. *Ibid.*, para. 123.

is alleged that numerous federal and state laws underline the 'total prohibition'.[51]

Some commentators[52] raise the question of how a violation of a GATS obligation, caused by the cumulative effect of a series of measures, each of which, in and of itself, does not amount to a full prohibition or a violation of a distinct GATS obligation, would be treated. The *China – Publications and Audiovisual Products* Panel report seems to indicate a possible answer to this question. It is true that for each piece of legislation or administrative document, the Panel examined, first, whether it is a 'measure' in the sense of GATS Article 3.3 DSU.[53] However, analyzing their effect in the context of GATT Articles XX[54] and XVII[55] and GATS Article XVII,[56] the Panel accepted, at least in the facts of that case, that a violation of these provisions may be caused by the cumulative effect of more than one measure.

The conclusion seems to be that the Appellate Body positions in *US – Gambling* and in *China – Publications and Audiovisual Products*, taken together, should be understood as requiring the presentation of all relevant legal *sources* of the measures at stake, but at the same time as not ruling out a possible cumulative *effect* of some measures which boils down to a violation of the agreement.

4.3.7.2 Examples of 'Measures'

GATS Article XXXIV(c) states:

> 'measures by Members affecting trade in services' include measures in respect of
>
> (i) the purchase, payment or use of a service,
> (ii) the access to and use of, in connection with the supply of a service, services which are required by those Members to be offered to the public generally;
> (iii) the presence, including commercial presence, of persons of a Member for the supply of a service in the territory of another Member;

---

51. *Ibid.*, para. 125. It should be noted that 'measure' in GATS is interpreted as broader than under 6.2 DSU: GATS commentary, n. 2, 545.
52. D. Irwin & J.H.H. Weiler, 'Measures Affecting the Cross-Border Supply of Gambling and Betting Services', *7 World Trade Review* (2008), 71, 81–82.
53. WT/DS363/R *China – Publications and Audiovisual Products*, n. 8, paras 7.162–7.226.
54. *Ibid.*, para. 7.792. The Panel said:

> In response to a question from the Panel, both parties expressed the view that a measure can be characterized as 'necessary' within the meaning of Article XX *even if it does not achieve the desired objective all by itself.* We see no need to take a position on whether this would be correct in all circumstances. In the specific circumstances facing us, however, we are able to agree with the parties.

55. WT/DS363/R *China – Publications and Audiovisual Products*, n. 8, para. 7.1039, 7.1048.
56. *Ibid.*, para. 7.1430.

The list of measures refers to three potential groups of measures that could be misused as disguised barriers to international trade in services:

4.3.7.2.1 Measures in Respect of the Purchase, Payment or Use of a Service

Measures in respect of the *purchase* of a service could restrict the amount of service activities a certain service supplier is allowed to supply to one customer or their total value; restrict the very ability of customer to acquire a service from a foreign source; or subject such transaction to very burdensome administrative requirements, that would make it less accessible or less worthwhile for the customer. In *EC – Bananas III*[57] the Panel mentioned examples such as licensing requirements,[58] numerical limitations and foreign exchange regulations.

Measures in respect of *payment* for a service could include limitations on the use of foreign currency, limitations on the use of payment means, like credit cards and bank transfers, higher tax rates on the purchase of foreign services, for example, purchase tax and VAT.

Measures in respect of the *use* of a service could include a complete ban on domestic customers to use foreign services, or certain foreign services (e.g., financial services such as insurance and banking); the use of such services could otherwise be subject to restricting conditions that would make it either inconvenient, more expensive, or practically inaccessible. The reference to 'use', namely to the consumption of services, is meant to prevent Members from escaping their commitments by imposing prohibitive legislation on consumption.[59]

4.3.7.2.2 Measures in Respect of the Access and Use of Public Ancillary Services

The ability to provide certain services relies on certain, ancillary services, provided by the country where the service is supplied. One cannot supply transportation services without having access to transportation infrastructure such as roads, railways, inland waterways, ports, airports, airlines, etc. Similarly, one cannot supply telecommunications services without having access to telecommunication networks (see, for example, the *Mexico – Telecoms*[60] case). Measures that prevent access of foreign services suppliers to such ancillary services, in effect, function as barriers to the supply of these services by them.

57. WT/DS27/R, AB/R/USA EC – Regime for the Importation, Distribution and Sale of Bananas, adopted on 25.9.1997, Panel report, para. 7.280.
58. The Appellate Body regarded a regime that allocated a certain share of import licenses to importers from certain states as 'affecting' international trade stressing, that in that case that regime was *inter alia* cross-subsidizing imports from the preferred sources. WT/DS27/AB/R, n. 57, Appellate Body report, para. 211.
59. GATS commentary, n. 2, 548.
60. WT/DS204/R Mexico – Measures Affecting Telecommunications Services, adopted on 1.6.2004.

4.3.7.2.3 Measures in Respect of the Presence of Foreign Persons

The first two groups mentioned are relevant to all modes of supply. The third group refers to Modes 2–4, because Mode 1 (cross border) does not require the presence of persons in another Member. Measures affecting the presence of foreign persons may apply to individuals as well as to legal entities, such as enterprises, affiliates, branches, service centers, etc. Such measures may effectively restrict the number of foreign persons allowed, or the manner of their incorporation; the professional qualifications and experience necessary to gain access to a market of a Members, etc.

4.3.7.2.4 The List Is Indicative

The list of 'measures' included in the definition of 'measures by Members affecting trade in services' is indicative. Other measures, which are not listed, may also well fit into this general definition. Here too, it seems that GATS drafters wanted to leave maximal flexibility, to ensure a maximal, current and future, scope of application. In *EC – Bananas III* the Panel, recognizing that the list including Article XXVIII(c)(i)–(iii) is merely illustrative, explains:

> In other words, the term 'in respect of' does not describe any measures affecting trade in services, but rather describes what such measures might regulate.[61]

The Panel further determined:

> no measures are excluded *a priori* from the scope of the GATS as defined by its provisions. The scope of the GATS encompasses any measure of a Member to the extent it affects the supply of a service regardless of whether such measure directly governs the supply of a service or whether it regulates other matters but nevertheless affects trade in services.[62]

In fact, a 'measure affecting trade in services' could be, in principle, any measure that does not correspond to a Member's legal obligations according to GATS.

4.3.7.2.4.1 Only Measures Affecting Services and Service Suppliers

The words 'affecting trade in services' are interpreted as referring to measures affecting services or service suppliers.

The 'supply of a service' is broadly defined in Article XXVIII(b) of GATS as including the production, distribution, marketing, sale and delivery of a service.

In order for GATS to apply to measures affecting service suppliers, it should be established that these measures affect them in their *capacity as* service suppliers.[63]

These terms are broadly interpreted by the WTO adjudicating bodies. Thus, for example, referring to 'distribution' the Appellate Body in *China – Publications*

---

61. WT/DS27/AB/R, n. 57.
62. WT/DS27/R, n. 57, para. 7.285.
63. M. Krajewski, n. 9, 68.

and Audiovisual Products noted that according to Article XXVIII(b) of GATS the meaning of this term applies to both tangible and intangible products.[64]

'Service supplier' is defined in GATT Article XXVIII(g) as 'any person that supplies a service'. Footnote 12 of GATS adds to this definition:

> Where the service is not supplied directly by a juridical person but through other forms of commercial presence such as a branch or a representative office, the service supplier (i.e., the juridical person) shall, nonetheless, through such presence be accorded the treatment provided for service suppliers under the agreement. Such treatment shall be extended to the presence through which the service is supplied and need not be extended to any other parts of the supplier located outside the territory where the service is supplied.

This definition is broad enough not to limit the discretion of the Members as to the types of juridical persons to be regarded as service suppliers according to the national standards and domestic traditions. Moreover, the functional approach of the agreement treats branches and representative offices which lack a legal personality equivalently to juridical persons, although the *real* natural or juridical person behind them might be located outside the territory of that Member, thus avoiding a requirement for full incorporation in the territory of the host state as a precondition for GATS application.[65]

GATS disciplines apply to measures affecting services *consumers* only as far as services or service suppliers are affected. Thus, a Member may apply restrictions on the consumption of its own consumers, taking place outside its jurisdiction.[66]

One question arising in GATS jurisprudence is whether, in order to determine if a measure affects service suppliers, only *actual* service suppliers should be considered, or also *potential* service suppliers, and how would the latter be defined. In *EC –Bananas III* the Panel decided that vertically integrated companies who were present at the market, but did not have an opportunity to supply wholesale services with respect to bananas, could enter at the market at any time and thus should be considered as potential service suppliers.[67] The Appellate Body in this case did not address this issue directly, although in principle it upheld the Panel's conclusion that vertically integrated companies may be considered 'wholesale service suppliers'.[68] This approach was criticized for stretching GATS disciplines

64. WT/DS363/AB/R *China – Publications and Audiovisual Products*, n. 8, paras 379, 395.
65. W. Zdouc, n. 4, 132–133.
66. S/L/92 Guidelines for the Scheduling of Specific Commitments Under the General Agreement on Trade in Services (GATS), published 28.3.2001, adopted by the Council for Trade in services on 23.3.2001, S/C/M/52, para. 30. See the text of the guidelines in <http://docsonline.wto.org>.
67. WT/DS27/R, n. 57, para. 7.346.
68. WT/DS27/AB/R, n. 57, para. 227. Although the EC explicitly questioned this Panel decision (para. 204) the Appellate Body referred only to the aspect that vertically integrated companies may be considered 'wholesale service suppliers' *to the extent that they engage* in such activities. Nevertheless, the Appellate Body concluded its reference to this subject by upholding the Panel's decision on this matter.

too much.[69] In *Canada – Autos* the Appellate Body criticizes the Panel for not having made a factual finding as to which companies actually provided wholesale trade services in that case.[70]

Nevertheless, this approach was followed in *China – Publications and Audiovisual Products*, as both the Panel and Appellate Body agreed that Chinese measures totally prohibiting foreign service suppliers from *engaging in* the supply of 'cultural goods' in the Chinese market form a violation of GATT and GATS provisions. Due to this prohibition, the entire analysis concerning these measures referred to their effect on *potential* suppliers.[71]

4.3.7.2.4.2 Two Explicit Exceptions

There are two a priori exceptions to this broad sectoral coverage of GATS: air transport services, excluded from GATS scope by the Annex on Air Transport (see Chapter 16); and services supplied in the exercise of governmental authority, according to Article I:3(b) of GATS, to be discussed below.

4.3.7.3 'By Members'

This wording implies that the measures subject to GATS should be conducted by the Members themselves, or at least under their instruction, direction or control. Past GATT Panels referred to different levels of government involvement, tending to interpret this requirement broadly, to include *inter alia*, action of private actors according to non-mandatory governmental guidance and informal administrative guidance, and even *ex post* authorization or endorsement by a government. The dividing line is drawn between acts encouraged or supported by the government that would be considered as 'measures', and private restrictive conduct merely tolerated by the government, who fails to act against it, which would escape this definition.[72]

4.3.7.4 Affecting

4.3.7.4.1 A Link between Measures and Trade

In the context of the equivalent GATT provision, Article III:4, this word was interpreted to serve 'as a link between the identified forms of government action, which are covered by the obligation, that is, laws, regulations or requirements, and the specific transactions, activities and uses relating to products in the marketplace ("internal sale, offering for sale, purchase, transportation,

69. W. Zdouc, n. 4, 135.
70. WT/DS139, 142/AB/R *Canada – Autos*, n. 5, para. 164.
71. See, for example, WT/DS363/R, AB/R *China – Publications and Audiovisual Products*, n. 8, paras 7.1429–7.1431.
72. W. Zdouc, n. 4, 112–114.

distribution or use")'.[73] Similarly, in GATS, this word should be seen as a link between the relevant measures and the specific services or service suppliers at stake.

4.3.7.4.2 *The Order of Examination*

In *Canada – Autos* the Appellate body set the stages for examination of whether a measure is 'affecting' trade in services, saying:

> We believe that at least two key legal issues must be examined to determine whether a measure is one 'affecting trade in services': first, whether there is 'trade in services' in the sense of Article I:2; and, second, whether the measure in issue 'affects' such trade in services within the meaning of Article I:1.[74]

This approach was criticized on the ground that the absence of actual trade might be the result of a WTO-inconsistent trade restriction, and therefore this examination is not logical. GATT jurisprudence does not reflect such a two-step test; according to it, the examination of a less favourable treatment claim logically presupposes that the measure involved affected trade in goods.[75]

4.3.7.4.3 *Broad Scope of Application*

EC – Bananas III was the first case that interpreted GATS. In its decision, the Panel chose to give this expression the broadest possible meaning which, combined with the entire wording of this provision would lead to GATS broadest scope of application:

> In accordance with Article 31 of the Vienna Convention on the Law of Treaties, we note that the ordinary meaning of the term 'affecting', in Article I:1 of GATS, does not convey any notion of limiting the scope of the GATS to certain types of measures or to a certain regulatory domain. On the contrary, Article I:1 refers to measures in terms of their effect, which means they could be of any type or relate to any domain of regulation. Like GATT, the GATS is an umbrella agreement which applies to all sectors of trade in services and all types of regulations.[76]

Faithful to this position, the Panel rejected the EC's interpretation that Article XXVIII(c) narrows the meaning of the term 'affecting' to 'in respect of'. It added:

> In accordance with Article 32 of the Vienna Convention, we note that the preparatory work of the GATS confirms the foregoing interpretation. In the

73. WT/DS108/AB/RW United States – Tax Treatment for 'Foreign Sales Corporations' – Recourse to Art. 21.5 of the DSU by the European Communities, adopted on 29.1.2002, Appellate Body report para. 208.
74. WT/DS139, 142/AB/R *Canada – Autos*, n. 5, para. 181.
75. W. Zdouc, n. 4, 119–120.
76. WT/DS27/R (USA), n. 57, para. 7.280.

> Uruguay Round, the drafters of the GATS were aware that the term affecting had been interpreted in prior GATT panel reports to cover not only laws and regulations which directly govern the conditions of sale or purchase but also any laws or regulations which might adversely modify conditions of competition between like domestic and imported products on the internal market. Another indication of the wish of the drafters to widen the scope of the GATS in terms of the regulatory measures it covers is the use of the concept of 'supply' of services rather than 'delivery'. The text of Article XXVIII(b) as well as the preparatory work indicate that the choice of the term 'supply of a service' involved the coverage of a wider range of activities than the case would have been had the drafters chosen to use the term 'delivery'. That has made a wider range of regulations subject to the application of the GATS. In sum, we believe that, consistently with their general approach, the drafters consciously adopted the terms 'affecting' and 'supply of a service' to ensure that the disciplines of the GATS would cover any measure bearing upon conditions of competition in supply of a service, regardless of whether the measure directly governs or indirectly affects the supply of the service.[77]

In that case the Appellate Body noted that the use of the term 'affecting' indicates that GATS has a broad scope of application, wider than such terms as 'regulating' or 'governing' could imply.[78] The necessary 'effect' may be caused cumulatively by more than one measure.

4.3.7.4.3.1 Not Necessarily Aiming Directly at Services

Following this logic, it was determined in *EC – Bananas III* that in order to be subject to GATS, a measure does not have to regulate or directly aim at trade in services. It could regulate other matters, nevertheless affecting trade in services:[79] the mere fact that a particular measure is essentially intended to govern trade in goods does not preclude the possibility that it also affects trade in services. Nevertheless, where the same measure can be scrutinized under both GATT 1994 and GATS, the focus of the enquiry under each of the agreements would be different. Under GATS 'the focus is on how the measure affects the supply of the service or the service suppliers involved'.[80] In *China – Publications and Audiovisual Products*, this interpretation was effectively broadened to apply even to an overlap

77. *Ibid.*, para. 7.281.
78. Note 57, para. 220.
79. W. Zdouc, 'WTO Dispute Settlement Practice Relating to the General Agreement on Trade in Services', in F. Ortino & E.U. Petersmann (eds) *The WTO Dispute Settlement System: 1995-2003*, London, Kluwer International Law (2004).
80. WT/DS27/AB/R *EC – Bananas III*, n. 57, Appellate Body report para. 221. This notion of overlap between GATT and GATS was addressed from different angles in WT/DS31/R, AB/R, *Canada* – Certain Measures Concerning Periodicals, adopted 30.7.1997, as well as in WT/DS139, 142/AB/R *Canada – Autos*, n. 5, Appellate Body report paras 160–161, reaching the same result.

between trade in services, covered by GATS and trade in goods, covered not by GATT but by China's Accession Protocol.[81]

4.3.7.4.3.2 Modification of Competitive Conditions

A measure affects trade in services when it 'modifies the conditions of competition in supply of a service'. According to the WTO jurisprudence,[82] it is not necessary to determine an *actual* 'effect'. It is enough to demonstrate a *potential* effect on trade,[83] as long as the 'measure' which is the source for this effect, or potential effect, is clearly identified.[84]

4.3.7.4.4 GATT Interpretation

The word 'affecting', or the entire expression 'measures affecting trade in services', was probably inspired, at least to some extent, by the wording of GATT Article III:4, applying the national treatment standard to 'laws, regulations and requirements affecting the internal sale…, purchase,…. distribution…' of goods. That wording was also interpreted by the WTO adjudicating bodies in a broad manner, as including measures beyond legislation directly regulating or governing the sale of domestic and like imported products.[85] It may be assumed, that GATS drafters were aware of this interpretation and relied on it in GATS phrasing. This interpretation was explicitly referred to by the WTO adjudicating bodies to base their broad interpretation of GATS provision. Thus, in *EC – Bananas III* the Appellate Body said:

> The ordinary meaning of the word 'affecting' implies a measure that has 'an effect on', which indicates a broad scope of application. This interpretation is further reinforced by the conclusions of previous panels that the term 'affecting' in the context of Article III of the GATT is wider in scope than such terms as 'regulating' or 'governing'.[86]

4.3.7.4.5 Decision Must Be Based on Facts

In *Canada – Autos*, the Appellate Body rejected the approach adopted by the Panel, which decided that the measures involved 'affected' trade in services, based

81. WT/DS363/R *China – Publications and Audiovisual Products*, n. 8, paras 7.542, 7.552, 7.555, 7.560.
82. In WT/DS139, 142/R *Canada – Autos*, n. 5, the panel held that a measure can be considered to be 'affecting' the internal sale of imported products even if it is not 'shown to have an impact under current circumstances on decisions of private firms' to buy imported products: paras 10.80, 10.84. The same logic draws from GATT 1947 panel report on *Italian Discrimination against Imported Agricultural Machinery*, adopted 23.10.1958 BIDS 7S/60 para. 12, where it was provided that the word 'affecting' refers, *inter alia*, to measures that *might* adversely modify the conditions of competition between like products.
83. F. Ortino, n. 36, 3.
84. WT/DS285/AB/R *US – Gambling*, n. 6, paras 120–126.
85. See WT/DS27/R *EC – Bananas III*, n. 57, paras 7.175–7.178, including n. 409 thereto.
86. WT/DS27/R n. 57, para. 220.

on its assumption, thus skipping a factual examination. The Appellate Body stressed:[87]

> The Panel failed to analyze the evidence on the record relating to the provision of wholesale trade services of motor vehicles in the Canadian market. It also failed to articulate what it understood Article I:1 to require by the use of the term 'affecting'. Having interpreted Article I:1, the Panel should then have examined all the relevant facts . . . *It is not enough to make assumptions.* Finally, the Panel should have applied its interpretation of 'affecting trade in services' to the facts it should have found. [Emphasis added].

4.3.7.5 Services: 'Except Services Supplied in the Exercise of Governmental Authority'

GATS lacks a generally accepted economic definition for services.[88] GATS Article I:3(b)[89] determines 'services' as including 'any service in any sector except services supplied in the exercise of governmental authority', thus drawing the line between services covered by GATS and services excluded from its scope of application, reflecting a delicate balance between what pertains to be 'commercial' activity and what pertains to be 'public', 'governmental' activity that does not effectively relate to trade and commerce.

Article I:3(c) determines that 'a service supplied in the exercise of governmental authority' as 'any service which is supplied neither on a commercial basis, nor in competition with one or more service suppliers'. This definition is broad and flexible,[90] excluding only a narrow portion of the governmental activity. Both conditions have to be fulfilled for a service to be excluded from GATS scope of application.[91] This cumulative nature of conditions limits the potential scope of activities that may be included in this definition. (See detailed analysis in 4.3.7.5.3 below.) It is assumed that 'the cumulative requirements of non-profitability and non-competitiveness are not fulfilled by many services.'[92] It should be noted, that

87. WT/DS139, 142/AB/R, n. 5, paras 164–166.
88. W. Zdouc, n. 4, 106.
89. For the negotiating history of Art. I:3(b),(c) see: M. Krajewski, 'Public Services and Trade Liberalization: Mapping the Legal Framework', *6 Journal of International Economic Law* (2003), 341, 357–358; E.H. Leroux, 'What is a 'Service Supplied in the Exercise of Governmental Authority' Under Art. I:3(b) and (c) of the General Agreement on Trade in Services?', *40 Journal of World Trade* (2006), 345, 355–357.
90. In this case, also, flexibility is achieved by ambiguity, which in turn deters Members from taking broader commitments: 'This situation may have prompted some governments to include in their schedules various limitations and footnotes with the purpose of clarifying the respective role of public and private services suppliers . . . or not to commit at all on relevant subsectors'. M. Cossy, n. 47, 127.
91. F. Ortino, n. 36, 4.
92. M. Krajewski, n. 9, 73; See also M. Krajewski, n. 89, 358–359. Krajewski criticizes this narrow concept 'which may not be the dominant understanding of all times and countries. This provision effectively blocks an interpretation of the agreement mindful of the changing concept of trade in services [i.e., privatization and outsourcing – N.M.]. GATS law therefore is at risk of

both these conditions are open for interpretation, thus implying flexibility of application and a scope of discretion for interpreters. This exclusion may be the result of political debates about the impact of GATS on public services,[93] and thus should be narrowly interpreted.

In the context of public utilities, frequently, governments prefer to retain ownership of a facility and contract out certain tasks to private companies. Such arrangements may include the so-called 'public-private-partnerships' (PPPs), making use of various instruments such as management, Built-Operate-Transfer (BOT) and concession contracts.[94] Due to the shared responsibility between government and private sector, it is unclear whether these arrangements will be considered as 'services supplied in the exercise of a governmental authority'.[95]

4.3.7.5.1 *'Supplied . . . on a Commercial Basis'*

The 'supply of a service' is broadly defined in Article XXVIII(b) of GATS as including the production, distribution, marketing, sale and delivery of a service.

The 'supply on commercial basis' test concentrates not on the supplier, but rather on the manner of supply. However, this definition is ambiguous. According to the ordinary meaning, *a commercial basis* could be interpreted as expressing the notion of financial return or profit.[96] Conversely, services exercised *not* on commercial basis could be interpreted narrowly as including only services provided *for free*, for example, environmental services. An interpretative question may arise as to services which are subject to a fee, which does not reflect their real cost: would such services be considered as provided for free? And what about services provided for a fee covering only their real cost, without any profit?[97] Or local services provided by a private service supplier, but are highly cross-subsidized?[98]

A broader interpretation may include any supply of service for non-profitable reasons, including services provided in a low, subsidized price or in exchange for

---

becoming static and unreceptive to the WTO Membership at large'. He calls for the Appellate Body to take a similar approach to that of the ECJ, determining that certain services, such as public education, are automatically excluded from the scope of the agreement since they do not constitute economic activity and therefore should not be considered 'services'. Nevertheless, he recognizes that differing opinions in different countries as to the nature of different services may undermine this idea. *Ibid.*, 366–367.

93. M. Krajewski, n. 9, 68.
94. M. Cossy, n. 47, 129.
95. A similar interpretative difficulty arises in the context of Art. XIII of GATS, referring to government procurement. See: M. Cossy, n. 47, 129–131.
96. E.H. Leroux, n. 89, 349–351. His interpretation is based on the dictionary meaning, the ordinary meaning, the context: 'commercial presence' definition and GATT jurisprudence interpreting GATT Art. XVII:1(b).
97. See the example of water: M. Cossy, n. 47, 126.
98. R. Adlung & A. Mattoo, 'The GATS', in A. Mattoo, R.M. Stern & G. Zanini (eds), *A Handbook of International Trade in Services*, Oxford University Press (2007), 48, 52.

an administrative fee.[99] A public monopoly will not always be covered by this definition, and this is another illustration of its vagueness.

As broad as the definition chosen is, the larger would be the scope of services excluded from GATS scope. On the other hand, if services would be considered to be supplied on commercial basis even in the absence of profit-seeking design and structure, Article I:3(b) and (c) could end up with minimal coverage, counter to the interpretative principle of effectiveness.[100]

4.3.7.5.2 'Competition'

In the context of services, '"competition" conveys the general idea of two or more service suppliers competing one with another in the same services market'.[101] The existence of competition is a fact-based determination, on a case-by-case basis, based on common economic and legal tests.[102] Where governmental authority is exercised, competition in this sense is generally absent.

The expression *services provided not in competition with service suppliers* could be thus interpreted as meaning services supplied where there is no elasticity of substitution. This fact is to be determined on a case-by-case basis and might vary from country to country.[103] A question may arise as to how to measure elasticity of substitution as to services which are supplied side-by-side by governmental and private entities, for example, education and health services; or alternatively, for services supplied for free.[104] Would this situation be considered 'competition'? The answer may depend on the terms of supply; that is, the comparative cost of the services, their availability to consumers, etc. Thus, for example, if the cost of a governmental service, for example, education, is much lower than the similar private service, elasticity of demand might not effectively exist. A similar result may occur where the comparatively cheaper service is not available to the general public but only to preferred group, for example, the low-income population.

The competition test raises particular difficulties in sectors where only one supplier can operate in the market. It happens in services which are still considered natural monopolies. In such cases:

> [c]ompetition may exist between private suppliers before accessing that market, in the bidding process for a concession contract for instance. But in this case, a public authority is not competing with private suppliers since it is in fact seeking to contract out certain activities. A competition test in a sector which is inherently non-competitive amounts to trying to square the circle.[105]

---

99. M. Krajewski, n. 9, 69–70. Krajewski prefers the latter, broader interpretation for being more compatible with the context of the agreement.
100. E.H. Leroux, n. 89, 354.
101. *Ibid.*, 362–384.
102. See elaboration on the legal and economic tests for the establishment of competition in Ch. 11.
103. M. Krajewski, n. 9, 71.
104. GATS commentary, n. 2, 67.
105. M. Cossy, n. 47, 127.

Yet another question to be asked is: is it realistic to expect competition among the markets of all Members, where consumers and producers will move across borders, between more than 150 markets,[106] or should it rather be examined in a single Member's market?

Finally, it should be asked whether competition should be examined only within the same mode of supply, or could rather be examined between different modes of supply. This idea is controversial in the literature, as the opponents argue that supply by different modes might have different end-users, and that if this notion is accepted, scheduling commitments by mode of supply are not necessary; while supporters of this idea mainly base their argument on practical trade considerations.[107]

4.3.7.5.3 *'Governmental Authority'*

Article I:3(c) provides: '"a service supplied in the exercise of governmental authority" means any service which is supplied neither on a commercial basis, nor in competition with one or more service suppliers'. As mentioned above, the test is *cumulative*: *both elements* need to be fulfilled for a service to be considered as supplied in the exercise of governmental authority. Thus, the test is *factual*: if a service is supplied either 'on a commercial basis' or 'in competition with other service suppliers' it will not be considered as supplied in the exercise of governmental authority. As to the former requirement, 'the essence of governmental authority relates to exercise of powers to regulate, control or supervise individuals or entities, or otherwise restrain their conduct, through the exercise of lawful authority'.[108] These functions do not bear a commercial character.

The latter condition may be ascertained by an objective parameter: whether market access for potential competitors is legally permitted, or alternatively by establishing that although such entry is theoretically permitted, no actual entry has in fact occurred.[109]

This phrasing makes it impossible to claim that certain services are a priori excluded from GATS because of their nature of public or governmental services.[110] In practice, it is thus likely that the scope of this exemption will differ from one country to another, depending on national policy choices and constitutional and administrative organization.[111]

---

106. GATS commentary, n. 2, 67.
107. *Ibid.*, 67–68.
108. E.H. Leroux, n. 89, 352.
109. W. Zdouc, n. 4, 108. The first parameter is also reflected in the wording of the Annex on Financial Services, (see Ch. 16) where the main criterion for delimitation from purely private entities is which type of activity an entity is principally engaged in *ibid.*, 109.
110. M. Krajewski, n. 9, 71–72. The author compares this definition with a different approach to the definition of governmental authority in Art. 1(b) of the Annex on Financial Services, referring to the supplier and to the nature of service.
111. M. Cossy, n. 47.

This definition may apply to current as well as to *future* services. Typical examples include police, fire-protection, monetary policy operations, mandatory social security and tax and customs administration.[112] It may further apply to services used as *inputs* in the production of goods or to services embodied in goods, like literature, recorded music or computer programs. As of now, WTO adjudicating bodies have not defined 'services' in general, and they may never do so if they wish to keep the maximal flexibility provided for by the agreement. Thus, they adopted a pragmatic approach, stating which service was possibly affected in fact.[113]

4.4 CONCLUSION

GATS drafters chose the broader, most flexible definition for its scope of application. Nevertheless, it comes on the expense of legal vagueness, affecting the entire agreement. In the few cases that were examined by the WTO adjudicating bodies till now, the clear tendency is to allow the application of GATS to the broadest possible scale of services and service suppliers. This interpretation corresponds to the general aim of this agreement, to achieve broad liberalization of trade in services.

---

112. WTO explanatory paper, WTO Secretariat, 29.3.2006 (3776.4), 5.
113. M. Krajewski, n. 9, 66.

Chapter 5
GATS Rules of Origin

5.1 INTRODUCTION

5.1.1 Rules of Origin and Their Role

Most international trade agreements have rules of origin.[1] Their major purpose is to ensure, that only goods and/or services (depending on the agreement's coverage) from the parties to the agreement will enjoy the benefits of that agreement. In other words, rules of origin are meant to define the 'nationality' of a product, a service or a service supplier, thus denying the benefits of the agreement from 'free riders'.[2]

Rules of origin practically determine market access: while liberal rules of origin encourage foreign import of services (but also benefit free riders), restrictive

1. Rules of origin also exist in other types of international agreements such as treaties for the avoidance of double taxation and investment protection treaties. Basically, all these groups of agreements refer to criteria such as incorporation, registration, nationality/citizenship of natural persons, or of the natural persons who own/control/have substantial interests in a legal entity, principal place of business, centre of administration or management. However, each category of agreements necessitates a different approach towards these rules.
2. Rules of origin may serve additional purposes, like being an instrument in the hands of governments for the encouragement of export by protecting input producers. Rules of origin may facilitate control over export and determination of exclusive jurisdiction rights for tax purposes, facilitate the collection of statistical data concerning trade investment flows, and the enforcement of health regulations, standards and sanitary requirements: B.M. Hoeckman, 'Rules of Origin for Goods and Services – Conceptual Issues and Economic Considerations', *27 Journal of World Trade* (1993), 81, 82; These rules may further facilitate the enforcement of international trade agreements' provisions, for example, provisions that suspend the application of agreements' concessions to a certain party, temporarily or permanently. A mistaken or a misleading declaration of origin may derive sanctions, applied by the customs authorities of the destination country: R. Bhala & K. Kennedy, *World Trade Law*, Lexis Law Publishing, Virginia (1998), 278, 346–348.

rules of origin would imply a more protectionist outcome. Thus, the choice of rules of origin depends on the objectives of the agreement. The effect of rules of origin is measured comparatively, by the costs they impose on service suppliers from non-Member countries, in terms of tax obligations and business transaction costs.[3]

In GATS, due to the permanent tension between domestic and multilateral interests, these rules must be flexible enough to offer references to divergent criteria in national legislation determining nationality.[4]

5.1.2 Rules of Origin as Barriers to Trade

In recent decades, the total number of international trade agreements – bilateral, multilateral and plurilateral – has grown considerably. Most of these agreements have rules of origin. Needless to say – each agreement has different rules of origin. Exporters of goods and services, particularly multinationals, wishing to benefit from globalization by exporting their products or services to many destinations, have to adapt them to differing rules of origin for each destination. This is a considerable burden for exporters. This situation is compared to a spaghetti bowl.[5]

5.1.3 Rules of Origin for International Trade in Goods

Rules of origin for trade in goods are relatively simple. Their simplest version exists where the goods are 'wholly obtained' in one state. For example, vegetables, minerals, live animals. In this case, it is clear that 100% of the product originates from the same country.

A more elaborated case occurs where the goods include some ingredients that are produced in different countries. For example, computers assembled from components produced in different countries, or shirts designed in one country and produced in another. In these cases, rules of origin usually set the threshold percentage of production in a certain country, out of the total 100% of the product involved, necessary to define a product as originating in that country. Usually, ancillary activities such as packing, washing and cleaning, stamping and labeling are not taken into account in the calculation of the threshold percentage of production in a country, necessary to define it as a country of origin. To be considered as part of this percentage, the actions taken concerning the goods have to substantially modify them.

3. C. Fink & D. Nikomborirak, 'Rules of Origin in Services: A Case Study of Five ASEAN Countries', *The World Bank Policy Research Papers 4130* (2007), 5–6, 8–9. <www-wds.worldbank.org>. The authors refer to FTAs but concerning the discussed subjects the same logic applies to GATS.
4. W. Zdouc, *Legal Problems Arising Under the General Agreement on Trade in Services – Comparative Analysis of GATS and GATT*, dissertation der Universität St. Gallen (2002), 141.
5. J. Bhagwatti, *Free Trade Today*, Princeton University Press (2000), 113.

5.1.4 GATT-WTO Rules of Origin

GATT 1947 did not include rules of origin. This subject was left to the discretion of the Contracting Parties. However, they were required by GATT Article IX not to use such rules as unnecessary or disguised barriers to trade. In the Uruguay Round, this approach changed and the WTO Agreement on Rules of Origin[6] was concluded. This agreement calls for harmonization of existing rules of origin for trade in goods, in a process conducted by the WTO Committee on Rules of Origin and the World Customs Organization (WCO). It further includes some disciplines to be applied until this goal will be accomplished.[7]

As to services, the different Uruguay Round approach is reflected by the fact that GATS includes rules of origin right from its beginning.

5.1.5 Rules of Origin for Trade in Services

Rules of origin for trade in services are more elaborated than rules of origin for trade in goods: they have to address not only the services, but also service suppliers; They have to take into consideration the personal aspect involved at least in personal services, which makes it difficult to compare between services; They have to take into consideration the four possible modes of supply, including commercial presence that actually means production and supply of the service in the country of destination; And finally, they have to be flexible enough to suit the wide variety of services, existing as well as services that might develop in the future. All these aspects make it even more difficult to determine rules of origin for trade in services, than for trade in goods.

Trade in goods is supplied by one mode of supply: cross border. At the time of crossing a border, it may be subject to examination of origin by the customs authorities. Services are supplied in four different modes of supply (see Chapter 1). In Modes 2 and 3 the foreign services supplied do not cross a border. This fact raises the question: where, by whom and at what time will the origin examination take place? However, even Mode 1 (cross-border) is different for services and goods in this respect, since services may be supplied electronically. By now, this form of trade is largely unrestricted. Accordingly, it might be difficult to follow such services, to see whether they are totally supplied by a service supplier of a Member, or are sub-contracted by the supplier to another supplier in a third country.[8]

---

6. See full text: <www.wto.org>.
7. Originally, the parties believed that such harmonization could be achieved within three years after the end of Uruguay Round. Until now, this goal has not yet been accomplished.
8. C. Fink & D. Nikomborirak, n. 3, 3.

5.2 GATS RULES OF ORIGIN

The purpose of GATS rules of origin is to avoid multiple attribution of service suppliers to several Members, a situation that may create confusion as to the rights and obligations which are relevant to that service supplier, and situations where a service supplier persuades one Member, which is its country of origin, to defend its rights against another Member, whose origin that person holds as well. It is also meant to prevent service suppliers lacking attribution to any Member that could defend its rights to trade in services before the WTO.[9]

Rules of origin for services and service suppliers may refer to the following criteria: For *companies (juridical persons)* – incorporation, substantive business operations, domestic ownership and control, and domestic employment.

For *individual service suppliers (natural persons)* – nationality, residence and center of economic interest.[10]

The rules of origin in GATS were formed in a flexible manner, establishing general principles, which are common to all kinds of services, modes of supply and service suppliers. They answer some questions:

- What is the country of origin?
- Who is an individual/legal entity from a Member, entitled to GATS benefits?

According to GATS, each service and service supplier of a Member is entitled to the agreement's benefits.[11]

The rules of origin are in fact embodied in the definitions included in GATS Article XXVIII. The general nature of the rules of origin, stemming from this provision, is open for the application and interpretation of the Members in each particular case.

5.2.1 Service of Another Member

Article XXVIII(f) provides:

> 'service of another Member' means a service which is supplied,
>
> (i) from or in the territory of that other Member, or in the case of maritime transport, by a vessel registered under the laws of that other Member, or by a person of that other Member which supplies the service through the operation of a vessel and/or its use in whole or in part; or

9. W. Zdouc, n. 4, 143–144. This rational is different from the rational underlying economic integration agreements, which are designed to limit the groups of beneficiaries under the agreement.
10. See elaboration on each criterion in C. Fink & D. Nikomborirak, n. 3, 7.
11. See, for example, Art. II (1): '. . . each Member shall accord . . . to services and service suppliers of any other Member treatment no less favourable . . .'.

(ii) in the case of the supply of a service through commercial presence or through the presence of natural persons, by a service supplier of that other Member;

5.2.1.1 Five Options

This provision covers five possible scenarios:

The first, and most simple one, is where a service is supplied *from or in the territory of the supplying Member.* This condition may be fulfilled by Mode 1: cross-border, for example, where a legal opinion is sent to a client abroad by fax or by mail. It may also be fulfilled by Mode 2: consumption abroad, for example, where a tourist from a Member enjoys tourism services in the territory of another Member.

The second case addressed by Article XXVIII(f)(i) is where a vessel registered under the laws of a Member supplies maritime transport services to individuals or commodities from another Member.[12]

The third option envisioned by this provision is similar to the second case, only the vessel is not necessarily registered in another Member, but the person operating it, wholly or partly, is a 'person of that other Member'. The 'person' may be an individual or a legal entity, fulfilling the terms of this definition. Its relative share in the operation of the vessel is not specified, and therefore could be even minimal. Thus, a vessel that is wholly or mostly owned by persons from non-Members, registered in a non-Member and mostly operated by persons from non-Members could enjoy GATS benefits because it is partly operated by a person from a Member.

The two last options complement the coverage of four modes of supply. The fourth option addresses the supply of services through commercial presence (Mode 3), for example, consulting services supplied through a branch in the country of destination. The service supplier may be an individual or a legal entity, fulfilling the conditions set forth by the respective definition.

The fifth option addresses the presence of natural persons (Mode 4), for example, medical services supplied by a physician from another Member, which is not permanently established in the country of destination. This mode refers only to individuals. Those individuals have to fulfil the conditions set forth by the definition of a 'natural person of another Member'.

In both these cases, the territory of the country of origin is not relevant since the service is supplied on the territory of the country of destination. Therefore, the focal point moves to the service supplier, who should be 'a service supplier of that other Member'.

12. This option was already known in GATT 1947 practice. See, for example, the Panel report DS/21R United States – Restrictions on Imports of Tuna, dated 3.9.1991 (unadopted), 39S/155, paras 5.43–5.44.

5.2.1.2 Cases of a Mixed Source

All the possibilities covered in this definition are based on a prospect of one source for the service or service supplier.

The definition does not cover cases were a service is produced through some 'stations', or supplied by some service suppliers together, for example, an elaborated consulting process, requiring the cooperation of some experts from different states. Such a case occurred, for example, in *Mexico – Telecoms*, where international telecommunication services were examined. The Panel found that the definition does not imply that the supplier of such services must itself own or control the entire network infrastructure over which the cross-border service is supplied, and that the cross-border supply of telecommunications services could take place even if elements of the service were sub-contracted or carried out with assets owned by another firm.[13]

5.2.1.3 Persons

A service supplied in these modes of supply may enjoy GATS benefits if it is supplied 'by a service supplier of that other Member'. Article XXVIII(g) provides: '"service supplier" means any person who supplies a service'. The words 'any person' refer to two kinds of 'persons' recognized by GATS: natural person and juridical person. While a natural person is an individual, Article XXVIII(l) provides:

> 'juridical person' means any legal entity duly constituted or otherwise organized under applicable law, whether for profit or otherwise, and whether privately-owned or governmentally-owned, including any corporation, trust, partnership, joint venture, sole proprietorship or association.

This provision is accompanied by footnote 12 to the agreement that broadens the scope of application of GATS even to indirect supply of a service by a juridical person:

> Where the service is not supplied directly by a juridical person but through other forms of commercial presence such as a branch or a representative office, the service supplier (i.e., the juridical person) shall, nonetheless, through such presence be accorded the treatment provided for service suppliers under the Agreement. Such treatment shall be extended to the presence through which the service is supplied and need not be extended to any other parts of the supplier located outside the territory where the service is supplied.

Despite the wording 'that supplies a service', which may be interpreted as implying supply in effect, GATS jurisprudence reflects an ambivalent approach as to the recognition of potential suppliers as 'service suppliers' to which the agreement

13. WT/DS204/R Mexico – Measures Affecting Telecommunications Services, adopted on 1.6.2004, paras 7.34, 7.42.

applies. (See discussion in Chapter 4 – 4.3.7.2.4.1). At least some of the adjudicating bodies' decisions (including the recent *China – Publications and Audiovisual Products* case), seem to support this notion. However, this approach is criticized on the grounds that:

> although the broader scope no doubt adds to trade liberalization, the Members' intention was certainly not to have an unidentifiable number of potential service suppliers when they bound themselves to specific commitments.[14]

5.2.2 Natural Person of Another Member

This definition is aimed at diminishing the problem of double citizenship.

Article XXVIII(k) provides:

> 'natural person of another Member' means a natural person who resides in the territory of that other Member or any other Member, and who under the law of that other Member:
>
> (i) is a national of that other Member; or
> (ii) has the right of permanent residence in that other Member, in the case of a Member which:
>   1. does not have nationals; or
>   2. accords substantially the same treatment to its permanent residents as it does to its nationals in respect of measures affecting trade in services, as notified in its acceptance of or accession to the WTO Agreement, provided that no Member is obligated to accord to such permanent residents treatment more favourable than would be accorded by that other Member to such permanent residents. Such notification shall include the assurance to assume, with respect to those permanent residents, in accordance with its laws and regulations, the same responsibilities that other Member bears with respect to its nationals;

This provision includes some options:

The first option is an *individual who resides in a Member, and is also its national.* On its face, while residence seems to refer to the factual situation, nationality seems to refer to the legal situation.[15] However, 'residence' may also reflect a legal status. In different contexts, residence may be differently defined. Thus, for example, in the context of direct taxation, residence is usually determined according to the centre-of- life test, which examines which country

14. R. Worfrum, P.T. Stoll & C. Feinäugle (eds), *WTO – Trade in Services*, Max Planck Commentaries on World Trade Law, Martinus Mijnhoff Publishers, Leiden, Boston (2008), 554 (hereby: 'GATS commentary'). It is noted there, that an explicit reference to potential suppliers is included in para. 5(b) of the Annex on Financial Services, which refers to persons *wishing* to supply financial services: 555–556.
15. GATS commentary, n. 14, 558.

may be considered as the centre-of-life of the individual taxpayer in term of the place where there is a permanent home available to him, where the centre of its vital interests is, where he has an habitual abode, etc.[16] No such tests are mentioned in GATS. The suggested reference to 'resides' as expressing the factual situation while seeing 'the right of permanent residence' as referring to the legal status is based on an interpretation according to which the chapeau of Article XXVIII(k) refers to 'a natural person who resides' while sub-paragraph XXVIII(k)(ii) adds another condition: 'has the right of permanent residence'.[17] However, since the word 'resides' in the chapeau refers not only to sub-paragraph (ii) it could also be understood as referring to a legal right for temporary residence. In any case, the wording of this provision does not solve this difficulty, neither does it specify how 'residence' would be determined: according to the laws of the Member involved, or by any other agreed legal/factual parameters?

The second option refers to an *individual who resides in a Member, and obtains the right of permanent residence in it*. Since this option reflects a weaker link between the individual and the state, compared to the former option, it is subject to two additional, alternative, conditions: One case where residence plus the right for permanent residence will suffice in order to define an individual as a 'natural person of another Member', is where the Member involved has no nationals. This seems a rare possibility, addressing WTO Members which are not states in international law.[18] The second case is more common: it refers to a Member according substantially the same treatment to its permanent residents as it accords to its nationals in respect of measures affecting trade in services. Such a Member has to notify its position in advance to the WTO Secretariat. It has to assure the Secretariat that it would assume, with respect to those permanent residents, the same responsibilities that it bears with respect to its nationals. Some Members have already submitted such notifications to the WTO.[19]

The term 'substantially the same treatment' is meant to ensure close proximity between nationals and the residents at stake, in terms of the treatment accorded to them by the Member in which they reside and obtain the right for permanent residence, while at the same time reflecting the understanding that the treatment accorded to them does not need to be identical to that accorded to nationals. However, this term may raise interpretative difficulties because it is not defined by GATS. The word *substantially* implies that GATS drafters wanted to emphasize substance over formalities, the treatment de facto over the treatment de jure and to ensure that such a resident will be de facto entitled to the same treatment like nationals of that Member regarding measures affecting trade in services, even if de

16. OECD Model Tax Treaty, Art. 4: <www.oecd.org>.
17. GATS commentary, n. 14, 558.
18. MTN.GNS/W/139 Definitions in the Draft General Agreement on Trade in Services – Note by the Secretariat, 15 Oct. 1991, para. 13.
19. *WTO Analytical Index* (2nd edn), Cambridge University Press (2007), 1004, See also: <www.wto.org>.

jure the relevant rights of such a resident may be defined differently, or separately. This word is also included in GATT Article XXIV and GATS Article V, both referring to economic integration agreements and their relationships with GATT and GATS, respectively. In these provisions, the word 'substantially' is used to ensure that economic integration agreements have a wide scope of coverage concerning the trade between the partners. In that context no definite interpretation of the word 'substantially' was developed, but it seems to be generally agreed that it refers to a considerable scope of coverage (see Chapter 10). In the current context, this word is not used to describe a *scope* of coverage, but refers to the *nature* of treatment. Therefore, the interpretative approach should be somewhat different. However, some of the interpretative questions that might arise are similar: will the comparison involve quantitative or qualitative parameters? What scope of exceptions to the rule would be allowed by this provision?

The '*treatment*' covered by this provision is 'in respect of measures affecting trade in services', namely measures that may act as barriers to trade in services (see Chapter 4). Thus, the purpose of this provision is to ensure, that such residents who have the right for permanent residence in a Member, are not discriminated against by their own country of residence by applying to them, barriers to trade in services. This is a precondition for their entitlement to GATS benefits. However, the language of this provision does not address the following questions: what is the level of effect necessary? Will measures with negligible or indirect effect on trade in services be taken into account? Should this condition be understood as implying a general observation of the treatment accorded by that Member, in all respects,[20] or alternatively, would a case-by-case approach, referring only to the 'treatment' relevant in a certain case, suffice?

Another precondition that should be fulfilled by the country of residence is *assuming the same responsibilities* in respect to these residents as that Member assumes in respect to its nationals. It seems that while the first precondition should be applied domestically, within the borders of the Member involved, the second precondition may have an international scope of application: the responsibilities that Members should assume in respect of their residents are responsibilities in the international level, towards the other Members. Such responsibilities could include, for example, securing compliance with GATS provisions and disciplines, as far as they affect individuals. Thus, the two preconditions are complementary.

Due to the relatively weaker link between the resident and its state of residence, GATS provides for a rule diminishing the obligations of the other Members towards such a resident, compared to their obligations towards nationals of other Members, providing: 'provided that no Member is obligated to accord to such permanent residents treatment more favourable than would be accorded by that other Member to such permanent residents'.

20. Such a 'holistic' approach may raise more difficulties, for example, how should this provision be interpreted where a Member does not discriminate residents with respect to certain measures, but discriminates them with respect to other measures? Is it feasible to examine all the 'measures' applied by a certain Member, to ensure the fulfilment of this condition?

This condition implies some mutuality between the Members involved, with regard to their treatment of the resident at stake. However, the expression 'more favourable' is another vague, undefined expression which appears in some GATS provisions. A similar expression is included in GATT. Both agreements also include the opposite expression 'less favourable treatment', *inter alia* in the national treatment provision, that provides for non-discrimination between imported goods or services and like domestic goods or services, respectively.[21] In that context, less favourable treatment is treatment undermining the equal competitive opportunities of the imported product or service. This legal test is applied on a case-by-case basis. While in that context, the standard of 'no less favourable treatment' is meant to prevent discrimination, in the context of the current provision, the standard of 'more favourable treatment' is meant to provide for allowed discrimination in the level and scope of benefits accorded to nationals compared to residents of a Member. However, drawing an analogy between the examined provisions could lead to the adoption of two elements from the interpretation of 'no less favourable treatment', in the context of national treatment, for the interpretation of the expression 'more favourable treatment' in the current context: firstly, it may be understood as implying that a Member may not be expected to grant a resident of another Member, who is entitled to permanent residence but is not a national in that other state, a treatment that includes improved competitive opportunities compared to the competitive opportunities accorded to him by his state of residence. Secondly, the equality of competitive opportunities test is concentrating on the essence of treatment, preferring it over formalities. The same approach could be adopted here.

Actually, the treatment accorded to such residents by their country of residence will reflect the best treatment they are entitled to and may expect to receive. According to this provision, the other Members will be entitled to accord these residents a 'less favourable' or a similar treatment compared to the treatment accorded to them by their country of residence. However, an interpretative question may arise concerning the relationship between this provision and GATS Article II:1 (MFN – see Chapter 6).[22]

21. GATT Art. III:4, GATS Art. XVII, see full interpretation in Ch. 8.
22. GATS Art. II:1 provides:

> With respect to any measure covered by this Agreement, each Member shall accord immediately and unconditionally to services and service suppliers of any other Member treatment no less favourable than that it accords to like services and service suppliers of any other country.

The MFN provision seems to determine a higher standard than that provided for in Art. XXVIII(k). The MFN standard applies, *inter alia*, to 'service suppliers'. 'Service supplier' is defined in Art. XXVIII(g) as 'any person that supplies a service'. 'Person' is defined in Art. XXVIII(j) to mean 'either a natural person or a juridical person.' This definition leads back to the definition of 'natural person of another Member' in Art. XXVIII(k)(ii)(2) who may be a service supplier who is entitled to MFN treatment which sets the standard of 'no less

5.2.3 Juridical Person of Another Member

Article XXVIII(l)–(n) provides:

(l) 'juridical person' means any legal entity duly constituted or otherwise organized under applicable law, whether for profit or otherwise, and whether privately-owned or governmentally-owned, including any corporation, trust, partnership, joint venture, sole proprietorship or association;

(m) 'juridical person of another Member' means a juridical person which is either:

(i) constituted or otherwise organized under the law of that other Member, and is engaged in substantive business operations in the territory of that Member or any other Member; or

(ii) in the case of the supply of a service through commercial presence, owned or controlled by:

1. natural persons of that Member; or
2. juridical persons of that other Member identified under subparagraph (i);

(n) a juridical person is:

(i) 'owned' by persons of a Member if more than 50 per cent of the equity interest in it is beneficially owned by persons of that Member;

(ii) 'controlled' by persons of a Member if such persons have the power to name a majority of its directors or otherwise to legally direct its actions;

(iii) 'affiliated' with another person when it controls, or is controlled by, that other person; or when it and the other person are both controlled by the same person.

GATS drafters chose a very broad and flexible definition of 'juridical person': in terms of purpose, it may either exist for profit or not. In terms of ownership, it may either be privately-owned or governmentally owned. As to the form of incorporation, the provision mentions 'any corporation, trust, partnership, joint venture, sole proprietorship or association'. The word 'including' indicates that this is an indicative list, and other incorporation forms could also be included in this provision. This definition does not prevent legal entities from holding multiple nationalities, thus enjoying rights emanating from this status in several jurisdictions. Current global reality, in addition to the regulatory framework in Members and to the type of juridical person, might make it very difficult in certain cases to follow the real ownership behind a corporate structure, since the information may not be publicly available, or even impossible to achieve without the assistance of the company

---

favourable treatment than that accorded to like . . . service suppliers *of any other country*'. To mediate these two provisions it may be determined that for the MFN purpose, Art. II:1 would be considered *lex specialis*, while for all other purposes the standard determined by Art. XXVIII(k)(ii)(2) would apply.

itself.[23] This broad definition may help to overcome these practical difficulties, in certain cases. However, at the same time this broad definition may complicate matters where a juridical person is attributable both to a country participating in an economic integration agreement and to a third party at the same time.[24]

In order to be considered as a 'juridical person' of another Member the juridical person examined has to fit into one of two scenarios:

According to the first one, it has to fulfil two cumulative conditions:[25]

(1) 'constituted or otherwise organized under the law of that other Member'.
(2) 'Is engaged in substantive business operations in the territory of that Member or any other Member'. While the first condition should be fulfilled in the country of origin, the second condition could be fulfilled in any Member.

The requirement that the entity involved will be *'constituted or otherwise organized under applicable law of that other Member'* emphasizes the necessity of the juridical person to be subject to the domestic law of its (Member) State of origin. The terms 'constituted' and 'otherwise organized' are not interpreted in the text. It may be suggested, that 'constituted' refers to entities that are established by formal processes, like incorporation of enterprises, or registration of registered partnerships, while 'otherwise organized' refers to entities or manners of business cooperation that could be established by contracts, like joint ventures.

The term *'substantive business operations'* is meant to ensure that a juridical entity would not enjoy the benefits of the agreement by only taking the formal steps of registration or incorporation or 'organization' in a Member, solely for this purpose, thus deterring countries from getting engaged in deeper regional integration. However, this expression is ambiguous and should be interpreted on a case-by-case basis. The major question would be: what 'substantive business operations' means? Is the establishment of an interests' office enough? Would constituting ancillary operations such as marketing or the operation of ancillary facilities for the major activities of the company be enough? Or does this expression necessitate actual import of services into the relevant Member? Is the share of the activities taken by the relevant juridical person in a certain state, out of its total activity, important for this matter?

What does the word 'substantive' mean? Since this is a relative term, according to what scale will it be measured? Will it depend on the size of the economy involved or of the business involved? Will 'substantiveness' be measured qualitatively or quantitatively? Will only current data be taken into account, or also

23. M. Molinuevo, 'Can Foreign Investors in Services Benefit from WTO Dispute Settlement? Legal Standing and Remedies in WTO and International Arbitration', *NCCR Working Paper No. 2006/17* (2006), 18, <http://papers.ssrn.com>.
24. W. Zdouc, n. 4, 224.
25. International law recognizes many alternative criteria to determine the origin of a juridical entity, including the place of registration, the place of incorporation, the place where the board of directors meet, the business centre, the headquarters, etc.

development potential, which might play an important role in the case of start-ups, for example? These interpretative questions were not yet addressed in this context.

This option applies to Modes 1, 2 and 4. For Mode 3 (commercial presence) there are other rules, included in the second alternative provided for.

A commercial presence may be defined as a 'juridical person of another Member' if it is owned or controlled by natural or juridical persons of a Member. This condition could be fulfilled if one of three alternative possibilities occurs:

- More than 50% of the equity interest in it is beneficially owned by persons of a Member.
- Persons of a Member have the power to name a majority of its directors.
- Persons of a Member have the power, otherwise, to legally direct its actions.

The three options reflect three stages of a gradually growing flexibility of approach, that is ready to recognize different arrangements as entitled to the agreement's benefits, being defined as a 'commercial presence'. The idea behind these options seems to be that holding a dominant position does not necessarily imply holding the majority of shares.[26]

The first two conditions are relatively specific and clear, because they stick to facts that may be easily proved. The scenario depicted by them is relatively simple if a person from a Member, whether an individual or a legal entity, directly holds more than 50% of the equity interest in the 'juridical person' involved, or has the direct power to name the majority of its directors, because in this case the source of control is clear and definite. However, the provision uses the word 'persons', namely: the 50% holdings or the power to name the majority of directors could be in the hands of more than one person, whether individuals or legal entities, or a combination of both. This is a more elaborated scenario. The internal power division in such a group is not specified, probably because the focal point of the provision is their effective power of control over the 'juridical person'. The provision neither implies that all the persons involved should be from the same Member. Therefore, each of them could be of another origin, as long as all of them are from Members.

GATS drafters chose a relatively high percentage of holdings (more than 50%) as a threshold to define 'ownership'. It narrows down the scope of application of GATS benefits. 'It could be regarded as an attempt to avoid "double" or "multiple" nationalities of service suppliers in order to ensure a relatively clear attributability of particular companies to particular WTO Member governments'.[27] However, this intention could be effectively undermined where a chain of legal entities, or rather 'juridical persons', is involved. One may imagine a

26. WT/DS363/R, AB/R China – Measures Affecting Trading Rights and Distribution Services for Certain Publications and Audiovisual Entertainment Products, adopted on 19.1.2010, Panel report, para. 7.1393.
27. W. Zdouc, 'WTO Dispute Settlement Practice Relating to the GATS', *Journal of International Economic Law* (1999), 295, 331.

'juridical person' from a Member, 'owned' by a juridical person of a Member, beneficially owning 51% of its equity interest. The latter juridical person of a Member is also 'owned' by a juridical person of a Member beneficially owning 51% of its equity interest, etc. As the chain is longer, the effective link to the Members, that the drafters wanted to ensure by this provision, is watered down. Yet, the 'juridical persons' in the chain will be entitled to the agreement's benefits, as well as to the diplomatic protection of the Member involved.[28] The same criticism may apply to the power to name the majority of directors, which is a relatively weaker link than the link of ownership.

The weakest link between persons from a Member and the 'juridical person' is where they can 'otherwise . . . legally direct its actions'. This expression is also vague, unclear and not defined in GATS. The word 'legally' is a key word here, excluding the exercise of illegal affect on the actions of such a juridical person. It may also be interpreted as enfolding a double meaning, the other meaning being 'by legal means', as opposed to mere economic pressure, for example.

The notion of affiliation, expressed in Article XXVIII(n)(iii), is based on the former definition of control. It describes the relationship of a close connection between juridical persons where one controls the other or both are controlled by a third juridical person. The close relationship between such juridical persons may affect their functioning as well as the competitive conditions in the market, and therefore should be taken into account in certain circumstances.[29]

Practical difficulties to prove ownership and/or control were reflected in *EC – Bananas III*:

- One EC claim, rejected by the Panel, was that in the case of transnational companies, the nationality of parent and subsidiary companies is usually not the same. The Panel in that case turned to Article XXVIII(n) contending that 'in order for the complainants to establish that there are non EC-owned or controlled service suppliers commercially present in the EC for GATS purposes . . . it would be sufficient for them to show that (i) entities of the Complainants' origin (ii) control subsidiaries in the EC that supply such services'.[30] This approach was followed in *Canada – Autos* where the Panel held that 'in order to define a "juridical person of another Member" Article XXVIII(m) of GATS does not require the identification of the ultimate controlling juridical or natural person: it is sufficient to establish ownership or control by a juridical person of another Member, defined according to the criteria set out in subparagraph (i)'.[31]

28. *Ibid.*
29. The notion of affiliation is relevant to Art. VIII on monopolies and exclusive service suppliers as well as to Art. 3(d) of the Annex on Telecommunication.
30. WT/DS27/R, AB/R European Communities – Regime for the Importation, Sale and Distribution of Bananas, adopted on 25.9.1997, Panel report, paras 7.328–7.329. The Panel justified its position, in the context of Art. XVII, that was the subject of dispute between the parties.
31. WT/DS139,142/R Canada – Certain Measures Affecting the Automotive Industry, adopted on 19.6.2000, Panel report, para. 10.257.

- Yet a second difficulty raised by the EU was the lack of formal records of shareholders and company registrations to support the complainants' claims. The Panel justified this lack of information, relying on GATS Article III*bis*, which provides: 'nothing in GATS requires any Member to provide confidential information, the disclosure of which . . . would prejudice legitimate commercial interests of particular enterprises'.[32] This may turn to be a permanent difficulty. Furthermore, Article III*bis* may be abused to require the application of GATS provisions to companies that do not fulfil the origin requirements. In the face of the lack of sheer evidence, the Panel will have to decide the cases based only on its confidence in the complainants' claims, as was the case in *EC – Bananas III.*

5.2.4 The Relationship between the Definitions of 'Service Supplier' and 'Commercial Presence'

It should be noted, that these definitions are overlapping but are not identical: 'commercial presence' is limited to Mode 3 while the definition of 'service supplier' may involve the four modes of supply (see Chapter 1). A 'service supplier' is defined as any *person* that supplies a service, thus including *natural* or *juridical* persons. 'Commercial presence' may include other forms than 'juridical person', that is, branches or representative offices that are subject to the non-discrimination disciplines of GATS due to footnote 12 to GATS Article XXVIII(g) (see in 5.2.1.3 above), entitling service suppliers supplying services indirectly, through different forms of commercial presence, to the benefits of the agreement.

This footnote is bridging the divergence between the relatively narrow definition of 'service supplier' and the wider definition of 'commercial presence', according to which the juridical person behind the commercial presence makes use of Mode 3.[33]

In cases of 'juridical persons' in their own right, the defining factors are:

(1) constitution or organization of the juridical person under the law of the relevant Member; and
(2) 'substantive business operation' in the territory of any WTO Member.

Cases of 'commercial presence' that do not enjoy legal personality in their own right are defined on the basis of the origin of the *juridical person* and/or *natural person* that *owns* or *controls* that commercial presence.[34]

32. WT/DS139, 142/R, n. 31, para. 7.331.
33. GATS commentary, n. 14, 555.
34. W. Zdouc, n. 27, 329–330.

5.3 THE CRITICISM ON GATS RULES OF ORIGIN

5.3.1 Narrow Scope of Application

In many cases, the rules chosen narrow the scope of application of GATS benefits compared to the possible scenarios. Thus, for example, the definition of 'service of another Member' does not cover a situation where the service is supplied through some 'stations'. Adopting a similar approach to that adopted for trade in goods, GATS could have determined that the relative contribution of each 'station' to the final service should be weighed in order to establish its share in the total process. However, the intangibility of services could make it difficult to receive and assess these data. Alternatively, it could be established, that a service shall be entitled to GATS benefits if the majority of 'stations' in which it was produced are in Members. A difficulty could, however, arise where the majority of 'stations' would be responsible to a relatively minor portion of the entire service, while the lion share of the service is produced in a source which is not entitled to GATS benefits. Anyhow, GATS drafters chose not to confront these difficulties at all.

Another example that contributes to the narrowing of GATS scope of application is the threshold of more than 50% in the definition of permanent establishment ownership.

The narrow scope of definitions is not compatible with the general purpose of GATS to enhance international trade liberalization in services. However, it could be understood in light of the need to balance between this purpose, on the one hand, and the prevention of abuse of the agreement by sophisticated business constructions, that do not promote the agreement's purposes in essence, as well as with other interests mentioned in the Preamble, on the other hand.

5.3.2 Unclear, Vague Language

GATS rules of origin suffer from a deficiency characterizing many provisions in WTO agreements, including GATS. These agreements include many vague expressions that have no agreed interpretation. The provisions examined include some such expressions: 'substantive business operations', 'more favourable treatment', 'or otherwise to legally direct its actions'.

Such expressions undermine the predictability and certainty of the rules of origin. In most cases, they will be interpreted by each Member, taking the risk that its interpretation will be retroactively rejected by the WTO dispute settlement mechanism.

In addition, not all cases are covered by these rules. Thus, for example, a foreign employee working for a domestically owned firm seems not to be covered by these rules. In principle, private parties are not entitled to the protection of the agreement. However, where foreign firms or independent service suppliers from Members are involved, their country of origin may intervene to obtain their rights. This is impossible where the affected 'service supplier' is considered to be of domestic origin.

5.4 THE RELATIONSHIP BETWEEN GATS RULES OF ORIGIN AND THE RULES OF ORIGIN OF MEMBERS

GATS does not address the relationship between its rules of origin and the rules of origin obliging its Members, being parties to other international trade agreements. GATS Article V, recognizing economic integration agreements as an exception to the MFN rule, subjects this recognition, *inter alia*, to a requirement that these agreements will not raise the overall level of barriers to trade in services in the respective sectors or sub-sectors in respect of any Member outside the agreement, compared to the level applicable prior to such an agreement.[35] The compliance of a certain economic integration agreement with GATS Article V conditions is examined by the CRTA. Allegedly, it could be claimed before it, in the course of examination of such an agreement, that rules of origin of that economic integration agreement infringe this rule. The question whether rules of origin could be viewed as barriers to trade was addressed in GATT 1947 context but not decided.[36] The immediate legal implication of such a determination could be a decision by CRTA that the economic integration agreement examined does not fulfil the conditions set forth by Article V, and therefore the agreement should not be recognized as an exception to the MFN principle included in GATS. (See full explanation of the MFN principle in Chapter 6. See full explanation of GATS Article V in Chapter 10.)

Such a decision may have far-reaching implications beyond the specific case involved, since this could be a decision establishing a general principle, based not on the examination of any specific rules of origin involved, but on the general idea that the proliferation of economic integration agreements, all including different rules of origin, creates this 'spaghetti bowl' of rules that in effect serve as barriers to trade. Such a decision could affect the overall policy of recognizing economic integration agreements as exceptions to the MFN rule and may limit their conclusion. It could further encourage some harmonization of rules of origin at the WTO-level. However, such an interpretation will deprive Article V:4 completely off any meaning, thus being incompatible with the provisions of the Vienna Convention.

The approach embodied in GATT 1947 that avoided including rules of origin and only provided that such rules formed by the Members, should not be used as unnecessary or disguised barriers to trade, saved the need to determine the relationship between two sets of rules: those of GATT and those of economic integration agreements. Nevertheless, the need for more certainty finally prevailed in GATT as well as in GATS contexts. The formation of rules of origin in GATS raises the need to address the relationship between the two sets of rules. In the current wording of GATS this subject is not addressed.

35. GATS Art. V:4.

36. See *Analytical Index – Guide to GATT Law and Practice*, the WTO, Geneva (1995), vol. 2, 802–803.

5.5 CONCLUSION

As with most international trade agreements, GATS includes rules of origin, aiming at ensuring that its benefits will not be accorded to 'free riders'. Nevertheless, the fact that GATS applies to services, which are intangible and supplied in four modes of supply, and furthermore to service suppliers, which may be individuals or legal entities, substantially complicates its rules of origin, compared to such rules for trade in goods. Additional difficulties arise where services serve as inputs for, or are incorporated into, goods or other services, where it should be decided whether they acquire the origin of the latter or retain their own origin.[37] Vague wording adds to these inherent difficulties.

37. W. Zdouc, n. 27, 328.

Chapter 6
The Most Favoured Nation Principle

6.1 INTRODUCTION

The MFN principle is one of the two non-discrimination principles included in GATS. It prevents discrimination among like services and service suppliers from different Members, thus complementing the national treatment principle (to be discussed in Chapter 8), that prevents discrimination between imported and domestic like services and service suppliers. The most favoured nation principle ensures that each Member shall accord to services and service suppliers from other Members the most favoured treatment it accords to like imported services and service suppliers from any other state, whether or not a WTO Member.[1] This principle balances the interests emanating from the fact, that each Member has, at the same time, a double role in GATS context: that of a rights-provider and that of a beneficiary.[2] This principle presumes that a Member indeed accords trade benefits to other states, otherwise having no meaning at all. Nevertheless, the MFN principle is neutral in the sense that it is aimed at abolishing differences, which may be equalized by lower or higher level to all. The MFN principle does not necessarily guarantee that the higher level of benefits is being preserved.[3]

The economic logic behind this provision is to eliminate discrimination in order to ensure the most efficient access for service suppliers to foreign markets, thus supporting the best allocation of resources.[4] In addition, prohibition of discrimination is believed to encourage the willingness of countries to give trade

1. As the number of WTO Members grows, the reference to concessions given to third countries becomes less important.
2. Y. Yang, 'Most Favored Nation Treatment Under the General Agreement on Trade in Services – and its Application in Financial Services', *30 Journal of World Trade* (1996), 91, 96.
3. R. Worfrum, P.T. Stoll & C. Feinäugle (eds), *WTO – Trade in Services,* Max Planck Commentaries on World Trade Law, Martinus Mijnhoff Publishers, Leiden, Boston (2008) (hereby: GATS commentary), 73.
4. GATS commentary, n. 3, 75.

concessions,[5] although it may act in the opposite direction as well, deterring a Member from according trade concessions in the WTO framework, due to their automatic application to more than 150 WTO Members.

The MFN requirement is a powerful instrument for small countries lacking the economic leverage or administrative resources to negotiate effectively with large trading partners:[6] it ensures that these countries will, nevertheless, enjoy the benefits embodied in the agreement.

The importance of this provision is reflected, *inter alia*, in Article X:2 of the WTO Agreement which provides that this provision may be amended only upon acceptance by all Members.

The MFN principle is embodied in GATS Article II,[7] providing:

Most-Favoured-Nation Treatment

1. With respect to any measure covered by this Agreement, each Member shall accord immediately and unconditionally to services and service suppliers of any other Member treatment no less favourable than that it accords to like services and service suppliers of any other country.
2. A Member may maintain a measure inconsistent with paragraph 1 provided that such a measure is listed in, and meets the conditions of, the Annex on Article II Exemptions.
3. The provisions of this Agreement shall not be so construed as to prevent any Member from conferring or according advantages to adjacent countries in order to facilitate exchanges limited to contiguous frontier zones of services that are both locally produced and consumed.

6.2 THE BURDEN OF PROOF

The WTO adjudicating bodies[8] developed a three phase examination[9] for the application of Article II:1 in a given case:

(1) Determination whether the measure examined is 'covered' by GATS, that is, 'affecting trade in services' (Article I:1).

---

5. WT/DS139, 142/AB/R Canada – Certain Measures Affecting the Automotive Industry, adopted on 19.6.2000, para. 84.
6. R. Adlung & A. Mattoo, 'The GATS', in A. Mattoo, R.M. Stern & G. Zanini (eds), *A Handbook of International Trade in Services,* Oxford University Press (2007), 48, 64.
7. An MFN provision exists in other WTO agreements as well, including Arts I:1, V:5 and IX:1 of GATT and Art. 4 of the TRIPS. For the legislative history of this provision see: GATS commentary, n. 3, 77–78.
8. In WT/DS27/R, AB/R European Communities – Regime for the Importation, Sale and Distribution of Bananas, adopted on 25.9.1997, Panel report, para. 7.344, the first two stages were mentioned. The third stage was added in the case of WT/DS139, 142/AB/R *Canada – Autos*, n. 5 paras 170–171, 180.
9. F. Ortino, 'Regional Trade Agreements and Trade in Services', in S. Lester & B. Mercurino (eds), *Bilateral and Regional Trade Agreements: Commentary, Analysis and Case Studies*, Cambridge CPU (2007), 6, <http://papers.ssrn.com>.

(2) Determination whether the services and/or service suppliers concerned are 'like', and establishment of the factual findings concerning the treatment of the imported service or service supplier, compared to the like domestic service or service supplier, respectively, in the case examined.
(3) Application of Article II:1 to the facts, to conclude whether the facts reflect a 'less favourable treatment' which is contrary to this Article.[10]

Application of these tests in practice may involve complex evidentiary problems, due to the necessity to ensure that the origin of the service/service supplier affected is in a Member, particularly in cases of de facto discrimination, and the necessity to investigate the particular situation of each and every private company that qualifies as a service supplier for the service at stake, which could be a very burdensome task considering the practice of dispute settlement under GATS, where a certain degree of aggregation is inevitable.[11]

6.3 SCOPE OF APPLICATION

6.3.1 MEASURES

Article II:1 provides that the MFN principle will apply to 'any measure covered by this agreement'. 'Measure' is defined in GATS Article XXVIII(a):

> 'Measure' means any measure by a Member, whether in the form of law, regulation, rule, procedure, decision, administrative action or any other form.

This definition is very wide and flexible, and should be read in conjunction with GATS Article I:1 which defines GATS scope of application, providing:

> 'This agreement applies to measures by Members, affecting trade in services' (see Chapter 4).

As a matter of fact, these definitions do not exclude, a priori, the application of GATS disciplines, including the MFN principle, to any possible measure.

Thus, the MFN principle implies that each Member shall apply, immediately and unconditionally, to all other Members:

- Its specific commitments (see Chapters 7–9).
- Any advantage, favour, privilege or immunity, beyond its schedule of specific commitments, accorded to services and service suppliers of other Members.

---

10. In GATT case WT/DS26/AB/R EC – Measures Concerning Meat and Meat Products (Hormones), adopted on 13.2.1998 it was established that the application of the law to the facts of a case constitutes an issue of law and thus, pursuant to Art. 17.6 DSU, is part of the Appellate Body's competence. This element is therefore potentially subject to examination by WTO adjudicating bodies.
11. W. Zdouc, *Legal Problems Arising Under the General Agreement on Trade in Services – Comparative Analysis of GATS and GATT,* dissertation der Universität St. Gallen (2002), 340.

– Any advantage, favour, privilege or immunity accorded to services and service suppliers of any non-Member – to like services and service suppliers from Members.

As a result:

> [t]his provision constitutes a general obligation which is, in principle, applicable across the board by all Members to all services sectors, not only in sectors or sub-sectors where specific commitments have been undertaken. Any exception to this general obligation would have to be provided for explicitly in accordance with the terms of the GATS.[12]

6.3.1.1 'Affecting'

This word does not explicitly appear in Article II:1, but is part of the scope of the agreement defined in Article I:1.

The MFN standard in GATT applies only to goods, not to their producers or suppliers. Thus, where a measure affects these producers or suppliers they have to prove an effect on the goods in order to gain the MFN standard protection. In GATS, the MFN applies to services *and to service suppliers*. Thus, where a measure violates the MFN standard with regard to service suppliers, they might have an easier burden of proof if this provision is interpreted to be fulfilled where a measure affects services *or* service suppliers. (See discussion in Chapter 4.)

In cases involving goods and services it is important not to mix between the factual proof concerning violation of the MFN principle in GATT with the factual proof concerning violation of that principle in GATS. In *Canada-Autos*, the Appellate Body reversed the Panel analysis and decision concerning the application of the MFN provision in GATS for that reason, contending:[13]

> the Panel has conducted a 'goods' analysis of this measure, and has simply extrapolated its analysis of how the import duty affects manufacturers to wholesale trade service suppliers of motor vehicles . . . the Panel failed to demonstrate how the import duty exemption, granted to certain manufacturers, but not to other manufacturers, affects the supply of wholesale trade services and the suppliers of wholesale trade services of motor vehicles.

6.4 'IMMEDIATELY AND UNCONDITIONALLY'

In GATS, the MFN principle applies immediately and unconditionally. It means that it applies automatically and without any delay once a Member joins GATS.

12. WT/DS27/R, AB/R/USA *EC – Bananas III*, n. 8, Panel report para. 7.298. Before GATS conclusion, the MFN principle for services was applied in bilateral or multilateral trade agreements to their parties. In GATS, for the first time, this principle is applied at once to more than 150 GATS Member States: Y. Yang, n. 2, 93.
13. WT/DS139,142/AB/R *Canada – Autos*, n. 5, para. 181.

It is impossible to subject this principle to any preconditions, or to permanently exclude any category of services or service suppliers from its scope of application. This treatment is not subject to the specific commitments made by Members, thus applying to all service sectors in which a Member gives any trade concession to any other state. Thus, a Member which did not take any specific commitment in legal services may maintain or apply any restriction in this sector. However, if it removes any restriction, or gives any privilege, with regard to the provision of such services from any country (whether a Member or a non-Member of GATS), it has to remove that restriction or give that privilege to all GATS Members.

Article II includes two exceptions to this principle: a list of individual exemptions (Article II:2) and exchanges of services in frontier zones (Article II:3), to be discussed below.

6.4.1 'Immediately'

The right of a Member to MFN treatment is established once any GATS Member accords a concession to any other state, whether a GATS Member or not. Article II:1 does not specify whether the MFN principle covers concessions given by a Member *before* joining GATS, but customarily, it is interpreted as covering these concessions. The reason is that the purpose of this provision is to put the Members who are entitled to the MFN treatment and the country that enjoys the concession on the same footing. Limiting the application of the equal treatment rule only to future benefits would have undermined this purpose.

The immediate application may take place either in cases where the services at stake were already traded between two Members before the concession was accorded to a third party, thus applying immediately, but not retroactively, between the two Members, or where trade in the relevant services between the two Members starts after the concession was given to the third party. In that case, the relevant concession will be accorded immediately between them, since the beginning of trade in the relevant service.[14]

6.4.2 'Unconditionally'

The unconditionality of this principle was adopted due to the fear, mainly, of developing countries that subjecting the MFN principle to conditions would create a 'selective' application of it, as Members would deny trade concessions to other Members for not satisfying a certain level of liberalization in return. This notion is driven from the equivalent GATT Article I. In that context, trade concessions subject to conditions were found to be inconsistent with the MFN principle, although meeting some origin-neutral requirements.[15]

14. GATS commentary, n. 3, 85–86.
15. See, for example, WT/DS54,55/R Indonesia – Certain Measures Affecting the Automobile Industry, adopted on 23.7.1998, paras 14.145–14.147.

In the discussions before GATS conclusion, certain countries expressed an expectation that the MFN principle would be conditional. Some Members reacted to its unconditionality by adding to their list of exemptions, according to Article II:2, conditions of mutual market access in certain sectors, such as financial services and maritime transport. Intensified use of the exemptions list undermines the unconditionality of the MFN principle. In order to balance the interest of promoting trade liberalization in services, on the one hand, with the fears of 'free riders',[16] on the other hand, it was determined, that the lists of exemptions would have temporary duration.

The unconditional MFN approach facilitates the development of rule-oriented, instead of power-oriented, relations. It enhances trade efficiency, affecting the costs of transactions, by ensuring access to cheaper costs and to the infrastructure necessary for the supply of services. Such benefits are prevented by an approach that subjects trade benefits to mutuality, thus distorting the effective allocation and use of resources, consequently raising consumers' costs.[17]

In *Canada – Autos* it was established, in the context of the equivalent GATT Article I:1, that the determination whether an advantage has been granted 'unconditionally' cannot be made independently of an examination of whether it involves discrimination between like products of different Members.[18]

In that case the Panel stressed that 'unconditionally', in the context of the equivalent GATT Article I:1, does not necessarily mean that the concession granted must not be subject to any conditions:

> In this respect, it appears to us that there is an important distinction to be made between, on the one hand, the issue of whether an advantage within the meaning of Article I:1 [of GATT 1994 – N.M.] is subject to conditions, and, on the other, whether an advantage, once it has been granted to the product of any country, is accorded 'unconditionally' to the like product of all other Members. An advantage can be granted subject to the conditions without necessarily implying that it is not accorded 'unconditionally' to the like product of the other Member.[19]

A different approach was expressed by the Panel in the later GATT case, *EC – Tariff Preferences,* where this term was interpreted more narrowly based on a dictionary definition, to mean 'not limited by or subject to *any* conditions'. [Emphasis added].[20]

---

16. Thus, for example, the United States withdrew its offer for trade liberalization in financial services claiming, that other Members did not present generous enough offers in return.
17. Y. Yang, n. 2, 123.
18. WT/DS139,142/R *Canada – Autos*, n. 5, Panel report, para. 10.22. This analysis was followed in WT/DS366/R Columbia – Indicative Prices and Restrictions on Ports of Entry, adopted on 20.5.2009, paras 7.361–7.367.
19. WT/DS139,142/R *Canada – Autos*, n. 5, para. 10.24.
20. WT/DS246/R, AB/R European Communities – Conditions for the Granting of Tariff Preferences to Developing Countries, adopted on 20.4.2004, Panel report para. 7.59.

The choice between these interpretative options in GATS context depends on the desired scope of application of this provision. While the broader interpretation tolerates certain conditions accompanying a concession, the narrower approach considers any condition to be an infringement of the MFN principle.

6.4.3 No Offset of More Favourable with Less Favourable Treatment

With regard to GATT 1947, dispute settlement Panels determined that more favourable treatment in one case could not be balanced with less favourable treatment in another case, and the standard of 'no less favourable treatment' should apply in each case separately. It was explained:[21]

> If such balancing were accepted, it would entitle a contracting party to derogate from the most-favoured-nation obligation in one case, in respect of one contracting party, on the ground that it accords more favourable treatment in some other case in respect of another contracting party. In view of the Panel, such an interpretation of the most-favoured-nation obligation of Article I:1 would defeat the very purpose underlying the unconditionality of that obligation.

The same approach was adopted in the context of GATS, in *EC – Bananas III*,[22] where the Panel cited this decision to reject an EC argument that their system of licensing for the importation of bananas gives the bananas of the complainants a certain advantage in the first stage that balances the disadvantage suffered by them in later stages.

6.4.4 List of Exemptions

According to Article II:2, each Member is entitled to submit a list of exemptions[23] to the MFN principle. This list can be only submitted once, when joining GATS.[24]

21. DS18/R US – Denial of Most-Favoured-Nation Treatment as to Non-Rubber Footwear from Brazil, adopted on 19.6.1992, 39S/128, 151, para. 6.10.
22. WT/DS27/R, n. 8, para. 7.239.
23. This arrangement was devised to capture special reciprocal rights already shared by certain Members before the conclusion of GATS: C. Arup, *The New World Trade Organization Agreements*, Cambridge University Press (2000), 111.

    According to the WTO, in 2006 more than eighty Members maintained such exemptions, which were mostly intended to cover trade preferences on a regional basis. The sectors predominantly concerned were road transport and audiovisual services, followed by maritime transport and banking services: WTO explanatory paper, WTO Secretariat, 29.3.2006 (3776.4), 7.
24. Although this is the common practice, it is not necessarily supported by the language of GATS. Art. II:2 subjects this practice to the terms provided for in the Annex on Art. II exemptions. The Annex refers only to one point in time: 'at the entry into force of the WTO Agreement'

It reflects concerns of some industries that MFN allowed competitors located in countries with relatively restrictive policies to benefit from their sheltered markets while enjoying a 'free ride' in less restrictive markets.[25]

The duration of the list of MFN exemptions is limited 'in principle' to a maximal period of ten years.[26] The words, 'in principle', open a way to deviate from this tenet, and indeed, many Members have indicated in their list that the duration of exemptions is 'indefinite'.[27] In fact, no Member is rushing to delete these measures. Thus, exemptions taken by most of the WTO Members in 1994, when GATS was concluded, still exist. These exemptions are subject to reviews[28] and to further negotiations in any subsequent trade round. As a result, even a Member willing to give up an exemption will not do so 'for free', but would rather prefer to negotiate a consideration for it. This provision reflects a compromise achieved by the end of the Uruguay Round between those who believed that MFN should be granted horizontally, across all services, and those who believed that it should only apply in sectors where specific commitments were undertaken.[29]

The lists are constructed according to rules included in the Annex on Article II Exemptions. There are no uniform criteria, agreed by all the Members,

---

(which took place in 1.1.1995). This provision is commonly interpreted as referring to the entry into force of the agreement towards a specific Member who joins it. But this seems to be an inaccurate interpretation, since where this was the drafters' intention, it was specifically pronounced. See, for example, Art. VII:4(a) which provides: 'each Member shall: (a) within twelve months from the date *on which the WTO Agreement takes effect for it...*'

25. B. Hoeckman, 'Tentative First Steps: An Assessment of the Uruguay Round Agreement on Services', *The World Bank Policy Research Working Papers* (1995), 7, <www-wds.worldbank.org>.
26. See additional procedural information in S/L/106 Procedures for the Certification and Terminations, Reductions and Rectifications of Art. II (MFN) Exemptions, 11.6.2002, <http://docsonline.wto.org>.
27. 'The General Agreement on Trade in Services (GATS): an Analysis', *OECD* (1994), 10, <www.olis.oecd.org>.
28. According to GATS, the exemptions that have been granted for periods of more than five years should have been reviewed. In conducting the review, the council for trade in services is mandated, under the Annex on Art. II Exemptions, to 'examine whether the conditions which created the need for the exemption still prevail; and determine the date of any further review'. By now, the exemptions were reviewed twice, in 2000 (S/C/M/44 Council for Trade in Services – Council Review of MFN Exemptions – Report of the Meeting Held on 29 May 2000 – Note by the Secretariat; S/C/M/45 Council for Trade in Services – Council Review of MFN Exemptions – Report of the Meeting Held on 5 Jul. 2000 – Note by the Secretariat; and S/C/M/47 Council for Trade in Services – Council Review of MFN Exemptions – Report of the Meeting Held on 5 Oct. 2000 – Note by the Secretariat) and in 2004 (S/C/M/76 Council for Trade in Services – Council Review of MFN Exemptions – Report of the Meeting Held on 30 Nov. 2004 – Note by the Secretariat; S/C/M/78 Council for Trade in Services – Council Review of MFN Exemptions – Report of the Meeting Held on 23 Feb. 2005 – Note by the Secretariat). Members decided to launch a third review not later than June 2010. In addition, the Hong Kong Declaration adopted on 18 Dec. 2005 commits Members to removing or reducing them substantially and to clarify the scope and duration of the remaining measures: <www.wto.org>.
29. R. Adlung, 'The GATS Turns Ten: A Preliminary Stocktaking', *WTO* (2004), 3, <www.wto.org>.

as to what exemptions are considered legitimate. Probably, it is due to the difficulty to find a common denominator to this end among all the Members.

The list of exemptions is limited to existing measures, although some of the measures included in the list are future measures presented as current ones.[30]

The MFN exemptions can only apply where a Member did *not* take any specific commitment: Article II:2 only allows exemptions from the MFN principle but not from the conditional market access (Article XVI) and national treatment (Article XVII) obligations, subject to the Member' specific commitments. The specific commitments should be thus granted to all Members, without exemptions:

> In other words, if a Member wants to maintain or introduce discriminatory treatment with respect to a certain liberalization measure, it cannot include that measure in its schedule of commitments (and therefore – that is the disincentive – it cannot offer that measure as a concession in the negotiation process).[31]

Some Members wished to allow market access of service suppliers, in their schedules, only *in addition to existing service suppliers* (a grandfathering clause). This practice is contrary to the MFN principle which should not be derogated by the specific commitments, but some Members have such commitments, for example, in financial services.

The MFN exemptions lists may principally cover existing or planned *reciprocity requirements*; namely, requirements for reciprocal procurement of services as a pre-condition for trade. It has been argued that such requirements, although legalized by the MFN exemptions lists, are contrary to GATS spirit, implying reciprocity over the overall balance of commitments and not on a specific measure basis. On the other hand, Members who maintain such provisions argued that they should not even be mentioned in the MFN exemption list, because the relevant law will not be considered as contrary to GATS as long as they provide for administrative discretion allowing the authorities not to apply discriminative sanctions, contrary to GATS, at the end of the procedure.[32]

Exemptions to the MFN principle which are not included in the list could only be obtained by the waiver procedure, according to Article IX:3 of the WTO Agreement (see Chapter 15).

30. See examples in Y. Yang, n. 2, 102, n. 45. Other commentators believe that the list may include future measures, as long as they are described clearly. This approach is justified, *inter alia,* since categories of measures which are not exempted by the list also include future measures. In any case, this maneuvering option between existing and future measure may form a basis for future different interpretations, making the list not completely 'closed' as it claims to be: GATS Analysis, n. 27, 11.
31. GATS Analysis, n. 27, 10.
32. *Ibid.*, 10–11.

6.4.4.1 Aspects of Examination in a Dispute Involving a Claim Concerning an MFN Exemption Listed in the Exemptions List

In disputes involving a claim concerning an exemption included in the exemption list, the following aspects should be ascertained:[33]

(1) Whether the Member involved has scheduled in its national MFN exemption list, an exemption with respect to the particular service sector or mode of supply at issue.
(2) The breadth of that Member's market access and national treatment commitments.
(3) As a separate question, the degree to which the commitments are within the Panel's terms of reference in the particular dispute.

6.4.5 Exchanges of Services in Frontier Zones

Article II:3 allows deviation from the MFN principle with regard to benefits accorded to facilitate exchanges of services, locally produced and consumed, between the two sides of a border in frontier zones. This provision is a result of a controversy that arose between Members concerning the possible inclusion in GATS Article V (economic integration agreements – see Chapter 10) of a provision equivalent to GATT Article XXIV:3, facilitating frontier traffic. This provision, reflecting the final decision of the drafters, narrows down this exception by imposing two strict conditions: (1) Privileged service exchanges are confined to contiguous frontier zones. (2) The potential services qualifying this exception must be locally produced and consumed.[34]

6.4.6 Additional Exceptions to the MFN Principle

In addition to the two exemptions/exceptions to the MFN principle mentioned in Article II:2 and II:3, GATS includes other ways to deviate from this principle, effectively diminishing its scope of application. They include:

- Article V (regional trade agreements) – discussed in Chapter 10.
- The general exceptions (Article XIV) and the security exception (Article XIV*bis*) – discussed in Chapter 15.
- Government procurements (Article XIII) – discussed in Chapter 2.
- Modification or withdrawal of benefits by a Member, affected by the modification of schedules of specific commitments by another Member, who

33. W. Zdouc, 'WTO Dispute Settlement Practice Relating to the GATS', *Journal of International Economic Law* (1999), 295, 322.
34. W. Zdouc, n. 11, 219.

does not comply with the findings of an arbitration concerning compensation (Article XXI:4(b)).
- The waiver process (Article IX:3 of the WTO Agreement).
- Non-application of the WTO agreements between particular Members, due to political or economic reasons (Article XIII of the WTO Agreement).

All discussed in Chapter 15.

- Recognition (Article VII) – discussed in Chapter 12, is also considered by some as belonging to this group.

Additional, sector-specific exemptions, discussed in Chapter 16, exist concerning:

- *Financial services* – according to the fifth protocol to GATS.[35]
- *Maritime transport* – according to the Decision on Maritime Transport Services adopted by the Council for Trade in Services at its meeting of 28 June 1996, which suspends negotiations on maritime transport services.[36]
- *Basic telecommunication* – see the Fourth Protocol to GATS, adopted by the Council for Trade in Services at its meeting of 30 April 1996.[37]

It should be noted that where no scheduled commitment exists in a sector or a mode of supply, an exemption from the MFN clause opens the possibility for complete discrimination.[38]

6.5 SERVICES AND SERVICE SUPPLIERS ENTITLED TO MFN TREATMENT

According to Article II:1, services and service suppliers of any other Member are entitled to MFN treatment. Such services and service suppliers are defined in GATS Article XXVII. (See in Chapter 4.) The application of this principle to services as well as to service suppliers implies a broad scope of application. Moreover, the MFN principle applies to the four modes of supply, including commercial presence (Mode 3) and presence of natural persons (Mode 4), where the service supplier supplies the service in the territory of another Member.

35. S/L/45 Fifth Protocol to the General Agreement on Trade in Services, adopted by the Committee on Trade in Financial Services, 14.11.1997 (S/L/44).
36. The Decision further states that such negotiations will resume with 'the commencement of comprehensive negotiations on Services' and that Art. II of GATS will enter into force with respect to 'international shipping, auxiliary services and access to and use of port facilities' when these negotiations have been concluded. S/L/24, WTO Decision on Maritime Transport Services, 3.7.1996 para. 4, <www.wto.org>.
37. S/L/19 Decision on Commitments in Basic Telecommunications – Adopted by the Council for Trade in Services on 30 Apr. 1996, para. 3.
38. GATS commentary, n. 3, 91.

6.6 THE 'NO LESS FAVOURABLE TREATMENT' STANDARD

The standard of treatment ensured by the MFN principle is 'treatment no less favourable than that it accords to like services and service suppliers of any other country'.

No less favourable treatment – this is a common standard in GATS, which is based on GATT language. In both agreements, it is not defined, thus being subject to interpretation. In both agreements, its interpretation raises the following difficulties: should the treatment be assessed formally or substantially? How should the comparison be conducted?

Unlike the language of GATT Article I that mentions sorts of measures to which the non-discrimination provision applies, the language of GATS Article II uses the general term 'measure'. The use of such a broad and flexible term may save arguments as to whether the measure involved in a certain case is subject to this standard.[39] On the other hand, interpretative questions may arise as to what would be considered a 'measure'.

It should be noted, that this standard does not prevent a Member from according another country treatment *more* favourable than that accorded to other countries. However, in such a case all the Members will be entitled to that benefit. Thus, this standard enhances trade liberalization in services.

Any other country – The subject of comparison for the application of the MFN standard is the treatment accorded to any other country, not necessarily a GATS Member.

The standard of 'treatment no less favourable' is also referred to in Article XVII (national treatment), but there the substance of this obligation is specified (see Chapter 8). Article II does not include paragraphs similar to paragraphs 2 and 3 of Article XVII, specifying that such treatment could be formally identical or formally different, subject to the modification of competitive conditions test. The lack of these provisions in Article II raises the interpretative question of whether this is a *lacuna* or rather a deliberate omission, implying a different line of interpretation of Article II.

6.6.1 Interpretation of 'No Less Favourable Treatment' by WTO Adjudicating Bodies

6.6.1.1 Broad Scope of Application

In GATT the 'no less favourable treatment' standard appears, for example, in Article II:1 (Schedules of Specific Commitments) and in Article III:4 (National Treatment), but not in Article I, addressing the MFN standard. GATT Article I provides:

> *[a]ny advantage, favour, privilege or immunity* granted by any contracting party to any product originating in or destined for any other country shall be

39. Y. Yang, n. 2, 97.

> accorded immediately and unconditionally to the like product originating in or destined for the territories of all other contracting parties. [Emphasis added].

Judging by its language, this provision differs from GATS Article II in the wording, scope of coverage, and substantive content. Generally speaking, it seems that GATS provision is spelled out in broader terms than GATT provision. In GATS, the 'no less favourable treatment' standard was preferred, being more general and flexible, thus implying a broader scope of application of the MFN discipline. Nevertheless, due to the broad interpretation of Article I GATT by dispute settlement jurisprudence, in practice its substance is not very different from the 'no less favourable' standard in GATS Article II.[40]

6.6.1.2 A Similar Standard: Preventing Discrimination De Facto and De Jure

The choice, in GATS Article II, of a different language from that used in GATT Article I has not gone unnoticed by the Panel in *EC – Bananas III*:[41]

> While the drafters of the GATS have been guided by GATT concepts, provisions and past practice, they have chosen to use identical operative language of 'treatment no less favourable' in both Articles II and XVII, *departing in the case of Article II from the formulation used in the GATT MFN clause in Article I*... Thus, the formulation of both Articles II and XVII of GATS derives from the 'treatment no less favourable' standard of the GATT national treatment provisions in Article III of GATT, which has been consistently interpreted by past panel reports to be concerned with conditions of competition between like domestic and imported products on internal markets. [Emphasis added].

Nevertheless, in that case,[42] the Panel determined that the words 'no less favourable treatment' in GATS Article II should be interpreted in a manner similar to their interpretation in GATS Article XVII (see Chapter 8) and in GATT Article III, as preventing discriminating treatment de jure as well as de facto. The Panel noted:

> If the standard of 'no less favorable treatment' in Article II were to be interpreted narrowly to require only formally identical treatment, that could lead in many situations to the frustration of the objective behind Article II which is to prohibit discrimination between like services and service suppliers of other Members. It would not be difficult for regulators to contemplate regulatory measures which are identical on their face while in effect provide less favourable competitive opportunities to a group of service suppliers to the advantage of others.

40. W. Zdouc, n. 11, 149.
41. WT/DS27/R, n. 8, para. 7.302.
42. *Ibid.*, Panel report, para. 7.303.

In *Canada – Autos,* the Panel found that discrimination de facto existed due to:

> a measure which, on the one hand, involves a limitation to certain importers of an advantage granted in connection with the importation of a product but which, on the other hand, does not impose conditions regarding the origin of the product which can benefit from such advantage.

The Panel rejected Canada's argument that only a denial of an import benefit based on origin would be considered discrimination, holding that this is too narrow an interpretation which is not supported by GATT Article I:1, contending alternatively that this provision should also apply where the limitation of the benefit 'may by itself have a discriminatory impact on the treatment of like products of different origins'. In the facts of that case, the Panel determined that the limitation of eligibility for the exemption from import duty to certain importers in Canada, who were affiliated with manufacturers in certain countries, affected the geographical distribution of the imports, thus de facto discriminating the importers who were not entitled to the benefit. [43] This conclusion was upheld by the Appellate Body.[44]

6.6.1.3 The Competitive Opportunities Test

The competitive opportunities test was developed in GATT and 'imported' into GATS with the use of the expression 'less favourable treatment' in GATS Articles II and XVII. This test defines as discrimination of imported services or service suppliers situations where their competitive opportunities in the market of import are undermined. GATS Article XVII:3 explicitly provides:

> Formally identical or formally different treatment shall be considered to be less favourable if it modifies the conditions of competition in favour of services and service suppliers of the Member compared to like services and service suppliers of any other Member.

Unlike Article XVII, GATS Article II does not include a similar language, namely: does not explicitly address the competitive opportunities test. Since there is no doubt that this test was known to GATS drafters, being included by them explicitly in GATS Article XVII, the interpretative question is: why did they refrain from explicitly referring to this test in Article II? Was it intentional? And if so – what was their intention? And what alternative test could be used?

The WTO adjudicating bodies seem to overlook this difficulty and apply to Article II the same test. The Panel in *EC – Bananas III* said:

> The absence of similar language in Article II is not, in our view, a justification for giving a different ordinary meaning in terms of Article 31(3) of the Vienna

43. WT/DS139,142/R *Canada – Autos*, n. 5, paras 10.37, 10.40, 10.47.
44. WT/DS139,142/AB/R *Canada – Autos,* n. 5, Appellate Body report, para. 78.

> Convention to the words 'treatment no less favourable' which are identical in both Articles II:1 and XVII:1.[45]

This decision was criticized by the EC in their appeal, on the ground that different language implies a different meaning.[46] The Appellate Body in the same case tried to disqualify this test literally, but in fact found it impossible to otherwise interpret this provision, and therefore returned to the same test 'through the back door':

> We find the Panel's reasoning on this issue to be less than fully satisfactory.
>
> The Panel interpreted Article II of the GATS in the light of panel reports interpreting the national treatment obligation of Article III of the GATT. The Panel also referred to Article XVII of the GATS, which is also a national treatment obligation. But Article II of the GATS relates to MFN treatment, not to national treatment. Therefore, provisions elsewhere in the GATS relating to national treatment obligations, and previous GATT practice relating to the interpretation of the national treatment obligation of Article III of the GATT 1994 are not necessarily relevant to the interpretation of Article II of the GATS. The Panel would have been on safer ground had it compared the MFN obligation in Article II of the GATS with the MFN and MFN-type obligations in the GATT 1994 . . .
>
> The GATS negotiators chose to use different language in Article II and Article XVII of the GATS in expressing the obligation to provide 'treatment no less favourable'. The question naturally arises: if the GATS negotiators intended that 'treatment no less favourable' should have exactly the same meaning in Articles II and XVII of the GATS, why did they not repeat paragraphs 2 and 3 of Article XVII in Article II? But that is not the question here. The question here is the meaning of 'treatment no less favourable' with respect to the MFN obligation in Article II of the GATS. There is more than one way of writing a de facto non-discrimination provision. Article XVII of the GATS is merely one of many provisions in the *WTO Agreement* that require the obligation of providing 'treatment no less favourable'. The possibility that the two Articles may not have exactly the same meaning does *not* imply that the intention of the drafters of the GATS was that a de jure, or formal, standard should apply in Article II of the GATS. If that were the intention, why does Article II not say as much? The obligation imposed by Article II is unqualified. The ordinary meaning of this provision does not exclude de facto discrimination. Moreover, if Article II was not applicable to de facto discrimination, it would not be difficult – and, indeed, it would be a good deal easier in the case of trade in services, than in the case of trade in goods – to devise discriminatory measures aimed at circumventing the basic purpose of that Article.
>
> For these reasons, we conclude that 'treatment no less favourable' in Article II:1 of the GATS should be interpreted to include de facto, as well as de jure, discrimination. We should make it clear that we do not limit our

45. WT/DS27/R, n. 8, para. 7.301.
46. WT/DS27/AB/R *EC – Bananas III*, n. 8, Appellate Body report, para. 48.

> conclusion to this case. We have some difficulty in understanding why the Panel stated that its interpretation of Article II of the GATS applied '*in casu*'.[47]

Based on this approach the Panel in *Canada – Autos* determined that a situation where measures reserve access to duty-free goods (cars) to a closed category of service suppliers, which were not mentioned in Canada's list of MFN exemptions, 'allow some wholesale trade service suppliers to import and resell under more favourable conditions, while putting at a *competitive disadvantage* other suppliers, who have to pay the tariff or buy licenses out of the tariff quota'.[48] [Emphasis added].

An alternative approach to this linguistic difference could be based on the assumption that indeed GATS drafters meant 'no less favourable treatment' to have a different meaning in these two provisions: a lesser degree of obligation under the MFN provision, since it is unconditional and has a broader scope than the national treatment provision, which is conditional.[49] The result of the interpretation chosen by the Appellate Body implies a stronger MFN obligation compared to the alternative approach.

6.6.1.3.1 *Vertical Integration, Exclusive Distribution Arrangements and Mutuality Agreements*

Vertical integration, exclusive distribution arrangements and mutuality agreements are three common commercial practices. Nevertheless, it is clear that these practices intrinsically imply some limitation of competition in the market where they apply. Therefore, the relationships between these practices and GATS non-discrimination provisions are not obvious, and should be questioned.

In *Canada – Autos,*[50] the Panel said:

> We therefore *find* that vertical integration and exclusive distribution arrangements between manufacturers and wholesalers in the motor vehicle industry do not rule out the possibility that treatment less favourable may be granted to suppliers of wholesale trade services for motor vehicles. We also *find* that vertical integration and exclusive distribution arrangements do not preclude potential competition among wholesalers for the procurement of vehicles from manufacturers and actual inter-brand competition for sales to retailers.

The Appellate Body reversed these findings, determining that they were 'pure speculation', providing that the Panel did not find any evidence defining the relationship between manufacturers and wholesalers in the Canadian market, did not examine the structure of competition in that market and failed to analyse whether and how the measure at stake affects service suppliers who benefit from the trade concessions compared to service suppliers who do not benefit from it.[51]

47. *Ibid*, paras 231, 233–234.
48. WT/DS139,142/R *Canada – Autos,* n. 5, Panel report, para. 10.246. See also para. 10.262.
49. W. Zdouc, n. 11, 187–188.
50. WT/DS139,142/R *Canada – Autos*, n. 5, Panel report, para. 10.254.
51. WT/DS139,142/AB/R *Canada – Autos*, n. 5, Appellate Body report, para. 174.

This decision reflects the difficulty of WTO adjudicating bodies to engage in a thorough fact-finding investigation.[52] The Appellate Body's decision may further be questioned against the willingness of WTO adjudicating bodies to recognize *potential* service suppliers as 'affected' by a measure. (See discussion in Chapter 4 – 4.3.7.2.4.1). It could be suggested that where a service supplier is practically affected, the evidence to this effect should be presented and weighed by the adjudicating bodies. Where there are service suppliers which *might potentially* be affected, it is clear that since the effect did not occur yet, there is no evidence to present. Nevertheless, the result of this interpretation is that a higher burden of proof is imposed in the former case than in the latter case. This result does not seem logical.

It seems that mutuality agreements between Members will also be considered as hampering the MFN principle, because they undermine the competitive conditions of Members which are not parties to them. A practical solution for Members who nevertheless wish to exercise this practice may be to accord minimal access to all Members in the relevant specific commitment, and exercise mutuality beyond this specific commitment.

6.6.1.3.2 The Aim-and-Effect Test

The aim-and-affect test was developed in GATT context and later examined in GATS context as an alternative to the competitive opportunities test. According to it, the aim of a measure is decisive in order to determine whether the measure examined is discriminating imported goods, services or service suppliers compared to domestic like ones. If the aim of the measure is not discriminatory – the measure will not be considered as discriminating, even if its result is discriminatory. This test was later rejected by the WTO adjudicating bodies for GATT as well as for GATS purposes, realizing that in order to fulfil the purpose of enhanced trade liberalization the final outcome should be preferred over the intention. If the outcome is discriminating, the agreements' purpose is undermined. Therefore, the competitive opportunities test prevailed.[53] Still, there are commentators who criticize this decision[54] and believe that this doctrine might be revisited in the future. (See additional discussion in Chapter 8 – 8.8).

6.6.1.4 Minimum Standard

The Secretariat 2001 guidelines for scheduling commitments (see details in Chapter 7) explain:

> A Member taking a national treatment or a market access commitment in a sector must accord the stated *minimum* standard of treatment specified in its schedule to all other Members. The MFN obligation requires that the most

52. W. Zdouc, n. 11, 340.
53. WT/DS27/AB/R, n. 8, Appellate Body report, para. 241.
54. See, for example, W. Zdouc, n. 11, 183.

> favourable treatment *actually* accorded in all sectors, whether the subject of a commitment or not, must also be accorded to all other Members. Where an MFN exemption has been granted for a measure, a Member is free to deviate from its Article II obligations, but not from its Article XVI and Article XVII commitments. Therefore, in such cases, a Member may accord treatment in that sector more favourable than the minimum standard to some Members, as long as all other Members receive at least that minimum standard of market access and national treatment appearing in its schedule. In such cases, it is not possible for a Member to accord less favourable treatment to certain Members than that specified in its schedule (for example, on grounds of reciprocity or the lack of it).[55] [Emphasis in the original].

The guidelines do not form an integral part of GATS, nor part of its context, but were recognized by the Appellate Body as an interpretative means according to Article 32 of the Vienna Convention.[56]

6.6.2 'Like' Services and Service Suppliers

Services and service suppliers from other Members are entitled to the MFN treatment by a Member, if they are 'like' the service or service suppliers compared to the services or to the service suppliers from another country, respectively, who are entitled to a more favourable treatment. In other words, the entitlement to the MFN principle depends on proving a resemblance between the service or service supplier accepting this treatment, and the one claiming to deserve it.

The word 'like' is not defined in GATS. The same word was used in GATT, similarly undefined. However, in GATT this word was interpreted in many dispute settlement cases, determining the following rules:

(1) The term 'like' is interpreted on a case-by-case basis.
(2) To determine 'likeness', the WTO adjudicating bodies addressed, *inter alia*, the following aspects: customs classification, end uses, physical characteristics and consumption habits.[57]

In principle, a similar approach could be adopted for the interpretation of 'like' services in GATS. Thus, 'likeness' could be addressed on a case-by-case basis, and

55. S/L/92 Guidelines for the Scheduling of Specific Commitments Under the General Agreement on Trade in Services (GATS), published 28.3.2001, para. 21; Adopted by the Council for Trade in services on 23.3.2001, S/C/M/52, para. 11. See the text of the guidelines in <http://docsonline.wto.org>.
56. WT/DS285/AB/R US – Measures Affecting the Cross-Border Supply of Gambling and Betting Services, adopted on 20.4.2005, Appellate Body report, paras 175–177.
57. WT/DS26/R/USA *EC – Hormones*, n. 10, Panel report, paras 4.261–4.266. In this case the EC claimed, that the MFN principle should be interpreted as allowing the discrimination of like products as long as the Members are not discriminated. The Panel abstained from addressing this claim and decided the case based on other provisions.

be determined *inter alia* addressing the classification of the service involved,[58] its end uses, modes of supply, and consumption habits.

However, in GATS context, an interpretative difficulty could stem from the unique characteristics of services: their intangibility prevents the use of the 'physical characteristics' test. In addition, it seems that aspects such as the practical ability or capacity to provide a service, as well as the size of incorporated service suppliers, number of employees, skills of the staff, the type of its assets, its technological equipment, and its traditional field of business[59] should be taken into account.

Both in GATT and in GATS contexts, the definition of 'likeness' requires a definition of the relevant market.[60] Some commentators[61] recommend doing so on the basis of cross-price elasticity demand, meaning that 'likeness' will be determined through comparison between the 'reference' service and all the other services that, if sold or made available in a Member at a global price, will lead to a decrease in the price of the 'reference' service by a certain percentage. However, this approach is criticized by others, suggesting that 'a state cannot be expected to regulate on the basis of second-guessing domestic consumer preferences'.[62] (See additional discussion in 8.5.3.2).

The language of Article II:1 addresses 'like services and service suppliers'. As for service suppliers, it would be even more difficult to assess 'likeness', taking into account personal differences, differences in the quality of the service provided, in the character, skills, attitude, talent, experience and reputation of the service suppliers compared.

Other questions arising in this context are: should the service supplier supply the service in the same mode of supply in order for it to be considered as 'like'?[63] It is suggested, for example, that 'stretching *likeness* across modes [of supply] may turn the GATS non-discrimination clauses into tools compelling Members to

58. For the purpose of constructing GATS schedules of specific commitments, a common classification method was developed. See explanation in Ch. 7.
59. W. Zdouc, n. 11, 333.
60. J.B. Goco, 'Non-Discrimination, "Likeness", and Market Definition in World Trade Organization Jurisprudence', *40 Journal of World Trade* (2006), 315, 332.
61. J.B. Goco, n. 60, 338; G. Verhoosel, *National Treatment and the WTO Dispute Settlement* Hart Publishing (2002). This suggestion is inspired by GATT jurisprudence on GATT Art. III (national treatment), which considered the role of this test in that context: WT/DS8,10,11/R Japan – Taxes on Alcoholic Beverages, adopted on 1.11.1996, Appellate Body report, 25; A more ambivalent approach is reflected in WT/DS75,84/AB/R Korea – Taxes on Alcoholic Beverages, adopted on 17.2.1999, Appellate Body report, para. 121.
62. R. Pillai, 'Review Article: National Treatment and the WTO Dispute Settlement', *1 World Trade Review* (2002), 321, 338.
63. This question was raised, for instance, during the discussions on GATS application to electronic commerce: should electronically delivered services and those delivered by other methods be considered 'like services'? No decision was accepted. See: S/L/74 Work Program on Electronic Commerce – Progress Report to the General Council, adopted by the Council for trade in services in 19.7.1999.

comprehensive harmonization of domestic legislation and economic integration of their market'.[64]

Is there any relevance to the fact that the service supplier is an individual or a juridical person? Should the 'likeness' requirement be fulfilled, in each case, for the service *and* the service supplier? These questions were not yet addressed particularly by the dispute settlement authorities. However, in *EC – Bananas III* and *Canada – Autos*[65] a very simplifying approach was taken by the Panels, both agreeing that 'to the extent that the service suppliers concerned supply the same services, they should be considered "like" for the purpose of this case'. It is not clear, whether this determination will stand in more elaborated cases that may occur in the future.

6.7 CONCLUSION

The MFN principle is a core principle in GATS, ensuring non-discrimination among different sources of import from Members. Ambiguous expressions included in it make it more flexible, on the one hand, but necessarily weaker on the other hand. Since no much jurisprudence interpreting this provision is available as yet, many interpretative dilemmas, presented in this chapter, still remain open. The time factor may raise additional difficulties to the interpretative difficulties already described above. Thus, it is questionable whether preferential market arrangements (e.g., monopoly status) that were made earlier to GATS could be challenged by the MFN provision. In addition, it is questionable to what extent the MFN requirement would oblige administrations developing new regulatory codes (e.g., building codes or safety requirements) to subject existing foreign-owned operations to the same standards as new start-ups.[66]

64. W. Zdouc, n. 11, 150.
65. WT/DS27/R *EC – Bananas III*, n. 8, Panel report, para. 7.322; WT/DS139,142/R *Canada – Autos*, n. 5, para. 10.248.
66. R. Adlung, n. 29, 11.

Chapter 7
Schedules of Specific Commitments

7.1 INTRODUCTION

Article XX:1 of GATS requires each Member that joins GATS to submit a schedule of specific commitments, annexed to the agreement and viewed as an integral part of it. The submission of a schedule of specific commitments is obligatory, as Article XX:1 starts with the words 'each Member *shall* set out in a schedule . . . '. Accordingly, each Member has to undertake at least some minimal commitments to apply the national treatment and market access obligations. However, no threshold is determined by GATS in terms of number or level of a Member's sectoral commitments. The agreement neither compels Members, even in sectors they include in schedules, to offer conditions that are more liberal than the prevailing trading conditions.[1] Therefore, a Member may do with some minimal commitments to that extent, and still enjoy the entire benefits of GATS and of the other WTO obligatory Agreements.[2]

The schedules submitted by the Members are lists that specify to which service sectors and modes of supply a Member chooses to apply the national treatment and

1. A. Carzaniga, 'The GATS, Mode 4 and pattern of Commitments', in A. Mattoo & A. Carzaniga (eds), *Moving People to Deliver Services*, The World Bank and Oxford University Press (2003), 21.
2. Indeed, the level of GATS commitments in the Uruguay Round is not considered to be relatively high. This outcome is explained by the cautious approach taken by many Members in the first round of negotiations, and by the expectation of further liberalization to emanate from future successive rounds of negotiations. However, it is also a result of political economy considerations: M. Roy, 'Endowment, Power, and Democracy: Political Economy of Multilateral Commitments on Trade in Services', WTO Economic Research and Statistics Staff Working Paper No. 2009-07 (2010), <http://papers.ssrn.com>.

market access obligations (as well as possible additional commitments) according to GATS, and subject to what conditions. Thus, the schedules represent a 'bottom up' or a 'positive list' approach applied by the agreement to these two disciplines.[3] The schedules may further specify additional specific commitments this Member undertakes. It is equivalent to the bound tariffs under GATT. The schedules thus represent the minimum level of trade concessions guaranteed by a Member. Members remain free to apply a more liberal regime than that described in the schedules, but may not, as a rule, apply a less liberal regime than that described in the schedules.

The schedules of specific commitments ensure transparency of market terms, and at the same time form the basis for further negotiations, aimed at improving access to that market.

As a rule, the schedules may be modified at the end of every round of negotiations committed under GATS Article XIX[4] as a result of a mutual process of give-and-take that takes place among the Members during the round. As a general rule, the schedules are subject to two rules: *standstill*, according to which a Member is not allowed to back off its commitments specified in the schedule; and *rollback,* according to which at each round of negotiations a Member is expected to improve its commitments, namely to enhance trade liberalization. However, GATS includes 'safety valves' allowing deviation from these rules in exceptional circumstances, to be discussed in Chapter 15.

---

3. This approach was criticized for achieving a narrower scope of service trade liberalization than a 'negative list' approach that could have applied GATS disciplines automatically to all sectors and modes of supply, but those explicitly excluded from its application. However, this approach does not only reflect the cautious approach which characterized the first round of services trade negotiations. It also solves some practical difficulties encountered by certain Members, who were:

   > not equipped to identify all national and local laws that might conflict with the national treatment and market access provisions. In some cases they did not have the personnel to do it. In other cases their regulatory systems did not evolve to a state where they could identify potential inconsistencies, and they did not want to constrain their future ability to develop their own regulatory approach, or to put themselves in the uncomfortable position of having to renegotiate their commitments.

   G. Feketakuty, 'Assessing and Improving the Architecture of GATS', in P. Sauvé & R. Stern (eds), *GATS 2000: New Direction in Services Trade Liberalization,* The Brookings Institution, Washington USA (2000), 85, 98.

   Some commentators define GATS approach as a positive/negative or a hybrid approach, due to the structure of market access commitments (see Ch. 9): F. Ortino, 'Regional Trade Agreements and Trade in Services', in S. Lester & B. Mercurino (eds), *Bilateral and Regional Trade Agreements: Commentary, Analysis and Case Studies*, Cambridge CPU (2007), 9, <http://papers.ssrn.com>.
4. R. Volfrum, P.T. Stoll & C. Feinäugle (eds), *WTO – Trade in Services,* Max Planck Commentaries on World Trade Law, Leiden/Boston, Martinus Mijhoff Publishers (2008) (hereby: GATS commentary), 427–444, <http://papers.ssrn.com>.

7.2 THE RELEVANT GATS PROVISIONS

Article XIX of GATS provides:

Negotiation of Specific Commitments

1. In pursuance of the objectives of this Agreement, Members shall enter into successive rounds of negotiations, beginning not later than five years from the date of entry into force of the WTO Agreement and periodically thereafter, with a view to achieving a progressively higher level of liberalization. Such negotiations shall be directed to the reduction or elimination of the adverse effects on trade in services of measures as a means of providing effective market access. This process shall take place with a view to promoting the interests of all participants on a mutually advantageous basis and to securing an overall balance of rights and obligations.
2. The process of liberalization shall take place with due respect for national policy objectives and the level of development of individual Members, both overall and in individual sectors. There shall be appropriate flexibility for individual developing country Members for opening fewer sectors, liberalizing fewer types of transactions, progressively extending market access in line with their development situation and, when making access to their markets available to foreign service suppliers, attaching to such access conditions aimed at achieving the objectives referred to in Article IV.
3. For each round, negotiating guidelines and procedures shall be established. For the purposes of establishing such guidelines, the Council for Trade in Services shall carry out an assessment of trade in services in overall terms and on a sectoral basis with reference to the objectives of this Agreement, including those set out in paragraph 1 of Article IV. Negotiating guidelines shall establish modalities for the treatment of liberalization undertaken autonomously by Members since previous negotiations, as well as for the special treatment for least-developed country Members under the provisions of paragraph 3 of Article IV.
4. The process of progressive liberalization shall be advanced in each such round through bilateral, plurilateral or multilateral negotiations directed towards increasing the general level of specific commitments undertaken by Members under this Agreement.

Article XX of GATS provides:

Schedules of Specific Commitments

1. Each Member shall set out in a schedule the specific commitments it undertakes under Part III of this Agreement. With respect to sectors where such commitments are undertaken, each schedule shall specify:
   (a) terms, limitations and conditions on market access;
   (b) conditions and qualifications on national treatment;
   (c) undertakings relating to additional commitments;

(d) where appropriate the time-frame for implementation of such commitments; and
(e) the date of entry into force of such commitments.
2. Measures inconsistent with both Articles XVI and XVII shall be inscribed in the column relating to Article XVI. In this case the inscription will be considered to provide a condition or qualification to Article XVII as well.
3. Schedules of specific commitments shall be annexed to this Agreement and shall form an integral part thereof.

7.2.1 'Specify' (Article XX:1)

In *Mexico-Telecoms* the Panel noted that the word 'specify' requires that the entry would describe each measure concisely, indicating the elements that make it inconsistent with the relevant discipline.[5]

7.2.2 'Terms', 'Limitations', 'Conditions', 'Qualifications'

These terms seem to reproduce the language of Articles XVI and XVII, respectively. The different language used in these provisions, as well as in the current paragraphs XX:1(a) and (b) 'does not seem to entail a difference between the elements to be inscribed under market access or national treatment'.[6] In essence, these paragraphs allow Members to subject their commitments to terms, limitations, conditions and qualifications as they wish.

7.2.3 Broad Interpretation of Article XX:2

Article XX:2 clearly refers to 'measures', thus being understood by certain Members not to apply where no commitment is undertaken ('unbound'). A broader interpretation of this provision, read together with Article XX:1 suggests that the commitments cover terms, limitations, conditions and qualifications, thus having a broader scope of coverage than 'measures'. This broader scope of coverage can be interpreted to also include situations where no commitment has been taken.[7] By now this controversy has not been decided, and both options are left open, thus contributing to the ambiguity of this provision.

5. WT/DS204/R Mexico – Measures Affecting Telecommunications Services, adopted on 1.6.2004, para. 7.76.
6. GATS commentary, n. 4, 450.
7. *Ibid.*, 459–460.

7.3 THE BINDING VERSION

The binding version of the schedules of specific commitments is the original version, attached as an annex to GATS, referred to as the 'treaty copy'. The WTO Secretariat created a computerized pool of all the schedules of specific commitments that may be viewed on the WTO internet site. This pool serves the accessibility and convenience of its users, but for legal purposes the binding version is still the 'treaty copy'.

7.4 GUIDELINES BY THE WTO SECRETARIAT

7.4.1 The 1993 and 1997 Guidelines

Most of the schedules submitted by the Members by the end of the Uruguay Round are based on guidelines published by GATT Secretariat in 1993 and in 1997.[8] These guidelines include more detailed instructions concerning the scheduling of specific commitments, aimed at specifying and clarifying the legal obligations embodied in the relevant GATS provisions. These guidelines have an official status in the sense that they reflect the agreement of the Members, and form the basis on which they relied in inscribing their specific commitments. However, paragraph 1 of the 1993 guidelines stresses that 'the note cannot answer every question that might occur to persons responsible for scheduling commitments; it does attempt to answer those questions which are most likely to arise. The answers should not be considered as an authoritative legal interpretation of the GATS'.

And indeed, the 1997 document reflects further questions that arose in the course of scheduling the specific commitments, after the publication of the 1993 guidelines.

7.4.2 The 2001 Guidelines

In 2001, new guidelines for the scheduling of specific commitments under GATS were published.[9] The new, improved guidelines are applicable as of the date of their adoption, thus not clearing up the situation concerning commitments taken before this date. Since most of the existing schedules were submitted by the end of the Uruguay Round and are therefore based on the 1993 guidelines, the 2001 guidelines are expected to gain full effect at the end of the Doha Round.

8. MTN.GNS/W/164, Scheduling of initial Commitments in Trade in Services: Explanatory Note, 3.9.1993, <http://docsonline.wto.org>.
   MTN.GNS/W/164/Add.1 Scheduling Guidelines: Background – Note by the Secretariat, 10.10.1997, <http://docsonline.wto.org>.
9. S/L/92 Guidelines for the Scheduling of Specific Commitments Under the General Agreement on Trade in Services (GATS), published 28.3.2001, adopted by the Council for Trade in services on 23.3.2001, S/C/M/52, para. 11. See the text of the guidelines in <http://docsonline.wto.org>.

It is anticipated, that their legal status will be similar to that of the 1993 guidelines, since paragraph 1 thereof also states that 'the answers should not be considered as a legal interpretation of the GATS'.

However, these guidelines are already criticized for being even less demanding than Article XX:1 and 2 of GATS on schedules of specific commitments. It is further alleged, that the guidelines provide for a technique of negotiations dictated by the developing countries, which in itself restricts the liberalizing outcome of negotiations.[10]

7.4.3 THE LEGAL STATUS OF THE GUIDELINES: CONTEXT OR SUPPLEMENTARY MEANS?

In *US – Gambling,* the Panel regarded these guidelines as part of GATS 'context', in the meaning of Article 31 of the Vienna Convention. The Appellate Body reversed this interpretation:

> Such documents can be characterized as context only where there is sufficient evidence of their constituting an 'agreement relating to the treaty' between the parties or of their 'accept[ance by the parties] as an instrument related to the treaty'.
>
> We do not accept, as the Panel appears to have done, that, simply by requesting the preparation and circulation of these documents and using them in preparing their offers, the parties in the negotiations have accepted them as agreements or instruments related to the treaty. Indeed, there are indications to the contrary . . . the Explanatory Note that prefaces the Scheduling Guidelines itself appears to contradict the Panel in this regard, as it expressly provides that, although it is intended to assist 'persons responsible for scheduling commitments', that assistance 'should not be considered as an authoritative legal interpretation of the GATS'.

Thus, the Appellate Body viewed these guidelines 'as interpretative tools in the interpretation and application of Members' scheduled commitments'[11] and used them accordingly. Hence, 'initially, these Guidelines were created in order to facilitate Members in the preparation of their schedules of commitments. Nevertheless, these documents also ended up constituting an interpretative instrument of the GATS and the obligations laid down therein'.[12]

10. S.M Stephenson, 'Can Regional Liberalization of Services go Further than Multilateral Liberalization Under the GATS?', *1 World Trade Review* (2002), 5, 8, <www.netamericas.net>.
11. WT/DS285/R, AB/R US – Measures Affecting the Cross-Border Supply of Gambling and Betting Services, adopted on 20.4.2005, Panel report paras 6.72–6.96, Appellate Body report paras 175–177. The Appellate Body referred not only to the Guidelines but also to the CPC – para. 176. See also WT/DS204/R, *Mexico-Telecoms*, Panel report, n. 5, paras 7.43–7.44.
12. P. Delimatsis, 'Towards a Necessity Test for Services: A Little Less Conversation, A Little More Action, Please!', *NCCR Working Paper No. 2006/16* (2006), 3, <http://papers.ssrn.com>.

7.5 THE STRUCTURE OF SCHEDULES

The schedules of specific commitments consist of a table, constructed as follows:

	Mode of Supply	*Market access limitations*	*National treatment limitations*	*Additional Commitments*
1. HORIZONTAL COMMITMENTS				
All sectors included in this Schedule				
2. SECTOR-SPECIFIC COMMITMENTS				
Sector or subsector	1. Cross-border			
	2. Consumption abroad			
	3. Commercial presence			
	4. Presence of natural persons			

The commitments included by Members in the schedules may be divided into two groups:

> *Horizontal Commitments (Part I of the schedule)* – in order to avoid double reference, most of the Members include, at the beginning of their schedules, horizontal commitments specifying measures applying to trade *across all scheduled* services sectors, for example, legislation affecting foreign direct investments, formation of corporate structures or land acquisition. In principle, Members may use this technique to make commitments (or introduce restrictions) for all services with one single entry.[13]

13. GATS commentary, n. 4, 452. It is noted there that some Members have listed commitments with regard to all services falling within a given sector or subsector in a sort of 'sectoral horizontal commitment'.

Such measures may affect a certain mode of supply. For instance, legislation concerning foreign direct investments, incorporation or land acquisition mainly affects commercial presence (Mode 3). Legislation setting requirements concerning access of individuals to a Member, their temporary stay and right to work there mainly affects the presence of natural persons (Mode 4).

Sector-Specific Commitments (Part II of the schedule) – this part includes commitments referring to specific sectors and modes of supply. It should be mentioned that the schedules reflect a positive list approach: only sectors and modes of supply which are specified are covered by the relevant disciplines. Scheduling by modes of supply is not provided for by GATS itself[14] and was criticized for distorting incentives and resource allocation by creating the opportunity for biasing incentives towards a particular mode of supply.[15]

7.6 THREE CATEGORIES OF COMMITMENTS

The schedules of specific commitments include three categories of commitments, each of which is scheduled in a separate column (Article XX:1):

- The *market access* obligation, in which each Member specifies the 'terms, limitations and conditions' subject to which it applies this discipline to services sectors and modes of supply it chooses; This category refers only to measures specified by the exhaustive list of six types of measures included in Article XVI (see detailed discussion in Chapter 9). It is explained by the Secretariat:

  > A Member grants full market access in a given sector and mode of supply when it does not maintain in that sector and mode any of the types of measures listed in Article XVI.
  >
  > The 'terms, limitations and conditions' to be specified in the Schedule may for example, refer to the conditions to form a corporate structure or to acquire land (relevant to Mode 3 – commercial presence), or to stipulate requirements concerning the entry, the duration of temporary stay and the right to work for natural persons who are service suppliers (relevant to Mode 4 – presence of natural persons).[16]

- The *national treatment* obligation, according to which each Member specifies 'conditions and qualifications' to which the application of this discipline to each services sector and mode of supply is subject. It should

---

14. B. Hoeckman & P. Sauvé, 'Liberalizing Trade in Services', *The World Bank Discussion Papers* (1994), 35, <www-wds.worldbank.org>.
15. B. Hoeckman, 'Tentative First Steps: An Assessment of the Uruguay Round Agreement on Services', *The World Bank Policy Research Working Papers* (1995), 27, <www-wds.worldbank.org>.
16. MTN.GNS/W/164, n. 8, para. 4; S/L/92, n. 9, para. 8.

be noted that 'limitations on national treatment cover cases of both de facto and de jure discrimination'.[17]

The 'conditions and qualifications' to be specified may refer, for example, to professional qualifications (relevant to Mode 4 – presence of natural persons).

- *Additional commitments*[18] – such commitments may be taken according to Article XVIII of GATS, providing:

> Additional Commitments
> Members may negotiate with respect to measures affecting trade in services not subject to scheduling under Articles XVI or XVII, including those regarding qualifications, standards or licensing matters. Such commitments shall be inscribed in a Member's Schedule.

To this extent, it is further explained by the Secretariat:[19]

> Additional commitments are expressed in the form of undertakings, not limitations. In the schedule, the Additional Commitments column would only include entries where specific commitments are being undertaken, and need not include those modes of supply where there are no commitments undertaken or any entries at all where no Article XVIII undertakings are made.

According to this provision, such commitments may refer, *inter alia,* to the use of standards, qualifications and licenses. Additional commitments have been included in schedules of specific commitments by some Members.[20] Additional commitments were also included by some seventy Members in the Reference Paper on telecommunication, incorporating into their schedules, certain competition and regulatory (self-) disciplines (see Chapter 16).[21] Members have also used this column to foreshadow

---

17. MTN.GTS/W/164, n. 8, para. 7; S/L/92, n. 9, para. 13.
18. This option did not appear in GATS draft until approximately 1991. The explanation for its inclusion refers to the aim of capturing all types of trade restrictions, beyond those covered by Arts XVI and XVII: J.B. Bigos, 'Contemplating GATS Article XVIII on Additional Commitments', *42 Journal of World Trade* (2008), 723, 731–732, 738.
19. MTN.GNS/W/164, n. 8, para. 12; S/L/92, n. 9, para. 19.
20. J.B. Bigos, n. 18, 724–725, divides existing commitments under this heading into five categories: non-discriminatory restrictions on market access other than the types of measures listed in Art. XVI:2; market access and national treatment undertakings independent of Arts XVI and XVII; regulatory principles, other than national treatment, binding domestic regulatory bodies and the regulations they promulgate; specific commitments relating to actions in the future; and inscriptions that should not have been scheduled as additional commitments because they do not meet the characteristics of additional commitments.
21. WTO explanatory paper, WTO Secretariat, 29.3.2006 (3776.4), 10. In WT/DS204/R *Mexico – Telecoms*, n. 5, the dispute referred to commitments made in the Reference Paper on telecommunications, that was incorporated in the schedules of both parties under Art. XVIII, involving measures regarding anticompetitive practices. However, in that case the Panel left unresolved questions referring to the relationship between Arts VI, XVI, XVII and Art. XVIII.

liberalization initiatives (e.g., the preparation and submission to the parliament, of a law that would terminate a monopoly regime), where they are able to control only the procedural steps, but not the final outcome. The binding aspect thus refers only to the obligation to take the procedural steps.[22] Unlike Articles XVI and XVII, Article XVIII covers commitments but does not mention the possibility of scheduling under it 'conditions and qualifications'.[23]

It is the common view that measures subject to scheduling under Articles XVI and XVII are excluded from the scope of Article XVIII.[24] In *Mexico-Telecoms* the Panel held that a limitation inscribed in either the market access or the national treatment column can limit the applicability of an additional commitment under Article XVIII.[25] Article XVIII is linked with Article VI, in particular Article VI:4, but the scope of the former is broader than the scope of the latter, since additional commitments are not restricted to domestic regulatory measures, and can also apply to the cross-border supply of services.[26]

Article XVIII does not contain any legal obligations in itself. Therefore, commitments inscribed under it must take the form of undertakings, with full description of the obligation established therein.[27] In addition, Article XVIII does not include any reference to a common method of

22. R. Adlung & A. Mattoo, 'The GATS', in A. Mattoo, R.M. Stern & G. Zanini (eds), *A Handbook of International Trade in Services*, Oxford University Press (2007), 48, 60.
23. This fact is explained in light of the open character of Art. XVIII: since unlike the other two articles it does not contain specific standards or obligations, there is no need for limitations and qualifications: GATS commentary, n. 4, 423. The drafting history of this provision explains the reasons for the 'open character' of it:

> the drafters realized that there might be other types of restrictions which would not be captured by Articles XVI and XVII. In other words, they would not be discriminatory and therefore escape the provisions of Article XVII, nor would they be of the six types of measures referred to in sub-paragraphs 2 (a) to (f) of Article XVI. It was considered that such measures would mainly, but not exclusively, relate to qualifications, standards and licensing matters. At the same time, it was not possible to arrive at a clear definition of the restrictive nature of such measures so that disciplines similar to those of Articles XVI and XVII could be established. It was therefore considered best to simply provide a legal framework for Members to negotiate and schedule specific commitments which they would define, on a case-by-case basis, in relation to any measures which do not fall within the scope of Article XVI or XVII. That framework was provided by Article XVIII . . .

S/CSC/W/34 Committee on Specific Commitments, Note by the Secretariat: Additional Commitments Under Art. XVIII of GATS, 30.7.2002, para. 3.
24. One open question seems to be: would Art. XVIII include, for example, government procurement excluded from the scope of Arts XVI and XVII by Art. XIII?– R. Adlung, 'Services Negotiations in the Doha Round: Lost in Flexibility?', 9 *Journal of International Economic Law* (2006), 856, 890.
25. WT/DS204/R *Mexico – Telecoms*, n. 5, para. 7.94.
26. For detailed interpretation of Art. XVIII and its relationship with these Articles see J.B. Bigos, n. 18, 750–762; GATS Commentary, n. 4, 421–426.
27. S/CSC/W/34, n. 23, para. 3.

scheduling. Thus, the commitments scheduled under this column vary considerably between sectors and Members.[28]

In *US – Gambling* the dispute did not directly involve Article XVIII. However, the Appellate Body's finding that the 1993 Guidelines should not have been treated by the Panel as falling within GATS context, but rather as a supplementary means of interpretation under Article 32 of the Vienna Convention, may indirectly affect the interpretation of commitments under Article XVIII and the relationship between this Article and Articles VI and XVII.[29]

7.7 THE TIME-FRAME FOR A COMMITMENT AND 'PRE-COMMITMENT'

Article XX:1(d) requires that where appropriate, the time-frame for implementation of commitments will be noted in the schedules of specific commitments. Generally, the entry into force of commitments cannot be individually established; the date of entry into force refers to the entire schedule. Usually, this date depends on the agreed conclusion of the negotiating round or on the date of a new Member's accession, and applies equally to all Members.[30] However, 'Article XX:1(d) permits Members who wish to depart from its general rule to specify a "time frame" within which they implement their commitments'.[31] The date of entry into force might be relevant to rights under Article XXI (modification of schedules – see Chapter 15), and to possible non-violation cases.[32]

The time-frame of a commitment was a subject of dispute in the case of *Mexico-Telecoms.*[33] In that case, Mexico made a market access commitment that was subject to a permit that would not be granted 'until the corresponding regulations are issued'. The Panel stressed, that the specification in a schedule of a time-frame for the application of a commitment should be made where the relevant Member wishes to implement a commitment *after* the entry into force of the schedule. However, such a delay must have a foreseeable, or a reasonable, time-frame, and could not be used as a cover to an ongoing omission. It was stressed, that this standard applies to commitments under either Articles XVI, XVII or XVIII (additional commitments). Thus, in *Mexico-Telecoms,* the Panel found that Mexico acted inconsistently with the market access commitment inscribed in its schedule, since Mexico did not initiate any process of regulating the relevant regulation five years after its schedule came into force.[34]

28. GATS commentary, n. 4, 424.
29. J.B. Bigos, n. 18, 746.
30. GATS commentary, n. 4, 457.
31. WT/DS204/R *Mexico – Telecoms*, n. 5, para. 7.368.
32. GATS commentary, n. 4, 457.
33. WT/DS204/R *Mexico – Telecoms*, n. 5.
34. WT/DS204/R, n. 5, paras 7, 368–7.371.

7.8 MEASURES INCONSISTENT WITH BOTH ARTICLES XVI AND XVII

Article XX:2 provides, that such measures will be inscribed in the column of market access limitations, and the inscription will be considered as referring to national treatment as well. This manner of inscription may lead to different misunderstandings, for instance:

- There could be a situation where no limitation concerning a specific service sector and mode of supply appears in the column of national treatment limitations, but in the submitting country such limitations exist, only they are inscribed in the market access column.
- In cases where, for the same sector and mode of supply, a full commitment ('none' – see 7.10 below) is inscribed in the national treatment column and no commitment ('unbound' – see 7.10 below) is inscribed in the market access column – which one prevails?[35]

(See detailed discussion in Chapter 9 – 9.5).

Therefore, a careful reading of the schedules is necessary. The 2001 guidelines suggest, that in such cases Members could 'indicate that this is the case (e.g., by stating "also limits national treatment" in the market access column)'.[36]

7.9 THE COVERAGE OF COMMITMENTS BY SECTOR AND MODE OF SUPPLY

In *US – Gambling* it was determined that a commitment in a service sector applies to all services within that sector, unless otherwise specified.[37] In *China-Publications and Audiovisual Products* it was further stressed that:

> a description of a service sector in a GATS schedule does not need to enumerate every activity that is included within the scope of that service and is not meant to do so. Article XXVIII(e) of the GATS defines 'sector' generally as 'the whole of that service sector, including all of its subsectors'. A service sector or subsector in a GATS schedule thus includes not only every service activity specifically named within it, but also any service activity that falls within the scope of the definition of that sector or subsector referred to in the schedule.[38]

35. GATS commentary, n. 4, 458. This overlap may occur in particular between market access and national treatment measures with regard to discriminatory quantitative restrictions covered both by Art. XVI:2(a)–(d) and Art. XVII.
36. S/L/92, n. 9, para. 19.
37. WT/DS285/AB/R, n. 11, Appellate Body report, para. 180. This practice was followed by the Panel in WT/DS363/R, AB/R China – Measures Affecting Trading Rights and Distribution Services for Certain Publications and Audiovisual Entertainment Products, adopted on 19.1.2010, Panel report, paras 7.968–7.969.
38. WT/DS363/R, n. 37, para. 7.1014.

7.9.1 Service Transactions Requiring the Use of More than One Mode of Supply

Where service transactions require the use of more than one mode of supply, it is stressed in the 2001 guidelines that coverage of the transaction will only be ensured when there are commitments in each relevant mode of supply,[39] for example, a legal opinion sent by fax or mail (Mode 1 – cross-border) followed by personal consultations (Mode 2 – consumption abroad or Mode 4 – presence of natural persons).

7.10 LEVELS OF COMMITMENT

The schedules of specific commitments reflect four possible degrees of commitment that could potentially be undertaken by a Member:

Full commitment, marked 'none' – implies that the Member involved does not limit market access or national treatment through measures inconsistent with Articles XVI or XVII in a specific service sector and mode of supply. However, any relevant limitations listed in the horizontal section of the schedule will still apply, so in fact the 'none' mark for a specific services sector and mode of supply should be read as 'none except the conditions set out in the horizontal section', unless explicitly provided otherwise.

Commitment with limitations, marked 'none, except . . . ' – in cases where a Member chooses to apply a measure inconsistent with Article XVI and/or Article XVII it must specify this measure in the correct column of its schedule, indicating the elements which make it inconsistent with Article XVI or XVII.

No commitment, marked 'unbound' – this inscription in a schedule implies that the relevant Member remains free to apply to the specific sector and mode of supply to which this mark is attached, any measure inconsistent with Article XVI and/or Article XVII.[40] This mark appears only where certain commitments have been made concerning another mode of supply in a specific services sector. Where all modes of supply are 'unbound', and no additional commitments have been undertaken in the sector, the sector should not appear on the schedule.

*Lack of technical feasibility, marked 'unbound'** – this mark will appear where it is technically impossible to supply a service in a certain mode of supply, for example, cross-border supply of house cleaning services. The asterisk should then refer to a footnote which states 'unbound due to lack of technical feasibility'.

---

39. S/L/92, n. 9, para. 35.
40. The 'unbound' inscription is criticized for not supplying any information about the barriers existing in the market, thus undermining transparency: B. Hoeckman, n. 15, 26.

7.11 WHAT SHOULD *NOT* BE SCHEDULED

Measures which are not incompatible with market access or national treatment obligations, and are not subject to any additional commitment a Member may want to take under Article XVIII, should not be scheduled. In other words, schedules should *not* provide legal cover for measures inconsistent with other provisions of GATS, for example, with the MFN obligation (Article II); with the obligation for reasonable, objective and impartial administration of measures of general application (Article VI:1); with trade-impeding effects associated with non-discriminatory domestic regulation, such as qualification requirements, minimum capital requirements for banks, mandatory liability insurance for personal service suppliers such as physicians, lawyers, accountants; with prudential measures aimed to ensure the stability and integrity of the financial services sector, as well as bans covered by the general exceptions or security exception (Articles XIV, XIV*bis*).[41]

7.12 INTERPRETATION OF THE SPECIFIC COMMITMENTS: THE DIFFICULTIES

7.12.1 THE RULES OF INTERPRETATION

The schedules of specific commitments were recognized by WTO adjudicating bodies as an integral part of the WTO agreements due to Article XX:3 of GATS, and are thus subject to interpretation according to Articles 31–32 of the Vienna Convention[42] pursuant to Article 3.2 DSU, the same as the text of the treaties.

Nevertheless, the unique structure and content of the schedules impose challenges to the interpreters using this approach. The Appellate Body expressly dismissed the idea of applying differential interpretative treatment to the schedules based on the need to guarantee the security and predictability to the multilateral trading system according to Article 3.2 DSU. This approach was first expressed in the context of trade in goods,[43] and then adopted to trade in services.[44] However, some commentators[45] raise doubts whether these schedules should be considered

41. The WTO explanatory paper, n. 21, 12.
42. The Panel report in *Mexico-Telecoms*, n. 5, paras 7.14–7.15, the Appellate Body report in WT/DS285/AB/R *US – Gambling*, n. 11, para. 160. In that case it was stressed by the Appellate Body (para. 159) that the schedules represent a commitment by one Member, but at the same time a common agreement by all Members.
43. WT/DS62,67,68/AB/R EC – Customs Classification on Certain Computer Equipment, adopted on 22.6.1998, paras 82, 85. The alternative approach considered by the Appellate Body and rejected according to this reasoning was interpretation of the schedules in light of the 'legitimate expectations' of the exporting Members.
44. WT/DS285/AB/R *US – Gambling*, n. 11, paras 159–160.
45. See, for example, I. Van Damme, 'The Interpretation of Schedules of Commitments', *41 Journal of World Trade* (2007), 1.

as a 'treaty' in the sense of Article 2(1)(a) of the Vienna Convention. One conceptual difficulty to treat the schedules as a 'treaty' is the process of their negotiating, drafting, and concluding which can be unilateral at various degrees, thus not corresponding to the common procedure of treaty drafting.[46] It is argued that, in fact, the Appellate Body 'is increasingly torn between its formal attachment to Articles 31, 32 and 33 VCLT [the Vienna Convention – N.M.] and the recognition that the VCLT offers only limited means of justification for interpretation',[47] thus developing different techniques to effectively broaden the scope of interpretative instruments used to analyse schedules beyond the strict options offered by the Vienna Convention, to adapt it to the unique character of schedules.[48]

7.12.1.1 Introductory Heading

The introductory heading of a commitment in a schedule may affect its interpretation: In *Mexico – Telecoms* the parties interpreted differently, the relevant introductory heading of Mexico's schedule and disagreed on its implications for the scope of the commitments undertaken. The Panel interpreted the meaning of the

46. I. Van Damme, n. 45, 7, 21, 23. Thus, for example, in WT/DS285/AB/R *US – Gambling*, n. 11, the United States, explicitly wrote on the cover page of the schedule that it is authentic in English only, thus deviating from the Spanish, as well as from the common interpretation rule of treaty law embodied in Art. 33(1) of the Vienna Convention, according to which 'when a treaty has been authenticated in two or more languages, the text is equally authoritative in each language, unless the treaty provides or the parties agree that, in case of divergence, a particular text shall prevail'. *Ibid.*
47. I. Van Damme, n. 45, 52. One example given is the reference of the Appellate Body in the case of WT/DS269, 286/R EC – Customs Classification of Frozen Boneless Chicken Cuts, adopted on 27.9.2005 to classification according to the Harmonized System of classification (HS) as a means of interpretation, although the HS is not part of the WTO agreements and many of the WTO Members are not contracting parties to the HS Convention. *Ibid.*, 30.
48. I. Van Damme, n. 45, examines alternative interpretative approaches for the schedules: interpretation as a unilateral declaration following the ICJ jurisprudence, (13–18) or as 'multilateral act of a special character' (19–21). It is shown, for example, that in WT/DS285/AB/R *US – Gambling*, n. 11, the Appellate Body referred to interpretative means such as W/120 and the 1993 Scheduling Guidelines, two instruments written by the secretariat and therefore not forming part of the WTO agreements, justifying their use under Art. 32 of the Vienna Convention as supplementary means of interpretation (Appellate Body report paras 175–177), and compared between US schedule and other Members' schedules, although it is not clear whether such comparison should take place considering the fact that 'each Schedule has its own intrinsic logic' (32). It is claimed that the Appellate Body tries to strive for an effective interpretation of schedules, giving effect to their object, purpose and practice of scheduling as well as, to a limited extent, to the process of negotiating, drafting and concluding Schedules (34). While it is recognized that the object and purpose of a specific treaty provision (in this case – a schedule or an entry thereof) should be in harmony with the general object and purpose of the treaty involved, the Appellate Body seems to present a cautious approach towards a too narrow interpretation of the object and purpose of a specific treaty provision, especially in the interpretation of tariff schedules and their detailed tariff headings. In addition, consideration is given to relevant decisions of international organizations, as well as to 'subsequent practice', reflecting an understanding about the interpretation of the agreement under interpretation, by its parties (38–40).

introductory heading as part of the process of determining the scope and content of Mexico's relevant commitments.[49]

7.12.2 Classification of Services

Members are assumed to use the common instruments: W/120 list by the WTO Secretariat, the Central Product Classification (CPC list by the UN) or an equally precise classification system and to follow the Scheduling Guidelines. However, since these instruments are not obligatory,[50] a Member deviating from them is expected to state it clearly.[51]

In any case, 'a specific service cannot fall within two different sectors or subsectors. In other words, the sectors and subsectors in a Member's Schedule must be mutually exclusive'. The Appellate Body stresses that any other interpretation would result in unclear commitments.[52]

7.12.3 New Services

Experience shows, that the schedules of specific commitments resist at least some years, since modification is only possible when a round of negotiations ends.

The modern world is characterized by rapid technological changes that in turn facilitate the creation of new services and/or modes of supply. This reality challenges the schedules of specific commitments that cannot be modified or adapted to these changes between and during rounds of negotiations. Some practical aspects of this difficulty were discussed among the Members, and the following principles were decided:

- The schedules of specific commitments will not be interpreted as applying to new services.
- This decision necessitates a decision, *whether a new technology forms a new service, or just a development of an existing service*, already included in the existing schedules. This question arose, at the time, concerning

49. WT/DS204/R *Mexico-Telecoms*, n. 5, Panel report, paras 7.53–7.72. The Panel in the GATT case WT/DS375,376,377/R *EC and its Member States – Tariff Treatment of Certain IT Products*, published 19.8.2010 (not adopted yet at the time of writing) followed that practice. See section E 4(a)(i-ii), F 4 (a)(i), of the Panel report.
50. This list did not become a part of GATS because this could have complicated the procedures for the modification of specific commitments undertaken by the Members. Its current status also allows for its easier adaptation to newly emerging types of services and services transactions: W. Zdouc, *Legal Problems Arising Under the General Agreement on Trade in Services – Comparative Analysis of GATS and GATT*, dissertation der Universität St. Gallen (2002), 107.
51. S. Wunch-Vincent, 'The Internet, Cross-Border Trade in Services, and the GATS: Lessons from *US – Gambling*', *5 World Trade Review*, 319, 328.
52. WT/DS285/AB/R *US – Gambling*, n. 11, Appellate Body report para. 180. This decision was cited and followed by the Panel in WT/DS363/R, AB/R *China – Publications and Audiovisual Products*, n. 37, Panel report, para. 7.1197.

internet services, for example. Such a decision is an interpretative decision that should balance between two conflicting interests:

On the one hand – preventing the possibility of undermining existing schedules of specific commitments by including a minor, negligible modification in a description of a service as a basis for arguing that this is a new service, to which the commitment does not apply. A vast use of this practice could considerably undermine the entire scope of specific commitments.

On the other hand – allowing flexibility and full discretion of the Members to decide whether, and to what extent, specific commitments should be made concerning new services. Where a new service is developed the Members may be justified arguing that this development could not be foreseen, and therefore when the specific commitments were engineered there was no intention to make a commitment concerning this service. One difficulty stems from the fact that despite updates that took place since 1994 in the CPC list used for services classification, as well as the publication of new scheduling guidelines, most of the schedules are based on the old versions of these instruments since they were written before 1994.

This is the major consideration why the negative list approach was preferred for shaping the specific commitments: if the positive list approach would have prevailed, any new service would have automatically included in it, unless explicitly excluded from the list.

In GATT context, some attempts were made to argue that the goods involved in a dispute were new and therefore the schedules of specific commitments did not apply to them. These attempts were not supported by the Panels, who tried to develop narrow legal interpretative tests for such cases, based on the principles of the Vienna Convention. The two elements that were examined by the Panels were the ordinary meaning of the *language* of the specific commitment involved, and the *legitimate expectations* of the parties. It was recognized, that these expectations may sometimes be 'based on other particular supplementary factors'. Denying them 'would be to rob such commitments of the reality of the context in which they clearly occur in Article II'.[53]

In GATS context, this question is more complicated than in GATT context due to the reference to service suppliers and modes of supply; is a service supplied by new technologies considered a 'new' service? Principally, GATS is claimed to be based on technological neutrality.

The need to answer these questions gives birth to additional, practical questions:

- Who will decide what a new service is, and what is an existing service, covered by the existing specific commitments? Under what procedure would such a decision be made? Since the final decision might be accepted

53. L/575 Greek Increase in Bound Duties, SR 11/12, 1956, 115, 116. See also WT/DS62,67,68/R EC-Customs Classification of Certain Computer Equipment (LAN), adopted 22.6.1998, <www.law.georgetown.edu>.

by the WTO adjudicating bodies retroactively, the certainty and predictability of the system are undermined.
- If the existing classification system does not cover a new service – how would it be classified?

These questions were faced by the Panel in *China – Publications and Audiovisual Products,* where the question arose whether a specific commitment made by China according to Article XVII, referring to 'sound recordings', may be interpreted as including sound recordings distributed by the internet. China argued that at the time China made its commitments, such services did not yet exist, and therefore China did not intend to include these services in its specific commitments, noting that in GATT case, *EC – Hormones,* the Appellate Body stated that 'one should not lightly assume that a sovereign state intends to impose upon itself the more onerous, rather than the less burdensome, obligation'.[54] However, the Panel, interpreting China's relevant specific commitment according to the ordinary meaning, the context and the object and purpose, rejected China's interpretation deciding that the relevant entries 'cannot be said to refer solely to physical products'. The Panel further rejected, on factual bases, China's argument that the electronic distribution of sound recordings and the legal framework for such business emerged only after the negotiation of its GATS Schedule and its accession to the WTO.[55] This conclusion was supported by the Appellate Body who said:

> having included a sector or subsector and having specified commitments for one or more modes of supply in its Schedule, a Member undertakes to liberalize 'the production, distribution, marketing, sale and delivery' of the service(s) falling within that sector or subsector and mode(s) of supply, unless it has specified otherwise by inserting conditions, limitations, or qualifications in the Schedule.[56]

The Appellate Body explains the reasoning behind this broad interpretation:

> interpreting the terms of GATS specific commitments based on the notion that the ordinary meaning to be attributed to those terms can only be the meaning that they had at the time the Schedule was concluded would mean that every similar or identically worded commitments could be given different meanings, content, and coverage depending on the date of their adoption or the date of the Member's accession treaty. Such interpretation would undermine the predictability, security, and clarity of GATS specific commitments. . . .[57]

This broad interpretation is far-reaching and if applied literally in other cases, out of the context of this case, might lead to far-reaching consequences: the will of the

54. WT/DS363/R *China – Publications and Audiovisual Products*, n. 37, para. 7.1165, referring to WT/DS26/R/USA European Communities – Measures Concerning Meat and Meat Products (Hormones), adopted 13.2.1998.
55. WT/DS363/R, n. 37, paras 7.1235–7.1247.
56. WT/DS363/AB/R, n. 37, Appellate Body report, para. 377.
57. *Ibid.*

Appellate Body to give GATS a dynamic, flexible interpretation that would keep it updated with new technologies might undermine certainty and stability, and may expose Members' schedules to unexpected interpretation. It might further deter Members from scheduling commitment, unable to predict how such commitments would be later interpreted in light of technological developments. It therefore seems that this approach of the Appellate Body needs some 'fine-tuning', through the development of legal tests that would help to determine, in each case, whether a technological innovation should be read into an existing schedule.

7.12.4 Specific Difficulties of Interpretation: Mode 4 Commitments

Mode 4 refers to the movement of natural persons. GATS intends to regulate only temporary movement of natural persons, thus refraining from intervening in immigration policies by the Members. However, there are different categories of natural persons, ranging from unskilled labour to senior managers. Neither GATS nor the scheduling guidelines provide for any classification of such natural persons. The specific commitments concerning this mode, which are not based on such uniform classification, are less clear and transparent and more difficult for comparative assessment.[58]

7.12.5 Scheduling Mistakes

The schedules of specific commitments form a technical instrument attached to GATS. However, they incorporate substantial, legally binding, commitments. Once submitted, they become an integral part of GATS, and are therefore subject to the rules of interpretation provided for in Articles 31–32 of the Vienna Convention. Thus, inscription mistakes having a technical nature may impose on a Member a legal obligation it did not mean to undertake. Scheduling in the Uruguay round suffered imprecision.[59] In the case of *US – Gambling,* it was determined that the United States discriminated foreign gambling and betting services in a manner inconsistent with its national treatment obligations in its schedule of specific commitments, interpreting GATS schedule of the United States to include specific commitments for gambling and betting services under the sub-sector entitled 'Other Recreational Services (except sporting)'.[60] The Appellate Body in this case interpreted United States' schedule based on the 1993 Guidelines (see above),

58. R. Chanda, 'Movement of Natural Persons and the GATS: Major Trade Policy Impediments', in B. Hoeckman, A. Mattoo & P. English (eds), *Development, Trade and the WTO: A Handbook, The World Bank* (2002), 304, 310.
59. R. Adlung, 'The GATS Turns Ten: A Preliminary Stocktaking', *WTO* (2004), 13–14, <www.wto.org>.
60. WT/DS285/AB/R, n. 11, paras 162–169; 179–213.

viewed as 'supplementary means of interpretation' according to Article 32 of the Vienna Convention, and compared the inscription of the relevant commitments by the United States to the inscription of similar commitments in the schedules of other Members, referring to them as 'context' in the meaning of Article 31 of the Vienna Convention.[61]

Once included in a schedule, such an obligation, borne by a technical mistake, will be subject to the standstill and rollback principles, thus becoming very difficult to modify. Therefore, each Member should draft its schedule in a careful manner, analyzing its implications thoroughly before formally submitting it to the WTO Secretariat. The 2001 guidelines stress:[62]

> Since schedules, including footnotes, headnotes and attachments, are a record of legal commitments, nothing should appear in them which a Member does not intend to be legally binding.

7.13 CONCLUSION

The technique of scheduling GATS commitments is criticized for creating documents which are not transparent, not user-friendly, and are vague and confusing in a manner that could subject the true substance, meant by the Members, to different interpretations as to their contents. But in addition, not all the schedules meet even the standards of precision set by the Guidelines on scheduling.[63] As a result, the scheduling Member may preserve some scope of maneuvering, while the stability and predictability the other Members should enjoy is hampered.

The schedules are based on two classification instruments: the W/120 list by the WTO Secretariat and the CPC classification. The level of specification possible under these methods seems to create inadequacies in the schedules, not always providing an adequate description to cover all range of services under consideration. In addition, both systems find it difficult to adapt to the dynamic evolution in sectors based on rapid technological changes. A new service is only covered by a country's schedule if it can be clearly identified under the sectoral classification. Thus, a new service will sometimes be uncovered by existing schedules, while in other cases vagueness and uncertainty will occur. This disadvantage seems to be 'built in' the system, since 'by definition static classification systems always run behind trade realities'. It should be noted, though, that neither of these classification methods are obligatory. Members could apply their own sub-sector definitions or refer to different classification schemes.[64] But such pluralism could further

61. *Ibid.*, paras 177, 196.
62. Note 9, para. 3.
63. G. Feketekuty, n. 4, 99. He notes, though, that schedules of new entrants received a great deal more scrutiny than the schedules of existing Members and therefore come closer to providing the desirable information.
64. A. Mattoo & S. Wunsch, 'Securing Openness of Cross-Border Trade in Services: A Possible Approach', *Center for International Development at Harvard University* (2004), 12–13, 19, <www.cid.harvard.edu>.

undermine transparency and certainty of schedules. Yet another alternative could be the exchange of the 'positive list' for a 'negative list' approach. This option, favoured in many regional trade agreements, is likely to be rejected by many Members for domestic political reasons.

It should be further noted, that the schedules of specific commitments do not reflect a full and accurate market picture; these schedules do not include measures which are not deliberately discriminating against imported services/service suppliers; minimum requirements such as common licensing criteria; and measures included in the general exceptions list.[65]

It is unclear:

> whether certain types of measures which are non-quantitative and non-discriminatory but which may have a restrictive impact on trade are to be scheduled or whether they are to be treated as exclusively falling under the purview of GATS Article VI on 'domestic regulation'.[66]

In addition to the technical deficiencies, the specific commitments are negotiated through the request-and-offer approach: trade partner by trade partner, sector by sector. This technique has many disadvantages. It implies high costs and extensive use of negotiating resources; does not necessarily produce an efficient result in economic terms, due to the differences in bargaining powers of the negotiating parties; affected by the free rider problem; and does not offer any credit to unilateral trade liberalization.[67]

All these uncertainties probably affected the approach taken by committing countries.[68] In many cases, instead of specifying the measure creating an exception to the national treatment provision, countries carved out all the activities covered by this measure.[69]

Due to all these reasons it is 'difficult, if not impossible, to find two identical schedules among the current . . . WTO Members'.[70]

The ambiguities embodied in the scheduling and classification system are considered as one factor that might affect the relatively poor level of offers for further service trade liberalization in the current Doha Round.[71]

---

65. *Ibid.*, 27.
66. S.M Stephenson, n. 10, 5–7.
67. A. Mattoo & S. Wunsch, n. 64, 2.
68. For analysis of GATS Uruguay Round commitments see: R. Adlung & M. Roy, 'Turning Hills into Mountains? Current Commitments under the GATS and Prospects for a Change', *WTO* (2005), 8–18, <www.wto.org>.
69. G. Feketekuty, 'Setting the Agenda for the Next Round of Negotiations on Trade in Services', in J.S. Schott (ed.), *Launching New Global Trade Talks: an Action Agenda,* Institute for International Economics (US) (1998), 91, 94–95.
70. R. Adlung, et al., 'The GATS: Key Features and Sectors', in B. Hoeckman, A. Mattoo & P. English (eds), *Development, Trade and the WTO: a Handbook, The World Bank* (2002), 259, 261, <www-wds.worldbank.org>.
71. R. Adlung, 'Services Liberalization from a GATS/WTO Perspective: in Search for Volunteers', *WTO Staff Working Paper ERSD-2009-05* (2009), 9–10. Still more factors that may have led to this outcome may be the lack of experience with international services agreements, the novelty

This system is further criticized on substantial grounds, suggesting that 'once governments are entitled to select, to some extant, the obligations and liberalization commitments it becomes increasingly difficult to ensure mutually balanced trade liberalization'. It is further suggested that 'sectoral approaches foster result-oriented, instead of rule-oriented and principle-oriented international arrangements'. Yet another claim is that 'regarding certain services sectors and modes of supply, the interest to ensure reciprocity between the level of commitments undertaken by Members prevailed over the interest to grant each Member the right to decide which sectors or supply modes to liberalize'.[72]

---

and apparent complexity of core concepts of GATS, insufficient knowledge of the economic situation in relevant sectors and ensuing uncertainties about what might constitute a 'national interest', absence of requests from trade partners, and possibly objection of incumbent suppliers to their governments offering access guarantees at international level: 'Services Negotiations under the GATS: Current State of Play (Request-and-Offer Process)', WTO Secretariat, Trade in Services Division, February 2006, 2, <www.wto.org>.

For analysis of commitments by 2004 see R. Adlung, 'The GATS Turns Ten: A Preliminary Stocktaking', *WTO* (2004), 6–10, <www.wto.org>; see also R. Adlung & M. Roy, n. 68, 19–25.

72. W. Zdouc, n. 50, 93, 104 respectively.

Chapter 8
National Treatment

8.1 INTRODUCTION

National treatment is a complementary discipline to the MFN discipline. While the latter ensures non-discrimination between or among similar services and/or service suppliers originating in different Members, the former ensures non-discrimination of 'like' services and/or service suppliers originating in other Members, in comparison to domestic services and/or service suppliers. This discipline sets a constraint on the ability of governments to accord preferential treatment to domestic services and service suppliers.[1]

Unlike the MFN discipline, and unlike the equivalent GATT Article III, which are unconditional,[2] national treatment in GATS does *not* apply immediately and

1. For the interaction between national policies and foreign direct investments see: B. Hoeckman & C. Saggi, 'National Treatment and the Choice between Exports and FDI', *3 Topics in Economic Analysis & Policy* (2003), *Article 13*, <www.bepress.com>.

   It should be noted that the differences among different domestic regulatory regimes may, by themselves, form barriers to trade, implying extra cost and administrative burden to adapt marketing for each target-market. See, for example, H. Kox & A. Lejour, 'Regulatory Heterogeneity as an Obstacle to International Services Trade', *CPB Netherlands Bureau of Economic Policy Analysis* (2005), <www.fep.up.pt/conferences/earie2005/cd_rom/Session%20I/I.G/Kox_Lejour.pdf>.

   H. Kox & H.K. Nordas, 'Services Trade and Domestic Regulation', *OECD Trade Policy Working Paper No. 49* (2007), <http://mpra.ub.uni-muenchen.de/2116/1/MPRA_paper_2116.pdf>.

   However, this aspect is not addressed by the national treatment principle, which recognizes the sovereignty of governments to regulate their markets as they prefer, as long as such regulation is not discriminating imported, compared to like domestic services. An attempt to direct the Members towards the adoption of international standards exists, to a limited extent, in other GATS provisions, such as Arts VI and VII on Administrative Standards and Recognition (see Ch. 12).
2. The reason is explained by the particular nature of services:

   > Universal national treatment for goods does not necessarily imply free trade. Imports can still be controlled by tariff which, in turn, may be bound in the country's tariff schedule. By

unconditionally to all imported services/service suppliers once a country joins this agreement. Its *actual* scope of application is rather subject to the discretion of each Member, and is reflected in the schedules of specific commitments.

Article XVII of GATS provides:

National Treatment

1. In the sectors inscribed in its Schedule, and subject to any conditions and qualifications set out therein, each Member shall accord to services and service suppliers of any other Member, in respect of all measures affecting the supply of services, treatment no less favourable than that it accords to its own like services and service suppliers.
2. A Member may meet the requirement of paragraph 1 by according to services and service suppliers of any other Member, either formally identical treatment or formally different treatment to that it accords to its own like services and service suppliers.
3. Formally identical or formally different treatment shall be considered to be less favourable if it modifies the conditions of competition in favour of services or service suppliers of the Member compared to like services or service suppliers of any other Member.

Unlike the equivalent GATT Article III, Article XVII GATS does not distinguish between fiscal and regulatory discrimination against domestic products.[3]

Unlike GATS Article XVI, providing for market access (see Chapter 9), Article XVII does not include any exhaustive list of measures inconsistent with national treatment.

8.2 THE PURPOSE OF ARTICLE XVII

Article XVII of GATS does not include a purpose provision. The equivalent GATT Article III:1 explicitly provides that domestic laws and regulations affecting trade 'should not be applied to imported or domestic products so as to afford protection to domestic production'. This provision was interpreted by the WTO adjudicating bodies, in many cases before and after the conclusion of GATS.[4]

It seems that interpretation according to the principles of the Vienna Convention, referring to the purpose and spirit of the agreement, expressed *inter alia* in

---

contrast, given the impossibility of operating tariff-type measures across large segments of services trade, the general extension of national treatment in services could in practice be tantamount to guaranteeing free access.

WTO explanatory paper, WTO Secretariat, 29.3.06 (3776.4), 10.

3. W. Zdouc, *Legal Problems Arising Under the General Agreement on Trade in Services – Comparative Analysis of GATS and GATT*, dissertation der Universität St. Gallen (2002), 150.
4. See *Analytical Index – Guide to GATT Law and Practice*, the WTO, Geneva (1995), 124–141; WTO Analytical Index (2nd edn), Cambridge University Press (2007) vol. 1, 137–177.

GATS Preamble, to encourage liberalization of trade in services among its parties and to eliminate discrimination, may lead to the same result.

8.3 BURDEN OF PROOF

Basically, the examination of this discipline is exercised through a test comprising of six cumulative elements, requiring the examination of whether: (1) the respondent Member took a commitment in the relevant services sector and mode of supply; (2) the relevant Member adopted or applied a measure which is the subject of dispute and the measure at issue is a '*measure*' according to GATS definition; (3) that measure is subject to *specific commitments* (horizontal and/or vertical) undertaken by the Member involved; (4) that measure *affects* services, or service suppliers of another Member; (5) the foreign and domestic services/service suppliers affected by that measure are '*like*'; and (6) the foreign services/service suppliers are granted *treatment less favourable* compared to the domestic like service/service supplier.[5]

A Member invoking Article XVII should make a prima facie case of the inconsistency of the measure at issue with Article XVII. It is then for the respondent Member to rebut these allegations. If the respondent does not present any argumentation concerning the claim, the WTO adjudicating bodies will only examine whether the prima facie case stands.[6]

8.4 SCOPE OF APPLICATION OF THE NATIONAL TREATMENT OBLIGATION

Article XVII has a much narrower scope of application than provided for by the general provision concerning GATS scope of application, Article I:1, referring to 'measures by Members, affecting trade in services' (see Chapter 4). This narrower scope is defined by two elements referred to in paragraph XVII:1; the first element, already mentioned, is its application subject to the specific commitments undertaken by Members. The second element is reflected in the words 'in respect of all measures affecting *the supply* of services', to be discussed below.

8.4.1 Application to Modes of Supply

The national treatment obligation in GATS may theoretically apply to each of the four modes of supply referred to by GATS, if the examined Member made a

5. WT/DS27/R EC – Regime for the Importation, Sale and Distribution of Bananas, adopted on 25.9.1997, para. 7.314. W. Zdouc, n. 3, 156. See also WT/DS363/R, AB/R China – Measures Affecting Trading Rights and Distribution Services for Certain Publications and Audiovisual Entertainment Products, adopted on 19.1.2010, Panel report para. 7.944.
6. WT/DS363/R *China – Publications and Audiovisual Products*, n. 5, para. 7.942.

specific commitment to apply this obligation to that mode of supply, in a specific sector, and subject to the conditions and qualifications set forth by that Member.

Article XVII:1 provides: 'In the sectors inscribed in its Schedule, and subject to any conditions and qualifications set out therein. . . .'

From the language of this provision, it is unclear whether this phrase provides that once a sector is included in a schedule of specific commitments the national treatment obligation applies to all its modes of supply, or whether it applies only to modes of supply specified in the schedule. These two interpretative options have different economic implications. If national treatment had applied automatically to all four modes, this would have considerably strengthened the protection of foreign suppliers against discriminating practices.[7] However, the schedules of specific commitments are constructed according to the latter option (see Chapter 7), which allows the Members more flexibility in determining the scope of their obligations.

8.4.2 Application to Services and Service Suppliers

While GATT disciplines apply only to goods, GATS disciplines apply to services as well as to service suppliers. This personal dimension represents a new perception, which considerably broadens the non-discrimination obligation embodied in this discipline. A service supplier may be entitled to this treatment, supplying services in each of the four modes of supply including consumption abroad, where the provider does not cross a border at all, and commercial presence, where the service is supplied from the territory of the 'importing' country. However, it should be noted that due to the wording of GATS Article XVII:1, a service supplier will be entitled to national treatments only concerning measures affecting the supply of services.

Without reference to the service suppliers, Article XVII would have required non-discrimination of two like services, overlooking differences in service suppliers that might imply different treatment from a regulatory point of view.[8] However, WTO jurisprudence reflects, in many cases, an approach that overlooks these differences. Thus, in *EC – Bananas III* it was established that as long as service suppliers provide the same service they should be considered 'like' service suppliers. This approach was supported in *Canada – Autos* and criticized by commentators (see detailed discussion in Chapter 6 – 6.6.2).

8.4.2.1 Potential Service Suppliers

Similar to the approach of the adjudicating bodies in the context of the MFN provision (see Chapter 6 – 6.6.1.3.1), in the context of GATS Article XVII, the

7. A. Mattoo, 'National Treatment in the GATS: Corner-Stone or Pandora's Box?', *31 Journal of World Trade* (1997), 14–17, <www.wto.org>.
8. M. Krajewski, *National Regulation and Trade Liberalization in Services*, Kluwer Law International (2003), 106.

Panel in *Canada – Autos* was also ready to refer to vertically integrated companies as potential service suppliers, and to apply this provision to such potential service suppliers, providing:

> In our view, vertical integration of production and distribution does not exclude the possibility of considering the distribution operator as a service supplier, which may be affected in its capacity as a service supplier... *regardless of whether actual competition exists* in the wholesale trade market.[9]

This approach seems also to be held in *China – Publications and Audiovisual Products*, where the Panel determined that 'the "like" service suppliers requirement in Article XVII is met as long as *there will, or can, be* domestic and foreign suppliers that, under the measure, are the same in all material respects except for origin'.[10] [Emphasis added]. This interpretation broadens the scope of this perception to include cases where to the understanding of the WTO adjudicating bodies, in given circumstances there could have been foreign services suppliers, but their participation in the market is blocked by the discriminating measure at stake. In *China – Publications and Audiovisual Products* the Panel did not ask for a *positive* proof of this element, but simply concluded that there are, or can be such service suppliers 'in the absence of any contrary evidence'.[11] This is a further broadening of this provision's scope.

This position of the Panel, which was not reversed by the Appellate Body, seems to strengthen the impression that WTO adjudicating bodies are, in principle, ready to consider the application of GATS to *potential* service suppliers (see discussion in Chapter 4 – 4.2.7.2.4.1).

8.4.3 Application to Measures

Article XVII of GATS applies the national treatment obligation 'in respect of all measures affecting the supply of services'.

Article XVII does not include any exhaustive list of measures to which this provision applies. In the absence of such a list, the general definition of 'measures' in Article XXVIII of GATS applies, providing:

> For the purpose of this Agreement:
>
> (a) 'Measures' means any measure by a Member, whether in form of law, regulation, rule, procedure, decision, administrative action, or any other form;

---

9. WT/DS139,142/R Canada – Certain Measures Affecting the Automotive Industry, adopted on 19.6.2000, Panel report para. 10.253.
10. WT/DS363/R *China – Publications and Audiovisual Products*, n. 5, para. 7.976.
11. *Ibid.*, para. 7.973.

(b) 'Supply of a service' includes the production, distribution, marketing, sale and delivery of a service;
(c) 'Measures by Members affecting trade in services' include measures in respect of
  (i) The purchase, payment and use of a service;
  (ii) The access to and use of, in connection with the supply of a service, services which are required by those Members to be offered to the public generally;
  (iii) The presence, including commercial presence, of persons of a Member for the supply of a service in the territory of another Member.

The equivalent GATT Article III:4 does not use the general term 'measures' but rather, specifically refers to 'laws, regulations and requirements'. This provision was broadly interpreted. Thus, it was determined that 'Article III:4 applies not only to mandatory measures but also to conditions that an enterprise accepts in order to receive an advantage, including in cases where the advantage is in the form of a benefit with respect to the conditions of importation of a product'.[12] In that case, it was stressed that actions by private parties can constitute 'requirements'. The Panel explained that 'to qualify a private action as a "requirement" within the meaning of Article III:4 means that in relation to that action a Member is bound by an international obligation, namely to provide no less favourable treatment to imported products than to domestic products'. The Panel provided that for a private action to amount to a 'requirement', a 'nexus between that action and the action of a government' must be established, which is 'such that the government must be held responsible for that action'. Nevertheless, it was stressed that, 'there is a broad variety of forms of government of action that can be effective in influencing the conduct of private parties'.[13]

It was further determined that the fact that a measure is imposed on the imported product as a condition to its importation, or at the time or point of importation, is not in itself an obstacle to its falling within the scope of Article III:4.[14] It seems that the same interpretation may apply to Article XVII, and similarly, the examination concerning national treatment concentrates on the substance and effect of the treatment at stake. (See also the detailed discussion on the interpretation of 'measures' in Chapter 4).

8.4.3.1 'Affecting'

The non-discrimination standard set forth by Article XVII refers to 'measures affecting trade in services'.

12. WT/DS139,142/R *Canada – Autos*, n. 9, Panel report para. 10.73.
13. *Ibid.*, Panel report para. 10.107. In that particular case it was established, that private parties made commitments with regard to the growth in the level of Canadian value added motivated by expectation to conclude a Pact with the Canadian government, and the level of Canadian government involvement in this process was such that the commitments included in these letters may be considered 'requirements': para. 10.122.
14. WT/DS363/R *China – Publications and Audiovisual Products*, n. 5, para. 7.1624.

In *EC – Bananas III*, the EU attempted to argue that where measures involved apply at the same time to goods and services, they should not be examined under GATS. This claim was rejected as the Panel explained that broad interpretation to this provision serves better the purpose of GATS to enhance trade liberalization in services, and that there is no provision in GATT or in GATS preventing the application of both agreements in the same circumstances.[15]

The Panel in that case combined a broad interpretation of the term 'affecting' with the broad definition of cross-border delivery and commercial presence to conclude that a system applied by the EC, dividing all banana suppliers to three groups according to their countries of origin, and applying different criteria for the eligibility of each group to import licenses in terms of quotas, administrative requirements and customs duties, was considered 'measures affecting trade' in distribution services.[16]

This broad interpretation is in accordance with the interpretative principles set forth by the Vienna Convention, since it promotes the spirit and purpose of GATS, to enhance international trade liberalization in services. The broader the basic expressions in the agreement are interpreted, the broader the scope of application for its disciplines is achieved.

In GATT case *India – Autos*, the Panel noted that: 'the fact that the measure applies *only to imported products* need not [be], in itself, an obstacle to its falling within the purview of Article III'. [Emphasis added].[17]

The most recent GATS case, *China – Publications and Audiovisual Products*,[18] also involved goods and services: it referred to a limitation applied by China, that content review exercised on all foreign-origin 'cultural goods', that is,

---

15. WT/DS27/R *EC – Bananas III*, n. 5, paras 7.316, 7.175-7.177. The same logic applies to the interpretation of this word in the equivalent GATT Art. III:4: WT/DS27/R *EC -Bananas III*, n. 5, Appellate Body report, para. 211; WT/DS139,142/R *Canada – Autos*, n. 9, Panel report paras 10.80, 10.84-10.85; WT/DS108/AB/RW United States – Tax Treatment for 'Foreign Sales Corporations' – Recourse to Art. 21.5 of the DSU by the European Communities, adopted on 29.1.2002, Appellate Body report para. 208.
16. The same approach applies concerning the equivalent GATT provision, Art. III. Art. III:2 prevents discrimination of goods from other Members by taxes in access, applied 'directly or *indirectly*'. These words, which do not explicitly appear in the GATS provision, were interpreted to mean that taxes applied to suppliers such as distributors and wholesalers (=service suppliers) indirectly affect the goods involved, thus violating this provision: WT/DS31/AB/R Canada – Certain Measures Concerning Periodicals, adopted on 30.7.1997, Appellate Body report, 18. The same approach is reflected in WT/DS155/R Argentina – Measures Affecting the Export of Bovine Hides and Import of Finished Leather, adopted on 16.2.2001, para. 11.159 were importers (=service suppliers) of goods were more heavily taxed than domestic producers of like goods. In that case the Panel explained the logic behind this interpretation, contending that acceptance of the argument that the discriminating taxed did not apply to the goods, 'it would also not be difficult for Members to introduce measures designed to circumvent the disciplines of Article III:2'. Despite of the difference in wording, it seems that the same logic lies behind GATS Art. XVII.
17. WT/DS146, 175/R, AB/R India – Measures Affecting Trade and Investment in the Motor Vehicle Sector, adopted on 5.4.2002, Panel report para. 7.306.
18. WT/DS363/R *China – Publications and Audiovisual Products*, n. 5.

books, newspapers, periodicals, music transferred through the internet, will be exercised only by wholly Chinese-owned entities. The complaint combined reference to the effect of this practice on the goods, thus referring to GATT, as well as on their distribution services, thus referring to GATS. Nevertheless, in light of the principle set forth in the *EC – Bananas III* case, the parallel application of GATT and GATS was taken for granted and the parties presented their claims accordingly.

In *EC – Bananas III* the term 'affecting' was given a broad scope, based on its interpretation in the context of the equivalent GATT Article III, determining that it 'is wider in scope than such terms as "regulating" or "governing" '.[19] Based on this interpretation, the Panel in *Canada – Autos* interpreted this word in the equivalent GATT Article III:4 to imply that:

> a measure which provides that an advantage can be obtained by using domestic products but not by using imported products has an impact on the conditions of competition between domestic and imported products and thus affects the 'internal sale . . . or use' of imported products, even if the measure allows for other means to obtain the advantage, such as the use of domestic services rather than products.[20]

In *China – Publications and Audiovisual Products* the Panel, based on the same interpretation in *EC – Bananas III*, decided that measures that were proved to 'regulate' or 'govern' trade in services should be considered as 'affecting' trade in services.[21]

8.4.3.1.1 'Affecting': Actual and Potential Effect

In *Canada – Autos* the Panel, referring to the equivalent GATT Article III:4 noted:

> it has been held that, since a fundamental objective of Article III is the protection of expectations on the competitive relationship between imported and domestic products, a measure can be found to be inconsistent with Article III:4 because of its *potential discriminatory impact* on imported products. The requirement of Article III:4 is addressed to 'relative competitive opportunities created by the government in the market, *not to the actual choices made* by enterprises in the market'.[22] [Emphasis added].

It seems that the same interpretation, due to the same logic, may apply to GATS Article XVII. However, it should be noted that this is a broad interpretation, encouraging trade liberalization, and a narrower interpretation that would refer

19. WT/DS139,142/AB/R *Canada – Autos*, n. 9, Appellate Body report, para. 220.
20. WT/DS139,142/R *Canada – Autos*, n. 9, Panel report paras 10.80, 10.82.
21. WT/DS363/R *China – Publications and Audiovisual Products*, n. 5, para. 7.971.
22. WT/DS139,142/R *Canada – Autos*, n. 9, Panel report para. 10.78, citing the Panel report on DS23/R United States – Measures Affecting Alcoholic and Malt Beverages, adopted on 19.6.1992, BIDS 39S/206, para. 5.31. In GATS context see the same approach in para. 10.304.

only to *actual* discrimination is also optional, depending on the discretion of interpreters and the desired balance of interests (See also Chapter 4 – 4.3.7.4).

8.4.3.2 'Supply of Services'

According to Article XVII:1, the national treatment obligation in GATS applies to 'measures affecting the *supply of services*'. This expression is defined by Article XXVIII(b) as including the production, distribution, marketing, sale and delivery of a service. This is a narrower scope of application than the general GATS scope of application provided for in Article I:1, which refers to 'measures affecting *trade* in services'. Thus, it is clear, for example, that measures affecting merely the consumption of services will not be included in this expression.[23]

The list of activities describing 'supply' of services in GATS Article XXVIII(b) resembles, to some extent, the list included in Article III:4 (the national treatment provision) of GATT, mentioning 'internal sale, offering for sale, purchase, transportation, distribution or use' of services in the country of import. A comparison between the two lists reveals that GATS list includes production, which is not mentioned in GATT list, since the latter refers only to the treatment accorded to imported goods in the country of destination, while the former covers services produced by commercial presence in the country of destination.

On the other hand, GATT list includes limitations on the purchase and use of goods, namely, on the purchaser. Equivalent limitations on the purchase and use of services are not explicitly mentioned by GATS list, making its scope of application allegedly narrower compared to the equivalent GATT list. However, it seems that this difficulty may be solved, at least partially, by interpretatively referring to such limitations, for GATS purposes, as limitations on the sale, distribution or supply of a service. This reference opens the door for GATS application, in many cases where basically goods are involved, since the sale of goods is accompanied, in most cases, by activities of distribution, supply etc. This was the case in *EC – Bananas III* (referring to the sale of bananas), *Canada – Autos* (referring to cars), *Mexico – Telecoms* (referring to telecommunication equipment and supply), and recently *China – Publications and Audiovisual Products* (referring to 'cultural goods' and their distribution). The only cases where goods and auxiliary services are involved but only GATT claims will arise are cases where no relevant GATS commitments exist, and vice versa. Thus, in *Canada – Periodicals* only GATT was invoked, while the *US – Gambling* case refers only to services.

In *China – Publications and Audiovisual Products*, it was noted that this term includes 'those measures affecting the establishment of commercial presence by "service suppliers of another Member"'.[24] The reference to commercial presence as subject to this discipline is another feature distinguishing GATS from GATT.

---

23. R. Worfrum, P.T. Stoll & C. Feinäugle (eds), *WTO – Trade in Services*, Max Planck Commentaries on World Trade Law, Martinus Mijnhoff Publishers, Leiden, Boston (2008) (hereby: GATS commentary), 399.
24. WT/DS363/R *China – Publications and Audiovisual Products*, n. 5, para. 7.974.

In that case, the meaning of 'distribution' in the context of GATT Article III:4 was discussed. Based on dictionary definitions, the Panel concluded that this term should be 'understood as meaning a process or series of transactions necessary to market and supply goods, either directly or through intermediaries, from the producer to the consumer'.[25] This interpretation was further supported by the object and purpose of this provision. In the context of import, the Panel noted that 'internal "distribution" is the portion of that process or series of transactions from the point of importation (i.e., the time when the goods enter the customs territory of the importing Member) until the good is received by the consumer'.[26] A similar interpretation may be applied, *mutatis mutandis*, to the distribution of services.

8.4.3.3 Three Possibilities to the Potential Domain of National Treatment

In terms of policy, three options[27] for interpreting the domain of national treatment are foreseen:

(1) *Strong national treatment* covering the right of establishment as well as post-establishment treatment. This option is supported by the broad wording 'all measures affecting the supply of services'.
(2) *Post-entry national treatment*, excluding the right of establishment from the scope of national treatment. It is assumed that this interpretation, also reflected by certain elements of negotiation history, might have formed the basis for the scheduling practice of at least some of the Members.
(3) *Limited national treatment* excluding all measures falling within the scope of Article XVI (market access) from the scope of national treatment obligation.

While the first option seems to be supported by the text and thus by the interpretative principles of the Vienna Convention,[28] and the second interpretation, which is not supported by the text, could nevertheless be treated as 'context' in the meaning of the Vienna Convention, being a basis for certain scheduling commitments, the third option seems to be neither intended nor acceptable.[29]

In the *China – Publications and Audiovisual Products* case, the first option seems to have been chosen. The Panel discussed the limitations on national treatment caused to foreign distributors of 'cultural goods' due to the Chinese requirement, that such foreign-origin goods would use only one distribution channel: designated publication import entities which are only Chinese state-owned. It was established that this requirement effectively prevented distribution of these

25. *Ibid.*, para. 7.1459.
26. *Ibid.*, para. 7.1465.
27. A. Mattoo, n. 7, 10–11.
28. Although this interpretation may turn Art. XVI or parts of it unnecessary: Mattoo, n. 7, 11.
29. Mattoo, n. 7, 11–12. Mattoo thinks that while the first option has a sounder legal basis, the second option seems to represent a neater division of disciplines between Art. XVI and Art. XVII.

services by foreign suppliers in any mode of supply, including commercial presence. The examination of these measures under national treatment was *additional* to the reference to market access obligations.[30]

8.4.3.4 Inherent Competitive Disadvantages of Foreign Service Suppliers

Footnote 10 of GATS, attached to Article XVII:1, clarifies:

> Specific commitments assumed under this Article shall not be construed to require any Member to compensate for any inherent competitive disadvantages which result from the foreign character of the relevant services or service suppliers.

To apply this provision, four steps should be followed:[31]

(1) Comparison between foreign and domestic like service suppliers to measure the 'inherent' competitive disadvantage of the former.
(2) Assessment of the restrictive impact of the domestic regulation at stake.
(3) Ascertainment of this restrictive impact.
(4) Quantification of the restrictive impact to establish one of three options:
   (a) Where this impact does not exceed what is justified under the inherent competitive disadvantage, footnote 10 applies.
   (b) Where the amount of the third variable is higher than the sum of the first and second variables, de facto discrimination occurs.
   (c) Where the amount of the third variable is *lower* than the sum of the first and second variables, an unusual case of 'reverse' discrimination to the advantage of the foreign services will occur.

In *Canada – Autos*,[32] the panel rejected a Canadian claim that all the alleged adverse effect caused to foreign service suppliers was caused by inherent disadvantages resulting from the foreign character of the relevant services and service suppliers. The measures examined were tax exemptions accorded only if the amount of Canadian value added in a manufacturer's local production of motor vehicles exceeded a certain level. One component of the Canadian measure was 'maintenance and repair work executed in Canada on buildings, machinery and equipment used for production purposes'.

The panel distinguished between inherent disadvantages, on the one hand, and disadvantages caused by the host country, on the other hand. It was determined, that where the disadvantage of the foreign service/service supplier is *caused by a measure* of the host Member, whether by law or by practice, this footnote will not

30. WT/DS363/R *China – Publications and Audiovisual Products*, n. 5, paras 7.956 *et seq.*
31. W. Zdouc, n. 3, 184.
32. WT/DS139,142/R *Canada- Autos*, n. 9, paras 10.298-10.301.

apply and the discipline of national treatment will apply, providing for non-discrimination.[33]

This approach is similar to the approach taken in *Dominican Republic – Cigarettes*, a decision on the equivalent GATT provision, Article III, where the Appellate Body stressed:

> the existence of a detrimental effect on a given imported product resulting from a measure does not necessarily imply that this measure accords less favourable treatment to imports if the detrimental effect is explained *by factors or circumstances unrelated to the foreign origin of the product, such as the market share of the importer* in this case.[34] [Emphasis added]

Other justifications explaining the disproportionate adverse impact on imports were also accepted in the cases of *Chile – Alcoholic Taxes* (GATT) and *EC – GMOs* (SPS).[35]

One inherent disadvantage might be the lack of a language, where its knowledge is required as a pre-condition for market access of service suppliers. This condition may be relevant, for example, to lawyers or teachers. The question whether such a requirement is undermining a national treatment obligation where it exists in a specific commitment should be decided on a case-by-case basis. The reason is that there are professions where the language is the major working tool, for example, tourist guide, taxi driver, etc. In such cases, a language requirement may be justified.

8.5 THE STANDARD OF TREATMENT: 'NO LESS FAVOURABLE'

Article XVII:1 requires that Members accord to foreign services and/or service suppliers, treatment no less favourable than that accorded to like domestic services or service suppliers, respectively. In paragraphs 2 and 3 to this Article it is explained, that 'no less favourable treatment' may be formally identical or different, as long as it does not modify the competitive opportunities in favour of domestic services and service suppliers. These paragraphs are based on GATT jurisprudence concerning the equivalent GATT Article III,[36] and their phrasing is criticized for not taking into account the differences between GATT and GATS

33. F. Ortino, 'The Principle on Non-Discrimination and its Exceptions in the GATS: Selected Legal Issues', *King's College London* (2006), 7, <http://papers.ssrn.com>.
34. WT/DS302/AB/R Dominican Republic – Measures Affecting the Importation and Internal Sale of Cigarettes, adopted on 19.5.2005, para. 96.
35. WT/DS110/R, AB/R Chile – Taxes on Alcoholic Beverages, adopted on 12.1.2000; WT/DS291, 292, 293/R EC – Measures Affecting the Approval and Marketing of Biotech Products (GMOs), adopted on 21.11.2006. See analysis in Ortino, n. 33, 12.
36. In particular, the GATT 1947 Panel reports on L/833 Italy – Agricultural Machinery BIDS 7S/60, adopted on 23.10.1958, para. 12, and L/6439 United States – Section 337 of the Tariff Act of 1930, adopted on 7.11.1989, 36S/345, para. 5.10.

substance, which is a source for many interpretative difficulties.[37] In *EC – Bananas III* the Panel regarded paragraphs 2 and 3 of Article XVII as not imposing additional obligations to those included in paragraph 1, but rather serving the purpose of clarifying and reinforcing the interpretation of 'treatment no less favourable'.[38]

Less favourble treatment may involve not only measures that impose costs or other competitive disadvantages on foreign services suppliers in the domestic market, but also measures that provide direct cost advantages to domestic suppliers, compared to their foreign competitors.[39]

The elements of GATS Article III were originally developed by dispute settlement cases interpreting the equivalent expression in Article III:4 of GATT.[40] In *EC – Bananas III* the Panel, interpreting these words in GATS context for the first time, noted that '[t]hese words are to be found throughout the General Agreement', noticing their origin in Article III:4 of GATT, drew direct conclusions from the interpretation of this GATT provision for the interpretation of the equivalent expression in GATS.[41]

In that case, an allocation system for licenses to import bananas into the EU according to different criteria for different groups of importers was recognized by both the Panel and Appellate Body as implying less favourable treatment for the complainants, *inter alia*, since a substantial percentage of the licenses were exclusively available only for EC and ACP suppliers, who could not only use them but also trade them, benefiting from the rent, while the complainants were not entitled to these licenses, unless purchasing them from original holders for a price up to the amount of the tariff quota rent. It was therefore concluded, that service suppliers of complainants' origin were subject to less favourable conditions of competition in their ability to compete in the wholesale services market for bananas than service suppliers of EC (or ACP) origin.[42]

8.5.1 A General Effect

In GATT context, it was determined that the comparison should take place between the *group* of relevant imported products and the *group* of relevant domestic products.[43] The same idea of examining the general approach, rather than a particular case, seems to apply in GATS context as well. In cases where factually

37. W. Zdouc, n. 3, 172–173.
38. WT/DS27/R, n. 5, para. 7.301.
39. P. Delimatsis, *International Trade in Services and Domestic Regulations – Necessity, Transparency and Regulatory Diversity*, Oxford University Press (2007), 141.
40. See: GATT Analytical Index, n. 4, vol. 1, 163–171; WTO Analytical Index, n. 4, vol. 1, 171–175. See also: F. Ortino, n. 31, 7–12.
41. WT/DS27/R, n. 5, para. 7.327, nn. 496, 497.
42. *Ibid.*, paras 7.341, 7.368, 7.393.
43. WT/DS135/AB/R European Communities – Measures Affecting Asbestos and Asbestos-Containing Products, adopted on 5.4.2001, Appellate Body report para. 100. See also WT/DS291, 292, 293/R *EC – GMOs*, n. 35.

only one domestic and one foreign service supplier operate in a market, this notion should be adapted to mean that the legal test would refer to the existence of a generally discriminating measure, which is not an inherent disadvantage covered by footnote 10, that could *potentially* modify the conditions of competition in the market for other potential foreign trade suppliers, if they join the market.[44]

8.5.2 'Formally Identical' or 'Formally Different' Treatment

Article XVII:2 provides, that discrimination could be achieved by formally identical or formally different treatment. In other words, this provision implies prohibition of discrimination de jure as well as de facto. While the former may refer to measures which openly link a difference in treatment to the origin,[45] for example, specifically promoting domestic services supply, such as subsidies, requirements for transfer of technology or local content rules, preferences in allocation of frequencies for transmission of audiovisual services to domestic suppliers, limitations on the duration of operating terms,[46] discriminating taxation,[47] or even to cases where the foreign service supplier is subject to the cumulative requirements of the home country and host country, the latter may include requirements of residency, prior experience within the country, or language requirements.[48]

GATT jurisprudence acknowledged that formally different treatment does not lead to less favourable treatment, if that treatment results in maintaining the competitive conditions for imported products as no less favourable than those of the like domestic products.[49]

---

44. Krajewski, n. 8, 116.
45. GATS commentary, n. 23, 410.
46. In WT/DS363/R *China – Publications and Audiovisual Products* one of the restrictions on foreign service suppliers discussed was an operating term limited to thirty years, compared to an unlimited operation term for like domestic suppliers. The Panel determined that the extension of this period was not mere formality since a positive decision of a competent authority was required, and three substantive conditions had to be met. It was further noted that within thirty years, the Chinese regulation might change in a way that would not enable the extension process anymore. It was recognized that although the risks are realized only towards the end of this time limit, they have a present value in terms of the willingness of potential partners to get engaged in business, in particular in the context of multi-year and supply contracts, with foreign suppliers subject to this time-limit, and this effect would grow towards the end of the operating term, thus potentially modifying the competitive conditions of foreign, compared to domestic, service suppliers. Note 5, paras 7.1136-7.1142.
47. Discriminating taxation is a common practice of discrimination for trade in goods, see reference to former GATT cases and decision in WT/DS366/R Columbia – Indicative Prices and Restrictions on Ports of Entry, adopted on 20.5.2009, paras 7.188-7.190, 7.195, 7.199, 7.201.
48. Krajewski, n. 8, 116; MTN.GNS/164, Scheduling of Initial Commitments in Trade in Services: Explanatory Note, 3.9.1993.
49. WT/DS161,169/R, AB/R Korea – Measures Affecting the Imports of Fresh, Chilled and Frozen Beef, adopted on 10.1.2001, para. 136; WT/DS2/R United States – Standards for Reformulated and Conventional Gasoline, adopted on 20.5.1996, Panel report para. 6.25.

The concept of subjecting de facto discrimination to the national treatment discipline is similar to the approach adopted concerning such discrimination in the context of MFN (see Chapter 6 – 6.6.1.3). It refers to cases where an allegedly 'neutral' criterion is applied, which nevertheless effectively discriminates (or, modifies the conditions of competition) between imported services/service suppliers and like domestic services/service suppliers, respectively. However, according to one opinion, under the national treatment clause this concept should be interpreted more broadly than under the MFN clause.[50]

Applying this provision to the case before it, the Panel report on *EC – Bananas III* said:

> according to Article XVII, formally identical treatment may, nevertheless, be considered to be less favourable treatment if it adversely modifies conditions of competition for foreign services or service suppliers.

This test may be interpreted narrowly, as referring only to measures which *can be expected* to adversely affect foreign services or service suppliers, excluding measures which only, *by coincidence*, adversely affect foreign services or suppliers or which are *more burdensome than necessary.*[51] It could be alternatively interpreted more broadly, referring only to the *result* of such measures; adverse effect. Judging according to the general spirit of WTO dispute settlement decisions, which neglected the 'aim and effect' test (see below) in favour of the competitive opportunities test which concentrates more on the results of a measure than on its motives, as well as by the tendency to prefer the trade liberalization achievement over domestic policy goals in certain cases,[52] it seems that the latter approach would prevail. This broad approach is further supported by the Panel decision on *Canada – Autos*[53] discussed above, where the Panel analysed the market condition caused by Canada, coming to a conclusion that the foreign services and service suppliers suffered adverse effect by Canadian measures that modified the competitive conditions in the market. However, at the same case the Appellate Body introduced some *narrowing* approach of this concept, criticizing the Panel for failing to analyse how the measure at issue, which was aimed at manufacturers of goods, affected service suppliers *in their capacity* as service suppliers. This 'fine-tuning' element is of particular importance where there is a partial overlap between measures affecting trade in goods and measures affecting trade in

50. W. Zdouc, n. 3, 158.
51. This interpretation is supported by M. Krajewski, n. 8, 114, allegedly allowing for more domestic regulatory autonomy.
52. See, for example, WT/DS161,169/R, AB/R *Korea – Beef*, n. 49; WT/DS332/R, AB/R Brazil – Measures Affecting Imports of Retreaded Tyres, adopted on 17.12.2007; WT/DS291,292,293/R *EC – GMOs*, n. 35. However, the reasoning in recent cases, such as WT/DS285/R, AB/R United States – Measures Affecting the Cross-Border Supply of Gambling and Betting Services, adopted on 22.5.2007 and WT/DS363/AB/R *China – Publications and Audiovisual Products*, n. 5, may reflect a more cautious approach, which may support the other interpretative option.
53. WT/DS139,142/R n. 9.

services, and the measures involved directly regulate trade in goods but indirectly affect trade in services.[54]

An interpretative difficulty may arise where a measure is proved to be formally identical but claimed to be substantially different, and vice versa. This may be specifically relevant where the measure involved is not quantifiable like taxes are, for example. This difficulty implies a heavier burden of proof on the defendant, who might bear a long period of uncertainty (involving a high economic cost) until the case is decided.

8.5.3 Modification of Competitive Conditions

This condition, explicitly included in Article XVII:3, is drawn from GATT jurisprudence, the context where its common interpretation was developed. In *EC – Bananas III* the Panel explained:

> The selection of the word '*affecting*' would imply, in the opinion of the Panel, that the drafters of the Article intended to cover in paragraph 4 [of GATT Article III – N.M] not only the laws and regulations which directly *governed* the conditions of the sale and purchase but also any laws or regulations which might *adversely modify the conditions of competition* between the domestic and imported products on the internal market... If the scope of Article III were limited... to a specific type of laws and regulations... the general rules of non-discrimination as between imported and domestic products could be easily evaded.[55]

In *Canada – Autos* it was stressed by the Panel, in the context of the equivalent GATT Article III:4, that:

> the equality of competitive opportunities... is affected if a measure accords an advantage to the sale or use of domestic products but not to the sale or use of the like imported products, *regardless of whether or not that advantage can also be obtained by other means.*[56] [Emphasis added].

In *China – Publications and Audiovisual Products*, it was stressed, in the context of the equivalent GATT Article III, that 'not every form of differential treatment has an impact on competitive opportunities'. The burden is on the complainant to demonstrate that a measure *adversely affects* the competitive opportunities of the foreign service or service supplier, or *may reasonably be expected to adversely modify* the conditions of competition.[57] Thus, the Panel further broadened the scope of this provision beyond its wording which seems to refer only to factual

54. W. Zdouc, n. 3, 180–181.
55. WT/DS27/R, n. 5, para. 7.237.
56. WT/DS139,142/R *Canada – Autos*, n. 9, Panel report para. 10.87.
57. WT/DS363/R *China – Publications and Audiovisual Products*, n. 5, paras 7.1469, 7.1471.

modification of competitive opportunities and does not mention reasonable expectations thereof.

However, in GATS context, a relatively simple set of facts was presented before the Panel in *China – Publications and Audiovisual Products*, who determined that where a measure 'deprives the foreign service supplier of *any* opportunity to compete with like domestic suppliers', such treatment 'modifies the conditions of competition in the most radical way, by eliminating all competition . . . ' [Emphasis in the original].[58]

8.5.3.1 Definition of Potential Competitors

In *Mexico – Telecoms*, the Panel recognized, with regard to the telecommunications sector, that competition between service suppliers in the international arena might take place *indirectly*:

> In domestic setting, it is true that two operators in the same geographic area and providing the same type of service will usually compete directly for the same customers. In international setting, two operators may however also compete for the same customers through subsidiaries of services offered in each others' markets.[59]

This difference may be relevant to the analysis of potential competitors in other services sectors as well.

8.5.3.2 Market Definition

The establishment of an argument that a measure modified the competitive opportunities in a market requires an assessment of the competitive opportunities in that market, before and after the application of the measure at issue. For that purpose, the relevant market should be defined. In the context of the equivalent GATT Article III the Panel, in a statement that was not addressed by the Appellate Body, explained that it is not necessary to use, for this purpose, the same criteria as under competition law:

> It is not illogical that markets be defined more broadly when implementing laws primarily designed to protect competitive opportunities than when implementing laws designed to protect the actual mechanisms of competition. In our view, it can thus be appropriate to utilize a *broader* concept of markets with respect to Article III:2, second sentence, than is used in the antitrust law. [Emphasis added].[60]

58. *Ibid.*, para. 7.979.
59. WT/DS204/R Mexico – Measures Affecting Telecommunications Services, adopted on 1.6.2004, para. 7.113.
60. WT/DS75,84/R, AB/R Korea – Taxes on Alcoholic Beverages, adopted on 17.2.1999, Panel report, para. 10.81.

Some idea concerning the parameters that should be examined to define the relevant market may be drawn from GATT jurisprudence:

Cross-price elasticity: one of the methods to assess whether compared services/service suppliers are competitive is the assessment of cross-price elasticity. This method attempts to predict the change in demand resulting from the change in price caused by the introduction of the 'affecting' measure. The use of this method, supported by some commentators,[61] was recognized by GATT jurisprudence,[62] but it was stressed that it should not turn to become *the* decisive criterion, since the 'quality' or 'nature' of competition should be assessed.[63] The same hesitation as to the correct weight that should be given to this test is expressed by other commentators[64] (see in Chapter 6 – 6.6.2).

Relevance of market situation in other countries: in the context of GATT Article III:2 the Appellate Body held that although not every other market would be relevant, since consumer responsiveness to a product may vary from country to county, evidence from other markets may contribute to the analysis of the examined market, 'particularly when demand on that market has been influenced by regulatory barriers to trade or competition', and 'if another market displays characteristics similar to the market at issue'. It was nevertheless stressed that the relevance of such information should be assessed 'on a case-by-case basis, taking account of all relevant facts'.[65]

Latent, extant and potential demand: in the context of GATT Article III:2 the Appellate Body held that since '[c]ompetition in the marketplace is a dynamic, evolving process . . . the competitive relationship between products is *not* to be analysed *exclusively* by reference to *current* consumer preferences'. In light of this understanding, the consideration of latent and extant demand was allowed.[66] The reason behind this position is that the discriminatory measure may affect the current demand, and therefore the object and purpose of Article III:2: discrimination prevention, may be defeated by an analysis referring only to the current demand.[67]

61. J.B. Goco, 'Non-Discrimination, "Likeness", and Market Definition in World Trade Organization Jurisprudence', *40 Journal of World Trade* (2006), 315, 338; G. Verhoosel, *National Treatment and the WTO Dispute Settlement*, Hart Publishing (2002).
62. WT/DS8,10,11/R, AB/R Japan – Taxes on Alcoholic Beverages, adopted on 1.11.1996, Appellate Body report, 25.
63. WT/DS75,84/AB/R *Korea – Alcoholic Beverages*, n. 60, para. 121.
64. R. Pillai, 'Review Article: National Treatment and the WTO Dispute Settlement', *1 World Trade Review* (2002), 321, 338.
65. WT/DS75,84/AB/R *Korea – Alcoholic Beverages*, n. 60, para. 137.
66. *Ibid.*, para. 116.
67. WT/DS8,10,11/AB/R *Japan – Alcoholic Beverages*, n. 62, Appellate Body report para. 120; WT/DS75,84/AB/R *Korea – Alcoholic Beverages*, n. 60, paras 122–124; WT/DS31/R, AB/R *Canada – Periodicals*, n. 14, Appellate Body report, 28.

8.5.3.3 Scope of the Test

The modification of the competitive conditions test, explicitly included in this provision, was developed through GATT jurisprudence. Its explicit inclusion in this provision thus saves future interpretative process of establishing this notion. On the other hand, it may limit the flexibility accorded in the equivalent GATT provision, to apply other, alternative tests, 'based on balancing or proportionality concerns, as to whether the domestic regulatory categories are appropriately justified by non-protectionist regulatory policy objectives'.[68] It also rules out any future use of the '*aim and effect*' test, which was rejected by WTO jurisprudence referring to GATT[69] and to GATS.[70] (See discussion in Chapter 6 – 6.6.1.3.2).

In addition, in certain circumstances this standard could compete with other GATS standards, which are also subject to interpretation. For example, where the issuing of a license requires prior residency, it could either be scheduled under Article XVII, being less likely to be met by foreign nationals, or totally prohibited for being 'unnecessarily burdensome' under Article VI (see Chapter 12).[71] Another example may be drawn from the *China – Publications and Audiovisual Products* case, where China was found, *inter alia*, to discriminate foreign service suppliers wishing to establish a commercial presence in terms of the registered capital requirement, which was fifteen times higher than the registered capital requirement from a domestic service supplier. Such a measure may be recognized as both modifying the competitive conditions under Article XVII and as a market access restriction under Article XVI(e).[72]

8.5.4 The Scope of Adverse Effect and the '*De Minimis*' Standard

In *Canada – Autos*, Canada was trying to argue, *inter alia*, that the minimal effect of the less favourable treatment should be taken into account. This argument was rejected by the Panel, who admitted that 'albeit that the actual trade effects of this different treatment may be minimal under current circumstances' the effect of the

68. J.P. Trachtman, 'Lessons for the GATS from Existing WTO Rules on Domestic regulation', in A. Mattoo & P. Sauvé (eds), *Domestic Regulation and Service Trade Liberalization*, the World Bank and Oxford University Press (2003), 57, 64.
69. WT/DS8,10,11/R *Japan – Alcoholic Beverages*, n. 62, Panel report para. 6.15.
70. WT/DS27/AB/R, n. 5, Appellate Body report, paras 216 and 241. The determined rejection of the 'aim and effect' test was criticized by some commentators who believe that it should be reconsidered. However, it may be argued that such reconsideration, if occurs, may be relevant only to GATS Art. II, where the modification of competitive conditions is not explicitly mentioned.
71. 'The General Agreement on Trade in Services (GATS): an Analysis', *OECD* (1994), 17, <www.olis.oecd.org>.
72. WT/DS363/R *China – Publications and Audiovisual Products*, n. 5, para. 7.1114. Art. XVI:2(e) refers to 'measures which restrict . . . specific types of legal entity . . . through which a service supplier may supply a service'. (See detailed analysis in Ch. 9.)

measure at stake should not be judged factually but according to the question of whether it has an impact on the conditions of competition.[73]

Similarly, in *China – Publications and Audiovisual Products* the Panel rejected the Chinese interpretation suggesting that only where a *significant* modification of competitive conditions occurs, will this provision apply, noting that 'the phrase "treatment no less favourable" is not quantified by a *de minimis* standard. Accordingly, *any* less favourable treatment . . . is contrary to the obligation in Article III:4 . . .'[74] [Emphasis in the original]. The same interpretation seems to apply to the equivalent GATS provision, which also lacks any reference to a *de minimis* standard.

Nevertheless, GATT jurisprudence and literature also reveal an alternative approach; thus, analysis[75] of the Panel and Appellate Body reports in GATT case *Dominican Republic – Cigarettes*[76] may lead to the conclusion that the scope of adverse effect suffered by the foreign supplier should be substantial and disproportionate. If this position is accepted, a *de minimis* adverse effect will not do as basis for the application of the equivalent GATT Article.

Both interpretative options may be applied, *mutatis mutandis*, to GATS article XVII. It is a matter of interpreters' discretion, based on desired policy goal, since it is clear that the first option enhances trade liberalization more than the second option, which seems to give a broader scope of maneuvering to domestic authorities.

8.6 'LIKENESS'

According to Article XVII, discrimination between or among domestic and foreign services and/or service suppliers is determined subject to their likeness. This perception is based upon the wording and tradition of GATT Articles III:2, III:4.[77]

73. WT/DS139,142/R *Canada – Autos*, n. 9, Panel report para. 10.84.
74. WT/DS363/R, n. 5, para. 7.1537.
75. F. Ortino, n. 33, 12–13.
76. WT/DS302/AB/R *Dominican Republic – Cigarettes*, n. 34.
77. See interpretation in the WTO Analytical Index, n. 4, vol. 1, 143–175. In previous GATT jurisprudence likeness in these two GATT paragraphs did not have the same meaning. In some cases, the Appellate Body ruled that 'like' in Art. III:2 should be interpreted narrowly considering its reference to the broader category of directly competitive or substitutable products: WT/DS8,10,11/AB/R *Japan – Alcoholic Beverages*, n. 62, WT/DS75,84/AB/R *Korea – Alcoholic Beverages*, n. 60, WT/DS121/AB/R *Chile – Alcoholic Beverages*, n. 35. Some change of attitude may be drawn from the WT/DS135/AB/R *EC – Asbestos* case, n. 43, where the Appellate Body ruled that Members would be induced to shift from fiscal to non-fiscal regulation if the coverage of 'like' in Art. III:4 is much narrower than in Art. III:2. The difference in the meaning of 'like' in these two provisions is further criticized for being difficult to reconcile with the ordinary meaning of the word 'like', but nevertheless, according to Zdouc it might serve as a precedent to suggest that 'like' could be differently interpreted in the context of GATS Arts II and XVII: W. Zdouc, n. 3, 152.

The 'likeness' requirement is also included in Article II (MFN), but its interpretation in these two provisions does not necessarily have to be the same.[78]

8.6.1 The Concept of 'Likeness'

Being vague, the concept of 'likeness' calls for interpretation. Traditionally, it does not have any single, general interpretation. Its interpretation is determined on a case-by-case basis, and may differ from one Article to another, subject to the context. Such a difference was recognized by the WTO adjudicating bodies in Article III:2 and III:4 of GATT, and may also apply to Articles II and XVII of GATS. This practice contributes to maximum flexibility and discretion of the WTO adjudicating bodies, but at the same time derogates from the predictability and certainty of GATS parties.

GATT jurisprudence gradually[79] developed some examinations that apply in each case, to determine likeness. Basically there are two alternatives to prove 'likeness' of domestic and foreign goods: 'either by demonstrating that they are "like" by applying the traditional criteria or by demonstrating that the measures at issue distinguish between imported and domestic products solely based on origin and that there can be or will be imported products that are "like" domestic products'.[80]

In *China – Publications and Audiovisual Products*, a case involving restrictions on the distribution of 'cultural goods' in China, the Panel applied the same approach to the national treatment provisions in GATT and in GATS. Thus, it accepted the United States' complaint that foreign-origin goods and services were treated differently solely due to their origin. Since China did not rebut this claim, the Panel concluded that in all other respects these goods and services were 'like'.[81] But usually, the proof of 'likeness' is more complicated. '[I]n cases where a difference of treatment is not exclusively linked to the origin of the service suppliers, but to other factors, a more detailed analysis would probably be required . . . '.[82]

78. W. Zdouc, n. 3, 158 relies on former GATT cases which interpreted the scope of 'likeness' in Arts III:2, III:4 GATT to suggest that the difference in context, in object and in purpose between the two provisions may justify a different meaning to the same wording in each of them.
79. The basic criteria for 'likeness' in GATT context were laid down by the Working Party on *Border Tax Adjustments*, then being the subject of many disputes concerning the equivalent GATT provision, referring *inter alia* to different alcoholic beverages (WT/DS8,10,11/R *Japan – Alcoholic Beverages*, n. 62); Periodicals originating in different Members, targeted at the same market (WT/DS31/R *Canada – Periodicals*, n. 16); Cigarettes (DS10/R Thailand – Restrictions on the Importation of and Internal Taxes on Cigarettes, adopted on 7.11.1990, 37S/200).
80. WT/DS363/R *China – Publications and Audiovisual Products*, n. 5, Panel report para. 7.1447; For the application of discrimination solely based on origin in GATT context see: WT/DS366/R *Columbia – Ports of Entry*, n. 47, paras 7.182-7.184.
81. WT/DS363/R *China – Publications and Audiovisual Products*, n. 5, para. 7.975. Origin-based discrimination also occurred in WT/DS27/R *EC – Bananas III*, n. 5, see Panel report para. 7322.
82. WT/DS363/R *China – Publications and Audiovisual Products*, n. 5, para. 7.975.

The 'traditional criteria' developed in GATT context, include the physical characteristics of the goods examined, the end uses, consumers' tastes and habits, customs classification of a product, or any combination thereof.[83] Of these criteria, which are actually subjective indicators of cross-price elasticity of demand,[84] physical characteristics seem less relevant to services[85] and classification methods for services (for instance, the CPC classifies the services, see Chapter 7) seem less accurate[86] for services than for goods, thus being a less precise source of indication to their 'likeness'.

Since 'likeness' in this context is included in a provision protecting the equality of competitive conditions between foreign and like domestic services and service suppliers, it is suggested that 'characteristics of services and service suppliers which reflect the *competitive relationship between foreign and domestic services and service suppliers* should be taken into account when determining likeness'.[87] [Emphasis in the original].

The choice of tests has to refer, undoubtedly, to the unique characteristics of services in general, but also of the particular services at stake.[88] It also depends on the perspective chosen. From the perspective of consumers, criteria such as 'consumers' tastes and habits' and 'end-uses in a given market' are definitely relevant. However, it is clear that both in GATT and in GATS contexts, the definition of 'likeness' requires a definition of the relevant market (see discussion in section 8.5.3.2 above).[89]

In the first GATS case ever brought before the WTO dispute settlement authorities, *EC – Bananas III*, the Panel faced a relatively easy case of origin-based discrimination. In its analysis,[90] the Panel referred to the classification of the services involved according to the CPC, but also to the 'nature' and 'characteristics' of the services transactions involved, without specifying.

This interpretation was repeated in *Canada – Autos*,[91] although the panel noted that it was applied 'for the purpose of the case', thus leaving the door open for different interpretation in the future. In *US – Gambling*,[92] the panel exercised judicial economy concerning this complaint.

83. See, for example, WT/DS135/AB/R *EC – Asbestos*, n. 43, para. 99.
84. J.B. Goco, n. 61, 332.
85. Although in WT/DS285/R, AB/R *US – Gambling*, n. 52, the parties' arguments came close to the physical test, referring, *inter alia*, to the differences between the characteristics of betting on the internet compared to physical betting paraphernalia: M. Cossy, 'Determining "Likeness" under the GATS: Squaring the Circle?', *WTO* (2006) <www.wto.org>, 19.
86. The CPC list was developed by the UN for statistical purposes and is not based on the competitive relationship between services. It is thus suggested to use it only as a first approximation to the likeness of services, but not as a decisive factor: GATS commentary, n. 23, 404.
87. GATS commentary, n. 21, 402.
88. See, for example, the unique characteristics of gambling and hairdressing services in GATS commentary, n. 23, 403.
89. J.B. Goco, n. 61, 315, 332.
90. WT/DS27/R, n. 5, para. 7322.
91. WT/DS139,142/R, n. 9, para. 10.307.
92. WT/DS285/R *US – Gambling*, n. 52, paras 3.149, 6.426.

End uses, and to a lesser extent, consumer tastes, could serve as more appropriate indications for 'like' services. In some cases, high estimates for cross-price elasticity of demand may create a presumption in favour of likeness.[93] However, to this end it would be difficult to distinguish whether the consumers' taste refers to the service or to the supplier. End uses and consumers' tastes were not yet discussed by the WTO adjudicating bodies in GATS context.[94]

Future cases may raise difficulties in this context, specifically, where likeness of personal service suppliers will be claimed. The personal aspect of confidence and personal relations, professionalism and professional experience of the service supplier characterize the personal services. All these aspects may make it more difficult to prove 'likeness' of service suppliers. Some commentators suggest referring, to that extent, to criteria such as skills, size of the company, number of employees, type of assets, technological equipment, traditional fields of business, experience and know how.[95] These criteria may raise interpretative questions. For example, where would one draw the line between 'small' and 'big' business? Why should difference in ownership justify a different treatment?[96] In addition, these criteria will not always suffice. Thus, while professional formal skills and education may be compared, it is much more difficult to compare talent and approach towards a professional assignment. Design, for example, is a matter of taste and thus difficult to compare.

The decision concerning 'likeness' in a specific case depends, to a large extent, on its scope of definition; the wider the definition of a 'like' service or service supplier, the wider will be the scope of measures deemed inconsistent with Article XVII. On the other hand, the narrower the definition of 'like' service or service supplier, the more likely that measures will escape Article XVII discipline.[97] Thus, from the WTO adjudicating bodies' point of view this definition involves more vast interests than solving the specific case before them.

8.6.1.1 Hypothetical Likeness?

In the context of the equivalent GATT Article III, the WTO jurisprudence continuously recognized the possibility of determining violation of the national treatment principle relying on the effect the measure at issue might have on hypothetical like products, where real like products are lacking. This practice is particularly common in cases of origin-based discrimination.[98] The same logic of analysis may apply to GATS Article XVII, realizing that this is a broad interpretation, facilitating the enhancement of trade liberalization.

93. A. Mattoo, n. 7, 25.
94. M. Cossy, n. 85, 22.
95. *Ibid.*, 20–21; W. Zdouc, n. 3, 166.
96. M. Cossy, n. 85, 20–21.
97. A. Mattoo, n. 7, 18.
98. WT/DS31/R *Canada – Periodicals*, n. 16, 20–21; WT/DS54,55/R Indonesia – Certain Measures Affecting the Automobile Industry, adopted on 23.7.1998, Panel report, para. 14.113; WT/DS155/R *Argentina – Hides and Leather*, n. 16, paras 11.168-1.170.

8.6.2 'Like Service Suppliers'

8.6.2.1 Technological Neutrality?

Theoretically, the concept of 'likeness' is supposed to ensure technological neutrality. However, in the case of GATS this is not full neutrality, since GATS allows parties to discriminate between the four modes of supply by attaching to them different commitments.[99] Due to this practice, the question of whether services supplied in different technologies, or modes of supply, are 'like', arises. This question does not seem to have a definite, uniform answer in GATS context.[100]

For instance, in *Canada – Autos* the Panel, determining that the measure at stake does not discriminate between domestic and foreign service suppliers operating in Canada under Modes 3 and 4, noted that 'for the purpose of this case' it is reasonable to recognize services supplied under Modes 1,2 as 'like', since the Canadian value added requirements provided:

> an incentive for the beneficiaries of the import duty exemption to use services supplied within the Canadian territory over 'like' services supplied in or from the territory of other Members through modes 1 and 2, thus modifying the conditions of competition in favour of services supplied within Canada.[101]

On the other hand, in the same case Canada argued that two companies compared were 'unlike', as one was a wholesaler of motor vehicles while the other was only a manufacturer. The Panel factually accepted this claim, thus rejecting the Japanese claim for breach of national treatment obligation with respect to this company.[102]

In *US – Gambling*, the claim of technological neutrality was implied by the Panel, who noted that this principle 'seems to be largely shared among WTO Members'.[103] In *China – Publications and Audiovisual Products*, the United States invoked this principle and China argued that it has never been formally accepted by Members.[104] The Panel cited the *US – Gambling* decision, accepting this principle, but noted that it did not have to invoke and discuss this principle in the circumstances before it.[105] Summing up this point, it seems that the adjudicating bodies reflect an ambivalent approach towards this notion: where accepting it, they stress that it is accepted in the circumstances of the case before them. Whenever possible, they refrain from ruling on it. This approach is criticized for restricting Members' flexibility in shaping their specific commitments.

Extension of the national treatment principle across modes might have economic unintended implications; it could further increase the tendency among

99. S. Wunch-Vincent, 'The Internet, Cross-Border Trade in Services, and the GATS: Lessons from *US – Gambling*', *5 World Trade Review* (2006), 319, 333.
100. *Ibid.*, 333–335.
101. WT/DS139,142/R, n. 9, para. 10.307.
102. *Ibid.*, paras 10.283-10.290.
103. WT/DS285/R *US – Gambling*, n. 52, para. 6.285.
104. WT/DS363/R *China – Publications and Audiovisual Products*, n. 5, para. 7.1249.
105. *Ibid.*, Panel report, para. 7.1257.

governments to favour producer over consumer subsidies. The application of the national treatment discipline to denial of governmental support for consumption abroad (Mode 4) could contrast with the Scheduling Guidelines provision that Article XVII does not require the extension of national treatment to suppliers located abroad, since there is no obligation on a Member to take measures beyond its territorial jurisdiction. It could have a particular effect on education and health services.[106]

An alternative, less extreme approach, that seems to have been exercised in *Canada – Autos*, implies that where a Member has taken national treatment commitments across some modes of supply, it would have to apply the same standard of treatment to all these modes and ensure equal competitive conditions. Yet another suggestion is to refer to the *means* of supply rather than to the *modes* of supply.[107]

In conclusion it seems, that despite the convenience of developing a general formula to approach this question, the most accurate way, which would also be the closest to the wording of Article XVII, that does not mention explicitly, neither supports, any of these interpretative options, would be to examine 'likeness' by comparing between or among the modes involved on a case-by-case basis.

8.6.3 Are 'Like Services' and 'Like Service Suppliers' Necessarily Linked?

While GATT standards refer only to goods, GATS standards refer to services and to service suppliers. Because the four different modes of supply might affect the nature and substance of service rendered, a double standard is set by Article XVII, requiring the examination of 'like services' and 'like service suppliers'. Some approaches are available concerning this question:

(1) *Evaluation of services' treatment should be separate from the evaluation of treatment of service suppliers*, thus allowing for justification of different regulations concerning different modes of supply of similar services. In other words, 'regulations applying to the service, as such, would only be evaluated to determine whether like services are treated alike, whereas regulations applying to the service provider, as such, would only be evaluated to determine whether like service providers are treated alike'. However, it is admitted that this interpretation is not supported by GATS language.[108] Moreover, sometimes separation between the service and service supplier might be difficult. At an early stage of the

106. R. Adlung, 'The GATS Turns Ten: A Preliminary Stocktaking', *WTO* (2004), 12, <www.wto.org>.
107. M. Cossy, n. 85, 13–14.
108. J.P. Trachtman, n. 68, 64; K. Nicolaides & J. Trachtman, 'Liberalization, Regulation, and Recognition for Services Trade', in S.M. Stephenson (ed.), *Services Trade in the Western Hemisphere: Liberalization, Integration and Reform*, General Secretariat/Organization of American States (2000), 43, 52–53.

Uruguay negotiations, negotiators acknowledged that 'the national treatment concept should recognize the inseparability between the service provider and the service itself'.[109] While the reference to service suppliers broadens the scope of application of national treatment, it could make the burden of proof more difficult.[110]

Yet another version of this disjunctive test suggests that the WTO adjudicating bodies will have to decide in each case, first, whether the measure in question affects a service or a service supplier, and then examine whether this foreign service or service supplier was treated less favourably. This interpretation is not precluded by the language of Article XVII.[111]

(2) Another approach is reflected in the WTO adjudicating bodies' decisions, which seem to *draw an automatic linkage between these two allegedly separated requirements.* In *EC – Bananas III*, the panel noted that 'to the extent that entities provide these like services, they are like service suppliers'.[112] The Panel in *Canada -Autos* repeated this notion.[113] The cumulative option may raise difficulties, particularly in cases where the different treatment of service suppliers is justified because they are unlike, but it affects the services provided by them, which are like.[114] Accordingly, this approach was criticized by various commentators, raising the following questions:

> Is it always the case that suppliers are *ipso facto* 'like' because they supply 'like' services? Can *a priori* unlike supplier provide 'like' service? Conversely, can it be assumed that like suppliers provide like services?[115]

On the other hand, the major advantage of this approach is simplification. Some claim that the result of this interpretation actually broadens the notion of likeness, since it overlooks the legal status (natural person? legal person?), the origin and the ability or capacity to supply the service in question, concentrating only the factual provision of services. However, it is clear that concentration on strictly service-based likeness or supplier-based likeness would lead to an extremely broad or narrow definition

109. MTN.GNS/10, Negotiation Group on Services, Note on the Meeting of 15–17 Sep. 1987, 15.10.1987.
110. M. Cossy, n. 85, 7.
111. M. Krajewski, n. 8.
112. WT/DS27/R, n. 5, para. 7.322.
113. WT/DS139,142/R, n. 9, para. 10.248.
114. M. Krajewski, n. 8.
115. See, for example, M. Cossy, n. 85, 7. It is further suggested, that the drafting history of this provision reveals an intention not to refer only to likeness of services: 'the December 1990 Draft Final Act solely focused on the likeness of services referring to "like domestic services and providers of like services", this formulation was finally dropped and replaced by the current text of Art. XVII': GATS commentary, n. 23, 408.

of likeness, and therefore some combination of the two should be aimed at.[116]

In *Canada – Autos*,[117] the Panel determined that 'in the absence of "like" domestic service supplier, a measure by Member cannot be found to be inconsistent with the national treatment obligation in Article XVII', thus totally disregarding the question whether like *services* existed.

In *US – Gambling*[118] the different Members involved in the dispute expressed different opinions concerning this question. Different opinions on this matter are also expressed by different commentators.[119]

(3) Yet another interpretative option, relying on the context of Article XVII, that is, on the definition of the modes of supply in Article I:2 of GATS as well as on the Scheduling Guidelines, is based on the fact that while the definitions of Modes 1 and 2 refer only to services, the definitions of Modes 3 and 4 refer also to service suppliers. It is thus suggested to follow this guidance and to apply the same approach in the interpretation of Article XVII concerning each of the four modes, the logic behind it being that the presence of a foreign supplier in the market may give rise to discriminatory treatment.[120] However, even in modes 1 and 2 foreign services suppliers may be discriminated against, for example, in terms of taxation. In addition, there does not seem to be any support to this different approach towards different modes in the text of Article XVII, and both sources for this idea are secondary interpretative sources to the text of this Article.

The 'likeness across modes' raises yet another problem: it could force regulatory harmonization since potentially, any domestic distinction between modes of supply, in particular with reference to Modes 3 (commercial presence) and 4 (movement of natural persons) could become subject to challenge under GATS non-discrimination clauses.[121]

Another dimension of this question is: will 'like' services provided by public as well as by private authorities (e.g., medical services, education services) be considered as 'like' for the purpose of this provision? Such an interpretation might have far-reaching consequences. For example, in the absence of disciplines

---

116. W. Zdouc, n. 3, 165. Presenting some additional supplier-related factors such as the size of companies, the number of employees, the skills of its staff, the type of its assets, its technological equipment and its traditional fields of business, Zdouc points that no two companies are *like* with reference to all the factors mentioned: *ibid.*, 166–167.
117. WT/DS139,142/R, n. 9, paras 10.283-10.289.
118. WT/DS285/R *US – Gambling*, n. 52, paras 3.148-3.163.
119. M. Cossy, n. 85, 8–10.
120. *Ibid.*, 10.
121. W. Zdouc, n. 3, 168–169. He points out that the drafters of the agreement were aware of this difficulty, but its implications were watered down substantially by the 'positive scheduling' approach, allowing each Member to decide its scope of commitments under this provision. However, he thinks that this is a shortsighted vision, and its implications are likely to become stronger in the future, as the scope of specific commitments grow.

concerning subsidies in the agreement, can a foreign hospital service supplier of a public service ask for the same subsidies given to a municipal hospital?[122] Such consequences might be contrary to the spirit of GATS and its Annexes, which usually accord public services a different status than private services.[123]

Needless to say, each approach may lead to a different result in a given case, and some of them disregard the explicit words of Article XVII. Nevertheless, although by now the WTO adjudicating bodies seem to stick to the second approach, the very existence of alternatives may lead, in the future where more elaborated cases are encountered, to an unexpected change in their approach, thus undermining the stability, predictability and certainty of potentially affected parties.

8.6.4 Relevance of Regulatory Purpose for 'Likeness' Determination

In GATT context, one interpretative question arising in this context is whether 'likeness' in a specific case should be decided taking into consideration the regulatory purpose behind the measure involved. In GATT, this option is considered due to Article III:1, prohibiting the application of a domestic measure 'so as to afford protection to domestic production'. This general requirement seems to affect the more specific provisions of Article III:2 and III:4 of GATT.[124] This wording is not included in GATS, which alternatively refers to the modification of competitive conditions. It is clear from the context that such modification, when caused by a Member, is aimed at 'affording protection' or improving market conditions for domestic services and/or service suppliers, compared to 'like' foreign services/service suppliers, respectively. Therefore, it seems that the interpretative question, whether the interpretation of 'likeness' should take into account the regulatory purpose, is relevant in GATS context as well. According to one commentator,[125] interpreting Article III of GATT, 'likeness' is not a detached, independent concept, but should be determined in the respects that are relevant to the purpose of making the comparison. Competition between the examined services/service suppliers means that they are viewed by the market as substitutes.[126] However, substitution could be determined in the narrow, technical sense, referring only to the direct function of the service involved, or in a wider sense, taking into account broader regulatory considerations, such as environmental effect. An example brought by that commentator refers to transportation services by a taxi

122. M. Krajewski, 'Public Services and Trade Liberalization: Mapping the Legal Framework', *6 Journal of International Economic Law* (2003), 341, 360–361.
123. See, for example, Art. I:3(b),(c) of the GATS, Art. 1(b) of the Annex on Financial Services, Art. 5(e) of the Annex on Telecommunications.
124. D.H. Regan, 'Regulatory Purpose and "Like Products" in Article III:4 of the GATT (With Additional Remarks on Article III:2)', *36 Journal of World Trade* (2002), 443.
125. D.H. Ragen, n. 124, 446.
126. *Ibid.*, 447.

operated with fuel, compared to the same service by a taxi operated with biofuel. In the narrow sense, both are 'like' transportation services, but in a wider sense each has a different environmental effect, and thus could be treated differently by the regulator, not for the purpose of domestic services protection but for another reason. It is thus suggested that GATT is more than an economic treaty, because it imposes restrictions and determines disciplines concerning government regulation. Therefore, this broader analysis of 'likeness', referring to the regulating purpose, should prevail. Accordingly, if it is proven that a measure has a disproportionate impact on foreign goods because they are disproportionately vulnerable to some public value, no discrimination will be determined.[127] In considering whether this broad approach should be applied to services, one interpretative question should be: Does the difference in language between the relevant provisions of GATT and GATS count?

Looking at the different language of these agreements, it may be argued that it implies a different meaning, thus excluding the broad interpretation possibility in GATS context. However, the drafting of GATS Article XVII is based on the interpretation developed in the context of GATT Article III jurisprudence that interpreted its language to imply the modification of competitive opportunities. This fact may cut both ways. On the one hand, it could be argued that if GATS drafters wanted to follow GATT, the same language could have been used. On the other hand, it may be argued that GATS drafters tried to do a 'shortcut' by explicitly referring to the legal test that was developed in the course of interpreting the equivalent GATT provision, and basically aimed at the same purpose. If this approach is accepted, the same interpretative approach should be applied to both these provisions, allowing for the broad interpretation of 'likeness' in GATS in a manner considering the regulatory purpose behind the compared measures, as suggested above in GATT context.

Another question that should be asked is, whether this concept could not return, to a certain extent, the rejected 'aim and effect' test (see 8.8 below) through the back door. Unlike that test, where the purpose of regulation is taken into account to determine whether a measure is discriminating, according to this suggestion it is taken into account only to determine 'likeness'. Nevertheless, indirectly, the determination of 'likeness' affects the decision whether discrimination exists. Thus, in certain cases the result may turn out to be the same.

8.6.5 Does 'Likeness' Include Directly Competitive or Substitutable Services/Service Suppliers?

The language of GATS Article XVII refers only to 'like' services and service suppliers. Thus, it resembles the language of Article III:2 and III:4 of GATT, also referring literally only to 'like' products. However, in GATT context, the WTO

127. *Ibid.*, 453–454 with reference to the GATT. The same view may be expressed with reference to GATS.

adjudicating bodies expanded this provision by interpretation to apply also where directly competitive or substitutable products where discriminated. This fact was known to GATS drafters, who nevertheless chose to refer in this provision only to discrimination of 'like' products. Despite this fact, some believe[128] that the broad interpretation developed in the context of the equivalent GATT Article III should be adopted in GATS context, to allow a broader scope of application of the national treatment discipline. This approach was adopted by the Panel and approved by the Appellate Body[129] in *EC – Bananas III*. However, this approach overlooks the lingual difficulty, stemming from the fact that GATS drafters were aware of this option and did not choose to include it in the language of this provision, as they explicitly did, for example, with the modification of competition test, another product of GATT interpretation, developed by the WTO adjudicating bodies.

In addition to this lingual difficulty, substantial doubts may arise as to the application of this interpretative approach to Article XVII of GATS: in services, particularly in personal services, the personal aspect is decisive: the goodwill of a service supplier, its professional experience, and the unique relationships developed between supplier and consumer, based on trust. This aspect necessarily weakens the claim concerning directly competitive or substitutable services, at least for this kind of services.

The interpretative dilemma stems from the temptation to opt for the broader interpretation, thus necessarily expanding the scope of application of this provision, on the one hand, and the narrow language that seems to be deliberately chosen by the drafters, on the other hand.

8.7 THE NON-DISCRIMINATION STANDARD: CONCLUSION

The application of this non-discrimination standard in GATS Article XVII simplifies this provision compared to the equivalent GATT provision,[130] and at the same time allows for maximal flexibility in the application of this standard on a case-by-case basis. Thus, in GATS, in order to determine whether a treatment is 'no less favourable', one may opt for examining only the purpose of a measure; protection of domestic production, or rather for a factual examination whether a treatment is formally identical or different and whether the result is of a discriminating nature for the imported service or a foreign service supplier (e.g., extra taxation). In each of these options, the final examination must refer to the effect of

128. See, for example, A. Mattoo, n. 7, 21.
129. WT/DS27/R, AB/R n. 5, panel report 7.322, 7.359, 7.379, Appellate Body report paras 223–228 (these paragraphs do not explicitly deal with the question of 'likeness', but nevertheless imply the same conclusion).
130. A similar standard to the non-discrimination provisions in GATT and in GATS is included in Art. 2.1 of the TBT Agreement.

the measure examined; does it modify the conditions of competition to the benefit of the domestic service/service supplier?

The relative simplification and flexibility of this standard come at the cost of some interpretative vagueness caused by the use of words and expressions like 'measures', 'no less favourable', etc.[131]

8.8 THE 'AIM AND EFFECT' TEST

In the context of the national treatment provision in GATT, an alternative approach to the competitive opportunities test was developed in two dispute settlement cases, known as the 'aim and effect' test. According to it, determination of discrimination depends on the aim of the measure examined: where no intention to discriminate is proved, the measure will not be considered as infringing the national treatment discipline, namely as discriminating imported goods to the benefit of like domestic goods, even where its effect is discriminating.

This approach raises some considerable interpretative difficulties:

- Where there was no intention to protect domestic production but the effective outcome is protective, could it be overlooked? How would that correspond with the purpose of the agreement to enhance trade liberalization?
- The difficulty to prove intentions, specifically where more than one interest is involved, and the risk of finding a retroactive justification to discriminatory measures.
- The fear that most measures could be justified in light of a legitimate intention.
- The tension between legitimate domestic policy goals and trade liberalization.

Some commentators believed that this approach had advantages over the competitive opportunities test approach since it took into consideration the *bona fide* intention of regulators, giving some more weight to regulatory considerations besides the limited scope allowing for their consideration under Article XIV.[132]

Nevertheless, this approach was rejected later in the context of GATT as well as in the context of GATS. The WTO adjudicating bodies shifted their focus from

131. An alternative, less vague option for a non-discrimination provision exists, for example, in Art. 2.3 of the SPS Agreement, containing no reference to the vague notions of 'less favourable treatment' and 'like products', alternatively simply prohibiting discrimination among Members, including the importing state. Art. 5.5 of this Agreement restricts 'arbitrary or unjustifiable distinctions' between 'different situations, if such distinctions result in discrimination or disguised restriction on international trade'. This phrasing is inspired by the chapeau of Art. XX of the GATT. See comparative analysis in J.P. Trachtman, n. 68, 61.

132. See, for example, R.E. Hudec, 'GATT/WTO Constraints on national regulation: Requiem of an "Aim and Effect" Test', *32 The International Lawyer* (1998), 619–649, 628, referred to the equivalent Art. XX of the GATT. Art. XIV of the GATS is even more limited, comparably (see Ch. 15).

the aim of the measure to its effect, deciding that the discriminating effect of a measure examined is the decisive condition for deciding that it infringes the national treatment principle. In *EC – Bananas III*, the Appellate Body said:

> We see no specific authority either in Article II or in Article XVII of the GATS for the proposition that the 'aims and effects' of a measure are in any way relevant in determining whether that measure is inconsistent with those provisions. In the GATT context, the 'aims and effects' theory had its origins in the principle of Article III:1 that internal taxes or charges or other regulations 'should not be applied to imported or domestic products so as to afford protection to domestic production'. There is no comparable provision in the GATS. Furthermore, in our Report in *Japan – Alcoholic Beverages* the Appellate Body rejected the 'aims and effects' theory with respect to Article III:2 of the GATT 1994. The European Communities cites an unadopted panel report dealing with Article III of the GATT 1947, *United States – Taxes on Automobiles*, as authority for its proposition, despite our recent ruling.[133]

However, some commentators believe that in the future the effect of different domestic regulation regimes might be revisited, finding some hints for that assumption in the Appellate Body's references to regulatory intentions.[134] This option might depend on two parameters: first, an interpretative decision that this test could be read into Article XVII. To this extent it should be remembered, as noted by the Appellate Body in *EC – Bananas III*, that GATS Article XVII lacks the wording 'so as to afford protection' which formed the textual basis for the aim and effect test in GATT. Second, an improvement of this test 'to ensure that only *bona fide* regulatory distinctions pass the test[135] and that the effect on foreign services and suppliers is not disproportionate'.[136] It is further suggested that the improved test will allow for a more objective assessment of the intent behind a measure, by considering only intentions that are reflected in the design, structure and application of the measure.[137]

133. WT/DS27/AB/R *EC – Bananas III*, n. 5, para. 241.
134. M. Cossy, n. 85, 23. See detailed analysis of this test *ibid.*, 24–28. Another alternative optional concept to 'like service and service supplier', 'like circumstances', was rejected by GATS drafters after consideration, but some echoes of it may still be found in discussions and argumentations in the WTO: *ibid.*, 32–38. Another hint may be found in the GATT case WT/DS110/R, AB/R *Chile – Alcoholic Beverages*, where the Appellate Body seemed to allow consideration of the measure's purpose albeit apparently only in order to rebut a finding of 'protective application' of an internal tax: n. 35, para. 71, as well as in WT/DS31/R *Canada-Periodicals*, n. 16, where the Appellate Body considered the *purpose* of a regulation to determine whether its 'design, structure and effect' were protectionist: W. Zdouc, n. 3, 183.
135. Meaning: the measure is not aimed at protecting domestic industry.
136. M. Cossy, n. 85, 39–45.
137. GATS commentary, n. 23, 415.

8.9 THE INTERPRETATION OF ARTICLE XVII OF GATS BASED ON ARTICLE III OF GATT

In *EC – Bananas III*, the first case involving GATS interpretation, the WTO adjudicating bodies explained that Article XVII:2,3 of GATS is based on the provision of Article III:4 of GATT and then automatically applied the common interpretation of Article III:4 of GATT, disregarding the difference in language and context.

To a certain extent, this approach was supported by the fact that before GATS conclusion, mixed cases of discrimination involving goods and services were treated under Article III:4 of GATT, due to the lack of legal framework to discuss the services aspect.[138]

This approach, automatically adopting GATT to GATS interpretation, raises some interpretative difficulties:

8.9.1 Relationships between Article III of GATT and Article XVII of GATS

In *Canada – Periodicals* (1996), some measures applied by Canada to imported periodicals targeted at the domestic market, were claimed to be discriminating against these periodicals in favour of their domestic competitors. The Panel solved the case relying on GATT provision, probably since there were no relevant specific commitments under GATS. Rejecting the claim that this was a GATS matter, and that such overlap should not be allowed, the Panel said:

> Overlaps between the subject matter of disciplines in GATT 1994 and in GATS are inevitable, and will further increase with the progress of technology and the globalization of economic activities. We do not consider that such overlaps will undermine the coherence of the WTO system. In fact, certain types of services such as transportation and distribution are recognized as a subject-matter of disciplines under Article III:4 of GATT 1994. It is also noteworthy in this respect that advertising services have long been associated with the disciplines under GATT Article III.[139]

The Panel did not address the question of whether it was prompt to continue to apply Article III of GATT to trade in services despite GATS conclusion and the change of *context* caused by it (as required by Article 31(1) of the Vienna Convention). Nevertheless, its interpretative position was not rejected by the Appellate Body examining that case.[140]

---

138. Thus, for example, in the case of *US – Section 337*, n. 36, a claim concerning discriminating taxation of import, marketing and distribution of tobacco was examined according to the GATT.
139. WT/DS31/R, n. 16, para. 5.18.
140. WT/DS31/AB/R, n. 16.

This approach disregards some differences between the national treatment provisions in GATT and in GATS:

- In GATT, national treatment applies immediately and unconditionally while in GATS, it is subject to the specific commitments of each Member.
- In GATT, this discipline applies to goods while in GATS it applies to services and service suppliers. Specifically concerning the latter, unique difficulties, which were not addressed in GATT context, arise.
- Article III of GATT refers to discrimination in general, while Article XVII of GATS specifically refers to the competitive opportunities test.

It should be determined whether these differences affect the interpretation of the national treatment provision in both agreements.[141]

If the answer to the former question is affirmative, should Article III of GATT be interpreted in the same way as before GATS conclusion, or should the difference in context, caused by GATS conclusion, affect its interpretation and potential application?

The deterring effect emanating from the disregard by the WTO adjudicating bodies of the literal differences between Article III of GATT and Article XVII of GATS is reflected in the discussions that took place in 1995 in the Council for Trade in Services, concentrating on an exceptions list to the national treatment principle, submitted by the United States, referring to the sub-federal taxation system. The list was criticized for including many hypothetical cases that might occur in the future, but did not reflect the legal situation in the United States at the time the list was submitted. The United States explained that the list reflected a cautious approach, emanating from a concern that in the future the national treatment principle will be interpreted in a manner which would not reflect its intentions, relying, *inter alia*, on the common interpretation of Article III of GATT.[142]

8.10 THE NECESSITY TEST

To balance between the national treatment discipline and the right of governments to regulate domestic policy goals it is suggested by some commentators to read into Article XVII, a necessity test implying that measures more discriminatory than necessary to achieve a legitimate objective would not be allowed. This test is neither based on the language of Article XVII, nor on the common interpretation of the equivalent Article III of GATT by WTO adjudicating bodies. Therefore, it does not seem currently applicable. It could be considered in the course of future negotiations,[143] but by now this option was not discussed.

141. For further discussion on the differences between these two provisions and their context, and the possible implications thereof on their respective interpretation, see: A. Mattoo, n. 7.
142. S/C/W/13 Interim Report on the Status of Consultations on Taxes and Subsidies at the Sub-Central Level, 30.1.96.
143. Mattoo, n. 7, 30–33; M. Cossy, n. 85, 45.

8.11 ALTERNATIVE INTERPRETATION OF ARTICLE XVII

An alternative approach[144] for the interpretation of GATS Article XVII suggests that an origin-neutral measure having an adverse effect on foreign services or service suppliers, compared to their domestic competitors, should not be automatically found in breach of this provision. Rather, a two-fold test should apply:

(1) Assessment of the legitimacy of the domestic policy objective put forth by the relevant Member, as a justification for the measure at stake.
(2) If the measure is found to be legitimate, a 'necessity test' will be applied, examining whether that measure is the least restrictive measure that could be applied to achieve the domestic policy objective.

If these two conditions are fulfilled, the measure involved should not be deemed to breach the national treatment obligation, despite the incidental inconvenience caused to the foreign service suppliers involved.

This approach integrates the necessity test, which already exists in Article XIV (general exceptions – see Chapter 15 and could be possibly included in disciplines to be developed for domestic regulation under Article VI:4 – see Chapter 12) into Article XVII. It further allows the WTO adjudicating bodies to legitimize *any* policy objective, not only those included in Articles XIV, thus allowing them to make judgment upon what policies a Member may or may not adopt. No criteria for this broad discretion are specified. To avoid any criticism implying that, due to this interpretation, the general exceptions in Article XIV will become redundant, it is further suggested that Article XVII, thus interpreted, will apply to discrimination de facto while Article XIV will apply to interpretation de jure.

On its face, this interpretative approach seems to have some advantages:[145]

- At the *micro level*, it resolves interpretative difficulties described above, stemming from the current interpretative approach. Thus, for example, *it reduces the importance of likeness assessments.*
- At the *macro level*, it *supports regulatory heterogeneity among Members.*

This suggested interpretation is not explicitly supported by GATS language.[146] However, this suggestion relies *inter alia* on the *good faith* obligation embodied in the Vienna Convention, assuming that a Member acting in good faith will not apply unnecessary restrictive regulation.

This suggested interpretation of Article XVII is heavily criticized for giving the adjudicating bodies a too-broad discretion to judge domestic policy objectives of the Members, thus undermining the delicate balance achieved in the exhaustive

144. G. Verhoosel, n. 61.
145. R. Pillai, n. 64, 327, 332.
146. Although Pillai sees some support in footnote 10 of the GATS which provides that no Member will be required to compensate for any inherent competitive disadvantages resulting from the mere fact that the service or service supplier is foreign. Pillai believes that this footnote embodies the same notion as his suggested interpretation of Art. XVII: the adverse effect born by foreign services/service suppliers is a possible price of regulatory autonomy.

list of policy objectives contained in Article XIV. 'The fear . . . is that the panelist [*sic*] might apply their own vision of the "average consumer", when considering a particular regulation'.[147] In addition, it may give Members a dangerous freedom, allowing them to circumvent the agreement.[148]

8.12 CONCLUSION

The national treatment standard in GATS is a complementary discipline to the MFN discipline. It provides for non-discrimination between imported and like domestic services and service suppliers, to the benefit of the latter. This discipline was developed in the context of GATT and adopted into GATS. The wording of Article XVII deviate from the wording of the equivalent GATT provision, Article III, since they reflect both some practical experience gained by GATT dispute settlement cases, and the adaptation of this discipline to the different environment of trade in services. Nevertheless, it seems that these differences are disregarded by the WTO adjudicating bodies interpreting Article XVII, who prefer to automatically adopt the interpretation developed in the context of Article III of GATT, without taking into account the language and context differences.

In addition, this provision includes many ambiguous expressions that are subject to further interpretation.

These two features create an ambiguous legal atmosphere which does not contribute to the creation of a stable and predictable environment, which would encourage Members to take specific commitments concerning this discipline.

147. R. Pillai, n. 64, 332.
148. *Ibid.*, 334.

Chapter 9
Market Access

9.1 INTRODUCTION

GATS refers to two major groups of trade barriers: *discriminatory and non-discriminatory* measures. The MFN and national treatment disciplines mainly cover *discriminatory* measures. Article XVI of GATS encompasses market-access disciplines which cover *quantitative restrictions and measures equivalent to them*, either *discriminatory or non-discriminatory*. Additional relevant disciplines are embodied in Article XI (payments and transfers) and in Article VII (recognition), also referring to market access of services and therefore will also be addressed in this chapter. However, GATS does not include any definition to the concept of 'market access'.

9.2 ARTICLE XVI

According to GATS, market access to services and service suppliers is not automatic. It is subject to commitments by Members, which provide market access to certain service sectors and modes of supply, in their schedules of specific commitments. Such access may be subject to conditions, specified in the schedules. Article XVI of GATS determines the Members' obligation to accord services and service suppliers from other Members, treatment no less favourable than that provided for in their schedules of specific commitments. To that extent, the scheduled commitments form a *minimum guarantee* of treatment. Members may accord foreign services/service suppliers better treatment, but not worse treatment, than that described in their schedules. It further specifies six groups of measures restricting market access, which should not be applied by a Member to services or service suppliers from other Members in sectors where specific commitments were undertaken by it, unless specified in its schedule of specific commitments.

Article XVI of GATS provides:

Market Access

1. With respect to market access through the modes of supply identified in Article I, each Member shall accord services and service suppliers of any other Member treatment no less favourable than that provided for under the terms, limitations and conditions agreed and specified in its Schedule.
2. In sectors where market-access commitments are undertaken, the measures which a Member shall not maintain or adopt either on the basis of a regional subdivision or on the basis of its entire territory, unless otherwise specified in its Schedule, are defined as:

   (a) limitations on the number of service suppliers whether in the form of numerical quotas, monopolies, exclusive service suppliers or the requirements of an economic needs test;
   (b) limitations on the total value of service transactions or assets in the form of numerical quotas or the requirement of an economic needs test;
   (c) limitations on the total number of service operations or on the total quantity of service output expressed in terms of designated numerical units in the form of quotas or the requirement of an economic needs test;
   (d) limitations on the total number of natural persons that may be employed in a particular service sector or that a service supplier may employ and who are necessary for, and directly related to, the supply of a specific service in the form of numerical quotas or the requirement of an economic needs test;
   (e) measures which restrict or require specific types of legal entity or joint venture through which a service supplier may supply a service; and
   (f) limitations on the participation of foreign capital in terms of maximum percentage limit on foreign shareholding or the total value of individual or aggregate foreign investment.

While the first four paragraphs refer to quantitative restrictions taking the form of the economic needs test, the last two paragraphs refer more specifically to foreign direct investment and establishment, which may form important contributions to the enhancement of the host country's economy.[1]

9.2.1 Article XVI:1: 'Treatment No Less Favourable'

Article XVI:1 of GATS provides that a Member will not accord services or service suppliers treatment less favourble than that specified in its commitments. This provision ensures the rights of services and service suppliers from other Members, relying on the schedules, thus turning the schedules into a source for legal obligations by the Member who submitted them.

1. A. Mattoo, 'Negotiating Improved Market Access Commitments', in B. Hoeckman, A. Mattoo & P. English (eds), *Development, Trade and the WTO: A Handbook, The World Bank* (2002), 280.

9.2.1.1 Application to Specific Commitments

It should be stressed that due to the general reference of this provision to treatment 'provided for under the terms, limitations and conditions agreed and specified in its Schedule', it may refer not only to MFN and national treatment commitments, but also to additional commitments included in Members' schedules, transforming them into irreversible undertakings. However, automatic application of Article XVI:1 to additional commitments, which do not express any specific obligation that could be violated on its own terms, may lead to a problematic outcome. In addition, the drafting history reveals that the Members did not intend that Article XVI:1 would apply to Article XVIII. Therefore, additional commitments 'should be phrased so as to describe and define the affirmative undertakings or obligations to which the Member is bound'.[2]

9.2.1.2 Application to Measures

Article XVI:1 provides that a Member may not accord, to a service or a service supplier, *treatment less favourble* than that provided for in its schedule. It is clear, that the general meaning of this provision is to ensure that concessions given in the schedules will not be derogated. In the 'Scheduling of Initial Commitments on Trade in Services: Explanatory Note'[3] Article XVI was interpreted to apply both to discriminatory and to non-discriminatory measures.[4]

9.2.1.3 The Competitive Opportunities Test

The expression 'no less favourble treatment' was originally developed in GATT context, where it was interpreted as applying the competitive opportunities test (see Chapters 6, 8). According to it, discrimination de facto or de jure may be considered 'less favourble treatment', and the test that proves discrimination is whether the competitive opportunities of the service or service supplier from another Member were adversely affected, compared to these of a 'like' domestic service or service supplier.

---

2. J.B. Bigos, 'Contemplating GATS Article XVIII on Additional Commitments', *42 Journal of World Trade* (2008), 723, 759–762.
3. MTN.GNS/164, 3.9.93, which forms the basis for many Uruguay Round specific commitments. It has a weaker interpretative weight than the wording of GATS itself, being part of the preparatory work of the agreement, thus being considered as a supplementary means of interpretation according to Art. 32 of the Vienna Convention. It provides: 'the answers should not be considered as an authoritative legal interpretation of the GATS'.
4. It thus covers both measures of the type 'only five new foreign banks will be granted licenses' and measures such as 'only 10 new foreign and domestic banks will be granted licenses': R. Adlung, et al., 'The GATS: Key Features and Sectors', in B. Hoeckman, A. Mattoo & P. English (eds), *Development, Trade and the WTO: A Handbook, The World Bank* (2002), 259, 262, <www-wds.worldbank.org>.

The language of Article XVI:1 raises a similar interpretative dilemma to that raised by the language of Article II of GATS, providing for the MFN treatment. It is clear, that when GATS was drafted, its drafters were fully aware of the competitive opportunities test. Moreover, they explicitly included it in Article XVII (national treatment, see Chapter 8). Nevertheless, this test was not literally included in Article II (MFN) and in Article XVI (Market Access). This language-gap raises some interpretative questions: what is the reason for this difference? Did GATS drafters want this expression to be differently interpreted in Articles I and XVI than in Article XVII? And if so – how? Allegedly, the requirement set by Article 31 of the Vienna Convention, for interpretation according to the 'ordinary meaning' of the text, implies a different meaning to different texts, one including the competitive opportunities test and the other – not.

The language of Article XVI, like that of Article II, does not supply any clue to this difference. Moreover, its interpretation without reference to the competitive opportunities test may substantially narrow its scope of application, if not undermine it at all: if the competitive opportunities test applies, it may be argued that services and service suppliers from a Member are entitled to treatment that would not undermine their competitive opportunities more than provided for by the relevant specific commitments of a Member in its schedule. Without this test, the right involved may be narrowly interpreted, so that treatment no less favourable de jure, but not necessarily de facto, might be considered as satisfying the requirements of Article XVI.

The interpretative dilemma, or choice, is between pragmatic considerations, supporting an interpretation according to the competitive opportunities test, which is already known, developed and successfully applied in GATS context, thus encouraging certainty and stability and complying with GATS purpose, on the one hand, and the interpretative considerations relying on the Vienna Convention, that is based on an assumption that the drafters of international agreements have a particular intention reflected in their language, on the other hand.

This conflict was not yet encountered by the WTO adjudicating bodies in the context of Article XVI, but based on their decisions in the context of Article II,[5] bearing the same difficulty, it seems that the pragmatic approach will prevail, and the competitive opportunities test will be applied to Article XVI.

9.2.1.4 'Terms, Limitations and Conditions'

Article XVI:1 subjects the standard of 'no less favourable treatment' to the 'terms, limitations and conditions' specified in the Members' schedules of specific commitments. The general intention of this provision is clear: it subjects the standard 'no less favourable treatment' to the specific commitments taken by the Members. However, interpretation of the words 'terms, limitations and conditions' raises some difficulties.

5. WT/DS27/R, AB/R EC - Regime for the Importation, Sale and Distribution of Bananas, adopted on 25.9.1997, Appellate Body report, paras 231, 233–234.

In *US – Gambling*,[6] the Panel noted that this language is parallel to that of:

> Article XX:1 of the GATS, which requires Members to set out in their schedules 'terms, limitations and conditions on market access'. This language, particularly the use of the word 'limitations', denotes the limitations identified in Article XVI:2(a),(b),(c),(d) and (f). The words 'terms' and 'conditions' refer to the 'measures' contemplated by Article XVI:2(e) and the chapeau of Article XVI:2 (i.e., the possibility to make a commitment on the basis of a regional subdivision of the territory).[7]

The Panel also mentioned footnote 2 of the 1993 Scheduling Guidelines,[8] stating:

> The term 'limitations' will be used throughout this Note to refer to the 'terms', 'conditions', 'limitations' and 'qualifications' used in Article XVI and XVII of the GATS.

The Panel thus concluded:

> Therefore, the 1993 Scheduling Guidelines would seem to indicate that *no difference* exists between the 'terms, conditions and limitations' contained in a Member's schedule and the 'limitations' and 'measures' that it is entitled to maintain if scheduled, pursuant to the second paragraph of Article XVI. [Emphasis added].

This is a somewhat odd interpretation, since the basic assumption of interpretation is that every word in the text should have a particular meaning. While the difference between 'limitations' and 'conditions' is well understood, referring to the ordinary meaning of these two words, the difference between 'terms' and 'conditions' is less clear.

This language is similar to the language of the equivalent GATT provision, Article XI. It seems that these words are meant to cover every possible variation of specific commitments phrasing, to give the Members maximal flexibility in drafting their schedules.

---

6. WT/DS285/R, AB/R United States - Measures Affecting the Cross-Border Supply of Gambling and Betting Services, adopted on 22.5.2007, Panel report paras 6.294–6.296.
7. According to another opinion, there is no textual or contextual justification for this interpretation: R. Volfrum, P.T. Stoll & C. Feinäugle (eds), *WTO – Trade in Services*, Max Planck Commentaries on World Trade Law, Leiden/Boston Martinus Nijhoff Publishers (2008) (hereby: GATS commentary), 372, n. 16, <http://papers.ssrn.com>.
8. The 2001 guidelines do not explicitly mention these three options, referring generally to 'limitations on market access': S/L/92 Guidelines for the Scheduling of Specific Commitments Under the General Agreement on Trade in Services (GATS), published 28.3.01, paras 8–12, <http://docsonline.wto.org>.

9.2.1.5 'Agreed and Specified'

These words stress the mutual nature of the specific commitments that, although made by each Member separately, reflect the common agreement of all the Members by the end of the last round of negotiations.[9]

9.2.1.6 Movement of Capital

Footnote 8 of GATS, referring to Article XVI:1, provides:

> If a Member undertakes a market-access commitment in relation to the supply of a service through the mode of supply referred to in subparagraph 2(a) of Article I [cross border supply – Mode 1 – N.M.] and if the cross-border movement of capital is an essential part of the service itself, that Member is thereby committed to allow such movement of capital. If a Member undertakes a market-access commitment in relation to the supply of a service through the mode of supply referred to in subparagraph 2(c) of Article I [commercial presence – Mode 3 – N.M.], it is thereby committed to allow related transfers of capital into its territory.

This note is meant to ensure the movement of capital resulting from trade in services that takes place either through Mode 1 (cross-border) or through Mode 3 (commercial presence).

In case of *cross-border* trade, protection by this note is given 'if the cross-border movement of capital is an *essential* part of the service itself'. This is a quite narrow condition. However, the word 'essential' is not interpreted by the text, thus being open to further interpretation. It is clear that the movement of capital would be an essential part of a financial transaction. However in other cases, this condition may be subject to conflicting interpretations. For example, is the movement of capital for the establishment of a commercial presence in a Member an 'essential part of the service itself'? And if it is – to what extent? In addition, an obvious question arising is: what about the consideration for a service given? Is it considered 'an essential part of the service' and thus guaranteed by this note? Theoretically, in terms of legal interpretation, a negative answer is also possible,[10] but if accepted, it could deter service suppliers from providing a service under such terms.

A similar interpretative question arises concerning the second part of this note, referring to the supply of services through commercial presence. In this case, the

9. In GATT context, this idea was expressed by the Appellate Body in WT/DS62,67,68/AB/R EC – Customs Classification of Certain Computer Equipment, adopted on 22.6.1998, para. 109, providing: 'Indeed, the fact that Members' Schedules are integral part of the GATT 1994 indicates that while each Schedule represents the Tariff commitment made by one Member, they represent a common agreement by all Members'.
10. See, for example, GATS commentary, n. 7, 373.

note provides that if a Member undertakes a market-access commitment in relation to the supply of a service through this mode of supply, it is committed to allow related *inward* transfers of capital. Here, again, it seems that the note does not refer to transfers of capital, stemming from the transaction, *outward.*

Some commentators are of the opinion that other restrictions on capital flows, for instance, repatriation of liquidation proceeds on other capital outflows may be covered where they *affect trade in services*, particularly foreign services suppliers' *competitive opportunity.*[11]

It is further suggested to read these obligations in conjunction with Article XI and the relevant references to the Members' rights under the IMF agreement.[12]

The specific reference in this note to Modes 1, 3 excludes Modes 2, 4, namely, in these two latter modes, the Members are not obliged to allow capital flows as should be allowed concerning the former two modes. Nevertheless, this freedom seems to be subject to Article XI disciplines (see section 9.4 below).[13]

9.2.2 Article XVI:2

Article XVI:2 consists of a chapeau providing for general principles, followed by six categories of limitations on market access, which are not allowed unless explicitly scheduled. These categories of measures describe quantitative restrictions or measures having an equivalent effect.

9.2.2.1 The Burden of Proof

In order to invoke Article XVI, a Member must put forward a prima facie case, showing:

(1) that the respondent Member made market-access commitments in its GATS schedule and
(2) identifying, with supporting evidence, that the challenged 'measures' of that Member constitute an impermissible limitation falling under one or more of the sub-paragraphs of this provision.[14]

It is then for the respondent Member to rebut these claims.

In *US – Gambling*, Antigua found it difficult to specify the 'measures' by which the United States was allegedly violating this provision. In the appeal, the United States claimed that it did not, therefore, establish a prima facie case, and

11. 'The General Agreement on Trade in Services (GATS): An Analysis', *OECD* (1994), 17, <www.olis.oecd.org>.
12. GATS commentary, n. 7, 373.
13. *Ibid.*, 373.
14. WT/DS285/AB/R *US – Gambling*, n. 6, Appellate Body report, para. 143.

that the Panel itself improperly made Antigua's prima facie case.[15] The Appellate Body determined:

> A prima facie case must be based on 'evidence and legal arguments' put forward by the complaining party in relation to each of the elements of the claim. A complaining party may not simply submit evidence and expect the panel to divine from it a claim of WTO-inconsistency. Nor may a complaining party simply allege facts without relating them to its legal arguments.

Examining the Panel decision in light of these principles, the Appellate Body came into conclusion that Antigua made a prima facie case only concerning part of the measures examined by the Panel, and reversed the Panel decision concerning the other measures.

9.2.2.2 The Chapeau

The chapeau of Article XVI:2 repeats the idea that the market-access obligations are subject to the schedules of specific commitments. It then stresses, that a Member should 'not maintain or adopt, either on the basis of a regional subdivision or on the basis of its entire territory', these prohibited (unless specifically scheduled) measures. This idea is not new because it is already provided for by Article I:3(a), defining 'measures by Members' as including all government levels (see Chapter 4).

It should be remembered, that the term 'measures' is very broadly defined by Article XXVII(a) of the agreement, to include any measure by a Member, 'whether in the form of law, regulation, rule, procedure, decision, administrative action or any other form' (see Chapter 4). Thus, *any* measure taken, resulting in one of the six specified limitations, would be subject to this provision. This interpretation leads to the conclusion that any alleged infringement of this provision would be decided subject to the actual *effect* of any measure taken.

Article XVI:2 applies to measures adopted *after* its conclusion, but also to measures adopted *before* its conclusion, that were maintained.[16]

To sum up the conditions set forth by the chapeau of Article XVI:2, the following elements should be established:

- Specific market-access commitments were made in the relevant services sector and mode of supply by the Member involved.
- Nevertheless, the Member involved applies to a service or to service suppliers thereof, in a specific mode of supply, measures included in the list of six groups specified in Article XVI:2(a)–(g).[17]

---

15. WT/DS285/AB/R, n. 6, Appellate Body report paras 137, 140, 147–155.
16. GATS Commentary, n. 7, 375.
17. In *US – Gambling* this list was interpreted as an exhaustive list of measures that complements Art. XVI:1 by specifying the measures considered as 'less favourable treatment' under this paragraph: WT/DS285/R, n. 6, Panel report, paras 6.298 and 6.318.

- The measures are applied either on the basis of a regional subdivision or on the basis of its entire territory.
- The measures were not specified in the schedule of the applying Member.

By specifying a measure of the kinds mentioned in Article XVI in its schedule, a Member thus commits itself only to *partial market access.*[18]

9.2.2.3 Six Limitations on Market Access

Article XVI:2 of GATS determines six groups of measures that are considered limitations to market access. These measures are often used to regulate public services such as health services, telecommunications, postal or rail transportation services. Sometimes they are used to reduce negative implications of over-supply on the quality of the service.[19]

A Member wishing to avoid claims of breaching this provision, must ensure that all measures applied by it, falling under any of the categories listed in Article XVI:2, are scheduled.

9.2.2.3.1 Technological Neutrality

Article XVI:2 does not refer to the *means* used for the supply of a service. In *US – Gambling*[20] it was, however, clarified, that:

> Market access commitment . . . implies the right for other Members' suppliers to supply a service through all means of delivery . . . unless otherwise specified in a Member's Schedule. We note that this is in line with the principle of 'technological neutrality', which seems to be largely shared among WTO Members.

Thus, market-access commitments form, in fact, a legal instrument recognized by the agreement, by which a Member may prevent the application of the technological neutrality principle, by specifying the terms and conditions for granting market access in its schedule. Such conditions may refer, *inter alia*, to the mode of supply and to the manner and means of supply.

Paragraphs (a)–(d) of Article XVI:2 refer to *origin neutral* limitations by numerical quotas. These criteria are based on the quantities of services and/or service suppliers.[21] They do not relate to the quality of the service supplied

18. F. Ortino, 'Treaty Interpretation and the WTO Appellate Body Report in *US – Gambling*: A Critique', *9 Journal of International Economic Law* (2006), 117, 121.
19. M. Krajewski, *National Regulation and Trade Liberalization in Services*, Kluwer Law International (2003), 95.
20. WT/DS285/R *US – Gambling*, n. 6, para. 6.285.
21. In some cases, limitation of the number of service suppliers may be justified either because of the nature of service, for example, services based on technical limited resources such as scarcity of radio frequencies or limited space for department stores in airports, or services based on economy of scale such as the supply of electricity, public transportation: A. Mattoo, n. 1, 281.

(i.e., technical standards), nor to the ability, reputation or professional experience of the supplier to supply the service (i.e., qualification of the supplier). According to the Scheduling Guidelines from 2001, 'numerical ceilings should be expressed in defined quantities in either absolute numbers or percentages'.[22]

According to these guidelines:

> It should be noted that the quantitative restrictions specified in sub-paragraphs (a) to (d) refer to maximum limitations. Minimum requirements such as those common to licensing criteria (e.g. minimum capital requirements for the establishment of a corporate entity) do not fall within the scope of Article XVI.[23]

Thus, if a Member wishes to allow more liberalized access than committed – it is, of course, possible.[24]

The second group (sub-paragraphs e–f) includes *qualitative* limitations, on the manner of incorporation.

9.2.2.3.2 Limitations on the Number of Service Suppliers

According to Article XVI:2(a), limitation on market access may be caused by measures 'in the form of numerical quotas, monopolies, exclusive service suppliers or the requirements of an economic needs test'.

This provision includes three types of measures:

- Measures forming a *numerical quota* – this standard may be expressed either by specification of the *number* of service suppliers or by the *form* of activity, which indirectly affects their number. Both these possibilities are based on the broad definition of 'service supplier' in Article XXVIII(g), referring to natural or juridical person (Article XXVIII(j)) (see Chapter 5). These measures may include annually established quotas for foreign medical practitioners; government or privately owned monopoly for labour exchange agency services; nationality requirements for suppliers of services (equivalent to zero quota).
- *Monopolies or exclusive service suppliers* – to be discussed below: section 9.2.2.3.2.1.
- Measures applying a *substantive, economic needs test*, for example, a license for a new restaurant based on an economic needs test – to be discussed below: section 9.2.3.

In *US – Gambling*,[25] a question arose whether a total prohibition on a cross-border supply of a service, in respect of which a full market access commitment was

---

22. S/L/92, n. 8, para. 9.
23. *Ibid.*, para. 11.
24. R. Adlung & A. Mattoo, 'The GATS', in A. Mattoo, R.M. Stern & G. Zanini (eds), *A Handbook of International Trade in Services*, Oxford University Press (2007), 48, 58; A. Mattoo, 'National Treatment in the GATS: Corner-Stone or Pandora's Box?' (1996), 3, 4, <www.wto.org>.
25. WT/DS285/R *US – Gambling*, n. 6.

undertaken (gambling and betting services), can be deemed a market-access limitation under paragraphs XVI:2(a) and (c), although this prohibition does not explicitly refer to *numbered units*. Referring to sub-paragraph XVI:2(a), the Appellate Body said: 'the thrust of sub-paragraph (a) is not on the form of limitations, but on their numerical, or quantitative, nature'. It was added, that the words *in the form of* should not be taken 'as prescribing a rigid mechanical formula'.[26] Hence, the Appellate Body accepted that a total prohibition, equivalent to zero-quota, is a measure of numerical nature, or rather a quantitative measure inconsistent with Article XVI:2(a).[27]

The correctness of this interpretation is disputed by some commentators: according to one opinion, this is a misinterpretation of Article XVI, if the prohibition in this case was considered by the Appellate Body to be origin-neutral (namely: the prohibition applies to domestic and foreign services at stake), based on a qualitative judgment rather on a protectionist motive. According to this opinion, such origin-neutral prohibitions are not prohibited by Article XVI, since a zero-quota is not a quota: a quota is usually regarded as providing for an allowed quantity which is more than zero. According to this opinion, an origin-neutral zero-quota is not the sort of measure Article XVI aims at, since it does not exclude anyone from an existing market in which other suppliers are allowed to do what the excluded supplier wants to do. A difference is drawn between Article XVI (Market Access) and XVII (National Treatment) as the latter refers to discrimination on a case-by-case basis, while the former establishes a formal criterion: the numerical quota criterion, to which the case at stake is a borderline case. It is argued that this interpretation allows Members to pursue their own agenda within the limits of the treaty, and therefore it is more wishful for long run considerations. It is stressed, that in the facts of this case, both parties could have strived for the scheduling of a more specific commitment. Nevertheless, for rare cases in which the inscription of an origin-neutral zero-quota might actually seem unfair, the use of the non-violation remedy under Article XXIII:3 is suggested.[28]

According to another opinion, the Appellate Body chose a middle-way between a formalistic and rather narrow approach endorsed by the United States, and the rather sweeping interpretation suggested by Antigua, the EC and Japan, by developing its own realistic interpretation, beyond the text.[29] According to this opinion, both the Panel and Appellate Body took seriously into consideration that the United States made a full market-access commitment with respect to gambling

26. WT/DS285/AB/R, n. 6, Appellate Body report, paras 231–232. A similar interpretation was accorded to para. XVI:2(c): para. 247.
27. WT/DS285/AB/R, n. 6 Appellate Body report, paras 227–238.
28. D.H. Regan, 'A *Gambling* Paradox: Why an Origin-Neutral "Zero-Quota" is not a Quota Under GATS Article XVI', *41 Journal of World Trade* (2007), 1297; see also: F. Ortino, n. 18, 133–134.
29. P. Delimatsis, 'Don't Gamble with the GATS – The Interaction between Articles VI, XVI, XVII and XVIII GATS in the Light of the *US – Gambling* Case', *40 Journal of World Trade* (2006), 1059, 1076.

and betting services that did not differentiate between modes of supply. At the same time, both tribunals

> were careful enough to avoid any statement that would allow measures that have the effect of limiting the number of service suppliers or the number of service operations and the total quantity of services output to be covered by the Article XVI:2 prohibition. This, however, had a negative effect on the clarity and overall coherence of the overall judgment . . .[30]

Thus, the choice of desired interpretation depends on the desired balance of interests: while the former option implies a narrower interpretation, giving a broader scope of discretion to the national authorities, the latter option of interpretation, which was opted for in *US – Gambling*, enhances trade liberalization.

9.2.2.3.2.1 Monopolies and Exclusive Service Suppliers

This sub-paragraph also refers to situations where *monopolies or exclusive service suppliers* dominate the market. Monopoly suppliers are broadly defined by Article XXVIII(h) of GATS to include 'any person, public or private, which in the relevant market of the territory of a Member is authorized or established *formally or in effect* by that Member as the sole supplier of that service'. [Emphasis added]. According to Article XXVIII(j) a person is either natural or juridical (defined in Article XXVIII(l)). Exclusive service suppliers are defined in Article VIII:5 of GATS:

> where a Member, *formally or in effect* (a) authorizes or establishes a small number of service suppliers and (b) substantially prevents competition among those suppliers in its territory. [Emphasis added].[31]

Based on the language of both provisions, examination of the two practices in form and in effect was provided for by the Appellate Body in *US – Gambling*.[32] The approach of the Appellate Body in that case was criticized[33] for interpreting limitations 'in form of monopolies or exclusive service suppliers' in Article XVI:2(a) to effectively also mean limitations being, *in effect*, monopolies or service suppliers, thus 'hinting that measures, which de facto operate as any of the market-access limitations listed in Article XVI:2, fall within the prohibition of Article XVI'.

The Appellate Body in this case opted for a broad interpretation, based on the language of the relevant provisions, facilitating the enhancement of trade liberalization.

30. P. Delimatsis, n. 29, 1067.
31. The word 'and' implies that the two conditions are cumulative.
32. These two options were stressed by the Appellate Body in WT/DS285/AB/R *US – Gambling*, n. 6, para. 230.
33. F. Ortino, n. 18, 135.

9.2.2.3.3 *Limitations on the Total Value of Service Transactions or Assets*

Article XVI:2(b) prohibits two kinds of restrictions:

- Restrictions on the total value of a service *transaction*, for example, limitation of the total value of lending operations that foreign banks may grant, expressed in a monetary figure.[34]
- Restrictions on the total value of *assets*, for example, foreign bank subsidiaries limited to per cent of total domestic assets of all banks.[35]

9.2.2.3.4 *Limitations on the Total Number of Service Operations or on the Total Quantity of Service Output*

9.2.2.3.4.1 'Total'

The term 'total', in this provision, was interpreted in a somewhat odd manner by the Panel in *US – Gambling*, as the Panel was striving to claim that it expresses the notion that the limitations specified in this provision are maximum limitations. The Panel found it difficult, however, to explain how it was that sub-paragraph (a) is also based on the maximum limitation standard, but nevertheless, does not include the word 'total'. The Panel said:

> Unlike subparagraph (a), subparagraph (c) of Article XVI:2 contains a reference to 'total' number of service operations and 'total' quantity of service output. The 1993 Scheduling Guidelines state that: 'It should be noted that the quantitative restrictions specified in subparagraphs (a) to (d) refer to maximum limitations.' This suggests that the word 'total' in Article XVI:2(c) serves the purpose of indicating that limitations covered by Article XVI:2(c) must impose maximum limits on services operation and/or service output.
>
> Accordingly, such differences as there are between the wording of subparagraphs (a) and (c) of Article XVI:2 do not warrant a different conclusion as to the impact of the two subparagraphs in the present case.
>
> The maintenance and enforcement of laws that prohibit the supply by remote means of a committed sector or sub-sector limits to zero the number of service operations in the sector or sub-sector for which the Member has made a commitment. It imposes a 'limitation on the total number of service operations . . . expressed . . . in the form of quotas' contrary to Article XVI:2(c) of the GATS.[36]

A simpler interpretation could suggest, that the word 'total' implies that the service operations or assets at stake are not limited specifically, but by a general quantity

34. GATS commentary, n. 7, 379.
35. An example drawn from schedules of Members: S/L/92, n. 8.
36. WT/DS285/R, n. 6, Panel report, paras 6.345–6.347.

'expressed in a form of quota', which is determined *ex ante* by the importing Member.

In *US – Gambling*, the ban on import of gambling and betting services, addressed by the Panel as a zero-quota, was considered by the Panel to be a limitation on the total number of service operators or on the total quantity of service output.[37]

9.2.2.3.4.2 'Services Operations', 'Services Output'

These terms are not defined by GATS, but in *US – Gambling*,[38] the Panel attempted to interpret them, determining that 'service operations' mean activities comprised in the production of a service, while 'service output' means the result of the production of the service. However, the Panel did not apply this distinction between the two options while referring to the facts of that case.[39]

The facts of *US – Gambling* show that there could be some overlap between these two categories, but it would not have any effective implications as long as at least one of them covers the case at stake, since the same provision covers both of them.[40]

An interpretative question arising from the practice of the Panel in *US – Gambling* is whether this provision covers cases where both kinds of limitations exist, in light of the language of this provision, using the word 'or', which implies alternative relations between the two categories. This is a matter of interpretation. A narrow interpretation would suggest that these two options should be approached as alternatives. However, the result of such an interpretation would be that while the application of each of the restrictions separately is prohibited, their combined application is allowed. This is an absurd result. Therefore, a more effective interpretation, taking into account the context, would read 'or' as also implying 'and'.

9.2.2.3.4.3 The Manner by which the Measures are Expressed

According to Article XVI:2(c) the measures covered by it may be 'expressed in terms of designated numerical units in the form of quotas or the requirement of an economic needs test'. An example to this category of limitations, drawn from schedules of Members, includes restrictions on broadcasting time available for foreign films.[41]

In *US – Gambling*, a question arose whether a total prohibition on a cross-border supply of a service in respect of which a full market access commitment was undertaken (gambling and betting services) can be deemed a market-access

37. *Ibid.*, Panel report, para. 6.355.
38. *Ibid.*, Panel report, paras 6.348–6.349. The Panel based this conclusion on the 1993 Scheduling Guidelines (MTN.GNS/W/164, n. 3) 'which provide the following example of a limitation on "service operations or quantity of service output" under Article XVI:2(c), namely restrictions on broadcasting time available for foreign films'.
39. In WT/DS285/R *US – Gambling*, n. 6, the Panel referred to both options together, see paras 6.355, 6.361, 6.369, 6.376.
40. GATS Commentary, n. 7, 380.
41. S/L/92, n. 8.

limitation under paragraphs XVI:2(a) and (c), although this prohibition does not explicitly refer to numbered units. Referring to sub-paragraph (c), similar to its reference to sub-paragraph (a), the Appellate Body explained that it refers to a quantitative restriction on market access, but it is not clear that such restrictions must take a particular form.[42] Hence, the Appellate Body reached a similar conclusion to that reached concerning sub-paragraph (a), that such limitation can be deemed a market access limitation under paragraphs XVI:2(c), although the prohibition does not explicitly refer to numbered units, because in effect it created a zero quota.[43]

The justification and the implications of this analysis are disputed among commentators.[44] Even if this approach is accepted in principle, yet another question arises about whether it will also apply where 'the effects of the measure are felt only "on part of the scheduled sector" or if the measure in question restricts only one means of delivery covered by Mode 1, leaving others unaffected'.[45] This question remains unresolved in the meantime. It is clear, that if these options are accepted by GATS jurisprudence, they will broaden the scope of application of this provision; and since this provision defines practices which are prohibited unless scheduled, such a broad interpretation would serve to enhance trade liberalization on the expense of domestic regulatory freedom.

9.2.2.3.4.4 Measures which Limit Input for the Supply of Service are Allowed

According to footnote 9 of GATS, 'subparagraph 2(c) does not cover measures of a Member which limit inputs for the supply of services'.[46]

Since limitations on the input necessarily affect the output, this footnote may have an indirect narrowing effect on the scope of application of this paragraph.

Since the term 'inputs for its supply' was not interpreted in GATS, this interpretation has far-reaching consequences, for example, if telecommunications and financial services were interpreted as 'inputs' to other business services.

The new Guidelines and Procedures for the negotiations on Trade in Services applying to the Doha Round negotiations, provide, to that extent:

> It is understood that market access and national treatment commitments apply only to the sectors or sub-sectors inscribed in the schedule. They do not imply a right for the supplier of a committed service to supply uncommitted services which are inputs to the committed service.

42. WT/DS285/AB/R, n. 6, Appellate Body report, para. 231.
43. WT/DS285/R, n. 6, Panel report, paras 6.331–6.332, Appellate Body report, para. 250–251.
44. See, for example, GATS Commentary, n. 7, 380–381; D.H. Ragen, n. 28; P. Delimatsis, n. 29.
45. D. Irwin & J.H.H. Weiler, 'Measures Affecting the Cross-Border Supply of Gambling and Betting Services', 7 *World Trade Review* (2008), 71, 86–87.
46. Historically, this footnote was conceived to allow Members to regulate zoning and floor space. In addition, it seems that Members wanted to make a clear separation between main services and services that are output to it: GATS commentary, n. 7, 381.

Thus, the status of services which may be considered as 'input' and where not clearly scheduled may be unclear. This is an undesirable situation, undermining predictability and certainty of foreign services suppliers.[47]

9.2.2.3.5 Limitations on the Total Number of Natural Persons

9.2.2.3.5.1 Scope of Coverage: Modes of Supply

Article XVI:2(d) prohibits restrictions on 'the total number of natural persons that may be employed in a particular service sector or that a service supplier may employ and who are necessary for, and directly related to, the supply of a specific service'.

According to this provision, such measures may have 'the form of numerical quotas or the requirement of an economic needs test'. While in principle this provision applies to all Modes of supply, it has particular implications concerning measures addressing Modes 3 (commercial presence) and Mode 4 (movement of natural persons). Examples to this category of limitations, drawn from schedules of Members, include provisions providing that foreign labour should not exceed x per cent and/or wages xy per cent of total.[48] On the other hand, a case where the establishment of a commercial presence is subject to the employment of *at least* a certain number of nationals would not be covered by this provision since the *total number of natural persons that may be employed* is not restricted.[49]

9.2.2.3.5.2 'Or'

The provision refers to restrictions on the total number of natural persons that may be employed either in a particular *service* or by a particular *service supplier*. Here, also, an interpretative question may arise where the two situations are combined into one case. According to the same logic of the analysis of sub-paragraph XVI:2(c) and the approach adopted by the Panel in *US – Gambling* in the context of that sub-paragraph, it seems that despite the word 'or' such a case would also be recognized as covered by this sub-paragraph.

9.2.2.3.5.3 'Necessary for, and Directly Related to'

This provision is restricted to measures 'necessary for, and directly related to' the supply of a specific service. This phrasing is narrowing the scope of this provision. It implies that other measures limiting the number of natural persons would not be prohibited by this provision, and thus, should not be scheduled to be allowed. However, the expressions 'necessary for' and 'directly related to' are not defined by the agreement, therefore allowing for flexibility of interpretation, but at the

47. A. Mattoo & S. Wunsch, 'Pre-empting Protectionism in Services: The WTO and Outsourcing', *The World Bank Policy research Working Paper* (2004), 15, <www-wds.worldbank.org>.
48. S/L/92, n. 8.
49. Such practice could, however, be challenged as a national treatment violation: GATS commentary, n. 7, 382.

same time creating uncertainty. It seems that these provisions would be interpreted on a case-by-case basis.

9.2.2.3.6 *Limitations on the Manner of Incorporation*

Article XVI:2(e) refers to 'measures which restrict or require specific types of legal entity or joint venture through which a service supplier may supply a service'. In fact, these are *not quantitative, but qualitative* entry controls, because they require certain services to be provided through particular legal entities.

Examples to this category of limitations, drawn from schedules of Members, include:[50]

- Commercial presence excluding representative offices.
- Foreign companies required to establish subsidiaries.
- In sector x, determination that commercial presence must take the form of a partnership.

Since this provision applies to legal entities, it does not refer to Mode 4 (presence of natural persons).

In *China – Publications and Audiovisual Products*, the Panel classified, under this heading, a Chinese measure that required foreign distributors who wished to engage in the distribution of audiovisual products in China to do so through established contractual joint ventures.[51]

9.2.2.3.7 *Limitations on the Participation of Foreign Capital*

Article XVI:2(f) refers to limitations 'in terms of maximum percentage limit on foreign shareholding or the total value of individual or aggregate foreign investment'. An example to this category of limitations, drawn from schedules of Members, includes foreign equity ceiling of x per cent for a particular form of commercial presence.[52] Some countries also limit the *minimum* foreign investments in a joint venture or a company. It seems that due to the precise wording of sub-paragraph (f), explicitly referring only to a *maximum* limit, this limitation will not be covered by it.[53]

According to one commentator,[54] many countries maintain limits on foreign or private ownership, or both, but it is not easy to find a sound economic rationale to this behaviour.

50. S/L/92, n. 8.
51. WT/DS363/R, AB/R China – Measures Affecting Trading Rights and Distribution Services for Certain Publications and Audiovisual Entertainment Products, adopted on 19.1.2010, Panel report, para. 7.1356.
52. S/L/92, n. 8.
53. Krajewski, n. 19, 94. The author suggests that such a limitation could either be subject to sub-para. (e) if accompanied by a limit on the manner of incorporation, or by Art. VI:4 of GATS, if it turns to be more burdensome than necessary.
54. A. Mattoo, n. 1, 282.

This is the only GATS provision referring to 'foreign investment' rather than to 'commercial presence'.[55] This perception is not defined in the agreement. Neither are the relationships between the two perceptions clear. It may be assumed that foreign investment represents a broader perception than commercial presence, the former also including cases where foreign capital is invested but the investor does not actively participate in the operation of the commercial presence, or cases where the investment is insufficient for the acquisition of ownership or control over a company. If this interpretation were to be accepted, it would imply that all foreign equity limitations should be scheduled.

In *China – Publications and Audiovisual Products* it was determined that a Chinese regulation containing a limitation on foreign equity participation, providing that the Chinese co-operator shall hold no less than 51% equity in a contractual joint venture (a form of incorporation obligatory in order for foreign distributors to engage in distribution of audiovisual products in China), that was not set out in China's schedule, was inconsistent with China's market-access obligations under Article XVI:2(f).[56]

9.2.3 The Economic Needs Test

The economic needs test, mentioned in some of the categories of Article XVI:2, is not further interpreted by the text of the agreement. According to it, a Member may prevent the import of a certain service from other Members or the supply of a service by a service supplier from another Member where its economic situation dictates so; namely, its market does not need, or cannot absorb, imported services or service suppliers. This is a very flexible test, which is completely subject to the discretion of decision-makers in each country. It may thus be abused to apply barriers to trade. For example, may a country prevent the import of certain services, or the access of service suppliers, claiming that their activity would enhance domestic unemployment? If this interpretation is accepted, it may considerably undermine the purpose of GATS. If this test would have been part of a provision that only prohibits the use of different categories of limitations, paradoxically, it should be broadly interpreted, in order to give this provision a maximal scope. However, since Article XVI is prohibiting certain unscheduled practices, but at the same time allows such practices, where scheduled, it is better to refer to this test on a case-by-case basis, thus allowing for maximum flexibility of interpretation.

9.2.4 A Measure May be Included in Some of the Groups

A measure examined may be included in more than one prohibited group of limitations according to Article XVI:2.

55. GATS commentary, n. 7, 389.
56. WT/DS363/R, n. 51, Panel report, para. 7.1367.

Thus, in the case of *Mexico – Telecoms*[57] the panel noted that Mexico's GATS schedule required that international telecommunications traffic 'must be routed through the facilities' of a Mexican concessionaire, and with respect to non-facilities-based services supplied cross-border, the routing requirement prohibited 'the cross-border supply upon termination within Mexico by means of the very "leased capacity" which defines this type of service'. In both cases, the panel determined that these measures were restrictions under Article XVI:2(a), (b) and (c). In *US – Gambling*,[58] a prohibition which did not explicitly refer to numbered units was nevertheless interpreted as a prohibition in the form of a zero-quota, prohibited under Article XVI:2(a) and (c).

9.2.5 Article XVI:2: An Exhaustive List

The measures included in Article XVI:2 comprise an exhaustive list. A Member which does not specify any limitation to the six possible categories in its schedule of specific commitment concerning a sector or a sub-sector ('none' – see Chapter 7), is deemed to allow full market access concerning this sector or sub-sector.[59] On the other hand, limitations that are not covered by any of the groups described in this list are not subject to this Article, and therefore may be applied to imported services and service suppliers from other Members, concerning services sectors and modes of supply for which specific commitments were taken (e.g., measures considered as 'domestic regulation', covered by Article VI:4,5 – see Chapter 12; fiscal measures, such as high non-discriminatory tax on a particular service which severely limits market access;[60] minimum-size requirements related to equity, capacity,[61] restrictions on the capital movements with respect to Modes 2 and 4;[62] and measures mentioned in Article XVIII, including, but not limited to, measures relating to qualifications, standards or market access).[63] In addition, the specifications on each of the categories are also exhaustive. Thus, limitations on the number of service suppliers are prohibited only if they take form of numerical quotas, monopolies, exclusive service suppliers or the requirements of an economic needs test.[64]

In the case of *Mexico – Telecoms*,[65] Mexico undertook a commitment to allow the access of certain telecommunications services from Members, subject to the

57. WT/DS204/R Mexico – Measures Affecting Telecommunications Services, adopted on 1.6.2004, Panel report, paras 7.85–7.86.
58. WT/DS285/AB/R n. 6, Appellate Body report paras 231–232.
59. MTN.GNS/W/164, n. 3, para. 4; S/L/92, n. 8, para. 8.
60. A. Mattoo, n. 24, 3.
61. R. Adlung & A. Mattoo, n. 24, 57–58.
62. Footnote 8 to GATS (see above).
63. P. Delimatsis, n. 29, 1064–1065. Delimatsis notes that this interpretation is in line with the principle of progressive liberalization as well as with the Members' right to regulate.
64. WT/DS285/R *US – Gambling*, n. 6, Panel report, paras 6.298, 6.325, 6.341.
65. WT/DS204/R, n. 57, paras 7.357–7.358.

issuance of corresponding regulation. Examining whether the implied delay of access is subject to Article XVI:2 and therefore prohibited according to it, the Panel said:

> none of the six categories relate to *temporal* limitations – such as dates for entry into force or for the implementation of commitments. This suggests that temporal limitations cannot constitute limitations on market access under Article XVI:2 of the GATS.

GATT 1947 case of *Japan – Trade in Semiconductors*[66] reflects the use of burdening administrative practices which, if applied to services, would not be covered by Article XVI:2. It was found that the Japanese government exercised powerful administrative pressure on the private sector, to stop exporting in prices below specific costs of the firm, *inter alia* by exercising governmental control on costs and prices and an ongoing requirement for the supply of information by the private sector on the relevant activities. In that case, it was determined, that in fact these measures were equivalent to mandatory limitations by law. Such limitations are uncovered by Article XVI:2.

Finally, limitations on inputs used for the production of a service, explicitly addressed by footnote 9 of GATS (see above) form another example to measures uncovered by this Article.

Sometimes, such measures will still be found to be prohibited according to another GATS provision.

To complete the picture, it should be mentioned that Article XVI ensures only non-discrimination of *foreign* services and service suppliers, thus overlooking possible discrimination of *domestic* services and service suppliers. This approach could be resulting from the assumption that governments will hardly ever treat domestic services or service suppliers less favourably, because of internal political pressures. Nevertheless, in fact, such practices exist, for example, in the case of harmful tax competition where domestic suppliers may be deprived of tax benefits accorded to foreign service suppliers in order to attract them to exercise economic activities in a country. In any case, the relationships between a government and its citizens/nationals are not covered by international agreements.

9.2.6 Interpretation Rules for the List

Article XVI must be interpreted as representing a balance between market access and domestic regulation.[67]

66. L/6309 The Panel report on Japan – Trade in Semiconductors, adopted on 4.5.1988, BIDS35S/116.
67. J. Pauwelyn, 'Rien Ne Va Plus? Distinguishing domestic Regulation from Market Access in GATT and in GATS', *Duke Law School Legal Studies Paper No. 85* (2005), 131, 158–159, 168, <http://papers.ssrn.com>.

According to one commentator, the underlying rationale of this article is the presumption that the measures listed in it lack any legitimate policy justification. This presumption may be rebutted.[68]

Article XVI has been interpreted[69] to cover both discriminatory and non-discriminatory measures. This interpretation has a far-reaching implication on governments' authority for domestic regulation, since it implies that a Member that has made full market-access commitments is not free to impose certain strictly non-discriminatory measures, unless they can be justified under the exemption provisions (see Chapter 15).[70]

In *US – Gambling*[71] the WTO adjudicating bodies gave a broad interpretation to the market access limitations included in the list of Article XVI, including in it any measure having an *effect similar* to that of any market-access limitations listed in Article XVI:2, regardless of form. This broad interpretation is criticized by some commentators for disregarding the object an purpose of this provision, which is drawing a 'line between "quantitative and qualitative" measures – the first forbidden, the latter permitted', or a 'balance between liberalization and the right to regulate',[72] referring, more specifically, to the current and future purpose and function of Article VI:4. According to this criticism, such interpretation could lead to a result where most domestic regulation would be prohibited under Article XVI, unless justified under the exceptions of Articles XIV and XIV*bis* (which also suffer from an interpretation that seems to narrow the autonomy of domestic regulator). Such an interpretation may thus undermine the purpose of Article VI:4.[73]

However, other commentators justify the WTO adjudicating bodies' decision concerning this matter.[74] This position is based on the following reasoning: at present, Article VI is very weak. Thus, Articles XVI and XVII serve as major instruments for the achievement of trade liberalization and should therefore be strengthened. Unlike the equivalent GATT Article XI, Article XVI of GATS refers to policy matters, although from a quantitative aspect. It embraces even *non-discriminatory* restrictive measures (while Article XVII embraces only

68. F. Ortino, n. 18, 142–143.
69. In MTN.GNS/164, n. 3.
70. A. Mattoo, 'Services in a Development Round', *The World Bank Policy Research Paper No. 3718* (2005), 10, <http://papers.ssrn.com>.
71. WT/DS285/R *US – Gambling* n. 6, paras 6338, 6355; WT/DS285/AB/R, paras 239 and 252. See interpretation by F. Ortino, 'Regional Trade Agreements and Trade in Services', in S. Lester & B. Mercurino (eds), *Bilateral and Regional Trade Agreements: Commentary, Analysis and Case Studies*, Cambridge CPU (2007), 9, n. 36, <http://papers.ssrn.com>.
72. D. Irwin & J.H.H. Weiler, n. 45, 92–99. They suggest the adoption of the EU approach, drawing the line between the quantitative and qualitative effects as follows: 'a State measure that has a quantitative effect will be caught by the Market Access provision only when the effect in question is such as totally to exclude the product from the marketplace. In addition, State measures will be scrutinized if they are discriminatory and protectionist'. *Ibid.*, 103.
73. J. Pauwelyn, n. 67, 161, <http://papers.ssrn.com>.
74. P. Delimatsis, 'The Interaction between GATS Articles VI, XVI, XVII and XVIII after the US – Gambling Case', *NCCR Trade regulation Working Paper No. 2006/9* (2006), <http://papers.ssrn.com>.

discriminatory policy measures). External provisions to Article XVI imply that measures *which are not covered* by the exhaustive list of six groups of prohibited practices provided for by this provision may still restrict trade. Such measures are mentioned in footnote 8 of Article XVI, for example, restrictions on capital movement with respect to Modes 2 and 4, as well as in Article XVIII, for example, measures relating to qualifications, standards or licensing. These measures could restrict services trade even in the absence of any limitation scheduled under Article XVI.

It is argued that the WTO adjudicating bodies chose an interpretative approach less sweeping than those suggested by Antigua, the EC and Japan, but also not narrowly formalistic. The aim of this approach is to prevent WTO Members, who took a full market-access commitment, from escaping this commitment, thus upsetting reasonable market-access expectations that other WTO Members developed in light of this unqualified market-access commitment. The WTO adjudicating bodies stressed that it is not the *form* of measure, but rather its *quantitative nature*, that determines the applicability of any of Article XVI:2 sub-paragraphs, irrespective of whether this quantitative nature is expressed in numbers.

Referring to the possible effect of this judgment on Article VI:4,5 it is argued, that this case is not relevant to these provisions, for two reasons: first, a total restriction on import can never ensure the quality of import, and second, the reasoning behind the restriction on the import of gambling and betting services was justified to protect minors, morality or public order or to avert fraud, thus being explained as legitimate domestic policy that could have been potentially covered by Article XIV exceptions.[75]

9.2.7 RELATIONSHIP BETWEEN ARTICLE XVI:1 AND XVI:2

The Panel in *US – Gambling*[76] described the relationship between the two paragraphs of Article XVI as follows: 'paragraph 2 of Article XVI exhaustively defines the limitations and measures that are prohibited by Article XVI, unless scheduled. In that sense, paragraph 2 of Article XVI complements the first paragraph of that Article'. However, the adjudicating bodies in this case did not give a clear answer to the question, 'whether a market access commitment undertaken by a Member would constrain that Member from introducing any measure that might inhibit market access even if that measure was not among those listed in Article XVI:2'.[77] Thus, the question remains open whether, in a case of full market-access commitment, a Member is also obliged to allow *total market openness* in a given sector.

75. P. Delimatsis, n. 74, 16.
76. WT/DS285/R *US – Gambling*, n. 6, para. 6.298.
77. P. Delimatsis, *International Trade in Services and Domestic Regulations – Necessity, Transparency and Regulatory Diversity*, Oxford University Press (2007), 132.

Some believe, that an affirmative answer would neglect important textual elements entrenched in the text of GATS.[78]

In addition to this aspect, paragraph 1 adds to paragraph 2 the reference to services and service suppliers of any other Member, thus excluding from the scope of this provision domestic services and service suppliers. Read together, the potential scope of paragraph 2 is narrowed by paragraph 1 in that respect. It further applies to such foreign services and service suppliers, the discipline of treatment no less favourable, subject to the scheduled specific commitments.

9.2.8 Does Article XVI Apply to Consumers?

The underlying presumption behind the six measures' categories included in Article XVI is that they are aimed at foreign services or service suppliers, inhibiting their access into the market of destination. In *US – Gambling*, Antigua argued that given its specific commitments on gambling services the United States could not have maintained certain domestic laws aimed at the *consumption* of such services. The Panel rejected these claims, concluding that these laws are not inconsistent with Article XVI:2(a)–(c). Antigua appealed this decision but the Appellate Body decided it did not have to address this question and these findings of the Panel have not been refuted.[79] This result allegedly implies that despite full specific commitments, a Member can still domestically regulate consumption as it wishes. Nevertheless, such measures may still be challenged under a non-violation cause (see Chapter 17), if they nullify or impair the benefits that can reasonably be expected to accrue under a commitment.[80]

Alternatively, another interpretation is suggested, reading other provisions of this Article, in particular paragraphs (b) and (c), as preventing restrictions on consumers. This interpretation relies on the fact that GATS applies to measures *affecting* services, defined broadly by Article XXVIII(c) to include 'the purchase, payment or *use* of a service'. In terms of policy, it is noted that such interpretation might be necessary to prevent Members, who took full commitments, from circumventing them by imposing restrictions on consumers rather than on suppliers of services. On the other hand, this approach 'would entail a questionable interpretative expansion of the terms of Article XVI, which, as noted by the Appellate Body, does not cover all measures that *have an effect* of limiting the number of

78. *Ibid.*, 133.
79. WT/DS285/R, n. 6, Panel report, paras 6.382–6.383 (Colorado), 6.397–6.398 (Minnesota), 6.401–6.402 (New Jersey), 6.405–6.406 (New York). The Appellate Body's avoidance from addressing this question emanated from its decision that no prima facie case was made by the complainant concerning the relevant measures, which followed by reverse of the Panel decision concerning these measures: Appellate Body report, para. 254.
80. S. Wunch-Vincent, 'The Internet, Cross-Border Trade in Services, and the GATS: Lessons from *US – Gambling*', *5 World Trade Review* (2006), 319, 338.

service suppliers or the total number of service operations, but only those that are *quantitative* in nature'.[81] [Emphasis in the original].

9.3 QUANTITATIVE RESTRICTIONS IN GATT: A COMPARISON

Prohibition of quantitative restriction in GATT is embodied in Article XI of GATT, prohibiting 'restrictions other than duties, taxes or other charges, whether made effective through quotas, import or export licenses or other measures'. Complementary provisions are found in GATT Articles III:5 and III:7, specifying different techniques for quantitative restrictions which are prohibited by GATT, as well as in GATT Article XIII, providing for non-discriminatory administration of quantitative restrictions. These provisions apply, in principle, to governmental measures, but may also apply to action of private parties 'if there is sufficient governmental involvement in it'. This should be determined on a case-by-case basis.[82] It was further recognized that 'governmental measures may enable private parties, directly or indirectly, to restrict trade, where those measures themselves are not trade restrictive'.[83]

GATT Article XI:1 explicitly recognizes that quantitative restrictions are often accompanied by licensing requirements. Although the equivalent GATS provision does not refer to licensing explicitly, the quantitative restrictions mentioned by it can be implemented by licensing requirements. GATT jurisprudence examined discretionary non-automatic licensing requirements under this provision.[84] Nevertheless, it was held that discretionary licensing used in conjunction with a quantitative restriction does not necessarily result in any additional restriction.[85]

Article XI of GATT is broadly interpreted by the WTO adjudicating bodies, through the interpretation of vague expressions in it such as 'restrictions'.[86]

Several differences may be noted between GATT and GATS provisions concerning this matter. The basic difference between the provisions of the two agreements emanates from their different subject matter: the trade restrictions referred to

81. GATS commentary, n. 7, 394. It is noted there, though, that the Scheduling Guidelines from 1993 as well as from 2001, reflecting the preparatory work of the agreement, could be interpreted to support both possible approaches.
82. WT/DS44/R Japan – Measures Affecting Consumer Photographic Film and Paper, adopted on 22.4.1998, Panel report, para. 10.56.
83. WT/DS155/R Argentina – Measures Affecting the Export of Bovine Hides and Import of Finished Leather, adopted on 16.2.2001, Panel report, para. 11.18.
84. WT/DS90/R India – Quantitative Restrictions on Imports of Agricultural, Textile and Industrial Products, adopted on 22.9.1999, paras 5.129–5.130.
85. WT/DS161,169/R Korea – Measures Affecting the Imports of Fresh, Chilled and Frozen Beef, adopted on 10.1.2001, Panel report, para. 782.
86. See analysis of former cases and decision in WT/DS366/R Columbia – Indicative Prices and Restrictions on Ports of Entry, adopted on 20.5.2009, paras 7.233–7.240, 7.249–7.254, 7.273–7.275.

by GATT provisions are different from these referred to by GATS provisions. The latter are more elaborated and adapted to the four modes of supply envisioned by GATS, and its application to service suppliers.

While Article XI of GATT applies to export as well as to import, Article XVI of GATS applies only to import. GATS concentrates on the enhancement of international trade, thus abstaining from interference in domestic regulation concerning domestic production. Therefore, Article XVI does not apply to restrictions on inputs used for the production of services, nor does it refer to the granting of trade or tax benefits only to foreign investors.

Article XI of GATT includes a list of exceptions, namely circumstances where the application of quantitative restrictions is allowed, in order to protect a domestic interest. Such a list is not included in Article XVI of GATS. The sovereign right of Members to regulate domestic policy matters is reserved by abstaining from reference to such matters as explained in the former paragraph, and by the general exceptions included in Articles XIV, XIV*bis* and other 'safety valves' included in the agreement (see Chapter 15).

Article XI of GATT automatically applies to all international trade in goods subject to the agreement. Unlike it, Article XVI of GATS applies selectively, only to services and service suppliers where specific commitments were undertaken.

While Article XI of GATT refers only to discriminatory practices, Article XVI of GATS refers to non-discriminatory, as well as to origin-neutral market limitations.[87]

Article XI includes a residual provision applying it to 'other measures'. This provision was given a broad interpretation by GATT panels.[88] Article XVI of GATS is confined to the six categories of measures specified in it.

Unlike Article XVI of GATS, Article XI of GATT does not include the 'no less favourble treatment' discipline. Nevertheless, in GATT 1947 case *US – Petroleum*,[89] it was explained that the purpose of Articles XI, III:5, and III:7 of GATT is to defend the expectations of the Members concerning the competitive relations between their products and the products of other Members. Both provisions are not only aimed at protecting current trade but also at ensuring the certainty and predictability necessary for planning future trade.

The differences between these two equivalent provisions imply a cautious interpretative approach for the adoption of GATT Article XI interpretation to GATS context. Nevertheless, despite the differences between GATT and GATS provisions, it seems that a similar approach for their interpretation is applied by the WTO adjudicating bodies.

87. In GATT, this kind of measures is covered by Art. III, due to *the Ad Note* to Art. III.

88. See: *Analytical Index – Guide to GATT Law and Practice*, the WTO, Geneva (1995), vol. 1, 220–225.

89. L/167 The Panel report on United States – Taxes on Petroleum and Certain imported Substances, adopted on 17.6.1987 34S/136, para. 5.2.2.

9.4 PAYMENTS AND TRANSFERS

Free flow of money is essential for international trade. Impossibility to transfer money into a country, to finance the supply of services there, or to take profits out of a country may form a decisive consideration not to trade with this country. Footnote 8 of GATS, (see full text above, 9.2.1.6) referring to Article XVI:1, applies to Mode 1 (cross-border) and Mode 3 (commercial presence). While for Mode 1 it provides for 'the cross-border movement of capital', which could be interpreted as implying both directions: in and out of the country, for Mode 3 it only provides for 'transfers of capital *into* its territory', thus ensuring the access of money into the territory of destination, where the commercial presence should be established, but not the ability to take profits out of the country.

On the other hand, while for cross-border supply, the footnote provides that the transfer of money should be allowed if it is 'an essential part of the service itself', an expression which is not interpreted in the text but implies a narrow scope, for commercial presence the note provides for what seems to be a broader criterion: 'related transfers', which is also not interpreted by the text and thus open for discretion.

It should be noted that Article XVI:2(f) also refers to commercial presence, prohibiting limitations on the participation of foreign capital.

According to Article XXVIII(c) of GATS, measures affecting payment for a service are covered by GATS. Thus, such measures are at least subject to the MFN principle. It is thus logical that GATS Article XI, referring to situations where specific commitments were undertaken, must go further beyond this general rule.

Article XI of GATS[90] includes some complementary disciplines to these included in other GATS provisions, providing:

Payments and Transfers

1. Except under the circumstances envisaged in Article XII, a Member shall not apply restrictions on international transfers and payments for current transactions relating to its specific commitments.
2. Nothing in this Agreement shall affect the rights and obligations of the members of the International Monetary Fund under the Articles of Agreement of the Fund, including the use of exchange actions which are in conformity with the Articles of Agreement, provided that a Member shall not impose restrictions on any capital transactions inconsistently with its specific commitments regarding such transactions, except under Article XII or at the request of the Fund.

This provision was not yet interpreted by the WTO adjudicating bodies. Its aim is clear, and corresponds to the aim of the former provisions specified: facilitating international transactions in services by eliminating barriers to transfer of the finance involved. Applying only to payments and transfers related to specific

90. For the history of this provision see GATS commentary, n. 7, 247.

commitments, this is a conditional provision, depending on the existence, in a certain case, of such commitments.

9.4.1 Article XI:1

The language of this provision raises some interpretative difficulties:

- The expression 'current transactions' was not defined, since its definition is subject to the IMF.[91] The IMF definition regards 'current transactions' as payments which are not for the purpose of transferring capital.[92] This definition includes transfer of profits, but firms might want to know whether it includes dividends, as well as sums transferred in order to cover operating expenses. The scope of this expression will also be determined by interpretation, subject to the considerations mentioned.
- Article XI does not specify whether it refers to outward or inward transactions (unlike GATS the footnote 8 – see above). Therefore, it may be assumed that it applies to both, as long as they are related to a specific commitment.[93]
- It is unclear whether the transfers and payments should be related to the specific commitments, or whether the current transactions should be related to them, or both. In other words: does this provision require a direct link between the payments and transfers and the specific commitments, or only a direct link between the payments and transfers and the current transactions, which are, in turn, related to the specific commitments?
- The nature of the necessary link between the transaction and the specific commitment involved, embodied in the word 'relating', is unclear. A narrow interpretation could require a direct link, namely, apply this provision only to a transaction accompanying the direct application a specific commitment. A more liberal approach may adopt a broader interpretation, applying this provision also to a transaction involved in ancillary activities. For example, in case of a foreign bank giving loans in another Member, a narrow interpretation would apply this provision to the transfer of money necessary for the loans only. A broader interpretation might also apply this provision to the money necessary for the conduct of all the ancillary activities involved in the administration of loans. An even broader interpretation may consider its application to the money necessary for the construction of the bank building, or for the rent paid for such a building. The interpretation chosen depends on the balance point that will be chosen between the interest of enhancing world trade liberalization, on the one

91. For further elaboration on the IMF and World Bank complementary contribution on these aspects see: A. Lehmann, N.T. Tamirisa & J. Wieczorek, 'International Trade in services: Implications for the IMF', *IMF Policy Discussion Paper* (2003), 18–19.
92. GATS commentary, n. 7, 249.
93. *Ibid.*, 250.

hand, and the will of Members to protect their domestic markets, on the other hand.

- The term 'restrictions' is also not defined by this provision. A broad interpretation of this term is suggested to include 'any measure that could negatively affect international transfers and payments', based on the interpretation of this term in the context of other GATT and GATS provisions.[94] However, this interpretation is also not very clear (what would be considered as 'could negatively affect'? would only measures *directly* affecting be included, or also measures with *indirect* effect? does the language of this provision refer only to *actual* effect, or rather, as suggested, also to *potential* effect?)[95] Therefore, it seems that this term will be interpreted on a case-by-case basis, subject to the policy of interpreters, whether to allow a broader or narrower scope of application of this provision.

According to one interpretation, the scope of this provision is limited, since it covers transfers into a Member (e.g., operating expenditure of a commercial presence), but not out of it. This is a result of a position held by the developing countries that were concerned about their ability to control capital movements, movement of firms abroad and investments abroad. Thus, this provision does not ensure that an investor will be able to take out its capital or profits from the country of investment. The result of such a narrow interpretation is that Article XI:1 does not add anything beyond the provision of footnote 8.

According to a broader interpretation, this provision may apply to the direct transfer of payments gained by a service supplier operating trough Mode 3 (commercial presence), who wishes such payments to be made directly to the mother company abroad, or operating according to Mode 4 (movement of natural persons), wishing its wages to be transferred directly to its home country.

Due to its general language, this provision could further prohibit any restrictions on currency exports intended to pay for consumption abroad under Mode 1 or 2, such as maximum amount of national currency that could be used for these purposes or limitations on the use of credit cards. It could further cover repatriation of profits, earnings, dividends and interest gained by service suppliers in the host country.[96]

In *US – Gambling*[97] Antigua argued, *inter alia*, that restrictions imposed by the United States on the payment for certain gambling services were violating Article XI. The Panel did not rule on that claim for reasons of judicial economy, but nevertheless recognized the importance of this provision to secure GATS purposes.

94. *Ibid.*, 251.
95. Examples to such measures include exchange restrictions, discriminatory currency arrangements and multiple currency practices: GATS commentary, n. 7, 251.
96. GATS Analysis, *OECD*, n. 11, 19.
97. WT/DS285/R, n. 6, Panel report, paras 6.441–6.442.

9.4.2 Article XI:2

Paragraph 2 of Article XI forms an exception to the rule set forth in paragraph 1 thereof. Where balance-of-payment difficulties occur, it allows the application of certain restrictions on the access of capital into a Member, in the circumstances specified in Article XII (see detailed analysis of this Article in Chapter 15). The words 'under Article XII' seem to refer not only to the balance-of-payment difficulties specified by this provision, but to the entire Article, including the conditions of application specified in it, that is, non-discrimination, proportionality etc. Despite these reservations, that considerably narrow the scope of application of this provision, it may still deter investors and service suppliers.

The scope of application of Article XI:2 is subject to the specific commitments taken by Members. Similarly to other exceptions to GATS principles, a cautious approach should be taken concerning the application of this exception, to prevent its use as a disguised barrier to trade.

To complete the picture it should be noted, that other exceptions to Article XI:1 may emanate from the following legal sources:

- Articles XIV and XIV*bis* – general and security exceptions (see Chapter 15).
- Paragraph 2(a) of the Annex on Financial Services – prudential measures (see Chapter 16).
- Rights reserved by Article XI under the IMF agreement – relating to current transactions only (see above).[98]

9.5 RELATIONSHIP BETWEEN MARKET ACCESS (ARTICLE XVI) AND NATIONAL TREATMENT (ARTICLE XVII)

Article XVII outlaws any form of discrimination between domestic and foreign like services and service suppliers. Thus, it covers the forms of discrimination mentioned in Article XVI, creating a potential overlap between these two provisions.[99] Both Articles are silent about their relationship, although in terms of substance, there might be an overlap in their application to measures. However, Article XX:2 of GATS, providing that measures inconsistent with both provisions shall be inscribed in the schedules of specific commitments, in the column referring to Article XVI, assumes that measures can be covered by both provisions. Thus, the following interpretative question arises: how is one to deal with measures

98. See detailed discussion in GATS commentary, n. 7, 254–256.

99. Thus, for example, in WT/DS363/R *China – Publications and Audiovisual Products* measures containing foreign equity participation limitations were claimed to be inconsistent with Art. XVI as well as with Art. XVII, but due to judicial economy the Panel, finding them to be inconsistent with Art. XVI, refrained from examining their inconsistency with Art. XVII. Note 51, Panel report para. 7.1412.

falling within both articles, if the commitments in market access and national treatment are different?[100]

In the lack of clear indication in the schedule if commitments were taken only concerning one discipline or concerning both, it is unclear whether the Member involved is entitled to introduce new discriminating restrictions, in conflict with the allegedly uncommitted discipline.[101]

This problem becomes even more acute since the united inscription provided for by the Scheduling Guidelines[102] and its implications may not clearly reflect the difference between Article XVII, which outlaws *any* form of discrimination, and Article XVI, which allows for certain discriminatory practices.

In *US – Gambling*, United States' prohibitions on internet gambling, applied to domestic and foreign service suppliers, were regarded by both the Panel and Appellate Body as inconsistent with its relevant commitments on market access (Article XVI), which precluded even non-discriminatory prohibitions (declaring 'none'). Since these measure were not inscribed in United States' schedule, it was concluded that 'a Member that has made full market-access commitments is not free to impose certain strictly non-discriminatory measures . . . unless they can be justified under the general exceptions provision of GATS'.[103]

Some optional interpretative solutions to this difficulty are suggested by commentators (considering GATS text would not be amended):

---

100. An example given by P. Delimatsis, n. 29, 1073: A Member having a full market access commitment but inscribed 'unbound' in the national treatment column. Another example given by R. Aldung:

> If a Member has undertaken no bindings under market access ("unbound") and full commitments on national treatment under the same mode, three options are conceivable. The Member may be permitted to operate: (i) all types of measures falling under the market access provisions of Article XVI:2(a)–(f), regardless of any discriminations that may be implied; (ii) all types of market access restrictions in their non-discriminatory form, except those that are discriminatory by nature (joint venture requirements and foreign equity ceilings); or (iii) only non-discriminatory market access restrictions, thus precluding the use of the two latter categories. Recent discussions in the Council for Trade in Services suggest that each option enjoys some support.

R. Adlung, 'The GATS Turns Ten: A Preliminary Stocktaking', *WTO* (2004), 13, <www.wto.org>.

101. A. Mattoo, n. 24, 9.
102. Article 8 of the Scheduling Guidelines from 2001 (S/L/92, n. 8) provides, *inter alia*, 'all measures falling under any of the categories listed in Article XVI:2 must be scheduled, whether or not such measures are discriminatory according to the national treatment standard of Article XVII'. The Guidelines are considered as negotiating documents, non-obligatory supplementary means of interpretation according to Art. 32 of the Vienna Convention: WT/DS285/AB/R *US – Gambling*, Appellate Body report, n. 6, paras 174–175; WT/DS204/R *Mexico-Telecom*, n. 57, paras 7.66–7.67.
103. B. Hoeckman, A. Mattoo & A. Sapir, 'The Political Economy of Services Trade Liberalization: A Case for International Regulatory Cooperation?', *23 Oxford Review of Economic Policy* (2007), 367, 386.

- To treat Article XVI as *lex specialis* to Article XVII. Consequently, measures falling within the scope of market access would be excluded from the scope of national treatment, even if they are discriminatory. In addition, any market-access limitation would apply to discriminatory and non-discriminatory form of the measure involved.[104] This interpretation is based on interpreting Article XX:2 not only as a scheduling rule but also as implying the substantial relationship between the two provisions.[105] This approach is criticized for creating a hierarchy between the two provisions without any legal basis.[106]
- To interpret any measure falling under Article XVI as having also to comply with Article XVII, which covers 'all measures affecting trade in services', unless the measure has been specifically scheduled as a limitation to Article XVI in both its discriminatory and non-discriminatory forms. This approach is criticized for rendering meaningless provisions such as Article XVI(e),(f) addressing market-access restrictions existing only in a discriminatory form.[107]
- To determine a rule that the national treatment provision (Article XVII) always prevail. Consequently, Article XVI would apply only to discriminatory measures, becoming irrelevant once a Member takes full national treatment commitment. It is criticized for disregarding the fact that under Article XVI, many non-discriminatory market-access restrictions are scheduled.[108]
- To determine a rule that an 'Unbound' entry always prevails over the commitments undertaken.[109]
- To determine that an entry containing a commitment would always prevail over an 'Unbound' entry.[110]
- To interpret these provisions in the following way: 'assuming a WTO Member has not granted national treatment to foreign suppliers, it cannot impose on them any of the measures featured in Article XVI GATS, unless it has indicated so in its schedule of concessions'.[111]

104. GATS commentary, n. 7, 418.
105. Krajewski, n. 19, 115.
106. P. Delimatsis, n. 74, 144.
107. GATS commentary, n. 7, 417.
108. *Ibid.*, 417.
109. P. Delimatsis, n. 74, 145–146. To his opinion this option corresponds to Art. XX:2 and to para. 18 of the revised Scheduling Guidelines and seems to support progressive liberalization.
110. P. Delimatsis, n. 29, 1074.
111. P. Mavroidis, 'Highway XVI Re-visited: the Road from non-Discrimination to Market Access in the GATS', *6 World Trade Review* (2007), 1, 9, 15–16, 22. This interpretation is based on the assumption that Art. XVI reflects the types of deviations from national treatment that WTO Members should abolish, unless they have clearly indicated their wish not to do so. It is suggested that in practice, if a Member accords national treatment to foreign services suppliers, Art. XVI would be irrelevant, in the sense that it will be impossible to apply such measures only against foreign suppliers due to the non-discrimination principle. If no national treatment is accorded – this will be indicated in the schedule under the column 'Art. XVII'. In that case,

The problem is that none of these alternatives is particularly supported by the text. This ambiguity undermines the legal security of service suppliers.

9.6 RELATIONSHIP BETWEEN MARKET ACCESS (ARTICLE XVI) AND DOMESTIC REGULATION (ARTICLES XIV AND VI)

GATS, like GATT, distinguishes between two categories to which domestic regulation may fall: one category includes domestic regulation subject to scheduling of specific commitments: national treatment (Article XVII) and market access (Article XVI).

Domestic regulation falling into one of the six categories mentioned in the market-access provision is *prohibited*, unless explicitly specified in the scheduled of specific commitments. Deviation from these commitments is allowed, subject to Articles XIV (general exceptions) and XIV*bis* (the security exception) (see Chapter 15).

The other category is domestic regulation subject to Article VI (recognition – see Chapter 12). Such domestic regulation is *allowed, as long as it is non-discriminatory.*[112]

Another difference between the two categories is that while market-access restrictions refer to the *quantitative* aspects, namely to the number of services/service suppliers, Article VI:4,5 refers to the *quality* of services/service suppliers, that is, to the professional education and skills of the service suppliers. In addition, while Article XVI imposes *maximum* limitations, Article VI:4,5 imposes *minimum* limitations on market access.[113]

Due to the contradictory implications of the two categories, the legal decision as to which of them the domestic regulation at stake belongs to, has far-reaching implications concerning its legality under GATS. For certain domestic regulation the distinction between the two categories is not very clear.

This dilemma was faced by the WTO adjudicating bodies in *US – Gambling*, which considered[114] whether restrictions imposed by the United States on imported gambling services were prohibited restrictions on market access, justified restrictions under one of the exceptions to this principle, or allowed domestic regulation under Article VI. The adjudicating bodies chose to give priority to

---

nothing prevents a Member from applying one of the instruments reflected in Art. XVI to foreign service suppliers only. It will be scheduled under the column 'Art. XVI'.

112. These two categories are also different in terms of the burden of proof and the scheduling commitment: J. Pauwelyn, n. 67, 138–139.

113. J. Pauwelyn, n. 67, 153. It should be noted, though, that domestic regulations under Art. VI:4,5 may substantially form market-access restrictions under Art. XVI: *ibid.*, 155.

114. P. Delimatsis, n. 29, 1069, notes that in fact, the United States never claimed that its measures examined fell under Art. VI, but rather under the abstract right of domestic regulation ascertained under GATS Preamble, seen by the United States as part of GATS object and purpose.

the market access provision over the domestic regulation provision, providing that 'Articles V:4 and V:5 on the one hand and XVI on the other hand are mutually exclusive',[115] meaning that a measure could qualify as falling under one of them only. This approach was criticized on the grounds that it was never supported, neither by the negotiating history nor by the discussions in Working Party on Domestic Regulation (WPDR), and that the Members seem to regard these provisions as *complementary*.[116] Both provisions can cover non-discriminatory measures and hence, may overlap.[117] However, this criticism is rejected by other commentators in light of the differences explained above between these two provisions. It should be further noted that a prohibition of the kind applied by the Untied States in that case cannot be regarded as a technical standard being total, thus not defining any requirements to be fulfilled in order to allow access.[118] The Appellate Body refrained from addressing the relationship between these provisions, providing: 'it is not necessary nor appropriate for us to draw, in the abstract, the line between quantitative and qualitative measures'.[119] The implication of this decision is narrowing the scope of regulatory autonomy.[120] Such a dilemma may arise, *inter alia*, concerning licensing requirements establishing minimum training levels, or driving tests keeping taxi drivers that do not pass it off the market.[121]

As a result of this interpretative controversy, domestic regulations under Article VI:4,5 may substantially form market-access restrictions under Article XVI, and it is unclear whether, in such a case, these two Articles are mutually exclusive or could they apply together. It is suggested that this question should not be decided upon by referring merely to the quantitative effect.[122]

One of the dilemmas reflected in *US – Gambling* was whether measures with a legitimate purpose, prevention of gambling, could have been considered under Article XVI. The Appellate Body abstained from examining this question by examining these measures in light of Article XIV, allowing for an exceptional recognition of such measures.[123]

---

115. WT/DS285/R, n. 6 Panel report, para. 6.305. The Panel based its decision on the Scheduling Guidelines and the attachment 4 thereto, which is an Informal Note by the Chairman of the WPPS on Matters Relating to Arts XVI and XVII of GATS, in connection with the disciplines on domestic regulation in the accountancy sector.
116. P. Delimatsis, n. 74, 14.
117. P. Delimatsis, n. 29, 1070.
118. P. Delimatsis, n. 74, 139.
119. WT/DS285/AB/R, n. 6, Appellate Body report, para. 250.
120. J. Pauwelyn, n. 67, 158.
121. S. Wunch-Vincent, n. 80, 340.
122. J. Pauwelyn, n. 67, 155, 157, 160. The example given is that if a country requires taxi derivers to pass a test, the mere fact that taxi drivers who did not pass the test are kept out of the market does not turn this measure into a prohibited market access restriction.
123. WT/DS285/AB/R, n. 6, para. 373 E (i).

9.7 CONCLUSION

Market access in GATS is subject to specific commitments made by a Member, as well as to disciplines dictated by Articles XVI and XI of GATS. Article XVI specifies six categories of prohibited restrictions to trade in services, applicable to services sectors and modes of supply where specific commitments were undertaken. This provision is aimed at diminishing quantitative restrictions, which are common in services trade.[124]

This is an exhaustive list, meaning that the application of restrictive measures which are not included in it is allowed, even for services sectors and modes of supply, where specific commitments were undertaken. Thus, restrictions emanating from labour legislation, tax regimes, restrictions on land availability, ownership or use, licensing and related fees, existence and reach of competition policies, regulation of monopolies and judicial enforceability of contracts are not caught by the market-access provision (although they may be subject to the national treatment principle). They may thus restrict the contestability of markets. If a Member introduces policies that are not prohibited by this provision, but have the effect of nullifying its specific commitments, it can be confronted with a non-violation complaint (see Chapter 17).[125]

Article XI refers to capital flows linked to services transactions, prohibiting their restriction. This prohibition is also not total; it may be deviated from in cases of balance-of-payment difficulties. Both provisions include vague expressions that may be given narrow or broad interpretation, thus affecting their scope of application, which is a matter of judicial discretion.

Finally, the legal relationships between Article XVI and Article XVII (national treatment), and Article XVI and Article VI (recognition) are not clearly determined by GATS. These unclear relations form a source for interpretative disagreements that undermine the certainty and predictability of these provisions.

124. Where the rents accrue to foreigners, these quotas resemble voluntary export restrains: A. Mattoo, n. 1, 282.

125. B. Hoeckman, 'Tentative First Steps: An Assessment of the Uruguay Round Agreement on Services', *The World Bank Policy Research Working Papers* (1995), 16, <www-wds.worldbank.org>.

Chapter 10
Economic Integration Agreements

10.1 INTRODUCTION

Form the perspective of a country, international trade liberalization may take place with three possible techniques:

(1) *Unilateral trade liberalization* – may be achieved by the unilateral removal of trade barriers. Such a step is based on a unilateral decision by a country, assessing that such liberalization would better serve the development of its market than protectionist policy. The advantage of such a step is the exclusive and comprehensive control over the process and its rhythm. At the same time, this is a disadvantage, because the exclusive control over the process forms a constant source of political pressure by domestic forces, adversely affected by trade liberalization, who may be interested in stopping, reversing or at least slowing down this process. Another disadvantage folded in this technique is a loss of at least part of the external bargaining power, in regional or multilateral negotiations for trade liberalization.

(2) *Bilateral or Regional trade liberalization (through 'economic integration agreements', in GATS language)* – is achieved by the conclusion of international trade agreements between or among relatively small groups of participants. In the past, regional trade agreements were common between or among countries sharing geographic proximity. However, in recent years, more and more of these agreements are concluded among countries that do not necessarily fulfil this condition. This process is probably enhanced by globalization as well as by the improvement of international transportation means and technological developments. This framework enjoys, on the one hand, the mutual sharing of benefits and the relative intimacy, allowing for the shaping of the agreement in a manner

reflecting the needs and expectations of its parties in the best way. The disadvantage of this technique lies in its relatively narrow scope of geographic application. In addition, where a party to such an agreement concludes many bilateral or regional trade agreements, the unique benefits accorded by them to its partners gradually erode.[1]

(3) *Multilateral trade liberalization* – is achieved by comprehensive, large-scale international trade agreements with many participants, such as the WTO agreements. The major advantage of this technique lies in its wide scope of geographic application. The many participants in the process and their different, sometimes conflicting, interests are a source of some disadvantages to this framework: a relatively slow process of liberalization; concentration on the lowest common denominator; and a relative ambiguity of drafting.

The WTO multilateral framework is based, *inter alia*, on the MFN principle, providing for non-discrimination between or among 'like' imports from different Members. Economic integration agreements, which provide for certain trade concessions to be granted only to their parties, are not corresponding to the MFN principle.

This difficulty was already encountered by the drafters of GATT 1947: when this multilateral trade agreement was first concluded, bilateral and regional trade agreements already existed. Therefore, in 1949 it was decided to recognize these agreements as an exception to the MFN rule in Article XXIV of GATT. Besides the need to confront an existing reality, GATT drafters believed, after World War II, that encouragement of regional economic alliances would enhance political stability.[2] In addition, they viewed such recognition as serving the general goal of GATT: the enhancement international trade liberalization, encouraging parties who wish to enhance this process in a relatively higher speed between or among them.[3] Thus, regional trade agreements are viewed by some as complementary, rather substitutable, instruments to GATS.[4]

Being a more intimate framework, with less participants and more like-minded partners, economic integration agreements have some advantages over the existing GATS framework: in many of them, an integrated set of disciplines was

1. For the economic implications of different liberalization techniques in services see: A. Mattoo & C. Fink, 'Regional Agreements and Trade in Services: Policy Issues', *The World Bank Policy Research Working Paper* (2002), <www-wds.worldbank.org>.
2. F.M. Abott, 'GATT and the EC: A Formula for Peaceful Coexistence', *12 Michigan Journal of International Law* (1990), 6.
3. See a research approving this view: S. Robinson & K. Thierfelder, 'Trade Liberalization and Regional Integration: The Search for Large Numbers', *46 Australian Journal of Agricultural and Resource Economics* (2002), 585–604. <http://ssrn.com>; For another, less definite view see: J.A. Crewford & S. Laird, 'Regional Trade Agreements and the WTO', *Credit (Center for Research and Economic Development and International Trade) Research Paper No. 3, University of Nottingham* (2000), <www.nottinghamdistancelearning.com>.
4. B. Hoeckman & P. Sauvé, 'Liberalizing Trade in Services', *The World Bank Discussion Papers* (1994), <www-wds.worldbank.org>.

developed, covering both goods and services, referring also to investment, government procurement, the movement of natural persons, monopolies, intellectual property rights and technical barriers to trade, avoiding the fragmented approach of GATS. This, in turn, allows for combined negotiations on all subjects involved, leading to a coherent legal structure covering all aspects involved; In some economic integration agreements, a 'negative list', rather than the 'positive list' approach of GATS, is adopted *a priori*, including in their scope all services sectors, unless specifically excluded. This approach is turning them into much more transparent legal instruments than GATS, since their schedules present a much more accurate and complete picture of market conditions; some of the agreements further oblige for the exchange of inventories of measures affecting trade in services among their parties. This specificity, in addition to a '*status quo*' provision included in some of these agreements, leaves much less room for maneuvering by presentation of new barriers to trade compared to GATS. In addition, many economic integration agreements adopt a more pro-active approach to recognition of professional record than GATS. Some of them even go beyond GATS in terms of the liberalizing content of their disciplines.[5] An empirical analysis of the substance of services economic integration agreements reveals considerable advantages in terms of trade liberalization level over GATS.[6]

Developing countries may prefer this framework over the multilateral framework, feeling that they risk less, face lower adjustment costs and are able to preserve some tariffs against non-members, thus gaining some revenue.[7]

5. S.M. Stephenson, 'Can Regional Liberalization of Services go Further than Multilateral Liberalization Under the GATS?', *1 World Trade Review* (2002), 8–17. It was however noted, that at the time of writing, despite of the substantive legal differences, the actual level of trade liberalization achieved by the examined economic integration agreements was not much higher than that achieved by the GATS. *Ibid.*, 19. One reason may be that the application of the process provided for by these agreements requires modification of domestic legislation, regulations, decrees and procedures, a time-consuming and costly process that in a small country setting will generally involve the same amount of work and the same generation of domestic consensus as carrying this out on a multilateral basis. *Ibid.*, 23. See also comparative legal analysis of regional trade agreements' provisions and the GATS: F. Ortino, 'Regional Trade Agreements and Trade in Services', in S. Lester & B. Mercurino (eds), *Bilateral and Regional Trade Agreements: Commentary, Analysis and Case Studies*, Cambridge CPU (2007), 11–29, <http://papers.ssrn.com>, <www.netamericas.net>.

   See suggestions for more liberalized disciplines, for example, a stronger MFN commitment, an absence of local presence requirement, elimination of technical and quantitative restrictions, enhanced transparency: F.J. Prieto & S.M. Stephenson, 'Multilateral and Regional Trade in Services', in R. Mendoza, P. Low & B. Kotschwar, *Trade Rules in the Making: Challenges in Regional and Multilateral Negotiations* (1999), 235, 254–257, <http://books.google.com>.
6. M. Roy, J. Marchetti & H. Lim, 'Services Liberalization in the New Generation of Preferential Trade Agreements (PTAs): How Much Further Than the GATS?', *WTO* (2006), 53–54. <www.wto.org>.
7. S. Laird, 'Regional Trade Agreements: Dangerous Liaisons?', *22 World Economy* (2002), 1179, 1189.

On the other hand, being a more intimate framework, these agreements might be easier to reverse the liberalization process, where necessary.[8] Like in the case of unilateral trade liberalization, this may be viewed as an advantage or as a disadvantage, since the governments involved might be more exposed to domestic pressures of interest groups.

To serve this goal in the best way at the GATS level, balancing between the interests involved, it was decided that the recognition of such agreements as exceptions to the MFN rule should be subject to conditions ensuring that the Members are engaging in a comprehensive liberalization process, and are not using this opportunity to liberalize only one narrow aspect of their trade. This manner of treatment, developed in GATT 1947 and reassured by GATT 1994, was adopted in GATS as well.

In recent years, a proliferation of economic integration agreements is being witnessed. It is explained, *inter alia*, in light of the disappointment from the slow rhythm of trade liberalization process in the multilateral system.[9] This proliferation implies the growing importance of GATS provisions referring to such agreements.

10.2 THE ECONOMIC ASPECT OF ECONOMIC INTEGRATION AGREEMENTS

Economically, it is difficult to assess the cost-advantage relations in an economic integration agreement, due to the elaboration and dynamic development of the trade pattern involved, and to the lack of accurate and complete statistical data.[10] In 1950, the economist J. Viner described the basic economic effect of such agreements, thus forming the basis for economic analysis of such agreements. His theory, expressed in '*The Customs Union Issue*'[11] proves that every economic integration agreement has positive and negative effects. The positive effects are recognized as *trade creating*: encouraging the replacement of an expensive source of trade with a cheaper source, thus improving the allocation of production factors. The negative effects are recognized as *trade diverting*: encouraging the replacement of a cheap source of trade with an expensive source, covered by the agreement. This effect emanates from the discriminating nature of economic integration agreements, granting preferential trade terms to their parties. As a result, the customers in the parties to such agreements pay cheaper prices for products or services originating in the parties to the agreements, but the governments involved are, in fact, paying higher prices for these products, since the loss of import duties and charges removed by the agreement has to be added to the effective price paid. Due to this trade diversion, third parties will

8. *Ibid.*, 1184.
9. M. Roy, et al., n. 6.
10. References to the statistical difficulties concerning international trade in services see in Ch. 1, n. 10.
11. J. Viner, 'The Customs Union Issue', in J. Bhagwati, P. Krishna & A. Panagariya (eds), *Trading Blocks: Alternative Approaches to Analyzing Preferential Trade Agreements*, Massachusetts Institute of Technology (1999), 105.

export less to the countries bound by economic integration agreements. Viner determines that therefore, the overall effect of an economic integration agreement on its parties cannot be pre-viewed, because it depends, in each case, on whether trade creation outweighs trade diversion. Since 1950, economic researchers developed economic methods to assess whether the overall effect of an economic integration agreement is trade creating or trade diverting.[12] However, due to the elaboration of this matter, no exhaustive method was yet developed.[13]

Economic integration agreements are criticized for distorting international markets by encouraging trade among their parties, thus implementing the comparative advantage principle on a regional, instead of global, basis.

Some fear that a tendency to overcome economic difficulties by economic integration agreements draws attention from the efforts to encounter them on a global basis.

Multinational enterprises feel threatened, to a certain extent, by economic integration agreements, being concerned that such agreements might worsen their market access conditions by applying protectionist policies to encourage the development of industries in their parties.

In the past, these agreements were criticized for being mainly concluded between or among developed countries, enhancing their trade advantages and thus enlarging the gap between developed and economically less developed countries. It was further argued that geographically isolated countries are threatened by these agreements because they are not attractive enough to become parties to them. In recent years it seems that this reality is somewhat changing.[14]

However, other considerations support economic integration agreements:

First, they are viewed as instruments for the enhancement of international trade, corresponding to the goal of the WTO agreements. They are viewed as interim measures for progress towards this goal, in a world where differences in level of development and interests among countries prevent the achievement of enhanced liberalization on a global basis. Thus, they are viewed as a motivating power for the development of the economies engaged in them.

Second, instead of conducting discussions among many countries, it is better that a relatively small number of trading groups of countries, bound by economic trade agreements, negotiates in the global level.

In 1995, a WTO research concluded that '. . . to a much greater extent than it is often acknowledged, regional and multilateral integration initiatives are complements rather than alternatives in the pursuit of more open trade'.[15]

This research found, that regional trade agreements fostered negotiations by groups of countries on rules and commitments that were far-reaching compared to those acceptable in the multilateral level at the time. Later, some of these rules, for

12. See, for example, Bhagwati et al., n. 11.
13. For explanation on the difficulties encountered see: Abott, n. 2, 7–8.
14. See: R.V. Fiorentino, L. Verdeja & C. Toqueboeuf, Discussion Paper No. 12: 'The Changing Landscape of Regional Trade Agreements: 2006 update', WTO 2007, 3–5, <www.wto.org>.
15. *Trading Into the Future*, WTO Publications (1997), 4.4.

example, rules concerning trade in services and protection of intellectual property rights, paved the way for the Uruguay Round agreements.

10.2.1 Cost of Economic Integration Agreement

Some reasons due to which preferential arrangements in services could potentially be less harmful than such arrangements for trade in goods are suggested:[16]

- reducing barriers to trade in services does not lead to loss of revenue since there are no import duties on services;
- since barriers to trade in services are mainly embodied in regulation, their modification, to the benefit of service suppliers from a preferential trade agreement countries, may affect other suppliers from other countries as well, since often governments will not put in place different sets of regulation for different countries;
- nevertheless, the most restrictive measures, such as measures affecting Mode 3 (commercial presence), may be applied on a preferential basis.

It should be born in mind, though, that economic integration agreements may bear considerable costs, due to their implication on third parties.[17]

10.3 ARTICLE V OF GATS

Article V of GATS is equivalent to Article XXIV of GATT. It grants coverage for preferential treatment of services trade in the framework of economic integration agreements, in derogation of the MFN obligation of GATS Article II.[18] It provides:

Economic Integration

1. This Agreement shall not prevent any of its Members from being a party to or entering into an agreement liberalizing trade in services between or among the parties to such an agreement, provided that such an agreement:
   (a) has substantial sectoral coverage, and
   (b) provides for the absence or elimination of substantially all discrimination, in the sense of Article XVII, between or among the parties, in the sectors covered under subparagraph (a), through:
      (i) elimination of existing discriminatory measures, and/or
      (ii) prohibition of new or more discriminatory measures, either at the entry into force of that agreement or on the basis of a reasonable

16. M. Roy, et al., n. 6, 184.
17. *Ibid.*, 185–187.
18. For the drafting history of this provision see: S.M. Stephenson, 'Regional Agreements on Services in Multilateral Disciplines: Interpreting and Applying GATS Article V', in S.M. Stephenson (ed.), *Services Trade in the Western Hemisphere: Liberalization, Integration and Reform*, General Secretariat/Organization of American States (2000), 86, 87–88.

time-frame, except for measures permitted under Articles XI, XII, XIV and XIV*bis*.

2. In evaluating whether the conditions under paragraph 1(b) are met, consideration may be given to the relationship of the agreement to a wider process of economic integration or trade liberalization among the countries concerned.
3. (a) Where developing countries are parties to an agreement of the type referred to in paragraph 1, flexibility shall be provided for regarding the conditions set out in paragraph 1, particularly with reference to subparagraph (b) thereof, in accordance with the level of development of the countries concerned, both overall and in individual sectors and subsectors.
   (b) Notwithstanding paragraph 6, in the case of an agreement of the type referred to in paragraph 1 involving only developing countries, more favourable treatment may be granted to juridical persons owned or controlled by natural persons of the parties to such an agreement.
4. Any agreement referred to in paragraph 1 shall be designed to facilitate trade between the parties to the agreement and shall not in respect of any Member outside the agreement raise the overall level of barriers to trade in services within the respective sectors or subsectors compared to the level applicable prior to such an agreement.
5. If, in the conclusion, enlargement or any significant modification of any agreement under paragraph 1, a Member intends to withdraw or modify a specific commitment inconsistently with the terms and conditions set out in its Schedule, it shall provide at least 90 days advance notice of such modification or withdrawal and the procedure set forth in paragraphs 2, 3 and 4 of Article XXI shall apply.
6. A service supplier of any other Member that is a juridical person constituted under the laws of a party to an agreement referred to in paragraph 1 shall be entitled to treatment granted under such agreement, provided that it engages in substantive business operations in the territory of the parties to such agreement.
7. (a) Members which are parties to any agreement referred to in paragraph 1 shall promptly notify any such agreement and any enlargement or any significant modification of that agreement to the Council for Trade in Services. They shall also make available to the Council such relevant information as may be requested by it. The Council may establish a working party to examine such an agreement or enlargement or modification of that agreement and to report to the Council on its consistency with this Article.
   (b) Members which are parties to any agreement referred to in paragraph 1 which is implemented on the basis of a time-frame shall report periodically to the Council for Trade in Services on its implementation. The Council may establish a working party to examine such reports if it deems such a working party necessary.

(c) Based on the reports of the working parties referred to in subparagraphs (a) and (b), the Council may make recommendations to the parties as it deems appropriate.

8. A Member which is a party to any agreement referred to in paragraph 1 may not seek compensation for trade benefits that may accrue to any other Member from such agreement.

10.3.1 Article V:1

Article V:1 of GATS determines two conditions that have to be fulfilled in order that GATS 'shall not prevent any of its Members from being a party to or entering into an agreement liberalizing trade in services between or among the parties to such an agreement'. This provision implies that where these two mandatory conditions are fulfilled, such an economic integration agreement would be recognized as an exception to the MFN principle, embodied in GATS Article II.[19] The words 'being a party to or entering into' imply that this provision applies to *current*, as well as to *future*, economic integration agreements. It is further implied that this provision applies to economic integration agreements, not only between or among Members, but also between or among WTO Members and *non-Members*. In that latter case, this provision will affect, of course, only the party which is a WTO Member.

The overall aim of these two conditions is to ensure that the examined economic integration agreement is comprehensive, and does not refer to only a narrow portion of the entire trade in services between or among its parties.

However, their language is not very clear; it includes some expressions that are subject to legal interpretation:

- What are the 'economic integration agreements' to which this provision applies?
- The agreement should have *substantial sectoral coverage*. While the general intention is clear: ensuring comprehensive coverage of trade in services, interpretative questions arise as to the meaning of the word 'substantial': will it be determined quantitatively or qualitatively? What will be considered as 'substantial' coverage: 51% of the entire trade? 90%? Should this condition be examined on a sector-by-sector basis, on a subsector-by-subsector basis or on a disaggregated basis? Should the parties to an economic integration agreement be expected to meet a higher standard than that set by GATS (under which much of the transport sector, including air transport and maritime transport services are effectively excluded at present)? Does this requirement allow the exclusion of a mode

19. The idea that Art. V may also justify deviation from other GATS provisions, such as transparency, domestic regulation and safeguard measures is controversial: R. Worfrum, P.T. Stoll & C. Feinäugle (eds), *WTO – Trade in Services*, Max Planck Commentaries on World Trade Law, Martinus Mijnhoff Publishers, Leiden, Boston (2008) (hereby: GATS commentary), 129.

of supply, or particular categories within one mode of supply, for one service sector only?[20]

- The agreement further provides for the absence or elimination of *substantially all discrimination*, between or among its parties. The word 'substantially' in this context gives rise to similar interpretative questions as in the former provision discussed: will it be determined quantitatively or qualitatively? What will be considered as 'substantial' coverage: 51% of the entire discrimination? 90%? One difficulty here is the difficulty of trade services measurement (see Chapter 2): when a service or a service sector is excluded from the scope of an economic integration agreement, it is thus difficult to determine its economic importance to the entire trade relations of the parties. Another difficulty stemming from this fact is: how to measure the extent of liberalization achieved?[21]
- The agreement further calls for the elimination of existing discriminatory measures, *and/or* prohibition of new or more discriminatory measures. The words and/or may motivate Members to opt for the 'or', thus leaving some of the discriminatory measures in place.
- The time for such elimination is either at the entry into force of that agreement or on the basis of a *reasonable time-frame.* This expression is also ambiguous, calling for further interpretation: should a uniform standard be determined in this context, or should 'reasonability' be determined on a case-by-case basis?

This Article was not yet thoroughly explored by the WTO adjudicating bodies. It was shortly addressed in the *Canada – Autos* case. However, some interpretative conclusions may be drawn from a comparison between this provision and the equivalent GATT Article XXIV,[22] as well as from the discussions on these questions in the relevant WTO forums.

10.3.1.1 Comparison to Article XXIV:1 of GATT

10.3.1.1.1 The Agreements Covered: 'Economic Integration Agreements'

Article XXIV of GATT applies to free trade area agreements and customs unions.

Unlike it, Article V of GATS does not refer to specific types of agreements, but uses the general term 'economic integration agreements'. This choice implies

20. S.M. Stephenson, n. 18, 91–92.
21. *Ibid.*, 92–93.
22. The Understanding on the Interpretation of Art. XXIV of GATT 1994 does not mention services, despite of the fact that it was negotiated simultaneously with the GATS. According to Zdouc, this is a sufficient reason to assume that the negotiators 'were implicitly opposed to interpreting GATS by cross-references to the "Understanding . . .".': W. Zdouc, *Legal Problems Arising Under the General Agreement on Trade in Services – Comparative Analysis of GATS and GATT*, dissertation der Universität St. Gallen (2002), 217. Nevertheless, in practice such cross-reference between GATT and GATS equivalent provisions is common.

maximum flexibility concerning the degree of economic integration chosen by the parties to such agreements and for full discretion concerning its content, as well as for maximal scope of application of GATS relevant disciplines to such agreements. This provision may cover free trade area agreements in services on the one hand, and economic union agreements such as the EU Treaties, on the other hand, subject to the conditions set forth by Article V, to be further specified and discussed below.

10.3.1.1.2 'Substantial Sectoral Coverage'

The general purpose of this expression in Article V:1 is to ensure a wide scope of coverage for economic integration agreements. It seems that the logic behind it is that if an exception to the MFN principle is recognized, it should at least be ensured that the general goal of international services trade liberalization is enhanced by it.[23] Therefore, this exception is designed to prevent the conclusion of economic integration agreements with a limited coverage, covering one or a few sectors, or exchanging preferential treatment in limited domains, such as foreign direct investments.

The drafting history[24] of this provision reveals that during GATS negotiations, a question arose whether the comprehensiveness of economic integration agreements' scope of coverage should be examined only in the context of trade in services, or rather in a wider context, of trade in goods *and* services. The compromise achieved was:

(a) economic integration agreements would be subject to more stringent conditions than those provided for in the December 1990 text (in particular, the interpretation of the 'substantial sectoral coverage' contained in footnote 1 to Article V:1(a) was added at that point of time); and
(b) Members, in evaluating the sectoral coverage of economic integration agreements, could give *consideration to whether such integration process included also goods sectors*. [Emphasis added].

Namely, according to the drafting history of this provision it allegedly seems that a partial services' trade liberalization, combined with a partial or comprehensive goods' trade liberalization, may suffice to satisfy this requirement.[25] Nevertheless, according to another interpretation this provision in GATS should be read separately from the context of trade in goods, so that economic integration agreements provide for comprehensive liberalization of trade in services only.

23. This notion indirectly protects the MFN principle, since it prevents its circumvention in all cases where the coverage of an economic integration agreement is not comprehensive: GATS commentary, n. 19, 132.
24. WT/REG/W/21/Rev.1 Committee on Regional Trade Agreements, Systemic Issues Related to 'Substantially All Trade' – Background Note by the Secretariat, 5.2.1998.
25. This view seems to be supported by W. Zdouc, n. 22, 221.

Footnote 1 of GATS provides:

> This condition is understood in terms of *number of sectors, volume of trade affected and modes of supply*. In order to meet this condition, agreements *should not provide for the a priori exclusion of any mode of supply*. [Emphasis added].

This footnote provides some indication concerning the elements that should be examined in order to achieve a conclusion as to the sectoral coverage of the agreement. The three relevant factors: number of sectors, volume of trade affected and modes of supply, seem to apply cumulatively.[26] Unlike the other elements, as to modes of supply, it is particularly emphasized that no mode should be *a priori* excluded from the scope of the economic integration agreement examined under this provision. Thus, an economic integration agreement recognized by Article V should potentially refer to all modes of supply.[27] Nevertheless, the degree of liberalization accorded by such an agreement in each mode of supply is completely subject to the discretion of its parties. Some commentators suggest to read Article V:1 and footnote 1 as implying that 'the lack of commitments with regard to one or more modes of supply does not impair the liberalization of substantial volumes of trade'.[28] However, this interpretation does not seem to reflect the wording of Article V and footnote 1, and the 'volume of trade' criterion is ambiguous in itself.

Footnote 1 is further weakened by the use of the words 'in terms of'.[29]

This footnote does not refer to the following questions:

- The rate of coverage necessary to apply this exception: 51% of the sectors of trade between the parties? 90%? Or any other percentage?
- The relations between the examined parameters: in case where the entire trade between two trade partners concentrates in five sectors, four of which are covered by the agreement but reflect only 20% of the entire trade between them, while the fifth sector, uncovered by the agreement, reflects 80% of the entire trade in services between them, which requirement prevails: 'substantial sectoral coverage' or 'substantially all trade'? Are these requirements cumulative or alternative?
- When an agreement does not allow for trade in a certain mode of supply, in a certain sector, how can the effect of this provision be measured? How is it possible to assess, to what extent the scope of trade between the parties could have been changed if trade would have been allowed?

---

26. F. Ortino, 'The Principle on Non-Discrimination and its Exceptions in the GATS: Selected Legal Issues', *King's College London* (2006), 26, <http://papers.ssrn.com>.
27. Labour mobility, in particular under Mode 4, is still not comprehensively covered by the GATS. Therefore, it seems that the exclusion of it in economic integration agreements would not amount to a violation of Art. V: GATS commentary, n. 19, 134–135.
28. GATS commentary, n. 19, 134.
29. W. Zdouc, n. 22, 229.

Article XXIV of GATT includes a similar expression to 'substantial sectoral coverage' in GATS: 'substantially all trade'.[30] This expression, that seems to be stricter than the equivalent GATS expression,[31] has a long history of interpretation. The common source of vagueness in both provisions is the word 'substantially', which probably reflects a scope which is narrower than the whole trade, but it is unclear to what extent.[32] Discussions in the CRTA reflect similar interpretative difficulties. The qualitative approach, which seems easier to apply at first glance, raises the following questions:[33]

- What percentage of the entire trade will be considered as 'substantially all trade'?
- Should a permanent rate be determined, or should a case-by-case approach be preferred?
- Can the examination be based on data prior to the agreement, considering the expected effect of the agreement in the long run? Should the effect of the agreement in the long run (reflecting rise or fall in the volume of trade) be taken into account, and if so – what period will be determined as the relevant period for examination?
- Should the effect of barriers to trade, existing before the agreement, be taken into account in calculating the percentage of trade that was liberalized?

In addition to these difficulties that are relevant to trade in services as well as to trade in goods, the determination of 'substantial sectoral coverage' for trade in services becomes more difficult than the determination of 'substantially all trade' in goods, due to specific statistical difficulties in this field:

- In services, the data collected are affected by the difficulty to follow transactions in certain modes of supply. Thus, transactions by commercial presence may be registered as economic activities of the country of destination, rather than of the country of origin. Cross-border transactions may be difficult to follow and register.
- Sometimes, data concerning the trade benefiting from trade concessions are not collected, or are not comprehensive, not referring to all the relevant concessions.
- Some of the concessions may be created due to a network of economic integration agreements, to which a country is a party, not only by a single agreement.

An alternative technical approach to examine whether the 'substantial sectoral coverage' condition is fulfilled in a specific case is based on classification: the

30. Article XXIV:8(a)(i), (b) of the GATT.
31. B. Hoeckman & P. Sauvé, n. 4, 57.
32. WT/REG/W/19 Committee on Regional Trade Agreements – Communication from Hong Kong, China, 17.11.1999, para. 14, <http://docsonline.wto.org>.
33. WT/REG/W/18 Committee on Regional Trade Agreements – Communication from Australia, 17.11.1997.

trade between the parties to an economic integration agreement is examined according to a classification list to determine whether the items covered by such trade amount to a percentage of covered items necessary to fulfil this condition (say, 90% or 95% of the entire trade), determined in advance.[34] According to this approach, it is unnecessary to refer to elements affecting trade. It is based on the low probability that a whole sector shall be withdrawn from the agreement. This method is specifically suitable for trade in goods.[35]

In the report of the CRTA examining the Treaty of Rome, 1957 which established the EEC, it was argued that the aim of this expression in GATT was to allow Members some flexibility concerning trade liberalization, so that liberalization in a certain sector could be avoided. Therefore, the expression 'substantially all trade' was preferred over the expression 'trade in substantially all products'. Nevertheless, the Committee could not reach an agreement on this subject.[36] This dilemma was not solved in later discussions.[37]

According to the qualitative approach, no major sector should stay out of the agreement, even if the volume of trade in this sector is relatively low.[38] This approach gives rise to the following difficulties:

- Should the consistency-assessment take into account the tendency of an economic integration agreement to facilitate trade expansion in a sector even though its provisions might not call for the elimination of trade barriers?
- Should the removal of trade barriers take place among all the parties in order for the liberalization to be factored into the assessment?[39]

Some believe that the best solution should combine elements of both, quantitative and qualitative, approaches.[40]

---

34. In the Committee on Regional Trade Agreements the representative of Australia argued, that in the past this expression was commonly interpreted as requiring 80%–90% coverage out of the entire trade between the parties to an economic integration agreement, and suggested to raise it to 95% on a six digit level of specification: WT/REG/W/22 Communication from Australia, 30.1.1998, para. 65; WT/REG/M/16 Note on the Meeting of 16–18 and 20 Feb. 1998, para. 110.
35. WT/REG/M/16, n. 34, para. 112.
36. L/1235 adopted on 4.6.1960, S/9, 83–85, paras 48–49, 51, 54.
37. *Analytical Index – Guide to GATT Law and Practice*, the WTO, Geneva (1995), 825–827.
38. In GATT context, the Understanding on the Interpretation of Art. XXIV of GATT 1994 recognizes, in the preamble, that the contribution to trade development in the world by economic integration agreements is diminished where a major sector is excluded from them. However, the Understanding does not provide for any legal obligation in this context, neither does it specify how the 'majority' of a sector would be determined: by quantitative criteria? Or rather by qualitative criteria?
39. WT/REG/M/16, n. 34, para. 40.
40. See WT/REG/W/15, Guidelines on Procedures to Improve and Facilitate the Examination Process – Note by the Chairman, 6.5.1997 para. 66 (The US position); WT/REG/W/18, n. 33, para. 12 (position of Australia); GATT Analytical Index, n. 37, 824–828.

It should be recognized, that due to the exceptions to the general principles recognized in each economic integration agreement (referring to general interests such as balance-of-payments difficulties, security, the life and health of human beings, plants and animals etc.) a total trade liberalization between the parties involved in such agreements never occurs.

In *Canada – Auto*, Canada tried to defend its policy of granting trade benefits selectively to certain importers, by justifying it in light of the existence of an economic integration agreement between Canada and the countries from where these imports originated, relying on GATT Article XXIV and GATS Article V. The Panel rejected Canada's arguments. Based on the factual analysis, the Panel rejected the Canadian argument regarding GATT Article XXIV, determining that the measure at stake granted duty-free treatment not only in respect of products imported from the parties to an economic integration agreement from Canada but also to third parties.[41] Concerning Article V GATS the Panel noted that only a narrow portion of trade between the relevant parties was covered by that agreement, since the trade benefits at stake were given only to some services and service suppliers. The Panel explained, that Article V is based on the presumption that:

> economic integration agreements are aimed at achieving higher levels of liberalization between or among their parties than achieved among WTO Members. Article V:1 further prescribes a certain *minimum level* of liberalization which such agreements must attain in order to qualify for the exemption from the general MFN obligation in Article II. In this respect, the purpose of Article V is to allow for ambitious liberalization to take place at a regional level, while at the same time guarding against undermining the MFN obligation by engaging in minor preferential arrangements ... it is not within the object and purpose of Article V to provide legal coverage for the extension of more favourbale treatment only to a few service suppliers of parties to an economic integration agreement on a selective basis, even in situation where the maintenance of such measures may explicitly be provided for in the agreement itself.[42] [Emphasis in the Original].

10.3.1.1.3 *'Substantially all Discrimination'*

Article V:1(b) of GATS requires that the economic integration agreement under examination would provide 'for the absence or elimination of substantially all discrimination'. This provision is aimed at ensuring a basis for fair competition between domestic and foreign services and service suppliers from the parties to an economic integration agreement. Therefore, it is based on reciprocity. Nevertheless, no complete symmetry of concessions is necessary.[43]

41. WT/DS139,142/R, AB/R Canada – Certain Measures Affecting the Automotive Industry, adopted on 19.6.2000, Panel report, paras 10.55–10.57.
42. WT/DS139,142/R *Canada – Autos*, n. 41, Panel report para. 10.271.
43. GATS commentary, n. 19, 135, in particular n. 21.

This provision raises some interpretative difficulties:

- What is 'substantially all discrimination'? Similarly, to the former provision examined, the root of ambiguity is the word 'substantially': should a quantitative or a qualitative approach be adopted towards this word? Moreover, what would be the essence of the chosen approach? For example, does this provision allow for an economic integration agreement to include a conditional MFN provision? Differential degrees of MFN treatment? MFN treatment with gradual implementation? Different conditional MFN towards third countries?[44]
- Sub paragraphs (i) and (ii) of Article V:1(b) provide that this expression refers to the elimination of existing discriminatory measures and to the prohibition of new or more discriminatory measures. The expression 'discriminatory measures' is ambiguous: does it refer to measures intended to discriminate or to effectively discriminating measures, or to both?[45] (see discussion below 10.3.1.1.3.3).

In the discussion held by the CRTA concerning the NAFTA agreement,[46] two different views were presented concerning the possible interpretation of these sub paragraphs. Referring to the meaning of the words 'and/or', one interpretation suggested reading these words as a requirement that Members entering into a regional arrangement with respect to services eliminate existing discriminatory measures. According to a second approach, this interpretation does not seem to be supported by the text, since it does not imply any meaning to the word 'or'. Thus, it was suggested that instead of understanding this provision as providing for the elimination of existing measures, it should be understood as obliging parties to eliminate the possibility to make existing measures more burdensome or to add new measures.[47] This dilemma was not solved. Although it seems that the latter interpretation is better supported by the text, the discussion reflects that this is not the obvious and only interpretative option for this provision.

The nature of trade barriers in services (see Chapter 2) makes it difficult to attach to them a quantitative value.[48]

In *Canada – Autos*,[49] in a finding subsequently not addressed by the Appellate Body, the Panel considered that, with respect to an import duty exemption

44. S.M. Stephenson, n. 18, 103.
45. The WTO adjudicating bodies rejected the aim and effect approach in GATT context, thus treating a measure as discriminating according to its effect, neglecting its aim (see Ch. 8 – in s. 8.8). A different approach was held by the European Court of Justice who differentiates between cases with similar facts according to the existence of a discriminating aim. See: M. Danusso & R. Danton, 'Does the European Court of Justice Look for a Protectionist Motive under Article 95?', *Legal Issues of European Integration* (1990/1991), 67.
46. North Free Trade Area Agreement among the US, Canada and Mexico, Concluded 1991.
47. WT/REG4/M/4, Examination of the North American Free Trade Agreement, Not of the Meeting of 24 February 1997, 16.4.97, paras 19–21.
48. S.M. Stephenson, n. 18, 96, presents some possible alternatives to this requirement, discussing their advantages and disadvantages.
49. WT/DS139,142/R *Canada – Autos*, n. 41, paras 10.269–10.272.

available to only a limited number of firms of manufacturers and wholesalers in the automotive industry, out of all the relevant firms in the NAFTA countries, Canada could not claim an exemption from its MFN obligation under Article II by invoking Article V:1. The Panel interpreted Article V:1(b) in a very broad manner, extending the non-discrimination obligation beyond the national treatment requirement:

> Although the requirement of Article V:1(b) is to provide non-discrimination in the sense of Article XVII (national treatment), we consider that once it is fulfilled it would also ensure non-discrimination between all service suppliers of other parties to the economic integration agreement. It is our view that the object and purpose of this provision is to eliminate all discrimination among services and service suppliers of parties to an economic integration agreement, including discrimination between suppliers of other parties to an economic integration agreement. In other words, it would be inconsistent with this provision if a party to an economic integration agreement were to extend more favourable treatment to service suppliers of one party than that which it extended to service suppliers of another party to that agreement.

10.3.1.1.3.1 'Substantially'

This term was not yet interpreted in the context of Article V of GATS. However, in the context of the equivalent Article XXIV:8 of GATT, it was noted by the Appellate Body in GATT case *Turkey – Textiles*, referring to GATT Article XXIV:8:

> Neither the GATT Contracting Parties nor the WTO Members have ever reached an agreement on the interpretation of the term 'substantially' in this provision. It is clear, though, that 'substantially all trade' is not the same as *all* the trade, and also that 'substantially all trade' is something considerably more than merely *some* of the trade.[50]

It was stressed, that although this word offers some flexibility, it is a limited degree of flexibility.

In that case the Appellate Body tended to agree that the term 'substantially' (in the context of 'substantially the same' in GATT Article XXIV:8(ii)) appears to provide for both quantitative and qualitative components.[51]

10.3.1.1.3.2 In the Sense of Article XVII

Article V:1 provides for the absence or elimination 'of substantially all discrimination, in the sense of Article XVII (national treatment), between or among the parties'. This language does not mention Article XVI (market access) restrictions, which are thereby not covered by it. Hence, economic integration agreements are not expected to eliminate 'substantially all discrimination' emanating from market access restrictions. It means that while the scope of coverage of these agreements,

50. WT/DS34/R, AB/R Turkey – Restrictions on Imports of Textile and Clothing Products, adopted on 19.11.1999, Panel report para. 9.146.
51. WT/DS34/AB/R *Turkey – Textile*, n. 50, Appellate Body report, paras 48, 49.

in terms of sectors, is expected to be broad, the depth of concessions is entirely left to the discretion of the parties. An interpretative question invoked by this provision is: would discriminatory measures listed under Article XVI:2, that is, joint venture requirements and foreign equity ceilings, be considered as measures 'in the sense of Article XVII', to which this provision applies?[52]

10.3.1.1.3.3 Elimination of Existing Discriminatory Measures, and/or Prohibition of New or More Discriminatory Measures

Subparagraphs V:1(b) provide some explanation to the former ambiguous provision by implying that elimination of substantially all discrimination may be achieved by '(i) elimination of existing discriminatory measures, and/or (ii) prohibition of new or more discriminatory measures'. In general, these two manners of behaviour are considered to be complementary. It is thus questionable why an alternative choice between them was also allowed, since it is clear that if a Member fulfills only one of these requirements, this provision may be circumvented through the other option. Therefore, in cases where the two options are feasible for a country, it is advisable not to interpret this provision as determining two alternatives, but as providing that in sectors where both ways of acting are necessary, both will be effectuated, while in sectors where only one way of acting is relevant, only this way of acting will be effectuated.

Article V:1(b)(i),(ii) is regarded by one commentator as illustrative explanations or examples for how the absence or elimination of substantially all discrimination may be accomplished, without diminishing or derogating from the general obligation.[53]

10.3.1.1.4 Elimination of Discrimination: When?

Article V:1 of GATS provides that the elimination of 'substantially all discrimination' shall be examined either at the entry into force of that agreement or on the basis of a *reasonable time-frame*. Usually, when an economic integration agreement is concluded, its application is gradual, in order to allow the adjustment of the market to the new terms of trade. Therefore, the latter alternative suggested is very commonly used. However, the expression 'reasonable time frame' is not defined by the agreement and therefore it is unclear: should a uniform, acceptable period be agreed by the CRTA? Or should at least some maximum boundaries be determined (five to ten years)?[54] Alternatively, should it be decided on a case-by-case basis?[55]

52. R. Adlung, 'The GATS Turns Ten: A Preliminary Stocktaking', *WTO* (2004), 13. <www.wto.org>.
53. W. Zdouc, n. 22, 234.
54. The Understanding on the Implementation of Art. XXIV of the GATT (1994) provides that the transitional period of such agreements should exceed ten years only in exceptional cases. In April 1999 in a meeting of the WTO Council for Trade in Services Japan made a proposal that this end would be met within five years: S.M. Stephenson, n. 18, 95, n. 9.
55. See, for example, discussion in WT/REG50/M/1, WT/REG51/M/1, WT/REG52/M/1, Examination of the EC-Hungary, Poland, Slovak Europe Agreements – Note of the Meeting of 18 February 1998, 19.3.98, paras 11,13,14, 15. Abott, n. 2, 33–34, referring to the equivalent

Some of the economic integration agreements pose even a greater difficulty to apply this provision, because they do not include a comprehensive timetable, referring not only to current, but also to future liberalization processes. In these agreements, the parties decide, from time to time, how and when to proceed. Thus, in the examination of such agreements according to Article V there is no way to determine whether 'a reasonable time frame' is followed for future processes.[56]

This difficulty is further reflected in the position of Article V towards the implications in case of breaching this provision:

> Article XXIV [of the GATT – N.M.], requires that if a Working Party finds that a plan or schedule for an interim agreement is not likely to result in a GATT-consistent customs union or a free trade area, its members 'shall not maintain or put into force . . . [an] agreement if they are not prepared to modify it in accordance with . . . the recommendations.' No such provision exists in Article V.[57]

10.3.1.1.5 *The Exception to the Obligation for Eliminating Discrimination*

Article V:1 excludes from the obligation to eliminate 'substantially all discrimination measures permitted under Articles XI, XII, XIV and XIV*bis*'. This exception is similar in concept to the one included in Article XXIV:8(b) of GATT: it excludes from that obligation measures recognized as 'safety valves' (see Chapter 15), aimed at protecting interests such as balance-of-payments stability (Articles XI, XII), security (Article XIV*bis*) and the general interests specified in Article XIV. The language of this provision in GATS is generally similar to the language of the equivalent GATT provision. However, in GATT, the security exception was not included in the list of exceptions mentioned in Article XXIV:8(b). It was therefore argued, that this could not possibly be an exhaustive list.[58] In GATS, the security exception was included in the list of Article V:1. In addition, GATS provision lacks the necessity condition to which the exemptions under GATT Article XXIV are subject. Thus, at least literally, for the purpose of Article V:1, no examination is necessary as to whether the least restrictive alternative was chosen. Otherwise, these provisions are similarly drafted, and therefore this interpretative claim may rise in GATS context too. Nevertheless, the language of GATS Article V:1 seems to

---

GATT provision (in an article written before GATS conclusion) suggests that the 'reasonability' of time frame will be subject to determination of the time necessary for the creation and operation of the agreement. He further suggests that the notification to the WTO authorities should include reference to the maximal duration of the discriminating measure, beyond which the Member involved shall be considered as infringing GATT provisions.

56. See, for example, WT/REG40/M/1 Examination of the Protocol on Trade in Services of the Australia – New Zealand Closer Economic relations Trade Agreement, 4.12.1997, paras 5–9.
57. B. Hoeckman & P. Sauvé, n. 4, 60.
58. See, for example, WT/REG/W/18, n. 33, paras 16–19.

indicate that its drafters meant an exhaustive list, since any other interpretation would undermine its purpose.

The list of exceptions specified by this Article does not include Articles VII (recognition), X (emergency safeguard measures), XIII (government procurement) and XV (subsidies).[59] It is true that in GATS context, these provisions are still not yet fully developed, being subject to further negotiations. However, their exclusion from the scope of this provision implies that where economic integration agreements do not eliminate discrimination between or among their parties in these omitted areas, or apply emergency safeguards, they can still be considered to fulfil the condition set forth by GATS Article V.

In addition, this provision does not require the parties to an economic integration agreement to abolish obstacles to market access in the meaning of GATS Article XVI. These obstacles are allowed subject to the limitations specified in Article XVI.[60]

10.3.2 Article V:2: Wider Process of Economic Integration

Article V:2 provides that in evaluating whether the conditions under paragraph V:1(b) are met, consideration may be given to the relationship of the agreement to a wider process of economic integration or trade liberalization among the countries concerned.

The intention behind this provision is to urge the interpreters of an economic integration agreement to see the wider picture. Thus, for instance, where agreements made in the context of countries joining the EU are examined, the final result and the essence of this economic integration alliance should be taken into account. It could be further construed to imply liberalization of trade in goods according to GATT Article XXIV:5,[61] thus supporting the suggested interpretation of 'substantial sectoral coverage' (see 10.3.1.1.2). Nevertheless, the provision does not specify precisely how the relationship between goods and services should be considered.[62]

The wording of this provision is broad and does not give the interpreters any direction: what should be the aim and result of such consideration? In what circumstances should it be exercised, and for what purpose?

In any case, the consideration of such a wider integration process is *optional* ('may be given'). There is no specification in this provision under which

59. S.M. Stephenson, n. 18, 93.
60. W. Zdouc, n. 22, 234.
61. WT/REG/W/37 Committee on Regional Trade Agreements – Synopsis of 'Systemic' Issues Related to Regional Trade Agreements – Note by the Secretariat, 2 Mar. 2000, para. 85.
62. GATS commentary, n. 19, 139. It is suggested there to interpret this provision as implying the lowering of the threshold, allowing remaining discriminatory measures among the parties to the economic integration agreement in services. Alternatively, it is noted that this condition might require a stricter reading of the liberalization commitments of the parties.

circumstances should it be considered. This phrasing may lead to a non-uniform application of this provision.

10.3.3 ARTICLE V:3: DEVELOPING COUNTRIES

When developing countries are involved in an economic integration agreement, Article V:3 provides for softer, more flexible conditions of the exception. Since the term 'developing countries' is not defined by the agreement (see Chapter 14), the scope of this provision is not definite.

Article V:3 uses an obligatory language: 'shall be provided', thus preventing any discretion from the Members concerning the entitlement of developing countries to special and differential treatment. However, Members have some discretion in terms of the *implementation* of this provision, through the shaping of their specific commitments.

Paragraphs V:3(a) and (b) form two independent cumulative means to grant special and differential treatment:[63]

The general idea of Article V:3(a) is clear: facilitating the application of Article V:1 to developing countries. It does not refer only to economic integration agreements *between developing* countries, but covers also economic integration agreements *to which a developing country is a party*, namely, economic integration agreements between developing and developed countries.[64]

Flexibility to facilitate the participation of developing countries in the multinational GATS framework could be achieved in terms of the contents of their specific commitments and in term of the transitional periods allowed to them.

Article V:3(b) allows, in cases of an economic integration agreements involving *only developing countries*, the grant of *more favourable* treatment 'to *juridical persons* owned or controlled by natural persons of the parties to such an agreement'. The notion of 'more favourable treatment' is not precisely explained, though. This provision allows for discrimination against firms owned or controlled by natural persons of non-parties, even if the latter are established in the territory of the parties to such an agreement.[65] This is an *exception* to the general rule of GATS, established by footnote 12 to the agreement (see Chapter 5), according

63. GATS commentary, n. 19, 143.
64. Some countries suggested that this provision would be interpreted to also benefit developed countries when concluding an economic integration agreement with a developing country. It is noted that although this interpretation could not be ruled out by the wording of this provision, it would lead to a result opposite to its object and purpose, as the developed countries would be allowed, in agreements with developing countries, to maintain a more restrictive regime than in agreements with developed countries: GATS commentary, n. 19, 142.
65. Article V:3 allows for the departure of developing countries, which are parties to economic integration agreements, from Art. V:6: B. Hoekman & P. Sauvé, n. 4, 60–61. It is suggested to read this provision 'in essence to allow for preferential treatment for small and medium sized enterprises and as a limitation to the liberal rules of origin of Article V:6'. GATS commentary, n. 19, 143.

to which in economic integration agreements which do not involve only developing countries, an established supplier (juridical person) of a third country in a WTO Member should be granted the same access conditions to other WTO Members as a juridical person of the Member where it is established.

It should be stressed, that this provision does not imply that the overall level of trade barriers may be raised.[66]

10.3.3.1 Juridical Persons

This relief is provided only to juridical persons, which are broadly defined in Article XXVIII(l), providing:

> 'juridical person' means any legal entity duly constituted or otherwise organized under applicable law, whether for profit or otherwise, and whether privately-owned or governmentally-owned, including any corporation, trust, partnership, joint venture, sole proprietorship or association.

This language is parallel to the definition in Article XXVIII(m), providing that a 'juridical person of another Member' means a juridical person which is either:

> (i) constituted or otherwise organized under the law of that other Member, and is engaged in substantive business operations in the territory of that Member or any other Member; or
> (ii) in the case of the supply of a service through commercial presence, owned or controlled by:
> 1. natural persons of that Member; or
> 2. juridical persons of that other Member identified under subparagraph (i);

Article XXVIII(n) further provides:

> A juridical person is:
>
> (i) 'owned' by persons of a Member if more than 50 per cent of the equity interest in it is beneficially owned by persons of that Member;
> (ii) 'controlled' by persons of a Member if such persons have the power to name a majority of its directors or otherwise to legally direct its actions.

See analysis in Chapter 5.

Summing up, the language of this provision is ambiguous and in fact gives full discretion to the interpreters of such an agreement, without establishing any minimum requirements for such countries. (See further discussion in Chapter 14; paragraph (b) will be discussed below, with paragraph 6.)

66. GATS commentary, n. 19, 143.

10.3.4 ARTICLE V:4: ADDITIONAL CONDITIONS

Article V:4 of GATS determines two additional conditions for an economic integration agreement to be recognized as an exception to the MFN rule:

(1) shall be designed to facilitate trade between the parties to the agreement and
(2) shall not, in respect of any Member outside the agreement, raise the overall level of barriers to trade in services within the respective sectors or subsectors compared to the level applicable prior to such an agreement.

Both these conditions are also pronounced in an obligatory language: 'shall/shall not', and are thus not subject to the discretion of the Members.

10.3.4.1 Scope of Application

10.3.4.1.1 Members and Non-Members

The language of Article V:4 may bear an application of its rules to an economic integration agreement between a WTO Member and a non-Member. This is probably the result of the experience gained in GATT context. The language of Article XXIV:5 of GATT refers to agreements 'between the territories of Contracting Parties', but it was systematically interpreted as also allowing recognition of agreements between a GATT Member and a non-Member State, read together with Article XXIV:10, which allows for the recognition of agreements that do not fully comply with the requirements of paragraphs 5–9, by a two third majority. GATT language did not explicitly provide whether this provision applies to agreements between developed and developing countries.[67] In GATS, this question was explicitly addressed in Article V:3. In GATT context, it was further unclear whether this provision refers to agreements between dependent territories. This question was not explicitly addressed by Article V of GATS, but an affirmative answer may be drawn from the general language of paragraph 4, read together with paragraph 1.

10.3.4.2 'Shall Not... Raise the Overall Barriers to Trade within the Respective Sectors or Subsectors'

This Provision:

> implies that countries participating in a free trade area may be permitted to raise some barriers against non-members, as long as the overall barriers of all the members of the agreement vis-à-vis non-members, for each of the relevant sectors or sub-sectors, does not increase. This option is clearly a significant difference with the GATT, which prohibits such 'rebalancing' for members of

67. See GATT Analytical index, n. 37, 798–800.

a free trade area, unless compensation is offered to affected GATT contracting parties.[68]

The overall aim of this condition is clear: the WTO, which is interested in trade liberalization at the *global* level, is ready to tolerate only economic integration agreements that enhance the achievement of this goal. However, the language of this provision holds some interpretative difficulties:

- Do the expressions 'to facilitate trade' and 'not to raise barriers to trade' represent a general statement of principles or additional conditions to be satisfied?
- Should this condition be applied by examining the effect of each barrier to trade, or should the effect of all the barriers involved be weighed together, allowing some offset of effects between them? This question was discussed in the CRTA regarding the accession of countries to the EU; while examination by sector, by country, revealed some cases where the level of barriers to trade towards third countries was raised, the counter-argument was that this negative effect should be weighed and offset against the benefits accruing from the accession of these countries to the EU, allowing third countries that are their trade partners to benefits from a huge single market.[69]
- How can the duties and regulations embodied in a new economic integration agreement, replacing an old one with an overlapping, or partly overlapping membership, be compared?
- To this extent, should a different approach be adopted where a new agreement is examined, compared to the examination of an extension of an existing agreement?
- Should the examination be affected by the degree of economic integration between or among the parties to an economic integration agreement?
- How will the overall level of barriers to trade be measured, particularly considering the statistical difficulties to measure accurately international trade flows in services?[70]
- How will the causal link between a reduction in trade volume and the agreement be established?
- Can administrative arrangements between parties to an economic integration agreement be considered as trade barriers toward third parties?

68. B. Hoeckman, P. Sauvé, n. 4, 58.
69. See, for example, WT/REG3/M/5 Examination of the Enlargement of the EC: Accession of Austria, Finland and Sweden – Note of the Meeting of 14 Jul. 1997, 12.8.1997, 3; WT/REG3/Add. 1, Enlargement of the EC – Accession of Austria, Finland and Sweden – Questions and Replies, Addendum, 23.4.1997, 2.
70. Paragraph 2 of the Understanding on the Interpretation of Art. XXIV of the GATT (1994), n. 54, includes some detailed instruction as to the evaluation of the overall effect of a customs union or free trade area agreement. It is mainly based on average tariff rates and statistics. Tariff rates are transparent and quantifiable, but they are not relevant to trade in services. Statistical data for trade in services are more difficult to achieve than for trade in goods.

- This provision provides for the examination of specific sectors or subsectors to see whether the overall level of barriers to trade has grown. Thus, it disregards the interaction that may take place due to the synergy *between* sectors or sub-sectors to this extent.[71]
- What is the purpose of this provision towards third party countries? Freezing the existing situation or creating a mechanism for future trade liberalization?
- When would a regulation be considered as a barrier to trade?[72]
- At what time should this provision be fulfilled, in light of the practice, common in international trade agreements, of gradual removal of trade barriers?[73]
- Should this evaluation procedure take place for agreements between GATS Members and third parties, which are not WTO Members?[74]

For the sake of certainty and predictability, it would have been better to determine clear criteria for the examination of the parameters set by this provision.

10.3.4.2.1 'Overall'

The concept of 'overall' evaluation in GATS recalls the 'on the whole' assessment in GATT Article XXIV. In terms of legislative history, the latter provides for a comparison between the whole level of tariffs in a customs union and the whole level of tariffs in the former constituent territories. This concept was clarified by

71. The equivalent GATT provision, Art. XXIV:4, provides that a customs union or free trade area agreement 'shall not to raise barriers to trade'. This is a more general concept, allowing to take into consideration synergies and cross-sector effects. Para. 2 of the Understanding on the Interpretation of Art. XXIV of the GATT, 1994, refers to Art. XXIV:5(a), providing that duties and other regulations of commerce will not be on the whole higher or more restrictive towards third countries than before the conclusion of the agreement. It provides, *inter alia*:

   > it is recognized that for the purpose of the overall assessment of the incidence of other regulations of commerce for which *quantification and aggregation is difficult*, the examination of *individual* measures, regulations, products covered and trade flows affected may be required. [Emphasis added].

   The same logic may explain GATS approach in this context.
72. In GATT context, for example, elaborated rules of origin were recognized as barriers to trade. See: GATT Analytical index, n. 37, 802.
73. GATT Understanding, n. 54, provides that only in rare cases the 'reasonable time frame' for the fulfilment of the equivalent GATT requirement will exceed ten years. This interpretation may give some indication as to the expectations of GATS Members concerning the maximal period, but the question yet unanswered is, in what circumstances a demand for shorter time limits should be justified.
74. In GATT, this option is specifically addressed by Art. XXIV:10, that was added later to the agreement (for the history of this provision see GATT Analytical Index, n. 37, 829; WT/REG/W/16 Committee on Regional Trade Agreements – Annotated Checklist of Systemic Issues – Note by the Secretariat, 26.5.1997, para. 53). Despite of the experience gained in GATT, such an explicit provision is not included in GATS, and therefore an interpretative question concerning the intention of its drafters rises.

the Understanding on Article XXIV of GATT 1994, due to which such assessment should be based upon weighted average in terms of quantity of import and value. Adapted to GATS context, the evaluation should also compare the situation before and after the formation of the economic integration agreement, but should concentrate on a sector or sub-sector comparison rather on a product-specific weighted tariff line basis in GATT context.[75]

10.3.4.2.2 Barriers to Trade

It is not specified which barriers are subject to this provision, but it seems that, read in conjunction with Article V:5, and in light of the object and purpose of this provision, preventing the abuse of such an agreement to raise the overall level of trade barriers. This expression should be interpreted broadly to include all trade barriers covered by GATS. Commentators disagree as to whether assessments according to this provision should refer to *potentially applicable* measures, and not only to measures effectively applied. While this notion is supported by one commentator, based on the same reasoning specified above,[76] according to another opinion, the evaluation should rely only on the actually applied levels of limitations, and not on the bindings in the schedules of specific commitments which might be higher.[77] This practice would make the examination more accurate, but at the same time might impose practical difficulties to find out the relevant information.

10.3.4.2.3 'Overall Level of Trade Barriers'

This ambiguous expression is not explained in the agreement. It is suggested that 'the assessment is to be made in comparison with the level of barriers applicable before the conclusion of the EIA [economic integration agreement-N.M.] and should take account of each sector and sub-sector covered by the agreement'.[78] Nevertheless, as explained above, the overall level of barriers to trade in services – before and after the agreement – is difficult to assess since barriers to trade in services are less quantifiable and transparent than barriers to trade in goods, and in addition, there are statistical difficulties to obtain the full data which is relevant for the assessment. Yet another difficulty stems from the lack of any indication how to weigh and balance barriers in a certain sector or sub-sector against barriers in another sector or sub-sector, particularly in light of the fact that different sectors or sub-sectors may bear different importance to different economies.

In the context of GATT Article XXIV:5, which provides that 'the effects of the resulting trade measures and policies of the new regional agreement shall not be

75. W. Zdouc, n. 22, 239–240.
76. GATS commentary, n. 19, 144.
77. W. Zdouc, n. 22, 239–240.
78. GATS commentary, n. 19, 143.

more trade restrictive, overall, than were the constituent countries' previous trade policies'. The Panel and Appellate Body in *Turkey – Textiles* agreed that this should by established by an economic test.[79]

10.3.4.2.4 'Facilitate Trade between the Parties'

This expression is equivalent to an expression included in Article XXIV:4 of GATT. The facilitation of trade between or among the parties is a purpose shared by economic integration agreements and GATS, and the reason for their recognition as an exception to the MFN rule in GATS. However, the word 'facilitate' is very general, and it is unclear what the essence of this word should be. Paragraph XXIV:4 of GATT is followed by paragraphs 5–8 thereof, that were regarded as specifying some conditions that must be fulfilled in order for an economic integration agreement to be covered by paragraph 4.[80] No such conditions are specified in Article V of GATS. This drafting allows full discretion of the interpreters of the agreement, thus potentially broadening the scale of agreements to be recognized as exceptions to the MFN provision. Any *mutatis mutandis* analogy from the equivalent GATT provision would raise the interpretative question: if this was GATS drafters' intention, why was it not specified, as in the equivalent GATT provision?

10.3.5 Article V:5: Compensation Due to Modification of Commitments

Article V:5 of GATS provides that Members engaging in an economic integration agreement, thus modifying their specific commitments in GATS, should compensate other Members affected by this modification. This provision was enacted in light of the experience gained in the application of the equivalent GATT Article XXIV:6, where it was argued that the modification of schedules mechanism, provided for in Article XXVIII of GATT, was drafted to apply only to situations where such modifications stem from the application of safeguard measures, and should not apply to cases of modification due to engagement in economic integration agreements.[81] Thus, Article V:4 explicitly provides for the application of Article XXI (see Chapter 15).

79. WT/DS34/R *Turkey – Textile*, n. 50, Panel report para. 9.121, WT/DS34/AB/R, Appellate Body report para. 55.
80. The Understanding on the interpretation of Art. XXIV of GATT (1994), n. 54, provides: 'Customs unions, free trade areas and interim agreements leading to the formation of a customs union or free trade area, to be considered with Article XXIV, must satisfy, *inter alia*, the provisions of paragraphs 5,6,7 and 8 of the Article'.
81. See, for example, WT/REG/W/16, n. 74, para. 47.

10.3.6 ARTICLE V:6: RIGHTS OF JURIDICAL PERSONS

According to Article V:6, the right of a service supplier, which is a juridical person constituted under the laws of a party to an economic integration agreement, to the benefits of the agreement, is subject to a condition '. . . that it engages in substantive business operations in the territory of the parties to such agreement'. Due to GATS rules of origin (see Chapter 5), the juridical person involved should be owned or controlled by natural or juridical persons from another GATS Member. Developing countries have been granted an exception to this rule under Article V:3(b).

The general aim of this provision is to ensure, that the benefits of the agreement shall not be abused by a juridical person without any real economic substance.[82] However, the wording of this provision raises some interpretative questions:

10.3.6.1 'Juridical Persons'

The definition of 'juridical persons' in Article XXVIII(l) (see Chapter 5) does not explicitly refer to non-incorporated entities such as branches and representative offices. It is therefore unclear whether such entities will be entitled to preferential treatment. It could be argued that these business forms are extensions of the home enterprise, which is not incorporated under the laws of the host country, and that these business forms are distinguished from 'juridical person' in Article XXVIII(d), which defines 'commercial presence'. On the other hand, it is argued that a reading which refers to the general context, as well as to the object and purpose of this provision, implies the inclusion of these entities under its scope.[83]

10.3.6.2 'Substantive Business Operations'

The expression 'substantive business operations' is ambiguous and calls for legal interpretation. It seems clear that this provision should be interpreted so as to prevent the abuse of the Agreements through the creation of a so-called 'letter-box' operation in one of the parties in order to circumvent controls imposed by the

82. The GATT does not include a similar provision. However, economic integration agreements include such provisions. For example, the term 'effective and continuous link' in the EU agreements: WT/REG39/1, Establishment of the EU, Services – Communication from the EC and their Member States, 24.4.1998, 7, para. 5; In Europe Agreements the expression used was 'real and continuous link': WT/REG50/2, WT/REG51/2, WT/REG52/2, Committee on Regional Trade Agreements – The European Communities-Hungary Europe Agreement, Services; the European Communities-Poland Europe Agreement, Services; The European Communities – Slovak Europe Agreement, Services, Communication from the Parties, 24.4.1998, 3. It is argued that this GATS provision 'appears basically to copy Art. 58 of the EC Treaty into the GATS': 'The General Agreement on Trade in Services (GATS): an Analysis', *OECD* (1994), 11, <www.olis.oecd.org>.
83. GATS commentary, n. 19, 146–147.

other on access by foreign nationals and companies to its market. The EU, for example, interprets similar requirements in its economic integration agreements examining, *inter alia*, the nationality of the partners, of the members of the management or supervisory bodies, or of the persons holding the capital.[84] However, the interest protected by this provision may conflict with other interests, including interests of GATS Members which are not parties of the economic integration agreement examined. According to one opinion this expression should be broadly interpreted, in equivalence to the determination of 'supply of a service' in Article XXVIII(b), to include 'the production, distribution, marketing, sale and delivery of a service'.[85] According to another opinion, the language of this provision is too broad, and therefore may justify different restrictions on the access of service suppliers to the markets of the Members, despite of other provisions of GATS.[86]

10.3.6.3 'In the Territory of the Parties'

According to Article V:6, substantive business operations have to take place 'in the territory of the parties' to an economic integration agreement. It should be noted that this provision does not restrict the place of activity only to the territory of one party, but allows the activity to take place at any of the territories of the parties to the agreement. This provision gains more importance as the number of parties to the agreement grows.

10.3.7 Article V:7: Notification

Article V:7 specifies the notification and reporting obligations of GATS Members to the WTO concerning economic integration agreements concluded by them. This provision is equivalent to Article XXIV:7 of GATT, and suffers from similar disadvantages:

It does not define 'prompt notification', nor in terms of form, neither in terms of timetable. Nevertheless, paragraph 3 of the 2006 Decision on a Transparency Mechanism for Regional Trade Agreements[87] provides that as a rule, notification will take place directly after ratification of the agreement and before the application of preferential treatment between or among the parties. Notification is made to the Council for Trade in Services, which might set up a working group to examine the agreement. Nevertheless, its impact is questionable since at this stage, it is

84. M. Danusso & R. Danton, n. 45.
85. GATS commentary, n. 19, 148.
86. See, for example, WT/REG50/M/2 Committee on Regional Trade Agreements – Examination of the European Communities-Hungary Europe Agreement, Services; the European Communities-Poland Europe Agreement, Services; the European Communities – Slovak Europe Agreement, Service, the Meeting of 18 Feb. 1998, 19.3.1998, 5 paras 20–25.
87. WT/L/671 General Council, Transparency Mechanism for Regional Trade Agreements, Decision of 14 Dec. 2006, 18.12.2006.

much harder to impose on the parties modifications in the agreement.[88] Indeed, this may be one reason why the right of the Council to make recommendations to the parties is based upon the working party report. Another reason is the consensus requirement.[89]

In practice, the examination of economic integration agreements is usually conducted by the CRTA. While the equivalent GATT provision, Article XXIV:7(b) provides that the Contracting Parties '*shall* make recommendations', GATS Article V:7(c) provides that the Council for Trade in Services '*may* make recommendations' [emphasis added]. In addition, while GATT Understanding on the implementation of Article XXIV from 1994 envisages review of the implementation of recommendations, GATS lacks such a provision. The disciplines provided for by GATS in this context seem weaker compared to GATT. It is suggested that the weak drafting of GATS may reflect the fact that GATT provisions were 'often mere law on the books'.[90] The weight of such a recommendation may be even weaker when an economic integration agreement includes Members and non-WTO-Members. In practice, however, examination of notified agreements usually takes place. The problem is that not all the agreements are properly notified.

10.4 ARTICLE V*BIS*: LABOUR MARKETS' INTEGRATION

Article V*bis* of GATS, which was included in it to the request of the Nordic countries[91] which had such agreements, applies to agreements creating labour market integration between or among their parties the same idea of Article V: recognition of agreements between or among a relatively small number of Members as an exception to the MFN rule. As a result of this provision, no listing of such agreements as MFN exemptions according to Article II:2 is necessary. This provision should be considered *lex specialis* concerning agreements which refer only to labour market integration, which in its absence could not have enjoyed the MFN exception embodied in Article V, requiring broader coverage of the economic integration than covered by them.

Movement of labour is considered a sensitive issue which has not yet found satisfactory coverage under GATS (see discussion on the modes of supply – Chapter 4, on regulation – Chapter 12 and on the Annex on Movement of Natural Persons – Chapter 16).

---

88. It should be noted, that discussion on drafts of agreements which might be changed is also inefficient, but maybe an examination of agreements after conclusion but before ratification would be more effective. See more information on the procedures, decisions and examination of specific economic integration agreements in the WTO Analytical index (GATS) paras 42–47 and annexes. <www.wto.org>.
89. GATS commentary, n. 19, 150.
90. W. Zdouc, n. 22, 246.
91. For its negotiations history see: GATS commentary, n. 19, 153–154.

It provides:

Labor Markets Integration Agreements
This Agreement shall not prevent any of its Members from being a party to an agreement establishing full integration of the labour markets between or among the parties to such an agreement, provided that such an agreement:

(a) exempts citizens of parties to the agreement from requirements concerning residency and work permits;
(b) is notified to the Council for Trade in Services.

This provision sets five cumulative conditions to be fulfilled in order for this exception to apply:

(1) *The existence of an agreement*– this provision could be interpreted to mean a binding international treaty, or rather a less formal form of international agreement, as acceptable in international public law.
(2) *A WTO Member is a party to that agreement* – this condition implies that other parties to the agreement may be non-WTO Members.
(3) *Establishing for full labour market integration* – the term 'establishing' is interpreted by some commentators as implying *current*, not *future* integration.[92] However, it is common practice that integration agreements are applied gradually, in order to allow market to adjust. Therefore, it seems more reasonable to opt for a similar approach to that exercised in Article V, which allows for integration to take place within a 'reasonable time frame' (see above).

The term 'full' is not defined in the agreement. In any case, it is clear that it implies agreements which do not provide for *partial* integration. 'Full' seems to be a stricter standard than the 'substantially all trade/substantial sectoral coverage' provided for by GATT and GATS. The term 'labour market' is also not defined in the agreement. It does not appear in any other GATS provision. A comparison with the term used in the Annex on Movement of Natural Persons shows that the English version of that Annex uses the term 'employment market' while the French and Spanish versions use the term equivalent to 'labour market' in Article V*bis*. It is thus suggested by some commentators that 'the two terms have no legal distinction'.[93]

Footnote 2, attached to this text, which is an integral part of the agreement, explains that typically, such integration provides citizens of the parties concerned with *a right of free entry* to the employment markets[94] of the parties and includes measures concerning *conditions* of pay, other conditions of employment and social benefits.

---

92. GATS commentary, n. 19, 158.
93. *Ibid.*, 156.
94. It is suggested by commentators to adopt the types of market restrictions which may not be maintained *mutatis mutandis* from Art. XVI:2: GATS commentary, n. 19, 157. However, it could be argued that the text does not imply such a restrictive interpretation, and allows for the application of this provision of other restrictive measures as well.

(4) *The agreement exempts citizens of parties to the agreement from requirements concerning residency and work permits* – in the circumstances to which this provision applies, residency may be a pre-condition to the ability to work in a market. In such cases, the relief from both procedures is complementary. The agreement should not ensure jobs. It neither disregards the fact that a foreign worker might need to obtain a 'residency permit', while its domestic competitor would not. However, it aims at ensuring free access to jobs by putting the foreign workers on as close as possible footing with their domestic competitors.

It should be noted, that the agreement does not explicitly refer to the relationship between visas and residency permits, which are different in different legal systems.[95]

(5) *The agreement is notified to the Council for Trade in Services*[96] – unlike the notification provision in Article V:7, this notification provision is phrased as one of the preconditions for the application of Article V*bis*. This phrasing is, no doubt, stronger than Article V:7, and might solve the difficulties stemming from the disregard of that provision by GATS Members, as specified above.

Article V*bis* provides that 'this Agreement shall not prevent any of its Members from *being a party to'* an agreement which fulfills these five conditions. This language is somewhat different from the language of Article V, using the words 'from being a party or *entering into'* an economic integration agreement. Despite of the first impression which might lead to a conclusion that Article V*bis* refers only to agreements existing at the time of its conclusion, its drafting history as well as a practical approach, based on the context, object and purpose call for its interpretation as applying to such agreements existing at the time of its conclusion as well as to future agreements.[97]

The conclusion of labour market integration agreements touches upon domestic policy sensitive issues such as concerns about job stability, wage and salary erosion and the loss of the associated social benefits.[98] This fact may explain why, by now, only a few such agreements were notified to the WTO.[99] Yet another

95. GATS commentary, n. 19, 160.
96. For the notification procedure see: S/L/5 Guidelines for Notifications under the General Agreement on Trade in Services – adopted by the Council for Trade in Services on 1 Mar. 1995, 4.4.1995
97. GATS commentary, n. 19, 163.
98. R. Self & K. Zutshi, 'Mode 4: Negotiating Challenges and Opportunities', in A. Mattoo & A. Carzaniga (eds), *Moving People to Deliver Services*, The World Bank and Oxford University Press (2003), 27, 42.
99. S/C/N/34 Council for Trade in Services, Notification pursuant to Art. V*bis* of the General Agreement on Trade in Services, Denmark, 2.12.1996; S/C/N/35 Council for Trade in Services, Notification pursuant to Art. V*bis* of the General Agreement on Trade in Services, Iceland, 2.12.1996; S/C/N/36 Council for Trade in Services, Notification pursuant to Art. V*bis* of the General Agreement on Trade in Services, Norway, 2.12.1996; S/C/N/37 Council for Trade in Services, Notification pursuant to Art. V*bis* of the General Agreement on Trade in Services,

explanation may stem from the fact that this provision is limited to agreements exclusively referring to this subject, while this subject is regulated in many regional trade agreements, covered by Article V.[100]

10.5 CONCLUSION

It seems that in recent years, services trade liberalization by economic integration agreements, as an alternative to GATS, is becoming more common. The reasons may be that these agreements are perceived by politicians as more focused and less resource consuming, an insight that might be encouraged by domestic political pressures from industries interested in a certain market. In addition, this approach avoids free riding and may be also fed by the Doha Round disappointment,[101] and may hold some advantages over the multilateral system (GATS) in terms of stability, transparency, depth of trade liberalization, great ease to achieve consensus and to apply commitments.[102]

GATS refers to these agreements as an exception to the MFN rule, subject to the fulfilment of criteria meant to ensure their comprehensiveness. The agreements are subject to examination by the CRTA, which was established in 1997 in the WTO and given the mandate for examining regional trade agreements (according to GATT) and economic integration agreements (according to GATS) in light of these criteria. However, this examination suffers from some systemic deficiencies:

- Many agreements are not notified to the WTO, thus escaping the examination provided for by the agreement.[103]
- The kinds of barriers that an economic integration agreement should eliminate, according to GATS, are unclear.
- The CRTA examines the agreements retrospectively, after their conclusion, and therefore has neither any effective power (nor the authority) to provide for their modification.
- The CRTA is not authorized to exercise any effective sanctions against agreements that do not fulfil the conditions set forth by GATS, except the procedure of examination that provides some political pressure.
- The CRTA is combined of the representatives of all the Members that are aware of the fact that their country's agreements will be examined by the same forum. Therefore, they prefer to adopt a moderate approach to the

Sweden, 2.12.1996; S/C/N/38 Council for Trade in Services, Notification pursuant to Art. V*bis* of the General Agreement on Trade in Services, Finland, 2.12.1996.

100. J. Nielsen, 'Labor Mobility in Regional Trade Agreements', in A. Mattoo & A. Carzaniga (eds), *Moving People to Deliver Services*, The World Bank and Oxford University Press (2003), 93.
101. M. Roy, et al., n. 6, 56.
102. S.M. Stephenson, 'Regional Versus Multilateral Liberalization of Services', *1 World Trade Review* (2002), 187.
103. S.M. Stephenson, n. 18, 96–98.

agreements examined by them, hoping for a mutual approach to be exercised in the examination of their agreements.
- The criteria set forth by Article V are ambiguous and subject to a case-by-case interpretation.
- Unlike in the case of goods, barriers to trade in services are much less quantifiable and transparent than customs duties and quotas. It is therefore much more difficult to examine whether the requirements set forth by Article V are met.
- Difficulties to achieve comprehensive statistical data affect the efficiency of examination.
- The CRTA published Guidelines on Procedures to Improve and Facilitate the Examination Process[104] but these guidelines do not solve all the difficulties mentioned. The Transparency Mechanism for Regional Trade Agreements of 14 December 2006[105] is inherently limited to an overall assessment of the agreements.
- Article V of GATS does not address difficulties stemming from the growing quantity of economic integration agreements: the relations between such agreements and GATS, legal implications, rules of origin, conflicting disciplines, priorities, relationship between dispute settlement mechanisms etc.

To sum up this point, it seems that the mechanism set forth by Article V suffers from four main deficiencies. One problem stems from the legal ambiguity of its provisions, created by the attempt to 'translate' a GATT concept into GATS context. The outcome proves to be difficult, because the barriers to trade in services are difficult to measure quantitatively and the degree of required liberalization ('substantial sectoral coverage', 'substantially all discrimination') is not uniformly understood and difficult to apply due to the variety of services and modes of supply. In addition, the rules governing services are unclear about the kind of barriers that economic integration agreements should be expected to eliminate, as well as about the degree of integration these agreements are supposed to provide for in areas such as foreign direct investment, labour mobility and the recognition of professional qualifications.[106]

The second deficiency stems from the fact that this provision does not refer to the status of safeguards in economic integration agreements: should they be applied on an MFN basis or selectively, between or among the economic integration agreement's parties as well as towards third parties.[107]

The third, practical problem stems from the lack of respect to this provision by the Members, avoiding notification to the WTO on economic integration agreements including services trade liberalization. This situation undermines transparency as well as the CRTA examination procedure provided for by the agreement.

A fourth weakness is the weak review procedure, taking place by the CRTA. Nevertheless, it is assumed that where a dispute arises due to the content of a

104. WT/REG/W/15, n. 40.
105. WT/L/671 n. 87.
106. S.M. Stephenson, n. 18, 90.
107. W. Zdouc, n. 22, 235–236.

specific economic integration agreement, dispute settlement procedures would be invoked.

It is unclear, to what extent the lack of notification of economic integration agreements stems from deterrence of the Members from examination under the ambiguous standards set by this provision, or rather from the feeling that the arrangement embodied in Article V does not correspond to the real economic needs, leading, for example, to the conclusion of stand-alone sectoral agreements,[108] effectively turning, maybe, into a trade barrier in itself. In addition, many Members have claimed wide-ranging exemptions for preferential trade agreements through notifying these under Annex II of their list of MFN exemptions, to avoid a CRTA examination, contrary to the purpose of Article II(1).[109]

Yet another source of difficulty could stem from the potential 'competition' between the dispute settlement forum which is in charge of the economic integration agreement, thus having the authority to rule according to the provisions of this agreement, and the WTO tribunals, the authority of which is confined to the WTO rules.[110]

It should be noted, that while GATT Article XXIV:10 allows for a waiver of economic integration agreements that do not fulfil all the requirements set forth by this provision, no such provision exists in GATS. This may be a sign for a stricter position of GATS drafters, who did not want to allow such an option, but on the other hand, this lack of flexibility seems to pay a price.

To complete the picture, it should be noted that in recent years many bilateral investment agreements are concluded between countries, including developing countries. These agreements are relevant to Mode 3 (commercial presence). Bilateral investment agreements do not seem to comply with the requirements set by Article V, since they cover only one aspect of trade. Unrecognized as an exception to the MFN rule, these agreements might be subject to this rule. 'While this extension may not cause problems in many cases, given generally liberal investment regimes and the focus of most treaties on protecting rather than liberalizing access, inconsistencies remain between the two frameworks'.[111]

Nevertheless, it should not be forgotten, that despite the benefits housed in the regional system, effective regulation of certain subjects must take place in the multilateral arena.

108. The legal status of these agreements is unclear: they obviously do not meet the requirements of Art. V and principally should have been object to a waiver request, but in most cases are not: S.M. Stephenson, n. 18, 100.

109. *Ibid.*, 101.

110. Such a dilemma arose in the GATT case WT/DS308/R, AB/R Mexico – Tax Measures on Soft Drinks, adopted on 24.6.2006, where Mexico asked the WTO Panel to decline from exercising jurisdiction claiming that only a NAFTA panel would be able to resolve the dispute, referring to Mexico's NAFTA claims and it could have procedural implications: W. Davey & A. Sapir, 'The *Soft Drink* Case: The WTO and regional Agreements', *8 World Trade Review* (2009), 5, as well as substantive implications, WT/REG4/M/4, n. 47.

111. R. Adlung & M. Molinuevo, 'Bilateralism in Services Trade: is There Fire behind the (BIT) Smoke?', *WTO Staff Working PaperERDS-2008-01* (2008), <http://papers.ssrn.com>.

Chapter 11
GATS and Competition Rules

11.1 INTRODUCTION

Protection of market players' expectations is a central principle in international trade enhancement. This principle is embodied in the WTO agreements, including GATS. These agreements do not prohibit the establishment or maintenance of state trading enterprises, or the formal or effective grant of exclusive or special privileges to enterprises. Nevertheless, these agreements include disciplines meant to ensure that measures affecting trade in services, applied by Members, will not undermine equality of competitive opportunities.

Anti-competitive practices, such as monopolies and cartels, form one category of measures restricting market access. The manner and degree of restriction depend, in each case, on the kind of practice involved, on the power the firms involved have in the market, and on additional factors.

Equality of competitive conditions may be undermined by governmental or private bodies. Both may undermine the certainty and predictability of the terms of trade, thus adversely affecting consumers' welfare. Private anti-competitive actions may sometimes be supported by governmental acts or omissions. However, the WTO agreements do not cover such private actions.[1]

In the international trade context, the important subject is not the protection of competition as such, but the protection of foreign competitors from structural restrictions or from restricting behaviour of domestic players in the domestic market.[2]

---

1. W. Zdouc, *Legal Problems Arising Under the General Agreement on Trade in Services – Comparative Analysis of GATS and GATT*, dissertation der Universität St. Gallen (2002), 267.
2. M.C. Malaguti, 'Restrictive Business Practices in International Trade and the Role of the World Trade Organization', *32 Journal of World Trade* (1998): 117, 119.

Thus, the WTO agreements do not form a general framework for regulation of competition. Nevertheless, their drafters found themselves forced to confront anti-competitive practices to the extent that they form a barrier to trade, undermining the purpose of these agreements.

In recent years, with the enhancement of globalization of international economy and the gradual removal of barriers to trade in the global level, the interrelations between trade and competition policy have grown. The two systems aim at the achievement of economic efficiency and welfare. Nevertheless, since the two systems, international trade rules and competition rules, use different instruments to achieve this goal, a conflict between them may occur; on the one hand, anti-competitive practices may undermine international trade, by restricting market access, to a certain extent. On the other hand, trade practices, such as safeguard measures, may form restrictions on market access and on competitive conditions in markets.

The difficulty in developing international competition rules stems from the fact that it implies an intervention in the sovereignty of states. As already explained, the WTO agreements are based on a delicate balance between international trade liberalization and domestic sovereignty. Thus, this matter must be cautiously approached.

11.2 GATS AND ANTI-COMPETITIVE PRACTICES

In the context of international trade in services,[3] the treatment of competition rules consists of two levels: application of existing disciplines and development of new disciplines. The disciplines provided for by GATS in this context are relatively weak.[4] In both cases, the determination of whether anti-competitive practices take place depends on the definition of the relevant market. This definition depends, *inter alia*, on the characteristics of each service sector and the manner of its operation. Thus, for example, it was established in *Mexico-Telecoms* that the relevant market for certain telecommunication services (voice, switched data and fax) is the country of termination of these services (Mexico).[5] The market definition for the purpose of these provisions does not necessarily correspond to the market definition for the MFN and national treatment provisions (see Chapter 6 – 6.6.2 and Chapter 8 – 8.5.3.2).

3. For the full picture of competition treatment by WTO agreements see B.M. Hoeckman & P.C. Mavroidis, 'Economic Development, Competition Policy, and the World Trade Organization', *The World Bank Policy Research Working Paper* (2002), 14, <www-wds.worldbank.org>.
4. Stronger disciplines concerning private restrictive business practices were included in the ITO charter that was finally not concluded: B.M. Hoeckman & P.C. Mavroidis, n. 3, 14.
5. WT/DS204/R, AB/R Mexico – Measures Affecting Telecommunications Services, adopted on 1.6.2004, Panel report, para. 7.152.

11.2.1 Application of Existing Disciplines

GATS includes two provisions, determining disciplines with regard to monopolies and exclusive service suppliers (Article VIII), and anti-competitive business practices (Article IX).

11.2.1.1 Monopolies and Exclusive Service Suppliers: Article VIII

Article VIII does not rule out the existence of monopolies and exclusive service suppliers, but rather is meant to ensure that they act according to GATS disciplines. The main concern covered by this provision is preventing monopolies from having control over infrastructure facilities, such as telecommunication and energy, thus abusing their position to circumvent specific commitments in other sectors of economic activity. This aim is relevant mainly to the protection of the interests of commercial operators. In addition, for public, basic services such as water and electricity, another aim that may be identified is the defence of consumers' interests against potential abuse from private enterprises, operating in a non-comparative environment.[6]

Article VIII provides:

Monopolies and Exclusive Service Suppliers

1. Each Member shall ensure that any monopoly supplier of a service in its territory does not, in the supply of the monopoly service in the relevant market, act in a manner inconsistent with that Member's obligations under Article II and specific commitments.
2. Where a Member's monopoly supplier competes, either directly or through an affiliated company, in the supply of a service outside the scope of its monopoly rights and which is subject to that Member's specific commitments, the Member shall ensure that such a supplier does not abuse its monopoly position to act in its territory in a manner inconsistent with such commitments.
3. The Council for Trade in Services may, at the request of a Member which has a reason to believe that a monopoly supplier of a service of any other Member is acting in a manner inconsistent with paragraph 1 or 2, request the Member establishing, maintaining or authorizing such supplier to provide specific information concerning the relevant operations.
4. If, after the date of entry into force of the WTO Agreement, a Member grants monopoly rights regarding the supply of a service covered by its specific commitments, that Member shall notify the Council for Trade in Services no later than three months before the intended implementation of

6. M. Cossy, 'Water Services at the WTO', in E. Brown Weiss, L. Boisson de Chazournes, N. Bernasconi-Osterwalder (eds), Fresh Water and International Economic Law, Oxford University Press (2005), 117, 128.

the grant of monopoly rights and the provisions of paragraphs 2, 3 and 4 of Article XXI shall apply.

5. The provisions of this Article shall also apply to cases of exclusive service suppliers, where a Member, formally or in effect, (*a*) authorizes or establishes a small number of service suppliers and (*b*) substantially prevents competition among those suppliers in its territory.

11.2.1.1.1 Monopolies and Exclusive Service Suppliers

This provision applies to monopolies and exclusive service suppliers who fulfil certain conditions. This is a narrow scope of application, implying that it does not apply to other restrictive practices, such as cartels and exclusive suppliers that do not fulfil the terms of this provision.

11.2.1.1.1.1 'Monopoly Supplier of Services'

'Monopoly supplier of services' is defined in Article XXVIII(h):

> any person, public or private, which in the relevant market of the territory of a Member is authorized or established formally or in effect by that Member as a sole supplier of that service.

The monopoly may be *private or public*. In some cases (e.g., sewerage services), a monopoly may consist of a public entity which delegates powers to a private entity by a concession contract.[7] Where such a case implies shared responsibility, an interpretative question may arise as to whether 'private *or* public' may also mean 'private *and* public'. In cases of full power delegation, it seems that the option of 'private' monopoly would cover the case.

This definition should be read together with the definitions of 'service supplier' (Article XXVIII(g)) and 'person' (Article XXVIII(j)), which, in turn, rely on the definitions of 'juridical person' (Article XXVIII(l), 'juridical person of another Member' (Article XXVIII(m)) and 'natural person of another Member' (Article XXVIII(k)) discussed in Chapter 5.

It should also be mentioned, that 'supply of a service' is broadly defined in Article XXVIII(b) to include 'production, distribution, marketing, sale and delivery of services'. Read together with the former definitions, the agreement implies that a monopoly may occur concerning all these activities.

7. Such cases are problematic in terms of the specific commitments: since they are not considered as government procurement as according to the definition of Art. XIII, they are covered by GATS. Nevertheless, since the access of foreign private service suppliers is subject to a concession agreement and is thus not automatic, there is a difficulty in phrasing the specific commitment accurately. One option is to ensure the access of such private entities to governmental bids in the specific commitments, but this is already a border-case similar to government procurement.

As a matter of principle, the ownership of an enterprise (private or public) is irrelevant to the existence of a monopoly according to Article XXVIII(h) of GATS.[8] This position rather depends on two cumulative conditions:

(a) 'In the relevant market of the territory of a Member it is *authorized or established formally or in effect by that Member*' – this definition rules out 'natural' monopolies, concentrating on monopolies created through governmental involvement.[9] The word 'authorizes' seem to reflect a more formal action, while 'established' seems to correspond more to 'in effect'. This broad wording thus covers both de jure and de facto monopolies created through active government involvement. Read with the other sub-paragraphs of this provision, it is suggested[10] that this provision requires government *action, not only tolerance;* but in any case, it is noted that this question would probably be decided on a case-by-case basis. According to another opinion,[11] acceptance of an existing monopoly may be also read into this wording.
(b) 'As a *sole* supplier of that service' – this definition is narrow, because it disregards all other forms of market dominance. Thus, it does not refer to 'gray area' cases where the monopoly controls *most* of the market. It affects the scope of application of this provision.

It should be stressed, that this provision does not cover 'services supplied in the exercise of governmental authority', which are excluded from GATS scope by Article I:3 (see Chapter 4).

11.2.1.1.1.2 Exclusive Service Suppliers

The application of this Article to certain exclusive service suppliers is provided for in Article VIII:5. According to it, 'exclusive service suppliers' have to meet two cumulative conditions:

> [w]here a Member, formally or in effect, (*a*) authorizes or establishes a small number of service suppliers and (*b*) substantially prevents competition among those suppliers in its territory.

(a) The first condition is that such an exclusive service supplier *has to be authorized or established, formally or in effect, by a Member.* This condition is similar to that provided for concerning monopolies in

8. This approach is different from GATT concept of 'state trading enterprises' established in GATT Art. XVII, although this approach was softened by the Understanding on the Interpretation of Art. XVII of GATT 1994, which clarifies that this concept may include non-governmental enterprises and even marketing boards.
9. This kind of practice is gradually disappearing with the expanding liberalization endeavors of diverse service sectors: R. Worfrum, P.T. Stoll & C. Feinäugle (eds), *WTO – Trade in Services,* Max Planck Commentaries on World Trade Law, Martinus Mijnhoff Publishers, Leiden, Boston (2008) (Hereby: GATS commentary), 223.
10. W. Zdouc, n. 1, 267; GATS commentary, n. 9, 209.
11. M. Cossy, n. 6, 127–128.

paragraph VIII:1. It is not clear what will be considered 'a small number' of service suppliers. It could be assumed that the 'ordinary meaning' of this wording envisages more than one exclusive service supplier, thus excluding such a case from the scope of this provision. But such a result does not seem to comply with the spirit and purpose of this provision. The expression 'a small number' is vague and relative, and it is unclear whether the determination of its fulfillment in a specific case should refer to the common situation in other countries in the same sector, or rather in other domestic or foreign services sectors, to the size of the country involved, to its geographic terms, etc. One option is to interpret this provision as implying that 'the number of suppliers must be so small that each of them has a dominant position that could be abused'.[12] However, these questions were never addressed by the WTO adjudicating bodies yet, and it seems that they will have to be decided on a case-by-case basis.

(b) The second condition that should be fulfilled is that the Member involved, *formally or in effect, substantially prevents competition among those suppliers in its territory.* While the words 'formally or in effect' imply a broad coverage of de jure as well as de facto practices taken by a Member, the words 'substantially prevents competition' imply a narrowing condition, according to which not *any* restriction would be covered by this provision. The word 'substantially' is not defined in GATS, and raises interpretative questions in other provisions as well, for example, Article V (see Chapter 10). Thus, in the context of GATT Article XXIV:8, it was interpreted by the Appellate Body in *Turkey – Textiles* that 'substantially all' is not the same as 'all', and is something considerably more than merely 'some'. It was stressed, that although this word offers some flexibility, it is a limited degree of flexibility. In that case the Appellate Body tended to agree that the term 'substantially' appears to provide for both quantitative and qualitative components.[13]

Read together with the rest of this sentence it is clear that it addresses cases where the government *prevents* competition, not only partially restricts it. Based on GATT experience, it is likely that the exact scope of this provision would to be decided on a case-by-case basis, taking into account that this narrow phrasing seems to reflect the balance achieved by GATS drafters between the interest of trade liberalization, on the one hand, and domestic sovereignty, on the other hand.

11.2.1.1.2 Manner of Acting

Article VIII:1 requires the Members to ensure that any monopoly supplier of a service in its territory does not, *in the supply of the monopoly service* in the relevant

12. GATS commentary, n. 9, 219.
13. WT/DS34/R, AB/R Turkey – Restrictions on Imports of Textile and Clothing Products, adopted on 19.11.1999, Appellate Body report, paras 48, 49.

market, act in a manner inconsistent with that Member's obligations under Article II (MFN) and specific commitments. Due to Article VIII:5, this requirement also applies to the exclusive service suppliers addressed in that provision.

11.2.1.1.2.1 'In the Supply of the Monopoly Service'

The scope of this provision is limited to acts of monopolies 'in the supply of the monopoly service'. Thus, it does not cover other services such monopolies may supply, in competition with other suppliers, as well as 'purchase or sale activities of such monopolies (either goods or services) in their input market or for their own consumption'.[14] Since this provision does not explicitly address exclusive service suppliers, but only applies to them due to Article VIII:5, it may be asked whether the same rule would apply, *mutatis mutandis*, to exclusive service suppliers, thus restricting the application of this provisions only to acts taken by them in the supply of services for which they hold exclusivity.

11.2.1.1.2.2 'In its Territory'

The scope of application of Article VIII is further limited by these words, which imply only a territorial application, thus excluding from the scope of application any extra-territorial anti-competitive practices of the monopolies involved.[15]

11.2.1.1.2.3 Application of Disciplines: MFN and Specific Commitments

According to Article VIII:1, a Member is obliged to ensure that, under the conditions mentioned, a monopoly and an exclusive service supplier covered by Article VIII accord to service suppliers and services from any other Member treatment no less favourable than that accorded by it to like services or service suppliers, respectively, from any other country, meaning that the monopoly does not discriminate service suppliers from Members de jure or de facto compared to like service suppliers from any other country. Take, for example, a case where a monopoly or an exclusive supplier which provides public services of strategic importance, for example, infrastructure services: water supply, electricity supply, public transport, and telecommunication. Where the supplier is a monopoly, it is clear that similar service suppliers will not be given access to the market, due to the strategic importance of the service involved. Where it is an exclusive service supplier, this supplier is one of a small group of suppliers authorized by the government to supply a certain service, without competition in the market (paragraph VIII:5). The position of the monopoly or exclusive supplier is not changed by this provision. The Member involved is only expected, according to this provision, not to discriminate as to services which are not connected to the rights of such a monopoly or exclusive supplier. For instance, transportation, general legal and accounting services, ancillary and input services used in the course of its functioning. Domestic and foreign services suppliers should have similar access to the supply of such services to a monopoly/exclusive service supplier. For example, in

14. GATS commentary, n. 9, 210.
15. W. Zdouc, n. 1.

the case of water or electricity supply – consulting services; in the case of telecommunication – advertising services; in the case of transport – financial services.

This obligation does not apply to sectors listed in the MFN exemption list (MFN – Article II – see Chapter 6). In addition, the relevant Member should ensure that this monopoly and/or exclusive service supplier accords to services and service suppliers from other Members treatment no less favourable than that provided for in its specific commitments. Such treatment may refer to national treatment commitments (Article XVI – see Chapter 8), to market access commitments (Article XVII – see Chapter 9) or to additional commitments (see Chapter 7).

The responsibility for the behaviour of monopolies/exclusive service suppliers according to these disciplines is on the governments involved, who authorized or established them, formally or in effect.

By mentioning explicitly the MFN obligation, which is generally applicable once a country joins GATS, and the specific commitments are undertaken, this provision seem to exclude the basic disciplines included in the national treatment and market access articles (Articles XVI and XVII), and all other GATS disciplines. It also implies effectively different levels of application of these standards in different Members, subject to their list of MFN exemptions and specific commitments.

11.2.1.1.3 Article VIII:2

Article VIII:2 extends the Members' responsibility to a situation where Members' monopolies or exclusive service suppliers engage, either directly or through an affiliated company, in the supply of services outside the scope of their monopoly or exclusive suppliers' rights, in a sector or a sub-sector subject to that Member's specific commitments. This provision is meant to prevent the monopoly/exclusive supplier's position from affecting market segments which are meant to operate under competitive conditions.[16] In this case also, the Member involved is responsible to ensure that such a supplier does not abuse its monopoly or exclusive supplier's position to act in its territory in a manner inconsistent with that Member's specific commitments.[17] Take, for example, a case where a monopoly or exclusive supplier's rights refer to some form of public transportation, for example,

16. *Ibid.*, 269.
17. The Panels interpreting the equivalent GATT 1947 Art. XVII consistently interpreted the 'non discrimination' principle in that provision as referring to MFN only: see, for example, G/32 The Panel report on 'Belgian Family Allowances', adopted on 7.11.52, 1S/59, 60 para. 4; L/5504 Canada – Administration of Foreign Investment Review Act, adopted on 7.2.1984, 30S/140, 163, para. 5.16. The interpretation of this provision in GATT 1994 seems to imply a broader understanding of this principle: in WT/DS161,169/R, AB/R Korea – Measures Affecting the Imports of Fresh, Chilled and Frozen Beef, adopted on 10.1.2001 the Panel, in a finding not reviewed by the Appellate Body, considered that the general principle of non-discrimination includes at least the provisions of GATT Arts I (MFN) and III (national treatment). In GATS Art. VIII it is clear that this principle also covers national treatment and market access, subject to the Members schedules.

by busses, and that monopoly or exclusive service supplier provides a service outside its monopoly rights, for example, tourists' transportation, where it competes with other companies, whether directly or by an affiliate. The relevant Member undertook specific commitments providing market access and national treatment to the service of tourists' transportation. According to Article VIII:2, this Member should ensure that the monopoly or exclusive service supplier does not abuse its position, for example, by offering this service at prices considerably lower than acceptable in the market, relying on cross-subsidization with its monopoly or exclusive service supplier's activities, thus undermining the competitive conditions in the market, or exercising pressure, based on its status, on the government ministry responsible for tourism or on municipalities responsible for areas including tourism attractions, in order to gain contracts for tourists' transportation avoiding competition with like service suppliers from other Members.

For the purposes of this provision it does not matter whether a monopoly or an exclusive service supplier abuses its position directly or through an affiliate, due to the broad definition of a juridical person in Article XXVIII(n)(ii-iii).[18]

Abusive act may occur de jure or de facto, for example, where a monopoly supplier exercises an equally abusive conduct against foreign and domestic services and service suppliers, but where such conduct is aimed at only domestic suppliers, it is not covered by this provision, since an international agreement does not cover purely domestic affairs.

Unlike Article VIII:1 which explicitly refers to MFN treatment, Article VIII:2 only refers to the specific commitments. As a result, while the exercise of monopoly rights is subject to the MFN treatment obligation, when the monopoly/exclusive service supplier competes outside the scope of its monopoly/exclusive supplier's rights, it is not subject to the MFN treatment obligation.[19]

11.2.1.1.3.1 'Affiliated Company'

The meaning of this term may be derived from the definition of 'juridical person' in Article XXVIII(n), which provides, *inter alia*:

> a juridical person is:
>
> . . .
>
> (ii) 'controlled' by persons of a Member if such persons have the power to name the majority of its directors or otherwise legally direct its actions.

18. W. Zdouc, n. 1, 269.
19. W. Zdouc, *ibid.*, 270, suggests two possible explanation for this situation:

> One answer to that question could be that the direct exercise of monopoly rights is more likely to have trade distortive effects than the abuse of monopoly rights in a market which is otherwise operating under competitive conditions. Another answer could be that GATS negotiators intended to create a staggered system of MFN obligations depending on whether or not a Member intends to enter into specific commitments in respect of a particular sector or mode of supply.

(iii) 'affiliated' with another person when it controls, or is controlled by, that other person; or when it and the other person are both controlled by the same person.

See detailed analysis in Chapter 4.

11.2.1.1.3.2 Scope of Monopoly Rights

Monopoly rights are derived from the definition of 'monopoly supplier of a service' in Article XXVIII(h) (see above). This definition refers to the 'relevant market', meaning that in order to determine the existence of a monopoly, the relevant market should be defined first. In the WTO context, the concepts of 'directly competitive' and 'substitutable' products were developed in GATT jurisprudence. The Panel in *Mexico-Telecoms* discussed this notion in the context of the Reference Paper on Basic Telecommunications (see Chapter 16), providing that substitution of products in the eyes of the consumer is central for market definition.[20] However, a different approach may develop in the context of this provision, or rather a case-by-case approach may be adopted. As broad as the definition of the market gets, the less dominant a position will this supplier have. For example, a monopoly supplier in the milk market might not be considered a monopoly if the relevant market is defined as the milk and milk products' market. The relevant market should be defined both in terms of the services supplied and in geographical terms.[21]

11.2.1.1.3.3 'Abuse of Monopoly Position'

This term is not defined in GATS. Nevertheless, it is clear that if a monopoly is 'the sole supplier' of a service and this position is supported by the government, abuse of it in the supply of a service outside the scope of its monopoly rights could amount to a behaviour that distorts competition, for example, by lowering the prices considerably due to cross-subsidization, by the use of competitors' information with anti-competitive results or by not denying access to information about essential facilities necessary to provide services.[22]

11.2.1.1.4 Article VIII:3

The relative weakness of this provision is revealed in Article VIII:3: no real sanction is applied to Members acting in a manner inconsistent with the former paragraphs. A Member which believes that another Member is acting inconsistently with Article VIII:1,2 may approach the Council for Trade in Services. Consequently, the Council 'may' (namely: is not obliged to) request from the Member establishing, maintaining or authorizing such suppliers, to provide

20. WT/DS204/R *Mexico – Telecoms*, n. 5, Panel report, para. 7.152.
21. GATS commentary, n. 9, 214.
22. *Ibid.*, 215–217.

specific information concerning the relevant operations. Such an act may impose on that Member some peer pressure, but no particular sanction is provided for.

11.2.1.1.5 Article VIII:4

Article VIII:4 provides for the notification[23] to the Council for Trade in Services of monopoly or exclusive supplier's rights as to services covered by the specific commitments, after the entry into force of GATS, no later than three months before their intended grant.

However, the grant, by Members of new monopolies or exclusive service suppliers' rights regarding the supply of a service covered by its specific commitments after joining GATS, is viewed by the agreement as a modification of such commitments, allowing some material compensation. Thus, the provisions of paragraphs 2, 3 and 4 of Article XXI, namely the procedure allowing the requirement for compensation due to modification of schedules (see Chapter 15) shall apply.

In conclusion, this is a relatively week provision, based on a cautious balance between the will to restrict monopoly and exclusive suppliers from undermining competition, on the one hand, and probably, the pressure and strong political power exercised by these influential bodies on their governments, on the other hand. The final outcome mainly provides for some transparency and subjects these bodies, through their governments, to the minimal standard of acting in compliance with the MFN discipline and the specific commitments on market access and national treatment taken by these governments.

Alleged violation under this provision may be challenged by requests for information (Article VIII:3) that may lead to dispute settlement.

11.2.1.2 Business Practices – Article IX

Article IX provides:[24]

> Business Practices
>
> 1. Members recognize that certain business practices of service suppliers, other than those falling under Article VIII, may restrain competition and thereby restrict trade in services.
> 2. Each Member shall, at the request of any other Member, enter into consultations with a view to eliminating practices referred to in paragraph 1. The Member addressed shall accord full and sympathetic consideration to

23. Notification is made according to the format determined by S/L/5 Council for Trade in Services Guidelines for Notifications under the General Agreement on Trade in Services, adopted by the Council for Trade in Services on 1 Mar. 1995, 4.4.1995.
24. This provision is based on a consultation procedure introduced by GATT Council decision on 'Arrangements for Consultations on Restrictive Practices' in 18.11.1960 (BIDS 9th Supplement, 20) and Art. 53:2 on 'special procedures with respect to services' of Ch. V on 'restrictive business practices' of the Havana Charter 1947/48: W. Zdouc, n. 1, 271–272.

> such a request and shall cooperate through the supply of publicly available non-confidential information of relevance to the matter in question. The Member addressed shall also provide other information available to the requesting Member, subject to its domestic law and to the conclusion of satisfactory agreement concerning the safeguarding of its confidentiality by the requesting Member.

This Article refers to business practices which are not covered by Article VIII, namely: service suppliers who maintain dominant positions in service markets but do not have a special status granted by the state. In this sense, Article IX is novel in the WTO law because it clearly concerns *private* business conduct.[25]

This Article recognizes that additional business practices, other than monopolies and exclusive service suppliers, may also restrict trade in services. However, since these practices are considered to be relatively less adversely affecting market competition, the obligations provided for by this Article are even weaker than these provided for in Article VIII, concerning monopolies and exclusive service suppliers.

11.2.1.2.1 'Certain Business Practices of Service Suppliers'

This language is very broad. It allows for an inclusive interpretation that could expand to literally any such practices of service suppliers that may somehow 'restrain competition.' In practice, this expression may cover horizontal anti-competitive practices such as cartels, price fixing, limiting output or dividing markets, but also, under certain circumstances, R&D joint ventures, consortia and cooperative arrangements for product standard setting procedures. It may further apply to horizontal, vertical and conglomerate mergers.[26] It may also cover vertical arrangements,[27] struck between undertakings involved in different successive stages of the production, distribution and marketing chain, for example, exclusive dealing, exclusive territories, tying arrangements and release price maintenance. Such a practice was the subject of the request for consultations in *Japan – Measures Affecting Distribution Services.*[28] The United States' complaint referred to the Japanese Large Scale Retail Store Law, which effectively formed a vertically integrated distribution system by regulating floor space, business hours and holidays of supermarkets and department stores. The United States claimed that this

25. W. Zdouc, n. 1, 296.
26. GATS commentary, n. 9, 227.
27. Such vertical arrangement were dealt with, although not in the context of this provision, in WT/DS27/R, AB/R, European Communities – Regime for the Importation, Sale and Distribution of Bananas, adopted on 25.9.1997, Panel report para. 7.346 referring to the bananas market, and in WT/DS139,142/R Canada – Certain Measures Affecting the Automotive Industry, adopted on 19.6. 2000, Panel report para. 10.253, referring to the automotive industry.
28. WT/DS45/1 Japan – Measures Affecting Distribution Services, request for consultations by the United States, 20.6.1996; WT/DS45/1/Add.1 Japan – Measures Affecting Distribution Services, request for further consultations by the United States, 26.9.1996; GATS commentary, n. 9, 226.

law linked the Japanese wholesale and retail distributors in a way having an exclusionary effect on foreign distribution service suppliers, but finally chose not to pursue a case under GATS but rather to pursue a more specific case on photographic film and paper under GATT.[29]

This provision may also apply to situations of abuse of dominant position in a market. Thus, in *Mexico – Telecoms,* the case dealt with the terms of connection between the foreign suppliers of certain telecommunications services with the domestic supplier in charge of the domestic infrastructure, which was necessary for the supply of the foreign service. In that context it was established that the Mexican domestic supplier was a 'major supplier', since it 'possessed the "ability to materially affect the terms of participation" in the relevant market, primarily through its ability to impose its negotiated settlement rate for an international route on its competitors'.[30] The determination of dominance requires an elaborated economic analysis on a case-by-case basis.

11.2.1.2.2 'May' [Restrain Competition]

The word 'may' also implies a broad interpretation: some anti-competitive practices, such as cartels, are subject to *ex post* review, while others, such as mergers and acquisitions, are subject to *ex ante* review. The expression 'may restrain competition' implies that the *potential* of doing so is enough, hence subjecting both categories to this provision.[31]

11.2.1.2.3 'Anti-competitive Practices'

The general idea behind this expression is clear: it refers to business practices that modify the competitive conditions in a market, to the benefit of domestic services/service suppliers, in a manner adversely affecting foreign services/service suppliers. However, being generally phrased, it is open to further interpretation on a case-by-case basis. Since it does not specify which practices are covered by it, this provision leaves a broad scope of discretion to the Member involved. A pro-liberalization reading of this provision would claim, that it would apply 'to practices of Members' service suppliers, as long as these have an effect restraining competition and restricting trade in services'.[32]

This expression was still not interpreted by the WTO adjudicating bodies in the context of Article IX. However, in *Mexico-Telecoms*[33] the adjudicating bodies interpreted the same expression in the Reference Paper on Telecommunications, aiming at preventing anti-competitive practices of major basic telecommunications

29. GATS commentary, n. 9, 226.
30. WT/DS204/R *Mexico-Telecoms*, n. 5, para. 7.158.
31. See comparative analysis of other international instruments, applying such a broad interpretation that includes potentially restrictive practices in GATS commentary, n. 9, 228.
32. GATS commentary, n. 9, 223.
33. WT/DS204/R, n. 5.

suppliers (see Chapter 16). Despite the difference in context, some conclusions may be drawn[34] from this decision concerning the possible interpretation of this expression in Article IX:

- The panel interpreted the expression 'anti-competitive practices' in the Reference Paper context in a wide manner, referring to the practices specified in it as merely indicative. It may be even easier to adopt a similar approach in the context of Article IX that does not even include an indicative list, and in addition provides for much less specific, and weaker obligations than the Reference Paper.
- Interpreting the specific examples referred to by the Reference Paper the panel in *Mexico – Telecoms* noted that this expression may include pricing actions,[35] horizontal coordination between undertaking operating in the same level of production and unilateral actions by major suppliers, which are not subject to any agreement.[36]
- In interpreting this expression the panel referred to the concept of anti-competitive practices embodied in other international instruments.[37]
- The panel stressed, that restrictive business practices could emanate from a provision of domestic law or regulation, and such practices would not be justified due to their source.[38]
- In examining whether the rates required by the domestic supplier for inter-connection of competitor foreign service suppliers to the domestic infra-structure held by it is a restrictive business practice, the Panel compared these rates, *inter alia,* to 'gray market' prices as well as to termination rates in other international routes, and also analysed financial compensation arrangements for the allocation of market share between domestic suppliers, that did not apply to foreign competitors. Analysis of all these factors made the Panel conclude that restrictive business practices existed in the relevant market.[39]

11.2.1.2.4 'Restrain Competition and Thereby Restrict Trade in Services'

Article IX applies only where two cumulative elements exist: (1) restraint of competition; (2) which causes to the restriction of trade in services, as trade restriction is foreseen to be *caused by* practices restraining competition. Therefore, it should be first established that a business practice restraining competition exists in

34. GATS commentary, n. 9, 228–230.
35. Such as cross-subsidization (n. 5, Panel report, para. 7.232), price-fixing cartel (n. 5, Panel report, para.7.262).
36. WT/DS204/R *Mexico-Telecom*, n. 5, para. 7.232.
37. Including the Havana Charter, the UN Set of Multilaterally Agreed Equitable Principles for the Control of restrictive Business Practices, the OECD Council Recommendation Concerning Effective Action against Hardcore Cartels, and the work of the WTO Working Group on the Interaction between Trade and Competition Policy.
38. WT/DS204/R *Mexico-Telecom*, n. 5, para 7.244.
39. *Ibid.*, paras 7.204–7.216, 7.264.

the market. Then, the restriction of trade in services should be proved. In fact, it seems that the complaining party would have to establish a causal link between these two elements to fulfil the requirement of this provision.

11.2.1.2.5 Practical Implications of Article IX

11.2.1.2.5.1 Consultations

This provision does not impose on the Members any obligation to maintain competition regulation. It only provides for consultations[40] between the Members involved, which may not be followed by any practical measures or sanctions. The consultations provided for by this provision are subject to two obligations:

(1) Full sympathetic consideration to the request for consultations should be accorded. This is an expression of the 'good faith' principle of public international law international law.[41]
(2) The supply of relevant information, which is divided to two categories:
   - *Publicly available non-confidential* information of relevance to the matter in question. The supply of this information is not subject to any conditions.
   - In practical terms, it seems that the decision about which information will, thus, be provided, will be, at least in the first stage, subject to the full discretion of the Member with which consultations are requested. Additional or complementary information may then be requested by the complaining party. In both cases, the supply or non-supply of information will be subject to the good faith standard.[42]
   - It seems from the language of this provision that the two conditions are cumulative, namely the information thus revealed should be both publicly available *and* non-confidential.
   - '*Other information*' available to the requesting Member – the supply of this kind of information is subject to the domestic law of the requested country, as well as to the conclusion of satisfactory agreement concerning the safeguarding of its confidentiality by the requesting Member.
   - The term 'other information' is not interpreted by the agreement but from the context it may be concluded that this is information which is not publicly available, and is confidential. Confidentiality in the business context may be a result of privacy protection rules, commercial secrets, etc.

40. M.C. Malaguti, n. 2, 131, believes that it is impossible that the only meaning of para. 1 is to enable consultations according to para. 2, because this option is already open for the Members due to Art. 4.2 of the DSU.
41. This principle is also reflected in Art. 4.3 DSU concerning consultations as a first stage to the initiation of dispute settlement procedures.
42. GATS commentary, n. 9, 231.

The supply of this kind of information is subject to two cumulative conditions:

(1) *The domestic law of the requested country* – if that law prohibits the supply of the information at stake it will not be supplied. If that law provides for conditions subject to which the information may be supplied, these conditions should be met.

(2) If the law of the requested country allows for the supply of the information requested, the information may be supplied *subject* to the conclusion of a satisfactory agreement concerning the safeguarding of its confidentiality by the requesting Member. The necessity for the conclusion of such an agreement is drawn from the word 'and'. Such an agreement is common, for example, in the context of bilateral treaties for the avoidance of double taxation, where it forms an integral part of the provision. Here it is provided that in order to obtain the information, a separate agreement should be concluded. This practice may complicate things, particularly since it will probably be considered in the course of consultations, where the parties already may be in conflicting positions. Thus, 'this leaves substantial leeway for the providing Member, which is not being bound by specific procedural rules, who may deny or delay indefinitely, the flow of information by claiming insufficient safeguarding of confidentiality or by requesting specific and/or elaborate preconditions in its domestic regulation'.[43]

It is interesting to note, that unlike other treaties (e.g., treaties for the avoidance of double taxation), high administrative burden and high costs are not mentioned as reasons for non-revelation of the information.

Consultations are obligatory, and may lead to further cooperation and coordination between the Members involved.

11.2.1.2.5.2 Sanctions

Since this Article is included in part II of GATS, and all the Members are committed to the MFN discipline as well as to their specific commitments on market access and national treatment, if it turns out that such a restrictive business practice is inconsistent with these obligations, the relevant procedures and sanctions attached to their non-compliance may be invoked.

11.2.1.2.5.3 Basis for Further Negotiations

The application of this provision should be examined on a case-by-case basis, and maybe if a certain restrictive practice will turn out to be common in many Members, a more specific treatment concerning it will be considered in future negotiations.

43. *Ibid.*, 232.

11.2.1.3 The Disadvantages of Existing Disciplines

Treatment of competitive conditions in a market according to existing disciplines reflects the following disadvantages:

- GATS relevant provisions do not apply to private restrictive business practices, which are not supported by governments.
- GATS provisions concentrate on competition in the domestic market. Practices affecting the export market or the lack of governmental regulation concerning the behaviour of firms under its jurisdiction in foreign markets are not covered by it.
- Even though GATS, unlike GATT, applies to suppliers, it does not include disciplines referring to the relation between competition and foreign direct investments.

11.2.2 The Development of New Disciplines in the WTO Context

The creation of conditions encouraging market competition, and thus encouraging international trade, is discussed in the WTO context in the Working Group on the Interaction between Trade and Competition Policy. These discussions are not specific to trade in services, but they refer to this aspect.

The development of multi-national competition rules requires harmonization, or at least approximation, of these rules by the countries involved.[44] It is difficult to lead such a move in the WTO context, which is based on the participation of many different countries with different rules, reflecting different approaches and policies to this subject. In the WTO, even common purposes or starting points concerning this matter were not defined.

The lack of common disciplines concerning this subject prevents the use of the violation cause in dispute settlement proceedings, since without disciplines there could be no violation thereof. Such practices may thus only be subject to dispute settlement based on the non-violation cause, which is much more difficult to prove and provides for substantially weaker remedies (see Chapter 17).

Another difficulty stems from the fact that the WTO agreements apply to the governmental authorities of the Members, and thus their effect on private practices of private entities will be limited in any case. Nevertheless, some minimum rules could be developed.[45] Such rules may refer to cross-subsidization, the development of common accounting standards concerning monopolies and exclusive service suppliers, common agreement on the services so supplied that would be subject to licensing requirements and the common requirements applicable. One successful attempt to develop pro-competitive rules in GATS context took

44. For suggestions for such disciplines see: A. Mattoo, 'Shaping Future GATS Rules for Trade in Services', *The World Bank* (2001), 14, <www-wds.worldbank.org>.
45. See Report (1998) of the Working Group on the Interaction Between Trade and Competition Policy to the General Council, 8 Dec. 1998.

place concerning basic telecommunications (see Chapter 16), and its lessons may form a basis for further such attempts.

The implementation of such rules by the Members, once developed, would require finance and skilled labour. Therefore, it would be particularly burdensome for developing countries.

GATS treatment of competition is common to its treatment in other WTO agreements,[46] due to the same reasons. In any case, GATS, like the other WTO agreements, lacks effective mechanisms for the exchange of information and enhancement of international cooperation concerning these subjects.

11.3 CONCLUSION

Monopolies and exclusive service providers are two common commercial practices, emanating, to some extent, from the comprehensive nature of some services, considered as 'essential facilities' to market development, as well as from the size of the country involved. Such practices may be developed regarding telecommunications, financial services, transportation services, energy services etc. GATS disciplines concerning this issue have a narrow scope of application. They seem to concentrate on 'reasonable' and 'cost oriented' conditions of access to networks and pricing of services, attempting to subject these restrictive practices to some competition rules. However, these disciplines are not comprehensive, and their further development might encounter difficulties emanating from the considerable variance and the highly technical issues raised across various sectors. This situation may call for the development of future sector-specific disciplines.[47]

46. See, for example, Art. 40 of the TRIPs (Trade Related Intellectual Property Rights) Agreement and Art. 9 of the TRIMs (Trade Related Investment Measures) Agreement.
47. A. Mattoo & P. Sauvé, *Domestic Regulation and Service Trade Liberalization*, The World Bank and Oxford University Press (2003), 225.

Chapter 12

Administrative Standards and Recognition of Professional Qualifications

12.1 INTRODUCTION

Domestic regulation is a major instrument to promote domestic policy goals. It is a means to achieve economic efficiency and improve allocation of resources. It may further serve to protect consumers, and in cases of natural monopolies, to ensure that any major supplier of essential facilities provides access to all new operators at cost-based rates, and that cost-effective prices are charged. Domestic regulation may intervene to achieve socially desirable levels of availability and continuity of a service, to promote re-distribution, to transfer income from economic rents forming unjustifiable extra profit, gained by producers or suppliers, back to the consumers, and to prevent discrimination in the regulated market.[1]

Regulation may assume the form of command-and-control, or rather set market incentives to follow them.[2]

At the same time, domestic regulation and their administrative exercise could form a barrier to international trade in services, either intentionally or non-intentionally[3] (see Chapter 1). From GATS point of view, it is important to prevent, or at least diminish, this option as much as possible. The underlying dilemma is,

1. P. Delimatsis, *International Trade in Services and Domestic Regulations – Necessity, Transparency and Regulatory Diversity*, Oxford University Press (2007), 87–90.
2. *Ibid.*, 92.
3. Concerning the impact of domestic regulation on the choice of servicing a foreign market see: H. K. Nordas & H. Kox, 'Quantifying Regulatory Barriers to Services Trade', *OECD Trade Policy Paper No. 85* (2008), <www.oecd.org>. S. Schwellnus, 'The Effect of Domestic Regulation on Trade in Services Revisited', *CEPII, Working Paper No. 2007-08*, <www.economie-internationale.fr>.

thus, 'how best to strengthen disciplines without unduly curtailing national regulatory freedom'.[4] In *US – Gambling* the Panel defined the limits of regulatory sovereignty providing that it 'ends whenever rights of other Members under GATS are impaired'.[5]

Two provisions in GATS deal directly with domestic regulation: Article VI, titled 'domestic regulation' and Article VII, titled 'recognition'.

Article VI:1-3,6 refers to administration and review of domestic measures covered by GATS, without addressing the instruments used and the goals pursued by domestic regulation.[6] Article VI:4 includes a mandate for the development of future multilateral disciplines referring to licensing, qualification and technical standards, and Article VI:5 sets a mechanism for provisional application for the main principles underlying the future disciplines.

Article VI of GATS provides:

Domestic Regulation

1. In sectors where specific commitments are undertaken, each Member shall ensure that all measures of general application affecting trade in services are administered in a reasonable, objective and impartial manner.
2. (a) Each Member shall maintain or institute as soon as practicable judicial, arbitral or administrative tribunals or procedures which provide, at the request of an affected service supplier, for the prompt review of, and where justified, appropriate remedies for, administrative decisions affecting trade in services. Where such procedures are not independent of the agency entrusted with the administrative decision concerned, the Member shall ensure that the procedures in fact provide for an objective and impartial review.
   (b) The provisions of subparagraph (a) shall not be construed to require a Member to institute such tribunals or procedures where this would be inconsistent with its constitutional structure or the nature of its legal system.
3. Where authorization is required for the supply of a service on which a specific commitment has been made, the competent authorities of a Member shall, within a reasonable period of time after the submission of an application considered complete under domestic laws and regulations, inform the applicant of the decision concerning the application. At the

4. A. Mattoo & P. Sauvé (eds), *Domestic Regulation and Service Trade Liberalization*, The World Bank and Oxford University Press (2003), 3. For a suggestion to adopt, in GATS context, standards employed in domestic US law to determine whether regulation unduly interfere with trade see: D. W. Leeborn, 'regulatory Discrimination in Domestic United States Law: A Model for the GATS?', in A. Mattoo & P. Sauvé, 43–55.
5. WT/DS285/R United States – Measures Affecting the Cross-Border Supply of Gambling and Betting Services, adopted on 22.5.2007, Panel report para. 6.316.
6. R. Worfrum, P. T. Stoll & C. Feinäugle (eds), *WTO – Trade in Services*, Max Planck Commentaries on World Trade Law, Martinus Mijnhoff Publishers, Leiden, Boston (2008) (hereby: GATS commentary), 168.

request of the applicant, the competent authorities of the Member shall provide, without undue delay, information concerning the status of the application.

4. With a view to ensuring that measures relating to qualification requirements and procedures, technical standards and licensing requirements do not constitute unnecessary barriers to trade in services, the Council for Trade in Services shall, through appropriate bodies it may establish, develop any necessary disciplines. Such disciplines shall aim to ensure that such requirements are, *inter alia*:
   (a) based on objective and transparent criteria, such as competence and the ability to supply the service;
   (b) not more burdensome than necessary to ensure the quality of the service;
   (c) in the case of licensing procedures, not in themselves a restriction on the supply of the service.
5. (a) In sectors in which a Member has undertaken specific commitments, pending the entry into force of disciplines developed in these sectors pursuant to paragraph 4, the Member shall not apply licensing and qualification requirements and technical standards that nullify or impair such specific commitments in a manner which:
      (i) does not comply with the criteria outlined in subparagraphs 4(a), (b) or (c); and
      (ii) could not reasonably have been expected of that Member at the time the specific commitments in those sectors were made.
   (b) In determining whether a Member is in conformity with the obligation under paragraph 5(a), account shall be taken of international standards of relevant international organizations applied by that Member.
6. In sectors where specific commitments regarding professional services are undertaken, each Member shall provide for adequate procedures to verify the competence of professionals of any other Member.

This article aims to create more transparent domestic regulatory decision making, implementation and administration. This aim has not been fully accomplished during the Uruguay Round. Therefore, this article includes a mix of disciplines for immediate application and disciplines to be developed in the future.

To a certain extent, Article VI forms a third, complementary dimension to Article XVI (market access) and to Article XVII (national treatment). However, the border between Article VI, on the one hand, and Articles XVI and XVII, on the other hand, is expected to be based on the fact that Article VI deals with *bona fide* regulatory measures, while the other two provisions deal with *discriminatory* measures.[7]

---

7. Fields of public policy objectives' regulation which are not interfered by GATS include: universal service, cross subsidies of services and service suppliers, quality requirements, prudential measures, price capping (minimum or maximum non-discriminating price), protection of natural resources.

12.2 SCOPE OF APPLICATION: ARTICLE VI:1

Article VI:1 establishes the general goal underlying the entire Article, specified by its other paragraphs, calling for reasonable, objective, and impartial administration of measures of general application affecting trade in services. Illuminating the other paragraphs of this provision, this goal may serve as an interpretative guide to them.

The term 'measures affecting trade in services' is broadly defined (see Chapter 4). The description '*of general application*' implies an unidentified number of cases, which are typically of an abstract nature.[8] In the context of the equivalent GATT Article X:1 this expression was interpreted as implying 'that the actions in question would have to have a significant impact on the overall administration of the law, and not simply on the outcome in a single case in question'.[9] This description characterizes laws, regulation, general administrative acts but seems to exclude, for example, legal acts aimed at specific persons. However, according to some commentators, such individual measures are also covered by this provision since they are typically the result of a general measure. This approach may be reflected by the Panel in GATT case *Japan – Film*, which held that this expression should cover 'administrative rulings in individual cases where such rulings establish or revise principles or criteria applicable in future cases'.[10] Others criticize this view, contending that it 'ignores the difference between the scope of application and its effect', suggesting that this description would apply to individual cases only 'in legal systems where courts or administration have the competence to establish a general principle by deciding an individual case'.[11] In the context of the equivalent GATT Article X:3, the United States challenged the EC customs administration 'as a whole or overall'. The Appellate Body agreed with the Panel that 'there is nothing in the DSU nor in other WTO agreements that would prevent a complaining Member from challenging a responding Member's system as a whole or overall'.[12] Nevertheless it was stressed that 'a panel request must identify, with sufficient degree of specificity, the measures that constitute or underline the legal system challenged "as a whole or overall", and must also provide the legal basis of the complaint (or the claims) so as to present the problem clearly'.[13]

8. GATS commentary, n. 6, 169.
9. WT/DS184/R, AB/R United State – Anti Dumping Measures on Certain Hot-Rolled Steel Products from Japan, adopted on 23.8.2001, Panel report, para. 7.268.
10. WT/DS44/R Japan – Measures Affecting Consumer Photographic Film and Paper, adopted on 22.4.1998, Panel report, para. 10.388.
11. GATS commentary, n. 6, 170.
12. WT/DS315/AB/R EC – Selected Customs Matters, adopted on 11.12.2006, Appellate Body report, para. 166.
13. *Ibid.* In that case the complaint concentrated on four legal instruments, administered collectively: *ibid.*, paras 174–175. In that case the Panel and Appellate Body seem to have agreed the principle, but not its application to the facts of the case, as the Panel dismissed the United States' claim concerning the 'design and structure' of the European Communities' customs system as a separate claim which did not refer to specific measures, while the Appellate Body viewed it as

This broad scope of application is narrowed by the reference to 'sectors where specific commitments were undertaken' by Members. Consequently, the scope of application of this provision varies from one Member to another, depending on the sectors where specific commitments were undertaken by each Member.

This language implies that the obligation to administer in reasonable, objective and impartial manner is not applicable to measures in sectors where no specific commitments were undertaken.[14] Due to this language, the obligation would apply to measures that were not included in the specific commitments, if they belong to a sector in which specific commitments were undertaken, and even if the scope of commitments taken in this sector is minimal.

12.3 THE LEGAL OBLIGATION

12.3.1 The Subject of Reference: Administration, not Substance

In sectors where specific commitments were undertaken, the relevant Member is required to ensure that all measures of general application affecting trade in services are administered in 'a uniform, impartial and reasonable manner'. It should be stressed, that these standards refer to the *administration, not to the substance*, of these measures.[15]

12.3.1.1 Comparison to Article X:3(a) of GATT

The equivalent GATT Article X:3(a) provides that 'each Member shall administer, in *a uniform, impartial and reasonable*' manner, all its laws, regulations, decisions and rulings referring to trade covered by this agreement.[16]

The adjudicative experience gained in the interpretation of this provision does not reflect a clear-cut distinction between the substance of measure at stake and its

---

part of the claim, referring to this claim as explaining why the specific measures were administered in a manner inconsistent with Art. X.

14. This approach deviates from the equivalent GATT provision, Art. X:3(a), where this obligation covers all measures specified in GATT Art. X:1. Comparably, GATS Art. VI:1 can be seen as both narrower and broader in scope, depending on the criteria used: P. Delimatsis, n. 1, 97.
15. WT/DS27/R, AB/R European Communities – Regime for the Importation, Sale and Distribution of Bananas, adopted on 25.9.1997. The Appellate Body repeated the line of analysis held in WT/DS69/AB/R European Communities – Measures Affecting the Importations of certain Poultry Products, adopted on 23.7.1998, para. 115.
16. According to P. Delimatsis, 'Due Process and "Good" Regulation Embedded in the GATS – Disciplining Regulatory Behaviour in Services Through Art. VI of the GATS', *10 Journal of International Economic Law* (2006), 13, 21, this provision has a broader scope of application than the parallel GATS provision, which applies these disciplines only in sectors where specific commitments were undertaken. On the other hand, Art. X:3(a) of GATT applies only to specific categories of measures, while Art. VI of GATS has a potential broader scope of application to 'measures of general application affecting trade in services' in sectors where specific commitments were undertaken.

administration: in *EC – Bananas III* the Appellate Body distinguished between the measures and their administration, holding that the measures themselves fall outside the scope of GATT Article X and should be examined according to other provisions in the agreement.[17] In *Argentina – Hides and Leather*[18] the Panel was of the opinion that a measure can be challenged under GATT Article X if its substantive content is administrative by nature. In *EC – Selected Customs Matters*[19] the Panel, repeating the distinction between *the measures* and *their administration*, warned of an approach that would blur this distinction. However, in the same case, the Appellate Body, although citing previous jurisprudence concerning Article X:3(a) making this distinction, effectively recognized that the substance of a measure, affecting the administration of *another* measure, such as penalty provisions and audit procedures, may be challenged under GATT Article X:3.[20]

This opinion of the Appellate Body might have far-reaching future consequences. It clearly seems to deviate from the rational of this provision, which applies legal standards, common in administrative law, to administrative acts. In the context of administrative domestic law, penalty provisions and audit procedures would seldom be considered as administrative acts. The same logic should apply here. The Panel analysis in this case seems to be more cautious and lead to a clearer distinction between the two categories of measures, preventing a possible blur of them. It would thus be preferable if the Panel's approach is adopted in the context of both GATT Article X:3 and GATS Article VI. However, in light of this decision, the adoption of this broader interpretation, developed in GATT context, to GATS context cannot be automatically ruled out.

12.3.2 The Burden of Proof

In the context of the equivalent GATT Article XI:3, it was determined that the complainant has to establish a *causal link* between the examined instrument and the lack of its uniform, impartial or reasonable administration.[21] Due to the similar phrasing of the equivalent GATS provision, it is likely that a similar analysis would be adopted in GATS context.

12.3.3 Uniform, Impartial, Reasonable

There is neither an indication in the language of either GATT or GATS provision as to the interpretation of these standards, nor any answer to the question of

17. WT/DS27/R, AB/R *EC – Bananas* III, n. 15; WT/DS69/R, AB/R *EC-Poultry*, n. 15.
18. WT/DS155/R, Argentina – Measures Affecting the Export of Bovine Hides and Import of Finished Leather, adopted on 16.2.2001, Panel report, paras 11.71–11.72.
19. WT/DS315/R *EC – Selected Customs Matters*, n. 12, Panel report, para. 7.113, 7.115.
20. WT/DS315/AB/R, *EC – Selected Customs Matters*, n. 12, Appellate Body report, para. 200.
21. *Ibid.*, 200–201.

whether a permanent, single interpretation to each of these words should be adopted to them, or rather should they be approached on a case-by-case basis.

Uniform – did the drafters mean formal or substantial uniformity? Bearing in mind that the former option may sometimes cause effective discrimination, maybe the latter option should be preferred.

Impartial – this standard is relatively the clearest of the three, providing for objectivity and neutrality of application of the specific commitments.

Reasonable – reasonability is always relative and depends upon the circumstances and the alternatives, as well as on the discretion of the person judging it.

Considering the nature of standards involved, the purpose of GATS: enhancement of trade liberalization in services and its expansion, and the sensitivity of the counter-interest of domestic regulation sovereignty, it seems preferable to opt for a general case-by-case approach in the application of these standards.

The meaning attributed to these words would be a function of the adjudicating bodies' policy. One possibility is that this provision would be employed and developed by them to impose a substantive obligation of proportionality in connection with the administration of domestic regulation.[22]

However, some indication concerning possible trends of interpretation may be found in the interpretation of equivalent standards in GATT Article XI:3.

Uniform – in the context of GATT 1947, this language was interpreted as preventing 'in the treatment accorded to imported goods, discrimination based on country of origin', as well as 'the application of one set of regulations and procedures with respect to some contracting parties and a different set with respect to the others'.[23] Dispute settlement decisions of GATT 1947 panels referring to this expression found the allocation of import licenses to competing domestic producers unreasonable.[24] However, minor, negligible differences in administrative treatment were overlooked.[25]

In the context of GATT 1994 this word was narrowly interpreted, not to be read as a broad anti-discrimination provision, but rather as implying uniform administration of measures between individual shippers and even with respect to the same person in different times and different places.[26]

It was provided that a Member cannot be considered to fulfil this requirement when its trade regulations vary, or every trade operator is treated differently over time, in different places and with respect to other trade operators. It was stressed

22. J. P. Trachtman, 'Lessons for the GATS from Existing WTO Rules on Domestic Regulation', in A. Mattoo & P. Sauvé, n. 4, 57, 65.
23. L/3149 A note by the Director General, dated 29.11.68, Analytical Index – Guide to GATT Law and Practice, Geneva (1995), 297.
24. L/5623 the Panel Report on 'Japanese Measures on Imports of Leather', adopted on 15/16.5.1984, 31S/94, 114.
25. L/6491, the Panel Report on 'EEC- Restrictions on Imports of Dessert Apples', adopted on 22.6.1989, 36S/93, para. 12.30.
26. WT/DS155/R *Argentina – Hides and Leather*, n. 18, Panel report, paras 11.81–11.84.

that a Member must ensure that its laws are applied consistently and predictably,[27] but not necessarily identically.[28] It was further determined, that there is no single concept of uniformity in the context of Article X:3(a), since the form, nature and scale of administration may vary from case to case. Thus, for example, the examination may refer to a single, specific legislative provision or rather to the administration of an entire system.[29] Moreover, uniformity can be achieved in a reasonable period of time, considering the number of products that cross a border every day and the number of officials involved, but even then, 'administration should not fall below certain minimum standards of due process, which encompass notions such as notice, transparency, fairness and equity'.[30]

Reasonable – in the context of GATT Article X:1, an administration of a measure was regarded 'reasonable' being in accordance with generally accepted standards of rationality and of sound judgment.[31] Thus, a product classification process that inherently contained the possibility of revealing confidential business information was considered as an unreasonable manner of administration.[32] According to one opinion, this standard is less advanced than 'necessary' or 'proportionate' and should not be interpreted as having the same meaning.[33]

Impartial – in GATT context, it was determined that where a party with a commercial interest, but no legal interest, is allowed to participate in an export transaction, there is an inherent danger for the application of customs laws, regulations and rules in a partial manner, potentially giving persons with adverse commercial interests access to confidential information for which they have no right.[34]

In *US – Shrimp*[35] the Appellate Body determined that:

> The non-transparent and *ex parte* nature of the internal governmental procedures . . . as well as the fact that countries whose applications are denied do not receive formal notice of such denial, nor of the reasons for the denial, and the fact, too, that there is no formal legal procedure for review of, or appeal from, a denial of an application, are all contrary to the spirit, if not the letter, of Article X:3 of the GATT 1994.

27. These notions fold the enhancement of greater confidence in the system, greater transparency in decision making, the promotion of greater efficiency through diminution of transaction costs: P. Delimatsis, n. 16, 28.
28. WT/DS315/R *EC – Selected Customs Matters*, n. 12, Panel report, para. 7.124; WT/DS155/R *Argentina – Hides and Leather*, n. 18, Panel report, paras 11.83, 11.84.
29. *Ibid.*, Panel report, para. 7.127.
30. *Ibid.*, Panel report, para. 7.134.
31. WT/DS302/R Dominican Republic – Measures Affecting the Importation and Internal Sale of Cigarettes, adopted on 19.5.2005, Panel report, para. 7.385.
32. WT/DS155/R *Argentina – Hides and Leather*, n. 18, Panel report, para. 11.94.
33. GATS commentary, n. 6, 171.
34. WT/DS155/R *Argentina – Hides and Leather*, n. 18, Panel report, para. 11.100.
35. WT/DS58/AB/R United States – Import Prohibition of certain Shrimp and Shrimp Products, adopted on 6.11.1998, Appellate Body report, para. 183.

12.3.3.1 Are the three Standards Cumulative or Independent?

Should all three standards be proved cumulatively in order for GATT Article X:3(a) and GATS Article VI:1 to apply?

Allegedly, their cumulative effect is drawn from the use of the word 'and'. Additionally, one would expect that the interrelations that may develop among these standards and their synergy should be taken into account. Nevertheless, in practice WTO case law (referring to GATT Article X:3(a)) examined each of these standards independently.[36] Thus, the complainant may introduce evidence only to breach of one of the standards, either by an active deed or by an omission.[37] The evidence should be solid and should 'reflect the gravity of accusations inherent in claims under Article X:3(a) of the GATT 1994'.[38] The Panel further stressed that the examination under this provision should refer to the *real effect* of a measure, explaining: '[t]his, of course, does not require a showing of trade damage . . . [b]ut it can involve an examination of whether there is a possible impact on the competitive situation due to alleged partiality, unreasonableness or lack of uniformity . . .'.[39]

In cases where these standards are invoked together, the WTO adjudicating bodies may examine them in any order they deem appropriate,[40] despite the fact that this difference in order may sometimes affect the final result.

12.4 REVIEW OF ADMINISTRATIVE DECISIONS: ARTICLE VI:2

Unlike the former provision, this provision applies not only to sectors where specific commitments were undertaken. The right of a trader who has been adversely affected by a decision of an administrative agency embodied in GATT Article X:3(b) was recognized by the Appellate Body as reflecting the due process objective.[41]

This review is initiated by the request of an affected service supplier. Thus, a service supplier who wants to initiate such a review has to establish:

- An administrative decision.
- An adverse effect on that service supplier.
- A causal link between the decision and the adverse effect.

---

36. WT/DS155/R, *Argentina – Hides and Leather*, n. 18, Panel report, para. 11.86.
37. WT/DS302/R *Dominican Republic – Cigarettes*, n. 31, Panel report, para. 7.379.
38. WT/DS268/AB/R United States – Sunset Reviews of Anti-Damping Measures on Oil Country Tubular Goods From Argentina, adopted on 17.12.2004, Appellate Body report, para. 217.
39. WT/DS155/R *Argentina – Hides and Leather*, n. 18, Panel report, para. 11.77.
40. *Ibid.*, n. 18, Panel report, para. 11.86.
41. WT/DS315/AB/R *EC – Selected Customs Matters*, n. 12, Appellate Body report, para. 302.

Beyond these basic elements, the Members are left with considerable discretion as to additional, procedural requirements they may introduce as a condition for the initiation of such a review.[42]

12.4.1 Administrative Decisions Affecting Trade in Services

This provision does not specify what are the 'administrative decisions affecting trade in services' that should be reviewed by such tribunals. One commentator suggests to understand 'administrative decisions', according to their ordinary meaning, as referring to 'a legally binding act by an authority, agency or other unit which is part of the administrative branch of government and which regulates a particular, individual, situation. Typically, an administrative action is the application of a general measure to a specific case with binding effect'.[43] The key for deciding the scope of this provision lies in the interpretative decision as to the difference between 'administrative decision' and 'administrative act'.

The interpretation of the expression 'affecting trade in services' may be based on its interpretation in Article I of GATS (see Chapter 4). It is clear from the context that this provision aims at administrative measures adversely affecting such trade, namely restricting it to some extent, either quantitatively or by applying a heavier administrative or financial burden, or by causing time delays to foreign services/service suppliers, compared to like domestic services/service suppliers. However, due to the lack of any specific guidance in the language of this provision, this expression, affecting the scope of legal obligation provided for by Article VI:2, will have to be determined on a case-by-case basis.

12.4.2 The Tribunals

Article VI:2 creates a mechanism for review of administrative decisions affecting trade in services. It requires each Member to have judicial, arbitral or administrative tribunals in charge of reviewing such decisions, providing for necessary remedies where appropriate. This provision is aimed at shielding foreign services suppliers from the abuse of discretion, or the omission to exercise such discretion, by administrative authorities in the country of destination.

This Article does not contain any requirement as to the institutional structure of such mechanism,[44] which is thus left to the discretion of the Members.

In the international level, enforcement of the legal rights accorded by GATS is open mainly to Members, who may approach the WTO adjudicating bodies.[45]

42. GATS commentary, n. 6, 174.
43. *Ibid.*, 173.
44. P. Delimatsis, n. 16, 29.
45. Individuals and organizations, including NGOs, may have limited access to the process according to the interpretation of Arts 13.1 and 17.9 to the DSU: M. Matsushita, T. J. Schoenbaum &

Since infringement of these rights mainly affects private parties, this provision reflects an attempt to create a forum where private parties could defend their rights according to the agreement, thus giving them an opportunity to personally see to GATS enforcement.

However, different countries have different approaches concerning the applicability of legal norms, developed by public international law, in their domestic law. Some countries apply a *monistic* approach, according to which legal norms emanating from international agreements concluded by these countries may be directly applicable by the domestic courts, being regarded as integral part of their legal system. Other countries apply a *dualistic* approach, requiring explicit domestic legislation providing for the application to private parties of a legal norm sourced in an international agreement. Article VI:2(a) attempts to cover both approaches, therefore providing that the review of administrative decisions in light of the agreement may be conducted by a judicial, arbitral or administrative tribunal. While in countries applying a monistic approach courts will be authorized to review such decisions, in countries applying a dualistic approach this review could be conducted by arbitral or administrative tribunals. Arbitral tribunals may be formed subject to the involved parties' consent. Where administrative tribunals are involved, a conflict of interests may occur. Therefore, it is provided that 'where such procedures are not independent of the agency entrusted with the administrative decision concerned, the Member shall ensure that the procedures in fact provide for an objective and impartial review'. However, in practice it seems that this standard would be difficult to follow.

12.4.2.1 The Tribunals' Scope of Authority

A tribunal acting according to Article VI:2, whether judicial, arbitral or administrative, is authorized by this provision to conduct a prompt review of administrative decisions at stake, and where justified, to provide for appropriate remedies to the affected party.

The term '*where justified*' leaves a broad scope of discretion to the reviewing authority, by not specifying in which circumstances a remedy might be justified. A decision based on a legal or factual mistake may establish such justification,[46] but a decision based on misjudgment, leading to an adverse effect, may form a 'gray area'.

The nature of possible remedies is not specified, it is only indicated that they should be 'appropriate.' It is therefore totally subject to the discretion of the reviewing authority and to its scope of authorities according to the domestic law. Thus, such remedies may vary considerably from one Member to another, referring to the replacement of the challenged administrative decision with a proper one,

P. Mavroidis, *The World Trade Organization – Law, Practice and Policy*, Oxford University Press (2003), 35–37.

46. GATS commentary, n. 6, 174.

compensating the affected service supplier for the damages caused, or combining both elements.

The equivalent GATT Article X:3(b), provides that such a tribunal will conduct a 'prompt review and *correction* of administrative action...' [Emphasis added]. Since not much experience was gained by the application of this provision in GATT 1947, in GATS, a more general language was used, leaving the choice of the most suitable remedy under the circumstances to the discretion of the competent authority. In GATS as well as in GATT context the decision of the competent authority should prevent a situation where an administrative authority may practically choose whether to act in compliance with this provision, or rather infringe it, and pay for its behaviour.

12.4.2.2 The Tribunals' Relations with the Administrative Authority: Independence?

One aspect where GATS reflects a weaker position than GATT refers to the relationships between the tribunal and the administrative authority involved. Article X:3(b) of GATT provides, that '[s]uch tribunals... shall be *independent* of the agencies entrusted with administrative enforcement'. [Emphasis added]. This provision was addressed by the Panel in *EC – Selected Customs Matters*,[47] determining that tribunals and procedures can be deemed independent only if they 'have the ability to conduct the review provided for under Article X:3(b)... with freedom in institutional and practical terms from interference by the agencies whose decisions are being reviewed'. In Article VI:2 of GATS a softer, and maybe more flexible approach prevailed, providing: 'Where such procedures are *not independent* of the agency entrusted with the administrative decision concerned, the Member shall ensure that the procedures in fact provide for an objective and impartial review'. [Emphasis added]. Namely, dependence is not completely overruled, but in this case it is the responsibility of the Member involved to ensure that the review is still objective and impartial. It is unclear to what extent this standard will be proved to be practical.

12.4.2.2.1 The Agencies Covered

In *EC – Selected Customs Matters* one question that arose about the tribunals' decision according to GATT Article XI:3(b) was: which government agencies would be subject to these decisions? While the Panel was of the opinion that it would be unreasonable to subject all the agencies across a territory of a federal Member to such a decision,[48] the Appellate Body presented a more liberal interpretation providing that GATT Article X:3(b) *allows, but does not require*, that such review decisions govern the practice of all relevant agencies within a

---

47. WT/DS315/R *EC – Selected Customs Matters*, n. 12, Panel report, para. 7.520.
48. *Ibid.*, para. 7.539.

Member's territory.[49] The same dilemma as to the desired interpretation may arise in the context of GATS Article VI:2.

12.4.2.3 Appeal on a Tribunal's Decision

There is no limitation in the language of GATS Article VI as to whether only a first instance tribunal may conduct the review, or rather could higher instances engage in such reviews as well.[50]

Article XI:3(b) of GATT explicitly refers to a possibility of appeal on a tribunal's decision: 'unless an appeal is lodged with a court or tribunal of superior jurisdiction . . .'. Such a possibility is not explicitly mentioned in Article VI:2 of GATS. It may be drawn from its general language, allowing Members to determine procedures (Article VI:2(a)), but thus could not be interpreted as obligatory, only as optional.

12.4.2.4 The Constitutional Exception

A complementary provision, included in Article VI:2(b), clarifies that 'the provisions of subparagraph (a) shall not be construed to require a Member to institute such tribunals or procedures where this would be inconsistent with its constitutional structure or the nature of its legal system'. This provision is a sort of a 'safety valve' for Members who may find themselves in a middle of a conflict between their international obligation and their constitutional structure. However, it may form an excuse for Members to ignore this provision, thus departing from Article 27 of the Vienna Convention, providing: 'A party may not invoke the provisions of its internal law as justification for its failure to perform a treaty'.

12.5 ADMINISTRATIVE AUTHORIZATION: ARTICLE VI:3

GATS Article VI:3 refers to cases where authorization is required for the supply of a service on which a specific commitment has been made. It provides that in these cases, the competent authorities of a Member shall, within a reasonable period of

49. WT/DS315/AB/R *EC – Selected Customs Matters*, n. 12, Appellate Body report, para. 304.
50. Based on the Panel decision in WT/DS315/R *EC – Selected Customs Matters*, n. 12, Panel report, paras 7.521–7.522, P. Delimatsis, n. 1, 106 suggests that GATT Art. X:3(b) covers only *first instance* bodies and procedures. It is further suggested that due to the similarity between GATT and GATS provisions and the drafting history, reflecting that GATS drafters were inspired by GATT provision, the same limitation could be read into GATS provision, although not specified by its language. However, the Panel decision concerning GATT Art. X:3 does not seem to be too definite, providing in para. 7.521 that the 'review required under Art. X:3(b) . . . *need not necessarily be the last instance review*'. [Emphasis added]. Even if this interpretation is correct for GATT, in GATS context an opposite conclusion can also be drawn from this drafting history: if the Members were aware of this option, why didn't they explicitly address it?

time after the submission of an application considered complete under domestic laws and regulations, inform the applicant of the decision concerning the application. In addition to the request of the applicant, the competent authorities of the Member shall provide, without undue delay, information concerning the status of the application.[51] This obligation applies only to committed sectors.

This provision serves some purposes. Firstly, it leads to *transparency* of the administrative procedure. Secondly, it supplies *information* that establishes a basis for service suppliers' decisions about their future steps. Thirdly, the information supplied may reflect *defects in the decision-making* process, thus forming a basis for procedures of the kind provided for in paragraph 2.

It should be noted, that this provision includes some uninterpreted expressions that should be analysed on a case-by-case basis: 'reasonable period of time', 'without undue delay'. The interpretation of these vague time frames may affect the scope and manner of the specific commitments' enforcement.

In terms of policy, interpreters of this provision should be aware that particularly under strict interpretation, this provision could potentially become an administrative burden on governments (particularly in developing countries) required to ensure the availability of an independent institutional framework, provided for by this provision.[52]

There is no parallel provision in Article X of GATT, and in this sense GATS provides for a higher standard.[53]

12.5.1 Article VI:1,3 in GATS Jurisprudence

To comply with this provision, a Member must have a mechanism of the kind presupposed by this provision. In *US – Gambling*[54] it was claimed, *inter alia*, that the United States had not put in place any procedure allowing the complainant's suppliers to file an application for an authorization to supply gambling services in a cross-border manner. The Panel determined that the complainant failed to identify the specific measures that impose such authorization requirements as well as to identify those authorization procedures that are allegedly accessible only to domestic suppliers. In addition, there was evidence that the complainant's suppliers had never applied for authorization to supply these services in the United States. Thus, these claims were dismissed.

51. According to Delimatsis, n. 1, and based on the Appellate Body report in WT/DS58/AB/R *US – Shrimp*, n. 32, para. 108, where the request is rejected, the competent authorities should give reason for this decision. However, this is not explicitly provided for in this provision.
52. M. Krajewski, *National Regulation and Trade Liberalization in Services*, Kluwer Law International, (2003), 195.
53. Nevertheless, similar provisions exist in Art. 5.2.2 TBT, Annex C:1(a) SPS and Art. 3.5(e),(f) Licensing Agreement.
54. WT/DS285/R, *US – Gambling*, n. 5, Panel report, para. 6.437.

12.5.2 The Purpose of Article VI:1-3

In *US – Shrimp*, the Appellate Body provided that GATT Article X:3 'establishes certain minimum standards for transparency and procedural fairness in the administration of trade regulations . . .'.[55] It seems that Article VI:1-3 of GATS shares the same purposes. To this multilateral level of scrutiny the establishment of private rights against national public administrators and regulators should be added.[56]

Accordingly, it is suggested that a violation of these provisions is sufficient to establish a violation complaint.[57]

12.6 FUTURE DISCIPLINES ON RECOGNITION OF PROFESSIONAL QUALIFICATIONS: ARTICLE VI:4,5

Article VI:4,5 concentrates on the development of future disciplines and determination of standards of behaviour for the time being.

12.6.1 Article VI:4

Article VI:4 reflects a shift from GATT model, which concentrated on negative regulation/integration, that is, what governments must *not* do, to positive regulation/integration – what governments must *do.*[58]

12.6.1.1 Scope of Coverage: 'Measures Relating'

Article VI:4 authorizes the Council for Trade in Services to develop disciplines ensuring that measures relating to qualification requirements and procedures, technical standards and licensing requirements[59] do not constitute unnecessary barriers to trade in services, subject to criteria specified by this provision. It thus provides an *indicative* list (using the words '*inter alia*') of *minimum* standards that such future disciplines should meet.[60]

55. WT/DS58/AB/R, n. 35, para. 183.
56. P. Delimatsis, n. 16, 34.
57. P. Delimatsis, n. 1, 112.
58. This approach is shared not only by GATS but also by the TRIPs, the TBT and the SPS agreements: P. Delimatsis, n. 1, 85. For the drafting history of this provisions see *ibid.*, 114–115.
59. Unlike qualification requirements, applying only to natural persons, licensing requirements apply to both natural and juridical persons.
60. P. Delimatsis, n. 16, 36–37. It is noted there, that the original intention of the drafters was that this provision would cover all services sectors and all types of services regulations, standards or qualifications, but the current language was chosen, realizing that the time was not yet ripe for this approach.

The term '*measures relating*' broadens the scope of coverage of this provision. It is not interpreted by the agreement and hence, it is open for future interpretation. The results may be unpredictable.[61]

One of the open questions in this context is whether Article VI:4 disciplines apply only to specific commitments, or rather to 'all services'. It is clear that the latter option decisively broadens the scope and potential effect of these disciplines. It is noted that 'the other clauses in Article VI clearly apply only to those services listed in a country's schedule of commitments, while Article VI:4 is written in a general obligation format. The WTO Secretariat believes that the different phrasing of Article VI:4 is "intentional".'[62]

In addition, the scope of this provision, in terms of *range of regulatory measures*, is narrow. Many services fall outside the scope of this provision, including the independence of the regulatory authority or universal service provisions, business advertising and marketing, access to networks as well as to essential facilities.[63]

12.6.1.2 'Qualifications', 'Technical Standards', 'Licensing', 'Requirements', 'Procedures'

Each of these words does not have a single meaning, acceptable to all GATS Members. In different states, and in different professional contexts, each of them may be interpreted differently.[64]

A certain indication to the meaning of these words may be found in a Note by the Secretariat[65] providing that *qualification requirements* 'normally relate to matters such as education, examination requirements, practical training, experience or language requirements' ensuring the quality of the service provider.

Licensing requirements are referred to in the Secretariat document as 'substantive requirements, other than qualification requirements, with which a service supplier is required to comply in order to obtain formal permission to supply a service', including 'residency requirements, fees, establishment requirements, registration requirements, etc.'.

---

61. P. Delimatsis, 'Towards a necessity Test for Services: A Little Less Conversation, A Little More Action, Please!', *NCCR Working Paper No. 2006/16* (2006), 4, mentions as other optional disciplines the reasonableness of license fees or the independence of the supervisory authority, 6, <http://papers.ssrn.com>.
62. S. Karmakar, 'Disciplining Domestic Regulation Under GATS and its Implications for Developing Countries: An Indian Case Study', *41 Journal of World Trade* (2007), 127, 140.
63. P. Delimatsis, n. 61, 6.
64. For different possible interpretations of these terms in the context of the legal profession see: L. S. Terry, 'But What Will the WTO Disciplines Apply to? Distinguishing Among Market Access, National Treatment and Art. VI:4 Measures When Applying the GATS to Legal Services', *American Bar Center for Professional Responsibility, 2003 Symposium, 83 The Professional Lawyer* (2003), 84, 98–100, <http://papers.ssrn.com>.
65. S/WPPS/W/9 Note by the Secretariat – The Relevance of the Disciplines of the Agreement on Technical Barriers to Trade (TBT) and on Import Licensing Procedures to Art. VI:4 of the GATS, 11 Sep. 1996, para. 4

Technical Standards are addressed in the Secretariat document as 'requirements which may apply both to the characteristics or definition of the service itself and to the manner in which it is performed'. The *US – Gambling*[66] case referred to US gambling laws, viewed by the WTO adjudicating bodies as market access limitations contrary to Article XVI. However, according to one opinion,[67] the WTO adjudicating bodies erred doing so, since these laws do not form market access restrictions *per se* but rather technical standards, imposed both on domestic and foreign suppliers and aimed at ensuring the *quality* of the service.

The different approach that may occur in different Members may add to the ambiguity concerning the scope of application of any disciplines developed under this provision. This fact has led to a lengthy discussion in the Working Party on Domestic Regulation (hereby: WPDR), attempting to produce an agreed list of examples to cases where the disciplines would apply.[68] The large number of drafts exchanged reflects the disagreement and the difference in views of different Members concerning this point.[69] In any case, agreement on this list would not solve disagreements on additional cases, which are not included in it.

12.6.1.3 The Criteria to Be Fulfilled by the Disciplines Developed

According to Article VI:4, the disciplines subject to it:

> shall aim to ensure that such requirements are, *inter alia*:
>
> (a) based on objective and transparent criteria, such as competence and the ability to supply the service;
> (b) not more burdensome than necessary to ensure the quality of the service;
> (c) in the case of licensing procedures, not in themselves a restriction on the supply of the service.

The words '*inter alia*' imply that these criteria form an indicative list of minimum characteristics that the prospective disciplines should have. The Members are free to introduce additional features into these disciplines.[70] Thus, for example, the WPDR has been reviewing further principles that could form a framework for regulatory development: *equivalence* – account should be taken of relevant qualifications and experience a supplier may have obtained abroad; *International*

66. WT/DS285/R, AB/R, n. 5.
67. J. Pauwelyn, 'Rien Ne Va Plus? Distinguishing domestic Regulation from Market Access in GATT and In GATS', *Duke Law School Legal Studies Paper No.* 85 (2005), 131, 161, <http://papers.ssrn.com>.
68. L. S. Terry, n. 64, 106–109.
69. See, for example JOB (02)/20/Rev. 10: WPRD, Examples for Measures to be Addressed by Disciplines Under GATS Art. VI:4, informal note by the Secretariat – revision, 31.1.2005.
70. P. Delimatsis, n. 61, 4, mentions as other optional disciplines the reasonableness of license fees or the independence of the supervisory authority.

standards – acceptance of international standards could facilitate the evolution of qualifications obtained abroad.[71]

12.6.1.3.1 Objective and Transparent Criteria

Article VI:4(a) provides for two cumulative requirements concerning the criteria on which regulation is based: these criteria should be *objective and transparent.*

The *objectivity* requirement refers to the *content* or essence of criteria. This standard is objective, and may therefore be assessed by all parties involved, including the WTO adjudicating bodies. This standard was chosen in order to ensure that domestic regulation will not be based on subjective considerations or standards that could form a basis for discrimination and prevent any objective assessment thereof, and in addition, undermine predictability.

The *transparency* requirement refers to the manner of publication. It implies that domestic regulation could not be expected to be followed without due publication. In the WPDR, relevant criteria to the fulfilment of this principle were discussed, including: reasonable advance notice before implementation, public availability to service suppliers, regulation being easy to find and to read, specification of reasonable time periods for responding to applications, information provided as to the reasons for declining an application, and provision of information on procedures for review of administrative decisions.[72]

However, these terms: 'objective' and 'transparent' are not defined by this provision, and therefore are subject to further interpretation. Such interpretation will have to determine, *inter alia*, whether they should have a common, permanent meaning or rather, should they be defined on a case-by-case basis.

12.6.1.3.2 The Necessity Test

Article VI:4 does not impose a direct necessity test on the Members. Rather, with respect to measures within its scope, it calls upon Members to *negotiate* any needed disciplines to ensure that such measures do not constitute unnecessary barriers to trade.[73] Article VI:4(b) specifies, that such measures should not be more burdensome than necessary to ensure the quality of the service.[74] This requirement reflects the intention of GATS drafters to balance between two important interests: on the one hand, preserving the Members' freedom to achieve domestic regulatory objectives through measures they choose, while, on the other hand, discouraging the Members from abusing this freedom to impose measures that unduly

71. Other principles that have been raised for discussion include: impartial application, proportionality (any penalties for non-performance should bear a reasonable relationship to the risks invoked), regular review process, minimization of the administrative burden involved: WTO explanatory paper, WTO Secretariat, 29.3.2006 (3774.6), 14.
72. WTO explanatory paper, n. 71, 14.
73. D. Honeck, The GATS and 'Necessity', WTO March 2004 (presentation), <www.wto.org>.
74. For comparison, see necessity tests in other WTO agreements: Delimatsis, n. 61, 10–24, in the accountancy disciplines, *Ibid.*, 29–32 and in regional trade agreements, *Ibid.*, 24–28.

restrict trade.[75] The necessity test requires that covered measures restricting trade *do not go beyond what is 'necessary'* to achieve the Member's policy objective.[76] Thus, three elements should be basically satisfied: a *measure* which is subject to the test, the *objective* that this measure seeks to achieve, and the *link of necessity* between the measure and the objective. GATT and WTO jurisprudence indicates that higher enforcement costs or an increased administrative burden of the alternative measure are not taken into account. This approach may be contrary to the explicit indication in the Preamble that different levels of Members' development (implying, *inter alia*, financial and administrative capacity), should be taken into account.[77]

In terms of essence, there are two interpretative approaches to the necessity test provided for by Article VI:4: the necessity test can be either interpreted as an *absolute requirement*, irrespective of the home regime, or *relative requirement*, referring to the home country regulatory regime, as a complementary measure.[78]

The *absolute requirement* approach concentrates on ensuring the quality of the service (its objective) and the link of necessity between the measure and that objective. According to this interpretation, no relative comparison to other measures that may achieve the same goal is made.

The *relative requirement* approach seems to interpret the necessity test in this provision as equivalent to the more severe proportionality test, embodied, for example, in GATT Article XX. According to this test, the measure at stake must be the *least trade-restrictive* measure reasonably available to achieve the regulatory goal. The adoption of this approach turns this provision into potentially 'very interventionist. It could restrict not just the means to attain a given regulatory goal but even the types of regulatory goals that might be achieved, as when the regulatory goal is not to maintain the quality of the service but to avoid some other externalization or regulatory harm by the service provider'.[79] It is further stressed that 'interventionism' could be reinforced by an interpretation applying the necessity test to measures falling under Article XVII (national treatment).[80] If this

75. D. Honeck, n. 73.
76. During the Uruguay Round there was an attempt to draft and objectivity and necessity test applying to domestic services regulation of all services sectors and all types of services regulations, standards and qualifications. This attempt did not work out and the current wording reflects the acceptable version of this notion: P. Delimatsis, n. 61, 5.
77. GATS commentary, n. 6, 188.
78. K. Nicolaides & J. Trachtman, 'Liberalization, Regulation, and Recognition for Services Trade' in S. M. Stephenson (ed.), *Services Trade in the Western Hemisphere: Liberalization, Integration and Reform*, General Secretariat/Organization of American States (2000), 43, 58.
79. J. P. Trachtman, n. 22, 68.
80. M. Cossy, 'Determining "Likeness" under the GATS: Squaring the Circle?', *WTO* (2006), 44, <www.wto.org>.

> Article V has been so far understood by Member States as applying only to *non-discriminatory measures.* The fact that GATS Articles V and XVII are mutually exclusive is not found in the GATS itself, but is expressed, for instance, in the Accountancy Disciplines which state that they 'do not address measures subject to scheduling under Articles XVI and XVII'. Arguably, nothing would prevent Members from modifying this

interpretation is accepted, the fulfilment of this criterion depends on the assessment of alternatives, as well as on the clear determination of purpose. Where no clear determination of purpose exists, assessment of necessity will be difficult.[81] According to this interpretation, different considerations could be involved: a less trade restrictive measure could be non-constitutional, or require restructuring parts of the legal system, or have financial or fiscal undesired implications. This difficulty, in turn, leads to the general question concerning the capability of the WTO dispute settlement authorities to evaluate legal, political, economic and social circumstances and considerations of diverging national regulatory systems.[82]

According to the Vienna Convention rules of interpretation, language differences between provisions providing for the *proportionality* test and provisions providing for the *necessity* test should be taken into account. Accordingly, it seems that in this case the first approach should prevail: this provision does not call for *proportionality*, but rather for *necessity* test. Thus, the measures at stake should not necessarily form the least restrictive option. They should rather be proved as necessary and at the same time not more burdensome than necessary to ensure the quality of the service.

Consultations between the Members took place in the WTO concerning the implementation of this provision.[83] By now, professional disciplines containing a necessity test in the form of obligation were developed for the accountancy sector.[84] The experience gained in this process arises some thoughts whether the

---

understanding and decide that the criteria contained in Article V:4, in particular its necessity test, can apply to measures falling under Article XVII.

81. WTO explanatory paper, n. 71, 4.
82. Krajewski, n. 52, 155.
83. See Analytical Index to the WTO (internet version), paras 132–135, <www.wto.org>.
84. The Accountancy Disciplines provide:

> Members shall ensure that measures not subject to Articles XVI or XVII of the GATS relating to licensing requirements and procedures, technical standards and qualification requirements and procedures *are not prepared, adopted or applied with a view to or with the effect of creating unnecessary barriers to trade in accountancy services.* For this purpose, Members shall ensure that such measures *are not more trade restrictive than necessary to fulfill a legitimate objective.* Legitimate objectives are, *inter alia*, the protection of consumers (which includes all users of accounting services and the public generally), the quality of the service, professional competence, and the integrity of the profession.

The disciplines developed are embodied in S/L/64 Disciplines on Domestic regulation in the Accountancy Sector, 17.12.1998, <http://docsonline.wto.org>. These disciplines would enter into force at the end of the current round of negotiations. (K. Iida & J. Nielson, 'Transparency in Domestic Regulation: Practices and Politics' in A. Mattoo & P. Sauvé (eds), *Domestic Regulation and Service Trade Liberalization*, The World Bank and Oxford University Press, (2003), 7, 9).

The disciplines are subject to two additional constraints that limit their impact: they apply only to Members that made commitments in the accountancy sector; and they do not apply to measures subject to scheduling under Arts XVI and XVII: J. Hegarty, 'Rules for Domestic regulations: the Experience with Accountancy', Box 29.3 in B. Hoeckman, A. Mattoo & P. English (eds), *Development, Trade and the WTO: a Handbook, The World Bank* (2002), 259, 295, <www-wds.worldbank.org>.

sector-specific approach is efficient, or should it be replaced, at least partially, with a horizontal approach for the development of such disciplines.[85] In any case, some interpretative questions concerning the necessity test and its application remain open:[86]

- 'Is it possible and, if so, is it necessary for Members to develop a list of legitimate objectives, either at the horizontal or sectoral level? Conversely, should Members instead focus on listing only "non-legitimate" objectives?
- How might such terms as "least trade restrictive", "not more restrictive than necessary", and "not more burdensome than necessary" be defined? What are their respective trade and legal implications . . .?
- Should the idea that a measure restricting trade be considered necessary only if there is no less-restrictive and reasonably available alternative measure to achieve the same policy objective be added to the necessity test . . .?'

It seems that these discussions are governed by 'a cautionary view to such proposals, which foresees challenges at the Dispute Settlement Body (DSB) *vis-à-vis* legitimacy and burdensomeness of regulations'.[87]

12.6.1.4 Potential Overlap with other GATS Provisions

It should be noted, that Article VI:4 belongs to the general part of GATS, which is not subject to specific commitments. Therefore, interpretative questions may arise concerning the relationships between disciplines developed under it and specific commitments under Articles XVI and XVII.[88] While these two provisions concentrate on discriminatory measures, paragraphs 4 and 5 of Article V are aimed at

For further discussion see: C. Trolliet & J. Hegarty, 'Regulatory Reform and Trade Liberalization in Accountancy Services', in A. Mattoo & P. Sauvé (eds) *Domestic Regulation and Service Trade Liberalization*, The World Bank and Oxford University Press (2003), 147–166; See considerations for the development of sectoral disciplines in financial services in J. Trachtman, 'Addressing Regulatory Divergence Through International Standards: Financial Services', in Mattoo & Sauvé, 27–41.

85. A. Mattoo, 'Shaping Future GATS Rules for Trade in Services', *The World Bank* (2001), 13, <www-wds.worldbank.org>.

The debate on the necessity of a necessity test is also relevant to the horizontal disciplines draft now discussed in the WPDR. See: P. Delimatsis, 'Concluding the WTO services Negotiations on Domestic Regulation – Walk Unafraid', *TILEC Discussion Paper DP-2009-032* (2009), 10–12, <http://papers.ssrn.com>.

For economic considerations supporting horizontal disciplines see: R. H. Snape, 'Regulating Services Trade: Matching Policies to Objectives' in T. Ito & A. O. Krueger (eds), *Trade in Services in the Asia-Pacific Region*, The University of Chicago Press (2003), 79.

86. D. Honeck, n. 73.
87. S. Karmakar, n. 62, 137.
88. R. Self & K. Zutshi, 'Mode 4: Negotiating Challenges and Opportunities', in A. Mattoo & A. Carzaniga (eds), *Moving People to Deliver Services*, The World Bank and Oxford University Press, (2003), 27, 56.

non-discriminatory regulation that could nevertheless be burdensome for international trade in services, exposing service suppliers to multiple, and possibly different, domestic regulation in different trade destinations. Adaptation to these different requirements may cause extra costs to the service suppliers involved.[89] However, an overlap between Article V:4,5 and Article XVII (national treatment) could take place where measures relating to qualifications, licensing or technical standards are discriminatory. One question might be: will such disciplines affect existing commitments? The WTO Members seem to attempt to prevent this option.[90]

The overlap between Article VI:4,5 and Article XVI (market access) may be more problematic. The dispute settlement decision in *US – Gambling* and the literature that followed reveal an interpretative controversy whether these provisions should be interpreted as complementary[91] or 'mutually exclusive'.[92] (See detailed discussion in Chapter 9.)

It should be further noted, that according to certain opinions, Article VI:4 disciplines will also not apply to measures covered by other GATS provisions, such as Article II (MFN), Article III (Transparency), Article VII (Recognition) and Article IX (Business practices).[93]

Yet another question arises as to the potential overlap between Article VI and Article XVIII. This Article does not contain legal obligations, but provides the legal basis for further negotiations and scheduling of commitments. Thus, this provision may encompass measures also covered by Article VI, although the latter concentrates mainly on developing long term, horizontal disciplines, while the former facilitates current commitments.[94]

These uncertainties might have growing practical implications as more disciplines would be developed under this article.

---

89. K. Nicolaides & J. Trachtman, n. 78, 44.
90. In the WPDR a draft horizontal disciplines of domestic regulations was developed. The draft is dated 20.3.2009 and includes a provision attempting to solve this difficulty by explicitly providing, in para. 10, that the disciplines included in the draft, if accepted, would not apply 'to measures to the extent that they constitute limitations subject to scheduling under Article XVI or XVII'. A similar provision is already included in the Accountancy Disciplines (not yet in force) and in S/L/92 Guidelines for the Scheduling of Specific Commitments Under the General Agreement on Trade in Services (GATS), published 28.3.2001, adopted by the Council for Trade in services on 23.3.2001, para. 10.
91. Delimatsis, n. 61, 8; L. S. Terry, n. 64, 97–98.
92. WT/DS285/R, *US – Gambling*, n. 5, Panel report, para. 6.305; Appellate Body report, para. 250.
93. L. S. Terry, n. 64, 106, referring to statements by the Chair of the Working Party on Domestic Regulation: S/WPDR/M/18 Report on the meeting held on 22 Oct. 2002, 3.12.2002, para. 8 and S/WPDR/M/19 Report on the meeting held on 4 Dec. 2002, 29.1.2003, para. 11.
94. That was the case with regulatory disciplines of the Reference Paper on Telecommunication which were inscribed as additional commitments in several Members' schedules: P. Delimatsis, 'The Interaction Between GATS Arts VI, XVI, XVII and XVIII After the US-Gambling Case', *NCCR Trade regulation Working Paper No. 2006/9* (2006), 21, <http://papers.ssrn.com>.
    See also: P. Delimatsis, 'Don't Gamble With the GATS – The Interaction between Articles VI, XVI, XVII and XVIII GATS in the Light of the *US – Gambling* Case', *40 Journal of World Trade* (2006): 1059, 1075.

12.6.1.5 The Doha Round Developments

In 1999 the Council for Trade in Services established the WPDR which is in charge of developing meaningful and coherent horizontally applicable disciplines on domestic regulation, according to Article VI:4. This is the only area of services trade negotiations in the Doha Round where the Members are willing to proceed. Such negotiations indeed take place, in an informal manner, in the WPDR, referring to *non*-discriminatory and *non*-quantitative domestic regulations. The draft discussed incorporates regulatory disciplines aimed at enhancing transparency of domestic measures relating to licensing, qualifications and standards, ensuring a due regulatory process, and ensuring that these measures would not be used as disguised barriers to trade. The disciplines discussed are horizontal and neutral, namely: should not be construed to prescribe or impose particular regulatory approaches or provisions in domestic regulation. The disciplines, if accepted, would apply only where specific commitments were undertaken. In an attempt to draw a line between Article VI and Articles XVI and XVII, the disciplines would apply to the manner the Members *administer or apply* these measures,[95] not to the measures themselves. Besides substance, the legal position of these disciplines and their relationships with GATS provisions, particularly with Article VI:5, would have to be decided.[96]

12.6.2 Nullification or Impairment: Article VI:5

Article VI:5 seeks to ensure that specific commitments are not nullified or impaired through regulatory requirements, or, in other words, 'to ensure that the standards that were set in Article VI:4(a)-(c) . . . will not be neglected or undermined by their absence while negotiations under Article VI:4 are taking place'.[97] This provision thus sets certain standards that should be followed by the Members in sectors where specific commitments were undertaken, to prevent their nullification or impairment.

95. The draft disciplines includes, *inter alia*, detailed instructions concerning transparency of measures; a less trade restrictive standard concerning residency requirement for licensing; detailed requirements concerning a due licensing procedure; due and undue requirements for qualification and qualification procedures; transparency of processes relating to the development and application of standards by non-governmental bodies and consideration of international standards; relieves for developing countries in the application of these disciplines.
96. P. Delimatsis, n. 61, 4–5, 16. See additional details on the draft in pages 5–10. Delimatsis predicts that if these disciplines are accepted, they would be followed by national regulatory audits to assess compliance thereto that might lead to considerable domestic regulatory reforms, <http://papers.ssrn.com>.
97. P. Delimatsis, n. 1, 117.

12.6.2.1 Scope of Application

Article VI:5(a) is applicable 'pending the entry into force of disciplines developed in these sectors pursuant to paragraph 4'. Thus, it ceases to apply once sector-specific disciplines such as these developed in the Accountancy sector come into force.

This provision applies to 'licensing and qualification *requirements*' and 'technical standards'. Despite the fact that it does not explicitly refer to licensing and qualification *procedures*, it seems that they are covered by this provision.[98]

Subparagraph (ii) implies that licensing and qualification requirements and technical standards that *could have been reasonably expected* at the time the specific commitments in the relevant sector were made, are excluded from the scope of this provision, that is, do not form basis for a nullification or impairment claim.

12.6.2.2 Burden of Proof

Article VI:5 provides that in sectors where specific commitments were undertaken and no disciplines on recognition of professional qualification were yet developed by the WTO:

> the Member shall not apply licensing and qualification requirements and technical standards that nullify or impair such specific commitments in a manner which:
>
> (i) does not comply with the criteria outlined in subparagraphs 4(a), (b) or (c); and
> (ii) could not reasonably have been expected of that Member at the time the specific commitments in those sectors were made.

A causal link between the application of the measure at stake and the adverse effect caused to the complainant should be demonstrated.

Limited Scope

Article VI:5 has a limited scope since it applies *only to sectors where specific commitments were undertaken and pending the entry into force of disciplines developed in these sectors pursuant to paragraph 4*. (Article V:5(a)).

Compliance with the Criteria specified in paragraph 4(a)–(c)

According to Article VI:5(a)(i), the complaining Member must show that a specific commitment was nullified or impaired through national regulation that does not comply with the criteria outlined in Article VI:4(a)–(c). One of these requirements,

98. *Ibid.*, 118.

incorporated in Article VI:4(b) is the *necessity test* discussed above, in one of its versions. This element will have to be proved by the complainant even if it is possible to show that a national measure nullifies or impairs service commitments.

Nullification or Impairment

Article VI:5(b)(ii), including a provision which is cumulative to that included in Article VI:5(a)(ii), due to the word 'and', is vaguely drafted and subject to interpretation on a case-by-case basis. Its language resembles to the requirement embodied in the non-violation cause[99] (see Chapter 17). Both provisions seem to incorporate a non-violation concept of nullification or impairment, which is aimed at providing protection of market access expectations. However, there is a controversy among different commentators whether this interpretation is correct.[100] Both provisions bear the same difficulty of proof. The proof requires both the ability to present evidence to the circumstances and intentions of the parties involved at the time the specific commitments in the relevant sector were made,[101] as well as an objective assessment as to the 'reasonability' of expectation that could rely on these facts and intentions. This is a relatively high burden of proof.[102] In addition it should be remembered that unlike in GATT, in Article VI:5, nullification and impairment are part of the prohibition itself, consequently placing the burden of proof on the complaining party, thus making it more difficult to use this provision.[103]

International Standards

Article VI:5(b) implies, *inter alia*, that account shall be taken of relevant international standards. The passive wording 'account shall be taken' does not provide for

99. Its drafting history seems to be based on GATT jurisprudence in non-violation cases: M. Cossy, n. 80, 43.
100. See, for example, K. Nicolaides & J. Trachtman, n. 78, 56–57, who support the non-violation interpretation. On the other hand see P. Delimatsis, n. 16, 43–44, and P. Delimatsis, n. 1, 122–124, who raises doubts about it.
101. WTO explanatory paper, n. 71, 8.
102. In GATT 1947 disputes under Art. XXIII mainly referred to subsidies which prevented a Member from enjoying tariff concessions. In the context of GATT 1994 case WT/DS44/R *Japan – Film*, n. 10, the United States, the complaining party, was required to demonstrate that the Japanese measures involved were not reasonably anticipated at the time concessions were granted. Where the measure at stake was issued after the tariff concession was granted, the Panel established a presumption, rebuttable by Japan, that the United States could not have reasonably anticipated the measure. In practice, this presumption has never been rebutted ever since: P. Delimatsis, n. 1, 120
103. In GATT as well as in the TBT and SPS agreements, the nullification or impairment requirement is not part of the prohibition itself: according to Art. 3(8) of the DSU, where a provision of one of these agreements has been violated, a prima facie nullification or impairment would result, and the respondent would bear the burden of rebutting it: J. P. Trachtman, n. 22, 67; K. Nicolaides & J. Trachtman, n. 78, 56–57.

an obligation[104] to base domestic regulations on international standard, thus providing a relatively weak incentive to apply such standards, unless seen as an interpretative guideline to the WTO adjudicating bodies, who may conclude that domestic regulation deviating from international standard forms an unnecessary trade restriction. According to the language of this provision, this interpretation is limited only to cases where the relevant international standard *was applied* by that Member.[105] In any case, the requirement to take international standards into account does not necessarily imply that these standards should be adopted. Thus, a Member may argue that the relevant international standards were considered and rejected, for any reasonable reason. For example, it is contended that 'it is essential for the international standards themselves to have adequate regard to transparency, necessity and proportionality' to justify the requirement for conformity with them.[106]

Another reference to international standards is found in Article VII:5, providing for their application to professional recognition.

In both cases the intention seems clear: it is assumed that it might be easier and faster to convince the Members to adopt a ready-made standard (which might probably be already recognized by some of the Members) than to develop a new standard. In addition, this practice could contribute, in the long terms, to some harmonization of international standards, to the benefit of international traders.

However, international standards are developed in different international forums, and there may be more than one relevant standard available. The agreement does not specify how to choose the most appropriate standard in such a case.[107] Unlike the TBT and SPS agreements of the WTO, Article VI:5(b) does not establish a presumption of compliance, according to which any measure which conforms to international standards is to be deemed necessary. This can be viewed both as a disadvantage, or a 'weaker' provision compared to the TBT and SPS provisions, and as an advantage, allowing the competent authorities more discretion.[108]

Moreover, membership in bodies developing international standards is not necessarily equivalent to GATS membership. Thus, international standards will not necessarily be open to all WTO Members.[109] Another difficulty stems from the fact that this mechanism may lead GATS Members to the adoption of standards for which they object, since their adoption is not subject to consensus.[110]

104. Relatively stronger references to international standards may be found in Arts 3.1, 3.2 of the SPS Agreement and in Art. 2.4 of the TBT Agreement.
105. Krajewski, n. 52, 152.
106. S. Karmakar, n. 62, 138.
107. The WTO expressed willingness to defer to action with functional organizations such as the ILO, the ITU and other specialized organizations. However, this initiative may prove ineffective due to the limitations on the applicability of non-WTO law in the context of WTO dispute resolution: K. Nicolaides & J. Trachtman, n. 78, 47–48.
108. P. Delimatsis, n. 1, 125–127.
109. GATS commentary, n. 6, 189.
110. *Ibid.*, 190.

In addition, since different standards involve economic and financial implications, and these provisions are phrased more in the spirit of a recommendation than of an obligation, it seems that the process of exercising these provisions will be long and elaborated.[111]

Finally, it should be noted that this provision does not provide for mutual recognition of equivalent conditions set by the home country of service suppliers. This idea does not seem to be recommended even by the WPDR.[112]

12.7 VERIFICATION OF PROFESSIONAL COMPETENCE

12.7.1 Scope of Application

Article VI:6 applies only to sectors *where specific commitments regarding professional services are undertaken.*

It is limited to the *procedure* and does not refer to the substance.

However, it seems that this provision 'has by and large not been discharged. One problem is the absence of any incentive for Members to accord such recognition in sectors where mutual benefit in terms of access is not apparent'.[113]

12.7.2 Purpose

Article V:6 provides that in sectors where specific commitments regarding professional services are undertaken, each Member shall provide for adequate procedures to verify the competence of professionals of any other Member. This legal obligation is a *minimum means*, affecting particularly the movement of natural persons for the supply of professional services (Mode 4), which is meant to prevent a situation whereby in the absence of a Mutual Recognition Agreement (MRA), a Member justifies the denial of access of professionals according to its specific commitments, relying on a technical excuse of not having an adequate procedure to verify their professional competence, combined with its responsibility to ensure the safety and well being of potential consumers of the service involved.

This provision may be seen as complementary to Article VII (recognition), facilitating its effective application.[114]

111. For comparative review of different standards and their application to the WTO agreements, including GATS, see: S. Charnovitz, 'International Standards and the WTO', *GWU Law School, Legal Studies research Paper No. 133* (2005), <http://papers.ssrn.com>.
112. See extended explanation in GATS commentary, n. 6, 190.
113. R. Self & K. Zutshi, n. 88, 51.
Nevertheless, one of the few Members who implemented this provision is New Zealand, with respect to verification of foreign engineers: P. Delimatsis, n. 16, 48, n. 139.
114. P. Delimatsis, n. 1, 128.

12.7.3 'Adequate Procedures'

Article VI:6 requires the Members to apply '*adequate procedures*'. This expression is not interpreted by the agreement, but should be interpreted in light of the general context and purpose of this provision as implying that 'adequate' means non-discriminatory, or procedures which would not undermine market access.

12.8 THE RELATIONSHIP BETWEEN ARTICLE VI AND ARTICLES XVI (MARKET ACCESS) AND XVII (NATIONAL TREATMENT)

This subject is mainly addressed in Chapters 8 and 9. While Articles XVI and XVII belong to Part III of the agreement (Specific Commitments) Article VI belongs to Part II (General Obligations and Disciplines). In part, this is a future provision. However, unlike the former provisions which are applied subject to specific commitments negotiated by the Members, the disciplines developed under Article VI are generally applicable. While the former provisions include *quantitative* provisions, Article VI disciplines are *qualitative*, intended to protect legitimate objectives. These three provisions are complementary in their functions: a measure scheduled under Article XVI or XVII may be scrutinized under Article VI regarding the regulatory, or administration aspects of it.[115]

12.9 DEVELOPMENT OF FUTURE DISCIPLINES CONCERNING RECOGNITION OF PROFESSIONAL QUALIFICATIONS

Article VII of GATS includes complementary[116] provisions on recognition of professional qualifications. This is particularly important for the supply of services under Mode 4. The basic difficulty concerning recognition is that the service supplier is, in fact 'a prisoner of its own past', not being able to alter its professional past and to develop new skills as might be required by the host country, within days or months.[117] It should be remembered, however, that market access of Mode 4 service suppliers is not only affected by recognition, but also by other regulatory interferes, such as regulated prices and salaries.[118]

---

115. *Ibid.*, 148–154.
116. J. P. Trachtman, n. 22, 75, says: 'the weak disciplines of Article VI:5, combined with potentially strengthened disciplines developed under Article VI:4, can provide incentives for recognition under Article VII, or under other circumstances they can accomplish the same goals as those sought under Article VII'.
117. R. Adlung, 'Services Liberalization from a GATS/WTO Perspective: in Search for Volunteers', *WTO Staff Working Paper ERSD-2009-05* (2009), 8, <www.wto.org>.
118. R. Adlung, n. 117, 13.

Article VII refers to the development of future disciplines on this subject. It provides:

> Recognition
>
> 1. For the purposes of the fulfillment, in whole or in part, of its standards or criteria for the authorization, licensing or certification of services suppliers, and subject to the requirements of paragraph 3, a Member may recognize the education or experience obtained, requirements met, or licenses or certifications granted in a particular country. Such recognition, which may be achieved through harmonization or otherwise, may be based upon an agreement or arrangement with the country concerned or may be accorded autonomously.
> 2. A Member that is a party to an agreement or arrangement of the type referred to in paragraph 1, whether existing or future, shall afford adequate opportunity for other interested Members to negotiate their accession to such an agreement or arrangement or to negotiate comparable ones with it. Where a Member accords recognition autonomously, it shall afford adequate opportunity for any other Member to demonstrate that education, experience, licenses, or certifications obtained or requirements met in that other Member's territory should be recognized.
> 3. A Member shall not accord recognition in a manner which would constitute a means of discrimination between countries in the application of its standards or criteria for the authorization, licensing or certification of services suppliers, or a disguised restriction on trade in services.
> 4. Each Member shall:
>   (a) within 12 months from the date on which the WTO Agreement takes effect for it, inform the Council for Trade in Services of its existing recognition measures and state whether such measures are based on agreements or arrangements of the type referred to in paragraph 1;
>   (b) promptly inform the Council for Trade in Services as far in advance as possible of the opening of negotiations on an agreement or arrangement of the type referred to in paragraph 1 in order to provide adequate opportunity to any other Member to indicate their interest in participating in the negotiations before they enter a substantive phase;
>   (c) promptly inform the Council for Trade in Services when it adopts new recognition measures or significantly modifies existing ones and state whether the measures are based on an agreement or arrangement of the type referred to in paragraph 1.
> 5. Wherever appropriate, recognition should be based on multilaterally agreed criteria. In appropriate cases, Members shall work in cooperation with relevant intergovernmental and non-governmental organizations towards the establishment and adoption of common international standards and criteria for recognition and common international standards for the practice of relevant services trades and professions.

This Article seeks 'to reduce potential trade distorting and restricting effects of recognition'[119] which is usually made towards certain countries, thus excluding the others. However, it does not provide for obligatory recognition of service suppliers' professional qualifications, but rather suggests doing so, either unilaterally or by agreement.

Article VII:1 This provision refers to all possible manners of recognition: unilateral, bilateral, multilateral and even, presumably, informal de facto recognition,[120] principally recognizing the right of Members to recognize education or experience obtained, requirements met, or licenses or certifications granted in a particular country.

Article VII:2 calls for Members engaging in a mutual recognition agreement (MRAs) to afford adequate opportunity for other interested Members to negotiate their accession to such an agreement or arrangement or to negotiate comparable ones with it.[121] This provision implies that recognition could be selective, thus effectively discriminating among Members, subject to the conditions set forth by paragraphs VII:2-5.[122] It does not restrict the discretion of the Members concerning the terms of recognition. The 'adequate opportunity' aims at balancing this tendency, preferring a multilateral or plurilateral approach towards recognition.[123]

In essence, this provision creates another exception to the MFN provision. It entails a broader vision than that reflected in Article V concerning regional trade agreements (see Chapter 10). However, unfortunately such recognition agreements are not subject to notification obligations similar to these provided for in Article V. This exception is balanced with disciplines embodied in paragraphs VII:2 and VII:3, designed to prevent this provision from completely undermining the MFN principle.[124]

The relationship between Article V and Article VII also raise an interpretative question: are MRAs concluded under Article V subject to Article VII?

> One view may be that Article V provides an exception to the fundamental non-discrimination (MFN) obligation in Article II and therefore an exemption also to similar obligations contained in other GATS provisions, including Article VII.
>
> Alternatively, it could be argued that all MRAs, regardless of whether they are concluded by parties to a regional integration agreement or other Members, are covered by Article VII and its disciplines cannot be circumvented by appealing to Article V.[125]

119. GATS commentary, n. 6, 199.
120. 'The General Agreement on Trade in Services (GATS): an Analysis', *OECD* (1994), 12, <www.olis.oecd.org>.
121. In practice only a few agreements were notified according to Art. VII. This fact seems to reflect the lack of interest in opening such agreements to the participation of third countries.
122. GATS Analysis, n. 120.
123. GATS commentary, n. 6, 201.
124. R. Adlung, 'The GATS Turns Ten: A Preliminary Stocktaking', *WTO* (2004), 5, <www.wto.org>.
125. A. Mattoo & D. Mishra, 'Foreign Professionals and Domestic regulation', The World Bank Policy Research Working Paper (2008), 13, <www-wds.worldbank.org>.

In practice, it seems that one obstacle to the creation of such mutual recognition agreements is the high transaction and regulatory costs involved in this process.[126]

Yet another practical obstacle may arise where MRAs are not concluded with the government of a Member but rather with entities which are not government entities, nor do they seem to exercise governmental powers. In such cases, these MRAs may totally escape from the scope of Article VII:2.[127]

According to Article VII:2(1), one way of achieving the goal of mutual recognition could be by harmonization of requirements. However, harmonization is a far-reaching step, likely to be taken between countries having a high degree of economic integration or similar systems of according professional diplomas.

One policy decision that should be taken in this context is: who decides about equivalence of professional qualifications?

> As long as this decision rests solely with the national authority and a WTO dispute settlement organ cannot question this decision, regulatory autonomy largely remains intact. If, however, dispute settlement organs determine whether there is equivalence or not, regulatory autonomy will be reduced.[128]

It is well known, that non-recognition of professional qualifications may be a serious obstacle to trade in services. At the same time, this is a sensitive issue, since it may involve protection of legitimate domestic interests such as consumer protection, public health and public safety.

In terms of substance, mutual recognition of professional qualifications and diplomas may be difficult and involve a considerable amount of knowledge. The process may be easier between countries with similar regime.[129]

Article VII:3 forbids Members from according recognition in 'a manner constituting a means of discrimination between countries . . . or a disguised restriction on trade in services'. It seems that due to the aforementioned substantive considerations, this provision has to be interpreted as implying substantial, rather than formal, non-discrimination.[130] Thus, based on the concept of non-discrimination developed in GATS Articles II (see Chapter 6) and XVII (see Chapter 8),

---

126. S.M Stephenson, 'Can Regional Liberalization of Services go Further Than Multilateral Liberalization under the GATS?', *1 World Trade Review* (2002), 14, <www.netamericas..doc>.
127. See examples for such agreements concluded by the United States: A. Mattoo & D. Mishra, n. 125, 13.
128. Krajewski, n. 52, 148.
129. For possible impact of future recognition disciplines on national regulations see: Krajewski, n. 52, 149–151.
130. An example given by Mattoo and Mishra refers to a physician from country x who wants to practice medicine in country y. Assuming that both are GATS Members, and the two stage approach for the examination of discrimination applies, if it is established that he is 'like' domestic physicians, according to the formal non-discrimination approach it will be impossible to impose on him any burden in terms of re-qualification which is not imposed on domestic physicians. Since this approach is hardly acceptable, it is preferred to opt for the practical, substantial non-discrimination, where the Members will have the right to impose extra requirements on foreign professional service suppliers to ensure domestic policy goals, subject to the necessity or proportionality test: n. 125, 14–15.

comparison as to the terms of recognition should take place subject to 'likeness' of circumstances.[131]

In some cases, though, a non-discrimination requirement alone might not suffice. These will be the cases where a non-discriminating requirement concerning professional qualifications, applying to domestic as well as to foreign services suppliers, is unduly intrusive.[132] Other barriers may stem from the cost of re-qualification or professional re-authorization process in the host country as well as from the necessity to cope with different requirements of different states (in the United States or in the EU).[133] The language of this provision does not cover such cases.

Article VII:4 refers to notification obligations by the Members to the Council for Trade in Services. According to it, recognition measures existing at the time of notification (twelve month after GATS entry into force for the relevant Member), new measures or significant changes in existing measures occurring thereafter, and the opening of negotiations on recognition agreements should be notified. Behind this provision there is an attempt to at least form transparency in this elaborated field. Transparency serves service suppliers in the short run, supplying the information about each Member's requirements and practice concerning recognition of professional qualifications. In the long run, it may create a database for further negotiations aimed at improving the current situation. The logic is similar to the logic behind the 'tariffication' process under GATT. However, similarly to other notification obligations in GATS, effective notification record is poor.[134] Infringement of the notification obligation undermines transparency, thus preventing other Members from proving that the requirements for recognition are fulfilled, hence undermining the MFN principle.

Unilateral recognition, without any MRA concluded, would also be subject to notification obligations.

While subparagraph VII:4(a) provides for a defined time-frame, the following subparagraphs: (b) and (c) refrain from doing so. However, the word 'promptly' included in them could be understood to imply, *inter alia*, a reasonable time frame that would be compatible to the achievement of transparency in relatively short-time objective of these provisions.

Article VII:5 repeats the same idea embodied in paragraphs VI:4(a) and VI:5(a), of potentially subjecting recognition to international standards, thus reflecting similar difficulties. The words 'where appropriate' leave discretion to the deciding authorities, thus turning this provision to non-obligatory, like the two provisions formerly mentioned.

131. GATS commentary, n. 6, 203.
132. Mattoo & Mishra give a far-fetched example, according to which a WTO Member requires all taxi drivers to be certified cardiologists because it is socially unacceptable in this country for people to die of hard attacks while trapped in traffic jams: n. 125, 16.
133. A. Mattoo & D. Mishra, n. 125, 17.
134. GATS commentary, n. 6, 204.

This provision attempts to strike a difficult balance between domestic policy needs and the trade liberalization interest of the agreement. One interpretative way to ensure that the disciplines developed under it would reflect this balance is to interpretatively read into it the necessity test, implying that the choice and level of measures applied by the Members in this respect will not be more burdensome than necessary. The interpretative difficulty in applying this test stems from the language of this article that does not mention it, unlike the explicit reference in the MFN and national treatment provisions.[135]

By now, this provision seems to be a dead letter.[136]

12.10 CONCLUSION

Provisions in GATS referring to administrative standards and recognition of professional qualifications (which is one specific case of administrative conduct) are meant to ensure that administrative functioning in the Members would not undermine the agreement's application and the fulfilment of its provisions in the Members.

The provisions referring to the application of specific commitments undertaken according to GATS are pronounced in a relatively much more definite manner, than the provisions referring to the application of domestic regulation concerning recognition of professional qualifications, which are more in the spirit of recommendations. This difference stems from both the lack of definite agreement among WTO Members as to the standards and methods that should apply in this context, and from the sensitive domestic interests involved in the process of recognition that should be guarded by the Members, for example, consumer protection, public health and safety.[137]

However, although the Members are not allowed to subject the obligations under Article VI to any scheduled limitations, and any deviation from these obligations would be considered a violation of this provision, the criteria set forth by this provision are so broad and vague that at least until more specific disciplines are developed according to Article VI:4, it would be very difficult to prove violation in fact.[138]

In fact, both groups of provisions are ambiguously drafted, *inter alia* to overcome an inherent conflict with domestic regulatory sovereignty.[139] This vague language is subject to interpretation by the WTO adjudicating bodies. Their future interpretation would thus determine the actual scope of these provisions, defining,

---

135. A. Mattoo, n. 85, 23.
136. P. Delimatsis, n. 16, 47.
137. Regional trade agreements referring to trade in services seem to adopt a much more pro-active approach to recognition: S.M Stephenson, n. 126, 13.
138. GATS Analysis, n. 120, 18
139. See suggestions to strengthen Art. VI: G. Feketekuty, 'Setting the Agenda for the Next Round of Negotiations on Trade in Services', in J. S. Schott (ed.), *Launching New Global Trade Talks: an Action Agenda*, Institute for International Economics (US) (1998), 91, 101.

at the same time, the division of powers between the WTO and its Members on this subject. In the meantime, this vagueness acts as an impediment to enhance commitments in this respect in the current Doha Round.[140]

The mechanism embodied in these provisions faces many difficulties, including the broad range of issues involved, the question of whether to apply these disciplines in the future also to sectors where no specific commitments were undertaken, and the complexity of issues involved with the sharing of competences between different government levels.[141]

The experience of developing sectoral disciplines to the accountancy sector, which reflected to what extent this process is time and effort consuming, encourages voices supporting return to the horizontal approach, based on the necessity test.[142]

To complete the picture of relationships between services trade liberalization and domestic regulation it should be noted, that these provisions reflect only part of the picture. An additional conflict of interest is reflected in Article XIV on general exceptions (see Chapter 15) as well as in the context of specific services sectors.[143]

---

140. R. Adlung, 'Services Liberalization from a GATS/WTO Perspective: in Search for Volunteers', *WTO Staff Working Paper ERSD-2009-05* (2009), 8, <www.wto.org>.
  For information of the poor application of these provisions, particularly Art. VII, until 2004 see: R. Adlung, *Ibid.*, 5–6.
141. P. Delimatsis, n. 16, 49.
142. P. Delimatsis, n. 61.
143. B. Hoeckman, 'Liberalizing Trade in Services: a Survey', *World Bank Policy Research Working Paper No. 4030* (2006), 37–39, <http://papers.ssrn.com>.

Chapter 13
Transparency

13.1 INTRODUCTION

Suppliers often find it difficult to do business in other countries, due to the laws and regulations applying in these countries, and sometimes even more – due to their non-transparency. Transparency of domestic laws and regulations is particularly decisive for trade in services, where regulation is a major instrument to restrict trade. In the short term, regulatory transparency is the minimum requirement for free trade in services, since it provides foreign service suppliers with more predictable conditions, for example, information about the costs and administrative burden they should expect in the country of destination. In practice, non-transparent information concerning market regulation is particularly burdensome for small service suppliers, who cannot afford to employ specialists to make the necessary inquiries.[1] Thus, transparency enhances competition. It may further contribute to dissemination of best practices and to to the reduction of disputes and improve monitoring of Members' behaviour, and encourage behaviour in a WTO consistent manner. Transparency can strengthen the supporters of liberalization against protectionists and reveal existing deficiencies that should be dismissed. In addition, 'regulatory transparency makes it more difficult for regulators to be captured by regulated firms, which helps protect the independence and autonomy that regulators need to do their jobs effectively'.[2] All these, in turn, may lead to an improvement of public confidence and a reduction of costs.[3]

1. R. Self & K. Zutshi, 'Mode 4: Negotiating Challenges and Opportunities', in A. Mattoo & A. Carzaniga (eds), *Moving People to Deliver Services*, The World Bank and Oxford University Press (2003), 27, 52.
2. K. Iida & J. Nielson, 'Transparency in Domestic Regulation: Practices and Politics', in A. Mattoo & P. Sauvé (eds), *Domestic Regulation and Service Trade Liberalization*, The World Bank and Oxford University Press (2003), 7–8.
3. P. Delimatsis, *International Trade in Services and Domestic Regulations – Necessity, Transparency and Regulatory Diversity*, Oxford University Press (2007), 255–257.

In the long term, the information thus revealed about regulatory practices in Members forms a factual basis for negotiations on better regulation, reflecting greater compliance with GATS disciplines, which could ultimately gain greater political legitimacy in the international trade arena. It may modify the patterns of services' supply and present higher standards for the operation of service suppliers.

It is for these reasons, that the notion and practice of transparency are inevitable to the development of the WTO agreements, including GATS. Transparency is particularly important in services areas where the role of regulation – as a trade protective instrument and/or as a domestic policy instrument – tends to feature more prominently than in most other segments of the economy.[4] However, GATS is not a transparent agreement,[5] in some aspects:

- The design of schedules, mainly the 'positive list' approach, implying that the schedules do not contain any information concerning service sectors which are not covered by them. This fact is combined with the relatively narrow scope of commitments made by some Members, particularly developing countries (see Chapter 7).
- Notification obligation in GATS Article III applies only to committed sectors.
- The scheduling technique leads to additional confusion and non-transparency (see Chapter 7).
- The discrepancy between Articles XVI and XVII, and to some extent between these provisions and Article VI:4 adds to this confusion (see Chapter 9).

In addition, in practice, the transparency obligation provided for by GATS is not always thoroughly followed by the Members. Moreover, transparency provisions in the WTO seem to be 'victims of judicial economy',[6] that is, neglected by WTO adjudicating bodies in favour of other provisions. Therefore, their interpretation is not intensively developed.

In GATS, transparency is mentioned in the Preamble, as well as in Article III and in Article VI:1-3 (domestic regulation concerning recognition, see Chapter 12).[7]

4. WTO explanatory paper, WTO Secretariat, 29.3.06 (3776.4), 7.
5. S.M. Stephenson, 'Regional Versus Multilateral Liberalization of Services', *1 World Trade Review* (2002) 187, 190.
6. R. Worfrum, P.T. Stoll & C. Feinäugle (eds), *WTO – Trade in Services,* Max Planck Commentaries on World Trade Law, Martinus Mijnhoff Publishers, Leiden, Boston (2008) (hereby: GATS commentary), 95.
7. Additional, sector specific and more enhanced provisions on transparency exist in the Reference Paper on Basic Telecommunications and in the disciplines developed on the Accountancy Sector, which are not yet in force.

Belonging to Part II of GATS, transparency is applicable to all service sectors and is unconditional.

Article III provides:

Transparency

1. Each Member shall publish promptly and, except in emergency situations, at the latest by the time of their entry into force, all relevant measures of general application which pertain to or affect the operation of this Agreement. International agreements pertaining to or affecting trade in services to which a Member is a signatory shall also be published.
2. Where publication as referred to in paragraph 1 is not practicable, such information shall be made otherwise publicly available.
3. Each Member shall promptly and at least annually inform the Council for Trade in Services of the introduction of any new, or any changes to existing, laws, regulations or administrative guidelines which significantly affect trade in services covered by its specific commitments under this Agreement.
4. Each Member shall respond promptly to all requests by any other Member for specific information on any of its measures of general application or international agreements within the meaning of paragraph 1. Each Member shall also establish one or more enquiry points to provide specific information to other Members, upon request, on all such matters as well as those subject to the notification requirement in paragraph 3. Such enquiry points shall be established within two years from the date of entry into force of the Agreement Establishing the WTO (referred to in this Agreement as the 'WTO Agreement'). Appropriate flexibility with respect to the time-limit within which such enquiry points are to be established may be agreed upon for individual developing country Members. Enquiry points need not be depositories of laws and regulations.
5. Any Member may notify to the Council for Trade in Services any measure, taken by any other Member, which it considers affects the operation of this Agreement.

The obligations to publish and notify measures affecting trade in services, dealt with in this provision, as well as the obligation to duly administer these measures, discussed in Chapter 12, are aimed at promoting a rule-oriented approach to trade policy in the national level.[8]

Article III distinguishes between the general obligation of *publication*, which applies to all services sectors and is unconditional (Article III:1), and the *notification* obligation (Article III:3) which refers only to trade in services affected by specific commitments of the notifying Member.

8. GATS commentary, n. 6, 94.

13.2 PUBLICATION OF RELEVANT MEASURES: ARTICLE III:1

Article III:1 provides that each Member should 'publish promptly . . . all relevant measures of general application which pertain to or affect the operation of this agreement'.

This provision applies to all services sectors, not only to sectors where specific commitments were undertaken.

This provision raises some interpretative questions:

- What is a 'prompt' publication?
- What are 'relevant measures of general application'?
- What does 'pertain to or affect the operation of this agreement' mean?
- What are 'emergency situations'?

13.2.1 Relevant Measures of General Application

The publication obligation refers to 'relevant measures of general application'. '*Measures*' are broadly defined by Article XXVII(a) of GATS (see Chapter 4). The *relevance* of a measure should be determined according to the circumstances, on a case-by-case basis. This broad definition may include measures in other sectors, for example, goods, which nevertheless affect trade in services.[9] The context of this provision clearly leads to a conclusion that it applies to 'measures affecting trade in services' in the broad meaning of Article I:1 of GATS (see Chapter 4). Nevertheless, the language of Article III:1 adds, that such measures should 'pertain to or affect the operation of this agreement'.

'Measures of general application', were interpreted by the WTO adjudicating bodies, in the context of the equivalent Article X of GATT, as measures affecting 'an unidentified number of economic operators'.[10] In the context of the equivalent GATT Article X it was further held 'that the actions in question would have to have a significant impact on the overall administration of the law, and not simply on the outcome in a single case in question'.[11] In principle, this interpretation should be understood as meaning that measures referring to specific economic operators or to specific situations will not be covered by this provision. This interpretation could

9. *Ibid.*, 97. However, in the context of the equivalent GATT Article X it was stressed that the determination whether a domestic measure corresponds to this definition is not in the hands of each individual Member, but is rather subject to the WTO law: WT/DS375,376,377/R *EC and its Member States – Tariff Treatment of Certain IT Products*, published 19.8.2010 (not adopted yet at the time of writing), para. 7.1023, citing former jursprudence. The same logic should apply in GATS context.
10. WT/DS24/R, AB/R United States – Restrictions on Imports of Cotton and Man-Made Fibre Underwear, adopted on 25.2.1997, Panel report, para. 7.65 and Appellate Body report, 21, DSR 1997:I, 3. at 29.
11. WT/DS184/R, AB/R United State – Anti Dumping Measures on Certain Hot-Rolled Steel Products from Japan, adopted on 23.8.2001, Panel report, para. 7.268.

either refer to the *nature* or to the *practical application* of the measure at stake. However, the former option seems preferable in terms of legal analysis, being more objective and predictable. Thus, in GATT case *Japan – Film,* the Panel established that administrative rulings in individual cases should be deemed measures of general application if they establish or revise principles or criteria applicable in future cases.[12]

While Article X:1 of GATT specifies the kind of measures it applies to: 'laws, regulations, judicial decisions and administrative rulings . . . ', Article III of GATS uses a much more general language, referring to 'all relevant measures of general application which pertain to or affect the operation of this agreement'. Compared to Article X:1 of GATT, Article III of GATS is a relatively short, comprehensive and flexible provision, that may cover additional future developments. It avoids a detailed list of measures that could always turn out to be non-comprehensive. On the other hand, the general drafting of GATS Article III suffers from some ambiguity.

13.2.1.1 'Pertain to or Affect the Operation of this Agreement'

This expression includes two categories of measures:

(1) Measures affecting the operation of the agreement.
(2) Measures pertaining to affect the operation of the agreement.

While the first category is based on facts, as the invoking party may prove that the measure involved affects the operation of the agreement, the second category is more flexible, since it refers to an assessment concerning future possibilities that did not yet take place. Therefore, the second option is subject to discretionary assessment, first by the relevant Member, and later, potentially, by other, challenging Members and by the WTO adjudicating bodies. GATS sets a substantially broad scope of obligation, to publish even such measures. In other words, it prevents the Members from using an excuse for non-publication arguing that the measure involved did not yet affect the operation of the agreement. This broad concept serves predictability.

13.2.1.2 Affect the Operation of the Agreement

There is no interpretation to this expression in the language of the agreement. It seems that the purpose of the provision in which it is included is to prevent a situation where a Member applies measures undermining the enhancement of liberalization of international trade in services, namely measures that impose barriers to trade or pertain to do so, without publishing them first, thus misleading foreign service suppliers to engage in transactions, believing that no barriers to trade exist, based on GATS and the specific commitments attached to it.

---

12. WT/DS44/R Japan – Measures Affecting Consumer Photographic Film and Paper, adopted on 31.3.1998, Panel report, para. 10.388.

However, it is unclear whether by the expression 'the operation of this agreement' the drafters meant that measures subject to the transparency requirement should be only these covered by GATS conditional and unconditional obligations, or also measures supporting the object and purpose of the agreement. Some commentators suggest[13] that this term should be regarded, for all practical purposes, as being the same as 'affecting trade in services'. However, this interpretation disregards the different language of the two provisions that should be taken into account according to the Vienna Convention.

13.2.1.3 Comparison to GATT Article X

Article X:1 of GATT requires, *inter alia,* the publication of 'agreements affecting international trade policy which are in force between the government or governmental agency of any Member and a government or a governmental agency of any other Member'.

Compared to this language, the language of GATS Article III extends the publication obligation by applying it not only to mutual agreements between or among Members, but also to agreements a Member may have with third parties.

GATT Article X:I, like GATS Article III:1, refers to measures *affecting* trade as well as to measures *pertaining* to affect it. But while Article III:1 of GATS does not specify the measures included in each category, Article X:1 of GATT divides the measures into two groups:

- '*pertaining* to the classification or the valuation of products for customs purposes, or to rates of duty, taxes or other charges, or to restrictions or prohibitions on imports or exports or on the transfer of payments; or'
- '*affecting* their sale, distribution, transportation, insurance, warehousing, inspection, exhibition, processing, mixing or other use . . . '

GATS drafting avoided this division, thus broadening the scope of measures to which the publication obligation applies.

In both agreements, this provision seems to be necessary in light of the growing numbers of regional trade agreements in the world.[14]

13.2.2 'Prompt' Publication

13.2.2.1 Time of Publication

Unlike GATS Article III:3, which explicitly requires an annual notification, Article III:1 does not specify any time limit for publication. On the one hand, this

13. GATS commentary n. 6, 96.
14. For data concerning this aspect see: R.V. Fiorentino, L. Verdeja & C. Toqueboeuf, Discussion Paper No. 12: 'The Changing Landscape of regional Trade Agreements: 2006 update', WTO (2007), 3–5, <www.wto.org>.

omission allows for full flexibility and a case-by-case analysis. On the other hand, it may lead to abuse of this full discretion by Members who would unduly delay publication, thus undermining the purpose of this provision.

Yet another question arising due to this omission is whether 'prompt' publication would be judged on equal basis for all Members, or rather, should their economic status (developed – developing – least developed) and their administrative capabilities be also taken into consideration.

Since this expression was not yet interpreted in GATS context, a lesson may be drawn from its interpretation in Article X of GATT, which seems to be its source, subject to the differences between these provisions, to be discussed below.

Rationally, it may be expected that publication would take place *before* the application of a measure. However, in the context of GATT 1947, in certain cases, *simultaneous* publication and entry into force would be allowed. In that context it was further established, that this provision does not imply that the measure involved should be published at the same time to domestic and foreign suppliers, neither does it requires a Member to publish trade regulations before their entry into force.[15] It was ruled that Article X:1 of GATT 1947 did *not* provide that domestic and foreign traders acquire access to information *at the same time*. In GATT 1994 case *US – Underwear,*[16] the Appellate Body's interpretation of Article X:2 does not seem to support this interpretation.[17] In the context of GATT 1947, 'promptly' was interpreted as preventing *retroactive* publication of a measure.[18] Nevertheless, the language of Article III:1 of GATS which, unlike Article X:1 of GATT 1947, does not explicitly provide otherwise, may tolerate even publications *after* the entry into force, in emergency situations. Due to this difference between the two provisions, GATS Article III may be considered theoretically weaker than GATT Article X. However, if GATT interpretation will be applied to GATS provision, this omission will not make a difference.[19]

In Article X:1 of GATT, the word 'promptly' is accompanied by some explanation: 'in such a manner as to enable governments and traders to become acquainted with them'. This explanation may assist the understanding of 'promptly' in GATS context as well, but since it was omitted by GATS drafters

---

15. DS17/R Canada – Import, Distribution and Sale of Certain Alcoholic Drinks by provincial Marketing Agencies, adopted on 18.2.1992, 39S/27, para. 5.34.
16. WT/DS24/R *US – Underwear*, n. 10, Panel report.
17. GATS commentary, n. 6, 98.
18. L/6491 The Panel Report on 'EEC – Restrictions on Imports of Dessert Apples, complaint by Chile', adopted on 22.6.1989, 36S/93, para. 12.29; L/6513 The Panel report on 'EEC – Restrictions on Imports of Apples, complaint by the United States', adopted on 22.6.1989, 36S/135, para. 5.23.
19. In the recent GATT case WT/DS375,376,377/R *EC and its Member States – Tariff Treatment of Certain IT Products*, n. 9, para. 7.1076 the Panel concluded that publication of measures in the official journal eight months after they were 'made effective' does not qualify as 'prompt' according to GATT Article X:1. P. Delimatsis, n. 3, 263–264, suggests not to take this omission as deliberate due to the nature and general function of the transparency principle. Nevertheless, since GATT formula was well known to GATS drafters, this omission raises interpretative questions as to their intention.

it is unclear whether they simply believed it to be obvious and therefore unnecessary to mention, or wanted to allow another interpretation.

Article III:1 implies that emergency situations may justify *retroactive* publication. In such cases, for example, in economic, financial or security crisis, it is obvious that publication is not in high priority, but once it becomes possible, it seems that retroactive publication is better than no publication at all. Nevertheless, in GATT context the Appellate Body stressed that '[w]here no authority exists to give retroactive effect to a restrictive governmental measure, that deficiency is not cured by publishing the measure sometimes before its actual application. The necessary authorization is not supplied by Article X:2 of the General Agreement'.[20]

Despite the necessary flexibility to cope with different situations as described above, the lack of clearer indications as to the time of publication undermines, at least to a certain extent, the purpose of this provision, to support the certainty and predictability of foreign service suppliers.

13.2.2.2 Place of Publication

Article III does not specify where the information should be published. It may be assumed that each publication will be examined due to the standard determined by this provision: 'promptly', on a case-by-case basis. Thus, an inaccessible publication shall not be acceptable.[21]

13.3 ARTICLE III:2

13.3.1 'Not Practicable'

Article III:2 provides that where publication as referred to in paragraph 1 is not practicable, such information shall be made otherwise publicly available. The term 'not practicable' is not defined by the agreement. It is unclear whether it provides for an objective, or rather a subjective standard; should it be considered according to a uniform standard, or may the economic status or development stage of a Member involved be taken into account? There is no answer to this question, neither in the language of this provision nor in GATT/WTO jurisprudence. According to one opinion,[22] 'this provision arguably allows WTO Members lacking the financial resources to publish all measures of relevant application the flexibility to avoid having to incur the full cost of publication (including the wide dissemination of certain material)'.

20. WT/DS24/AB/R *US – Underwear*, n. 10, Appellate Body report, 21.
21. In GATT context, for example, publication in the Official Journal of the EU was recognized as 'prompt': L/6491 *EEC – Dessert Apples*, n. 18, para. 12.29.
22. F. Ortino, 'Regional Trade Agreements and Trade in Services', in *S. Lester and B. Mercurino (eds), Bilateral and Regional Trade Agreements: Commentary, Analysis and Case Studies*, Cambridge CPU (2007), 6, <http://papers.ssrn.com>.

13.3.2 'Publicly Available'

Article III:2 provides, that where publication as referred to in paragraph 1 is not practicable, such information shall be made otherwise publicly available. This provision raises yet more interpretative questions: where and why publication according to paragraph 1 will not be practicable? And what is the alternative presented by the words 'shall be made otherwise practically available'?

The spirit of this provision is clear: it is meant to eliminate any opportunity of a practical obstacle for publication from supporting non-publication according to the agreement. Thus, if the Official Journal is not published for some reason – the Member involved could not rely on this fact for not fulfilling its legal obligation for transparency – it should rather find another way to achieve this end, whether by publishing in daily newspapers, or at the relevant ministry's internet site, or by making a public announcement.

However, since this provision does not determine any rules as to the circumstances where it will apply or to the ways by which the information will be made 'publicly available', it is not clear whether it will be considered to be fulfilled by putting one copy of the information in the relevant government ministry, thus enforcing every interested person to come and see it there.

It is unfortunate that the agreement does not determine that in such cases (that may occur at least in developing countries, who might not have enough resources to publish in a more efficient way), the Member involved will at least be obliged to publicly announce that such information exists and could not be otherwise published, for example, due to its length, and the way to gain access to it.

13.3.3 Language of Publication

Except in the case of formal notification obligation addressed above, the agreement does not determine any specific language of publication for the information.[23] Thus, the purpose of this provision may be totally or partially undermined, as the publication will not be understood or as alternatively, the interested party will be enforced to translate it, bearing an extra burden in terms of time and money.

13.4 ARTICLE III:3

Article III:3 contains the transparency obligations that Members have towards the WTO, that is, a yearly notification obligation.

This provision, like former paragraphs, includes some ambiguous, uninterpreted expressions: 'promptly', 'significantly affect', etc.

23. The use of specific languages (the WTO official languages), is provided for, e.g., in the transparency provision of the Government Procurement Agreement (GPA): Art. XVII:1(b).

13.4.1 Scope of Application

The scope of application of this notification provision is narrowed by its language, in some respects:

Firstly, the notification obligation applies only to measures significantly affecting trade in services, covered by *specific commitments*. Measures which do not affect services covered by specific commitments are thus excluded from the scope of this obligation, and should not be notified.[24] Nevertheless, this provision applies to measures which are not *scheduled* according to GATS (e.g., covered by GATT) if they *affect* trade in services covered by specific commitments.

Secondly, the notification obligation does not apply to *any* 'measure' (in the broad sense of Article XXVII(a) of GATS), but only to the categories specified in this provision: *laws, regulations or administrative guidelines*.

Thirdly, these categories of measures should only be notified being *new, or changing* existing laws, regulations or administrative guidelines. Thus, measures *existing* at the time of the conclusion of GATS should not be notified, unless being amended.[25] This provision significantly narrows the impact of this sub-paragraph, and may also undermine the thorough understanding of the meaning of later changes notified. Since the word 'changes' in neutral, changes improving a given situation, as well as changes escalating it, should be notified.[26]

Fourthly, measures should only be notified if they *significantly affect* trade in services covered by specific commitments. This condition would be judged by the Member applying such measures,[27] but its discretion could naturally be further challenged by other Members. It should be noted, there is no indication in this provision as to the relevant considerations that should be taken into account.

13.4.2 'Prompt' Notification

Similarly to Article III:1, this word is not defined by Article III:3, either. However, considering the context, it seems that the interpretation of this word in this provision should be different, and more flexible, than in paragraph 1.[28]

In terms of time, usually, the first publication of improved terms of trade is included in the schedules of specific commitments submitted to the Council for

24. Various Members believed that extending the notification obligation to measures *not* covered by the specific commitments would impose an unbearable administrative burden on certain Members: GATS commentary, n. 6, 99.
25. GATS commentary, n. 6, 100.
26. *Ibid.* If these measures also affect market access or national treatment commitments, they are subject to another notification obligation, under Art. XXI:1(b), that may start a modification of schedules' procedure (see Ch. 15).
27. GATS commentary, n. 6, 100.
28. *Ibid.*, 102.

Trade in Services. Following updates, including new legislation and regulation, have to take place at least annually.[29]

In terms of format, notification under this provision is subject to guidelines adopted by the Council for Trade in Services.[30] These guidelines dictate a standard format[31] for notification. The Trade Policy Review Body is the repository of all notifications by the Members. Notification made according to this format is submitted in the three official languages of the WTO: English, French and Spanish. It has to include an explanation referring to the essence of the measure involved and its effect. Notification is required even concerning measures that do not affect market access or national treatment in a certain sector. Notification is required whether the new measure improves, or worsens, the existing situation.

Where a Member intends to apply to a sector, in which specific commitments were undertaken, a measure affecting market access or national treatment, it should notify its intention at least three months before the date of application, and such notification will start the procedure provided for in Article XXI (modification of specific commitments – see Chapter 15).

13.5 ARTICLE III:4: ENQUIRY AND CONTACT POINTS

Article III:4 provides for the establishment, by the Members, of enquiry points to deal with requests for information. To facilitate their function it was provided, that the requests for information will be submitted by governments only, but this practice complicates access to the information by the private sector. Considering the difficulties encountered by developing countries mentioned before, these countries are entitled to a delay in establishing such enquiry points.[32]

It is determined, that 'enquiry points need not be depositories of laws and regulations'.

Article III:4 provides that 'each Member shall respond promptly to all requests by any other Member for specific information on any of its measures of general application or international agreements within the meaning of paragraph 1'. This provision does not specify what the term 'respond promptly' means: does it refer to the time frame, preventing undue delay? Does it refer to the content of response? For example, could an obligation to supply all the information concerning the relevant measure, in a commonly used language, be read into this provision? It

---

29. In practice, it seems that the Members do not fulfil this obligation: GATS commentary, n. 6, 101.
30. WT/TC/NOTIF/GATS1, Technical Cooperation Handbook on Notification Requirements – GATS, 15.10.96. See also Guidelines for Notifications under the General Agreement on Trade in Services, S/L/5 approved by the council for trade in services on 1.3.1995, S/C/M/1, paras 10–11.
31. This standard format is also applicable to notifications under Arts V, V*bis*, VII, VIII, X, XII, XIV*bis*, XXI and the para. 7 of the Annex on Art. II exemptions.
32. This provision is complemented by GATS Art. IV:2 requiring developed countries to establish, in addition, contact points serving services suppliers from developing countries (see Ch. 14).

seems that this provision should not be given a too broad meaning, undermining the balance of interests achieved by the other relevant provisions referring to this subject. It should be read in its context, namely in the context of Article III as a whole. So read, it may bear a narrow interpretation, confining its scope of application only to the manner of response, implying that it should take place within a reasonable time frame and should supply relevant details without creating an exceptional administrative burden on the competent authority. Nevertheless, even this approach may prove problematic, due to the substantial differences between competent authorities of the different Members, in terms of availability of labour, budget, availability of technological devices etc.

Article IV:2 of GATS further provides, that in addition to the enquiry points developed countries, and 'to the extent possible', other Members should establish contact points. Access to information from these points is direct.[33] These points should supply business information, particularly concerning access to services' technology, commercial and technical aspects of trade in services, registration, recognition and authorization procedures for service suppliers.[34] (For implication of this provision on developing countries see Chapter 14).

By now, these practices seem to have been barely used, being accessible only to governments while the private sector, which is the sector most interested in the information, has no access to them.[35]

13.6 REVERSE NOTIFICATION: ARTICLE III:5

This paragraph provides that any Member may notify to the Council for Trade in Services, any measure, taken by any other Member, which it considers as affecting the operation of GATS.

This provision opens another channel for notification: not only by the Member applying the restrictive measures, but also by the other Members. The right of a Member to notify a measure taken by another Member is not subject to it being affected by it, or to any prior consultations. The only condition for such notification is that the notifying Member feels that the notified measure 'affects the operation of GATS'. This is a broader scope of application than that provided for in paragraph 3, in two respects:

(1) Notification is not limited only to laws, regulations and administrative guidelines, but may refer to 'any measure'.

---

33. Article XXV:1 of GATS.
34. On 28.5.1996, the Council for Trade in Services adopted the Decision on the Notification of the Establishment of Enquiry and Contact Points, which calls upon Members to notify the establishment of enquiry points pursuant to para. 4 of Art. III: S/C/M/10, paras 9–10. The decision can be found in S/L/23 Council for Trade in Services, Decision on the Notification of the Establishment of Enquiry and Contact Points, adopted by the Council for Trade in Services on 28 May 1996, 27.6.1996.
35. P. Delimatsis, 'Concluding the WTO services Negotiations on Domestic Regulation – Walk Unafraid', *TILEC Discussion Paper DP-2009-032* (2009), 14, <http://papers.ssrn.com>.

(2) The effect of the notified measure is not limited to specific commitments, but refers to the entire GATS.

In terms of effectiveness, this provision may raise the chances for such notification by permitting other Members to interfere. Thus, a Member having a well established system following the legal situation of other Members may contribute to the general level of transparency from which all Members benefit. At the same time, it should be borne in mind that such notification totally depends on the discretion of the notifying Member, which may misjudge a measure by another member to affect trade in services, for example, due to lack of sufficient information concerning the domestic legal context of that measure.

At any rate, according to this provision such notification does not have any operative implications beyond spreading the information and drawing the attention of the Council for Trade in Services to that practice. In order to achieve more operative results concerning this measure, additional steps, based on other provisions in the agreement, should be taken.

13.7 COMPARISON TO ARTICLE X OF GATT

Article III of GATS and the equivalent Article X of GATT both establish a bottom-up approach, where the Members should supply the necessary information to the WTO.[36] However, a comparison between the two reflects some differences in the concept of drafting, which should be taken into account to prevent an automatic application of the interpretation developed in GATT context to GATS context. Some of the differences were discussed above. Yet other differences between the two provisions should be considered:

- Article X of GATT does not use the term 'transparency', used by Article III of GATS.
- While Article X of GATT incorporates all three obligations of which transparency commonly consists in the WTO agreements: publication, notification and due administration, in GATS the transparency obligations are shared by Article III and Article VI on domestic regulation (see Chapter 12).

13.8 THE EXCEPTION TO THE TRANSPARENCY RULE

Article III*bis* forms an exception to the general rule of transparency. Its general aim is to balance the interest of transparency discussed above with other legitimate interests. It could not be invoked by a Member as a basis for refusal to reveal

36. Top-down transparency is achieved by the periodic survey of Members' policies by the WTO in the Trade Policy Review Mechanism (TPRM): P. Delimatsis, n. 3, 259.

information in dispute settlement procedures, when the information is sought by a panel pursuant to Article 13 DSU.[37]

It provides:

> Disclosure of Confidential Information
>
> Nothing in this Agreement shall require any Member to provide confidential information, the disclosure of which would impede law enforcement, or otherwise be contrary to the public interest, or which would prejudice legitimate commercial interests of particular enterprises, public or private.

Such an exception is common in international agreements, for example, agreements for the avoidance of double taxation. However, this provision arises some interpretative difficulties.

13.8.1 Scope of Application

Article III*bis* forms an exception to GATS obligations, in particular to the transparency obligations specified in Articles III and VI. However, stating 'nothing in this agreement' implies that its application is broader and applies to *any* revelation of information according to GATS, including the professional Annexes considered an integral part of the agreement (see Chapter 16). If the accountancy disciplines will be annexed to GATS it will also apply to them.[38]

13.8.2 Circumstances where Article III*bis* may be Invoked

Article III*bis* does not define what should be considered 'confidential' information.[39] Alternatively, it defines the interests for the guarding of which it may be invoked. Three alternative interests are defined:[40]

37. See detailed analysis in GATS commentary, n. 6, 110–111.
38. In this sense its scope of application is broader than that provided for by the exception included in the equivalent GATT Art. X:1, which is confined to that article.
39. In WT/DS166/R US – Definitive Safeguard Measures on the Imports of Wheat Gluten from the EC, adopted on 19.1.2001, para. 8.20, the Panel, interpreting the term 'confidential' in Art. 3.2 of the Safeguard Agreement which is also not interpreted by that agreement, to mean that the competent authorities 'enjoy a certain amount of discretion in determining whether or not information is to be treated 'confidential'. However, this interpretation, even if applied *mutatis mutandis* to Art. III*bis* of GATS (as suggested in GATS commentary, n. 6, 109) does not determine the scope of reasonable discretion, neither does it specify the qualities of information necessary to render it confidential.
40. A different, more specific definition of interests to be protected by confidentiality exists in other WTO agreements: Art. 6.5 Anti Dumping Agreement, Art. 12.4 SCM Agreement. Confidentiality provisions are also included in Annex B:11(b) of the SPS Agreement, in Art. 5.2.4 of the TBT Agreement and in Art. 12.11 of the Safeguards Agreement.

(1) *The disclosure of the information would impede law enforcement* – the term 'law' is not defined in GATS. However, it is broad and seems to encompass all elements which determine legal disciplines in the domestic legal system, as well as international legal norms having domestic implication. It should be noted that this provision is not confined to commercial or trade law, but applies to law enforcement in general. This provision may be invoked, for example, to prevent the revelation of a planned enforcement operation.

(2) *The disclosure of the information would otherwise be contrary to the public interest* – this is an even broader category. The 'public interest' is not defined in the agreement, and would be probably decided on a case-by-case basis, and may change from one Member to another, as well as over time. This concept seems to be even broader than the interests defined in Articles XIV and XIV*bis* (see Chapter 15). While the former category pre-supposes the existence of 'law', a fact which should be established in a specific case in order to invoke that category, this category is more flexible, and may be invoked in cases where no relevant 'law' exists, but nevertheless, public interest is assessed to be threatened.

    Thus, for example, it is unclear whether the need to allocate substantial resources to fulfil transparency requirements in a poor country is 'contrary to the public interest', since the money could be used for other purposes, that would better serve the public interest? How would a poor country be defined for that matter?

(3) *The disclosure of the information would prejudice legitimate commercial interests of particular enterprises, public or private* – in order to use this argument, a legitimate commercial interest of particular, public or private enterprises should be established. The word 'legitimate' is not defined by this provision. Moreover: a conflict may occur between what is domestically considered as a 'legitimate' interest and the 'legitimacy' of an interest under GATS.

The burden of proof that these circumstances take place lies on the Member applying confidentiality. At the first stage, a Member invoking one of these arguments to avoid the disclosure of information exercises its own discretion. However, this discretion may be later challenged by another Member, being finally subject to the judgment of the WTO adjudicating bodies.

13.9 CONCLUSION

Transparency is a minimum requirement for creating a sound informative basis for foreign services suppliers, allowing them to take correct business decisions, as well as for preventing, or at least diminishing, trade barriers. Transparency may be achieved by different levels of obligations, for example, binding disciplines, 'best endeavours' disciplines, etc. Article III of GATS reflects a rather flexible approach to transparency requirements, reflected, *inter alia,* in some vague components thereof. Transparency disciplines embodied in Article III of GATS should be seen and interpreted as part of a larger context, including transparency requirements in other GATS provisions, for example, Article VI (see Chapter 12), as well as in other WTO agreements. To complete the discussion on this subject, it should be noted that part of the transparency difficulties encountered by foreign service suppliers emanate not from the incomplete legal framework of disciplines on this subject, but rather from poor implementation of existing disciplines or from the necessity for their greater precision, to which Article III may form an example.[41] In addition, these transparency obligations do not cover deficiencies emanating from the design and pursuit of schedules of specific commitments, including the information concerning access conditions to the markets of the Members. The schedules are subject to the 'bottom up' or 'positive list' approach (see Chapter 7), thus resulting in unequal commitments. The national schedules do not include information on services/service sectors where no commitment was made by a Member, neither for sectors marked 'unbound'. Moreover, the transparency obligation in Article III applies only to committed sectors. These deficiencies are particularly decisive in cases of countries that avoided taking too many commitments, for example, developing countries.[42] Probably for all these reasons, the Members have poor notification records.[43] However, it should be remembered, that transparency alone cannot eliminate more deeply embedded inefficiencies, and that its pursuit in greater quantities may be costly, thus necessitating a cost-benefit analysis before application.[44] Due to its importance, transparency is one of the prioritized subjects in the WPDR discussions.[45]

41. For further comparative information about transparency provisions in the multilateral, regional and domestic levels, and for suggestions of enhancing transparency see: K. Iida & J. Nielson, n. 2, 8–24.
42. S.M Stephenson, 'Can Regional Liberalization of Services go Further Than Multilateral Liberalization under the GATS?' *1 World Trade Review* (2002), 5, <www.netamericas.net>.
43. R. Adlung, 'Services Liberalization from a GATS?WTO Perspective: in Search for Volunteers', *WTO Staff Working Paper ERSD-2009-05* (2009), 5, <www.wto.org>.
44. Mattoo & Sauvé, n. 2, 224.
45. P. Delimatsis, n. 3, 270–271.

Chapter 14
GATS and the Developing Countries

14.1 INTRODUCTION

Developing countries form the majority of the WTO Members. About two-thirds of WTO Members are developing or least-developed countries. While least-developed countries are defined, according to Article XI:2 of the WTO Agreement, as those recognized as such by the UN,[1] developing countries are not defined according to any agreed criteria. Each Member decides whether to define itself as developing or developed.[2] Some indication to the profile of developing countries may be found in GATT Article XVIII:1 which refers to Members, 'the economies of which can only support low standards of living and are in the early stages of development'.

In Chapter 1, the suspicious position of developing countries towards the conclusion of GATS, and its reflection in GATS language, were already mentioned.

Compared to developed countries, the share of developing countries in international trade in services is minor. In addition, for some of them, the scope of international trade in services is substantially lower, compared to the scope of their international trade in goods. On the other hand, other developing countries rely on the profits gained from international trade in services, to offset deficits caused by their international trade in goods. According to the IMF, services account for about half of value-added and employment in developing countries.[3]

In recent decades, in some developing countries, particularly in Asia, a more rapid growth of trade in commercial services occurred than in developed countries.

---

1. See the UN list of countries recognized as LDCs: <www.un.org>.
2. Nevertheless, the definition must have some reasonable basis and it may hold further implications concerning the position of that state in other international economic forums, like the OECD.
3. A. Lehmann, N.T. Tamirisa & J. Wieczorek, 'International Trade in services: Implications for the IMF', *IMF Policy Discussion Paper*(2003), 2, <www.tessproject.com>.

By and large, developing countries tend to export tourism services and other labour-intensive services, such as private nursing and construction.[4] However, in recent years some developing countries also export services exercised by skilled workers, who join the global market, offering their services in relatively attractive prices. This trend is explained, *inter alia,* by the growing portion of the aging population in developed countries, which creates a need for young, skilled professional workers.[5] Examples for such services include information technology related services such as back-office processing and call centres.[6] The most famous example is that of Indian software engineers.[7]

Despite these facts and concerns mentioned in Chapter 1, trade in services is important for the development of developing countries.[8] Trade in services substantially affects development; services have a strong intermediate role. Therefore, gains from their trade include both the direct effect on the sector itself and the indirect effect on other sectors in the economy, making use of these services. In addition, this trade currently faces very high barriers to trade in comparison to trade in goods. The elimination of such barriers, thus, folds potentially higher gains.[9] However, concerns by leaders prevent, in many cases, the access of foreign service suppliers to these markets.[10]

4. In this sector developing countries have clear comparative advantage but trade is limited by trade barriers in many countries: J. Hodge, 'Liberalization of Trade in Services in Developing Countries', in B.M. Hoeckman, A. Mattoo & P. English, *Development, Trade and the WTO: A Handbook, The World Bank* (2002), 221, 223.
5. A. Mattoo & D. Mishra, 'Foreign Professionals and Domestic regulation', *The World Bank Policy Research Working Paper* (2008), 2, <www-wds.worldbank.org>.
6. J. Hodge, n. 4, 224.
7. V.N. Balasubramanyam, & A. Balasubramanyam, 'International Trade in Services: The Case for India's Computer Software', *20 The World Economy* (1997), 829. See also: T.W. Hertel, B.M. Hoeckman, & W. Martin, 'Developing Countries and the New Round of WTO Negotiations', *The World Bank Working Paper* (2000), 13, <www-wds.worldbank.org>.

   According to another opinion, success of developing countries in services export is only limited to country-episodes such as the Indian computer and data processing services, since these countries do not benefit yet from innovations in information technology sectors: R.J. Langhammer, 'Developing Countries as Exporters of Services: What Trade Statistics Suggest', *17 Journal of Economic Integration (2002),* 297–310. For an analysis of trade barriers faced by services suppliers from developing countries (in particular India) and an assessment of the effect of disciplines proposed in Doha Round on their market access options see: S. Karmakar, 'Disciplining Domestic Regulation Under GATS and its Implications for Developing Countries: An Indian Case Study', *41 Journal of World Trade* (2007), 127.
8. For specific difficulties in services trade encountered by these countries see: 'Service Delivery in Fragile Situations: Key Concepts, Findings and Lessons', *OECD, 9 Journal of Development* (2008), <www.oecd.org>.
9. J. Hodge, n. 4, 224.
10. See detailed analysis of anti-competitive practices and the importance of competition to the development of LDCs' markets: R.S. Khemani, 'Competition Policy and Promotion of Investment, Economic Policy and Poverty Alleviation in Least Developed Countries', *Working Paper 41334, the IBRD and the World Bank* (2007), <www-wds.worldbank.org>.

Some of the domestic services of developing countries, protected by governments, serve as inputs in the production of final products, for example, banking or insurance services. Their protection may adversely affect the final product's price.[11]

International trade liberalization in services is viewed as a growth and development engine for developing countries. It could contribute to their industrialization, by promoting investments, innovations[12] and integration of factor and product markets.[13] It could prevent, at least to some extent, the cost of protection.[14] Of particular importance to these countries are infrastructure services, ensuring better transportation, telecommunication, financing, health and education. In addition, trade in services bears important balance-of-payment implications for these countries.

Some even believe that due to the benefits enfolded in trade liberalization in services for developing countries, they should initiate unilateral acts to achieve it,[15] and indeed, some developing countries took such steps.[16]

Nevertheless, developing countries are still considered to have more restrictive trade regimes than developed countries.[17]

Economists believe that the comparative advantage theory applies to trade in services as much as it applies to trade in goods.[18]

The comparative advantage of a country is defined by the endowment of capital, natural resources and labour. Developed countries are often characterized by capital and skilled labour endowment, while developing countries are characterized by labour endowment.

Infrastructure is one important factor that differentiates between developed and developing countries in terms of the capacity to produce services. While the former enjoy developed infrastructure, as well as the ability to improve it in terms of knowledge and capital, the lack of due infrastructure in many of the latter

11. J.N. Bhagwati, 'Trade in Services and the Multilateral Trade Negotiations', *1 The World Bank Economic Review* (1987), 549, 561.
12. The import of innovations to these countries may be achieved by technology transfer: S. Miroudot 'The Linkages Between Open Services Markets and Technology Transfer', *OECD Trade Policy Working Paper No. 29* (2006), <www.olis.oecd.org>.
13. H.G. Broadman, 'GATS: The Uruguay Round Accord on International Trade and Investment in Serices', *17 The World Economy (1994),* 283; J. Whalley, 'Assessing the Benefits to Developing Countries of Liberalisation in Services Trade', 27 *The World Economy* (2004), 1223–1253; Lehmann et al., n. 3, 10–11.
14. J.A. Marchetti, 'Developing Countries in the WTO Services Negotiations'. *WTO* (2004), 4–8, <www.wto.org>.
15. B. Hindley, 'Service Sector Protection: Considerations for Developing Countries', *2 The World Bank Economic Review* (1988), 205.
16. Lehmann et al., n. 3, 12.
17. *Ibid.*, 3–4. It is noted, that in recent years some openness is seen in these countries concerning financial and telecommunication services, but commercial presence still seems to be the most restrictive mode of supply in them. While developed countries seem to be interested in more openness of this mode in developing countries, the latter seem to be more interested in more openness of temporary movement of natural persons by the former. (*Ibid.*, 8.)
18. A. Sapir, 'North-South Issues in Trade in Services', *8 The World Economy* (1985), 27, 32.

prevents the development of modern services industries, such as transportation or financial services. This, in turn, affects the quality and efficiency of trade in goods, thus affecting the capital gained as well as the import of skills and technologies that could improve the situation.

However, developing countries may modify the pattern of trade. East Asian countries like Korea, Singapore and Thailand succeeded in creating physical and human capital. Such a result may be achieved, for example, by acquiring services that embody technologies, thus acquiring not only the services, but also capital embodied in them, that may affect the future terms of trade.[19]

As such steps require investment of capital, which is not available in many developing countries, two alternatives may be considered: the first – encouragement of foreign investors. This alternative is not clean of disadvantages: foreign investors bring with them foreign cultures, which may be anticipated by the leaders of the importing developing country as threatening its unique culture and/or religion. In addition, their control over the capital implies power that may lead to loss of control by the developing country's government in important strategic industries like telecommunication, transport, basic infrastructure. In a less extreme scenario, such investors may disregard any responsibility to the environment and to reasonable labour conditions. Yet in a more moderate scenario, they may simply refuse to share with domestic workers their know-how, professional skills and technologies. The second, alternative option of developing countries is to initiate or encourage deliberate 'export' of potential labour to gain education in developed countries. This option requires a considerable capital investment or alternatively, reliance on the generosity of the host country. In any case, many of the skilled and educated minds will not return to their homeland, preferring to benefit from the improved conditions offered to them in the host country or in other countries.

Massive international services trade liberalization would make it necessary for these countries to lead intensive regulatory reforms. These may be assisted by the IMF and the World Bank.[20]

It is already well known, that the participation of developing countries in international trade is not only in *their* best interest. It is also the interest of the developed countries.[21] Participation of developing countries in international trade improves the global efficient allocation of production factors, allowing developed countries to concentrate on their comparative advantages, benefiting, at the same time, from the comparative advantages of developing countries.

To help developing countries overcome this vicious-circle, developed countries may *eliminate trade barriers*, including: *market access* limitations, for example, limitations on working licenses; *National treatment* limitations, for example, discrimination of foreign workers; limitations on *commercial presence,*

19. *Ibid.*, 36.
20. Lehmann et al., n. 3, 20–21.
21. See potential gains for the two groups: J. Nielson & D. Taglioni, 'Services Trade Liberalization: Identifying Opportunities and Gains', *OECD Trade Policy Working Paper No. 1* (2003).

for example, access to infrastructure, limitations on the ability to hire foreign workers.[22]

The elimination of barriers to trade in the framework of international organizations is still an important instrument for these countries to achieve their goals. In the WTO, for example, the developing countries already discovered their cumulative power when acting together, forming a majority, and they use it successfully to promote their goals. Despite this fact, the scope of their specific commitments under the agreement is still modest.[23]

14.2 GATS AND DEVELOPING COUNTRIES

GATS reflects the general approach that characterizes the WTO position towards developing countries. Unlike the IMF and the World Bank, the WTO does not contribute financially to these countries. It also doesn't believe in granting them permanent exemptions from legal obligations set forth by the WTO agreements. Instead of feeding the poor with fishes, the WTO prefers to teach them how to fish. Thus, the benefits offered to developing countries consist mainly of longer timeframes, administrative and technical assistance to fulfil the same obligations applying to all Members. The specific provisions referring to developing countries in GATS should be read together with its general, flexible provisions, allowing for broad discretion to its Members concerning the scope of commitment under the agreement.[24] It should be further noted, that while developing countries are treated by GATS individually, thus being entitled to individual reliefs and having to negotiate individually, least developed countries (LDCs) are treated more as a group.[25]

14.2.1 The Preamble

The Preamble to GATS defines the development of developing countries as one of its two major goals.[26] The Preamble further identifies some elements important for the developing countries:

- The will of developed Members to encourage their participation in international trade in services.

22. B. Ghosh, *Gains from a Global Linkage* (in Association with the IMO), Geneva (1997).
23. P. Egger & R. Lanz, 'The determinants of GATS Commitment Coverage', *31 The World Economy* (2008), 1666–1694; See detailed analysis of developing countries' Uruguay Round GATS commitments in J.A. Marchetti, n. 14, 8–16.
24. 'Special and Differential Treatment Under the GATS', *OECD Trade Policy Working Paper No. 26* (2005), 7–9, <www.olis.oecd.org>.
25. SDT Under the GATS, n. 24, 10. On 5.9.2003 the Council for Trade in Services, in a Special Session, adopted NT/S/13 Modalities for the Special Treatment for Least Developed Country Members in the Negotiations for Trade in Services, intended to ensure maximal flexibility for LDCs in the Doha Round negotiations.
26. The other major goal is the promotion of economic growth: R. Worfrum, P.T. Stoll & C. Feinäugle (eds), *WTO – Trade in Services,* Max Planck Commentaries on World

- Recognition of the special needs and conditions of developing countries, as well as of their 'particular need' to exercise their right to regulate trade in services in light of their domestic policy goals.[27]
- An expressed desire 'to facilitate the increasing participation of developing countries in trade in services and the expansion of their service exports including, *inter alia*, through the strengthening of their domestic services capacity and its efficiency and competitiveness'.[28]
- The inclusion of these elements in the framework of principles and disciplines for trade liberalization in services.
- Recognition of the special needs of the least-developed countries.

This 'declaration of intentions' may be used as an interpretative instrument to interpret the application of operative provisions of GATS to developing countries.

14.2.2 Specific provisions

14.2.2.1 Facilitating Terms

Article IV of GATS[29] recognizes the existing asymmetry of development of the service industry in developed countries, compared to the developing countries, and the need to take it into account in the negotiations for liberalization of trade in services, providing:

Increasing Participation of Developing Countries

1. The increasing participation of developing country Members in world trade shall be facilitated through negotiated specific commitments, by different Members pursuant to Parts III and IV of this Agreement, relating to:
   (a) the strengthening of their domestic services capacity and its efficiency and competitiveness, *inter alia* through access to technology on a commercial basis;

Trade Law, Martinus Mijnhoff Publishers, Leiden, Boston (2008) (hereby: GATS commentary), 22.

27. This reference is assessed as having a little legal value: GATS commentary, n. 26, 27.
28. The word 'its' is claimed to be 'clearly a drafting error', and a comparison to the French version leads to the conclusion that efficiency and competitiveness refer to 'the service sector' of developing countries: GATS commentary, n. 26, 28–29. However, since the words 'the service sector' are not mentioned in this paragraph, the interpretative option that 'its' refers to 'domestic services capacity' seems more reasonable. It is true that GATS does not deal with domestic affairs, but in the case of developing countries, as explained in this chapter, strengthening of their domestic services capacity may be achieved, for example, by improvement of their access to foreign markets that would encourage the development of export industries in them, the share of know-how with the domestic market by foreign investors, etc. This phrasing formula also appears in GATS Art. IV:1(a), and therefore it is not likely that a drafting error occurred more than once.
29. For the drafting history of this provision see: GATS commentary, n. 26, 115–116.

(b) the improvement of their access to distribution channels and information networks; and
(c) the liberalization of market access in sectors and modes of supply of export interest to them.

2. Developed country Members, and to the extent possible other Members, shall establish contact points within two years from the date of entry into force of the WTO Agreement to facilitate the access of developing country Members' service suppliers to information, related to their respective markets, concerning:
(a) commercial and technical aspects of the supply of services;
(b) registration, recognition and obtaining of professional qualifications; and
(c) the availability of services technology.
3. Special priority shall be given to the least-developed country Members in the implementation of paragraphs 1 and 2. Particular account shall be taken of the serious difficulty of the least-developed countries in accepting negotiated specific commitments in view of their special economic situation and their development, trade and financial needs.

14.2.2.1.1 Article IV:1: Principles Underlying Negotiations

This paragraph mentions a goal already addressed by the Preamble: the increasing participation of developing country Members in world trade, specifying the means for its achievement: negotiated specific commitments. This provision reflects the strategy chosen by GATS Members and discussed above, not to assist these countries through alternative means such as financial support, exemptions from the agreement's obligations, etc. In order to fulfil this goal, Article IV:1 suggests that such negotiations would be based on three principles:[30]

- The strengthening of the developing countries' domestic services capacity and its efficiency and competitiveness, *inter alia* through access to technology on a commercial basis.[31] In *Mexico – Telecoms* Mexico tried to use this provision and the fifth paragraph of the Preamble to justify existing measures in the telecommunication sector that were proved to be discriminatory towards foreign competitors. This attempt was rejected by the Panel, explaining: 'these provisions describe the types of commitments that Members should make with respect to developing country Members; they *do not*

30. These principles may be interpreted as describing three different types of commitments: GATS commentary, n. 26, 119, or rather be regarded as general principles that should be reflected, cumulatively or separately, by the specific commitments, viewed as a whole.
31. Article IV:1(a) of GATS. The words '*inter alia*' imply that access to technology is an example. Other such means may include training and education, logistical and organizational support and foreign direct investments. The words 'on commercial basis' imply that the developing countries are expected to compete according to the commercial terms set by the market: GATS commentary, n. 26, 119.

provide an interpretation of commitments already made by those developing country Members'.[32] [Emphasis added].
- Improvement of their access to distribution channels and information networks.[33]
- Priority in market access liberalization to services sectors and modes of supply which are of interest to developing countries as services exporters.[34]

Nevertheless, this provision lacks a specific mechanism that would render it operative.[35] Therefore, despite its being included in the operative part of the agreement, in essence it is more a declaration of intentions, which repeats, to a certain extent, what is already known from the Preamble.

Some of these concepts are further repeated by the Guidelines and Procedures for the services negotiations agreed by the Council for Trade in Services in Special Session (March 2001) (see Chapter 7) and in the Modalities for the Special treatment for Least Developed Country Members in the Negotiations on Trade in Services (September 2003).

14.2.2.1.2 Article IV:2: Contact Points

Article IV:2 provides that developed Members shall establish contact points within two years from the date of entry into force of the WTO Agreement.[36] The establishment of a contact point must be notified to the Council for Trade in Services.[37] 'Other Members' are expected to do so only 'to the extent possible'. 'Other' Members should be understood as Members which are not categorized as 'developed', thus being considered as emerging markets, developing and least developed countries.

The explicit goal of the contact points according to this provision is: 'to facilitate the access of developing country Members' service suppliers to information'. The information that should be provided by the contact points is described

32. WT/DS204/R Mexico – Measures Affecting Telecommunications Services, adopted on 1.6.2004, Panel report, para. 7.214.
33. Article IV:1(b) of GATS. Distribution channels are decisive for the marketing of a service. They may consist of physical networks, for example, in case of telecommunication, or of a regulatory environment such as the environment which formed basis to *EC-Bananas III* case (WT/DS27/R, AB/R European Communities – Regime for the Importation, Sale and Distribution of Bananas, adopted 25.9.1997). Access to information networks is complementary to Art. IV:2 provision on contact points.
34. Article IV:1(c) of GATS.
35. P. Delimatsis, *International Trade in Services and Domestic Regulations – Necessity, Transparency and Regulatory Diversity,* Oxford University Press (2007), 32.
36. Since the WTO agreement entered into force in 1.1.1995, this provision should have been fulfilled by its original Members by 1.1.1997.
37. S/L/23 Council for Trade in Services, Decision on the Notification of the Establishment of Enquiry and Contact Points, adopted by the Council for Trade in Services on 28 May 1996, 27.6.1996. The Council then publishes them in a list: S/ENQ/78/Rev.11 Council for Trade in Services – Contact and Enquiry Points Notified to the Council for Trade in Services – Note by the Secretariat – Revision, 26.10.2009.

in this provision as 'related to their respective markets'. The word 'related' may imply that the information expected to be provided does not only directly refer to the market of the Member providing the information, but may also indirectly relate to that market. Thus, it may refer to the contacts between this market and other markets; or to economic integration agreements with other partners affecting market terms. This interpretation may be further reinforced by the reference, in subparagraph IV:2(a) to 'commercial aspects'.

The Article further specifies the three subjects to which the information provided in the contact point should refer:

(a) commercial and technical aspects of the supply of services;
(b) registration, recognition and obtaining of professional qualifications; and
(c) the availability of services technology.

The information should refer to all services sectors and to all modes of supply.

It should be noted, however, that the broad and flexible phrasing of these categories leaves a great deal of discretion to the Members involved. It may further result in great diversity in terms of quality and degree of specificity of the information provided by different Members through their contact points.

This provision should be read together with other provisions in the agreement establishing transparency (see Chapter 13).

14.2.2.1.3 Article IV:3: Least Developed Countries

Article IV:3 requires that special priority would be given to least developed countries in accepting negotiated specific commitments, taking their special situation, interests and needs into account.

Due to this provision, LDCs are neither expected to undertake very comprehensive and deep commitments, nor 'to go beyond their institutional and administrative capacities on regulatory issues'. Furthermore, developed countries are to exercise restraint in seeking commitments from LDCs, and are not to seek removal of conditions attached to commitments by LDCs according to Article IV.[38]

Article IV implies certain rights to least developed countries. However, these are not very strong and definite rights, and their exhaustion requires some active work on behalf of the beneficiaries.

Thus, according to this provision, developing countries may require foreign service suppliers, interested in establishing permanent establishments in their territory, to establish a joint venture or to give domestic firms access to their channels of information and distribution. This provision was used by some developing countries that subjected this mode of supply to the economic needs criterion, as well as to a requirement for domestic participation in the management of the commercial presence of foreign enterprises. Some required that foreign service suppliers would use due technology and have enhanced professional experience, that foreign suppliers train domestic staff in new technologies and hire, where

38. GATS commentary, n. 26, 123.

possible, domestic labour. Foreign service suppliers were further required to supply full and accurate reports concerning their activities as well as for technological, accounting, economic and administrative data.[39]

14.2.2.2 Specific Commitments: Articles XIX and XXV

14.2.2.2.1 Article XIX

Article XIX:2 (progressive liberalization) is considered to 'operationalize' Article IV,[40] providing for some relief to developing countries in the scheduling process:

> There shall be appropriate flexibility for individual developing country Members for opening fewer sectors, liberalizing fewer types of transactions, progressively extending market access in line with their development situation and, when making access to their markets available to foreign service suppliers, attaching to such access conditions aimed at achieving the objectives referred to in Article IV.

The specific commitments attached to GATS allow developing countries to control the scope of trade liberalization, liberalizing only the services sectors they wish to, while protecting the more sensitive sectors or sectors with strategic importance. They may liberalize fewer sectors and fewer types of transactions, extending market access progressively, in line with their stage of development. At the same time, the schedules of specific commitments may be used by developing countries as a leverage to gain better terms of trade from their trade partners in each round of negotiations: they may subject their offered market access concessions to conditions promoting the achievement of the objectives referred to in Article IV.

Article XIX:3 provides, that the negotiating guidelines to be developed for each successive round of negotiations should provide for the special treatment of LDCs, as requested in Article IV:3.[41] It further provides that these negotiation guidelines 'shall establish modalities for the treatment of liberalization undertaken autonomously by members since previous negotiations'.[42] The guidelines and modalities which are adopted before each round of negotiations and form a basis thereto, thus reflect the flexibility accorded to developing Members by Articles IV

39. *Business Guide to the Uruguay Round,* International Trade Centre (WTO/UNCTAD) and Commonwealth Secretariat (1995), 277.
40. GATS commentary, n. 26, 433.
41. Originally, LDCs wished that developed countries will grant them full market access and national treatment in sectors of interest to them in Doha Round, but this position was not accepted by the Council for Trade in Services since due to the MFN principle such commitments should have applied to all WTO Members: GATS commentary, n. 26, 439.
42. See T/N/S/6 Modalities for the Treatment of Autonomous Liberalization, adopted by the Council for Trade in Services in a Special Session, 10.3.2003.

and XIX. In addition, subsequent reviews on the progress of negotiations should take these provisions into account to ensure their effective implementation.[43]

14.2.2.2.2 Article XXV

Article XXV complements Article IV, providing:

> Technical Cooperation
>
> 1. Service suppliers of Members which are in need of such assistance shall have access to the services of contact points referred to in paragraph 2 of Article IV.
> 2. Technical assistance to developing countries shall be provided at the multilateral level by the Secretariat and shall be decided upon by the Council for Trade in Services.

Article XXV:1 refers to the contact points, the establishment of which is provided for by Article IV.

Article XXV:2 establishes the right of developing countries to technical assistance by the Secretariat, subject to a decision by the Council for Trade in Services. Such a decision was accepted by the Council on 28 March 2001.[44] An additional, specific decision applying technical assistance to LDCs was accepted by the Council for Trade in Services in 3 September 2003.[45]

The Secretariat assists developing countries in terms of information exchange, assessment of trade in services and the establishment of negotiations guidelines and procedures. In addition, six international agencies cooperate to supply technical assistance to these countries: the WTO, UNCTAD, the International Trade Centre (ITC), the World Bank, the IMF and the UN Development Assistance Programme (UNDAP).[46]

14.2.2.3 Economic Integration Agreements

Economic integration agreements are recognized as an exception to the MFN rule, subject to certain conditions, meant to ensure their comprehensiveness (see Chapter 10). In the past, developing and least developed countries were not considered attractive partners to such agreements, but this trend seems to have changed in recent years.[47] Such agreements could be viewed by these countries as an

43. GATS commentary, n. 26, 436–437.
44. S/L/93 Guidelines and Procedures for the Negotiations on Trade in Services, adopted by the special session of the Council for Trade in Services on 28 Mar. 2001, 29.3.2001, para. 14, <http://docsonline.wto.org>.
45. TN/S/13 n. 25.
46. GATS commentary, n. 26, 522.
47. M. Roy, J. Marchetti & H. Lim, 'Services Liberalization in the New Generation of Preferential Trade Agreements (PTAs): How Much Further Than the GATS?' *WTO* (2006), 7–8, <www.wto.org>.

alternative to GATS for the achievement of desired services trade liberalization in certain cases, perhaps with the advantage of being more specific in geographical terms and less effort consuming in terms of negotiations (see Chapter 10).

In order to encourage the participation of developing countries to such agreements, GATS provides for some flexibility concerning the conditions for recognition of economic integration agreements to which a developing Member is a party as an exception to the MFN principle.[48] Article V:3, referring to economic integration agreements, provides for flexibility concerning the conditions for recognition of such agreement as an exception to the MFN principle where developing countries are parties to such an agreement (see Chapter 10 – 10.3.3):

> 3. (a) Where developing countries are parties to an agreement of the type referred to in paragraph 1, flexibility shall be provided for regarding the conditions set out in paragraph 1, particularly with reference to subparagraph (b) thereof, in accordance with the level of development of the countries concerned, both overall and in individual sectors and subsectors.
>
> (b) Notwithstanding paragraph 6, in the case of an agreement of the type referred to in paragraph 1 involving only developing countries, more favourable treatment may be granted to juridical persons owned or controlled by natural persons of the parties to such an agreement.

This flexibility refers particularly to the requirements concerning 'substantial sectoral coverage' and the 'elimination of substantially all discrimination'. This flexibility may encourage economic integration agreements by developing countries, *both with other developing countries and with developed countries.*

As an exception to the general MFN rule, it further allows developing countries to accord more favourable treatment to juridical persons owned or controlled by natural persons of the parties to an agreement involving *only developing countries.*[49]

14.2.2.4 Balance of Payment Difficulties

A particular reference to developing countries is included in Article XII of GATS, titled 'restrictions to safeguard the balance of payment'. In general, this provision allows taking measures restricting trade 'in the event of serious balance-of-payments and external financial difficulties or threat thereof' (see Chapter 15 – 15.2.5.1.3). However, more flexible terms allow taking such measures where developing countries or transition economies are involved. Article XII:1 provides:

> It is recognized that particular pressures on the balance of payments of a Member in the process of economic development or economic transition may necessitate the use of restrictions to ensure, *inter alia*, the maintenance of a

48. Unlike the equivalent GATT provision, Art. XXIV, which does not take into account developmental aspects of regional trade agreements.
49. Article V:3(b) of GATS.

level of financial reserves adequate for the implementation of its program of economic development or economic transition.

Namely, developing countries may restrict trade for balance-of-payments reasons, not only where serious difficulties or a threat thereof occurs, but also to maintain an existing situation, preventing it from escalating, where particular pressures are suffered by the Member involved.[50] This provision applies only where relevant specific commitments where undertaken. This relief is based on the recognition that the financial system in such countries might be more fragile and exposed to instability than in developed countries.[51]

14.2.2.5 Subsidies

GATS recognizes that in certain circumstances, subsidies may distort trade in services and calls for the development of multinational disciplines to prevent this result. At the same time, the role of subsidies in promoting development programmes of the developing countries is recognized. It is therefore provided, that the need for flexibility in this aspect should be taken into account.[52] As a matter of fact, this provision calls for a more forgiving approach towards subsidies applied by developing countries, recognizing their role in enhancing development programmes. In reality, though, subsidies stand, in recent years, at the centre of an ongoing debate between developed and developing Members of the WTO, where developing countries require that developed countries diminish the heavy subsidization of their exporting industries, claiming that it distorts competition, considering that developing countries are too poor to equivalently subsidize their own exporting industries. This debate may raise doubts as to the effectiveness of this provision.

14.2.2.6 Telecommunications Networks

Telecommunications networks are decisive for the development of trade in services, both in terms of services activities and as a mode of supply. The Annex on Telecommunications Services (see Chapter 16 – 16.3.1) is the only Annex specifically referring to the interests of developing countries. It applies to measures affecting the access to and use of telecommunications transfer networks (except for measures affecting the cable or broadcast distribution of radio or television programming).[53] It requires developed countries to abstain from subjecting the access to, or use of, these networks to conditions, unless such conditions are necessary to safeguard the availability of the service to the public, to protect the technical integrity of the networks or to prevent supply of the service to countries

50. Such pressures may emanate from an increased level of imports, a high level of foreign debt, particularly short-term debt, etc.: GATS commentary, n. 26, 263.
51. GATS commentary, n. 26, 263.
52. Article XV of GATS.
53. Article 2(b) of the Annex on Telecommunications.

that did not take specific commitments concerning this service.[54] A developing country, on the other hand:

> may, consistent with its level of development, place reasonable conditions on access to and use of public telecommunications transport networks and services necessary to strengthen its domestic telecommunications infrastructure and service capacity and to increase its participation in international trade in telecommunications services. Such conditions shall be specified in the Member's Schedule.[55]

Such extra-conditions placed by developing countries may be discriminatory, as long as they are 'reasonable' and necessary to obtain the three purposes mentioned in this provision:

- to strengthen its domestic telecommunications infrastructure;
- to strengthen its service capacity;
- and to increase its participation in international trade in telecommunications services.

The word 'and' implies that these purposes are cumulative.[56]

Two additional conditions should be met, according to this provision: the conditions put forward by a developing Member should be consistent with the level of development of that Member (this condition may be reflected in the 'reasonableness' analysis in a specific case), and must be specified in that Member's schedule. Where such conditions were not specified in a schedule, a Member will be able to use this provision only subject to modification of their schedules according to Article XXI (see Chapter 15).[57]

The annex foresees technical cooperation with the developing countries by enhanced participation of telecommunication suppliers in the development of development-programmes for international and regional organizations. It provides that developed countries should act to enhance cooperation in this field between developing countries in the international, regional and bilateral level and to assist, in cooperation with international organizations, the strengthening of telecommunications services and the development of telecommunications and information technology.[58] Concerning least developed countries, the Annex provides that foreign telecoms suppliers should be encouraged to transfer technology, to train personnel and to engage in other activities for the development of telecoms infrastructure and the expansion of such services in these countries.[59]

54. Article 5(e) of the Annex on Telecommunications.
55. Article 5(g) of the Annex on Telecommunications.
56. Nevertheless, in Art. VI, for example, the word 'and' does not prevent an interpretation by the WTO adjudicating bodies which refers to each element independently. See Ch. 12 – 12.3.3.1.
57. GATS commentary, n. 26, 706.
58. Article 6 of the Annex on Telecommunications.
59. During the discussions on this Annex it was suggested that developed countries would initiate short training programmes for professionals from developing countries: MTN.GNS/25, Note of the Meeting of 18–22 Sep. 1989, 23.10.1989, 79.

14.3 THE MEANING OF GATS PROVISIONS FOR THE DEVELOPING COUNTRIES

As already mentioned, GATS does not create a specific arrangement for developing countries, but includes them in the international liberalization framework, as active participants. They are not exempted *a-priori* from any general obligation in the agreement, and cannot enjoy liberalization as 'free riders'. This approach holds advantages, as well as disadvantages for the developing countries. The advantages include a framework of time delays and technical assistance that should encourage these countries to engage in the process, while supported by the developed Members as well as by the WTO Secretariat.[60] The engagement in the process is expected to enhance the economic benefits for these countries, discussed at the beginning of this chapter. However, the disadvantage of this mechanism lies in its total dependence on the negotiation process. Since the developing countries find it difficult to consolidate their negotiation offers, hesitate to take courageous steps for liberalization of their services markets due to considerations mentioned in Chapter 1, and suffer from a relatively weak position during such negotiations, their ability to exhaust the benefits held for them in GATS is limited. Therefore, the effect of GATS on these countries will be determined, to a large extent, by their own position towards trade liberalization in services.[61]

A decision to exhaust the process could improve the access of developing countries to cheaper imported inputs for their services industries, to improve the quality and prices of services offered to the public, and a chance that know-how and technologies imported by foreign investors would be absorbed by the domestic industry. Trade liberalization in services may improve the allocation of production factors. Developing countries could further profit from the development of disciplines in the field of competition and the prevention of anti-competitive practices.

However, in the short term a rapid liberalization process could cause unemployment and lead to a collapse of domestic industries; the exposure to foreign markets could cause a brain drain process where young educated people would choose to exhaust the liberalization benefits by offering their services in other countries, thus contributing to a loss of investment made by their home developing country which financed their education. An incautious approach to trade liberalization could further cause the loss of government control on strategic services industries that would fall into the hands of private foreign suppliers. All these risks should be taken into account and fully weighed before irreversible steps are taken.

---

60. Such technical assistance could facilitate the scheduling of specific commitments process, but also help them improve domestic standards, implement the agreement, strengthening regulatory agencies, etc.: B. Hoeckman, 'Been there, not [Quite][Yet] Done That: Lessons and Challenges in Services Trade', *NCCR Trade Regulation Working Paper No. 2006/18* (2006), SSRN 29–30, <http://papers.ssrn.com>.
61. For analysis of current participation of developing countries in GATS see: SDT Under the GATS, n. 24, 12–22.

This may be the reason why most of the developing countries do not rush into this process.

14.4 CONCLUSION

In principle, developing countries are recognized as entitled to special and differential treatment in GATS. In this respect, GATS reflects a similar approach to the general approach towards these countries embodied in the WTO agreements. Nevertheless, a thorough examination of the effective provisions in WTO agreements in general, and in GATS in particular, applying this approach, draws a relatively poor picture.

The legal framework of reliefs is probably not solid enough to attract deep and comprehensive commitments by these countries. Combined with their defensive position, it leads to relatively poor commitments in the Uruguay Round, and relatively poor offers in current negotiations.[62] By now, the Doha Round negotiations do not seem to reflect any serious mutual effort to change the situation.[63]

Some commentators believe that one of the future potential developments from which developing countries could profit is the development of strengthened multilateral disciplines on domestic regulation, for two reasons: first, it can play a significant role in promoting and consolidating domestic regulatory reform in these countries. Second, such disciplines can help exporters in developing countries address potential regulatory barriers to their exports in foreign markets.[64] On the other hand it should be remembered that the development of such disciplines could restrict, to some extent, the discretion concerning enhancement of domestic policy goals enjoyed by these governments, and to imply a greater burden of costs in order to comply with these disciplines. Developing and Least Developed Countries seem to suffer more than other Members from the general deficiencies of GATS discussed in this book. Hence, there are further suggestions in literature how to strengthen GATS disciplines to support developing countries' interests.[65] In addition, gradually, developing countries become parties to economic integration agreements, as well as to bilateral investment treaties, by which more

62. See detailed analysis of developing countries' participation in the Doha Round in J.A. Marchetti, n. 14, 21–37.
63. Towards the beginning of negotiations in the Doha Round, some developing countries expressed their disappointment over the process in its first four years. These countries argued that the application of the agreements raised practical difficulties that were not foreseen when GATS was concluded. They further claimed that the developed countries did not exercise any policy of liberalization towards them. The developed countries, on the other hand, argued that developing countries did not do enough by joining GATS, and they should improve their regulation and domestic infrastructure to exhaust GATS benefits: PRESS/122, 19.2.1999, The New Multilateral Trade Negotiations, the EU and its Developing Country Partners: an Agenda for Action.
64. A. Mattoo & P. Sauvé, *Domestic Regulation and Service Trade Liberalization*, the World Bank and Oxford University Press (2003), 229.
65. See, for example, J. Hodge, n. 4, 221–234; B. Hoeckman, n. 60.

advanced liberalization may be achieved by the partners.[66] All these considerations will be finally reflected by the schedules of specific commitments of these countries.[67]

The special status of Least Developed Countries was recognized in the current Doha round as the Hong Kong Ministerial Declaration[68] acknowledged that these countries are not expected to undertake new commitments and as the Negotiation Guidelines were complemented in 2003 by the Modalities for the Special Treatment for Least-Developed Country Members,[69] intended to ensure 'maximum flexibility' for LDCs in the negotiations, as well as to ensure the special reference of the other Members to these countries and to their needs.

66. See: S.M. Stephenson (ed.), *Services Trade in the Western Hemisphere: Liberalization, Integration and Reform,* General Secretariat/Organization of American States (2000).
    R. Adlung, M. Molinuevo, 'Bilateralism in Services Trade: is There Fire behind the (BIT) Smoke?' *WTO Staff Working PaperERDS-2008-01* (2008), <http://papers.ssrn.com>.
67. Read more about the necessary incentives to expand the specific commitments of developing countries in B. Hoeckman & A. Mattoo, 'Policy Arena: Services, Economic Development and the Next Round of negotiations on Services', *12 Journal of International Development* (2000), 283–296.
68. <www.wto.org>.
    The special needs of these countries are also mentioned in the Annex to the report of the chair of services negotiations issued on 26.5.2008, see: <www.wto.org>.
69. TN/S/13 n. 25.

Chapter 15
The Safety Valves of GATS

15.1 INTRODUCTION

In principle, the legal obligations set forth by GATS are shaped to enhance trade liberalization, by creating an irreversible process.

However, it was recognized by GATS drafters that some flexibility should be accorded in this context, to meet circumstances unforeseen at the time of its conclusion.

Thus, GATS and the WTO Agreement include some 'safety valves' that may be effectuated in different circumstances, allowing Members to temporarily or permanently deviate from commitments undertaken by them according to the agreement.

15.2 TEMPORARY 'SAFETY VALVES'

15.2.1 Waiver: WTO Agreement

Article IX:3 of the WTO Agreement allows a Member to ask the Ministerial Conference to waive an obligation made according to GATS. It is stressed that such a step shall be taken in exceptional circumstances, and subject to consensus, and if consensus in not achieved during a given time-frame – by a decision of three-fourths of the Members.[1] A request to initiate this process should be submitted to the Committee on Trade in Services, reviewing it within a time period that should

1. Certain waiver decisions may be accepted only in consensus, due to footnote 4 of the WTO Agreement, providing: '[a] decision to grant a waiver in respect of any obligation subject to a transition period or a period for staged implementation that the requesting Member has not performed by the end of the relevant period shall be taken only by consensus'.

not exceed ninety days, then submitting a report to the Ministerial Council, which is in charge of decision making. The decision by the Council should 'state the exceptional circumstances justifying the decision, the terms and conditions governing the application of the waiver, and the date on which the waiver shall terminate'. A waiver given is subject to an annual review by the Ministerial Conference.

This is a relatively tough procedure, originating in GATT 1947, which became tougher to exercise as the number of WTO Members grew. Therefore, its implementation is expected to be rare. By now, the only country who asked and got a waiver for trade in services was Albania, who could not fulfil its obligation to open the telecom market according to its specific commitments, despite its intensive efforts.

15.2.2 The Opt-out Clause: WTO Agreement

Recognizing the international political reality, Article XIII of the WTO Agreement enables the non-application of the WTO Agreements, including GATS, between Members, if one of them 'does not consent to such application'. The motive for such objection may be either political or economic.[2] A notice concerning this position may be given by the Member to the Ministerial Conference before acceding to the WTO.

The Ministerial Conference may review the operation of this Article in particular cases, at the request of any Member and make appropriate recommendations.

15.2.3 General Exceptions: GATS

Article XIV of GATS includes a list of interests, recognized by all the Members as justifying deviation from the general rules of GATS as well as from specific commitments. According to the common interpretation of GATS, a Member that has made full market access commitments is not free to impose certain non-discriminatory measures, such as prohibitions, unless they can be justified by the exceptions provisions,[3] the most important of which is Article XIV. When one of the interests mentioned in Article XIV is in danger, a Member is allowed to stop or restrict trade flows temporarily, in order to guard this interest. This Article is meant to insert an element of flexibility into the agreement, allowing the Members to

2. The source of this provision is in Art. XXXV of GATT 1947. For its history see: J. H. Jackson, *The World Trading System*, 2nd edn the MIT Press, Cambridge, Massachusetts and London, England (1997), 55–57.
3. A. Mattoo, 'Services in a Development Round', *The World Bank Policy Research Paper No. 3718* (2005), 10, <http://papers.ssrn.com>.

protect certain domestic policy interests.[4] Thus, it is invoked by the respondent as a defence claim after the complainant has established a prima facie case of inconsistency with the substantive obligations under GATS.

This defence should be invoked at an early stage of the Panel proceedings, subject to the particular circumstances of a given dispute.[5]

The equivalent GATT Article XX was described by the Appellate Body in *US – Shrimp*[6] as reflecting a balance between the *right* of a Member to invoke an exception under this provision and the *duty* of that Member to respect the treaty rights of other Members. This principle should also lead the interpretation of GATS Article XIV.

The ambiguous language of Article XIV leaves a broad scope of discretion to the WTO adjudicating bodies.

Article XIV provides:

> General Exceptions
> Subject to the requirement that such measures are not applied in a manner which would constitute a means of arbitrary or unjustifiable discrimination between countries where like conditions prevail, or a disguised restriction on trade in services, nothing in this Agreement shall be construed to prevent the adoption or enforcement by any Member of measures:
>
> (a) necessary to protect public morals or to maintain public order;
> (b) necessary to protect human, animal or plant life or health;
> (c) necessary to secure compliance with laws or regulations which are not inconsistent with the provisions of this Agreement including those relating to:
>   (i) the prevention of deceptive and fraudulent practices or to deal with the effects of a default on services contracts;

---

4. It is assessed, though, that since GATS obligations, in particular Arts XVI and XVII, are flexible compared to the equivalent GATT provisions, this provision will be of less use than its equivalent in GATT: R. Worfrum, P. T. Stoll & C. Feinäugle (eds), *WTO – Trade in Services*, Max Planck Commentaries on World Trade Law, Martinus Mijnhoff Publishers, Leiden, Boston (2008) (hereby: GATS commentary), 291.
5. WT/DS285/R, AB/R United States – Measures Affecting the Cross-Border Supply of Gambling and Betting Services, adopted on 22.5.2007, Appellate Body report, para. 272. In that case Antigua argued, *inter alia*, that the United States did not invoke this claim early enough. Despite the fact that this claim was only invoked in the second hearing, the Appellate Body upheld the Panel decision to allow it, due to three reasons: '[f]rom the outset, Antigua was apparently aware that the United States might argue that its measures satisfy the requirements of Art. XIV. Antigua admitted that it raised no objection to the timing of the United States defence before the panel. Antigua also acknowledged that it did have an opportunity to respond adequately to the United States defence, albeit at a late stage of the proceeding': *ibid.*, para. 276. It was stressed that the first consideration mentioned should be read together with the other two considerations. If used independently, it may always be adopted, undermining, to a large extent, the requirement to invoke this defence in a stage, as early as possible, which is important in terms of good faith and due process: *ibid.*, para. 272.
6. WT/DS58/R, AB/R United States – Import Prohibition of certain Shrimp and Shrimp Products, adopted on 6.11.1998, Appellate Body report, para. 156.

(ii) the protection of the privacy of individuals in relation to the processing and dissemination of personal data and the protection of confidentiality of individual records and accounts;

(iii) safety;

(d) inconsistent with Article XVII, provided that the difference in treatment is aimed at ensuring the equitable or effective imposition or collection of direct taxes in respect of services or service suppliers of other Members;

(e) inconsistent with Article II, provided that the difference in treatment is the result of an agreement on the avoidance of double taxation or provisions on the avoidance of double taxation in any other international agreement or arrangement by which the Member is bound.

15.2.3.1 Article XIV: General Structure and Order of Analysis

Article XIV (like the equivalent Article XX of GATT) is combined of a *chapeau*, determining some general principles, followed by a list of specific public policy objectives. The *chapeau* applies to each of these specific objectives and should be read together with them. Thus, the Appellate Body determined in *US – Gambling*,[7] that a two-tier analysis developed in the context of the equivalent Article XX of GATT could apply, *mutatis mutandis*, to this provision:

(1) *Assessment whether the challenged measure falls within the scope of one of the paragraphs of Article XIV.* It should be noted that each paragraph might call for different degree of connection between the measure at issue and the relevant policy objective. This difference could be drawn from the use of different words, such as 'relating to', 'necessary to', 'aimed at', 'the result of', included in each of the paragraphs of Article XIV.[8] For this stage of analysis, it is suggested[9] to proceed in two steps:

(a) Determination of the content and scope of the listed objective.

(b) Analysis of whether trade in services, under the given circumstances, impairs or jeopardizes the achievement of the relevant policy objective.

It is stressed, however, that these analytical steps need to be distinguished from the Members' right to determine their own level of protection for each of the interests involved.

If the answer to the question specified in (1) is affirmative, the second stage would be

7. WT/DS285/AB/R *US – Gambling*, n. 5, Appellate Body report para. 292. This analysis is based on the analysis of the equivalent GATT Art. XX. See, for example: WT/DS2/AB/R United States – Standards for Reformulated and Conventional Gasoline, adopted on 20.5.1996, Appellate Body report, 22; WT/DS161,169/R, AB/R Korea – Measures Affecting the Imports of Fresh, Chilled and Frozen Beef, adopted on 10.1.2001, Appellate Body report, para. 157.
8. WT/DS285/AB/R *US – Gambling*, n. 5, Appellate Body report, para. 292.
9. GATS commentary, n. 4, 294–295.

(2) Assessment of whether the challenged measure satisfies the requirements of the *chapeau* of Article XIV.

Therefore, the *chapeau* will be analysed after the review of the specific objectives.

15.2.3.2 Application of GATS Article XIV to Other WTO Agreements

In *China – Publications and Audiovisual Products*, China tried to use one of the equivalent GATT Article XX exceptions to defend measures applied by it, otherwise considered contrary not to GATT, but to its Accession Protocol. The Panel noted that this question involves 'complex legal issues', since GATT Article XX contains the phrase 'nothing in this agreement', with the term *agreement* referring to GATT 1994. The Panel adopted a suggestion by the United States, to examine China's claim in essence, and only if it is found justified, to return to the systemic issues involving the applicability of this provision to other WTO agreements. The United States relied on the practice of analysis exercised in *US – Custom Bond Directive*,[10] where GATT Article XX(d) was invoked in defence of measures found to be inconsistent with the WTO Agreement on Anti-Dumping.[11] In both cases it turned out that there was no need to revert to the issue of the availability of an Article XX defence to other WTO Agreements, since the measures examined did not fulfil the conditions of the first stage examination and thus, the conduct of the second stage of the analysis was spared.[12] This practice, exercised by the Panel, was heavily criticized by the Appellate Body in *China – Publications and Audiovisual Products*, on the grounds that it 'may detract from a clear enunciation of the relevant WTO law and create difficulties for implementation'.[13] The Appellate Body further explained that the Panel's

> analysis of the appropriate restrictive effect to be taken into account, depended, at least to some extent, on the availability of Article XX(a) as a defence to a violation of China's trading rights commitments. Thus, these parts of the Panel's analysis rest upon an uncertain foundation as a result of the absence of a ruling on the applicability of Article XX(a) in this case.[14]

The Appellate Body thus concluded that the use of this technique 'could be at odds with the objective of promoting security and predictability through dispute settlement'[15] and consequently turned to the examination of the applicability of this

10. WT/DS345/R, AB/R US – Customs Bond Directive for Merchandise Subject to Anti Dumping/ Countervailing Duties, adopted on 1.8.2008.
11. WT/DS363/R China – Measures Affecting Trading Rights and Distribution Services for Certain Publications and Audiovisual Entertainment Products, adopted on 19.1.2010, paras 7.743–7.745.
12. WT/DS363/R *China – Publications and Audiovisual Products*, n. 11, Panel report para. 7.912.
13. WT/DS363/AB/R *China – Publications and Audiovisual Products*, n. 11, Appellate Body report, para. 213.
14. *Ibid.*, para. 214.
15. *Ibid.*, para. 215.

provision in the given circumstances. the Appellate Body concluded that GATT Article XX is applicable to these provisions, since they 'have a clearly discernable, objective link' to China's 'right to regulate trade' which implies, also, the right to take regulatory action that derogates from obligations under the relevant WTO agreement, that is, to relevant exceptions.[16]

Based on this experience it may be assumed that if a similar doubt concerning the applicability of Article XIV is raised, this question should be addressed first, and the *arguendo* technique should be abandoned in favour of a concrete analysis of the agreement involved and the applicability of Article XIV to these provisions.

15.2.3.3 Extraterritorial Effect

A relatively simple case occurs where Article XIV is used to protect *domestic* policy objectives, such as the prevention of import of gambling services, to protect public morals or to maintain public order, or the prevention of import of retreaded tyres, considered an environmental nuisance. More difficult cases involve the ban on import in order to indirectly prevent the application of a measure taken with regard to that import *in the country of origin*. For instance, in GATT 1947 context, in the *US – Tuna* case,[17] the United States refused to allow import of tuna from Mexico due to the violent fishing method of the tuna, which according to the United States endangered the life of other species in the sea. This position was rejected by the dispute settlement Panel, which preferred the interest of free trade over the prevention of a violent fishing practice. Such a policy, aimed at an extraterritorial effect, may occur in the context of trade in services as well. Imagine, for example, a ban on services' import due to human rights considerations. Such practice may have one of two purposes: one – trade *restrictions:* the refusal to 'import' into a country services produced through harming human life or health. Yet a second motive may be the application of trade *sanctions* on such practice. While, based on current GATT and GATS[18] experience, it seems that the support of the WTO adjudicating bodies for the first purpose is not ensured, it is even less likely that their support would be granted to measures aimed at the achievement of the second purpose, since Article XIV is not aimed at being an instrument for the application of sanctions.[19]

16. WT/DS363/AB/R *China – Publications and Audiovisual Products*, n. 11, Appellate Body report paras 215–223, 230–233.
17. DS21/R Report of GATT Panel, United States – Restrictions on Imports of Tuna, (*Tuna I – 1991*), dated 3.9.1991 (unadopted) 30 I.L.M 1594, 39S/155; See also DS/29R Report of GATT Panel, United States – Restrictions on the Import of Tuna, dated 16.6.1994 (unadopted) 33 I.L.M 839 (*Tuna II – 1994*).
18. In WT/DS285/R, AB/R *US – Gambling*, n. 5, the decision of WTO adjudicating bodies, rejecting United States' claim concerning the protection of public morals and public order, was largely based on the fact that domestic gambling services were allowed. Therefore, it is hard to assess what would have been the chances of such a claim if such domestic services were forbidden.
19. See reference to this question in the context of the equivalent GATT Art. XX: L. Bartels, 'Article XX of GATT and the Problem of Extraterritorial Jurisdiction', *36 Journal of World Trade* (2002), 353.

15.2.3.4 The List of Exceptions Allowed by Article XIV of GATS

Article XIV specifies a list of policy objectives, for the guarding of which it is justified to deviate from the services' trade liberalization policy provided for by GATS. Thus, it allows the application of measures necessary to protect public morals and public order as well as of human, animal or plant life or health; to secure compliance with laws or regulations which are not inconsistent with GATS; and deviation from the MFN and national treatment principles to allow the enforcement of certain tax laws and treaties. This list is *exhaustive*. Therefore, other regulatory policy objectives pursued by governments, such as consumer protection, redistribution of income or bargaining power, or ensuring universal access to basic services, which are not included in this list, may not justify deviation from GATS disciplines.[20]

Thus, although this list is exhaustive, it is hard to tell to what extent it is comprehensive, and reflecting a systematic approach.[21]

The equivalent GATT provision, Article XX,[22] includes some exceptions which are not included in Article XIV of GATS, stemming from its application to trade in goods.[23] On the other hand, Article XIV of GATS refers, in paragraphs (d) and (e), to direct tax matters which are not covered by GATT provision, emanating from its personal application to service suppliers, who may be subject to such taxes.

15.2.3.4.1 'Measures Necessary…'

The first three exceptions in the list of exceptions recognized by Article XIV (paragraphs a-c) begin with the words 'measures necessary…', followed by the recognized interests to be protected.

---

20. M. Krajewski, *National Regulation and Trade Liberalization in Services*, Kluwer Law International (2003), 196. Thus, for example, this list lacks an equivalence to GATT Art. XX(g) concerning measures relating to the conservation of exhaustible natural resources. Some coverage of may be offered by Art. XIV(b) on measures necessary to protect human, animal and plant life: W. Zdouc, *Legal Problems Arising Under the General Agreement on Trade in Services – Comparative Analysis of GATS and GATT*, dissertation der Universität St. Gallen (2002), 201–202.
21. It should be noted that the entire WTO system does not provide for a global-welfare economic analysis, and it is doubted whether this legal system is sufficient to respond to global challenges such as the environmental challenge: C. P. Bown & J. P. Trachtman, '*Brazil – Measures Affecting Imports of Retreaded Tyres*: A Balancing Act', *8 World Trade review* (2009), 85, 133–134.
22. Article XX of GATT and the jurisprudence interpreting it was recognized by the WTO adjudicating bodies in WT/DS285/R, AB/R *US – Gambling*, n. 5, as relevant and potentially useful for the interpretation of Art. XIV of GATS, due to the textual and conceptual similarities between them: See the Panel report, para. 6.448.
23. See Art. XX of GATT, paras (c) and (e)–(j). This Article includes ten legitimate objectives, while Art. XIV of GATS includes only five legitimate objectives.

The word 'measures' is interpreted by Article XXVII(a) of GATS (see Chapter 4). But the necessity requirement is not interpreted by the agreement. What are 'measures necessary' to protect each of the following interests? Does it mean any possible measure? Or rather one of some possible measures? Or the most proportional measures?

In GATT 1994 case *US – Gasoline*, it was stressed that 'necessary' in the equivalent GATT Article XX does *not* refer to the necessity of the policy goal at issue, but to the *measure* at stake, which has a restrictive effect on trade.[24]

The necessity requirement implies that the Member wishing to use this provision to defend measures taken by it, which would otherwise be considered as violating its obligations according to GATS, must establish a *link* between the measure taken and its contribution to the achievement of the protected policy goal included in Article XIV.[25]

The burden of proof

In *US – Gambling*, the Appellate Body provided that the basic burden of proof concerning the 'necessity' of a measure is on the responding party. However, this party is not expected to 'identify the universe of less trade restrictive alternative measures and then show that none of these measures achieves the desired objective'. Rather, it has to put forward a prima facie case,[26] supported by arguments and evidence, that the measure at stake is necessary. This stage might then be followed by two other stages: at the *first stage*, the complainant may present an alternative *concrete*, WTO – *consistent (or less-inconsistent)* measure that should be taken, in its view, showing that this alternative measure can achieve the level of protection sought by the respondent. In that case, at the *second stage*, the respondent should refer to that measure and justify its challenged measure, taking into account the interests and values at stake and the respondent's desired level of protection.[27] According to one commentator,[28] this interpretation leaves the

24. WT/DS2/R *US – Gasoline*, n. 7, Panel report, para. 6.22.
25. In WT/DS363/AB/R *China – Publications and Audiovisual Products*, n. 11, China's claim for the public morals defence according to the equivalent GATT Art. XX(a) was rejected since China did not establish this link. See, for example, WT/DS345/AB/R, n. 10, Appellate Body report, para. 269.
26. WT/DS285/AB/R *US – Gambling*, n. 5, Appellate Body report, para. 360. This standard is considered very low: D. Irwin & J. H. H. Weiler, 'Measures Affecting the Cross-Border Supply of Gambling and Betting Services', *7 World Trade Review* (2008), 71, 84. See further discussion in Ch. 17. However, it was repeated in WT/DS363/AB/R *China- Publications and Audiovisual Products*, n. 11, see for example Appellate Body report, para. 288.
27. WT/DS285/AB/R *US – Gambling*, n. 5, Appellate Body report, para. 309–311; WT/DS363/R *China – Publications and Audiovisual Products*, n. 11, Panel report, paras 7.785 (Panel description of this process), 7.794–7.807 (China's prima facie claims), paras 7.873–7.785 (United States' WTO-consistent alternatives), 7.876–7.881 (China's reaction to the alternatives suggested by the United States, explaining why they would not reach the same level of protection).
28. F. Ortino, 'The Principle on Non-Discrimination and its Exceptions in the GATS: Selected Legal Issues', *King's College London* (2006), 14, 19, <http://papers.ssrn.com>.

question concerning the substance of first stage burden of proof by the respondent unclear.

The role of adjudicating body

In *US – Gambling*[29] and in *China – Publications and Audiovisual Products*[30] the Appellate Body determined, that the 'necessity test' implied by Article XIV is *objective*, and should be *independently* decided by the Panel based on the evidence before it, namely – it is decided *on a case-by-case basis.*[31] This authority to determine 'necessity', given to the WTO adjudicating bodies by the agreement, involves considerable discretion that could be used to 'intervene too greatly in national regulatory autonomy'.[32]

This position is well understood from an overall – WTO perspective, wanting to enhance services trade liberalization and thus narrowly and uniformly interpret the exceptions to GATS rules. However, for the Members involved, it implies that their discretion concerning the domestic policy goal, in each case, is potentially subject to a WTO dispute settlement review, with an *ex post* implication. This fact may deter Members from using the exceptions. While in the short run such an outcome may correspond to the general interest for trade liberalization enhancement, in the long run it could affect the readiness of Members to take deep and broad commitments under GATS, knowing that the result of using this safety valve may be unexpected. Accordingly, this intervention by the adjudicating bodies should take place cautiously and subject to clear tests. Unfortunately, these tests are gradually developing through GATT and GATS jurisprudence, which still reflects a puzzling picture.

The purpose of necessity requirement

In GATT 1947 case *Thailand – Cigarettes,*[33] the panel explained, that the necessity requirement is used:

> to allow contracting parties to impose trade restrictive measures inconsistent with the General Agreement to pursue overriding public policy goals *to the extent that such inconsistencies are unavoidable*. [Emphasis added].

29. WT/DS285/AB/R n. 5, Appellate Body report, para 304.
30. WT/DS363/AB/R, n. 11, Appellate Body report, para. 288.
31. Such evidence may include '(a) the respondent's characterization of the objectives of the measure and of the effectiveness of the regulatory approach adopted by the respondent; (b) the structure and operation of the measure; (c) the contrary evidence submitted by the complainant. An important part of this assessment is the panel's examination of whether the respondent already applies a *WTO–consistent* measure to a like or similar kind of illegal behaviour to attain the same objectives as the *WTO–inconsistent* measure at issue'. [Emphasis in the original]. GATS commentary, n. 4, 314.
32. C. P. Bown & J. P. Trachtman, n. 21, 119.
33. DS10/R Thailand – Restrictions on Importation of and Internal Taxes on Cigarettes, adopted on 7.11.1990, 37S/200, para. 74.

In that case, the Panel thus concludes

> that the import restrictions imposed by Thailand *could be considered to be 'necessary' in terms of Article XX(b) only if there were no alternative measure consistent with the General Agreement, or less inconsistent with it, which Thailand could reasonably be expected to employ to achieve its . . . objectives.* [Emphasis added].[34]

In other words, it seems that the panel applied the proportionality test. This test was also adopted (in GATT 1947 context) by the chairman's recommendations document titled *Streamline Mechanism for Reconciling the Interests of Contracting Parties in the Event of Trade Damaging Act.*[35] The Council took note of these recommendations, which included guidelines to be used in the event of a trade-damaging act. This document provides, *inter alia*: 'a measure taken by an importing contracting party should not be any more sever, and should not remain in force any longer, than necessary' to protect the interest involved.

The essence of necessity and its examination

In GATT 1994 *Korea – Beef*[36] case, referring to the equivalent provision in GATT 1994, the Appellate Body determined that 'necessary' is 'located significantly closer to the pole of "indispensable" than to the pole of "making a contribution to"'. The Appellate Body in *Brazil – Retreaded Tyres*, also referring to the equivalent GATT Article XX, viewed this test as weighing and balancing three factors: (a) The importance of the common interests or values protected by these measures; (b) The contribution made by the measure under review to the achievement of specified goal; (c) The accompanying (restrictive) impact of the measure on imports or exports.[37] The Appellate Body further acknowledged:

> If this analysis yields a *preliminary* conclusion that the measure is necessary, this result must be confirmed by comparing the measure with possible *alternatives*, which may be *less trade restrictive* while providing an equivalent contribution to the achievement of the objective. This comparison should be carried out *in light of the importance* of the interests or values at stake.[38] [Emphasis added].

In *US – Gambling*,[39] referring to GATS, the Panel implemented this sequence of analysis developed in GATT context, mentioning two elements that should be

34. DS10/R *Thailand – Cigarettes*, n. 33, para. 75.
35. C/M/236, 11.10.89, 6–7; 36S/67.
36. WT/DS161, 169/R, AB/R *Korea – Beef*, n. 8, Appellate Body report, para. 161. See also paras 162–166, 172.
37. In GATS commentary, n. 4, 316 it is noted that this list is meant to be *illustrative*, but 'the WTO judiciary appears to be satisfied when a measure at stake is tested against these three factors'.
38. WT/DS332/R, AB/R Brazil – Measures Affecting Imports of Retreaded Tyres, adopted on 17.12.2007, Appellate Body report, para. 178.
39. WT/DS285/R, AB/R, n. 5, Appellate Body report para. 306; Panel report, para. 6.455.

demonstrated by a Member to justify a measure under Article XIV: the measure is designed to achieve the specified goal, and is 'necessary' to achieve it.

This sequence was also accepted by the WTO adjudicating bodies in *China – Publications and Audiovisual Products.*[40]

It is noted by some commentators that this test is drawn from GATT Article XX, but while one of GATT's long term objectives is the elimination of discriminatory treatment in international trade in goods, no such objective is mentioned in GATS Preamble, which merely calls for progressive liberalization. This difference should be taken into account in the application of this element.[41]

Yet, the adjudicating bodies in both cases *US – Gambling* and *China – Publications and Audiovisual Products* did not seem to refer to this difference, applying the same manner of analysis as in *Korea – Beef.*

A review of the dispute settlement cases applying this test reveals some ancillary rules to this 'weighing and balancing' process:[42]

- 'The more vital or important those interests are, the easier it would be to accept as 'necessary' a measure designed as an enforcement instrument'.
- 'The greater the contribution [to the realization of the end pursued], the more easily a measure might be considered to be "necessary".'
- 'A measure with a relatively slight impact upon imported products might more easily be considered as "necessary" than a measure with intense or broader restrictive effects'.[43] For instance, in *China – Publications and Audiovisual Products*, measures *a-priori* excluding certain enterprises from engaging in the importation of relevant products were considered most restrictive.[44]

However, the Appellate Body declined to refer to the *relationship* among these variables and their *effect* on the final determination of necessity, as well as to their

40. WT/DS363/R, n. 11 Panel report, paras 7.782–7.793; WT/DS363/AB/R, Appellate Body report, paras 240–241, although in practice the Panel in that case proceeded in a somewhat odd order of examination: it examined, first, whether, and if so – to what extent, each of the examined measures *contribute to the protection of the interest involved* (public morals) (paras 7.768–7.781). Thereafter, the Panel proceeded to examine whether each of these measures is '*necessary*' to the protection of this interest. The examination of contribution of each measure to the promotion of the interest involved should be part of the necessity examination, and not a preliminary stage.

    In that case China argued that there was a difference between the Appellate Body's approach to this test between WT/DS285/AB/R *US – Gambling*, n. 5, and WT/DS332/AB/R *Brazil–Retreaded Tyres*, n. 38, but the Appellate Body rejected this claim, saying that 'although the language used is not identical, both reports articulate the same approach'. *Ibid.*, para. 242.
41. GATS commentary, n. 4, 318.
42. WT/DS161,169/AB/R *Korea–Beef*, n. 8, paras 162–163, as recited by C. P. Bown & J. P. Trachtman, n. 21, 121.
43. In *China– Publications and Audiovisual Products* it was noted concerning this last point: 'Consequently, if a Member chooses to adopt a very restrictive measure, it will have to ensure that the measure is carefully designed so that the other elements to be taken into account... will "outweigh" such restrictive effect'. WT/DS363/AB/R n. 11, para. 310.
44. WT/DS363/AB/R, n. 11, Appellate Body report, para. 310.

relations with the former *least trade restrictive alternative* test, to be discussed below.[45]

The Panel in *China – Publications and Audiovisual Products* suggested to expand the examination of the third element mentioned above, to 'weigh not only the restrictive impact the measures at issue have on imports of relevant products, but also *the restrictive effect they have on those wishing to engage in importing, in particular on their right to trade*'.[46] Although the Panel in that case limited its suggestion to the case before it, this practice may be well applicable in other cases as well. It is logical to assume that trade restrictive measures not only affect goods or services practically imported, but also deter importers from exercising their right to import. The practical difficulty in many such cases would be to prove and quantify this potential import. This manner of interpretation corresponds to a tendency also revealed in the interpretation of other GATS provisions, such as Article II (MFN, see 6.6.1.3.1) and Article XVII (national treatment, see 8.4.2.1).

A failure to apply this test to the facts of the case would render the Panel's decision unacceptable.[47]

The factors mentioned in *Korea – Beef* would be now analysed in details:

(a) The importance of the common interests or values protected by these measures

The procedural aspect: In *China – Publications and Audiovisual Products* some measures that were claimed to protect the same interest were challenged, and the Panel chose, at that stage, to refer collectively to all these measures, and to take only the later stages of analysis separately for each measure. This practice was approved by the Appellate Body.[48]

The substantive aspect: It is commonly assessed, that the 'weighing and balancing' process may further depend on the relative weight of the interests involved, with interests such as human life prevailing over other interests, thus potentially raising a higher degree of judicial deference and self-restraint,[49] while economic and environmental considerations are treated with less judicial self-renstraint. This approach, with seems to have gained an explicit reference in GATT cases *Korea – Beef*[50]

45. C. P. Bown & J. P. Trachtman, n. 21, 122.
46. WT/DS363/R n. 11, Panel report, para. 7.788.
47. In *China– Publications and Audiovisual Products* the Appellate Body found that the Panel erred in exercising this process concerning one of the measures at stake since 'the Panel did not cite any evidence in support of its assumption' and 'did not explain why the contribution made by the presumed limitation [caused by this measure-N.M] ... would be a 'material' one'. It was thus determined that 'the Panel neither addressed quantitative projections nor provided qualitative reasoning based on evidence before it to support that finding'. The Appellate Body thus determined that since the Panel's decision was based on a wrong assumption that the measure at stake 'imposes a limitation on the number of import entities, the inferences that the Panel drew from this assumption have no basis'. WT/DS363/AB/R n. 11, paras 292, 294, 296.
48. WT/DS363/AB/R n. 11, Appellate Body report, para. 249.
49. GATS commentary, n. 4, 316. WT/DS135/AB/R European Communities – Measures Affecting Asbestos and Asbestos-Containing Products, adopted on 5.4.2001, para. 172.
50. WT/DS161,169/AB/R n. 8, Appellate Body report para. 162.

and in *Brazil – Retreaded Tyres*[51] decisions, seems to be somewhat blurred by the *US – Gambling*[52] decision, where the Appellate Body cites the *Korea – Beef* decision to stress the freedom of domestic regulation embodied in this provision.[53] Displaying sensitivity to domestic regulatory concerns, both the Panel and Appellate Body in that case, avoided ruling directly on the legitimacy of US regulatory objectives,[54] pointing instead to cultural differences in policy choice.[55] The same approach seems to have been taken by both the Panel and Appellate Body in *China – Publications and Audiovisual Products*, as the Panel repeated, time and again, its recognition that 'the protection of public morals is a highly important value or interest',[56] adding: '[w]e do not consider it simply accident that the exception relating to 'public morals' is the first exception identified in the ten subparagraphs of Article XX'.[57] These decisions may reflect a shift in the approach of WTO tribunals, opting for a more cautious approach than in *Korea – Beef* and *Brazil – Retreaded Tyres*, following the criticism on these decisions.

Alternatively it may be suggested that the real importance of an interest in the eyes of the WTO tribunals, weighed and balanced against the free trade interest, should be judged according to the dispute's result. According to this test, both *US – Gambling* and *China – Publications and Audiovisual Products* could be included in the former category, because in both cases the WTO adjudicating bodies did not accept the Articles XX GATT/XIV GATS defence claims, thus practically intervening in a domestic policy decision/practice of the respondent Members.

(b) The contribution made by the measure under review to the achievement of specified goal

This aspect is viewed in two, complementary, perspectives: in the first stage, the contribution and the effectiveness of the measure at stake should be considered. In the second stage, the measure at stake should be compared to the alternatives.

The measure

Referring to the measure at stake, a means-end analysis is conducted to see to what extent the measure contributes to the achievement of the policy objective. The greater contribution by such a measure, the more likely it is that the measure shall be deemed necessary.[58]

51. WT/DS322/R, AB/R *Brazil –Retreaded Tyres*, n. 38.
52. WT/DS285/R, AB/R *US – Gambling*, n. 5.
53. D. Irwin & J. Weiler, n. 26, 107.
54. WT/DS285/AB/R *US – Gambling*, n.5, para. 327.
55. S. Wunch-Vincent, 'The Internet, Cross-Border Trade in Services, and the GATS: Lessons from *US – Gambling*', *5 World Trade Review*, 319, 348.
56. WT/DS363/R n. 11, Panel report, paras 7.759, 7.763.
57. WT/DS363/R n. 11, *ibid.*, Panel report, para. 7.817.
58. GATS commentary, n. 4, 317; WT/DS308/AB/R Mexico – Tax Measures on Soft Drinks, adopted 24.6.2006, para. 74; WT/DS285/R *US – Gambling*, n. 5, Panel report, para. 6.494.

This element could either be established on *quantitative projections* based on data, or on *qualitative reasoning* based on a set of hypotheses that are tested and supported by sufficient evidence.[59]

In *Brazil – Retreaded Tyres*, it was found that quantification of risk, of the contribution of the measure, or of the alternative measures is not always necessary.[60] But this may not be the case in other cases, particularly where all other elements are equal.

The *qualitative assessment* 'does not require quantification, but it requires judgment based on facts and inevitably requires estimation of magnitudes'.[61] This approach seems to have been followed in *China – Publications and Audiovisual Products*, where the Panel exercised its fact-analysis, noting, on certain occasions, the lack of sufficient information.[62] In that case, this approach was approved by the Appellate Body who foresaw situations where a qualitative, rather than a quantitative, assessment might take place, at least for the establishment of the contribution of the measure to the realization of the ends pursued by it.[63] The Appellate Body determined that the burden of proof lying on the responding party, is to put forward 'evidence and arguments that enable the panel to assess the challenged measure in light of the relevant factors to be "weighed and balanced" ',[64] thus not necessarily requiring a proof which consists of data.

A measure may be deemed necessary *even if there is no guarantee that it would achieve the policy objective in absolute certainty*.[65]

In GATT context, in the *Korea – Beef* case, it was clarified that although not only measures which are 'indispensable', but also measures 'making a contribution' to the pursued objective may be considered, a 'necessary' measure is 'located significantly closer to the pole of 'indispensable' than to the opposite pole of simply 'making a contribution to'.[66]

To that extent, where it is proved that the risk is decreasing due to other reasons, the 'necessity' of the measure examined may be doubted.[67]

In *US – Gambling*, Antigua argued that the unwillingness of the United States to engage in consultations demonstrates, in itself, that the United States did not consider the measures at stake 'necessary'. This argument was accepted by the Panel,[68] but rejected by the Appellate Body.[69]

59. WT/DS363/AR/R n. 11, Appellate Body Report para. 253.
60. WT/DS322/AB/R n. 38, Appellate Body report, para. 146. Former cases where quantification was required were mentioned, but the Appellate Body contended that the analysis of contribution may be done either in quantitative or in qualitative terms.
61. C. P. Bown & J. P. Trachtman, n. 21, 125, 130.
62. WT/DS363/AB/R n. 11, paras 7.834, 7.856.
63. WT/DS363/R n. 11, para. 253.
64. *Ibid.*, para. 288.
65. WT/DS308/AB/R *Mexico – Soft Drinks*, n. 58, Appellate Body report, para. 74; WT/DS285/R *US – Gambling*, n. 5, Panel report para. 6.494.
66. WT/DS363/AB/R n. 11, para. 161.
67. WT/DS246/R European Communities – Conditions for the granting of tariff preferences to developing countries, adopted on 20.4.2004, Panel report, paras 7.211–7.213.
68. WT/DS285/R n. 5, paras 6.526, 6.533–6.534.
69. WT/DS285/AB/R n. 5, para. 325.

In *China – Publications and Audiovisual Products* both parties suggested that a measure can be characterized as 'necessary' according to GATT Article XX even if it does not achieve the desired objective *all by itself.*[70] The Panel was willing to agree with the parties that this determination was right in the circumstances of the case before it, since the purpose of guarding public morals was cumulatively achieved by a series of measures. However, the Panel stressed: 'we see no need to take position on whether this would be correct in all circumstances'.[71]

Alternative measures

In GATT case *Korea – Beef*, it was reiterated that the Panel will examine whether WTO-*consistent alternatives* to the WTO-inconsistent measure exist, and where applied by responding party in other cases. If the answer is positive, it serves as a strong indication to the existence of a legal alternative that the respondent was reasonably expected to use in the case under dispute. In GATT case *Canada – Wheat Exports and Grain Imports*[72] the Panel specified three considerations that should be taken into account in weighing and balancing alternative measures:

(1) *The extent to which the alternative measure contributes to the realization of the end pursued* – the alternative measure must be able to achieve the same level of protection, namely: be equally effective.[73]
(2) *The difficulty of implementation.*
(3) *The trade impacts of the alternative measure compared to that of the measure for which justification is claimed.*[74]

Additionally, the alternative measure should be *precise and concrete.*[75]

The alternatives should be *reasonably available.* Thus, in *US – Gasoline* the Panel found that a measure may be considered 'reasonably available' even in the existence of administrative difficulties.[76] However, weighing the other reasonably

70. Thus, for example, wide geographic distribution of the branches of import entities was recognized as complementary to the efficiency of the import process, preventing delays and saving costs: WT/DS363/R, n. 11, Panel report, para. 7.833.
71. WT/DS363/R, n. 11, para. 7.792.
72. WT/DS276/R Canada – Measures Relating to Exports of Wheat and Treatment of Imported Grain, adopted on 27.9.2004, Panel report, para. 6.226.
73. WT/DS161, 169/R, n. 7, para. 665; This approach was adopted in WT/DS363/AB/R *China– Publications and Audiovisual Products*, n. 11, para. 319.
74. An example given by C. P. Bown & J. P. Trachtman, n. 21, 103, 117: examination of the alternative of a complete trade ban in the circumstances of *Brazil–Tyres* over the import tariff effectively applied, shows that the former option is less effective than the latter, being more trade restrictive, while the latter option would be more effective if complemented with a domestic-consumption tax on all tyres.
75. In WT/DS285/AB/R *US – Gambling*, n. 5, para. 317 the Appellate Body rejected the Panel's determination that consultations fulfil these criteria, reiterating that consultations for a process with uncertain and non-concrete results.
76. WT/DS2/R *US – Gasoline*, n. 7, paras 6.26–6.28. This conclusion was supported by the Appellate Body in WT/DS135/AB/R *EC – Asbestos*, n. 49; Effectively, the result of WT/DS363/R n. 11, *China – Publications and Audiovisual Products* may imply the same conclusion: the Panel was not convinced by China that the alternative suggested by the United States bears substantial

available options, the *practical* availability is stressed.[77] Thus, theoretical options: options the responding Member is not capable of pursuing or measures imposing an undue burden on a Member, will not be taken into account.[78] Also, difficulties of implementation, high administrative burden, costs, technical difficulties and lack of expertise can render an alternative reasonably unavailable.[79] This interpretation has substantial implications in favour of countries with limited resources. Some commentators point out that in GATT case *EC – Asbestos,* the Appellate Body interpreted 'reasonably available' as allowing the consideration whether the alternative measure 'contributes to the realization of the end pursued',[80] while in *US – Gambling*, the Appellate Body interpreted these words as implying that the alternative measure must preserve the right of the Member involved to achieve its desired level of protection with respect to the objective pursued,[81] noting that this contradiction is not yet settled.[82] This contradiction reflects the conflict between the two interests and its reflection in the developing WTO jurisprudence, discussed above.

The determination of protection level pursued by a Member, which is not easy in itself, will affect the decision to what extent other regulatory alternatives are reasonably available.[83]

Finally, it should be noted that the *mode of supply* may affect a decision about whether a measure forms an 'alternative' to the measure which is subject of dispute. Thus, a claim that remote supply of gambling and betting services raised concerns that were specific to this mode of supply was accepted by WTO adjudicating bodies in *US – Gambling*.[84]

---

administrative and financial burden: paras 7.902–7.906. As a result, China was practically faced with two alternative options: either to accept the alternative suggested by the United States, which was claimed by it to bear administrative and financial difficulties, or to look for another alternative practice that would be consistent with GATS provisions and with its commitments according to GATS. See also WT/DS363/AB/R, n. 11, Appellate Body report, para. 335.

77. For example, analyzing the alternative option of Brazil to subsidize domestic retreaded tyres instead of restricting trade of imported ones, brings to the conclusion that due to administrative and economic difficulties, as well as due to the high probability that such subsidy would be deemed to violate Art. III (national Treatment) and Art. XI of the GATT this option does not seem 'reasonably available': C. P. Bown & J. P. Trachtman, n. 21, 100.
78. WT/DS285/R, *US – Gambling*, n. 5, Appellate Body report paras 308, 320; WT/DS363/AB/R *China– Publications and Audiovisual Products*, n. 11, Appellate Body report, paras 318, 327, stressing that a claim concerning undue burden should be supported by sufficient evidence.
79. WT/DS135/R *EC – Asbestos*, n. 49, Panel report paras 8.207–8.217, WT/DS135/AB/R, Appellate Body report, para. 174.
80. WT/DS135/AB/R n. 49, para. 172.
81. WT/DS285/AB/R n. 5, para. 308; This rule is repeated in WT/DS363/R *China– Publications and Audiovisual Products*, n. 11, Panel report paras 7.836, 7.849, 7.836, 7.868.
82. C. P. Bown & J. P. Trachtman, n. 21, 122.
83. F. Ortino, n. 28, 16.
84. WT/DS285/R, n. 5, Panel report paras 6.497–6.498, WT/DS285/AB/R Appellate Body report para. 347.

Alternatives' assessment: the substance of the test

'The term "necessary", in the abstract, refers to a range of degrees of necessity'.[85] According to one interpretative option, based on a GATT 1947 case: *US – Section 337*,[86] it implies the *least-trade-restrictive alternative*, namely, the examination of some possible instruments pursue a policy objective, to determine which of them is the least trade restrictive. 'Within this calculation, the policy objective pursued by the Member, as well as the level of protection determined by the Member itself, is not called into question'.[87]

This is a relatively narrow interpretation, compared to the other option, according to which the WTO adjudicating bodies may 'weigh and balance' different societal values, which is much wider and more intrusive in the Members' regulatory autonomy.[88] It lacks the reference to the value of achievement of the regulatory goal.[89] Some commentators suggest that in post-Uruguay Round case law referring to GATT, a less rigid and more flexible position towards domestic regulation is adopted by the WTO adjudicating bodies.[90] Others argue that the *Brazil – Rretreaded Tyres* decision concerning GATT Article XX might be interpreted as a reversion to the *least-trade-restrictive alternative* test, while yet others regard this decision as reflecting a mere suitability test, simply asking 'whether the national measure seems reasonably designed to achieve the purported legitimate goal'. It is argued that this position of the WTO adjudicating bodies reflects a difficulty to evaluate the different implications involved, and moreover, the failure of these tribunals to define the measure to be evaluated and evaluate its contribution, and to define the chosen level of protection.[91]

The 'weighing and balancing' process must distinguish between:

- The *objective*, which is the basic value referenced in the relevant subsection of GATT article XX (and seemingly – GATS Article XIV).
- The *chosen level of protection* which is the degree for which that basic value is fulfilled.
- The *means* by which protection is achieved, namely the alternative that should be weighed against other alternatives.[92]

There is no indication in WTO jurisprudence what relative weight should to be attributed to each element. However, it seems that the relative weight of each element may differ on a case-by-case basis. Thus, for example, in *China – Publications and Audiovisual Products* the Panel seems to have attributed a decisive

85. The Appellate Body in WT/DS363/AB/R *China– Publications and Audiovisual Products*, n. 11, para. 251, quoting the Appellate Body in WT/DS161,169/AB/R *Korea–Beef*, n. 8.
86. L/6439 US – Section 337 of the Tariff Act of 1930, adopted on 7.11.1989, 36S/345.
87. F. Ortino, n. 28. See a table summarizing all the factors addressed under this test up to and including the *Brazil–Tyres* decision in C. P. Bown & J. P. Trachtman, n. 21, 118.
88. F. Ortino, n. 28, 14.
89. C. P. Bown & J. P. Trachtman, n. 21, 120.
90. GATS commentary, n. 4, 315.
91. C. P. Bown & J. P. Trachtman, n. 21, 87, 90, 98, 126.
92. *Ibid.*, 124–125.

weight to the third element, since the importance of the two first elements was not questioned by it.

(c) The trade (restrictive) impact of the measure on imports or exports

This aspect should be also examined referring to the intrinsic qualities of the measure at stake, as well as in comparison to the available alternatives, if there are any. Less trade-restrictive alternatives used by other Members may be considered, but should not automatically render the measure at issue unnecessary.[93]

The degree of trade-restrictiveness of a measure should be weighed against the importance of the objective pursued by it. In GATT case *Korea – Beef*, the Appellate Body determined that the measure at stake involved higher costs for imported beef and retailers thereof, while alternative WTO-consistent measures would not have such an effect.[94]

The trade restrictive impact of the measures at stake seems to have played a pivotal role in the Panel decision in *China – Publications and Audiovisual Products*. Despite recognizing the importance of the interest involved (public morals' protection) the Panel, examining the intrinsic qualities of the different measures involved,[95] came to the conclusion that many of these measures did not contribute to the protection of public morals,[96] while others could have been replaced with less restrictive alternatives.[97]

A measure may also be considered not 'necessary' due to intrinsic qualities, where it is too broad, applied through an unreasonably burdening administrative process (e.g., in terms of time or where 'the measures do not correspond to the commercial realities' of the relevant industry).[98] In fact, this means that the 'necessity' of a measure is subject, *inter alia*, to the proportionality test.

Is cost-effectiveness relevant?

One interpretative question raised in this context is: should less trade restrictive measures be weighed against less costly (or less onerous in any other manner) measures, and which measure would prevail. If the cost-effectiveness test is implied in GATS relevant language, could this imply that other costs incurred both by private (e.g., compliance costs) and public (e.g., administrative and enforcement costs) parties could be taken into consideration?[99] This notion may stem from the Appellate Body's decision in GATT case *Korea – Beef*,[100] implying

93. GATS commentary, n. 4, 318.
94. WT/DS161,169/AB/R n. 7, Appellate Body report para. 181.
95. WT/DS363/R n. 11, paras 7.821–7.867.
96. *Ibid.*, paras 7.842, 7.857, 7.865.
97. *Ibid.*, paras 7.886–7.909.
98. WT/DS339,340,342/R, AB/R China – Measures Affecting Imports of Automobile Parts, adopted on 12.1.2009, Panel report paras 7.361–7.362.
99. Ortino, n. 28, 17.
100. WT/DS161,169/AB/R n.7.

that Members may have to adopt measures which are *less trade restrictive* even though they may involve higher administrative or enforcement costs.[101] This notion seems to be repeated in *China – Publications and Audiovisual Products.* Although the Appellate Body stressed that China is not obliged to adopt the alternative suggested by the United States, it recognized that 'adopting any alternative measure will, by definition, involve some change, and this alone does not suffice to demonstrate that the alternative would impose an undue burden'. It was likely that any modification of the existing system of content review, to meet the decision of the dispute settlement report, would result in substantive additional costs for China. Nevertheless, the Appellate Body stressed its need to bring its measures into compliance with the agreement.[102]

Cost-benefit considerations are provided for by a somewhat different phrasing of a necessity test, included in Article 2.2 of the TBT agreement and in Article 5.6 of the SPS agreement. However, the difference in wording and context of GATS provision should be taken into account in the interpretation of this test in GATS context.[103]

The *balancing tests*, taking into account the administrative and enforcement costs, may set an alternative to the narrower cost-effectiveness test.[104]

In any case, there is still no definite choice of the test to be applied, thus undermining the expectancy of the Members.

The restrictive effect: on imports or also on importers?

In the case of *China – Publications and Audiovisual Products* the Appellate Body, analyzing the equivalent GATT Article XX(a), noted:

> The text of Article XX(a), however, refers only to measures 'necessary to protect public morals'. It does not, therefore, provide explicit guidance on the question of whether, in assessing 'necessity', a panel may take into account only the restrictive effect the measures have on *imports* of relevant products, or whether the panel may also consider the restrictive effect of the measures on *importers or potential importers.*[105]

101. D. H. Regan, 'The Meaning of 'Necessary' in GATT Art. XX and GATS Art. XIV: the Myth of Cost-Benefit Balancing', *6 World Trade Review* (2007), 347. The 'less trade restrictive alternative' is followed in later GATT cases: WT/DS135/AB/R *EC–Asbestos*, n. 49, WT/DS302/AB/R Dominican Republic – Measures Affecting the Importation and Internal Sale of Cigarettes, adopted on 19.5.2005, as well as by GATS case WT/DS285/AB/R *US – Gambling*, n. 5.
102. WT/DS363/AB/R n. 11, Appellabe Body report, paras 328, 335.
103. J. P. Trachtman, 'Lessons for the GATS from Existing WTO Rules on Domestic regulation', in A. Mattoo & P. Sauvé, *Domestic Regulation and Service Trade Liberalization*, the World Bank and Oxford University Press (2003), 57, 65–66.
104. C. P. Bown & J. P. Trachtman, n. 21, 86.
105. WT/DS363/AB/R n. 11, para. 303.

In GATT context, the Appellate Body answered this question in the affirmative, based on the general reference to 'international trade' in the *chapeau* and to 'international commerce' in the Preamble, saying that such an assessment

> may, in appropriate cases, extend beyond an assessment of the restrictive effect on imported products, as this assessment must be undertaken in the light of the measure at issue, the specific obligation of the covered agreements that the measure infringes, and the defence being invoked.[106]

This conclusion would be all the more correct if adopted to GATS context, due to the fact that GATS generally applies not only to measures affecting services but also to measures affecting service suppliers.

15.2.3.4.2 Measures Necessary to Protect Public Morals or to Maintain Public Order (Article XIV(a))

15.2.3.4.2.1 'Public Morals' and 'Public Order'

15.2.3.4.2.1.1 Scope

'Public morals' and 'public order' are relative expressions that may be interpreted differently in each country, as well as by the same country in different periods.[107] Thus, for example, the *China – Publications and Audiovisual Products* case presents a very strict approach towards foreign publications, totally subjecting them to 'content review' as a precondition for import. Although this is not a common practice in other WTO Members, the right of China to engage in such 'content review' was not questioned. The Panel recognized that 'the content and scope of 'public morals' can vary from Member to Member, as they are influenced by each Member's prevailing social, cultural, ethical and religious values'.[108] The Panel in that case further recognized that 'public morals is a highly important value or interest'.[109] The disagreement rather concentrated on the measures applied to achieve this end. In *US – Gambling*, the Panel (the finding of which were unchanged by the Appellate Body) noted that the two concepts may vary in *time* and *space*.[110] The term *public morals*, was defined by the Panel as referring to 'standards of right and wrong conduct maintained by or on behalf of a community or nation'.[111] The term *public order* was defined by the Panel as referring 'to the

106. *Ibid.*, para. 306.
107. Such an exception, including similar uninterpreted expressions, is common in other trade and economic agreements, for example, the EC Treaty and treaties for the avoidance of double taxation.
108. WT/DS363/R n. 11, Panel report para. 7.763. See also WT/DS285/R *US – Gambling*, n. 5, Panel report, para. 6.461, 6.467, 6.487, Appellate Body report, paras 299, 323.
109. WT/DS363/R n. 11, *ibid.*, paras 7.814–7.817. This determination seems unnecessary since the importance of this interest was already recognized by the agreement's drafters as an important interest and thus included in GATT Art. XX and GATS Art. XIV.
110. WT/DS285/R *US – Gambling*, n. 5, Panel report, para. 6.461.
111. *Ibid.*, Panel report, para. 6.465. This term is interpreted to encompass measures referring to alcohol, sex, gambling, slavery, torture of animals and drugs: GATS commentary, n. 4, 298.

preservation of the fundamental interests of the society, as reflected in public policy and law. These fundamental interests can relate, *inter alia*, to standards of law, security and morality'.[112] In that case, the Panel noted that under-age gambling and pathological gambling may fall under both concepts.[113]

The Panel further recognized that 'to the extent that both concepts seek to protect largely similar values, some overlap may exist'.[114] However, under the circumstances of that case, the Panel did not see any reason to develop this subject, determining that the measures at stake (preventing gambling and betting services) could have been considered to protect either public morals and/or public order.[115]

'Public morals' and 'public order' are very broad expressions which are not interpreted by GATS text, probably due to the different views of the Members as to their substance, implying the necessity to allow maximal flexibility in their interpretation. The reference to public order broadens the scope of this provision compared to the equivalent GATT provision (Article XX(a) thereof), referring only to 'public morals.'

According to some commentators,[116] 'public order' is broader and includes 'public morals' and other interests, which are not included in 'public morals', such as standards of safety, fight against organized crime and access to essential facilities.

Nevertheless, the Panel in *China – Publications and Audiovisual Products* drew a direct analogy from the interpretation of 'public morals' in GATS Article XIV(a) to GATT Article XX(a), providing:

> Since Article XX(a) uses the *same concept* as Article XIV(a), and since we see no reason to depart from the interpretation of 'public morals' developed by the panel in *US – Gambling*, we adopt the same interpretation for purposes of our Article XX(a) analysis.[117] [Emphasis added].

Two legal instruments narrow the potential scope of this exception, that is, the ability of the importing country to restrict the access of service suppliers into their territory due to this reason.

The first legal instrument is the *necessity test* that imports into this provision the proportionality standard, as explained above.

The second instrument is included in footnote 5 of GATS, which narrows only the scope of 'public order', determining:

> The public order exception may be invoked only where a genuine and sufficiently serious threat is posed to one of the fundamental interests of society.

---

112. WT/DS285/R n. 5, Panel report, para. 6.467. The word 'security' in this context does not imply that this provision refers to national security interests, covered exclusively by Art. XIV*bis* (see below): GATS commentary, n. 3, 299.
113. *Ibid.*, Panel report para. 6.469–6.470.
114. *Ibid.*, Panel report, para. 6.468.
115. *Ibid.*, Panel report, para. 6.469.
116. GATS commentary, n. 4, 300.
117. WT/DS363/R n. 11, Panel report para. 7.759.

The expressions 'genuine and sufficiently serious threat' and 'fundamental interests of the society' are subject to further interpretation on a case-by-case basis. One crucial question, for example, would be: should these elements be objectively or subjectively defined? Opting for a subjective definition implies more discretion to the Members, while opting for an objective definition would subject any decision by a Member to an *ex post facto* decision of the WTO adjudicating bodies, thus necessarily undermining certainty and creating a deterring effect to use this provision.

In *US – Gambling* the Appellate Body abstained from providing for a too strict form of application of this footnote, by rejecting Antigua's claim that the Panel failed to assess whether the interest served by the United States measures examined (federal statutes) satisfied the footnote's criteria. The Panel said:

> Having defined 'public order' to include the standard in footnote 5, and then applied the definition to the facts before it to conclude that the measures 'are designed to "protect public morals" and/or "to maintain public order", the Panel *was not required, in addition, to make a separate, explicit determination that the standard of footnote 5 had been met*'.[118] [Emphasis added].

It is thus suggested[119] to proceed in two stages: first, see if the measure could be protected under 'public morals' and only if not – try the 'public order' protection, which is subject to stricter terms.

15.2.3.4.2.1.2 Content – Who Defines It?

The Panel in *US – Gambling*[120] adopted an approach developed concerning the equivalent GATT Article XX to determine, that the content of 'public morals' and 'public order' is subject to the level of protection applied by each Member, and hence may be *unilaterally* defined.

15.2.3.4.2.1.3 The Procedure

Based on the analysis developed in the context of the equivalent GATT Article XX, *mutatis mutandis*, it seems that the respondent Member invoking this provision has to satisfy a three-tier test:[121]

(1) The policy in respect of the measures for which the provision was invoked fell within the range of policies designed to protect public morals and/or public order; For this purpose, the respondent has to establish a prima facie case, presenting evidence that tend to reflect the existence of risks to these interests.
(2) The inconsistent measures, for which the exception was being invoked, were *necessary* to fulfil the policy objective; and

118. WT/DS285/AB/R n. 5, Appellate Body report, para. 298.
119. GATS commentary, n. 4, 300.
120. WT/DS285/R n. 5, Panel report, para. 6.461.
121. WT/DS2/R *US – Gasoline*, n. 7, Panel report, para. 6.20.

(3) The measures were applied in conformity with the requirements of the *introductory clause* (*chapeau*) of Article XIV.

It is then for the complaining party to rebut this claim.

15.2.3.4.3 Measures Necessary to Protect Human, Animal or Plant Life or Health (Article XIV(b))

15.2.3.4.3.1 Scope

GATS Article XIV(b) justifies measures necessary to protect human, animal or plant life or health. This provision may be used to protect the public in the country of import from spreading diseases, from criminals who may endanger their lives, from the unlimited import of dangerous materials such as drugs, etc.

The equivalent GATT provision, Article XX(g), includes *inter alia* an explicit reference to measures 'relating to the conservation of exhaustible natural resources'. Such an explicit reference is not included in Article XIV(b) of GATS. This fact should be taken into account in the interpretation of Article XIV(b) in relation to GATS-inconsistent measures aimed at the protection of the environment.[122]

15.2.3.4.3.2 The Procedure

In GATT practice concerning the equivalent provision (Article XX(b)), which may form an indication to the procedure to be taken concerning GATS Article XIV(b) that was never a subject of dispute yet, the responding party is required to satisfy a three-tier test:[123]

(1) The policy in respect of the measures for which the provision was invoked fell within the range of policies designed to protect human, animal or plant life or health; For this purpose, the respondent has to establish a prima facie case, presenting evidence that tend to reflect the existence of health risks.

(2) The inconsistent measures for which the exception was being invoked were *necessary* to fulfil the policy objective; and

(3) The measures were applied in conformity with the requirements of the *introductory clause* (*chapeau*) of Article XIV.

It is then for the complaining party to rebut this claim.[124]

15.2.3.4.3.3 Territorial Scope of Application

Unlike public order and public morals, which may be defined differently by different Members, the interests protected by this provision seem to be more universally-defined. Therefore, one interpretative question concerning this provision

122. GATS commentary, n. 4, 302, 304–306.
123. WT/DS2/AB/R *US – Gasoline*, n. 7, Appellate Body report, para. 6.20.
124. WT/DS285/R n. 5, Panel report, para. 6.514.

refers to its territorial/extra territorial scope of application. In GATT 1947 context, the Panel in *US – Tuna*[125] rejected a US claim suggesting that this provision allows each Member to apply restrictions on import for the reasons specified in it even out of its territory. Examining the history of drafting of the equivalent GATT exception (Article XX(b)), its purpose and the results of the suggested, broad interpretation the Panel said:

> the panel considered that if the broad interpretation of Article XX(b) suggested by the United States were accepted, each contracting party could unilaterally determine the life and health protection policies from which other contracting parties could not deviate without jeopardizing their rights under the General Agreement. The General Agreement would then no longer constitute a multilateral framework for trade among all contracting parties but would provide legal security only in respect of trade between a limited number of contracting parties with identical internal regulations.

The same logic could be adopted concerning GATS provision, taking into account the resemblance of the two exceptions, their similar purpose and their context: being exceptions to the general purpose of the two agreements, which is the enhancement of trade liberalization.

15.2.3.4.3.4 Content

Restrictions according to the equivalent GATT exception refer, *inter alia*, to medicines, poisons and diseases, allowing border quarantine, examinations and vaccinations.

In services, the outcome of implementing this provision would be the prevention of access of imported services or foreign services suppliers by measures necessary to protect human, animal or plant life or health. One possible scenario could take place in case of an international disease, where the prevention of such access is meant to stop its distribution. Another possible scenario may take place where the imported services or service suppliers are suspected of being able to cause damage to the life or health of human beings, plants or animals.

Nevertheless, questions may arise as to the application of this provision to 'gray area' situations such as certain mental disorders[126] or controversial medical services such as the conduct of abortions in certain countries, controversial genetic engineering practices etc. It is suggested by some commentators that when a health concern may also qualify as a matter of public morals/order, Article XIV(b) will be regarded as *lex specialis* as compared to Article XIV(a), and all health concerns will be exclusively examined under it. However, when health is only *one* of a group of elements that may be examined under paragraph (a), it would be examined under paragraph (a).[127]

125. DS21/R, n. 17, para. 5.27.
126. In WT/DS285/AB/R *US – Gambling*, the parties disputed, *inter alia*, whether pathological gambling should fall within 'public morals' (Art. XIV(a)) or 'health' (Art. XIV(b)): n. 5, Appellate Body report, paras 75, 94.
127. GATS commentary, n. 4, 303.

Here, too, the word 'necessary' narrows the scope of the provision, subjecting it to the proportionality standard, as explained above.

15.2.3.4.3.5 Health and Health Concerns

The term 'health', relatively clear in itself, may overlap with other concepts included in Article XIV. Thus, it may overlap, to some extent, with the concept of 'life' embodied in the same subparagraph. It may further overlap, to some extent, with the concepts of 'public morals' and 'public order' embodied in subparagraph (a), since pathological addiction to alcohol, drugs, sex and even gambling may form a 'health concern'. This issue was examined in the *US – Gambling* case. However, neither the Panel (which addressed this issue through subparagraph (a)), nor the Appellate Body (which did not explicitly address this issue) gave any indication as to the possible or desired distinction between the two.[128] The reason may be that in that case the choice of any of the possible options would have borne the same implications.

15.2.3.4.3.6 Assessment of Risk (to Human, Animal or Plant Life or Health)

The necessity to take a measure to protect human, animal or plant life or health implies the existence of a risk. Consequently, some interpretative questions arise:

– Who is in charge of assessing the risk? Is it a sovereign decision of each Member, like in the case of 'public morals' or 'public order'?
It seems that Members do not have complete discretion on this matter (unlike in Article XIV*bis* which explicitly provides '*it* considers', referring to the Member involved – see below). Usually, such a claim should rely on scientific evidence, since unlike 'public morals' or 'public order', health and life matters are not matters reflecting values, but matters based on facts. Thus, it seems that *some* scientific basis would be necessary to establish a prima facie case.

However, Members still have considerable discretion: thus, they may decide which cases form negligible or minor injury. In addition, they are not obliged to follow a majority scientific opinion and may rely on scientific resources representing divergent opinions to establish their prima facie case. In the context of the equivalent GATT Article XX(b) the Appellate Body in *EC–Asbestos* determined:

> In justifying a measure under Article XX(b) of the GATT 1994, a Member may also rely, in good faith, on scientific sources which, at that time, may represent a divergent, but qualified and respected, opinion. A Member is not obliged, in setting health policy, automatically to follow what, at a given time, may constitute a majority scientific opinion. Therefore, a panel need not, necessarily, reach a decision under Article XX(b) of the GATT 1994 on the basis of the 'preponderant' weight of evidence.[129]

128. WT/DS285/AB/R n. 5, Appellate Body report, paras 75, 94.
129. WT/DS135/AB/R, n. 49, para. 178.

The problem here, as in many GATS/WTO other aspects, is that this discretion may be later exposed to controversy between Members, thus being finally judged *ex post* by WTO adjudicating bodies, who 'enjoy a margin of discretion in assessing the value of the evidence, and the weight to be ascribed to the evidence'.[130] The situation turns all the more complex where the scientific subject matter is complex for the understanding of non-scientists who have to decide on the matter.[131] Therefore, any discretion applied by a Member in this context involves a risk. This reality undermines stability and predictability.

Another difficulty may arise referring to the validity of the scientific evidence. Doubts may arise, *inter alia*, as to the date of scientific examination as well as to the method of examination. In *US – Continued Suspension*, the Panel addressed these matters in the context of scientific evidence required to base a risk assessment under Article 5 of the SPS Agreement, noting:

> the experts agree that data do not become invalid only because they are old, but that more recent measurement or analytical methods may be more accurate. The Panel notes, however, that a problem relates to accuracy is likely to occur with respect to results at the level of the detection limits of the older methods. Outside this particular situation, what matters is whether the method has been validated. The Panel thus concludes that whether a study is old or is not per se a criterion to put in doubt the validity of this study.[132]

Despite the difference between GATS and SPS provisions, this rational seems to be valid in GATS context as well.

– What is the degree of risk justifying action: would any risk suffice, or should a serious threat be established, as required by footnote 5 concerning 'public order'? Article XIV(b) is not accompanied by a provision similar to footnote 5. Therefore, there is no reason to assume that it is deemed to be activated only in serious cases of threat. On the other hand, its activation in minor and negligible cases may be considered as an infringement of the *good faith* principle. Between these two poles,

130. *Ibid., EC – Asbestos*, n. 49, Appellate Body report, para. 161.
131. Thus, for example, in GATT context, in *EC–Asbestos*, there was no dispute between the parties that the policy objective: prevention of lung cancer, was covered by the health exception. However, there was no agreement between the parties as to whether products containing asbestos constitute a risk to human health: WT/DS135/AB/R, n. 49, paras 19, 157–163. The complexity of scientific matters to the understanding of non-scientists, including Panel members, was discussed in WT/DS320/R, AB/R United States – Continued Suspension of Obligations in the EC-Hormones Dispute, adopted on 14.11.2008, Panel report, para. 4.720, and is also reflected in WT/DS291,292,293/R European Communities – Measures Affecting the Approval and Marketing of Biotech Products, adopted on 21.11.2006, referring to the SPS Agreement. The question whether a comprehensive, proper risk assessment was conducted also stands in the center of the dispute in WT/DS367/R Australia – Measures Affecting the Importation of Apples from New Zealand, published 9.8.10 (not adopted yet at the time of writing), see for example paras 7.904–7.905.
132. WT/DS320/R, n. 131, para. 7.427. See detailed explanation on the risk assessment under the SPS agreement in the Appellate Body report WT/DS320/AB/R, paras 525–532, 534.

it seems that the Members have discretion to decide how to act, a decision which, of course, would be subject to a potential *ex post* review by the WTO adjudicating bodies. It seems that, as for the former subparagraph, 'Members are free to determine their desired level of protection, which may entail measures that aim to reduce health risks to zero. While such an *objective* cannot be challenged, the chosen *instruments* will be subject to judicial review'.[133] From the analysis of the Appellate Body concerning Article 5 SPS, a conclusion may be drawn that 'a 'risk assessment' involves an identification of potentiality, even though this need not be expressed in numerical terms or as a minimum quantification of the level of risk'.[134]

– A necessary link between the risk and its cause

In *Japan – Apples*, in the context of risk assessment under Article 5 of the SPS agreement, the Appellate Body required the establishment of a causal link between the risk and the measure at issue, noting:

> Indeed, we are of the view that, as a general matter, 'risk' cannot usually be understood only in terms of a disease or adverse effects that may result. Rather, an evaluation of risk must connect the possibility of adverse effects with the antecedent cause. For example, the abstract reference to the 'risk of cancer' has no significance, in and of itself, under the SPS Agreement; but when one refers to the 'risk of cancer from smoking cigarettes', the particular risk is given content.[135]

Despite the difference between GATS and SPS provisions, this rational seems to be valid in GATS context as well.

15.2.3.4.4 Measures Necessary to Secure Compliance with Laws or Regulations which are not Inconsistent with the Provisions of This Agreement (Article XIV(c))

15.2.3.4.4.1 Scope and Content

This provision aims at allowing governments to stop or restrict the import of services or the access of service suppliers into their market, in order to secure compliance with laws or regulations which are not inconsistent with the provisions of GATS. The provision includes an *indicative* list of examples, referring to the prevention of four groups of problems: deceptive and fraudulent practices; a default on services contracts; the protection of the privacy of individuals; and safety.

133. GATS commentary, n. 4, 306.
134. WT/DS320/AB/R, n. 131, Appellate Body report, para. 574. In that case the Appellate Body reversed the Panel decision, on the grounds that it was based on the too general 'magnitude' concept.
135. WT/DS245/R, AB/R Japan – Measures Affecting the Importation of Apples, adopted on 10.12.2003.

The first group, *deceptive and fraudulent practices*, gives the government an instrument to ensure consumer protection. This is particularly important concerning trade in services, where fraudulent practices may expose the consumer to false physicians, lawyers and architects but also to frauds concerning financial services transactions or cross-border insurance services.

The second group, *a default on services contracts*, allows the protection of services consumers from unjust conditions in standard contracts as well as from default contracts for the supply of infrastructure services such as water, electricity, public transport etc.

The third group, *the protection of the privacy of individuals*, refers to services undermining this privacy, whether by photographing private premises, publication of private affairs, detection, listening-in etc. One of the difficulties encountered in recent decades is that some of these services may be exercised without any physical presence in the country of destination, but rather through the internet or through space devices, which makes it more difficult to prevent them. Confidentiality and privacy are also covered by GATS Article III*bis*. This provision mainly covers the outer limits of transparency and notification requirements applying to governments of the Members (see Chapter 13). To that extent, Article XIV(c) provides another layer of protection to private aspects of these data and information.[136]

The fourth group, *safety*, may allow the prevention of import of unsafe services, for example, where service suppliers are unable to guarantee the supply of clean water, safe gas or electricity supply, or the safety of cellular communication. It may also cover services based on unsafe facilities, such as unsafe amusements-park or extreme sports devices, as well as unsafe transportation measures. There is no equivalence to this norm in GATT Article XX. Safety standards concerning trade in goods need to be compatible with the non-discrimination requirements in GATT and with the relevant TBT requirements, while safety standards concerning trade in services need to follow the non-discrimination GATS provisions, Article XIV(c)(iii) and Article VI on domestic regulation (see Chapter 12).

The fact that this list is *indicative* may be concluded from the words 'including those relating to . . .'. The drafting history of the equivalent Article XX(d) of GATT supports this interpretation. In the discussions of the preparatory committee in Geneva, before its conclusion, it was explained:

> these examples given under sub-paragraph (g) [XX(d)] are, in fact, *only examples* . . . if any law or regulation is consistent with Chapter V, then any measure which is necessary for the enforcement of that law is taken care of here . . . [Emphasis added].[137]

This provision includes many vague expressions that are not interpreted by it, and raises some interpretative questions:

- What are 'laws or regulations which are not inconsistent with the provisions of GATS'?

136. W. Zdouc, n. 20, 206.
137. EPCT/A/PV 33 12–13.

- Should the interpretation of such laws/regulations by domestic courts be taken into consideration?
- Do 'the provisions of this agreement' include the specific commitments?

It seems that the answer to these questions will be revealed, in gray area cases, only retroactively, by the decision of the WTO adjudicating bodies. Thus, like in the other exceptions discussed, a country applying this exception is necessarily interpreting it in a certain manner, taking the risk that its interpretation will be later rejected.

15.2.3.4.4.2 The Procedure

The equivalent GATT provision, Article XX(d), was narrowly interpreted by GATT 1947 jurisprudence, based on the proportionality standard embodied in the word 'necessary'.[138] The factors to be considered in order to determine whether a measure is 'necessary' to secure compliance, developed by WTO jurisprudence, were summed up by the Panel in GATT 1994 case *US – Shrimp (Thailand)*, and upheld by the Appellate Body:[139]

> (i) the relative importance of the values or objectives the law or regulation is intended to protect; (ii) the extent to which the measure contributes to the realization of the end pursued – the securing of compliance with the law or regulation at issue; and (iii) the restrictive impact of the measure at issue.

To these tests another test should be added: the 'laws and regulations' with which compliance is being secured are in themselves 'not inconsistent' with the provisions of GATS.[140]

These legal tests were adopted and implemented by the Panel in GATS context in *US – Gambling*,[141] where the Panel came to the conclusion that although the laws at issue made a significant contribution to the law enforcement, they had a significant restrictive impact, and since the United States did not explore and exhausted WTO-consistent alternatives it could not justify them under this provision.

After a prima facie case is established by the respondent according to these tests, it is for the complaining party to rebut this claim.

---

138. See L/5333 US – Imports of Certain Automotive Spring Assemblies, adopted on 26.5.1983, 30S/107, para. 58; L/6439, US – Section 337, n. 80, 36S/345, paras 5.26–5.35; L/5504 Canada – Administration of Foreign Investment Review Act, adopted on 7.2.1984, 30S/140, para. 5.6.
139. WT/DS343/R, AB/R United States – Measures Relating to Shrimp from Thailand, adopted on 1.8.2008, Appellate Body report para. 316; WT/DS345/AB/R *United States – Customs Bond Directive*, n. 10, para. 316. See also: WT/DS31/R, AB/R Canada – Certain Measures Concerning Periodicals, adopted on 30.7.1997, Panel report, para. 5.11; WT/DS2/R *US – Gasoline*, n. 7, Panel report, para. 6.31. See implementation of the entire sequence of legal tests relevant to the equivalent GATT Art. XX(d) in WT/DS366/R Columbia – Indicative Prices and Restrictions on Ports of Entry, adopted on 20.5.2009.
140. WT/DS161,169/AB/R *Korea – Beef*, n. 7, Appellate Body report, para. 157.
141. WT/DS285/R *US – Gambling*, n. 5, Panel report, paras 6.557–6.565. This analysis was appealed by the United States, but the Appellate Body exercised judicial economy on this subject: Appellate Body report, para. 337.

15.2.3.4.4.3 'Laws and Regulations'

In the context of the equivalent GATT Article XX(d) the Appellate Body broadly interpreted 'laws and regulations' to include:

> rules that form part of the domestic legal system of a WTO Member, including rules deriving from international agreements that have been incorporated into the domestic legal system of a WTO Member or have direct effect according to that WTO Member's legal system.[142]

It was stressed by the Appellate Body, that these words do not include obligations of another WTO Member under an international agreement.[143]

15.2.3.4.4.4 'Secure Compliance'

The term 'secure compliance' implies that the laws or regulations at issue 'must "enforce" the relevant GATS-consistent laws and regulations'.[144]

In the context of GATT 1947, the words 'to secure compliance' were narrowly interpreted as referring only to compliance to the laws and regulations, not merely to the achievement of the same purposes. It was determined, that if these words were broadly interpreted, as implying the enforcement of obligations under laws and regulations

> the main function of Article XX(d) would be to permit contracting parties to act inconsistently with the General Agreement whenever such inconsistency is necessary to ensure that the obligations which the contracting parties may impose consistently with the General Agreement under their laws or regulations are effectively enforced. If the qualification 'to secure compliance with laws and regulations' is interpreted as 'to ensure the attainment of objectives of the laws and regulations', the function of Article XX(d) would be substantially broader. Whenever the objective of a law consistent with the General Agreement cannot be attained by enforcing the obligations under the law, the imposition of further obligations inconsistent with the General Agreement

142. WT/DS308/AB/R *Mexico – Soft Drinks*, n. 58, Appellate Body report, para. 79.
143. This determination was not explained by the Panel in that case. The Appellate Body based this interpretation on three arguments: (1) Arts X:1 and XX of GATT included a reference, in another part of the provision, to international agreements or obligations, thus indicating that the drafters of the agreement distinguished between international agreements, on the one hand, and 'laws' and 'regulations' on the other hand. (2) If the other interpretation was accepted, a WTO Member could invoke Art. XX(d) to justify measures taken to secure compliance with another Member's obligations – without complying with the detailed rules specified in Arts 22 and 23 of the DSU. (3) If the other interpretation would have been accepted, it would mean that the WTO dispute settlement system would have to assess whether the international agreement involved was violated, thus inappropriately becoming adjudicators of a non-WTO dispute. WT/DS308/AB/R *Mexico – Soft Drinks*, n. 58, Appellate Body report, paras 71, 77, 78 (respectively). According to Davey and Sapir, this interpretation corresponds to the 'ordinary meaning' of these words, since it is generally acceptable to refer to the international *law*, and not '*laws and regulations*': W. Davey, A. Sapir, 'The *Soft Drink* Case: The WTO and Regional Agreements', *8 World Trade Review* (2009), 5, 10–11.
144. GATS commentary, n. 4, 307.

> could then be justified under Article XX(d) on the grounds that this secures compliance with the objectives of the law. This cannot, in the view of the panel, be the purpose of Article XX(d) . . .[145]

In the same spirit it was explained in GATT 1994 case *China – Auto Parts*, that a Member wanting to use this provision must first demonstrate *specific obligations* that the measures at issue try to enforce and/or actions considered inconsistent under its domestic law that the measures at issue aim to prevent.[146] It is further reiterated by the Panel: 'there is nothing that prevents WTO Members from having a 'preventive' measure, as opposed to a 'responsive' measure, against actions considered inconsistent under their domestic laws or regulations'.[147]

However, some deviation from this narrow interpretation, in GATS context, can be seen in the decision recognizing a measure as 'securing compliance' even if it is only securing *partial* compliance, as in *US – Gambling*,[148] or (in GATT context) even if securing compliance by the measure examined cannot be guaranteed. In GATT 1994 case *Mexico – Soft Drinks* the Appellate Body rejected the use of coercion of a measure to 'secure compliance', stressing that compliance should be secured by the *design of the measure itself.*[149] It was further determined that the measure sought to be justified does *not* have to result in securing compliance with *absolute* certainty.[150]

Concerning the relationship between the words 'necessary' and 'secure compliance' it was determined in the context of GATT 1994 that where a measure does not 'secure compliance' with a domestic law or regulation, there is no need to examine whether it is 'necessary', since the two conditions are accumulative.[151]

15.2.3.4.5 Measures Inconsistent with Article XVII (National Treatment) (Article XIV(d))

15.2.3.4.5.1 Purpose

This subparagraph allows the deviation from the national treatment principle (non-discrimination of imported services and/or foreign services suppliers compared to like domestic services/service suppliers, respectively) in certain conditions. The conditions set forth by this provision are the following:

> provided that the difference in treatment is aimed at ensuring the equitable or effective imposition or collection of direct taxes in respect of services or service suppliers of other Members.

145. L/6657 EEC- Regulation on Imports of Parts and Components, adopted on 16.5.1990, 37S/195–197, paras 5.14–5.18.
146. WT/DS339,340,342/R *China – Auto Parts*, n. 98, Panel report para. 7.315.
147. *Ibid.*, para. 7.337.
148. WT/DS285/R, n. 5, Panel report, para. 6.539.
149. WT/DS308/AB/R, n. 58, Appellate Body report, para. 74.
150. *Ibid.*, para. 79.
151. WT/DS31/R *Canada – Periodicals*, n. 139, Panel report, para. 5.11.

The purpose of this provision is to prevent tax evasion by service suppliers or service consumers of foreign origin, who are not permanent residents in the Member applying the measure at issue, and are engaged in economic operations in several jurisdictions.[152]

15.2.3.4.5.2 The Procedure

A Secretariat document provides:

> Tax measures affecting service suppliers require no justification under Article XIV unless they violate an obligation or commitment under the Agreement. The two relevant provisions in this respect are Article XVI (National Treatment) and Article II (MFN).[153]

Where such a violation occurs, the responding party will invoke this provision and will thus bear the burden of proof, to demonstrate that the tax measure at stake is covered and justified by Article XIV(d). The complaining party will then have to rebut this claim.

15.2.3.4.5.3 'Direct Taxes'

Usually, direct taxes differ from indirect taxes, the former being imposed on income and capital, while the latter being imposed on consumption. In GATS context, direct taxes are defined in Article XXVIII(o) of the agreement:

> 'direct taxes' comprise all taxes on total income, on total capital or on elements of income or of capital, including taxes on gains from the alienation of property, taxes on estates, inheritances and gifts, and taxes on the total amounts of wages or salaries paid by enterprises, as well as taxes on capital appreciation.

This is a quite broad definition, which broadens the scope of the exception referring to direct taxes.

15.2.3.4.5.4 'Measures Aimed at Ensuring the Equitable or Effective Imposition or Collection of Direct Taxes'

The terms 'equitable' and 'effective' are ambiguous. They are not interpreted by the agreement. However, footnote 6 to the agreement includes a list of measures that would be deemed to fulfil this requirement:

> Measures that are aimed at ensuring the equitable or effective imposition or collection of direct taxes include measures taken by a Member under its taxation system which: (i) apply to non-resident service suppliers in recognition of the fact that the tax obligation of non-residents is determined with respect to taxable items sourced or located in the Member's territory; or (ii) apply to

152. W. Zdouc, n. 20, 208.
153. MTN.GNS/49, Informal GNS Meeting – 10.12.93, Chairman's Statement, 11.12.1993, n. 158, 1.

non-residents in order to ensure the imposition or collection of taxes in the Member's territory; or (iii) apply to non-residents or residents in order to prevent the avoidance or evasion of taxes, including compliance measures; or (iv) apply to consumers of services supplied in or from the territory of another Member in order to ensure the imposition or collection of taxes on such consumers derived from sources in the Member's territory; or (v) distinguish service suppliers subject to tax on worldwide taxable items from other service suppliers, in recognition of the difference in the nature of the tax base between them; or (vi) determine, allocate or apportion income, profit, gain, loss, deduction or credit of resident persons or branches, or between related persons or branches of the same person, in order to safeguard the Member's tax base. Tax terms or concepts in paragraph (d) of Article XIV and in this footnote are determined according to tax definitions and concepts, or equivalent or similar definitions and concepts, under the domestic law of the Member taking the measure.

It is unclear whether this is an exhaustive, or rather indicative, list of measures.[154] This question will have to be solved by future interpretation. If the list is merely indicative, this exception may have a wider scope than reflected by the list. The future interpretation will have to balance between the two interests: on the one hand, a broad as possible scope of application for the rules of the agreement and a narrow as possible scope of application for its exceptions, and on the other hand, effective tax collection. The common interpretative rule, providing that additional items to these included in an indicative list should be of the same nature, narrows the potential additional possibilities.

With respect to *option (i)* of the footnote it was indicated by the Secretariat: 'it would cover cases in which a tax measure would be applied not directly to a service supplier, because he is outside the jurisdiction, but rather through a consumer acting as a withholding agent'.[155]

The possibility included in *option (iv)* of the note seems somewhat far-reaching: it allows the application of measures to service *consumers* where the services are supplied in or from the territory of another Member, in order to ensure the imposition or collection of taxes on such consumers derived from sources in the Member's territory. It is understood that the consumers may be non-citizens and

154. On the one hand, the word 'include' seems to imply an *indicative* list. In the discussions that took place before GATS conclusion, the Secretariat replied to this question, raised by Members, providing that this is an *exhaustive* list. However, the reasoning held by the Secretariat was, 'in the absence of a term specifically indicating that the list is indicative, *such as "including"*' [emphasis added]: MTN.GNS/W/178 Taxation Issues Related to Art. XIV(d) – Note by the Secretariat, 15.11.1993. In a later discussion it was noted that there probably was a former version of this footnote, as well as that, there are many examples for cases that could come under this provision: MTN.GNS/49, n. 153. Since in the final version of this footnote the word 'include' appears, maybe the conclusion should be that this is an *indicative* list.

155. MTN.GNS/49, n. 153, 2.

even non-residents in the country where they are taxed. It is all the more far-reaching since taxes on consumption are usually considered indirect taxes, uncovered by this provision, while direct taxes are usually applied on suppliers.

15.2.3.4.5.5 Definition of Tax Terms or Concepts – Under Domestic Law

Footnote 6 of GATS further determines:

> Tax terms or concepts in paragraph (d) of Article XIV and in this footnote are determined according to tax definitions and concepts, or equivalent or similar definitions and concepts, under the domestic law of the Member taking the measure.

This provision is meant to prevent disagreements emanating from different interpretation of perceptions such as 'residence', 'source of income' etc. among the Members. It thus implies that such definitions and concepts may vary from one state to another,[156] based on their tax definitions and concepts, 'or equivalent or similar definitions and concepts'. While the former option may ensure some resemblance of perceptions among Members, assuming that the logic behind direct tax systems, as well as their mechanism, is basically similar, the latter option considerably broadens the scope of possibilities, particularly since the terms 'equivalent or similar definitions and concepts' are not defined, therefore seeming to be completely subject to the discretion of each Member. Thus, in fact, the implication of this exception may vary subject to the countries involved in a specific case where it is activated. This determination significantly facilitates the burden of proof as well as the invocation of this provision.[157] Despite the flexibility thus achieved, this practice somewhat undermines the uniform application of the agreement, as well as certainty and predictability.

15.2.3.4.5.6 Interpretation Rules for Article XIV(d)

Some interpretation rules for this provision were indicated by the WTO Secretariat:[158]

(1) 'The listing in the footnote of types of measures which governments may find it necessary to take is without prejudice as to whether any of them would necessarily be inconsistent with Article XVII'.
(2) 'Measures found to be justified under the footnote would normally be expected also to meet the requirement in the *chapeau* to Article XIV that they should not constitute a disguised restriction on trade.'

156. See interpretation in: MTN.GNS/W/178/Add. 1 Taxation Issues Related to Art. XIV(d) – Note by the Secretariat – Addendum, 30.11.1993.
157. W. Zdouc, n. 20, 208.
158. MTN.GNS/49, n. 153, 2.

15.2.3.4.6 Measures Inconsistent with Article II (MFN) due to Double Taxation Treaties (Article XIV(e))

15.2.3.4.6.1 Purpose

Deviation from the MFN principle (non-discrimination between sources of import from Members) is allowed:

> provided that the difference in treatment is the result of an agreement on the avoidance of double taxation or provisions on the avoidance of double taxation in any other international agreement or arrangement by which the Member is bound.

This provision is justified due to the unique position of treaties for the avoidance of double taxation, which are, by nature, bilateral, express mutual benefits given by the parties and engineered to conform to the direct tax systems of the parties.[159] Applying the MFN principle to measures resulting from these agreements would have undermined them completely, thus creating a group of 'free riders' who did not contribute any concession to the agreed framework but would nevertheless enjoy its benefits. This provision is essential considering the application of GATS to services and service suppliers who are directly taxed.[160]

15.2.3.4.7 Scope of Application: Subparagraphs XIV(d), (e)

The exceptions referring to tax measures affecting trade in services, justified under subparagraphs XIV(d), (e), would be invoked in reaction to claims that these measures are either incompatible with the MFN or with the national treatment obligation. In either case, the establishment of a discrimination claim against foreign services/service suppliers caused by such tax measure is subject to establishing that the relevant measure modifies the competitive conditions in the market. This test necessarily narrows the potential cases to be considered under these subparagraphs.[161]

---

159. The unique status of these treaties is also recognized by other WTO Agreements, including the WTO Agreement and the SCM Agreement. For further discussion see: GATS commentary, n. 4, 312–313.
160. Violations of Art. XVII (national treatment) arising from agreements on avoidance of double taxation are in principle within the ambit of GATS, but these matters are not subject to the general dispute settlement mechanism. They are rather subject to a specific procedure provided for by Art. XXII:3, where the matter may be brought to the attention of the Council for Trade in Services by any Member. The Council has to submit the matter to arbitration for a final and binding resolution. According to W. Zdouc, the existence of special derogation rules on MFN and national treatment means that other claims under GATS provisions against such agreements would be subject to the general dispute settlement procedures applicable to trade in services: W. Zdouc, 'WTO Dispute Settlement Practice Relating to the GATS', *Journal of International Economic Law* (1999), 295, 313.
161. GATS commentary, n. 4, 310.

15.2.3.5 The *Chapeau* (Introductory Clause) of Article XIV

The *chapeau* of Article XIV implies that the permission given in this article to guard certain, domestic interests at the expense of free trade flows should not be abused. Such measures should not be applied in a manner which would constitute:

- a means of arbitrary discrimination between countries where like conditions prevail;
- or a means of unjustifiable discrimination between countries where like conditions prevail;
- or a disguised restriction on trade in services.

These three standards serve 'to ensure that Members' rights to avail themselves of exceptions are exercised reasonably, so as not to frustrate the rights accorded other Members by the substantive rules of the GATS'.[162] They further reflect the general public international law *good faith* principle.[163]

These standards address 'not so much a challenged measure or its specific content, but rather the manner in which that measure is applied...'[164]

These standards are assessed after a prima facie case has been established, concerning the application of one of the specific objectives addressed in Article XIV to the measure at issue.

These standards seem to be *alternative* in nature. This conclusion is drawn from the use of the word 'or'. However, in practice the WTO adjudicating bodies sometimes examine all the three options together. Sometimes, these standards may overlap.[165] In the context of the equivalent GATT Article XX it was recognized that sometimes it may be difficult to separate these standards, when applied to the relevant facts.[166]

Thus, for example, in GATT case *US – Gasoline* the Appellate Body provided:

> 'Arbitrary discrimination', 'unjustifiable discrimination' and 'disguised restriction' on international trade may, accordingly, be read side-by-side; they impart meaning to one another'.[167]

If these standards are interpreted as cumulative, the order of their examination is insignificant.[168]

162. WT/DS285/AB/R *US – Gambling*, n. 5, Appellate Body report, para. 339.
163. WT/DS58/AB/R *US – Shrimp*, n. 6, Appellate Body report, para. 158, referring to the equivalent GATT provision.
164. WT/DS285/R *US – Gambling*, n. 5, Panel report, para. 6.581. This analysis is based on WT/DS58/AB/R *US – Shrimp*, n. 6, para. 150, referring to the equivalent GATT Art. XX.
165. WT/DS285/R *US – Gambling*, n. 5, Panel report para. 6.580. The Panel explained that such an overlap may occur since 'a "disguised restriction" includes disguised discrimination in international trade and a "disguised restriction" may be read as embracing restrictions amounting to arbitrary or unjustifiable discrimination in international trade'.
166. See, for example, the analysis of these elements in WT/DS58/AB/R *US – Shrimp*, n. 6, paras 166–177.
167. WT/DS2/AB/R *US – Gasoline*, n. 7, para. 25.
168. GATS commentary, n. 4, 322.

The three standards fold both substantive and procedural requirements.[169]

These standards are ambiguously phrased. In GATT case *US – Shrimp* the Appellate Body noted the significance of GATT Preamble as 'context' for the interpretation of the equivalent *chapeau* of GATT Article XX, reflecting the intentions of negotiators and giving 'colour, texture and shading to the rights and obligations of the Members . . . under the GATT 1994 . . .'[170]

15.2.3.5.1 The Burden of Proof: The Chapeau

In *US – Gasoline*[171] it was determined that the party invoking the exception bears the burden of proof to demonstrate that the measure involved is not applied in a discriminatory or restrictive manner as described in one or more of these three options. However, the standard of necessary proof of this element is different than the standard of proof required for showing that one of the specific exceptions in this Article encompasses the measure at issue, and is recognized by the Appellate Body as 'a heavier task.' This is a 'prima facie' burden of proof which may be based, *inter alia*, on the neutral wording of the measure, on the consistency of application of the measure at stake to foreign and domestic services/service suppliers, on the overall number of service suppliers, and on the patterns of enforcement or the reasons for non-enforcement.[172]

15.2.3.5.2 'A Means of Arbitrary or Unjustifiable Discrimination between Countries where like Conditions Prevail'

This condition aims at preventing the abuse of these exceptions for discrimination among like services and service suppliers from other members, where like conditions prevail. However, it consists of ambiguous expressions, undermining its certainty:

Does it refer to formal or substantial discrimination, and how would it be determined? What is 'arbitrary or unjustifiable' discrimination? What are the 'like conditions' that should exist in order for this provision to apply? Is formal or substantial 'likeness' required, and if substantial likeness is necessary – how will it be determined?

The *chapeau* of the equivalent GATT provision, article XX, refers to 'a means of arbitrary of unjustifiable discrimination between countries where the same conditions prevail'. The only difference between GATT and GATS provisions is that GATS provision refers to 'like' conditions while GATT refers to 'the same' conditions. Literally, GATS requirement seems more flexible than the equivalent GATT requirement.

169. WT/DS58/AB/R *US –Shrimp*, n. 6, Appellate Body report, para. 160.
170. *Ibid.*, paras 153–155.
171. WT/DS2/AB/R *US – Gasoline*, n. 7, para. 23.
172. GATS commentary, n. 4, 323.

GATT article XX was interpreted by the WTO adjudicating bodies in a relatively small number of cases, on a case-by-case basis.[173] Assuming that a similar interpretative approach would be applied to GATS provision, it will suffer from the same disadvantage: uncertainty and non-predictability.

In GATT context, in the case of *US – Shrimp*,[174] the Appellate Body, considered as 'unjustifiable discrimination', a situation where the United States (the importing country) required all exporting Members, wishing to exercise their GATT rights, to adopt essentially the same policy as that applied to, and enforced on, the United States' economic operators. The Appellate Body mentioned three elements that must exist for a measure to be applied in a manner which would constitute 'arbitrary or unjustifiable discrimination between countries where the same conditions prevail':

(1) The application of the measure must result in discrimination.
(2) The discrimination must be arbitrary or unjustifiable in character.
(3) This discrimination must occur between countries where the same conditions prevail.

These conditions will be now addressed in detail:

(1) The application of the measure must result in discrimination

This condition should be proved by evidence, on a case-by-case basis.[175] in *US – Gambling*, for example, the Panel found that the United States negotiated with some Members but not with others, and enforced an internet ban selectively against domestic suppliers, thus determining that the United States failed to prove 'that it applies its prohibition on the remote supply of these services in a consistent manner'.[176] The Appellate Body overruled this conclusion of the Panel, upholding only a discrimination finding concerning an exemption of domestic suppliers according to a state act, that allowed internet gambling of horseracing, without allowing foreign websites to participate.[177]

In *US – Gambling* the panel also ruled that the United States failed to demonstrate non-discrimination in the enforcement of its laws prohibiting the remote supply of gambling and betting services. This decision was reversed by the Appellate Body, contending:

> In our view, the proper significance to be attached to isolated instances of enforcement, or lack thereof, cannot be determined in the absence of evidence allowing such instances to be placed in their proper context. Such evidence might include evidence on the overall number of suppliers, and on the

---

173. *Analytical Index – Guide to GATT Law and Practice*, the WTO, Geneva (1995), 564–565 (hereinafter: GATT Analytical Index), *WTO Analytical Index* (2nd edn), Cambridge University Press (2007) (hereinafter: WTO Analytical Index), 260–280.
174. WT/DS58/AB/R, n. 6, Appellate Body report, para. 150.
175. See discussion in GATS commentary, n. 4, 322–325.
176. WT/DS285/R, n. 5, para. 6.607.
177. WT/DS285/AB/R, n. 5, para. 369.

> patterns of enforcement, and on the reasons for particular instances of non-enforcement. Indeed, enforcement agencies may refrain from prosecution in many instances for reasons unrelated to discriminatory intent and without discriminatory effect.
>
> Faced with the limited evidence the parties put before it with respect to enforcement, the Panel should rather have focused, as a matter of law, on the wording of the measures at issue.[178]

In GATT context, the *US – Shrimp* case raises a dilemma which is also relevant in GATS context: to what extent the production and processing method is relevant to the determination of 'likeness', which is the basis for a discrimination claim? However, the Appellate Body was silent in this point.[179]

(2) The discrimination must be arbitrary or unjustifiable in character

A measure shall be deemed inconsistent with the *chapeau* only if it forms 'arbitrary' or 'unjustifiable' discrimination. These seem to be high standards, implying severe discrimination. If these standards are not met, discrimination shall be tolerated by this provision.[180] Nevertheless, these standards are not interpreted by the agreement. Thus, full discretion for their interpretation is given to the WTO adjudicating bodies.

The *chapeau* of article XIV is discussed after a measure has been proved to be violating one of GATS provisions, after the respondent invoked Article XIV as a defence claim and the case seems to be covered under one of the specific exceptions of this Article. At that stage, the standard of 'discrimination' provided for by the *chapeau* must have a different meaning from the standard of discrimination provided for in other GATS articles, such as MFN (Article I) and National Treatment (Article XVI). The Appellate Body arrived at this conclusion while interpreting the *chapeau* of the equivalent GATT article XX, holding that applying the same standard of discrimination to that applied in the National Treatment provision 'would be both to empty the *chapeau* of its contents and to deprive the exceptions in paragraphs (a) to (j) of meaning'.[181]

The term '*arbitrary*' may describe the subjective perspective of the disputing parties in the case at stake, or a more wide and objective perspective, expressing the common views concerning the disputed measure.

Similarly, the term '*unjustifiable*' raises the obvious questions: so determined by whom? According to which standard? These questions imply that the answers will be relative and would depend upon the interests and values involved.

---

178. *Ibid.*, paras 356–357, referring to the Panel report, para. 6.589.
179. W. Zdouc, n. 20, 212–214.
180. WT/DS155/R Argentina – Measures Affecting the Export of Bovine Hides and Import of Finished Leather, adopted on 16.2.2001, Panel report para. 11.315, referring to the equivalent GATT Art. XX.
181. WT/DS2/AB/R *US – Gasoline*, n. 7, Appellate Body report, 23; WT/DS58/AB/R *US – Shrimp*, n. 6, para. 150.

The answers may change subject to the relevant time and place. It seems, therefore, that these standards will be addressed on a case-by-case basis.

In GATT case *EC – Tariff Preferences*, the Panel determined that the European Communities' drug arrangements, claimed to be justified under Article XX(b), were 'arbitrary' and 'unjustifiable' according to the *chapeau*, since no objective criteria were presented to explain the selection process between beneficiary countries and other countries.[182]

In *US – Shrimp* the Appellate Body further provided that in order to avoid arbitrary or unjustifiable discrimination, the importing Member had to make comparable efforts to provide all exporting Members similar opportunities to negotiate an international agreement.[183] It was also found that the certifying process of potential importers was discriminatory, since certain countries were certified as meeting United States' standards while others had limited opportunities to be heard and no right to appeal against denial of certification.[184]

In that case, the Unietd States attempted to argue that discrimination between countries where the same conditions prevail would not be 'unjustifiable' 'where the policy goal of the Article XX exception being applied provides a rationale for the justification'. This argument was rejected by the Appellate Body, contending that the policy goal should be examined under the specific paragraph, and if not found to be justified under it, cannot be justified under the *chapeau*.[185]

In *Brazil – Retreaded Tyres*, the Panel was of the opinion that 'the determination of whether discrimination is unjustifiable depends on the quantitative impact of this discrimination on the achievement of the objective of the measure at issue'.[186] The Appellate Body overruled this analysis for overlooking the rationale of the measure at issue, which should be examined in light of the rationale behind the relevant specific policy objective in one of the subparagraphs of GATT article XX/GATS article XIV.[187]

However, the Appellate Body did not completely rule out the relevance of trade flaws analysis, providing:

> Having said that, we recognize that in certain cases the effects of the discrimination may be a relevant factor, among others, for determining whether the cause or rationale of the discrimination is acceptable or defensible and, ultimately, whether the discrimination is justifiable. The effects of discrimination might be relevant, depending on the circumstances of the case, because, as we indicate above, the *chapeau* of Article XX deals with the manner of application of the measure at issue. Taking into account as a relevant factor, *among others*, the effects of the discrimination for determining whether the rationale of the discrimination is acceptable is, however, fundamentally different from

182. WT/DS246/R *EC – Tariff Preferences*, n. 67, paras 7.228–7.229, 7.232 and 7.234.
183. WT/DS58/AB/R, n. 6, Appellate Body report, para. 166.
184. *Ibid.*, para. 173.
185. WT/DS58/AB/R *US – Shrimp*, n. 6, para. 148.
186. WT/DS332/AB/R *Brazil – Retreaded Tyres*, n. 38, Appellate Body report, para. 229.
187. In that case, the Appellate Body referred to Art. XX(b): *Ibid.*, paras 228, 234.

> the Panel's approach, which focuses *exclusively* on the relationship between the effects of the discrimination and its justifiable or unjustifiable character. [Emphasis added].[188]

While the two other elements are mainly factual, this element is more a matter of discretion, decided on a case-by case basis. It seem to embody a 'balancing test' referring to the different interests involved, but which may entail 'complex factual determinations and social-policy prioritization that may be difficult for judicial bodies'.[189] The same interpretative dilemma, arising in *Brazil – Retreaded Tyres* in GATT context, may arise in the context of the *chapeau* of GATS Article XIV, the structure of which was inspired by GATT article XX. Each of the approaches taken – that of the panel or that of the Appellate Body, may lead to a different result, or rather to a different 'balance of interests', and although the approach of the Appellate Body seems to prevail, none of these approaches is clean of doubts.[190]

(3) This discrimination must occur between countries where the same conditions prevail

In GATT context, it was determined that the comparison may take place not only between different exporting Members, but also between exporting Members and the importing Member concerned.[191]

In *US – Shrimp*,[192] the Appellate Body noted that:

> It is not acceptable, in international trade relations, for one WTO Member to use an economic embargo to require other Members to adopt essentially the same comprehensive regulatory program to achieve a certain policy goal, as that in force within that Member's territory, *without* taking into consideration different conditions which may occur in the territories of those other Members. [Emphasis in the original].

Since it is rather likely that it would be difficult to find identical conditions between compared countries, the key for activating this provision seems to be flexibility of analysis.[193] It should be kept in mind, though, that such flexibility implies vast discretion of the deciding authority, and that naturally, the choice of a broader definition of like conditions would imply a broad scope of this provision, and vice versa. Thus, this provision undermines legal certainty and predictability.

188. WT/DS332/AB/R, n. 38, para. 230.
189. C. P. Bown & J. P. Trachtman, n. 21, 132.
190. See also A. Davies, 'Interpreting the Chapeau of GATT Art. XX in Light of the 'New' Approach in *Brazil–Tyres*', 43 *Journal of World Trade* (2009), 507.
191. WT/DS2/AB/R *US – Gasoline*, n. 7, Appellate Body report, paras 23–24. This conclusion was supported by WT/DS58/AB/R *US – Shrimp*, n. 6, paras 150, 164, 166–175, 177, 179–181.
192. *Ibid.*, para 164.
193. GATS commentary, n. 4, 324.

15.2.3.5.3 A Disguised Restriction on Trade in Services

In *US – Gambling*[194] the Panel noted that ' "disguised restriction" includes disguised discrimination in international trade and a "disguised restriction" may be read as embracing restrictions amounting to arbitrary or unjustifiable discrimination in international trade', thus pointing for a certain degree of overlap between these expressions.

In *US – Shrimp*, in the context of the equivalent GATT Article XX, the Appellate Body determined that having established that the measures at stake consisted 'arbitrary' and 'unjustifiable' discrimination, it is unnecessary to examine whether they also formed 'disguised restriction to international trade'.[195]

The key word, differentiating between this standard and the former two, is 'disguised', which may imply concealment of the real, trade restrictive, objectives of a measure.[196]

This interpretation does not solve the following basic questions: What is a 'disguised restriction' and how will it be measured? Could it be determined in advance or only in terms of result? How would the difference between a measure protecting a legitimate domestic interest and a measure being a disguised restriction to trade be determined, and by whom?

The economic and legal cost of this uncertainty is clear: a Member has no way to verify, in advance, whether an exception exercised by it fulfills these conditions, and therefore it takes a risk applying this provision, because its domestic policy goal may be later interpreted as an infringement of the *chapeau* of Article XIV by the WTO adjudicating bodies, in a time-consuming process, involving a considerable cost.

The equivalent *chapeau* to Article XX of GATT includes a similar expression: 'disguised restrictions on international trade.' The wording difference compared to the wording of GATS (the additional words 'on international trade') does not seem significant and is explained on the ground that in the context of GATT 1947, the drafters saw no need to specify that the agreement would apply only to trade in goods.[197] In GATT 1947 case *US – Automotive*,[198] the Panel contended that 'the preamble of Article XX made it clear that it was *the application of the measure* and not the measure itself that needed to be examined'. [Emphasis added]. In that case the Panel determined that since the measure was duly publicized and was not applied before its publication, it could not be considered as 'disguised'. This interpretation considerably narrows the meaning of the *chapeau*. A wider interpretation could have interpreted the *chapeau* as prohibiting situations where the measure was duly publicized, but yet its application forms a disguised restriction to

194. WT/DS285/R, n. 5, Panel report para. 6.580, based on the Appellate Body analysis in WT/DS2/AB/R *US – Gasoline*, n. 7, para. 25.
195. WT/DS58/AB/R, n. 6, para. 184.
196. WT/DS135/R *EC–Asbestos*, n. 49, para. 8.236, referring to the equivalent GATT Art. XX.
197. W. Zdouc, n. 20, 214.
198. L/5333 US – Imports of Certain Automotive Spring Assemblies, adopted on 26.5.1983, 30S/107, 125, para. 56.

trade. The equivalent GATS provision was not yet interpreted, but if interpreted similarly, it could be subject to the same criticism.

15.2.3.5.3.1 The Restrictive Effect Is Relevant in More than One Context

In *China – Publications and Audiovisual Products* China suggested, with reference to the equivalent GATT Article XX, 'that the restrictive effect of a measure could be relevant to a panel's analysis of whether a measure is consistent with an obligation, *or* its analysis of whether that measure can be justified under an exemption, but that *it could not be relevant to both questions*'.[199] [Emphasis added]. This notion was rejected by the Appellate Body, who stressed that:

> The fact that the restrictive effect of a measure is relevant in one context does not preclude that it may also be relevant in the other . . . the Panel assessed *whether* the provisions restrict the enterprises that may engage in importing . . . *to what extent* the provisions restrict those wishing to engage in importing, as well as *how* the restrictive effect comports with the degree of contribution to the achievement of the objective, and the societal importance and value of legitimate objective concerned. The restrictive effect of the provision was relevant to each of these distinct analytical inquiries. [Emphasis in the original].[200]

15.2.4 The Security Exception: GATS Article XIV*bis*

Article XIV*bis*[201] of GATS allows GATS Members to suspend obligations according to GATS due to state security reasons. It provides:

> Security Exceptions
> 1. Nothing in this Agreement shall be construed:
>
> (a) to require any Member to furnish any information, the disclosure of which it considers contrary to its essential security interests; or
> (b) to prevent any Member from taking any action which it considers necessary for the protection of its essential security interests:
>   (i) relating to the supply of services as carried out directly or indirectly for the purpose of provisioning a military establishment;
>   (ii) relating to fissionable and fusionable materials or the materials from which they are derived;
>   (iii) taken in time of war or other emergency in international relations; or
> (c) to prevent any Member from taking any action in pursuance of its obligations under the United Nations Charter for the maintenance of international peace and security.

199. WT/DS363/AB/R, n. 11, para. 308.
200. *Ibid.*
201. For negotiating history of this provision see: GATS commentary, n. 4, 332–334.

> 2. The Council for Trade in Services shall be informed to the fullest extent possible of measures taken under paragraphs 1(b) and (c) and of their termination.

This provision is based on the equivalent GATT provision, Article XXI. Although the motive behind it seems to be non-economic, or political, the means to achieve it, provided for by this provision, are economic:[202] this provision was invoked by Members to justify economic embargoes on other Members, and may further be used to justify restrictions on transportation and on the right to transit, prohibition or limitation of financial transactions or the 'freezing' of another country's assets.

There are no dispute settlement decisions interpreting this provision in GATS context.[203] In the context of GATT 1947, where a dispute referring to this provision occurred, the terms of reference were narrowly drafted, thus effectively preventing the Panel from examining the discretion of the Member implementing this provision as to the existence of 'time of war or other emergency in international relations'.[204]

The general impression is that in GATT context, this subject was treated cautiously by GATT 1947 and by the WTO adjudicating bodies, due to its sensitive nature and the recognition of the sovereign rights of the Members.[205] It is expected that the same approach would be taken in GATS context.

However, the use of some general interpretative instruments which are common in the WTO jurisdiction is suggested,[206] to improve the potential scope of judicial scrutiny provided for by this Article:

- Based on GATT experience, the use of standard terms of reference included in the DSU instead of particularly narrow terms of reference as those phrased in *US – Nicaragua Trade*[207] would substantially strengthen the power of WTO adjudicating bodies in assessing such a complaint.
- The general public international principle of *good faith* could also be used for this matter.

202. GATS commentary, n. 4, 331.
203. In GATT history, the rare use of the equivalent provision is explained by some reasons: 1. During the Cold War, sanctions on political grounds were mainly applied to non-Members of GATT; 2. GATT Members refrained abusing this provision, not wanting other Members to react similarly towards them. 3. The limitations embodied in Art. XXI of GATT, engineered to balance between the domestic interest of security and the general interest of trade liberalization. Under GATT 1947, Members were not obliged to notify the invocation of this provision. An alleged abuse of the security exception is reported to have occurred only once: GATS commentary, n. 4, 331–332.
204. L/6053 the panel report on US – Nicaragua Trade, dated 13.10.1986 (unadopted), para. 5.17.
205. See GATT Analytical Index (1995), n. 178, 600–606. Some Members believed, already in the context of GATT 1947, and still believe, that these provisions in GATT and in GATS entail political questions that should not be subject to judicial scrutiny: GATS commentary, n. 4, 334.
206. GATS commentary, n. 4, 336.
207. L/6053, n. 204.

- In *EC – Hormones*[208] the Appellate Body stressed that an exception should not be automatically interpreted in a stricter or narrower manner. It is rather subject to the general rules of treaty interpretation pursuant to Article 3.2 DSU.
- Like the interpretation of the general exceptions provision, any measure taken according to this provision should be subject to the proportionality rule.

15.2.4.1 Burden of Proof – Article XIV*bis*

Article XIV*bis* (security exception) follows the same pattern, in terms of the burden of proof, as Article XIV (general exceptions). It would be invoked after the complaining party has established a prima facie case of inconsistency with a substantive GATS obligation. At this stage, the responding party, invoking one of these provisions, has to convince that the measure at stake comes within the alleged Article, fulfilling all the necessary requirements in it, that there is no abuse[209] of the exception involved, and that it is subject to the proportionality rule.

15.2.4.2 Disclosure of Information Contrary to Essential Security Interests

Article XIV*bis*:1(a) provides that nothing in GATS shall be construed to require a Member to disclose information 'the disclosure of which it considers contrary to its essential security interests'. This provision is aimed at balancing between two interests: on the one hand, enhancement of trade liberalization and on the other hand, the protection of domestic security interests. Protection of security interests is common in international agreements, including economic agreements such as regional trade agreements. In this provision, this goal is achieved by the permission given for confidentiality of information. However, this permission is limited only to cases where *essential security interests* are involved.[210] This language has no common interpretation and therefore, it is open to interpretation on a case-by-case basis. It seems that the requirement for involvement of an *essential* security interest narrows the scope of potential confidentiality allowed by this provision, thus indirectly serving the enhancement of trade liberalization.

The wording of this provision allows for maximal flexibility, but at the same time undermines predictability and certainty: while at first the application of this provision seems to be based on a *subjective* decision by a Member, whether the

---

208. WT/DS26,48/R, AB/R European Communities – Measures Concerning Meat and Meat Products (Hormones), adopted on 13.2.1998, Appellate Body, para. 104.

209. In the context of the equivalent Art. XX of GATT the Appellate Body noted that the necessity of the measure is considered to be more difficult to prove than showing that an exception encompasses the measure at issue: WT/DS2/AB/R *US – Gasoline*, n. 7, paras 22–23; WT/DS285/AB/R *US – Gambling*, n. 5, Appellate Body report paras 282, 309.

210. In cases uncovered by this provision, Art. III *bis* of GATS, which includes broader options for avoiding disclosure of information, may apply (see Ch. 13).

terms included in this provision are fulfilled,[211] later this Member may find itself dragged into a dispute settlement procedure, where the final decision on this subject is in the hands of the WTO adjudicating bodies. They also 'have jurisdiction to assess whether the *right of invocation* has been abused, taking into account the overall context. They are to examine whether security interests are *manifestly* absent'. [Emphasis in the original].[212]

This provision does not seem to overrule Article 13 DSU, providing for disclosure of information in dispute settlement procedures. This interpretation makes sense for two reasons:

(1) Otherwise, dispute settlement procedures referring to security matters covered by this provision could be undermined, and in fact this provision would be rendered unnecessary, contrary to the principles of interpretation according to the Vienna Convention.
(2) The dispute settlement process ensures confidentiality of the information revealed in the process.

It should be stressed though, that this information is exposed only to the eyes of the participants of such procedure, subject to its rules, and in certain cases may be revealed only to the judiciary or be submitted only as a summery.[213]

15.2.4.2.1 'Essential Security Interest'

This expression is shared by both GATT and GATS provisions,[214] and in Article XIV*bis* it is shared by paragraphs (a) and (b). But while in paragraph (a) the list of such potential interests is not limited, in paragraph (b) it is limited to three options. This fact is explained on the grounds that GATS drafters did not deem it necessary to limit the scope of the transparency provision (paragraph a), but did so referring the positive action provision (paragraph b).[215] The balance of interests embodied in Article XXI of GATT, is explained by its drafters:

> We cannot make it too tight, because we cannot prohibit measures which are needed purely for security reasons. On the other hand, we cannot make it so broad that, under the guise of security, countries will put on measures which really have a commercial purpose.[216]

The same balance of interests should be taken into account in the context of GATS, and it should be used as a starting point for its interpretation. Some commentators suggest that this provision would cover measures serving an essential security

211. GATS commentary, n. 4, 335.
212. *Ibid.*, 338.
213. DSU Arts 13.1 and 14.
214. It is also included in the voluntary Government Procurement Agreement (GPA) in Art. XXIII.
215. GATS commentary, n. 4, 340.
216. ECPT/A/PV/33, 20–21 and Corr. 3.

interest of a Member only in part, to the extent that these measures contribute to securing essential security interests.[217]

15.2.4.3 Action Necessary for the Protection of Essential Security Interests

Article XIV*bis*:1(b) allows each Member to take any action which *it considers* necessary for the protection of *its essential* security interests, if this action could be classified into one of the three categories mentioned in this provision:

- It is relating to the supply of services as carried out directly or indirectly for the purpose of provisioning a military establishment.
- It is relating to fissionable materials or the materials from which they are derived.
- It is taken in time of war or other emergency in international relations.

The authority given in this paragraph is of a stronger nature than the former one: while the permission for confidentiality of information is of a passive nature, this paragraph allows a Member to take action. The words 'which it considers necessary' give the Member involved full discretion over the *circumstances* in which measures will be taken, as well as concerning the *measures* chosen. In the context of trade, such action probably means the application of trade restrictions in the circumstances specified. However, despite this broad language it should be noted, that any such decision or action of a Member will be subject to the general *good faith* obligation of public international law, which may be interpreted to include some proportionality test.

15.2.4.3.1 Who Defines 'Necessity'

Unlike other GATS provisions, Article XIV*bis explicitly* accords full discretion to a Member applying the trade restrictive measure to decide, whether an essential security interest is threatened. This conclusion is drawn from the words 'it considers' in paragraphs XIV:1(a) and (b). Allegedly, this discretion could not be subjected to an objective necessity test assessment by the WTO adjudicating bodies, who may only examine 'whether the right of invocation has been abused, taking into account the overall context'. For this purpose, the words 'necessary' and 'essential' may form an indirect conduit for inserting some objective assessment by the WTO adjudicating bodies, despite the allegedly full discretion given to the Members.[218]

15.2.4.3.2 Three Categories of Action

The concept of 'necessity' in Article XIV*bis*:1(b) refers to three categories of positive action, where a Member is allowed to take action *in order to protect its*

217. GATS commentary, n. 4, 339.
218. *Ibid.*, 343.

essential security interests. This condition should be read together with each option, thus narrowing their potential scope:

15.2.4.3.2.1 Provisioning a Military Establishment

The first group refers to the supply of services as carried out directly or indirectly for the purpose of provisioning a military establishment. It is unclear from the language of this provision what a 'military establishment' means (one tent? a camp?); whether it should be permanent or temporary; is it an establishment of a domestic or foreign military?

The reference to services carried out indirectly for that purpose considerably broadens the scope of this provision, and opens it to interpretation, implying a broad authority to restrict trade in such cases. Therefore, it should be approached cautiously.

15.2.4.3.2.2 Fissionable and Fusionable Materials

The second group of circumstances concentrates on the dangerous character of fissionable or fusionable materials or materials from which they are derived. Since such materials are goods and thus subject to the equivalent GATT provision, GATS provision may apply to the services involved in the supply of such goods: shipment and transport, distribution, packing etc.

15.2.4.3.2.3 War or Other Emergency in International Relations

The third group concentrates on the circumstances: war or other emergency in international relations. The situation of war may be easier to define, although in recent years acts of terrorist groups replace, to a large extent, the common notion of war between countries. The expression 'emergency in international relations' may cover the other possibilities. It may, for example, apply to situations like the terrorist attack on the United States in 11 September 2001. The vagueness of this expression allows some flexibility, but on the other hand raises interpretative doubts: should this expression be interpreted to cover only a global crisis, or also minor scale, local disputes between countries?

Another interpretative question may be, whether the general expression 'emergency in international relations' refers only to defence or may also refer to economic crises. GATT experience shows, that most of the cases where this provision was used concentrated on this justification, which seems to be the most generally phrased justification. According to some commentators, there may be a greater incentive to use this provision in GATS due to the lack of another, economic emergency safeguard mechanism (allowing for measures to be taken against trade restrictive practices such as dumping and subsidies).[219] However, it seems that if the *context* of this provision is considered, a narrow interpretation, referring only to defence crises, should be adopted, unless due to the scope and depth of a global economic crisis it is assessed, in a high degree of probability, that a defence crisis may evolve out of it.

219. *Ibid.*, 338.

Yet another interpretative question arises concerning the application of this provision to measures that serve an essential security purpose only in part. In this case, it seems that the WTO adjudicating bodies will have to decide, subject to the application of a balancing test, weighing the relative weight of this consideration in the general scope of relevant considerations.[220]

15.2.4.3.3 The Relationship between the Chapeau *and Subparagraphs*

Article XIV*bis*:1(b) is combined of a *chapeau*, referring to the right of Members to take action to protect their essential security interests, followed by the three sets of circumstances specified above. An interpretative question that may arise is whether the *chapeau* may be read independently, thus detaching this right of Members from the three sets of circumstances specified and broadening considerably its authorization to restrict trade in services for this purpose. It seems that the language of this provision does not support such an interpretation; neither is it supported by the general aim and spirit of the agreement, encouraging trade liberalization. For the same reason, it seems that an interpretation suggesting that the three sets of circumstances specified do not form an exhaustive list should be rejected.

15.2.4.4 Maintenance of obligations according to the UN Charter

Article XIV*bis*:1(c) provides, that nothing in GATS shall be construed as preventing any Member from taking any action in pursuance of its obligations under the UN Charter for the maintenance of international peace and security. This provision implies that the legal obligations and specific commitments taken in GATS may be suspended to apply trade-embargoes and other economic sanctions imposed by the UN Security Council under Chapter VII of the UN Charter. Although the WTO adjudicating bodies are not authorized to review these decisions, they may review measures taken by the Members in the following aspects:[221]

- ensure that there is a *relevant* UN decision.
- ensure that the measure at stake corresponds to this decision.
- ensure that the measure did not exceed the severity of measure provided for by the UN decision.

This examination may rely on the *good faith* principle of conducting international trade agreements, as well as on the *proportionality* principle.

15.2.4.5 Notification Obligations

Article XIV*bis*:2 subjects actions according to paragraph 1(b) and (c) to notification obligation to the Council for Trade in Services, including 'their termination'. This language implies the temporary character that such actions should have.

220. *Ibid.*, 339.
221. *Ibid.*, 345–346.

This provision implies transparency towards the Council of the actions taken, and implies some control by the Council on the actions taken.

15.2.4.5.1 Standard of Notification: 'To the Fullest Extent Possible'

It is provided that 'the Council for Trade in Services shall be informed *to the fullest extent possible*'. This standard is not interpreted to be absolute, allowing the Members some discretion.[222] It seems to refer to the substance of notification and not to the time factor. The fulfilment of this standard could be achieved by a combination of following the Guidelines for Notification Under GATS adopted by the Council for Trade in Services on 1 March 1995[223]and full reference to the different relevant elements addressed by this provision.

15.2.4.6 Potential Threat and Extra Territorial Threat

There is no clear reference to the application of this provision to potential threat and/or extra-territorial threat in its language. However, these possibilities may occur in practice. The adoption or rejection of an interpretation recognizing the right of a Member to apply trade restrictive measures under such circumstances is a matter of interpretative policy, drawing directly from the scope the WTO adjudicating bodies wish to give this provision, considering the political status of the agreement and the sensitivities of the Members. One may guess that claims concerning a totally theoretical threat would not be accepted, but gray area cases might require careful consideration.[224]

15.2.5 Balance-of-Payments Difficulties

Article XII of GATS allows a Member to impose trade restrictions on trade in services regarding which specific commitments were undertaken by it, where that Member suffers from serious balance-of-payments difficulties, external financial difficulties or threat thereof, subject to conditions specified in it. It provides:

> Restrictions to Safeguard the Balance of Payments
>
> 1. In the event of serious balance-of-payments and external financial difficulties or threat thereof, a Member may adopt or maintain restrictions on trade in services on which it has undertaken specific commitments, including on payments or transfers for transactions related to such commitments. It is recognized that particular pressures on the balance of payments of a Member in the process of economic development or economic transition may necessitate the use of restrictions to ensure, *inter alia*, the maintenance of a

222. *Ibid.*, 346. It is noted that the Members should equally notify the termination of such measures.
223. S/L/5 Guidelines for Notifications under the General Agreement on Trade in Services – Adopted by the Council for Trade in Services on 1 Mar. 1995, 4.4.1995.
224. GATS commentary, n. 4, 341.

level of financial reserves adequate for the implementation of its programme of economic development or economic transition.

2. The restrictions referred to in paragraph 1:

   (a) shall not discriminate among Members;
   (b) shall be consistent with the Articles of Agreement of the International Monetary Fund;
   (c) shall avoid unnecessary damage to the commercial, economic and financial interests of any other Member;
   (d) shall not exceed those necessary to deal with the circumstances described in paragraph 1;
   (e) shall be temporary and be phased out progressively as the situation specified in paragraph 1 improves.

3. In determining the incidence of such restrictions, Members may give priority to the supply of services which are more essential to their economic or development programmes. However, such restrictions shall not be adopted or maintained for the purpose of protecting a particular service sector.

4. Any restrictions adopted or maintained under paragraph 1, or any changes therein, shall be promptly notified to the General Council.

5. (a) Members applying the provisions of this Article shall consult promptly with the Committee on Balance-of-Payments Restrictions on restrictions adopted under this Article.

   (b) The Ministerial Conference shall establish procedures for periodic consultations with the objective of enabling such recommendations to be made to the Member concerned as it may deem appropriate.
   (c) Such consultations shall assess the balance-of-payment situation of the Member concerned and the restrictions adopted or maintained under this Article, taking into account, *inter alia*, such factors as:
      (i) the nature and extent of the balance-of-payments and the external financial difficulties;
      (ii) the external economic and trading environment of the consulting Member;
      (iii) alternative corrective measures which may be available.
   (d) The consultations shall address the compliance of any restrictions with paragraph 2, in particular the progressive phaseout of restrictions in accordance with paragraph 2(e).
   (e) In such consultations, all findings of statistical and other facts presented by the International Monetary Fund relating to foreign exchange, monetary reserves and balance of payments, shall be accepted and conclusions shall be based on the assessment by the Fund of the balance-of-payments and the external financial situation of the consulting Member.

6. If a Member which is not a member of the International Monetary Fund wishes to apply the provisions of this Article, the Ministerial Conference shall establish a review procedure and any other procedures necessary.

There is no agreement among the Members whether this provision covers capital outflows and inflows. Since this subject is not specifically addressed by this provision, and due to this controversy, it is suggested by one commentator that Article XII would also cover difficulties caused by capital inflows.[225]

This provision is equivalent to the balance-of-payments exception in GATT Article XII, clarified by the Understanding on Balance-of-Payments Provisions of GATT 1994. The recognition of additional flexibility necessary for developing countries in their early stages was recognized in GATT Article XVIII:B. These provisions, and the experience gained in the implementation of the relevant GATT 1947 provisions[226] influenced the design and contents of GATS Article XII.

15.2.5.1 Article XII:1

15.2.5.1.1 'Serious Balance-of-Payments and External Financial Difficulties or Threat Thereof'

This 'safety valve' may be effectuated where 'serious balance-of-payments and external financial difficulties or threat thereof' occur.[227] This condition includes some vague expressions that were not interpreted by the agreement: 'serious balance-of-payment difficulties', 'serious financial difficulties', 'threat thereof'.

It is explained by one commentator: '[b]alance-of-payment difficulties arise if a country is unable to obtain sufficient financing on affordable terms to meet its international payment obligation'. This may result in shortage of foreign exchange.[228]

The word 'serious' implies a narrow interpretation. However, no criteria for judgment of the situation are specified in this provision. Should this determination be based on an objective or some subjective assessment? Who would be in charge of this assessment: the Member applying this provision? An international organization such as the World Bank?

Since no such authority is specified in this provision, it seems that like in the other GATS exceptions discussed above, the determination concerning the existence of such a situation would be made, first, by the relevant Member, but might then be subject to potential *ex post* scrutiny by the WTO adjudicating bodies.

Another interpretative question is, whether the 'seriousness' requirement refers only to the balance-of-payment situation, or also to the external financial difficulties.

225. *Ibid.*, 262.
226. For GATT Art. XII, see GATT Analytical index, n. 173, 356–395. For Art. XVIII:B, see: GATT Analytical Index, n. 173, 501–508, WTO Analytical Index, n. 173, 240–248.
227. The equivalent GATT provision, Art. XVIII:B is more specific, defining two purposes for which this exception may be exercised: '(a) to forestall the threat of, or to stop, a serious decline in its monetary reserves, or (b) in the case of a Contracting Party with inadequate monetary reserves, to achieve a reasonable rate of increase in reserves'.
228. GATS commentary, n. 4, 262.

It is further unclear, whether the serious balance-of-payment and external financial difficulties are cumulative or independent requirements.

Yet another interpretative question refers to the word 'threat': what is a 'threat' according to this provision and how would it be measured? Subjectively by the country involved, or according to some objective criteria? What is the degree of threat allowing for the application of this provision: any threat or only a serious, probable threat?

While the determination concerning the existence of balance-of-payment or external financial difficulties should be based on monetary acceptable criteria, a 'threat thereof' is even more vague, calling for an assessment which is more open for discretion of the Member involved, first, but might be more exposed to controversy later. This situation undermines certainty and predictability.

All these interpretative questions have no answer in the language of this provision. However, being an exception to GATS rules, this provision should be interpreted according to the general principles for the interpretation of exceptions, developed by GATT/WTO adjudicating bodies:

- The general public international principle of *good faith* could also be used for this matter.
- In *EC–Hormones*[229] the Appellate Body stressed that an exception should not be automatically interpreted in a stricter or narrower manner. It is rather subject to the general rules of treaty interpretation pursuant to Article 3.2 DSU.
- Like the interpretation of the general exceptions provision, any measure taken according to this provision should be subject to the proportionality rule.

15.2.5.1.2 The Measures Allowed

Where the conditions specified in this provision are fulfilled, the Member involved may 'adopt or maintain restrictions on trade in services on which it has undertaken specific commitments, including on payments or transfers for transactions related to such commitments'.

The reference to 'services on which it has undertaken specific commitments' is necessary, since these services are subject to the disciplines set forth by GATS. Services which are not subject to specific commitments are not subject to market access and national treatment disciplines, and thus may bear restrictions contrary to these disciplines, without breaching the agreement. GATS also includes unconditional disciplines, such as the MFN discipline, but it seems that these disciplines would be less affected by the measures that should be taken to recover the balance-of-payments, which may take the form of limitations on the number of service suppliers, the total value of service transactions, etc.

229. WT/DS26,48/AB/R *EC–Hormones*, n. 208, para. 104.

This provision raises the following interpretative questions: what is the meaning of 'payments or transfers for transactions related to such commitments'? What sort of link is necessary? Would only a direct connection be considered, or an indirect connection as well, for example, payment for inputs used in the production process of a service, payments for auxiliary services such as advertisement services? Any choice of interpretation would affect the scope of this provision. A narrow interpretation, opting only for direct connection, would imply a narrow scope of this exception.

15.2.5.1.3 Member in the Process of Economic Development or Economic Transition

As further elaborated in Chapter 14, these two categories of countries are not defined in GATS. It is thus a decision of a Member to claim for this status and its implications, taking the risk that this claim may be challenged by other Members.

Paragraph XII:1 recognizes the unique sensitivity of developing countries or transition economies.

This provision may be regarded either as a declarative provision, or as an operative provision, implying some relief in the application of the balance-of-payment exception, where developing countries or transition economies are involved. There is no guidance in the language of the provision which interpretation prevails. However, the word '*maintenance*' may hint that while other Members may use this provision only where 'serious difficulties . . . or threat thereof' occur, developing countries and transition economies may apply it even where no such situation exists, to maintain the level of financial reserves adequate for the implementation of their programme for economic development or transition.

In addition, the words '*particular pressure*' imply that, for the application of this provision, it is not necessary for a substantial crisis to occur; 'particular pressure'

> may result from the increased level of imports, a high level of foreign debt, particularly short-term debt, or heightened exposure to volatile short-term investments, which may be called off at the first sign of an impending economic crisis . . .[230]

This provision does not specify what programme is at stake, who should be responsible for it, to whom should it be presented, by whom should it be authorized in order for this relief to apply.

It is further unclear who determines what is the 'adequate level' of financial reserves, should it be determined according to some objective parameter or subjectively by the Member involved?

Currently, there are no universally applicable standards for assessing the adequacy of reserves, and the assessment whether a particular pressure on the

230. GATS commentary, n. 4, 263.

balance-of-payments necessitates the use of restrictions according to this provision relies substantially on the information and assessment provided by the IMF.[231]

The answers to the interpretative questions are not specified in the language of this provision, and will therefore have to be established by its future interpretation.

The equivalent GATT provision, Article XVIII:SECTION B, allows developing countries with balance of payment difficulties, emanating from 'a rapid process of development', 'arising mainly from their efforts to expand their internal market as well as from the instability of their terms of trade', to maintain, under certain conditions, temporary import restrictions for balance-of-payment purposes.[232]

15.2.5.2 Article XII: 2

Article XII:2 subjects the provisions of paragraph 1 to a list of conditions. These conditions further narrow the scope of this exception, by balancing between the interest of monetary stability protected by it and other important interests. However, this list of conditions raises some interpretative difficulties:

Article XII:2(a): '*shall not discriminate among Members*' – discrimination is not defined in this provision. The use of the general term 'discrimination' leaves room for a flexible, case-by-case interpretation. It is neither specified whether the provision refers to non-discrimination de facto or de jure. However, the interpretation of non-discrimination in other GATS and WTO agreements' provisions is broad, including both de facto and de jure discrimination, and concentrating specifically on the discriminating effect of the measures examined (See, *inter alia*, MFN – 6.6.1.3, national treatment – 8.5.2).

Article XII:2(b): '*shall be consistent with the Agreement of the International Monetary Fund*'[233] – relevant provisions in that agreement may be Article VII, setting forth the terms for the authorization of the fund to impose limitations on the freedom of exchange operations in a scarce currency; Article VIII:2(a), prohibiting Members from imposing, without the approval of the fund, restrictions on the making of payments and international transfers for current international transactions; and Article XIV:3, providing for consultations with the fund on the retention of restrictions on payments and transfers on current international transactions already in force when the relevant country became a IMF Member.[234]

Article XII:2(c): '*shall avoid unnecessary damage to the economic, commercial and financial interests of any other Member*' – the words 'unnecessary damage' and 'economic, commercial and financial interests' are not defined, thus allowing flexibility and adaptability to different situations. It seems that they should be interpreted on a case-by-case basis.

231. *Ibid.*, 264.
232. See interpretation of this provision in GATT Analytical Index, n. 173, 501–508.
233. This agreement was concluded in 1944 and entered into force in 1945. Like GATT, it is one of the Bretton Woods agreements concluded after the end of World War II. For full text of the agreement see: <www.imf.org>.
234. GATS commentary, n. 4, 266.

Article XX:2(d): '*shall not exceed those necessary to deal with the circumstances described in paragraph 1*' – this is another condition subject to interpretation on a case-by-case basis. The difficulties mentioned in the definition of circumstances invoking the necessity to take measures make it even more difficult to define proportionality.

Article XII:2(e): '*shall be temporary and be phased out progressively, as the situation specified in paragraph 1 improves*' – the provision does not specify any time limits, thus allowing full flexibility subject to the specific circumstances involved. No standards or criteria for the definition of any time-frame, or for the examination whether the time-frame implemented in a specific case is due, are specified.

15.2.5.3 Article XII:3

Article XII:3 allows Members, in determining the incidence of restrictions according to this Article, to give priority to the supply of services which are more essential to their economic or development programmes. However, it is stressed that in any case, such restrictions shall not be adopted or maintained for the purpose of protecting a particular service sector. It is clear that this provision is aimed at supporting development programmes of developing countries and transition economies. Nevertheless, it is unclear from this provision what would be defined as an 'economic or development programmes what scope should it have, who will have the authority to define such a programme: is it entirely under the discretion of the Member involved? Should some international authority intervene? Should this definition, which in fact opens the way to apply the relief provided for by this provision, be subject to any common international criteria?

These interpretative questions, which are not answered by the language of this provision, may affect its scope of application.

15.2.5.4 Article XII:4

Article XII:4 provides for a notification obligation to the Council for Trade in Services, concerning the measures taken under this provision. The notification obligation serves transparency, and may form some deterrence from taking extreme measures. However, this provision does not specify what kind of reporting would be considered 'prompt', and whether the reporting should take place before the measures are taken or retroactively. Retroactive reporting may be considered less effective in term of the Council's control. On the other hand, the Council is not given any specific authorities in this context, and an emergency situation may require quick action. Maybe the best solution could be a rule requiring prior reporting with the exception allowing retroactive reporting in emergency cases. However, this solution is not reflected by the language of this provision. Another question unanswered by this provision concerns the manner of reporting: should it be submitted in a certain manner? In a certain format? According to what level of specification? Needless to say, the level of specification would affect the quality of control applied by the Council. Nevertheless, this information is not included in this provision.[235]

In practice, notification under this provision is subject to the Guidelines for Notification under GATS.[236] However, the general problem of poor notification under GATS seems to be reflected in the exercise of this obligation as well.

15.2.5.5 Article XII:5

Article XII:5(a) provides that Members applying this Article would 'consult promptly with the Committee on Balance-of-Payments Restrictions'. The standard of consultation: 'promptly' is ambiguous, and therefore subject to a case-by-case interpretation.

Article XII:5(b) further authorizes the Ministerial Conference to establish procedures for periodic consultations, that could result in recommendations to a Member involved. The connection between these to paragraphs in unclear: do the consultations depend on reporting and exercised as a result thereof? If not – what is the mechanism to start consultations? Can a Member report measures taken by another Member according to this Article and ask for consultations?[237] If this is possible – what is the procedure that should be followed? If not – can the Member applying the measures control the starting time of consultations by choosing the reporting date (regarding the lack of instructions concerning this matter in the provision), thus postponing consultations for as much as it wishes?

Article XII:5(c)–(e) specify the substance of consultations, including the considerations and information (the financial situation of the relevant Member, its general trading position) that should be weighed in such consultation. The Ministerial Conference is authorized to establish the procedure for the conduct of consultations. The consultations should be held periodically. It is understood by the Members that consultations that the procedure addressed by Article XII:5(b) shall be the same as GATT 1994 procedure referring to the equivalent provision.[238]

Article XII:5(d) provides that the consultations shall address the compliance of any restrictions with paragraph 2, thus determining some standard according to which measures by Members should be judged.

Article XII:5(e) distinguishes between *factual findings* of statistics and other facts presented by the IMF, relating to foreign exchange, monetary reserves and balance of payments, which 'shall' be accepted by the parties, having no discretion in this context, and *the assessment* of the fund of the balance-of-payments and external financial situation of the consulting Member, which is not binding, but would form a basis for the Committee's conclusions.

---

235. In GATT, the equivalent provision was interpreted to include a detailed report in writing, submitted to the Secretariat. The reports were then distributed to the Members.
236. S/L/5, n. 223.
237. Such a procedure was recognized, in the context of GATT 1947: L/4904, adopted on 28.11.1979, 26S/205, 207, para.3.
238. GATS commentary, n. 4, 268–269.

Consultations are concluded with a report by the Committee on Balance-of-Payments Restrictions to the General Council, which might include proposals for recommendations, to be addressed by the General Council to the relevant Member. Nevertheless, the committee is not given any stronger authorities to enforce the implementation of its conclusions or to apply any sanctions to Members deviating from its instructions.

Thus, a Member may have to turn to dispute settlement procedures to defend its rights which might be impaired by a measure which is practically unjustified under Article XII. In *India – Quantitative Restrictions*[239] the equivalent GATT provision was invoked by India to justify trade restrictions. India argued that dispute settlement Panels should not have an authority to make findings on whether balance-of-payments measures are justified under GATT Article XVIII:B, due to the risk of conflicting decision with the BOP committee. This claim was rejected by the Panel, in a decision upheld by the Appellate Body, on substantial grounds, but the Panel also noted that if it would have been accepted, other WTO Members would have been deprived of their right to effective protection of their substantial rights by the dispute settlement system.

15.2.5.6 Article XII:6

This provision authorizes the Council for Trade in Services to determine procedures for examination of the application of this provision by a Member which is not a Member of the IMF. It implies that for such countries, the procedure would be different. This provision is criticized for being hardly practical due to the major contribution of the IMF to such consultations, which would be missing where a non-IMF Member is involved.[240]

15.2.6 Emergency Safeguard Measures and Subsidies

GATT includes two additional temporary safety valves, allowing the implementation of emergency safeguard measures in cases of unfair trade practices such as dumping and export subsidization.[241] In GATS there are no such options, because at the end of the Uruguay Round the Members could not reach agreement whether they are necessary and applicable to trade in services, and if they are – how should they be adapted to the unique characteristics of trade in services. Therefore, Articles X and XV provide for future negotiations on these subjects. These negotiations were not yet concluded.

239. WT/DS90/R India – Quantitative Restrictions on Imports of Agricultural, Textile and Industrial Products, adopted 22.9.1999, Panel report paras 5.92–5.97, 5.114.
240. GATS commentary, n. 4, 271.
241. GATT Art. VI.

15.2.7 General Interpretative Approach for GATS Exceptions

In GATT 1994 *EC – Hormones* case, it was provided that exceptions should be interpreted under the same rules as other provisions of an international trade agreement (basically the customary treaty interpretation rules provided for by Article 3.2 DSU), by which the definition as 'exception' should not automatically lead to narrower or stricter interpretation.[242] Such broad interpretation of the exceptions supports the ability of the Members to use the exceptions to achieve other domestic policy objectives, sometimes at the expense of less trade liberalization.

However, at the same time such an approach narrows the scope of discretion accorded to the WTO adjudicating bodies to promote, by interpretation, the declared purpose of the agreement: enhanced trade liberalization.

The correct balance between these two conflicting interests is the subject of a long debate in the WTO context. It is politically understood, that these exceptions serve as safety valves for the Members, allowing them to exercise sovereignty of domestic regulation to protect interests recognized as important by all Members, and without these exceptions the agreement could not have been concluded. However, effectively the WTO adjudicating bodies sometimes tend to interpret them narrowly, thus preferring the liberalization of trade over the domestic protected interest.[243] Striking the right balance between these interests may also depend on the level of economic integration provided for by the agreement.[244]

15.3 PERMANENT 'SAFETY VALVES': MODIFICATION OF SCHEDULES

The schedules of specific commitments, determining the scope of application of GATS by each Member, are dominated by two rules: the *standstill* and the *rollback*. According to the former, normally a specific commitment may not be withdrawn. According to the latter, in future rounds of negotiations each Member is expected to improve its specific commitments, to deepen trade liberalization.

However, there are cases where a Member may have no choice, but to withdraw its specific commitments. The withdrawal may be temporary, thus treated according to the temporary exceptions discussed above. Sometimes, this withdrawal is permanent. One common reason for it may be an accession of a Member into an alliance based on harmonization of external trade law and policy by its

242. WT/DS26,48/AB/R *EC–Hormones*, n. 208, para. 104.

243. See, for example, WT/DS161,169/AB/R *Korea – Beef*, n. 6, WT/DS332/AB/R *Brazil – Retreaded Tyres*, n. 38 and the discussion in 15.2.3.4.1 (a).

244. In GATS commentary, n. 4, 337 it is claimed that similar exceptions included in the EC Treaty are interpreted narrowly by the European Court of Justice. However, this narrow interpretation of the ECJ may be justified due to the high level of economic integration provided for by the Treaty on the Functioning of the EU (TFEU), while in the context of GATS a more cautious approach is justified due to the relatively law degree of economic integration provided for by it.

participants. This process took place, for example, in the EU enlargement processes. The countries acceding to the EU had to give up their independent external trade policy in order to adopt the EU policy instead. For this purpose, these countries had, *inter alia*, to modify their GATS schedules of specific commitments.

GATS thus includes a safety valve allowing for such modification, to adjust to new circumstances or policy considerations.[245] It is constructed to balance between the interest of the country who has to modify its commitments for the reasons explained above, and the interests of the other countries affected by this modification.

Article XXI of GATS provides:[246]

Modification of Schedules

1. (a) A Member (referred to in this Article as the 'modifying Member') may modify or withdraw any commitment in its Schedule, at any time after three years have elapsed from the date on which that commitment entered into force, in accordance with the provisions of this Article.
   (b) A modifying Member shall notify its intent to modify or withdraw a commitment pursuant to this Article to the Council for Trade in Services no later than three months before the intended date of implementation of the modification or withdrawal.
2. (a) At the request of any Member the benefits of which under this Agreement may be affected (referred to in this Article as an 'affected Member') by a proposed modification or withdrawal notified under subparagraph 1(b), the modifying Member shall enter into negotiations with a view to reaching agreement on any necessary compensatory adjustment. In such negotiations and agreement, the Members concerned shall endeavour to maintain a general level of mutually advantageous commitments not less favourable to trade than that provided for in Schedules of specific commitments prior to such negotiations.
   (b) Compensatory adjustments shall be made on a most-favoured-nation basis.
3. (a) If agreement is not reached between the modifying Member and any affected Member before the end of the period provided for negotiations, such affected Member may refer the matter to arbitration. Any affected Member that wishes to enforce a right that it may have to compensation must participate in the arbitration.
   (b) If no affected Member has requested arbitration, the modifying Member shall be free to implement the proposed modification or withdrawal.

245. For a review of the practical implementation of this provision see: GATS commentary, n. 4, 476–478.
246. See the history of this provision in GATS commentary, n. 4, 467.

4. (a) The modifying Member may not modify or withdraw its commitment until it has made compensatory adjustments in conformity with the findings of the arbitration.
   (b) If the modifying Member implements its proposed modification or withdrawal and does not comply with the findings of the arbitration, any affected Member that participated in the arbitration may modify or withdraw substantially equivalent benefits in conformity with those findings. Notwithstanding Article II, such a modification or withdrawal may be implemented solely with respect to the modifying Member.
5. The Council for Trade in Services shall establish procedures for rectification or modification of Schedules. Any Member which has modified or withdrawn scheduled commitments under this Article shall modify its Schedule according to such procedures.

15.3.1 The Terms of Modification

The scope of Article XXI:1 is limited to situations in which new schedules provide less favourable treatment than the old schedules. It does not apply to new commitments, improvements of existing commitments and technical changes that do not change the substance of commitments.[247]

Article XXI allows for the *modification or withdarwal* of commitments. It covers partial or complete modification. It refers to *any* specific commitment.

Modification according to this provision may take place at any time after three years have elapsed from the date on which the modified commitment entered into force. This provision is meant to ensure a minimal time of application for agreed schedules.

15.3.2 The Rules for Modification of Schedules

15.3.2.1 Prior Notification

According to Article XXI:1(b) the modification of commitments should be notified to the Council for Trade in Services at least three months in advance. Such notification implies sufficient time for the Secretariat to circulate the information, and for other Members, who may be affected by this step, to react in due time in order to protect their rights according to the agreement. The intention of a Member to modify or withdraw scheduled commitments will then be included in the agenda of the next meeting of the Council for Trade in Services. The form of notification is determined in the Guidelines for Notifications under the General Agreement on Trade in Services.[248]

247. GATS commentary, n. 4, 468.
248. S/L/5, n. 223.

The modification process is held according to the procedure adopted by the Council for Trade in Services.[249]

15.3.2.2 Negotiations

Article XXI:2(a) defines as an 'affected Member' 'any Member the benefits of which under this agreement may be affected by the proposed modification or withdrawal'. This definition is broader than that of the equivalent GATT provision, Article XXVIII, referring to contracting parties with an initial negotiating interest or to those with a 'principal supplying interest', thus excluding many small countries from participation in this process. Under GATS, *any* affected Member may participate in compensation negotiations. This difference allegedly acts to the benefit of potential affected Members. But in fact this provision is less invoked than its GATT equivalent. According to one commentator,[250] its general language makes it difficult to predict 'the number of Members allowed seeking compensation under Article XXI, and hence the final 'cost' of withdrawal of commitments'. This may deter Members from using this procedure.

It should be stressed that in any case this provision covers only the relationship between Members, and does not fold any compensation for private parties – firms or individual service suppliers who might be affected by such withdrawal.

An affected Member is entitled to negotiate with the modifying Member 'with view of reaching agreement on any necessary compensatory adjustment'.

This provision does not specify within what time-frame should the affected Members ask for such negotiations, nor does it specify how long should such negotiations last. These details are specified in the procedure adopted by the Council for Trade in Services.[251] Article XXI:3(a) refers to 'the period provided for negotiations'. However, there is no specification in any of the other paragraphs of this Article what is this time frame. Article XXI:5 authorizes the Council for Trade in Services to determine the procedure for such negotiations. Therefore, it might have been assumed by GATS drafters that this detail shall be determined in this framework.

This provision does not refer to the *level* or *rate* of effect for which a Member may be entitled for compensation (even not in terms of defining *de minimis* effect). Moreover, it does not refer to the manner of measuring the effect, neither to the necessary ratio between the adverse effect and compensation. In addition, GATS, unlike the equivalent GATT provision, does not include any 'balancing' provision.[252]

249. S/L/80 Procedures for the Implementation of Art. XXI, the General Agreement on Trade in Services (modification of Schedules), adopted by the Council for Trade in Services 19.7.1999, <http://docsonline.wto.org>.

250. M. Cossy, 'Water Services at the WTO', in E. Brown Weiss, L. Boisson de Chazournes & N. Bernasconi-Osterwalder (eds), Fresh Water and International Economic Law, Oxford University Press (2005), 117, 139.

251. S/L/80, n. 249, para. 19.

252. Article XXIV of GATT provides that due account be taken of reductions of duties on the same tariff line made by other members of a customs union.

It is not explicitly provided, that the burden of proof concerning the adverse effect should be borne by the complaining Member, but this conclusion seems logical and corresponding to the purpose of this provision.

15.3.2.3 The Standard of Compensation

A pre-condition for compensation is a demonstration by a Member, contending to be 'affected' by the modification, of the extent to which it is affected. Without a clear establishment of such effect, compensation would not be justified.[253]

GATS is silent about the kind of compensation that may stem from this process. However, Article XXI:2(a) further provides for some guidance concerning the purpose of such compensation:

> the Member concerned shall endeavor to maintain a general level of mutually advantageous commitment not less favourable to trade than that provided for in the Schedules of Specific Commitments prior to such negotiations.

The general intention is clear: this provision aims at defending the reliance interest of the affected Member. However, it is full with vague expressions difficult to interpret: how does one measure the 'general level of mutually advantageous commitment' to ensure that it is not 'less favourable' than before?

In this provision, a similar approach to that applied in other provisions of GATS was applied: the use of ambiguous expressions, allowing maximal flexibility of interpretation, on a case-by-case basis. The flexibility and full discretion of negotiators were preferred over the interest of certainty and predictability. The measurement of each benefit's effect, to compare them one against another, to see whether the general level of benefits is preserved may be difficult for two reasons: first, sometimes there are no satisfactory statistical data to support this comparison. Second, the same modification of benefits may affect different countries in different manners. It is unclear whether the withdrawal or partial withdrawal from one benefit could be offset against another benefit.

The experience gained by the discussions on the effect of regional trade agreement in the Committee on Regional Trade Agreements shows that, for example, during the discussions on the accession agreements of east European countries to the EU, claims concerning the adverse effect of these agreements on third parties where rejected by the EU and candidate countries, claiming that their accession into the EU would allow their trade partners to benefit from the free circulation and the other benefits embodied in the EU as a trade partner, and thus in fact their situation was positively, not negatively, affected by this move. (See discussion in Chapter 10.) Such claims are very difficult to prove, considering the huge amount of details involved, the limitations of available data and the lack of agreed method of weighing the existing data.

253. GATS commentary, n. 4, 470.

15.3.2.4 The Compensation: Scope of Application

Article XXI:2(b) provides that the compensation agreed by the Members involved in negotiations will apply to all Members, on an MFN basis.

This provision has a double purpose: first, deterring Members from modifying their commitments, being aware of the broad effect of such a step. Second, ensuring non-discrimination where a modification is taking place.

However, the provision is unclear. Does it refer to formal non-discrimination, where the same compensation will be given to all Members, or rather to substantial non-discrimination, where each Member is compensated according to the effect of modification on its market, according to equal terms and criteria? Considering the interpretative experience gained with regard to other GATS provisions, it is likely that this provision will also be interpreted to cover both options. In this case, how will the MFN treatment be practically applied to other Members? These questions are not answered by the language of this provision.

15.3.2.5 Arbitration

Article XXI:3(a) provides, that if the parties do not reach agreement within a given time frame (which is not specified in the agreement, but is defined as a three months period following the last date on which such claim may be made in the procedure adopted by the Council for Trade in Services),[254] they may turn to arbitration. Any other Member, wishing to enforce a right that it may have for compensation, may join this procedure.[255] The arbitration decision should be submitted to the parties within three months from the appointment of the arbitration body.[256]

This is a new approach compared to the equivalent GATT provision, Article XXVIII:3, providing for reference of the matter to the DSB, without any arbitration option, but it folds some difficulties:

First, arbitration is expensive. Its cost may deter countries from engaging in it. Second, if many Members would join this process, each having to prove its damages and reach agreement on compensation, this could turn into a long, elaborated process. Assuming that the modifying Member had an immediate need for modification of schedules, such a delay may cause this country a substantial economic damage. On the other hand, the threat of arbitration may urge the modifying country to reach agreement with its trade partners, to avoid it.

Article XXI:3(b) determines, that if no affected Member has requested arbitration, the modifying Member shall be free to implement the proposed modification or withdrawal. However, since no provision concerning the time frame is included, a practical question arises: how long should the modifying Member wait before implementing the modification? Some hint may be drawn from Article XXI:3(a), providing that arbitration may take place if no agreement is

254. S/L/80, n. 249, paras 4, 7.
255. The procedure for this process is also specified in S/L/80, n. 249.
256. S/L/80, n. 249, para. 14.

achieved by 'the end of the period provided for negotiations', which is not specified. In any case, another question is, whether the request for arbitration should take place before the end of this period or afterwards, and if afterwards – until when? It is likely that in practice, the time frame will be judged in terms of reasonableness, on a case-by-case basis.

15.3.2.6 Compliance with the Decision of the Arbitration

Where arbitration takes place, Article XXI:4(a) provides that the modifying Member may not modify or withdraw its commitments until it has made compensatory adjustments in conformity with the findings of the arbitration. Article XXI:4(b) further provides, that if the modifying Member disregards this provision, any affected Member who participated in the arbitration may modify or withdraw substantially equivalent benefits in conformity with those findings, but only towards the modifying Member. This is an exception to the MFN principle. The purpose of this provision is to give the affected Member an effective sanction against the modifying Member. Such a step is subject to prior notification of one month to the Council for Trade in Services.[257] However, the language of this provision is unclear: what are 'substantially equivalent benefits'? How would their effect be measured and by whom? How can the affected Member applying them be sure that it does not infringe this provision?

Additional difficulties arise from the perspective of the modifying Member: How should it act if the arbitration decision is open to some interpretations and it applies it as understood by it, but the affected Member claims that it 'does not comply with the findings of the arbitration'? These questions are not answered by the language of this provision, and the practical implication of this fact is that they would have to be solved in time and money consuming legal procedures.

15.3.2.7 Procedures by the Council for Trade in Services

Article XXI:5 authorizes the Council for Trade in Services to determine procedures for the modification of schedules.

Such procedures were adopted by the Council for Trade in Services in 1999.[258] These Procedures are to be implemented whenever a Member intends to modify or withdraw a scheduled commitment. Other procedures were adopted by the Council for Trade in Services in 2000, to be implemented whenever a Member intends to undertake new commitments, improve existing ones, or introduce rectifications or changes of a purely technical nature that do not alter the scope or the substance of the existing commitments.[259]

257. *Ibid.*, para. 18.
258. *Ibid.*
259. S/L/84 Procedures for the Certification or Rectifications or Improvements to Schedules of Specific Commitments, adopted by the Council for Trade in Services 20.4.2000, <http://docsonline.wto.org>.

15.4 CONCLUSION

Being an international agreement, dealing with a very elaborated subject that enfolds many sensitivities of the Members, GATS includes different kinds of safety valves. These valves allow deviation from the legal obligations undertaken by the Members under this agreement, in exceptional circumstances, mostly unforeseen at the time of its conclusion. The safety valves provide for temporary, as well as for permanent solutions. While the temporary solutions are subject to further review, as well as to the proportionality standard, the permanent modification of schedules is subject to compensation of the adversely affected Members. All these safety valves are subject to the general *good faith* principle.

It is clear that these safety valves, which are similar to those included in GATT, were decisive to the conclusion of GATS and are vital for its further existence. Nevertheless, since they include an ambiguous language, open for interpretation, the interpretative dilemma concentrates on the desired scope of these provisions. While it might be expected that, as a general rule, exceptions would be narrowly interpreted, this is not always the policy or practice of the WTO adjudicating bodies. The lack of clear interpretative policy concerning these provisions, added to their ambiguous language, creates an uncertain environment where the Members find it difficult to anticipate the result of using these provisions.

Chapter 16
GATS Sector-Specific Instruments

16.1 INTRODUCTION

Sector-specific instruments in the context of WTO instruments for trade in services fulfil two major functions:

(1) *Specification of detailed rules for the application of GATS disciplines to certain, specific sectors* – this goal is mainly achieved by GATS Annexes, regarded as part of GATS due to Article XXIX, providing: 'the Annexes to this Agreement are an integral part of this Agreement', and in some cases also by other forms of legal instruments.

(2) *The creation of voluntary frameworks for the enhanced services' trade liberalization in the sectors involved* – by the end of the Uruguay Round, in 1994, it became clear that differences in view and interests among the Members may prevent enhancement of trade liberalization in certain sectors of services and aspects concerning trade in services, having decisive importance to the development of global economy as well as to improvement of domestic growth and welfare.

    It was therefore decided to add to GATS certain specific arrangements, including legal norms which are not considered to be in a lower normative status, over the legal norms included in GATS, but the participation in them is voluntary.

The sector-specific instruments of the two groups refer to movement of natural persons supplying services under the Agreement; telecommunications and basic telecommunications; financial services; air transport services; maritime transport services; professional services; e-commerce in services.

This chapter does not include a thorough legal analysis of each of these instruments, but rather depicts the road-map of sector-specific instruments, that should be taken into account in any legal analysis referring to these sectors.

16.2 MOVEMENT OF NATURAL PERSONS SUPPLYING SERVICES UNDER GATS

GATS does not refer to foreign workers who seek access to a Member's employment market on permanent basis, and to the processes involved, including the obtainment of residence or nationality in these countries.[1]

The Annex[2] on Movement of Natural Persons Supplying Services under the GATS[3] substantially limits the potentially broad effect of Article I:2(d) (Mode 4 – movement of natural persons, see Chapter 1) on immigration and domestic market regulation. In it, the Members express their agreement to accord temporary access to individuals, such as managers and experts – whether independent service suppliers or employees of a service supplier – who are not their nationals, in order to allow the supply of services under Mode 4.[4] The Annex refers to two categories: self employed persons from a Member, receiving their remuneration directly from consumers in the host country, and 'natural persons employed by a service supplier of a Member'. The Annex does not define the criteria establishing employment relations.[5] These criteria may differ from one Member to another. It is not clear whether this expression covers only foreign employees of service suppliers from other Members, or also foreign employees of firms from the host Member.[6]

---

1. Article 2 of the Annex on Movement of Natural Persons Supplying Services under the GATS. The Sub-Committee in Services discussed the question, on what basis the distinction between 'permanent' and 'temporary' stay should be made, but decided to avoid conclusion. See G/C/1, para. 6, adopted by the Council for Trade in Services in 1.3.1995, S/C/M/1, para. 14.
2. For comprehensive legal analysis see: R. Worfrum, P.T. Stoll & C. Feinäugle (eds), *WTO – Trade in Services*, Max Planck Commentaries on World Trade Law, Martinus Mijnhoff Publishers, Leiden, Boston (2008) (hereby: GATS commentary), 573–595.
3. This Annex is the result of conflicting interests between developing countries, who were interested in liberalization of natural persons' movement, and developed countries who opposed. For negotiation history of the annex see: R. Self & K. Zutshi, 'Mode 4: Negotiating Challenges and Opportunities', in A. Mattoo & A. Carzaniga (eds), *Moving People to Deliver Services*, The World Bank and Oxford University Press (2003), 27, 32–34, <http://books.google.com>.
4. Article 1 of the Annex on Movement of Natural Persons Supplying Services under the GATS.
5. GATS commentary, n. 2, 580–581.
6. According to A. Carzaniga, 'The GATS, Mode 4 and pattern of Commitments', in A. Mattoo & A. Carzaniga (eds), *Moving People to Deliver Services*, The World Bank and Oxford University Press (2003), 23, this provision refers to both employees in their home country which are present at the host country to supply a service, and to foreign employees of a domestic supplier in the host country.

   According to other commentators, the answer to this question is not clear: R. Self & K. Zutshi, n. 3, 34, <http://books.google.com>.

   S. Chaudhari, A. Mattoo & R. Self, 'Moving People to Deliver Services', *The World Bank Policy Research Working Paper* (2004), 6–7, <www-wds.worldbank.org>.

Article 1 of the Annex stresses that GATS does not apply to measures affecting persons seeking access to the labour market of the host country on permanent basis. But GATS does not define 'temporary' stay beyond the reference to permanent immigration, so this issue is left to the discretion of the Members.[7] Accordingly, Article 2 of the Annex narrows the scope of GATS application to movement of natural persons, providing: '[t]he Agreement shall not apply to measures affecting natural persons seeking access to the employment market of a Member, nor shall it apply to measures regarding citizenship, residence or employment on a permanent basis'. Another interpretative question may refer to the relationships between this Annex, which excludes permanent access to labour markets, and GATS Article V*bis*, recognizing labour market integration agreements, which are meant to allow such access, as an exception to the MFN principle (see Chapter 10).[8] However, since Article V*bis* allows this access only in the framework of a labour market integration agreement, it may be regarded as *lex specialis* compared to the Annex, which provides the general rule.

Article 3 of the Annex allows Members to undertake specific commitments 'applying to the movement of all categories of natural persons supplying services under the Agreement'. This provision does not add to the general GATS provisions, but was probably considered necessary as a clarification, in light of the former provision. The words 'all categories of natural persons' may either be interpreted to mean that commitments should be comprehensive and generally applicable, or alternatively as supporting category-specific measures, thereby introducing an additional element of flexibility.[9]

Article 4 of the Annex provides that the Agreement shall not prevent[10] Members from regulating the entry of natural persons, in order, *inter alia*, to protect the integrity of, and to ensure orderly border-cross by these individuals, providing that the arrangements made will not be 'applied in such a manner as to nullify or impair the benefits accruing to any Member under the terms of a specific commitment'. This sentence is also open to legal interpretation: first, it should be established that a specific commitment folds benefits for a complaining Member. Then, it should be established that this benefit is nullified or impaired by a regulatory requirement by the complainant Member. Due to footnote 13 attached to this Annex, the application of visa requirements only to natural persons from certain states, but not from others, for example, is not considered as nullifying or impairing such benefits.[11] A violation of Article II:1 as such would also not constitute a nullification or

7. S. Chaudhari et al., n. 6, 6–7.
8. R. Self & K. Zutshi, n. 3, 35.
9. A. Carzaniga, n. 6, 23.
10. The words 'shall not prevent' were interpreted by the Appellate Body in the context of GATT Art. XXIV:5 to mean 'shall not make impossible:' WT/DS34/AB/R Turkey – Restrictions on Imports of Textile and Clothing Products, adopted on 19.11.1999, para. 45.
11. This is specifically problematic taking into account the length of the visa obtaining process: R. Self & K. Zutshi, n. 3, 52.

impairment of this provision, since this provision covers only specific commitments, while Article II:1 is a general obligation.[12]

Another legal instrument attached to GATS, referring to the movement of natural persons, which should be mentioned here, is the *Third Protocol to the General Agreement on Trade in Services of 24 July 1995*, which entered into force on 30 January 1996. This protocol includes some advanced commitments on this matter by certain Members, which replaced or supplemented entries in the schedules of the relevant Members.

Following the Uruguay Round a working group was established for further development of rules in this context. The working group concluded its work in 1995, and the rules developed were included in the third protocol of GATS.[13]

16.3 TELECOMMUNICATIONS

The telecommunications sector has a dual role, as a distinct sector of economic activity and as infrastructure for the transmission of other economic activities. The telecommunications market forms about 2% of the world GDP and it is growing rapidly.[14] This sector is decisive for the development of countries with telecommunications industry, as well as to countries who are consumers thereof. It is inevitable for the development of value added industries such as electronic mail and vocal announcements, online data, databases and data processing. These services are usually supplied in two modes: cross border (Mode 1) or commercial presence (Mode 3).[15] Commercial presence is often more open than cross-border supply.[16] However, the reliance of these services on networks that should be constructed first turns this sector into a high capital intensity sector, leading in many cases to a 'natural' monopoly, although the improvement of technology gradually improves this situation.[17] This sector is characterized by cross-subsidization, which enables universal service. In recent years, it is undergoing substantial structural and technological changes.[18]

---

12. GATS commentary, n. 2, 593.
13. S/L/28, Decision on the Acceptance of the Second and Third Protocols to the GATS (1996).
14. The US, the EU, Canada, Japan and Australia account for 77% of the world market: C. Woll, *The Politics of Trade preferences: Business Lobbying on Service Trade in the US and in the EU*, (PhD dissertation), Institut d'Etudes Politiques de Paris und Wirtschafts – und Sozialwissenschaftliche Fakultät der Universität zu Köln (2004), 160, <http://kups.ub.uni-koeln.de>.
15. In WT/DS204/R Mexico – Measures Affecting Telecommunications Services, adopted 1.6.2004, para. 7.121.
16. R. Adlung, A. Carzeniga, B. Hoeckman & M. Kono, 'The GATS: Key Features and Sectors', in B. Hoeckman, A. Mattoo & P. English (eds), *Development, Trade and the WTO: a Handbook, The World Bank* (2002), 259, 276, <www-wds.worldbank.org>.
17. C. Woll, n. 14, 163–164. In WT/DS204/R *Mexico – Telecoms*, n. 15, para. 7.113 the Panel recognized the incentive to major suppliers in this sector 'to set interconnection rates at anti-competitive rates, and not to provide optimal service to the other suppliers in terms of quality and timelines.'
18. GATS commentary, n. 2, 687–688.

Some specific instruments were developed in the Uruguay Round[19] to multilaterally regulate 'the rules of the game' in this sector.[20]

16.3.1 The Annex on Telecommunications

The Annex on Telecommunications,[21] which forms an integral part of GATS, ensures reasonable and non-discriminatory access of service suppliers to public telecoms networks, including a reasonable, non-discriminatory possibility to use these networks and entitlement to the auxiliary services. It applies to all Members, regardless of the degree of monopolization, liberalization or deregulation in their respective telecommunications sectors, and to all networks or services, irrespective of their ownership, whether public, private or mixed.[22]

Suppliers of enhanced telecoms services create international networks by leasing lines from suppliers or basic telecoms services. The former supply the services, for example, electronic mail or databases, to customers who connect them by their personal computers. Paragraph 2(a) to the Annex provides that it applies to all measures affecting the access to and use of 'public telecommunications transport networks and services'.[23] 'Public telecommunications transport networks and services' are defined in paragraph 3 of the Annex. This provision was broadly interpreted by the Panel in *Mexico – Telecoms*,[24] to include '. . . *all* measures that affect access to or use of public telecommunications transport networks and services with regard to *all* services, including basic telecommunications services'. [Emphasis in the original].

The Panel further explained the reason behind this interpretation:

> If the Annex did not apply to measures affecting access to and use of public telecommunications transport networks and services for basic telecommunications services, Members could effectively prohibit any supply other than

---

19. This Annex is a result of the complexity of this sector and of the fact that at the time of its conclusion, this sector was largely dominated by state monopolies. The US, for example, refused to accord MFN treatment in this sector. For the history and dynamics of negotiations on this subject see: C. Woll, n. 14, 185–192.
20. For further analysis of these instruments, as well as assessment of their impact on domestic regulation and suggestions for their future development see: D. Roseman, 'Domestic Regulation and Trade in Telecommunications Services: Experience and Prospects Under the GATS', in A. Mattoo & P. Sauvé (eds), *Domestic Regulation and Service Trade Liberalization*, The World Bank and Oxford University Press (2003), 83–107.
21. See detailed legal analysis in GATS commentary, n. 2, 690–714.
22. W. Zdouc, *Legal Problems Arising Under the General Agreement on Trade in Services – Comparative Analysis of GATS and GATT*, dissertation der Universität St. Gallen (2002), 283.
23. Footnote 14, attached to this provision, determines:

    > This paragraph is understood to mean that each Member shall ensure that the obligations of this Annex are applied with respect to suppliers of public telecommunications transport networks and services by whatever measures are necessary.

24. WT/DS204/R *Mexico – Telecoms*, n. 15, para. 7.278–7.286.

> that which originated and terminated within the same suppliers' network, even where commitments were undertaken, thereby rendering most basic telecommunications commitments without economic value.[25]

However, measures affecting the cable or broadcast distribution of radio or television programming, and telecommunications transport networks or services not offered to the public generally, are excluded from the scope of the Annex by paragraph 2(b). It is further stressed, in paragraph 2(c), that nothing in this Annex shall be construed to require a Member to authorize a service supplier of any other Member to establish, construct, acquire, lease, operate, or supply telecommunications transport networks or services, other than as provided for in its schedule, or to require a Member (or to require a Member to oblige service suppliers under its jurisdiction) to establish, construct, acquire, lease, operate or supply telecommunications transport networks or services which are not offered to the public generally.

The Annex includes disciplines specific to this sector, applying to Members subject to their specific commitments in this sector. For example:

- *Transparency* – paragraph 4 requires Members to make information on the conditions affecting access to this market available to the public. It includes an illustrative list of matters that should be published, such as tariffs and other terms and conditions of service; specifications for technical interfaces with such networks and services; information on bodies responsible for the preparation and adoption of standards affecting such access and use; conditions applying to attachment of terminal or other equipment; and notifications, registration or licensing requirements, if any. Unlike GATS Article III, this provision does not specify any format and time frame for publication. It should be read together with the rules on confidentiality specified in Article III*bis*.[26]
- *Market Access* – paragraph 5(a) of the Annex includes a requirement that each Member ensures non-discriminatory market access and the use of public telecoms transport networks and services (defined in paragraph 3(b) and (c)) by 'any service supplier from any other Member' (a broad terminology), thus allowing the exercise of the right for international service. Access by this provision is limited to the supply of services included in the schedule of the relevant Member. In *Mexico-Telecoms* the Panel determined that the right provided for by this provision is subject to the conditions and limitations specified in that schedule.[27]

  This provision is accompanied by footnote 15, providing:

  > The term 'non-discriminatory' is understood to refer to most-favoured-nation and national treatment as defined in the agreement, as well as

25. *Ibid.*, para. 7.286.
26. GATS commentary, n. 2, 696.
27. WT/DS204/R *Mexico – Telecoms*, n. 15, para. 7.317.

> to reflect sector-specific usage of the term to mean 'terms and conditions no less favourable than those accorded to any other user or like public telecommunications transport networks or services under like circumstances'.

The two ambiguous 'likeness' requirements seem to narrow the potential scope of this provision.[28]

It is provided, that the access and use should be 'on reasonable . . . terms and conditions'. However, 'reasonableness' is not defined. The word 'terms' was interpreted by the Panel in *Mexico – Telecoms* to include the rates charged for access to a telecom network, thus being subject to the 'reasonability' test provided for by this provision.[29] Applying this test to the given circumstances in that case the Panel concluded:

> We find that rates which exceed cost-based rates to this extent, and whose uniform nature excludes price competition in the relevant market of the telecommunications services bound under Mexico's Schedule, do not provide access to and use of public telecommunications transport networks and services in Mexico 'on reasonable... terms'.[30]

This provision specifies practices that should be taken to achieve this goal.[31] This provision was broadly interpreted by the Panel in *Mexico – Telecoms* to apply to basic telecommunications as well.[32] Paragraph 5(a) should be read together with paragraphs 5(b)-(f), which specify aspects of non-discrimination. In *Mexico – Telecoms* the Panel explained the interrelations between the different subparagraphs of Article 5 of the Annex, particularly between paragraph 5(a), referring to market access, and paragraph 5(e), referring to safeguard measures:

> We determined earlier that paragraph (a) should be read together with the other paragraphs of Section 5. We note that paragraph (a) addresses 'terms and conditions' for access to public telecommunications transport networks and services, which must be 'reasonable and non-discriminatory'. Paragraph (e) requires that no condition other than as necessary to achieve any of three policy objectives contained in subparagraphs (e)(i) to (iii) shall be imposed by a Member. We infer that whenever a condition is 'necessary' under paragraph (e), it must, in addition, be 'reasonable and non-discriminatory' under paragraph (a). Conversely, if a condition is not 'necessary' to fulfil at least one of the three policy objectives set out under subparagraphs (i) to (iii),

28. W. Zdouc, n. 22, 284.
29. WT/DS204/R, n. 15, paras 7.325, 7.333.
30. *Ibid.*, para. 7.334–7.335.
31. Article 5 of the Annex on Telecommunications.
32. WT/DS204/R, n. 15, para. 7.281.

> paragraph (e) *prohibits* the imposition of such a condition, which suggests that there may be no need to analyse [sic] in that case whether that condition would otherwise be 'reasonable and non-discriminatory' . . .
>
> We conclude that the obligation contained in Section 5(a) informs the other paragraphs of Section 5, and is likewise informed by elements of these paragraphs. We cannot therefore examine what constitutes 'reasonable terms and conditions' for access to and use of public telecommunications transport networks and services in isolation from the question of whether or not a particular condition may be imposed, an issue that is addressed in paragraph (e).[33]

The Panel discussed the meaning of the word 'necessary' in this context, and came to a conclusion that the meaning of 'necessary' in paragraph (e) was closer to 'making a contribution' to a policy goal, since then 'an examination under paragraph (a) of whether that rate was also 'reasonable' would still have meaning'.[34]

- *Relief for developing countries* – paragraph 5(g) of the Annex on Telecommunications allows developing countries to protect domestic networks by measures forbidden to be taken by developed countries, subject to their specification in their schedules of specific commitments.[35] Paragraph 6 of the Annex encourages technical cooperation among developed, developing and least-developed countries.
- Paragraph 7 of the Annex calls for *enhancement of use of international standards* by cooperation with relevant international organizations.

Compared to the general GATS Article VIII (see Chapter 11), the Annex guarantees access to foreign service suppliers and includes substantive obligations that are much broader than those included in Article VIII:2. From these aspects, the Annex fosters trade liberalization.

However, it is criticized for dealing only with the rights of users to access and use public telecommunications transport networks, but not establishing rights to provide and supply such services.[36] It is further criticized for freezing the market structure and not tackling the deregulation of national monopolies and oligopolies in this sector.[37]

33. *Ibid.*, paras 7.306 and 7.309.
34. *Ibid.*, para. 7.342.
35. In WT/DS204/R *Mexico – Telecoms*, n. 15, the Panel noted that a developing Member wishing to benefit from this relief should specify the limitation according to this provision in its schedule. If it does not do so – this provision will not permit departure from its specific commitments, explicitly and voluntarily scheduled. See: n. 23, para. 7.388.
36. GATS commentary, n. 2, 710.
37. W. Zdouc, n. 22, 285.

16.3.2 The Annex on Negotiations on Basic Telecommunications

This Annex postponed the application of the MFN provision in GATS and the submissions of exceptions concerning the basic telecommunications sector to a later date. This delay did not refer to specific commitments made by the Members concerning this sector that had the same date of application like GATS. This delay expired with the conclusion of the Forth Protocol, which came into force in 5 February 1998.

16.3.3 The Fourth Protocol: The Agreement on Basic Telecommunications

This sector includes domestic and international voice telephony, data transmission, telex, telegraph, facsimile, private leased circuit services (i.e., the sale or lease of transmission capacity), fixed and mobile satellite systems and services, cellular telephony, mobile data services, paging, and personal communications systems. It is mostly concentrated in the hands of the developed countries. It forms a global market worth over USD 1.5 trillion in revenue. Mobile services account for roughly 40% of this.[38] During the Uruguay Round, many countries hesitated about whether to open this market for external competition, one of the major difficulties being the need to privatize governmental monopolies in many Members. The Members completed their negotiations on 15 February 1997. GATS Article XXI on the modification of schedules could not have been effectuated before three years had elapsed since GATS conclusion, and its operation would have further implied a long and costly procedure, whereby each Member modifying its commitments would have had to compensate other Members.[39] Therefore, a specific agreement on this subject was concluded in 1997 by sixty-nine countries holding 90% of the world telecommunications market.[40] The agreement entered into force in 1998 and was annexed to GATS as its Fourth Protocol.[41] The agreement refers to one sector of services and the rules established by it are constructed to encourage competition. It includes a protocol, schedules of specific commitments and a List of Exemptions from Article II concerning basic telecommunications annexed to it. It either supplements or modifies the schedules of specific commitments of its parties, referring *inter alia* to market access, investment and regulative principles encouraging competition, based on competition-enhancing rules, embodied in a Reference Paper from 1996 (see below).[42]

38. <www.wto.org>.
39. GATS commentary, n. 2, 715–716.
40. PRESS/80, 'Services in a Borderless Economy', a speech by Renato Ruggiero, Director General of the WTO, in the 2nd DEBIS conference in Berlin, 23.10.1997, 6.
41. S/L/20 Fourth Protocol to the General Agreement on Trade in Services, 30.4.1996.
42. <www.wto.org>. See comparison between the reference paper commitments and the Annex on Telecommunications obligations in the Panel report of WT/DS204/R *Mexico – Telecoms*, n. 15, paras 7.331–7.332.

16.3.4 The Reference Paper

The reference paper builds upon GATS Article VIII and the Annex on telecommunications, determining rules to protect users and service suppliers (but not suppliers, producers or traders of goods involved) from the abuse of market power by major suppliers in this sector. In *Mexico-Telecoms* it was explained:

> An analysis of the Reference Paper commitments shows that Members recognized that the telecommunications sector, in many cases, was characterized by monopolies or market dominance. Removing market access and national treatment barriers was not deemed sufficient to ensure the effective realization of market access commitments in basic telecommunications services. Accordingly many Members agreed to additional commitments to implement pro-competitive regulatory framework designed to prevent continued monopoly behaviour, particularly by *former* monopoly operators, and abuse of dominance by these or any other major suppliers.[43] [Emphasis in the original].

The Reference Paper thus specifies competition safeguards and conditions for interconnection.[44] It provides a set of principles for the Members to follow in formulating their own regulatory frameworks. It is further made flexible by providing only for minimum rules and by not indicating the entity to be responsible for the implementation of these obligations.[45] There is a controversy between commentators as to whether the regulatory principles specified in the Reference Paper apply only to basic telecommunications services, or also to value-added services.[46]

Paragraph 1 of the Reference Paper provides for the prevention of anti-competitive practices in telecommunications. This provision should be read together with the general GATS Articles VIII and IX (see Chapter 11). 'Anti-competitive practices' were interpreted by the Panel in *Mexico – Telecom* to include horizontal practices related to price-fixing and market-sharing agreements.[47] This implies that anti-competitive behaviour may be taken by either one service supplier or by some service suppliers together. Examining whether this expression also covers cases of major suppliers, which is required by a Member's law, the Panel concluded that since the Reference Paper commitments are designed to limit the regulatory powers of Members, they could not be unilaterally eroded by a domestic law of a Member.[48]

Paragraph 2 of the Reference Paper specifically establishes the obligation to allow interconnection to networks. This provision should be read together with paragraph 5 of the Annex on Telecommunications.

---

43. WT/DS204/R *Mexico – Telecoms*, n. 15, para. 7.237.
44. For detailed analysis see W. Zdouc, n. 22, 288–293; GATS commentary, n. 1, 719–747.
45. GATS commentary, n. 2, 721.
46. *Ibid.*, 723–724.
47. WT/DS204/R *Mexico – Telecoms*, n. 15, para. 7.230.
48. *Ibid.*, para. 7.244.

Paragraph 3 of the Reference Paper provides for the right of Members to impose universal service obligations. Universal service may be defined as 'the provision of telecommunications permitting access to a defined minimum service of specified quality to all users anywhere and at an affordable price'.[49]

Paragraph 4 of the Reference Paper provides for the public availability of licensing criteria. In fact, this is a specific transparency requirement. It applies when a license is required. However, the Reference Paper does not specify in which situations a license would be required and does not provide for any mutual recognition arrangements.[50]

Paragraph 5 of the Reference Paper sets out the disciplines meant to ensure the independence of regulator, providing both that the regulator should be separate from and not accountable to any supplier, and that its operational procedures and decisions must be impartial.[51]

Paragraph 6 of the Reference Paper sets out disciplines regarding the allocation and use of scarce resources. The disciplines do not interfere with the system of allocation chosen by a Member, but rather require that the procedures involved be exercised in an objective, timely, transparent and non-discriminatory manner. This paragraph further provides for governments to make available to potential users the current state of allocated frequency bands, except for detailed information frequencies reserved for security, rescue and civilian authorities.[52]

In many countries, it allows the activity of foreign companies through commercial presence or participation in the ownership of domestic companies.

In recent decade competition was introduced into this market. Since the conclusion of this agreement, commitments have been made by new Members, upon accession to the WTO, or unilaterally at any time. According to the WTO:

> A total of 108 WTO members have made commitments to facilitate trade in telecommunications services. This includes the establishment of new telecoms companies, foreign direct investment in existing companies and cross-border transmission of telecoms services. Out of this total, 99 members have committed to extend competition in basic telecommunications (e.g. fixed and mobile telephony, real-time data transmission, and the sale of leased-circuit capacity). In addition, 82 WTO members have committed to the regulatory principles spelled out in the 'Reference Paper', a blueprint for sector reform that largely reflects 'best practice' in telecoms regulation.[53]

This trend continues in the Doha Round, according to the WTO data, as of July 2008, thirty-nine governments had made offers to improve their existing commitments or to commit for the first time in the telecommunications sector.

49. GATS commentary, n. 1, 741.
50. *Ibid.*, 745.
51. GATS commentary, n. 2, 746.
52. *Ibid.*, 747.
53. Footnote 42.

16.3.5 Supplementary Documents for the Interpretation of Telecoms Commitments

Finally, following the *Mexico – Telecoms* case, attention should be drawn to some documents by the WTO Secretariat, which formed part of the preparatory work of the treaty and the circumstances of its conclusion, and therefore were used by the Panel, explicitly recognizing their high interpretative value, as supplementary means for the interpretation of Mexico's relevant commitments on telecommunication services: the Draft Model Schedule, the related Note by the Chairman, the Scheduling Guidelines[54] and the Understanding.[55]

16.4 FINANCIAL SERVICES

This sector includes banking, insurance and financial markets: three backbone services which are important to the development of economies. Differences in the levels of liberalization in this sector, in different countries, are affected, *inter alia*, by macro-economical and institutional factors such as GDP growth, the growth and performance of the banking sector and the size of the country.[56] The WTO Members could not reach an agreement on this sector within GATS,[57] and therefore, by the end of the Uruguay Round, concluded five additional agreements: the annex on financial services; the second annex on financial services; the decision on financial

54. WT/DS204/R *Mexico – Telecoms*, n. 15, paras 7.53–7.72, referring to the following supplementary documents, which served as guidance for the scheduling of specific commitments: Draft Model Schedule of Commitments on Basic Telecommunications, Informal Note by the Secretariat, Job No. 1131, 12.4.1995; S/GBT/W/2/Rev.1 Note for Scheduling Basic Telecommunications Services Commitments, Note by the Chairman, 16.1.1997; S/L/92 Guidelines for the Scheduling of Specific Commitments under the General Agreement on Trade in Services (GATS) adopted on 23.3.2001, 28.3.2001.
55. The Understanding is contained in a Report by the Group on Basic Telecommunications of 15.2.1997, issued at the close of negotiations on the Fourth Protocol (the instrument which contained Members' new commitments on basic telecommunications). The Report appended the draft schedules of Members. The Understanding is included in para. 7 of the Report and provides, *inter alia*, that the application of differential accounting rates to services and service suppliers of other Members, and would not give rise to WTO dispute settlement procedures. This Understanding should have been reviewed by 1.1.2000. However, the Panel noted that this Understanding concerns only procedural rights, and 'seeks to exempt a very limited category of measures, temporarily and on a non-binding basis, from the scope of WTO dispute settlement' and thus cannot affect directly the scope of a Member's obligations: paras 7.122–7.139.
56. N. Valckx, 'WTO Financial Services Commitments: Determinants and Impact on Financial Stability', *IMF Working Paper* (2002), 18. According to this paper, current level of financial liberalization under GATS 'did not contribute very strongly or robustly to financial vulnerability although the results tend slightly to favour the view that higher liberalization and more openness may be associated with a higher risk of financial stability'. These considerations may explain the different positions of Members concerning this matter, <www.imf.org>.
57. Concerning the history of negotiations see: R. Adlung et al., n. 16, 259, 265–267; E.H. Leroux, 'Trade in Financial Services under the World Trade Organization', *36 Journal of World Trade* (2002), 413, 426–427. In addition, a Committee on Trade in Financial Services was established by the Decision on Institutional Arrangements for GATS: <www.wto.org>.

services, the understanding on commitments in financial services and the Fifth Protocol. The first three documents allow, in effect, for deviations from the MFN rule of GATS, while the Understanding provides an approach to scheduling which deviates from Part III of GATS, leading to deeper commitments in this sector. The Fifth Protocol, concluded after the end of the Uruguay Round, expands the scope of commitments in this sector beyond those made under GATS, thus resulting in the full integration of this sector into GATS. Nevertheless, 'the commitments undertaken did nothing else than locking in the status quo in most markets during this period'.[58] The second annex and the decision included temporary provisions until June 1995, when the end of negotiations was anticipated. All in all, the effective results of these agreements in terms of commitments' level is modest, but their major importance stems from permanently subjecting the financial services sector to a comprehensive set of rules and disciplines that limit the ability for Members to adopt and maintain protectionist measures.[59]

16.4.1 The Annex on Financial Services

The Annex on Financial Services[60] is an *integral part* of GATS, thus binding on all Members, supplementing the general GATS provisions. It has a broad scope of application, achieved by broad definitions of terms such as 'measures affecting trade in financial services', 'financial services', 'service supplier' etc., specified in Article 1 of the Annex. It is explicitly noted in this paragraph, that references to the supply of financial services in the annex mean the broad concept of 'supply of a service' in Article I:2 of GATS (see Chapter 4).

'Financial services' are broadly defined in paragraph 5(a) of the Annex, thus determining, in fact, its scope of application:[61]

> A financial service is any service of a financial nature offered by a financial service supplier of a Member. Financial services include all insurance and insurance-related services, and all banking and other financial services (excluding insurance).

The definition specifies an indicative list of specific services in the banking and insurance sectors.

A financial service supplier is also broadly defined, in paragraph 5(b) of the Annex:

> A financial service supplier means any natural or juridical person of a Member wishing to supply or supplying financial services but the term 'financial service supplier' does not include a public entity.

58. P. Delimatsis, 'Financial Innovation and Climate Change: the Case of Renewable Energy Certificates and the Role of the GATS', *8 World Trade review* (2009), 439, 443.
59. E.H. Leroux, n. 57, 428.
60. See detailed legal analysis in GATS commentary, n. 2, 618–639.
61. Paragraph 5(a) of the Annex.

Unlike the general definition of 'service supplier' in GATS, this definition explicitly includes potential service suppliers, by using the words 'wishing to supply'. This is a relatively broader definition. As explained in Chapter 4, even the narrower GATS definition for 'service supplier' is sometimes interpreted by the adjudicating bodies to include potential suppliers. In both cases, this approach is based on the view that a potential supplier might be prevented from supplying a service due to the barriers to trade which the agreement aims to abolish.

16.4.1.1 Prudential Carve-out

In terms of substance, paragraph 2(a) of the Annex provides that prudential measures are meant to ensure stability of financial institutes, in the banking, insurance and financial markets. Prudential measures are considered an exception to GATS disciplines. These rules are necessary since the sectors involved, which underline the entire international trade, are sensitive, connected to governmental activities and decisive for the economic and monetary stability of states (the 'prudential curve out'). This exception applies to governmental authorities or entities conducting governmental function in the field of financial services.[62]

A public entity is defined as:[63]

(i) a government, a central bank or a monetary authority, of a Member, or an entity owned or controlled by a Member, that is principally engaged in carrying out governmental functions or activities for governmental purposes, not including an entity principally engaged in supplying financial services on commercial terms; or

(ii) a private entity, performing functions normally performed by a central bank or monetary authority, when exercising those functions.

The term 'principally engaged' is not defined in the text, and may raise interpretative questions as to the necessary scope of activity embodied in it. As to the private entities mentioned, this Annex will apply only to functions performed by them, which are normally performed by a central bank or monetary authority, while other functions would be subject to the general GATS rules.

The Annex further specifies, in paragraph 1(b) what the expression 'services supplied in the exercise of governmental authority' in Article I:3(b) and (c) (see Chapter 4) means, in the context of trade in financial services:[64]

(i) activities conducted by a central bank or monetary authority or by any other public entity in pursuit of monetary or exchange rate policies;

62. According to para. 1(b) of the Annex, central bank activities and activities forming part of the statutory system of social security or public retirement and all other activities conducted by a public entity for the account or with the guarantee or using the financial resources of the government are excluded from GATS scope of coverage.

63. Paragraph 5(c) of the Annex.

64. Paragraph 1(b) of the Annex.

(ii) activities forming part of a statutory system of social security or public retirement plans; and
(iii) other activities conducted by a public entity for the account or with the guarantee or using the financial resources of the Government.

Unlike Article I:3(c) of GATS, this definition is not based on the circumstances of supply, rather emphasizing the supplier and the nature of the service. Article I:3(b) of GATS, adding the condition 'neither on commercial basis nor in competition' further narrows this list of activities, some of which could be supplied in a competitive environment.[65]

It is further determined in paragraph 1(c), that if a Member allows any of the activities referred to in subparagraphs (ii) or (iii) to be conducted by its financial service suppliers in competition with a public entity or a financial service supplier, GATS obligations will apply.

These authorities are thus allowed to impose restrictions on international trade in financial services by regulation, to protect investors, depositors, policy holders or persons to whom a fiduciary duty is owed by a financial service supplier, or to ensure the integrity and stability of the financial system.

The Annex does not define which prudential measures may be taken by governments, thus leaving them a broad scope of discretion and flexibility. The measures taken may be discriminating. They are not registered in the schedules of specific commitments, since if they were so inscribed, they could have been considered as limitations on national treatment or market access.

However, to balance this interest with the interest of trade liberalization it is stressed, that such measures shall not be used as a means of avoiding the Member's commitments or obligations under the Agreement.[66] This provision, which was still not interpreted by the WTO adjudicating bodies, is interpreted as imposing on the Members a good faith obligation.[67]

The interpretation of this provision should be cautious and narrow, in order to ensure that no prudential measures will be taken where no substantial damage or threat for damage to the domestic market exists, in order to avoid the undermining of international competition.[68]

---

65. M. Krajewski, 'Public Services and Trade Liberalization: Mapping the Legal Framework', *6 Journal of International Economic Law* (2003), 341, 355.
66. Paragraph 2(a) of the Annex.
67. E.H. Leroux, n. 57, 431.
68. By way of analogy, jurisprudence referring to GATT Art. XX, providing that measures applied for the protection of general interests specified in it should not be applied in 'a manner which would constitute a means of arbitrary or unjustifiable discrimination between countries where the same conditions prevail' and its equivalence in GATS Art. XIV (see Ch. 15) may supply some guidance for the interpretation of this provision.

16.4.1.2 Confidentiality

Another exception to the rule set by this Annex refers to the confidentiality of information about financial activities of individuals. Paragraph 2(b) explicitly specified:

> Nothing in the Agreement shall be construed to require a Member to disclose information relating to the affairs and accounts of individual customers or any confidential or proprietary information in the possession of public entities.

This provision refers only to information possessed by public entities, but should be read with GATS Articles III*bis* and XIV(c)(ii) which include similar provisions, protecting the confidentiality of individual records and accounts.

16.4.1.3 Recognition

The territorial scope of prudential measures subject to this Annex is limited, in terms of enforcement, to the territory of the Member applying them. Enforcement is particularly difficult for Mode 1 (cross border) and Mode 2 (consumption abroad). To overcome this difficulty, there were attempts by Members to initiate recognition of prudential measures agreements. This option is foreseen by Article VII of GATS, as well as by paragraph 3 of the Annex,[69] and is subject to some legal obligations.[70] Thus, selective treatment based on such recognition is allowed, and would not be considered as a breach of the MFN obligation.

16.4.1.4 Dispute Settlement

Paragraph 4 of the Annex includes a specific provision concerning dispute settlement, requiring a Panel dealing with such matters to have the necessary expertise in this field. This is the only sector for which such a provision was specified.

16.4.2 The Understanding on Financial Services

Unlike the Annex, the Understanding on Financial Services[71] is *not an integral part of GATS*, but is a part of the Final act of the Uruguay Round.

---

69. Paragraph 3 of the Annex appears to go further than Art. VII of GATS, since liberalization measures themselves may be applied in a different manner, depending on the origin of financial service or service supplier: 'The General Agreement on Trade in Services (GATS): an Analysis', *OECD* (1994), 22, <www.olis.oecd.org>.
70. Notification to the WTO; providing equal opportunity to other Members to participate if they fulfil the participation conditions; allowing maximal liberalization possible, considering the prudential measures; the agreement is subject to the standards existing in the laws of the parties to the agreement.
71. See detailed legal analysis in GATS commentary, n. 1, 647–666.

The Understanding is a result of an initiative by the OECD countries. Suggesting an 'alternative approach', it is aimed at harmonizing the construction of the schedules of specific commitments on financial services, by forming a 'model schedule'.[72] Its application is *optional*, and does not require any formal 'adherence' by the Members. Its application must not conflict, under any circumstances, with GATS: it could only be used to enhance liberalization further. In the WTO system the Understanding has no legal force *per se.*[73] Its provisions are binding only on the Members adhering to it, gaining a binding effect since the schedules of specific commitments of these Members incorporate the rules and disciplines of the Understanding into the schedule by reference, either through insertion of a specific head-note in the financial services section or by inscription as an additional commitment according to Article XVIII (see Chapter 7). The Members who adhered to the Understanding must apply the rules and disciplines of it on an MFN basis, namely: also to non-adhering Members.[74]

16.4.2.1 Standstill

The Understanding includes an explicit *standstill* obligation, according to which the Members may refer, in their financial services' schedules, only to existing measures. This is a narrower approach than that provided for by Article III of GATS, interpreted by certain Members as allowing the schedules to refer to *future* measures as well (see Chapter 7 – 7.7). Another aspect by which this approach differs from that of GATS is, that GATS allows Members to inscribe in their schedules, restrictions that represent less than the regulatory *status quo*, thus opening an option for future effective regulatory rollbacks, while the Understanding fixes the regulatory *status quo* as a minimum.[75]

In addition, the Understanding provides for a 'top down' approach, formulating the ideal standards for liberalization, from which the parties are expected to take only limited reservations. The understanding includes the following obligations, beyond which the Members may take additional and complementary commitments according to the general approach of GATS.

16.4.2.2 Market Access

Section B of the Understanding modifies the list of prohibited market access restrictions of GATS Article XVI:2 (see Chapter 9) with respect to financial services.

72. GATS commentary, n. 2, 650.
73. *Ibid.*, 651.
74. E.H. Leroux, n. 57, 433.
75. *Ibid.*, 433.

16.4.2.2.1 Monopoly Rights

Paragraph B(1) of the understanding adds to the provisions of GATS Article VIII (transparency) by providing for the listing in the schedules of monopoly rights, to achieve transparency in the short term, endeavouring to reduce or eliminate them in the long term. This obligation applies to activities conducted by public entities for the account or with the guarantee of using the financial resources of the government. Such services usually fall outside GATS scope of application. Thus, the Understanding implicitly questions the political and economic legitimacy of such monopolies.[76]

16.4.2.2.2 Financial Services Purchased by Public Entities

Notwithstanding GATS Article XIII (government procurement), paragraph B(2) of the Understanding provides for the granting of MFN and national treatment to *established* foreign financial service suppliers, concerning government procurements of financial services. The Understanding does not specify, though, what 'established' means: does it necessitate the establishment of a subsidiary in the host country, or would a representative office do?[77] According to the general GATS approach, government procurements are excluded from such benefits (unless the Government Procurement Agreement applies). It should be noted that the meaning of this word, appearing in paragraphs B(5), B(6) and B(9)(a), should be weighed against 'commercial presence' which is defined in paragraph D(2). Some commentators suggest to 'assume that "established" financial supplier means those with a commercial presence in the territory of the host Member'.[78]

16.4.2.2.3 Cross-Border Trade

Paragraph B(3) of the Understanding provides for its Members to permit non-resident suppliers of financial services (defined in paragraph D(1)) to offer and supply, through an intermediary or as an intermediary, certain financial services such as insurance services in the field of maritime and air transport, goods in international transit, reinsurance, retrocession and for suppliers of certain information, advisory and other auxiliary services. In so permitting, the Members must afford national treatment. However, the Members may subject this permit to conditions. This obligation is considered rather limited, the reason largely being the fact that cross-border financial service suppliers are not directly subject to the supervision and regulatory powers of the host Member's financial regulator.[79]

76. *Ibid.*, 434.
77. *Ibid.*, 435. It is unclear what the relations are between this word and 'commercial presence' mentioned in the Understanding, which is broadly defined in para. D.2 of the Understanding, including subsidiaries, branches, agencies and representative offices.
78. GATS commentary, n. 2, 657.
79. E.H. Leroux, n. 57, 435.

On the other hand, paragraph B(4) provides that Members who adhered to the Understanding should allow residents to purchase abroad the listed financial services. In fact, this is 'consumption abroad' (Mode 2). The coverage of this paragraph is broader than the former, since this mode of supply does not give rise to regulatory concerns as the former.[80]

16.4.2.2.4 Commercial Presence

In order to facilitate the establishment of a financial commercial presence, either through internal growth or through acquisition of other institutions, the right of *establishment* and of further investment by established firms is recognized in Paragraph B(5) of the Understanding, requiring Members not to use authorization procedures as a means to circumvent this obligation. At the same time, this provision does not prevent a Member from imposing terms, conditions and procedures for the authorization of the establishment and expansion of such commercial presence, in so far as they do not circumvent the obligation according to paragraph B(5) or other GATS obligations. The term 'circumvent' is not interpreted by the Understanding, and some commentators suggest that it should be interpreted as equivalent to 'avoid'.[81] 'Commercial presence' is determined in paragraph D(2) in a broader manner than the general definition in GATS Article XXVIII(d). This definition is also relevant to paragraphs B(6) and B(9).

16.4.2.2.5 New Financial Services

Paragraph B(7) requires the Members who adhered to the Understanding to allow foreign services suppliers *established* (see the interpretative difficulty above) in the host Member, to supply in it 'new financial services', even if domestic suppliers cannot yet provide them. A 'New financial service' is defined in paragraph D(3), meaning services which did not exist anywhere before, but rather services already supplied in the territory of one WTO Member.

16.4.2.2.6 Transfer and Processing of Information

Paragraph B(8) of the Understanding prohibits Members from taking measures to prevent transfer of information, the processing of financial information or even transfer of equipment which are necessary for the conduct of ordinary business of financial service suppliers. This obligation does not restrict Members' right to protect personal data, personal privacy and confidentiality of individual records and accounts, as long as this right is not abused by the Member at stake to *circumvent* (see interpretative difficulty above) its obligations under GATS. Thus, this provision balances the interests of service suppliers and the Members involved. The confidentiality provision here should be read together with the confidentiality

80. *Ibid.*, 436.
81. GATS commentary, n. 2, 657.

provisions in paragraph 2(b) of the Annex on Financial Services and GATS Articles III*bis* and XIV(c)(ii).

16.4.2.2.7 Temporary Entry of Personnel

Paragraph B(9) of the Understanding obliges the Members who adhered to it to allow the temporary entry of foreign personnel, mainly intra-company transferees, such as senior managers and specialists necessary for the establishment and operation of a foreign commercial presence supplying services. Subparagraph (a) allows the entry of financial service suppliers 'that is establishing or has established a commercial presence'.

According to subparagraph (b) the access of computer, telecommunications, accounting, actuarial and legal specialists is allowed subject to the availability of qualified personnel in the country concerned. However, this provision only allows such entry where a commercial presence was already established in the host Member. These obligations do not prevent Members from applying measures to regulate this temporary entry, as long as such measures are not used to *circumvent* (see interpretative difficulty above) this obligation.[82]

For both subparagraphs, the description of permissible personnel is vague, and so is the notion of 'temporary entry'. It is further unclear whether the term 'personnel' requires the establishment of employer-employee relationship.[83]

16.4.2.2.8 Non-discriminatory Measures

Paragraph B(10) of the Understanding includes a 'best effort' obligation (expressed by the word 'endeavour') to remove or limit 'any significant adverse effect' (an expression which is not defined) of certain, mostly non-discriminating measures, possibly consistent with the other obligations of the Understanding and GATS applied to financial services. This obligation only applies to the extent that any action taken by a Member would not unfairly discriminate against its own financial service suppliers.[84] Paragraph B(11) complements this provision by providing for a 'best effort' obligation ('endeavour') not to limit or restrict the present degree of market opportunities or the benefits already enjoyed by financial service suppliers from other Members 'as a class' (meaning: generally)[85] in the territory of that Member, provided that this commitment does not result in unfair discrimination against domestic service suppliers. The words 'unfairly discriminate' are not defined by the Understanding.

---

82. Annex on Movement of Natural Persons Supplying Services Under the Agreement (see above), para. 4.
83. GATS commentary, n. 2, 659–660.
84. The effect of these provisions is doubtful, considering the fact that the schedules could include more far-reaching commitments and that the Understanding is subject to the agreement: *GATS Analysis*, *OECD*, n. 69, 25.
85. Some commentators suggest that 'market access benefits enjoyed *exceptionally* by the service suppliers of select Members may presumably be eliminated': GATS commentary, n. 2, 662.

16.4.2.2.9 National Treatment

Section C of the Understanding includes specific national treatment provisions, expanding on Article XVII. Paragraph C(1) provides for the access of foreign service suppliers *established* (see the interpretative difficulty above) in a Member to payment and clearing systems and to official funding and refinancing facilities, but not to lender of the last resort facilities,[86] and to self-regulatory bodies such as stock exchanges, professional associations etc., if necessary for supply of a service.[87] According to paragraph C(2), financial service suppliers of other Members who *reside* in a host Member are entitled to national treatment when membership or participation in, or access to, any organization or association is required by the host Member as a condition for the entitlement of financial service suppliers of other Members to supply financial services on equal basis with the host Member's financial service suppliers, or when the host Member provides to those entities privileges or advantages, directly or indirectly. Similar to the concept of 'establishment', the concept of 'residence' is not clear and raises interpretative questions as to the relations between it and 'commercial presence'.[88]

16.4.3 The Fifth Protocol: The Financial Services Agreement (1997)

This is an agreement within the scope of Article II:2 of the WTO Agreement, concluded after the end of the Uruguay Round, and entered into force in March 1999. The Members have annexed schedules of specific commitments and lists of MFN (Article II) exemptions to it. The commitments annexed to it cover 95% (in terms of income)[89] of international trade in banking, insurance, securities and financial information. This agreement includes, *inter alia*, specific commitments taken by its parties concerning market access in Mode 1 (cross border) or Mode 3 (commercial presence) for all sorts of insurance; commercial presence of banks; and the right to establish foreign securities firms.[90] Nevertheless, its effect

86. The lender of last resort is usually the central bank of a Member. This provision clarifies that it is under no obligation to act on behalf of a foreign financial service supplier, for example to help it overcome a financial crisis: E.H. Leroux, n. 57, 440.
87. This provision is also identified as a 'strange leftover' to previous drafts: *GATS Analysis, OECD* n. 69, *Ibid.*
88. E.H. Leroux, n. 57, 440.
89. R. Bhala & K. Kennedy, *World Trade Law*, LEXIS, Law Publishing, Charlotesville, Virginia, 1998, 1296. See additional information on the scope and content of these commitments in GATS commentary, n. 1, 643–646.
90. All the developed countries undertook commitments in all sub-sectors of financial services. Developing countries mainly undertook commitments relating to insurance and banking sectors: P. Delimatsis, n. 58, 442. For review of financial services sector developments and future prospects for further regulation in GATS framework see: S. Claessens, 'Regulatory Reform and Trade Liberalization in Financial Services', in A. Mattoo & P. Sauve (eds), *Domestic*

on international trade liberalization in these sectors is not assessed to be substantial.[91]

16.5 AIR TRANSPORT

Air transport services comprise of all non-military air transport, both passengers and mail or transport cargo. This is one of the fastest growing sectors in the global economy.[92] It is a sector particularly important to some developed countries, including the United States and the EU,[93] but other countries also consider it to be strategically important. Landing rights are subject to an elaborated and synchronized network of more than 3,000 bilateral agreements, based on the Chicago Convention from 1944, establishing the sovereign rights of countries in the air above their territory.[94] This network of agreements is inherently discriminatory. Domestic air transport services are relatively protected against foreign competitors.[95] Since aviation industry supplies working places to skilled domestic workers, and involves substantial export possibilities, many developing countries established national aviation industries. The governments are often involved in these industries. Even where the ownership of such industries is private, the owners depend, to a large extent, on the security and defence industries in order to survive. Thus, these industries enjoy direct or indirect government support that was a subject for trade disputes, being regarded as subsidy.

In recent years this sector is experiencing changes, including price reduction and privatization, and the creation of regional civil aviation markets.

16.5.1 The Annex on Air Transport

The Annex on Air Transport[96] forms an integral part of GATS.

Article 1 of the Annex on air transport[97] seems to define a broad scope for its application, providing:

> This Annex applies to measures affecting trade in air transport services, whether scheduled or non-scheduled, and ancillary services. It is confirmed that any specific commitment or obligation assumed under this Agreement

---

Regulation and Service Trade Liberalization, The World Bank and Oxford University Press (2003), 129–146; W. Brown, 'WTO Negotiations in Financial Services: Standing Offers Disappoint', *41 Journal of World Trade* (2007), 1259.

91. GATS commentary, n. 2, 627.
92. C. Woll, n. 14, 247.
93. *Ibid.*, 243.
94. For developments in international regulation of this sector see C. Woll, n. 14, 259–261.
95. R. Adlung et al., n. 16, 259, 278.
96. For detailed explanations about the operation of this market and legal analysis of the Annex see: GATS commentary, n. 2, 598–617.
97. For the history of the negotiations on this subject in GATS see C. Woll, n. 14, 270–275.

> shall not reduce or affect a Member's obligations under bilateral or multilateral agreements that are in effect on the date of entry into force of the WTO Agreement.

The terms 'trade in air transport services' and 'ancillary services' are not defined, thus allegedly allowing an interpretation implying a broad scope of coverage.

However, Article 2 excludes from the scope of this Annex traffic rights and services directly related with their exercise. 'Traffic rights' are defined in Article 6(d) of the Annex as:

> the right for scheduled and non-scheduled services to operate and/or to carry passengers, cargo and mail for remuneration or hire from, to, within, or over the territory of a Member, including points to be served, routes to be operated, types of traffic to be carried, capacity to be provided, tariffs to be charged and their conditions, and criteria for designation of airlines, including such criteria as number, ownership, and control.

However, 'services directly related to the exercise of traffic rights' are not defined by the Annex, thus causing some ambiguity. An additional interpretative question is 'whether *services not directly related to the exercise of traffic rights* within the meaning of para. 2 of the Annex are potentially *covered* by GATS *or* whether the *coverage* is *restricted to the subsectors* explicitly listed as covered by GATS *in para. 3 of the Annex . . .*'[98] [Emphasis in the original].

Article 3 of the Annex explicitly provides that it applies to aircraft repair and maintenance services, the selling and marketing of air transport services and computer reservation system (CRS) services.

Article 4 of the Annex restricts the use of the dispute settlement mechanism only to cases where specific commitments were undertaken, and the procedures according to other bilateral and multilateral agreements or arrangements were exhausted.

Article 5 of the Annex authorizes the Committee on Trade in Services to examine this subject every five years, in orders to consider broadening of GATS scope of application concerning this sector.[99]

16.5.2 The Agreement on Trade in Civil Aircraft

The Agreement on Trade in Civil Aircraft is a voluntary plurilateral framework, concluded already in 1980 and attached to GATS as Annex 4(a). It now has

98. GATS commentary, n. 2, 612.

99. The first review took place between September 2000 and November 2003. The second review began in September 2006: S/C/M/50 Council for Trade in Services, Report of the third session of the review mandated under para. 5 of the Air Transport Annex, held on 9 Oct. 2001 – Note by the Secretariat, 5.3.2001; S/C/M/89 Council for Trade in Services, Report of the second session of the review mandated under para. 5 of the Annex on Air Transport Services held on 2 Oct. 2007 – Note by the Secretariat, 19.11.2007.

thirty signatories. It eliminates import duties on all civil aircraft, civil aircraft engines and their parts and components, all other parts, components, and sub-assemblies of civil aircraft and all ground flight simulators and their parts and components. It contains disciplines on government-directed procurement of civil aircraft and inducements to purchase, as well as on government financial support for the civil aircraft sector.[100]

16.6 MARITIME TRANSPORT

Maritime transport[101] is a central and one of the oldest services sectors, involving substantial income and supporting trade in other, goods and services, sectors. It includes transport of commodities, final products and individuals. In this sector, all trade takes place according to Mode 1 (cross border). However, in recent years the issues of establishment and of commercial presence are becoming very important in this sector, particularly with regard to the supply of ancillary services and to multimodal transport services. This service depends, to a large extent, on port facilities and services. Most of the ports used for it in the world are owned by governments. This sector is less regulated than air transport, but likewise, it is characterized by many distortive and anti-competitive practices, such as unilateral, bilateral and plurilateral market sharing agreements, as well as subsidies, fiscal incentives, measures relating to cargo reservations, the existence of cartels or vertical and horizontal integration of trans-national corporations.[102] The Uruguay Round participants could not reach an agreement concerning this sector, which involves strategic, commercial and security interests. Therefore, the Annex on Negotiations on Maritime Transport Services, although forming an integral part of GATS, does not include any provisions which enhance trade liberalization in this sector. Rather, it postponed the application of the MFN principle to this sector, including maritime transport, auxiliary services, access to and use of port facilities, until agreement is achieved and if it could not be achieved – until the last report of the Negotiation Group, established for this purpose, was submitted. It was thus determined that before the implementation date, Members may improve, modify or withdraw all or parts of their specific commitments in this sector without offering compensation, notwithstanding the provisions of Article XXI. The working group could not reach an agreement. Therefore, the discussions were postponed to the next Round of discussions.[103] Some of the Members included specific commitments in this sector in their schedules of specific commitments, covering the three main areas in this sector: access to and use of port facilities; auxiliary services; and ocean transport,[104] but most of this sector is excluded from the liberalization disciplines of GATS.

---

100. <www.wto.org>.
101. See detailed analysis of this Annex in GATS commentary, n. 2, 668–682.
102. MTN.GNS/24, Note on the Meeting of 17 – 21 Jul. 1989, 28.8.1989, 26, paras 67–83.
103. S/L/24, WTO Decision on Maritime Transport Services, 3.7.1996.
104. <www.wto.org>.

In recent years, due to globalization, many restrictive practices in this sector ceased to be applied. This reality affects the new proposals discussed for further liberalization of this sector, in the Doha Round, taking place since 2000.[105]

16.7 E-COMMERCE

E-commerce is a relatively new form of trade that developed in recent decades. Its exercise raises difficulties in terms of the ability to follow transactions; the proper way to regulate and tax it; the ways to achieve effective customer protection as well as to ensure its privacy; encouragement of developing countries to engage in e-commerce, considering the lack of due infrastructure in these countries. Electronic supply of services is subject to GATS and may take place in all four Modes of supply. A specific difficulty arises concerning the distinction between Mode 1 (cross border) and Mode 2 (consumption abroad), which is unclear concerning this sector. Measures affecting the electronic transmission of a service are 'measures affecting trade in services' in the sense of Article I of GATS. In principle, GATS is technologically neutral. Nevertheless, an interpretative question arises concerning the application of the MFN and national treatment standards, based on the 'likeness' concept: could a service supplied electronically be considered to be 'like' a service supplied by other means? Since e-commerce further raises questions concerning competition policy, safeguard measures, customs duties, domestic taxation etc., the WTO initiated an overall programme to deal with all the aspects of this subject.[106] The programme identified three categories of e-commerce: ordering goods through the internet and their conventional supply – there was broad agreement that this aspect should be treated under GATT: Supply of services over the internet, for example, telecommunications services, medical services, financial and tourism services – there was broad agreement that this category should be treated under GATS. A dilemma arose concerning the correct framework of treatment to be chosen for the third category: trade in e-products such as books, music, software and video films, which were used to be traded in tangible versions but are now traded in electronic versions as well. Another question is, whether the Annex on Telecommunications Services should apply to access-to-internet services.

---

105. For the proposals see: <www.wto.org>. For further discussion on the relationship between regulation of different forms of public transportation and GATS see: R. Janda, 'GATS Regulatory Disciplines Meet Global Public Goods: the Case of Transportation Services', in A. Mattoo & P. Sauvé (eds), *Domestic Regulation and Service Trade Liberalization*, The World Bank and Oxford University Press (2003), 109–127.

106. S/L/74, WTO Work Programme on Electronic Commerce, progress report to the General Council, 27.7.1999.

16.8 CONCLUSION

This chapter refers to subjects that are still in an earlier stage of development, compared to other subjects dealt with by GATS. For certain matters, it was decided not to apply GATS at all, while for others, interim arrangements that is, plurilateral agreements were achieved. These subjects are expected to be further negotiated in the future, and maybe become integral parts of the multilateral arrangements.

Chapter 17
The Legal Instruments for GATS Enforcement

17.1 INTRODUCTION

GATS is a legal document: an international agreement among countries. It is therefore subject to the rules of public international law. The enforcement of GATS in the international level is exercised by the WTO dispute settlement mechanism. Formally, since GATS is an international agreement, the procedures of dispute settlement may only take place between or among its parties, namely: the Members. According to Article XII of the WTO Agreement, 'Members' may be states or autonomous customs territories. However, in fact these proceedings serve the interests of private parties, such as service suppliers, investors, importers who are active behind the veil.[1]

Pursuant to Article IX:2 of the WTO Agreement, the Ministerial Conference and the General Council of the WTO have the exclusive authority to adopt interpretations of GATS. This authority is exercised on the basis of a recommendation by the Council for Trade in Services. The decision to adopt an interpretation is subject to a three-forth majority of the Members. The general provisions concerning WTO dispute settlement mechanism are contained in the WTO and the Understanding on the Rules Governing the Settlement of Disputes (DSU).

Additional provisions referring to a dispute settlement process, involving GATS, are specified in Part V thereof.

The mechanism dealing with issues between GATS Members basically consists of several stages: consultations, dispute settlement procedure which is completed by a final DSB decision, and enforcement of this decision.

1. M. Molinuevo, 'Can Foreign Investors in Services Benefit from WTO Dispute Settlement? Legal Standing and Remedies in WTO and International Arbitration', *NCCR Working Paper No. 2006/17* (2006), 14–19, <http://papers.ssrn.com>.

17.2 CONSULTATIONS

Article XXII of GATS provides:

Consultations

1. Each Member shall accord sympathetic consideration to, and shall afford adequate opportunity for, consultation regarding such representations as may be made by any other Member with respect to any matter affecting the operation of this Agreement. The Dispute Settlement Understanding (DSU) shall apply to such consultations.
2. The Council for Trade in Services or the Dispute Settlement Body (DSB) may, at the request of a Member, consult with any Member or Members in respect of any matter for which it has not been possible to find a satisfactory solution through consultation under paragraph 1.
3. A Member may not invoke Article XVII, either under this Article or Article XXIII, with respect to a measure of another Member that falls within the scope of an international agreement between them relating to the avoidance of double taxation. In case of disagreement between Members as to whether a measure falls within the scope of such an agreement between them, it shall be open to either Member to bring this matter before the Council for Trade in Services. The Council shall refer the matter to arbitration. The decision of the arbitrator shall be final and binding on the Members.

Article XXII of GATS provides for consultations with respect to 'any matter affecting the operation of this Agreement', and for the application of the DSU[2] to such consultations. Such consultations form a first step, aimed at clarifying the dispute between or among the parties involved, attempting to solve it. Thus, only if this stage fails to solve the dispute may dispute settlement procedures be launched. Consultations embody the diplomatic approach which characterized the entire dispute settlement mechanism of the WTO until 1995.[3]

17.2.1 Bilateral Consultations

GATS Article XXII:1 refers to *bilateral* consultations between or among Members, providing that each Member shall 'accord sympathetic consideration to, and shall afford adequate opportunity for, consultation . . .'. This wording, which is similar to the equivalent GATT Article XXII:1, except for the last sentence, does not seem to create a very strict legal obligation. However, the similar

2. For detailed description see: <www.wto.org>.
3. The change of approach that took place since 1995 is marked, *inter alia*, by the recognition of an automatic right to a panel where consultations fail: R. Worfrum, P. T. Stoll & C. Feinäugle (eds), *WTO – Trade in Services*, Max Planck Commentaries on World Trade Law, Martinus Mijnhoff Publishers, Leiden, Boston (2008) (hereby: GATS commentary), 482.

wording of Article 4.2 DSU was interpreted by the WTO adjudicating bodies as establishing an absolute duty to consult.[4] Needless to say, this formal obligation cannot affect the substance of consultations, although the general *good faith* principle drawn from the Vienna Convention will apply.

A request for consultations may be 'with respect to any matter affecting the operation of this Agreement'. This broad wording is somewhat narrowed, read together with Article 4.4 of the DSU which provides: 'any request for consultations . . . shall give reasons for the request, including identification of the measures at issue and an indication of the legal basis for the complaint'.

According to Article 4.7 of the DSU, a complaining party may ask for a panel 'if the consultations fail to settle a dispute within sixty days after the date of receipt of the request for consultations' or 'during the sixty day period if the consulting parties jointly consider that consultations have failed to settle the dispute'.

17.2.2 Multilateral Consultations

GATS Article XXII:2, the wording of which is similar to that of the equivalent GATT Article XXII:2, foresees as a second stage, a possibility for *multilateral* consultations, lead by the Council for Trade in Services or the DSB, only where it has not been possible to reach a satisfactory solution through bilateral consultations.[5] The DSU does not include a similar option for multilateral consultations. The option for multilateral consultations is not obligatory, and therefore a complaining Member may skip it and ask for the establishment of a panel where consultations under Article XXII:1 failed. However, it is suggested by some commentators that once a panel was established, the option of multilateral consultations will not be available anymore. This interpretation is based on the reading of Article XXII:2 'which only refers to the consultations under Article XXII:1 but not to the panel procedures'.[6] On the other hand it may be assumed that regarding the strong determination of DSU Article 3.7: 'a solution mutually acceptable . . . is clearly to be preferred', and considering the fact that even where a panel was established, this step has been taken after the conduct of bilateral consultations according to Article XXII:1, an interpretation allowing multilateral consultations during the panel process may be acceptable, if it is believed that under the circumstances, it might lead to a mutually acceptable solution.

Since this procedure has no equivalence in the DSU, it is suggested that the Council for Trade in Services or the DSB, whichever is in charge of the multilateral consultations, would determine whether and when the consultations have failed.[7] In the absence of an equivalent provision to that of Article XXII:1, subjecting the

4. WT/DS22/AB/R Brazil – Measures Affecting Desiccated Coconut, adopted on 20.3.1997, para. 28.
5. This stage is regarded as an escalation of the dispute: GATS commentary, n. 3, 486.
6. GATS commentary, n. 3, 486, n. 15.
7. *Ibid.*, 487.

consultations to the procedures of the DSU, this procedure is subject to the full discretion of the Council for Trade in Services or the DSB, whichever is in charge of conducting the consultations.

17.2.3 THE EXCEPTION: DOUBLE TAXATION MEASURES

Measures by Members falling within the scope of an international agreement on the avoidance of double taxation between Members are excluded from this procedure under Article XXII:3. This provision, which has no equivalence in GATT, is meant to prevent benefits accorded by such agreements to be challenged under the MFN and national treatment obligations. This provision is thus recognized as an exception to the scope of application of the DSU by Article 1.2 and Appendix 2 to the DSU.

However, since it is recognized that a disagreement between Members as to whether a measure falls within the scope of such an agreement between them may occur, it is provided that either Member may bring this matter before the Council for Trade in Services. The Council is obliged ('shall') to refer the matter to arbitration. The decision of the arbitrator shall be final and binding on the Members. This provision does not specify the procedure by which the arbitration will take place.

Footnote 11, attached to this provision, adds:

> With respect to agreements on the avoidance of double taxation which exist on the date of entry into force of the WTO Agreement, such a matter may be brought before the Council for Trade in Services only with the consent of both parties to such an agreement.

17.2.4 DISPUTE SETTLEMENT

Under both procedures: bilateral or multilateral consultations, where no result is achieved within a given period,[8] the Members involved are allowed to turn to a dispute settlement procedure,[9] where the dispute is examined first by a Panel of experts, the decision (concerning legal questions) of which may be appealed before the Appellate Body. The decisions of both forums are subject to a reversed consensus authorization by the DSB, combined of the representatives of all Members.

---

8. For bilateral consultations, the relevant period is provided for in Arts 4.7 and 4.8 DSU. Multilateral consultations are not foreseen by the DSU, but these provisions may apply to them, *mutatis mutandis.*
9. Although the procedure established in Art. XXII:2 has no equivalence in the DSU, the DSU rules still apply. This conclusion is drawn from Art. 1.1 DSU and Appendix 1 to the DSU, subjecting GATS to its provision: GATS commentary, n. 3, 483.

The *Decision on Certain Dispute Settlement Procedures for the GATS*[10] provides that panels dealing with complaints concerning trade in services should be composed of panellists who have experience in trade in services and in particular sector-specific expertise.[11]

The legal standing to bring a dispute under GATS stems from GATS Articles XXII and XXIII. These Articles cover disputes arising under GATS and its Annexes, subject to the exceptions specified in Article XXII:3 and in paragraph 4 of the Annex on Air Transport Services.[12]

Article XXIII of GATS provides:

Dispute Settlement and Enforcement

1. If any Member should consider that any other Member fails to carry out its obligations or specific commitments under this Agreement, it may with a view to reaching a mutually satisfactory resolution of the matter have recourse to the DSU.
2. If the DSB considers that the circumstances are serious enough to justify such action, it may authorize a Member or Members to suspend the application to any other Member or Members of obligations and specific commitments in accordance with Article 22 of the DSU.
3. If any Member considers that any benefit it could reasonably have expected to accrue to it under a specific commitment of another Member under Part III of this Agreement is being nullified or impaired as a result of the application of any measure which does not conflict with the provisions of this Agreement, it may have recourse to the DSU. If the measure is determined by the DSB to have nullified or impaired such a benefit, the Member affected shall be entitled to a mutually satisfactory adjustment on the basis of paragraph 2 of Article XXI, which may include the modification or withdrawal of the measure. In the event an agreement cannot be reached between the Members concerned, Article 22 of the DSU shall apply.

17.2.4.1 Dispute Settlement Causes

GATS Article XXIII determines two causes[13] that start the dispute settlement mechanism: violation and non-violation.

---

10. <www.wto.org>.
11. A similar, sector-specific provision is included in the Annex on Financial Services, para. 4. In essence, the roster of GATS experts was integrated into a general list of all potential panelists, indicating their specific expertise: GATS commentary, n. 3, 495.
12. Providing: 'the dispute settlement procedures of the Agreement may be invoked only where obligations or specific commitments have been assumed by the concerned Members and where dispute settlement procedures in bilateral and other multilateral agreements or arrangements have been exhausted'.
13. The equivalent GATT provision, Art. XXVIII, includes another cause: any other situation impairing benefits ('situation complaint'). This cause was never invoked in GATT context, and this is probably the reason for its omission from GATS.

The general structure of causes in GATT and in GATS is similar. In both agreements, for both causes, one should prove

– a certain behaviour by the defendant Member.
– a causal link.
– a result that adversely affects the complaining Member.

17.2.4.1.1 The Violation Cause

The violation cause is applicable where a Member considers that any other Member has failed to carry out its obligations or specific commitments under GATS.

Naturally, a violation cause may be invoked only between or among 'Members', since where non-Members are involved, one may not argue that GATS applies, and was violated. However, this implies a particularly broad scope of application concerning foreign direct investors, since a WTO Member may launch a case for the benefit of any foreign investor in services, independently of its country of origin, as long as the investor comes from a WTO Member.[14] Other interests, such as those of private parties or NGOs might be represented by way of *amicus curiae* briefs.

In principle, the violation cause refers only to claims concerning GATS and the specific commitments taken under it. This conclusion emanates from the words 'this Agreement'. Other claims, concerning other WTO agreements, should be based on causes specified in these agreements. Nevertheless, it should be borne in mind that in *China – Publications and Audiovisual Products* the Appellate Body was ready to accept a defence claim by the respondent, based on GATT Article XX (the equivalent to GATS Article XIV), invoked to rebut a claim concerning the violation of another agreement: China's Accession Protocol.[15]

The procedures to be followed to bring up a violation complaint are specified in the DSU.

It should be noted that Article XXIII:1 stresses that a complaint should be filed 'with a view to reaching a mutually satisfactory resolution of the matter'. Like in other WTO agreements, such a solution is preferred over a dispute settlement procedure, and therefore, due to Article 3.7 DSU the procedure may be stopped at any stage before a Panel decision is given, where a mutually satisfactory solution is found.

17.2.4.1.1.1 Violation: The Burden of Proof

A violation cause must prove three elements:

(1) A 'Member fails to carry out its obligations or specific commitments under this Agreement'.

---

14. Hence, both Arts II (MFN) and XVII (national treatment) refer to 'service supplier of another Member', not necessarily the complaining Member: M. Molinuevo, n. 1, 15, 17.
15. WT/DS363/R, AB/R China – Measures Affecting Trading Rights and Distribution Services for Certain Publications and Audiovisual Entertainment Products, adopted 19.1.2010, Appellate Body report, para. 213.

(2) A causal link.
(3) A result that adversely affects the complaining Member.

17.2.4.1.1.2 Obligations and Commitments

A complaint should refer either to a legal obligation established by the agreement, that is, one of the general obligations such as MFN, transparency, or to a specific commitment, which is not respected by a Member.

17.2.4.1.1.3 The Failure to Comply

The failure by a Member to carry out an obligation or a specific commitment may take the form of an omission (including partial omission) or of an action. Such a failure may be under the responsibility of any government level (see Chapter 4) and due to the broad definition of 'measure' in GATS Article XXVII(a) and in Article 3.3 DSU, it may take different forms.

17.2.4.1.1.4 Comparison to GATT Article XXIII

17.2.4.1.1.4.1 'Directly or Indirectly'

According to GATT Article XXIII the benefit claimed to be nullified or impaired may be accruing to the complaining Member directly *or indirectly*. Allegedly, this is a broader wording than that chosen in GATS Article XXIII, referring to a failure to carry out obligations or specific commitments under GATS. However, since the content of such obligations or commitments is subject to interpretation, the interpretation given to them in a certain case could reach the same result as provided for by GATT language, by recognizing an indirect right accruing to a Member due to these obligations or specific commitments. The determination of the interpretative scope of such rights and obligations is a matter of policy: a broad interpretation would lead to a broad application of GATS provisions, and vice-versa. In certain cases, a broad interpretation may serve the object and purpose of this provision better, although the difference in language between GATT and GATS allegedly implies that this was not the intention of GATS drafters.

17.2.4.1.1.4.2 The Results' Presumption

According to the common interpretative practice concerning this provision in GATT 1947:[16]

> . . . [t]here is normally a presumption that a breach of the rules has an adverse impact on other contracting parties, and in such cases, it is up to the Member State against whom the complaint has been brought to rebut the charge.

Such a presumption does not literally exist in the equivalent GATS violation cause, which is therefore regarded by certain commentators as implying that 'Members are granted the right to bring a dispute regardless of the potential of economic effect that the challenged measure may or may not have on the other Members',

16. L/6175 US – Taxes on Petroleum and Certain Imported Substances, adopted on 17.6.1987, para. 5.1.5.

and 'in this sense, the legal standing to bring a violation complaint on services matters has de jure a broader scope of application than disputes related to goods'.[17] However, this presumption has been codified in Article 3.8 of the DSU, providing:

> In cases where there is an infringement of the obligations assumed under a covered agreement, the action is considered *prima facie* to constitute a case of nullification or impairment. This means that there is normally a presumption that a breach of the rules has an adverse impact on other Members parties to that covered agreement, and in such cases, it shall be up to the Member against whom the complaint has been brought to rebut the charge.

Practically, it has never been possible to rebut this presumption. It is therefore suggested that this is the reason for the omission, in GATS provision, of the requirements that violation depends on proving nullification or impairment of a benefit or the impeding of a treaty objective.[18]

This presumption affects the burden of proof concerning the causal link between the behaviour of the defendant Member and the adverse effect caused to the complaining Member, required by Article XXIII of GATS. Without the presumption, the proof of the causal link would be more difficult. The application of this presumption in GATT context was examined in *EC – Bananas III*, as the European Communities attempted to rebut the presumption of nullification or impairment with respect to the Panel's findings of violations of GATT 1994 on the basis that the United States has never exported a single banana to the European Communities, and therefore could not possibly suffer any trade damage. On this basis, the Panel extended the scope of the presumption in Article 3.8 of the DSU to claims made under GATS as well as to claims made by the Complaining Parties other than the United States, and the Appellate Body determined that the Panel erred doing so.[19] This decision reflects a cautious approach, not to extend the effect of this presumption beyond necessary, and may be justified on the grounds that in the absence of 'nullification or impairment' language in GATS Article XXIII:1, 'DSU Article 3.8 is probably of greater relevance for trade in goods than for trade in services'.[20] Such an approach diminishes the effect of the presumption on the respondent, by diminishing the scope of matters for which the burden of proof is transferred to it due to the presumption, and there is no definite indication that it should be preferred.

17.2.4.1.1.4.3 'Prima Facie' Case and the Role of the Dispute Settlement Tribunals

In *US – Gambling*, Antigua challenged United States' 'total prohibition' of cross-border supply of gambling and betting services, caused by some State laws it

17. M. Molinuevo, n. 1, 14.
18. GATS commentary, n. 3, 494.
19. WT/DS27/AB/R *EC- Bananas III*, n. 18, Appellate Body report, para. 250.
20. W. Zdouc, 'WTO Dispute Settlement Practice Relating to the GATS', *Journal of International Economic Law* (1999): 295, 298.

mentioned, without specifying the exact link between the State law challenged and the obligation alleged to be infringed. The Panel assumed an active role by going over these laws, trying to establish the necessary link, rather than rejecting Antigua's complaint for not establishing a prima facie case. This approach was later criticized by the Appellate Body.[21] It was also criticized by commentators, asking whether this approach may be justified where a developing country is involved, to ensure equality of arms, or rather when a substantive lacuna is found in the Statement of claim, considering the fact that the 'prima facie raff is very low', or otherwise, should it be considered a violation of Article 11 DSU.[22] These questions are yet unresolved.

17.2.4.1.1.5 The Remedies

According to GATS Article XXIII:2, where violation is established, and the DSB considers that the circumstances are serious enough to justify such action, it may allow for the suspension of obligations and specific commitments by the complaining Member, towards the defendant Member, in accordance with Article 22 of the DSU, that sets the rules for compensation and suspension of obligations for all WTO agreements.[23]

Article XXIII:2 of GATS recalls the language of Article XXIII:2 of GATT.

17.2.4.1.1.5.1 'Circumstances Serious Enough'

Suspension of obligations and specific commitments according to both GATT and GATS is subject to a DSB assessment, that the circumstances are serious enough to justify such action. This condition should balance between the possibility given to an affected Member to ask for a remedy, on the one hand, and the prevention of abuse of this mechanism, on the other hand. The discretion given to the DSB is broad. According to some commentators it includes 'not just the object and the gravity of the violation, but also the potentially negative effects of the suspension

21. WT/DS285/R, AB/R United States – Measures Affecting the Cross-Border Supply of Gambling and Betting Services, adopted on 22.5.2007, Appellate Body report, paras 147–148, 151–152.
22. D. Irwin, J. H. H. Weiler, 'Measures Affecting the Cross Border Supply of Gambling and Betting Services', *7 World Trade Review* (2008): 71, 84.
23. This provision allows temporary compensation and suspension of obligations (para. 1) while negotiations between the parties involved take place, with a view to developing mutually acceptable compensation. If no satisfactory compensation has been agreed within twenty days after the date of expiry of the reasonable period of time, any party having invoked the dispute settlement procedures may request authorization from the DSB to suspend the application to the Member concerned of concessions or other obligations under the covered agreements (para. 2). This provision further specifies the considerations that should lead the DSB in its decision, which concessions or other obligations should be suspended (paras 3–5), as well as the time-frame for such measures (paras 6, 8). An interim arbitration process may take place where a Member objects to the level of suspension, or claims that the principles and procedures set forth by para. 3 were not followed, where a complaining party has requested authorization to suspend concessions, or other obligations, pursuant to para. 3(b) or (c) (paras 6, 7). These provisions may be invoked in respect of measures affecting their observance, taken by regional or local governments or authorities within the territory of a Member (para. 9).

on trade relations between the Members and on services trade in general'.[24] The question whether, and to what extent, broader considerations concerning general trade policy and the global effect of each decision should be taken into account in this context, remains open. In both agreements, the language leaves this question entirely to the discretion of the DSB, which should, undoubtedly, take into account the considerations specified in Chapter 3.

The DSB has to apply both quantitative and qualitative considerations to reach this conclusion, on a case-by-case basis. It seems clear, that the damage caused to the complaining Member should be substantial and not negligible. This conclusion is supported by Article 22.4 DSU, providing that the complaining Member may be authorized to suspend concessions up to a level 'equivalent to the level of nullification or impairment'. This logic may thus prevent a Member from bringing a dispute in favour of a foreign commercial presence of another Member in its territory, if it is unable to prove that any damage or adverse effect was suffered by it. The decisive legal test would be effectiveness of this sanction, as provided for in Article 22.3(c) DSU.[25] It is further clear that the will to recover the situation would be a decisive consideration.

In this context it should be noted, that Article 22.3 of the DSU, allowing for the suspension of concessions as a sanction to non-compliance, is to be imposed primarily 'with respect to the same sector' where non-compliance occurred. In GATS context, it may therefore theoretically apply to service suppliers of the defendant country established in the complaining country as commercial presence. In such cases, it may turn out that these same foreign investors aided up in bringing the claim. The result may also have adverse effects on domestic employees of this foreign commercial presence. These considerations should be taken into account in the exercise of this provision.[26]

Some commentators are of the opinion that despite all these drawbacks, 'Article 22.6 DSU regulates the power of the DSB to authorize the suspensions of concessions under GATT and GATS in a manner which gives the complaining Member a semi-automatic right to counter-measures'.[27]

17.2.4.1.1.5.2 'Any Member or Members'

In GATS, like in GATT, Article XXIII:2 explicitly specifies, that such suspension could apply to any Member or Members. This provision stresses that the application of remedies is country-specific and is not subject to the MFN principle. It is subject to the proof of responsibility of a certain Member to the adverse effect caused to another Member due to its behaviour, and to the establishment of a causal link between this behaviour and the result.

---

24. GATS commentary, n. 3, 496.
25. M. Molinuevo, n. 1, 26.
26. *Ibid.*, 26.
27. GATS commentary, n. 3, 497. It is argued that words 'shall' and 'grant' in this provision are interpreted as obligatory, thus turning the DSB authorization into a formal act, without discretion.

17.2.4.1.1.5.3 No Authority for Complete Abolishment of a Measure

In GATS, like in GATT, the remedy allowed is 'suspension' of benefits or concessions, but not a complete abolishment thereof. This is part of the general WTO approach that remedies should be temporary, and in the long run the violating Member should be encouraged to bring its practices into conformity with the provisions of the relevant agreement. However, no time frame is determined, in order to allow full flexibility and discretion to the DSB, on a case-by-case basis.[28] Suspension of benefits is regarded as a last resort, and therefore should be considered very cautiously.[29]

17.2.4.1.1.5.4 Cross-Retaliation

Suspension of obligations may refer to trade flows under the same agreement ('standard retaliation measures'). Cross-retaliation measures are measures referring to trade concessions under *other* WTO agreements. Such measures might be allowed when it is not 'practicable' or 'effective' for a Member to impose penalties under violated agreement. In 2000, a right for such cross-retaliation measures was accorded to Ecuador in the *EC – Bananas III* case. Ecuador was allowed to suspend some of its obligations under the TRIPs involving patents and copyrights, but finally chose not to avail itself of these rights.[30] In the *US – Gambling* case, Antigua was allowed by the arbitrator to ask the DSB for cross-retaliation rights in the field of intellectual property rights, claiming that due to disproportion of economic size between the parties, retaliation against US exports would have no impact, while interruption of intellectual property right might create a strong lobby by affected industries to press the United States to abide by the DSB decision.[31]

17.2.4.1.1.6 Violation Complaints under GATS

By now,[32] most of the complaints filed under GATS were violation complaints. This tendency mirrors GATT 1947 history. The facts of these complaints will be shortly presented below:

Canada – Certain Measures Concerning Periodicals[33] – on 11.3.1996, the United States requested for consultations with Canada. The United States claimed for discriminating taxation imposed by Canada on advertisements published in periodicals originating in the United States, compared to advertisements in like

28. Article 22.8 DSU also does not specify any time frame for this procedure, indicating only:

> the suspension of concessions or other obligations shall be temporary and shall only be applied until such time as the measure found to be inconsistent with a covered agreement has been removed, or the Member that must implement recommendations or rulings provides a solution to nullification or impairment of benefits, or a mutually satisfactory solution is reached.

29. For GATT 1947 interpretation in this context see: *Analytical Index – Guide to GATT Law and Practice*, the WTO, Geneva (1995), 692–700.
30. G. Hufbauer & S. Stephenson, 'Services Trade: Past Liberalization and Future Challenges', *10 Journal of International Economic Law*, 605, 616–617.
31. <www.wto.org>.
32. This review is based on information published in <www.wto.org.>
33. WT/DS31/R, AB/R Canada – Certain Measures Concerning Periodicals, adopted on 30.7.1997.

periodicals originating in Canada. The United States' complaint concentrated on violation of GATT 1994, but one of Canada's defence claim was that it did not take on any commitment concerning advertising services under GATS, and restrictions on advertising (services) could not be considered as a violation of GATT. This claim was rejected by the WTO adjudicating bodies in a decision adopted on 30.7.1997, on the grounds of possible overlap between GATT 1994 and GATS.

EC – Regime for the Importation, Sale and Distribution of Bananas[34] – on 28.9.1995, Guatemala, Honduras, Mexico and the United States requested for consultations with the EC concerning the European Communities' system of Bananas' import licenses allocation. Ecuador joined this complaint at a later stage. In a Panel and Appellate Body decisions adopted on 25.9.1997, this system was found to violate GATS Articles II and XVII, as well as other WTO agreements' provisions, since an allocation of a substantial part of available import licenses for bananas to EC and ACP countries was proved.

US – The Cuban Liberty and Democratic Solidarity Act[35] – on 3.5.1996, the EC requested for consultations with the Unietd States due to a US Congress Act that imposed trade sanctions against Cuba, but also against companies or individuals from states who traded with Cuba. The sanctions included possible refusal of visas and the exclusion (or threat thereof) from United States' territory of persons that did business with Cuba. These measures were claimed to violate of Articles I, III, XI, XVI and XVII of GATS, the Annex on Movement of Natural Persons Supplying Services, and some GATT provisions. A Panel was established but the parties finally reached a mutually agreed solution.

Japan – Measures Affecting Distribution Services[36] – on 13.6.1996, the United States filed a complaint against Japan's measures affecting distribution services through the operation of Large Scale Retail Store Law that regulated the floor space, business hours and holidays of supermarkets and department stores. The United States claimed, *inter alia*, violation of Articles III and XVI of GATS. Later, the United States extended its complaint to additional measures affecting distribution services that concerned enterprise reform, commerce integration, small and medium enterprises and retailers and the adjustment of retail business. It also extended its claims to violation of GATS Articles VI and XVII. Finally, the United States did not pursue its GATS case against Japan and concentrated on a GATT violation and non-violation case: Japan – Measures Affecting Consumer Photographic Films and Paper,[37] where all its complaints were rejected by the Panel, without appeal.

---

34. WT/DS27/AB/R, n. 18. Another similar complaint was later filed by Panama (WT/DS105 European Communities – regime for the Importation, Sale and Distribution of Bananas) who could not join the original complaint since its accession process to the WTO was not completed at the time: W. Zdouc, n. 20, 300.
35. WT/DS38.
36. WT/DS45.
37. WT/DS44/R, adopted on 22.4.1998.

Belgium – Measures Affecting Commercial Telephone Directory Services[38] – on 2.5.1997, the Unietd States requested for consultations with Belgium in respect of measures taken by Belgium, who imposed conditions for obtaining licenses to publish commercial telephone directories, and the regulations, acts, policies and practices of the national Belgian telephone company, Belgacom N.V., with respect to telephone directory services. The United States claimed *inter alia* violation of GATS Articles II, VI, VIII and XVII. Finally, no Panel was established.

Canada – Measures Affecting Film Distribution Services[39] – on 20.1.1998, the EC initiated consultations in respect of Canadian measures affecting film distribution services, alleged to be violating Articles II and III of GATS. Finally, no Panel was established.

Canada – Certain Automotive Industry Measures[40] – on 3.7.1998, Japan requested for consultations with Canada, claiming that under Canadian law only a limited number of motor vehicle manufacturers are eligible to import vehicles into Canada duty-free and to distribute the vehicles in Canada at the wholesale and retail distribution levels. Japan claimed that the measures so providing were inconsistent *inter alia* with GATS Articles II, VI and XVII. The Canadian system was further the subject of complaint by the EC, and the two complaints were examined together. The Panel found that the Canadian measures violated, *inter alia*, Articles II and XVII of GATS. The Appellate Body considered that the Panel failed to examine whether the measure at issue affected trade in services as required under Article I:1 of GATS and reversed the Panel's conclusion that the import duty exemption was inconsistent with Article II:1 of GATS. The DSB adopted the reports on 19.6.2000.

Mexico – Measures Affecting Telecommunications Services[41] – on 17.8.2000, the United States requested for consultations with Mexico, claiming that since the entry into force of GATS, Mexico has adopted or maintained anti-competitive and discriminatory regulatory measures, tolerated certain privately-established market access barriers, and failed to take needed regulatory action in Mexico's basic and value-added telecommunications sectors. The United States considered that the alleged action and inaction on the part of Mexico may be inconsistent with Mexico's GATS commitments and obligations, including Articles VI, XVI, and XVII; Mexico's additional commitments under Article XVIII as set forth in the Reference Paper inscribed in Mexico's schedule of specific commitments; and GATS Annex on Telecommunications.

The Panel report ruled that Mexico violated its commitments according to Articles 1.1 and 2.2(b) of the Reference Paper and to Article 5(a) and (b) of GATS Annex on Telecommunications.

38. WT/DS80.
39. WT/DS117.
40. WT/DS139,142/R, AB/R adopted on 19.6.2000.
41. WT/DS204/R, adopted on 1.6.2004.

US – Measures Affecting the Cross-Border Supply of Gambling and Betting Services[42] – on 21.3.2003, Antigua and Barbados requested for consultations with the United States regarding measures applied by central, regional and local authorities in the United States which affect the cross-border supply of gambling and betting services. Antigua and Barbuda considered that the cumulative impact of the United States measures is to prevent the supply of gambling and betting services from another WTO Member to the United States on a cross-border basis. According to Antigua and Barbuda, the measures at issue might have been inconsistent with the United States obligations under GATS, and in particular Articles II, VI, VIII, XI, XVI and XVII thereof, and the United States' schedule of specific commitments annexed to GATS.

The United States was found to violate Article XVI:1,2 of GATS, by the Panel and Appellate Body reports adopted on 22.5.2007.

China – Value-Added Tax on Integrated Circuits[43] – on 18.3.2004, the United States requested for consultations with China concerning China's preferential value added tax (VAT) for domestically produced or designed integrated circuits, gained by a partial tax refund, to which only domestic enterprises producing integrated circuits, and integrated circuits domestically designed, are entitled. The United States considered these measures to violate, *inter alia*, Article XVII of GATS. Later on, the EC, Japan, Mexico and the separate customs territories of Taiwan, Penghu, Kinmen and Matsu requested to join the consultation. This dispute was solved by mutual agreement.

China – Measures Affecting Trading Rights and Distribution Services for Certain Publications and Audiovisual Entertainment Products[44] – on 10.4.2007, the United States requested for consultations with China concerning certain measures that reserves trading rights with respect to imported films for theatrical release, audiovisual home entertainment products (e.g., video cassettes and DVDs), sound recordings and publications (e.g., books, magazines, newspapers and electronic publications) to certain Chinese enterprises, and measures restricting market access for, or discriminate against, foreign suppliers of distribution services for publications and foreign suppliers of audiovisual services (including distribution services) for audiovisual home entertainment products. China was found to violate, *inter alia*, GATS Articles XVI and XVII, by the Panel and Appellate Body reports adopted on 19.1.2010.

China – Measures Affecting Financial Information Services and Foreign Financial Information Suppliers[45] – on 20.6.2008, Canada requested for consultations with China with respect to measures affecting financial information services and foreign financial information services suppliers in China. According to Canada, a dozen legal and administrative measures in China required foreign financial information suppliers to supply their services, and service consumers

42. WT/DS285/AB/R, n. 21.
43. WT/DS309.
44. WT/DS363/R, AB/R, adopted on 19.1.2010.
45. WT/DS378.

to acquire their services, through an entity designated by Xinhua News Agency. In addition, Canada claimed that China prevents foreign financial information service suppliers from establishing any commercial presence in China, other than limited representative offices. Canada considered this Chinese practices violate Articles XVI, XVII and XVIII of GATS, the horizontal standstill commitment contained in China's schedule of specific commitments and China's Accession Protocol. Later, the United States made a request to join the consultations. This dispute was finally solved by mutual agreement.

17.2.4.1.2 Non-violation

The non-violation cause, which seeks to protect the overall balance of concessions under GATS, is more general than the violation cause. This cause, provided for by Article XXIII:3, concentrates on the impediment of parties' expectations. It is concerned with nullification or impairment of reasonably expected benefits arising from specific commitments undertaken by the Members, as a result of the application of any measure which does not conflict with the provisions of GATS.[46] Such specific commitments may be taken regarding national treatment or market access, or may be additional commitments (see Chapter 7).

This cause was first developed under GATT 1947 'in response to the widely felt need for some form of "equity law jurisdiction" as a means of allowing for multilateral decision-making in times of unforeseen crisis'.[47] The language of GATS Article XXIII:3 is based on the relevant GATT 1947 jurisprudence. This source of interpretation continues to be decisive, since no non-violation complaint has been yet decided under GATS. In GATT 1994 case *Japan-Films* the Panel made a general statement, holding that:

> the non-violation nullification or impairment remedy should be approached with caution and treated as an exceptional concept. The reason for this caution is straightforward. Members negotiate the rules that they agree to follow and only exceptionally would expect to be challenged for actions not in contravention of those rules.[48]

However, the scope of this cause under GATS seems to be narrower than under GATT, where a non-violation complaint may be invoked where a Member considers that any benefit accruing to it directly or indirectly under the agreement is nullified or impaired.[49] This cautious approach seems to be desirable in view of the

46. In the context of the equivalent GATT Art. XXIII:1(b) this purpose was explained by the Panel in WT/DS44/R Japan – Measures Affecting Consumer Photographic Film and Paper, adopted on 22.4.1998, para. 1050.
47. GATS commentary, n. 3, 498.
48. WT/DS44/R *Japan – Film*, n. 37, para. 10.36. This view was supported by the Appellate Body in WT/DS135/AB/R European Communities – Measures Affecting Asbestos and Asbestos-Containing Products, adopted on 5.4.2001, para. 186.
49. GATT Art. XXIII. Under GATT the 'benefits accruing have traditionally been the reasonable expectations arising from tariff concessions, although the text of GATT Art. XXIII and DSU

large potential scope of measures that may upset the competitive relationship between domestic and like foreign services or service suppliers, as well as due to the ambiguity of the concepts involved, for example, national treatment, market access, 'likeness', which are not defined in the agreement and maybe would be better developed through the violation cause first.[50]

17.2.4.1.2.1 The Burden of Proof for the Non-violation Cause

In principle, Article 26.1(a) of the DSU and GATT jurisprudence[51] confirm that a non-violation complaint is an exceptional remedy for which the complaining party must provide a more detailed justification in support of its complaint. In general, four conditions should be established:

(1) The specific commitments of a Member give rise to benefits and concessions reasonably anticipated at the time when the relevant specific commitment was negotiated.
(2) A measure imputable to a government exists, which is not, in itself, contrary to the agreement.
(3) Nullification or impairment: the competitive relationship between foreign and like domestic services and service suppliers are upset as a result of this measure.
(4) This result was not reasonably anticipated at the time when the relevant specific commitment was negotiated.

17.2.4.1.2.2 Benefit and Concession

The non-violation cause is based on an expectation that a benefit or a concession will accrue. The term 'benefit' in this context 'does not refer to any legal right or interest,[52] but to the *improved competitive opportunities* which the complainant may legitimately expect to result from the concessions made at the end of the multilateral round of trade negotiations'.[53] In GATT case, *EC – Asbestos*, the Appellate Body rejected an EC argument that it is possible to have 'legitimate expectations' only regarding a purely 'commercial measure'. Based on the words '*any* measure', which also appear in GATS Article, the Appellate Body concluded: '[t]he use of the word "any" suggests that measures of all types may give rise to

---

Art. 26.1 in theory also permit redress against governmental measures that impede the attainment of any objective of any WTO agreement': W. Zdouc, n. 20, 303 (n. 15). It is further noted by Zdouc, that the omission of the word 'indirectly' in GATS provision may imply for a narrower scope than the equivalent GATT provision, although this option was hardly ever used in GATT context.

50. W. Zdouc, n. 20, 304.
51. WT/DS44/R *Japan – Film*, n. 37, paras 10.32, 10.41, WT/DS135/R *EC – Asbestos*, n. 49, para. 8.283.
52. In WT/DS44/R *Japan – Film*, n. 37, Panel report, para. 10.49, the Panel rejected Japan's argument that a 'measure' must provide a benefit or impose a legally binding obligation, contending that a 'measure' can even be a non-binding action that 'can potentially have adverse effect s on competitive conditions of market access'.
53. GATS commentary, n. 3, 499.

such a cause of action. The text does not distinguish between, or exclude, certain types of measure'.[54]

In GATT case *Japan – Film*[55] the Panel determined that the non-violation remedy is limited to measures that are currently being applied, based on the present tense language of this provision.

17.2.4.1.2.2.1 The Source of Benefit or Concession

The source of expected benefit or concession according to GATS is the specific commitments. In this sense this is a stricter requirement than that imposed on violation complainants. In GATT this source is more widely determined, as 'any objective of the Agreement'.[56] Thus, in GATS, the scope of this cause was diminished, and made more specific, and as a result – more difficult to prove. The more specific GATS language is meant to prevent unfocused, general claims that could, where abused, impede its purposes, creating unnecessary barriers to trade. Specific commitments which could be nullified or impaired may refer to market access, national treatment, or additional commitments under Articles XVI, XVII and XVIII, respectively.

17.2.4.1.2.3 The Cause of Adverse Effect: 'Application of any Measure'

'Application'

This expression was interpreted, in GATT context, as allegedly requiring an *active* behaviour by a government, such as interference in the market by the application of subsidies, taxes or barriers to trade, not only a *passive* agreement to the occurrence of certain circumstances, such as practical deviation from the rules of competition or their non-enforcement.[57] The same interpretative dilemma would rise in GATS context: should the non-violation cause be interpreted as referring to passive behaviour of governments as an 'application of any measure', or should this expression be interpreted as referring only to active behaviour? It seems that the 'ordinary meaning' of the word 'application' would support the latter possibility for GATS, similarly to the equivalent GATT provision. But another opinion supports the wider interpretation that recognizes passive behaviour as 'application of any measure'.[58] The choice made is a matter of policy, because it would naturally affect the scope of the non-violation cause. It should be remembered, that the violation cause applies only to measures already regulated by the general provisions of GATS or the schedules of specific commitments attached to it. Trade restrictions which are

54. WT/DS135/AB/R, n. 48, para. 188.
55. WT/DS44/R, n. 37, Panel report, para. 10.57.
56. Nevertheless, in practice the Panel in WT/DS44/R, *Japan – Film*, n. 37, para. 10.66, analyzing GATT cases, came to the conclusion that '[t]he conclusion that benefits accruing from concessions granted during successive rounds of tariff negotiations may separately give rise to reasonable expectations of improved market access is consistent with the past panel reports'.
57. B. M. Hoeckman & P. C. Mavroidis, 'Competition, Competition Policy and the GATT', *17 The World Economy* (1994): 21, 141.
58. B. M. Hoeckman & P. C. Mavroidis, n. 57, 141.

not yet covered by these legal instruments may be only treated according to the non-violation cause. A narrow interpretation, excluding passive behaviour of governments, effectively restricting trade flows, from the scope of this provision would totally prevent any possibility to prevent this behaviour according to GATS, thus undermining its purpose, to some extent. Even if this wider interpretation is accepted, it will not cover any extra-territorial effect of the 'measure', or any passive behaviour involved, but only practices preventing market access opportunities in the domestic market.[59]

'Any measure'

According to the provisions defining GATS scope of application a measure imputable to a government may refer to all government levels, as well as to private entities exercising governmental authorities (see Chapter 4). The scope of interpretation of this expression affects the scope of application of the non-violation cause: the broader interpretation given to it – a broader scope of application will follow. However, the difficulty in proving the other elements of this cause may balance this result.

'Which does not conflict with the provisions of this Agreement'

It should be established that the measure at stake does not, in itself, violate the provisions of GATS or the specific commitments undertaken under it, otherwise a violation complaint may be filed. Nevertheless, it should be proved that the measure at stake adversely affects the competitive opportunities in the market for services/service suppliers from other Members.

17.2.4.1.2.4 Nullification or Impairment

Nullification or impairment are proved where it is established that the competitive relationship between foreign and like domestic services and service suppliers are upset as a result of this measure.

17.2.4.1.2.4.1 The Causal Link

The causal link should establish a connection between the measure undertaken by a Member and its effect on competitive relationship between like foreign and domestic service suppliers.

In the context of the equivalent GATT provision it was determined by a GATT 1947 case:

> Impairment and nullification in the sense of Article XXIII does not arise merely because of the existence of any measure; the nullification or impairment must relate to benefits accruing to the contracting party 'under the General Agreement'.[60]

59. *Ibid.*, 141.
60. L/1923 Uruguayan Recourse to Art. XXIII adopted on 16.11.1962, 11S/95, para. 14.

This bond is explicitly recognized as necessary by the language of Article XXIII:3 of GATS, providing:

> any benefit it could reasonably have expected to accrue . . . is being nullified or impaired *as a result* of the application of any measure . . . [Emphasis added].

While a measure does not have to be the only reason for nullification or impairment, it has to have more than a *de minimis* effect.[61]

In GATT case *Japan – Film*, the Panel divided 'causality' into four separate issues:

- *The degree of causation* – whether the measure made more than a *de minimis* contribution to nullification or impairment.
- *Origin-neutrality of the measure at issue* – where the measure is origin-neutral (de facto discrimination), the complaining Member has to make a detailed showing of any claimed disproportionate impact on imports resulting from that measure.
- *The relevance of intent with respect to causality* – Article XXIII:1(b) does not require a proof of intent, only a proof of the impact of the measure, that is, whether it upset competitive relationships. However, in that case the Panel noted that if a measure which appears, on its face, to be origin-neutral is shown to have been intended to restrict imports, it may help to establish the causal link.
- *The extent to which measures may be considered collectively in an analysis of causation* – the Panel said:

  > It is not without logic that a measure, when analysed in isolation, may only have very limited impact on the competitive conditions in a market, but may have a more significant impact on such conditions when seen in the context of – in combination with – a larger set of measures. Notwithstanding the logic of this theoretical argument, however, we are sensitive to the fact that the technique of engaging in a combined assessment of measures so as to determine causation is subject to potential abuse and therefore must be approached with caution and circumscribed as necessary.[62]

The 'results' presumption' developed concerning the violation cause in GATT context (see paragraph 17.2.4.1.1.4.2), differentiates, in GATT context, between the violation and non-violation causes, applying only to the former.[63] If adopted in GATS context, (due to Article 3.8 DSU) an interpretative question would arise, whether it may apply only to violation or also to non-violation, since Article 3.8

61. GATS commentary, n. 3, 500.
62. WT/DS44/R, n. 37, Panel report, paras 10.83-10.88.
63. Article 5 of the Annex: Agreed Description of the Customary Practice of the GATT in the Field of Dispute Settlement (Art. XXIII:2), specifically refers to 'infringement of obligations assumed under the General Agreement'. This Annex is annexed to the Understanding on Notification, Consultation, Dispute Settlement and Surveillance of 28 Nov. 1979, 26S/210. See full text in GATT Analytical Index, n. 29, 634–636.

DSU refers to 'infringement of obligations', while the non-violation cause concentrates on benefits reasonably expected to accrue to a Member. If this presumption will not be applied to the non-violation cause under GATS, this interpretation would further weaken the non-violation cause, because without the presumption the burden of proof for the complaining party would be more difficult.

17.2.4.1.2.4.2 The Comparison between 'Like' Foreign and Domestic Suppliers

The notion of 'likeness' and 'competitive relationship' would have to be given meaning on a case-by-case basis.

17.2.4.1.2.4.3 The Proof of Adverse Effect

In the context of GATT 1947, it was determined that it is unnecessary to present statistical data concerning the trade flows between the Members involved in a non-violation case in order to prove the damage caused to the complaining party.[64] Thus, for example, in *EEC – Canned Peaches*,[65] it was determined that the governmental aids given to domestic production undermined the cost and price advantages of the competing imported products, thus undermining their competitive advantage. The subject of statistical data necessity did not arise yet in GATS context, but due to statistical difficulties to achieve such data it seems that a practical approach would adopt this policy in GATS context as well.

17.2.4.1.2.4.4 This Result Was Not Reasonably Anticipated at the Time When the Relevant Specific Commitment Was Negotiated

In the context of GATT 1947, most of the disputes based on the non-violation cause referred to nullification or impairment of customs concessions by subsidies that the complaining party could not have reasonably expected during the negotiations on tariff bindings.[66] It was determined by the WTO adjudicating bodies, that lacking evidence to the contrary, it may be assumed that a Member negotiating with another Member on concessions according to Article II of GATT has a reasonable expectation that the value of concessions accorded to it following this negotiations will not be nullified or impaired by its trade partner by subsidizing domestic production.[67] However, commentators believe that these are not the only kind of cases that could be covered by this cause.[68] Thus, for example, in GATT 1994 case *EC-Asbestos*, the Panel noted that the increasing evidence about the hazardous nature of asbestos and the growing number and Community decisions concerning its use 'could not do other than create *climate* which should have led Canada to anticipate a change in the attitude of the importing countries, especially

64. GATT Analytical Index, n. 29, 665–666.
65. L/5778 EEC – Production Aids Granted on Canned Peaches, Canned Pears, Canned Fruit Cocktail and Dried Grapes, 1985 (unadopted), paras 55, 80.
66. B. M. Hoeckman & P. C. Mavroidis, n. 57, 140.
67. L/334 The Working Party on 'Other Barriers to Trade', adopted on 3.3.1955, 3S/222, 224, para. 13.
68. B. M. Hoeckman & P. C. Mavroidis, n. 57, 140.

in view of the long-established trend towards ever tighter restrictions on the use of asbestos'.[69] Nevertheless, it seems that due to the difficulties to prove this cause, it is commonly used in factual cases, where there are available numerical data (like the rate of customs duty or of subsidization) that makes the proof of damage, and maybe of the causal link, easier.

In GATT context, it was established, that all measures of a party making the relevant commitment, that could have been reasonably anticipated, should be taken into account.[70] The difficulty may arise concerning measures, the effects of which are not straightforward and/or difficult to assess.

17.2.4.1.2.4.5 Intentions and Expectations

Unlike the equivalent GATS cause, GATT does not explicitly refer to the proof of intentions, expectations or any other mental motives. Therefore, allegedly the burden of proof in GATT is easier compared to GATS. But a brief look at the history of the interpretation of this GATT provision shows, that its common interpretation 'imported' these mental elements into it.

Thus, for example, GATT 1947 Panel report on *Japan – Agricultural Products*[71] relied, in order to prove this element, on the Council minutes, on Japan's claims concerning the customary behaviour in other countries, on the status of international negotiations and on the unique characteristics of the Japanese agriculture. In the report of the Working Group concerning 'The Australian Subsidy on Ammonium Sulphate' from 1950[72] the working group relied on the resemblance between two fertilizers that were subsidized during the war, while after the war the subsidy for one of them was stopped, to determine that it was reasonable to expect that after the war the subsidy for both of them will stop. The definition of reasonable expectation is an interpretative decision, based on the will to *preserve the balance of concessions* achieved by the agreement.[73] The Members may reasonably expect that this balance of concessions will not be nullified or impaired in the absence of opposite evidence. The recognition of the legitimacy of such expectation is the basis for recognizing the affected Member's right to request for permission to suspend the application of concessions or other obligations under the agreement.[74]

'Reasonable expectations' are usually interpreted on a case-by-case basis.[75] For this purpose, the date of application of the measure involved is relevant: if it

69. WT/DS135/R, n. 48, paras 8.297.
70. WT/DS44/R, *Japan – Film*, n. 37, para. 10.61.
71. L/6253 Japan – Restrictions on Imports of Certain Agricultural Products, adopted on 22.3.1988, 35S/163, 241.
72. GATT/CP.4/39, adopted on 3.4.1950, 11/188, 193–194, para. 12. See also the case of Treatment by Germany of Imported Sardines (1952), G/2, adopted on 31.10.1952, 1S/53, 58, para. 16.
73. L/6627 EEC – Payments and Subsidies Paid to Processors of Oilseeds and Related Animal-Feed proteins, adopted on 25.1.1990, 37S/86, 126–127, para. 144.
74. L/6627 *EEC – Oilseeds*, n. 73, para. 148.
75. See, for example, L/6631 US – restrictions on the Importation of Sugar and Sugar-Containing Products Applied Under the 1955 Waiver and Under the Headnote to the Schedule of Tariff Concessions, adopted on 7.11.1990, 37S/228, para. 5.21.

was applied *before* the agreement was signed, it is assumed that the complaining Member should have been aware of it and should have taken it into consideration in the negotiations, and vice versa.[76]

A Policy question to be asked is: should any general rules be determined in this context, or should it be decided on a case-by-case basis?

In GATT context, it was suggested to adopt the rule according to which, in the lack of evidence proving otherwise, presented by the respondent, the complaining party would be considered to have established its reasonable expectancy.[77]

Theoretically, this approach may be adopted for the interpretation of Article XXIII of GATS, too. However, for both agreements, it seems a far-reaching interpretation, transferring the burden of proof from the complaining party to the respondent, to prove that during the negotiations on the respective agreement the complaining party should have had reasons to believe that the agreed level of competitive conditions would escalate in the future. It seems that this was not the drafters' intention, and it is hardly supported by the language of the respective GATT and GATS provisions. In addition, this interpretation does not comply with the purpose of the two agreements, to enhance global services trade liberalization: it allegedly makes it easier for complaining parties to abuse this procedure, thus undermining trade liberalization.

In light of this interpretative experience, the drafting of Article XXIII:3 does not seem more elaborated than the equivalent GATT provision anymore. On the contrary, it seems more clear and transparent because it explicitly refers to the mental aspects that should be proved, although this clearer phrasing does not make the necessary proof easier.

17.2.4.1.3 The Remedies

The relevant instructions concerning remedies in GATS are contained in Article XXIII:3. While there is no obligation to withdraw a measure that causes nullification or impairment, the Member adversely affected by it is entitled to mutually satisfactory adjustment, subject to Article 26.1(b)–(c) DSU.

In GATT, the possible remedies in a non-violation case are similar to the remedies offered for a violation case: the DSB is entitled to allow the complaining Member to suspend the concessions or obligations according to the agreement where the circumstances are serious enough to justify this remedy.

Unlike it, in GATS, the obtainment of remedies depends on a two-stage process: in the first stage, the complaining party is only entitled to start a negotiations procedure for compensation according to Article XXI (see Chapter 15). No time frame is determined for this stage. However, it is subject to Articles 21.3 and 22 DSU, according to which it has to enter the negotiations at the latest on the expiry of reasonable period of time as determined pursuant to Article 21.3 DSU, and

76. L/5778 *EEC – Canned Peaches*, n. 65, para. 52.
77. B. M. Hoeckman & P. C. Mavroidis, n. 57, p.21.

conclude them within twenty days after that date.[78] Only if no agreement is achieved, may the second stage start, where the DSB is entitled to provide for complainant's suspension of obligations towards the respondent. This permission is subject to the reversed consensus principle (Article 22 DSU). The proper subject of suspension would be determined according to Article 22.3 DSU and the extent of suspension would be determined according to Article 22.4 DSU. This process weakens the non-violation cause even compared to its GATT equivalent.

Article XXI:2(a) distinguishes between the 'modifying' Member and affected Members. In the context of the non-violation cause it seems that the Member initiating the measures that nullify or impair the benefits accruing to another Member under the specific commitments of the former would be considered as the 'modifying' Member.[79]

Article XXI:3–4 provides for a special arbitration procedure if an agreement on a necessary compensatory adjustment cannot be reached, but Article XXIII:3 applies Article 22 DSU to cases of disagreement. Consequently, the special arbitration procedure provided by Article 22.6 DSU would prevail over the procedure provided for in Article XXI:3–4.[80]

17.2.4.1.4 Non-violation Complaints under GATS

Non-violation complaints are relatively rare. Since GATS conclusion, some non-violation complaints were initiated, but all of them ended up without a panel decision.[81]

US – The Cuban Liberty and Democratic Solidarity Act[82] – on 3.5.1996, the EC requested for consultations against a US Congress Act that imposed trade sanctions against Cuba, but also against companies or individuals from states who traded with Cuba. These measures were claimed to be inconsistent with some GATT and GATS provisions, but a non-violation complaint was also included, as the EC claimed that the interruption of financial services, the threat of seizure of assets for the purposes of satisfying compensation claims in respect of 'trafficking' and the harassment of its citizens through the denial of visa or exclusion from the United States, or a threat thereof, nullified and impaired the benefits the EC could expect to have accrued to it under the specific commitments of the United States and Cuba under GATS. After the establishment of a Panel the parties reached a mutual agreement.

Japan – Measures Affecting Distribution Services[83] – on 13.6.1996, the United States filed a complaint against Japan's measures affecting distribution services through the operation of Large Scale Retail Store Law that regulated the floor space, business hours and holidays of supermarkets and department stores.

78. GATS commentary, n. 3, 503.
79. W. Zdouc, n. 20, 310.
80. *Ibid.*, 311.
81. This review is based on information published in <www.wto.org>.
82. WT/DS38, n. 35.
83. WT/DS45, n. 36.

The United States claimed, *inter alia*, a non-violation GATS claim, suggesting that the vertically integrated distribution sector that linked Japanese manufacturers, wholesalers and retailers exerted and exclusionary effect on foreign services suppliers, thus nullifying and impairing benefits which the United States could reasonably have expected to accrue to it under Japan's specific commitments on market access and national treatment, *inter alia*, on distribution services. Finally, the United States did not pursue its GATS case against Japan and concentrated on a GATT violation and non-violation case: Japan – Measures Affecting Consumer Photographic Films and Paper,[84] where all its complaints were rejected by the Panel, without appeal.

Belgium – Measures Affecting Commercial Telephone Directory Services[85] – on 2.5.1997, the United States requested consultations with Belgium in respect of measures taken by Belgium, who imposed conditions for obtaining licenses to publish commercial telephone directories, and the regulations, acts, policies and practices of the national Belgian telephone company, Belgacom N.V., with respect to telephone directory services. The United States claimed *inter alia* non-violation nullification and impairment of benefits accruing to it under specific GATS commitments made by the EC on behalf of Belgium.[86] This case was solved between the parties, without the establishment of a Panel.

17.3 THE RELATIONS BETWEEN THE VIOLATION AND NON-VIOLATION CAUSES

17.3.1 Comparison

The non-violation cause, which protects reasonable expectations, is relatively weaker than the violation cause, in some respects:

- First, *the burden of proof is more difficult*: the violation cause calls for an objective, empirical proof of a legal obligation that was violated by a party. Due to the somewhat ambiguous drafting of certain GATS provisions, the very existence of a legal obligation, as well as its content, may stand in the centre of the dispute, but once this question is settled, the proof of violation is relatively simple, empirical and objective. The non-violation cause is based on a *proof of intentions*, of thoughts and of the parties' understanding and scope of reasonable expectations in the course of negotiations. These elements are naturally more difficult to prove, since often there will be no objective evidence to support them.
- Second, *the scope of application of a non-violation cause is narrower* than that of the violation cause: while the latter may apply to the general obligations set by GATS, like the MFN obligation, *and* to the obligations set by

84. WT/DS44/R, n. 37.
85. WT/DS80, n. 38.
86. W. Zdouc, n. 20, 302.

the specific commitments, the former may apply *only* to legal obligations set by specific commitments.

- Respectively, *the remedy* offered by GATS due to this cause is relatively weaker than the remedy given in cases of violation: if the measure involved has to be determined by the DSB to have nullified or impaired such a benefit, the Member affected shall be entitled to a mutually satisfactory adjustment on the basis of paragraph 2 of Article XXI. This procedure is usually applied to compensate Members affected by modification of schedules of specific commitments. It may include the modification or withdrawal of the measure. The procedure set forth by this provision is a three-fold procedure: first, the DSB has to be approached and convinced that the non-violation cause is fulfilled in the specific case brought before it. If the DSB so decides, the affected Member 'shall be entitled' to remedies according to Article XXI:2. However, this procedure does not allow the affected Member to take any unilateral steps, but only measures mutually agreed by the parties. Namely, at this stage the remedy depends upon consent of the other party. Only where an agreement cannot be reached between the Members concerned, Article 22 of the DSU shall apply, namely the DSB interference may be asked, in order for it to allow the affected Member to finally take unilateral steps against the other party.[87] This is a much longer and substantially more elaborated process than the one applying to the violation cause.

17.3.2 Non-violation for Cases where no Disciplines Were yet Developed

The violation cause requires proof that the governmental act or omission is contrary to its legal obligations under the agreement. This condition will not be fulfilled concerning aspects of trade in services for which no disciplines were yet developed in GATS. Thus, this cause will not be applicable to anti-competitive practices of private entities.[88] In these cases, the non-violation cause may apply.

17.3.3 Violation for Active Behaviour, Non-violation for Passive Behaviour

In GATT, most of the violation cases are cases where active action was taken by the government, while most of the non-violation cases refer to passive action thereof.[89]

87. Annex on Art. XXIII:2, n. 63.
88. Subject to the obligation of governments to ensure that the behaviour of monopolies and exclusive service suppliers corresponds to its obligations under GATS according to Art. VIII thereof (see Ch. 11).
89. B. M. Hoeckman & P. C. Mavroidis, n. 57, 143.

In GATS there is still no practice concerning this matter, but where passive behaviour could not form a basis for the violation cause, it should at least be covered by the non-violation cause.

17.3.4 The Procedural Relationship between Violation and Non-violation

Despite the fact that in some cases the two causes were claimed alternatively before GATT panels, where panels reached a conclusion that there was a violation of GATT, they abstained from examining the non-violation cause.[90] However, where the Panel rejected the violation complaint, it proceeded to examine the non-violation complaint.[91] Based on this GATT experience, it seems advisable to refer to both options alternatively in GATS context, too.

17.4 CONCLUSION

Despite the relatively long time that passed since GATS conclusion, only in a few dispute cases concerning this agreement a WTO procedure was opened. Even less cases completed the dispute settlement process. Thus, not much experience has been gained with these procedures. As a result, many open questions remain to be solved in the future. Some questions refer to the authority of the DSB concerning matters of substance. For example:

> Pursuant to the annex to GATS, could the DSB take up disputes concerning the termination or continuation of Article II (MFN Exemptions)? What are the rules and principles applicable to the fees, charges, and taxes levied on services included in the schedules of specific commitments?[92]

Other questions refer to more procedural aspects:

> Does the consideration of disputes in services sectors require specialized expertise as provided in the Decision on Certain Dispute Settlement Procedures for GATS?[93] Or is the integration of the roster established under GATS into the Indicative List of Governmental and Non-Governmental Panelists

90. See, for example, WT/DS2/R US – Standards for Reformulated and Conventional Gasoline, adopted on 20.5.1996, para. 642.
91. L/6627 *EEC – Oilseeds*, n. 73, para. 142.
92. H. A. Millan Smitmans, 'Dispute Settlement in the Services Area Under GATS', in S. M. Stephenson (ed.), *Services Trade in the Western Hemisphere, Liberalization, Integration and Reform*, Organization of American States and Brookings Institution Press, Washington DC (2001), 136.
93. S/L/2 dated 4.4.1995.

> satisfactory? What are the consequences for GATS . . . of cross retaliation under Article 22.3 (c) of the DSU?[94]

It may be assumed that the ambiguities embodied in the legal process discussed in this chapter may form at least one of the causes for the small number of GATS complaints. Thus, their importance is expected to grow as the level of liberalization provided for by GATS commitments will grow. This is particularly so since GATS is an international agreement having a character that does not seem to support direct application, even in Members such as the EU, the legal system of which recognizes this option in principle.[95]

---

94. H. A. Millan Smitmans, n. 91.
95. Case 266/81 *SIOT v. Ministro del Finanze,* ECR[1983] 731. In this case, GATT was examined by the ECJ, which concluded that it should not be directly applicable being an agreement based, *inter alia,* on mutuality and based on the negotiations principle, balancing the interests of its parties, with a separate dispute settlement mechanism, which many of its provisions are vaguely phrased and are thus not 'self executing'. It seems that the same analysis may apply to GATS, <http://eurlex.europa.eu>.

98. [illegible]

Concluding Remarks

The conclusion of GATS, in 1994, did not mark the end, but rather the beginning, of a long process of multilateral services trade liberalization. For the first time, a multilateral mechanism for such liberalization was presented. However, the hesitation and concern of different countries and groups of interests is reflected in its design, as well as in its contents. Therefore, GATS in its current shape is far from being perfect. It suffers from many deficiencies, including an ambiguous language open for interpretation, an incomplete set of disciplines that should further develop, and an incomplete, and in fact, voluntary scope of coverage for certain disciplines, which are subject to the national schedules of specific commitments. The schedules themselves are criticized for being vague and unclear, not user-friendly and not transparent enough.

There are many suggestions for the improvement of this multilateral framework. In 1995, B. Hoeckman, envisioning the future prospectus of international services trade liberalization services, wrote:

> Much can be done if the willingness to do so is there. The basic elements have been identified earlier: (1) adopt a negative list approach to scheduling for transparency purposes, with a transition period that gives Members sufficient time to do this; (2) eliminate all overlap between national treatment and market access, ensuring that the latter applies only to non-discriminatory measures; (3) seek to agree to horizontal disciplines on modes of supply, and eliminate mode-of-supply-specific limitations in the schedules; (4) expand the reach of the market access article by including the term 'or measures with equivalent effect'; (5) convert QR-like market access restrictions to price-based equivalent measures by auctioning them off, thus ensuring that MFN and national treatment are satisfied; (6) make all framework disciplines generally applicable by eliminating all instances where rules are currently conditional upon the scheduling of specific commitments; and (7) agree to

a formula-based approach for future liberalization and expansion of the sectoral coverage of the GATS.

He then added to this long list the three groups of disciplines that were not yet developed, on government procurement, subsidies and safeguard measures, and mentioned that complementary disciplines, external to GATS, should be developed on labour movements and foreign direct investments.[1]

The same recommendations, to go beyond GATS, are still relevant. Even the mechanism for the enhancement of international trade liberalization, embodied in GATS itself, is still not fully exhausted: commitments under GATS are still modest, and a substantial change is not expected during the Doha Round, based on the shallow level of offers submitted by the Members, and only a few WTO dispute settlement cases, interpret GATS.

The current dead lock in GATS development is explained, *inter alia*, by a lack of political momentum, segmentation of policy competencies across ministries, agencies and government level, definitional difficulties associated with the diversity of sectors, modes and measures covered by services agreements and a related lack of precision, the cost of reforms to domestic markets and the lack of public understanding, and thus support, concerning the effect of reforms in certain services sectors.[2]

In 2000 G. Feketekuty wrote:

> An international trade agreement such as the GATS should be assessed on the basis of at least four criteria: whether the negotiation procedures achieve a reduction of trade barriers, whether the disciplines built into the agreement restrain the introduction of new trade barriers, whether the legal framework and dispute settlement procedures facilitate the settlement of dispute arising over the interpretation of the commitments, and whether the agreement establishes a transparent and stable environment for enterprises engaged in international trade in services.[3]

No doubt, in all these respects there is still a long way to go. This conclusion may be drawn from the history of GATT development. However, despite all its deficiencies, GATS has highlighted the importance of multilateral commitment in the pursuit of domestic reform,[4] thus starting an international process that would substantially contribute to the enhancement of international trade in services in

1. B. Hoeckman, 'Tentative First Steps: An Assessment of the Uruguay Round Agreement on Services', *The World Bank Policy Research Working Papers (1995)*, 31–33, <www-wds.worldbank.org>.
2. R. Adlung, 'Services Liberalization from a GATS/WTO Perspective: in Search for Volunteers', *WTO Staff Working Paper ERSD-2009-05* (2009), 8–10.
3. G. Feketekuty, 'Assessing and Improving the Architecture of GATS', in P. Sauve & R. Mitchell (eds), *GATS 2000: New Direction in Services Trade Liberalization*, The Brookings Institution, Washington USA (2000), 85, 86.
4. J. Roberts, 'Issues in the Liberalization of Trade in Services', *12 Journal of International Development* (2000), 257–264.

the years to come, enhancing global growth and welfare. It should be stressed that even supporters of the regional framework admit that certain liberalization steps are only effective in the multilateral framework. By now, GATS seems to mark three modest achievements: providing a framework of basic rules for services trade liberalization at the multilateral level; being successful in resolving trade disputes involving services through the WTO panel process; and inspiring negotiators at the regional level to improve upon both its rules and liberalizing mechanisms.[5]

The literature referring to GATS includes many suggestions for the improvement of its language. Nevertheless it should be realized that such improvements are very difficult to achieve. It should be recognized that it was hard enough to achieve agreement on the current text, and therefore, far-reaching changes in this text are not likely to occur in the near future. Therefore, it is better to concentrate on the development of legal interpretation, facilitating the implementation of GATS and contributing to its best exhaustion, as the major multilateral instrument for the regulation for international trade in services. Such an approach, combined with expected future deepening of the level of specific commitments under GATS, would best serve the enhancement of the important economic process of global services' trade liberalization, foreseen by the drafters of this agreement.

5. G. Hufbauer & S. Stephenson, 'Services Trade: Past Liberalization and Future Challenges', *10 Journal of International Economic Law* (2007), 605, 612–621.

Bibliography

Books

Business Guide to the Uruguay Round, International Trade Center (WTO/UNCTAD) and Commonwealth Secretariat (1995).

Analytical Index – Guide to GATT Law and Practice, the WTO, Geneva (1995).

WTO Analytical Index (2nd edn). Cambridge University Press (2007).

WTO Appellate Body Repertory of Reports and Awards 1995-2006 (3rd edn). WTO, Cambridge University Press (2007).

Trading Into the Future, WTO Publications (1997).

Yearbook of the International law Commission, vol II (1966), <http://untreaty.un.org>.

Arup, C. *The New World Trade Organization Agreements*, Cambridge University Press (2000).

Aaronson, J.D. & P.F. Cowhey, *Trade in Services – A Case for Open Markets*, American Enterprise Institute for Public Policy Research, USA (1984).

Bhagwati, J.P. Krishna & A. Panagariya (eds). *Trading Blocks: Alternative Approaches to Analyzing Preferential Trade Agreements*, MIT Press (1999), <http://books.google.co>.

Bhagwatti, J. *Free Trade Today*, Princeton University Press (2000).

Bhala, R. & K. Kennedy, *World Trade Law*, LEXIS Law Publishing, Virginia (1998).

Delimatsis, P. *International Trade in Services and Domestic Regulations – Necessity, Transparency and Regulatory Diversity*, Oxford University Press (2007).

Ghosh, B. *Gains from Global Linkages* (in association with IMO), Geneva (1997).

Hoeckman, B. A. Mattoo & P. English (eds). *Development, Trade and the WTO: A Handbook, The World Bank* (2002), <www-wds.worldbank.org>.

Hoeckman, B. 'Liberalizing Trade in Services: A Survey', *World Bank Policy Research Working Paper No. 4030* (2006), <http://papers.ssrn.com>.

Ito, T. & A.O. Kruegger (eds). *Trade in Services in the Asia-Pacific Region*, University of Chicago Press, Chicago USA (2003), <http://books.google.com>

Jackson, J.H. *The World Trading System*, 2nd edn, the MIT Press, Cambridge, Massachusetts and London, England (1997).

Krajewski, M. *National Regulation and Trade Liberalization in Services*, Kluwer Law International (2003).

Matsushita, M. T.J. Schoenbaum & P. Mavroidis, *The World Trade Organization – Law, Practice and Policy*, Oxford University Press (2003).

Mattoo, A. & A. Carzaniga (eds). *Moving People to Deliver Services*, The World Bank and Oxford University Press (2003), <http://books.google.com>.

Mattoo, A. & P. Sauvé (eds). *Domestic Regulation and Service Trade Liberalization*, the World Bank and Oxford University Press (2003).

Mattoo, A. R.M. Stern & G. Zanini (eds). *A Handbook of International Trade in Services*, Oxford University Press (2007).

Nicolaides,P. *Liberalizing Services Trade: Strategies for Success*, Tylor and Francis e-Library (2005), <http://books.google.com>.

Sauvé, P. & R. Stern (eds). *GATS 2000: New Direction in Services Trade Liberalization*, The Brookings Institution, Washington USA (2000), <http://books.google.com>.

Sims, M. L. & R.R. Rivers. *The International Trade* in *Services Agenda: Origins, Revolution and Agenda*, Canada (1987).

Sorsa, P. *The GATS Agreement on Financial Services – A Modest Start to Multilateral Liberalization*, IMF, Geneva (1997).

Stephenson, S.M. (ed). *Services Trade in the Western Hemisphere: Liberalization, Integration and Reform*, General Secretariat/Organization of American States (2000), <http://books.google.com>.

Verhoosel, G. *National Treatment and the WTO Dispute Settlement*, Hart Publishing (2002).

Woll, C. *The Politics of Trade preferences: Business Lobbying on Service Trade in the US and in the EU*, (PhD dissertation), Institut d'Etudes Politiques de Paris und Wirtschafts- und Sozialwissenschaftliche Fakultät der Universität zu Köln (2004), <http://kups.ub.uni-koeln.de/volltexte/2005/1345/pdf/Dissertation_Woll.pdf>.

Worfrum, R. P.T. Stoll & C. Feinäugle (eds). *WTO – Trade in Services*, Max Planck Commentaries on World Trade Law, Martinus Mijnhoff Publishers, Leiden, Boston (2008).

Zdouc,W. *Legal Problems Arising Under the General Agreement on Trade in Services – Comparative Analysis of GATS and GATT*, dissertation der Universität St. Gallen (2002).

Essays

Abeyratne, R. 'Ground Handling Services at Airports as a Trade Barrier', *42 Journal of World Trade* (2008): 261.

Abott,F.M. 'GATT and the EC: A Formula for Peaceful Coexistence', *12 Michigan Journal of International Law* (1990): 6.

Adlung, R. 'The GATS Turns Ten: A Preliminary Stocktaking', *WTO* (2004), <www.wto.org>.

Adlung, R. 'Services Negotiations in the Doha Round: Lost in Flexibility?', *9 Journal of International Economic Law* (2006), 856.

Adlung, R. 'Services Liberalization from a GATS/WTO Perspective: In Search for Volunteers', *WTO Staff Working Paper ERSD-2009-05* (2009), <www.wto.org>.

Adlung, R. & M. Molinuevo, 'Bilateralism in Services Trade: is there Fire behind the (BIT) Smoke? *WTO Staff Working PaperERDS-2008-01* (2008), <http://papers.ssrn.com>.

Adlung, R. & M. Roy, 'Turning Hills into Mountains? Current Commitments under the GATS and Prospects for a Change', *WTO* (2005), <www.wto.org>.

Adlung, R., A. Carzeniga, B. Hoeckman & M. Kono, 'The GATS: Key Features and Sectors', in B. Hoeckman, A. Mattoo & P. English (eds). *Development, Trade and the WTO: A Handbook, the World Bank* (2002), <www-wds.worldbank.org>.

Altinger, L. & E. Enders, 'The Scope and Depth of GATS Commitments', *19 The World Economy* (1996): 307.

Balasubramanyam, V.N. & A. Balasubramanyam, 'International Trade in Services: The Case for India's Computer Software', *20 The World Economy* (1997): 829.

Banga, R. 'Trade in services: A Review', *5 Global Economy Journal* (2005), Article 3, 16, <www.bepress.com>.

Bartels, L. 'Article XX of GATT and the Problem of Extraterritorial Jurisdiction', *36 Journal of World Trade* (2002): 353.

Bebr, G. 'Agreements Concluded by the Community and Their Possible Direct Effect: From International Fruit Company to Kupfeberg', *20 CMLR* (1983): 35.

Bhagwati, J.N. 'Trade in Services and the Multilateral Trade Negotiations', *1 The World Bank Economic Review* (1987): 549.

Bhatnagar, P. & C. Manning, 'Regional Arrangements for Mode 4 in the Services Trade: Lessons from the ASEAN Experience', *4 World Trade Review* (2005): 171.

Bigos, J.B. 'Contemplating GATS Article XVIII on Additional Commitments', *42 Journal of World Trade* (2008), 723.

Blyde, J. & N. Sinyavskaya, 'The Impact of Liberalizing Trade in Services on Trade in Goods: An Empirical Investigation', *11 Review of Development Economics* (2007): 566–583.

Borchert, I. & A. Mattoo, 'The Crisis-Resilience of Services Trade', *The World Bank Policy Research Working Paper* (2009), <www-wds.worldbank.org>.

Bown, C.P. & J.P. Trachtman, '*Brazil – Measures Affecting Imports of Retreaded Tyres*: A Balancing Act', *8 World Trade Review* (2009): 85.

Broadman, H.G. 'GATS: The Uruguay Round Accord on International Trade and Investment in Services', *17 The World Economy* (1994): 283.

Broude, T. 'Principles of Normative Integration and the Allocation of International Authority: The WTO, the Vienna Convention on the Law of Treaties, and the Rio Declaration', the Hebrew University of Jerusalem, Faculty of Law, International Law Forum Research Paper no. 07–08 (2008), <http://papers.ssrn.com>.

Brown, W. 'WTO Negotiations in Financial Services: Standing Offers Disappoint', *41 Journal of World Trade (2007)*: 1259.

Burri-Nevona, M. & S.Z. Bigdeli, 'Commentary on GATS Article IX: Business Practices', in R. Wolfrum, P.T. Stoll & C. Feinaugle (eds). *Max Plank Commentaries on World Trade Law, Volume 6: Trade in Services*, Leiden/Boston, Martinus Nijhoff Publishers (2008), 4, <http://papers.ssrn.com>.

Carzaniga, A. 'The GATS, Mode 4 and pattern of Commitments', in A. Mattoo & A. Carzaniga (eds). *Moving People to Deliver Services*, The World Bank and Oxford University Press (2003), 21, <http://books.google.com>.

Chanda, R. 'Movement of Natural Persons and the GATS', *24 The World Economy*, Blackwell Publishers Ltd (2001), 631.

Chanda, R. 'Movement of Natural Persons and the GATS: Major Trade Policy Impediments', in B. Hoeckman, A. Mattoo & P. English (eds). *Development, Trade and the WTO: A Handbook, The World Bank* (2002), 304, <http://books.google.com>.

Charnovitz, S. 'International Standards and the WTO', *GWU Law School, Legal Studies research Paper No. 133* (2005), <http://papers.ssrn.com>.

Chaudhari, S. A. Mattoo & R. Self, 'Moving People to Deliver Services', *The World Bank Policy Research Working Paper* (2004), <www-wds.worldbank.org>.

Claessens, S. 'Regulatory Reform and Trade Liberalization in Financial Services', in A. Mattoo & P. Sauvé (eds). *Domestic Regulation and Service Trade Liberalization*, the World Bank and Oxford University Press (2003), 129.

Clark, T. 'International Services: Perspective at Century's End', *13 Journal of Services Marketing* (1999), 298–310.

Cloninger, P. & B. Oviatt, 'Measuring services Content: A Scale development', *48 Thunderbird International Business Review* (2006), 643–665.

Cossy, M. 'Water Services at the WTO', in E. Brown Weiss, L. Boisson de Chazournes & N. Bernasconi-Osterwalder (eds). Fresh Water and International Economic Law, Oxford University Press (2005), 117.

Cossy, M. 'Determining "likeness" under the GATS: Squaring the Circle?', *WTO* (2006), <www.wto.org>.

Crewford J.A. & S. Laird, 'Regional Trade Agreements and the WTO', *Credit (Center for Research and Economic Development and International Trade) Research Paper No. 3, University of Nottingham* (2000), <www.nottinghamdistancelearning.com>.

Danusso M. & R. Danton, 'Does the European Court of Justice Look for a Protectionist Motive Under Article 95?' *Legal Issues of European Integration* (1990/1991), 67.

Davies, A. 'Interpreting the Chapeau of GATT Article XX in Light of the 'New' Approach in *Brazil-Tyres*', *43 Journal of World Trade* (2009), 507.

Davey, W. 'The WTO Dispute Settlement System: the First Ten Years', *8 Journal of Economic International Law* (2005), 17, <http://papers.ssrn.com>.

Davey, W. & A. Sapir, 'The *Soft Drink* Case: The WTO and regional Agreements', *8 World Trade Review* (2009), 5.

Deardorff, A.V. 'International Provision of Trade Services, Trade, and Fragmentation, *9 Review of International Economics* (2002), 233–248.

Dee, P. 'Modeling the Policy Issues in Services Trade', *94–95 Economie Internationale* (2003), 283–300, <www.cairn.info/article.php>.

Delimatsis, P. 'Don't Gamble With the GATS – The Interaction between Articles VI, XVI, XVII and XVIII GATS in the Light of the *US – Gambling* Case', *40 Journal of World Trade* (2006), 1059.

Delimatsis, P. 'The Interaction Between GATS Articles VI, XVI, XVII and XVIII After the *US-Gambling* Case', *NCCR Trade regulation Working Paper No. 2006/9* (2006), <http://papers.ssrn.com>.

Delimatsis, P. 'Towards a Necessity Test for Services: A Little Less Conversation, A Little More Action, Please!', *NCCR Working Paper No. 2006/16* (2006), <http://papers.ssrn.com>.

Delimatsis, P. 'Concluding the WTO Services Negotiations on Domestic Regulation – Walk Unafraid', *TILEC Discussion Paper DP-2009–032* (2009), <http://papers.ssrn.com>.

Delimatsis, P. 'Financial Innovation and Climate Change: The Case of Renewable Energy Certificates and the Role of the GATS', *8 World Trade review* (2009), 439.

Egger P. & R. Lanz, 'The Determinants of GATS Commitment Coverage', *31 The World Economy* (2008), 1666–1694.

Feketekuty, G. 'Setting the Agenda for the Next Round of Negotiations on Trade in Services', in J.S. Schott (ed). *Launching New Global Trade Talks: an Action Agenda*, Institute for International Economics, USA (1998), 91, <http://books.google.com>.

Feketakuty, G. 'Assessing and Improving the Architecture of GATS', in P. Sauvé & R. Stern (eds). *GATS 2000: New Direction in Services Trade Liberalization*, The Brookings Institution, Washington USA (2000), 85, 98, <http://books.google.com>.

Fink C. & D. Nikomborirak, 'Rules of Origin in Services: A Case Study of Five ASEAN Countries', *The World Bank Policy Research Papers 4130* (2007), 3, <www-wds.worldbank.org>.

Fiorentino, R.V. L. Verdeja & C. Toqueboeuf, Discussion Paper No. 12: 'The Changing Landscape of Regional Trade Agreements: 2006 update', *WTO* (2007), 3. <www.wto.org>.

Freund, C. & D. Weinhold, 'The Internet and International Trade in Services', 92 *The American Economic Review* (2002), 236–240.

Goco, J.B. 'Non-Discrimination, "Likeness", and Market Definition in World Trade Organization Jurisprudence', *40 Journal of World Trade* (2006), 315.

Harrison, A. & T. Britton, 'Providing Services to Foreign Nationals', *Report of the OECD Round Table on Sustainable Development* (2003), <www.oecd.org>.

Hegarty, J. 'Rules for Domestic Regulations: The Experience with Accountancy, Box 29.3 in B. Hoeckman, A. Mattoo & P. English (eds). *Development, Trade and the WTO: A Handbook, the World Bank* (2002), 259, <www-wds.worldbank.org>.

Hertel, T. W. & B.M. Hoeckman, and W. Martin, 'Developing Countries and the New Round of WTO Negotiations', *The World Bank Working Paper* (2000), 13, <www-wds.worldbank.org>.

Hodge, J. 'Liberalization of Trade in Services in Developing Countries', in B. Hoeckman, A. Mattoo & P. English (eds). *Development, Trade and the WTO: Handbook, The World Bank* (2002), 221–234.A, <www-wds.worldbank.org>.

Hoeckman, B.M. 'Rules of Origin for Goods and Services – Conceptual Issues and Economic Considerations', *27 Journal of World Trade* (1993), 81.

Hoeckman, B. 'Tentative First Steps: An Assessment of the Uruguay Round Agreement on Services', *The World Bank Policy Research Working Papers* (1995). <www-wds.worldbank.org>.

Hoeckman, B. & C.A. Primo Braga, 'Protection and Trade in Services: A Survey', *World Bank Policy Research Working Paper No. 1747* (2004), 2–4, <http://papers.ssrn.com>.

Hoeckman, B. 'Been there, not [Quite][Yet] Done That: Lessons and Challenges in Services Trade', *NCCR Trade Regulation Working Paper No. 2006/18* (2006), SSRN 29–30, <http://papers.ssrn.com>.

Hoeckman, B. & A. Mattoo, 'Policy Arena: Services, Economic Development and the Next Round of Negotiations on Services', *12 Journal of International Development* (2000), 283–296.

Hoeckman, B., A. Mattoo & A. Sapir, 'The Political Economy of Services Trade Liberalization: a Case for International Regulatory Cooperation?', *23 Oxford Review of Economic Policy* (2007), 367.

Hoeckman, B. & A. Mattoo, 'Services Trade and Growth', *Policy Research Working Paper 4461, The World Bank* (2008), <http://books.google.com>.

Hoeckman, B.M. & P.C. Mavroidis, 'Competition, Competition Policy and the GATT', *17 The World Economy* (1994), 21.

Hoeckman, B.M. & P.C. Mavroidis, 'Economic Development, Competition Policy, and the World Trade Organization', *The World Bank Policy Research Working Paper* (2002), 14, <www-wds.worldbank.org>.

Hoeckman, B. & P. Sauve, 'Liberalizing Trade in Services', *The World Bank Discussion Papers* (1994), <www-wds.worldbank.org>.

Hindley, B. 'Service Sector Protection: Considerations for Developing Countries', *2 The World Bank Economic Review* (1988), 205.

Hirsch, S. 'A Service or not A Service', *11 The World Economy* (1988), 565.

Horn, H. & J.H.H Weiler '*European Communities – Trade Description of Sardines*: Textualism and its Discontent' in H. Horn & P.C. Mavroidis (eds). *The WTO Case Law of 2002*, Cambridge, CUP (2005), 252, <http://books.google.co>.

Hudec, R. E. 'GATT/WTO Constraints on National Regulation: Requiem of an "Aim and Effect" Test, *32 The International Lawyer* (1998), 619–649.

Hufbauer, G. & S. Stephenson, 'Services Trade: Past Liberalization and Future Challenges', *10 Journal of International Economic Law* (2007), 605.

Iida, K. & J. Nielson, 'Transparency in Domestic Regulation: Practices and Politics', in A. Mattoo & P. Sauvé (eds). *Domestic Regulation and Service Trade Liberalization*, the World Bank and Oxford University Press (2003), 7.

Irwin, D. & J. Weiler, 'Measures Affecting the Cross-Border Supply of Gambling and Betting Services', *7 World Trade Review* (2008), 71.

Janda, R. 'GATS Regulatory Disciplines Meet Global Public Goods: the Case of Transportation Services, in A. Mattoo & P. Sauvé (eds). *Domestic Regulation and Service Trade Liberalization*, the World Bank and Oxford University Press (2003), 109.

Jansen, M. & R. Piermartini, 'The Impact of Mode 4 on Trade in Goods and Services', *WTO Staff Working Paper No. ERSD-2004-07* (2004).

Jara A. & M.D.C. Domingez, 'Liberalization of Trade in Services and Trade Negotiations', *40 Journal of World Trade* (2006), 113.

Karmakar, S. 'Disciplining Domestic Regulation under GATS and its Implications for Developing Countries: An Indian Case Study', *41 Journal of World Trade* (2007), 127.

Karsenty, G. 'Assessing Trade in Services by Mode of Supply', in P. Sauvé & R. Mitchell (eds). *GATS 2000: New Direction in Services Trade Liberalization*, the Brookings Institution, Washington USA (2000), 33, <http://books.google.com>

Khemani, R. S. 'Competition Policy and Promotion of Investment, Economic Policy and Poverty Alleviation in Least Developed Countries', *Working Paper 41334, the IBRD and the World Bank* (2007), <www-wds.worldbank.org>.

Kox, H. & A. Lejour, 'Regulatory Heterogenity as an Obstacle to International Services Trade', *CPB Netherlands Bureau of Economic Policy Analysis* (2005), <www.fep.up.pt>.

Kox, H. & H. K. Nordas, 'Services Trade and Domestic Regulation', *OECD Trade Policy Working Paper No. 49* (2007), <http://mpra.ub.uni-muenchen.de>.

Krajewski, M. 'Public Services and Trade Liberalization: Mapping the Legal Framework, *6 Journal of International Economic Law* (2003), 341.

Laird, S. 'Regional Trade Agreements: Dangerous Liaisons?', *22 World Economy* (2002), 1179.

Langhammer, R. J. 'Developing Countries as Exporters of Services: What Trade Statistics Suggest', *17 Journal of Economic Integration* (2002), 297–310.

Lawson-Remer, T. 'Values under Siege: NAFTA, GATS, and the Propertization of Resources', *NYU 14 Environmental Law Journal* (2006), 481, <http://papers.ssrn.com>.

Leal-Arcas, R. 'The GATS in the Doha Round: A European Perspective', in K. Alexander & M. Andenas (eds). *The World Trade Organization and Trade in Services*, Brill/Nijhoff (2008), <http://papers.ssrn.com>.

Leeborn, D.W. 'Regulatory Discrimination in Domestic United States Law: A Model for the GATS?', in A. Mattoo & P. Sauve (eds). *Domestic Regulation and Service Trade Liberalization*, the World Bank and Oxford University Press (2003), 43.

Lehmann, A. N. T. Tamirisa & J. Wieczorek, 'International Trade in Services: Implications for the IMF', *IMF Policy Discussion Paper* (2003), <www.tessproject.com>.

Lennon, C. 'Trade in Services and Trade in Goods: Differences and Complementarities', *Working Paper No. 52 Paris School of Economics* (2008), <www.pse.ens.>.

Leroux, E.H. 'Trade in Financial Services under the World Trade Organization', *36 Journal of World Trade* (2002), 413.

Leroux, E.H. 'What is a "Service Supplied in the Exercise of Governmental Authority" Under Article I:3(b) and (c) of the General Agreement on Trade in Services?', *40 Journal of World Trade* (2006), 345.

Malaguti, M.C. 'Restrictive Business Practices in International Trade and the Role of the World Trade Organization', *32 Journal of World Trade* (1998), 117.

Mattoo, A. 'National Treatment in the GATS – Corner-Stone or Pandora Box?', *31 Journal of World Trade* (1997), 107.

Mattoo, A. 'Shaping Future GATS Rules for Trade in Services', *The World Bank* (2001), <www-wds.worldbank.org>.

Mattoo, A. 'Negotiating Improved Market Access Commitments', in B. Hoeckman, A. Mattoo & P. English (eds). *Development, Trade and the WTO: A Handbook, the World Bank* (2002), 280, <http://books.google.com>.

Mattoo, A. 'Services in a Development Round', *The World Bank Policy Research Paper No. 3718* (2005), <http://papers.ssrn.com>.

Mattoo, A. & C. Fink. 'Regional Agreements and Trade in Services: Policy Issues', *The World Bank Policy Research Working Paper* (2002), <www-wds.worldbank.org>.

Mattoo, A. & D. Mishra. 'Foreign Professionals and Domestic regulation', *The World Bank Policy Research Working Paper* (2008), <www-wds.worldbank.org>.

Mattoo, A. R. Rathindran & A. Subramanian, 'Measuring Services Trade Liberalization and its Impact on Economic Growth: an Illustration', *21 Journal of Economic Integration* (2006), 64–98.

Mattoo, A. & S. Wunsch, 'Securing Openness of Cross-Border Trade in Services: A Possible Approach', *Center for International Development at Harvard University* (2004), <www.cid.harvard.edu>

Mattoo, A. & S. Wunsch, 'Pre-empting Protectionism in Services: The WTO and Outsourcing', *The World Bank Policy research Working Paper* (2004), <www-wds.worldbank.org>

Maurer, A. & P. Chauvet, 'The Magnitude of Flows of Global Trade in Services', in B. Hoeckman, A. Mattoo & P. English (eds). *Development, Trade and the WTO: A Handbook, the World Bank* (2002), 235, <www-wds.worldbank.org>

Mavroidis, P. 'Highway XVI Re-visited: the Road from non-Discrimination to Market Access in the GATS', *6 World Trade Review* (2007), 1.

Meltzer, J. 'Comment: Interpreting the WTO Agreements – A Commentary on Professor Pauwelyn's Approach', *25 Michigan Journal of International Law* (2004), 917.

Millan Smitmans, H.A. 'Dispute Settlement in the Services Area Under GATS', in S.M. Stephenson (ed.). *Services Trade in the Western Hemisphere, Liberalization, Integration and Reform*, Organization of American States and Brookings Institution Press, Washington DC (2001).

Miroudot, S. 'The Linkages between Open Services Markets and Technology Transfer', *OECD Trade Policy Working Paper No. 29* (2006), <www.olis.oecd.org>.

Molinuevo, M. 'Can Foreign Investors in Services Benefit from WTO Dispute Settlement? Legal Standing and Remedies in WTO and International Arbitration', *NCCR Working Paper No. 2006/17* (2006), <http://papers.ssrn.com>

Nayyar, D. 'Some Reflections on the Uruguay Round and Trade in Services', *22 Journal of World Trade* (1988), 35.

Nielsen, J. 'Labor Mobility in Regional Trade Agreements', in A. Mattoo & A. Carzaniga (eds). *Moving People to Deliver Services*, the World Bank and Oxford University Press (2003), 93, <http://books.google.com>

Nielson, J. & D. Taglioni, 'Services Trade Liberalization: Identifying Opportunities and Gains', *OECD Trade Policy Working Paper No. 1* (2003), <www.olis.oecd.org>.

Nicolaides, K. & J. Trachtman, 'Liberalization, Regulation, and Recognition for Services Trade' in S.M. Stephenson (ed.). *Services Trade in the Western Hemisphere: Liberalization, Integration and Reform*, General Secretariat/ Organization of American States (2000), 43.

Nordas, H. K. & H. Kox, 'Quantifying Regulatory Barriers to Services Trade', *OECD Trade Policy Paper No. 85* (2008), <www.oecd.org>

Ortino, F. 'Treaty Interpretation and the WTO Appellate Body Report in *US – Gambling*: a Critique', *9 Journal of International Economic Law* (2006), 117.

Ortino, F. 'The Principle on Non-Discrimination and its Exceptions in the GATS: Selected Legal Issues', *King's College London* (2006), <http://papers.ssrn.com>

Ortino, F. 'Regional Trade Agreements and Trade in Services', in *S.* Lester & B. Mercurino (eds). *Bilateral and Regional Trade Agreements: Commentary, Analysis and Case Studies*, Cambridge CPU (2007), <http://papers.ssrn.com>.

Pauwelyn, J. 'The Role of Public International Law in the WTO: How Far Can We Go?', *95 American Journal of International Law* (2001), 535.

Pauwelyn, J. 'Rien Ne Va Plus? Distinguishing domestic Regulation from Market Access in GATT and In GATS', *Duke Law School Legal Studies Paper No. 85* (2005), 131, <http://papers.ssrn.com>.

Pillai, R. 'Review Article: National Treatment and the WTO Dispute Settlement', *1 World Trade Review* (2002), 321.

Regan, D.H. 'Regulatory Purpose and "Like Products" in Article III:4 of the GATT (With Additional Remarks on Article III:2)', *36 Journal of World Trade* (2002), 443.

Regan, D.H. 'A *Gambling* Paradox: Why an Origin-Neutral "Zero-Quota" is not a Quota Under GATS Article XVI', *41 Journal of World Trade* (2007), 1297.

Regan, D.H. 'The Meaning of "Necessary" in GATT Article XX and GATS Article XIV: The Myth of Cost-Benefit Balancing', *6 World Trade Review* (2007), 347.

Remirez Robles, E. 'Working Paper No. 9: Political & Quasi-Adjudicative Dispute Settlement Models in European Union Free Trade Agreements', *WTO* (2006). <www.wto.org>

Roberts, J. 'Issues in the liberalization of trade in services', *12 Journal of International Development* (2000), 257.

Robinson, S. & K. Thierfelder, 'Trade Liberalisation and Regional Integration: The Search for Large Numbers', *46 Australian Journal of Agricultural and Resource Economics* (2002), 585. <http://ssrn.com>.

Roseman, D. 'Domestic Regulation and Trade in Telecommunications Services: Experience and Prospects Under the GATS', in A. Mattoo & P. Sauvé (eds). *Domestic Regulation and Service Trade Liberalization*, the World Bank and Oxford University Press (2003), 83.

Roy, M. 'Endowment, Power, and Democracy: Political Economy of Multilateral Commitments on Trade in Services', WTO Economic Research and Statistics Staff Working Paper No. 2009–07 (2010), <http://papers.ssrn.com>.

Roy,M. J. Marchetti & H. Lim, 'Services Liberalization in the New Generation of Preferential Trade Agreements (PTAs): How Much Further Than the GATS? *6 World Trade Review* (2007), 155; WTO (2006), <www.wto.org>.

Sapir, A. 'North-South Issues in Trade in Services', *8 The World Economy* (1985), 27, 31.

Schwellnus, S. 'The Effect of Domestic Regulation on Trade in Services Revisited', *CEPII, Working Paper No. 2007–08* (2007), <www.economie-internationale.fr>.

Self, R. & K. Zutshi, 'Mode 4: Negotiating Challenges and Opportunities', in A. Mattoo, A. Carzaniga (eds). *Moving People to Deliver Services*, the World Bank and Oxford University Press (2003), 27, <http://books.google.com>.

Snape, R.H. 'Regulating Services Trade: Matching Policies to Objectives', in T. Ito & A.O. Krueger (eds). *Trade in Services in the Asia-Pacific Region*, The University of Chicago Press (2003), 79.

Stephenson, S. M. 'Regional Agreements on Services in Multilateral Disciplines: Interpreting and Applying GATS Article V', in S.M. Stephenson (ed.). *Services Trade in the Western Hemisphere: Liberalization, Integration and Reform*, General Secretariat/Organization of American States (2000), 86, 87–88.

Stephenson, S.M. 'Can Regional Liberalization of Services go Further than Multilateral Liberalization Under the GATS?', *1 World Trade Review* (2002), <www.netamericas.net>.

Stephenson, S.M. 'Regional Versus Multilateral Liberalization of Services', *1 World Trade Review* (2002), 187.

Stern, R.M. 'Quantifying Barriers to Trade in Service', *Discussion Paper No. 470, University of Michigan* (2000), <www.fordschool.umich.edu>.

Stern, R.M. & B.M. Hoekman, 'Issues and Data Needs for GATT Negotiations on Services', *10 The World Economy* (1987), 39.

Terry, L.S. 'But What Will the WTO Disciplines Apply to? Distinguishing Among Market Access, National Treatment and Article VI:4 Measures When Applying the GATS to Legal Services', *American Bar Center for Professional Responsibility, 2003 Symposium, 83 The Professional Lawyer* (2003), 84, 97–98, <http://papers.ssrn.com>

Trachtman, J.P. 'Lessons for the GATS from Existing WTO Rules on Domestic regulation', in A. Mattoo & P. Sauvé, *Domestic Regulation and Service Trade Liberalization*, the World Bank and Oxford University Press (2003), 57.

Trolliet, C. & J. Hegarty, 'Regulatory Reform and Trade Liberalization in Accountancy Services', in A. Mattoo & P. Sauvé (eds). *Domestic Regulation and Service Trade Liberalization*, the World Bank and Oxford University Press (2003), 147.

Valckx, N. 'WTO Financial Services Commitments: Determinants and Impact on Financial Stability', *IMF Working Paper* (2002), 18, <www.imf.org>.

Van Damme, I. 'The Interpretation of Schedules of Commitments', *41 Journal of World Trade* (2007), 1.

Viner, J. 'The Customs Union Issue', in J. Bhagwati, P. Krishna & A. Panagariya (eds). *Trading Blocks: Alternative Approaches to Analyzing Preferential Trade Agreements*, Massachusetts Institute of technology (1999), 105, <http://books.google.co.uk>

Whalley, J. 'Assessing the Benefits to Developing Countries of Liberalisation in Services Trade', *27 The World Economy* (2004), 1223.

Warren, T. & C. Findlay, 'Measuring impediments to trade in Services', in P. Sauvé & R. Mitchell (eds). *GATS 2000: New Direction in Services Trade Liberalization*, The Brookings Institution, Washington USA (2000), 57, <http://books.google.com>.

Weiler, J.H.H. 'The Rule of Lawyers and Ethos of Diplomats – Reflections on the Internal and External Legitimacy of WTO Dispute Settlement', *35 Journal of World Trade* (2001), 191.

Woll, C. *The Politics of Trade Preferences: Business Lobbying on Services Trade in the US and in the EU*, Institut d'Etudes Politiques de Paris, und Wirtschafts- und Sozialwissenschaftliche Fakultät der Universität zu Köln (2004), <http://kups.ub.uni-koeln.de>

Wong, C.Y.P. J. Wu & A. Zhang, 'A Model in Trade Liberalization of Services', *14 Review of International Economics* (2006), 148.

Wunch-Vincent, S. 'The Internet, Cross-Border Trade in Services, and the GATS: Lessons from *US-Gambling*', *5 World Trade Review* (2006), 319.

Yang, Y. 'Most Favoured Nation Treatment Under the General Agreement on Trade in Services – and its Application in Financial Services, *30 Journal of World Trade* (1996), 91.

Zdouc, W. 'WTO Dispute Settlement Practice Relating to the GATS', *Journal of International Economic Law* (1999), 295.

Zdouc, W. 'WTO Dispute Settlement Practice Relating to the General Agreement on Trade in Services', in F. Ortino & E.U. Petersmann (eds). *The WTO Dispute Settlement System: 1995–2003*, London, Kluwer International Law (2004).

OECD Papers and Publications

'The General Agreement on Trade in Services (GATS): an Analysis', *OECD* (1994), <www.olis.oecd.org>.

'The Service Economy', *OECD, STI Business and Industry Policy Forum Series* (2000), <www.oecd.org>.

'Special and Differential Treatment Under the GATS', *OECD Trade Policy Working Paper No. 26* (2005), <www.olis.oecd.org>.

'Service Delivery in Fragile Situations: Key Concepts, Findings and Lessons', *OECD, 9 Journal of Development* (2008), <www.oecd.org>.

'Structure and Trends in International Trade in Services', *OECD* (2007), <www.oecd.org>.

Presentations

'Measuring Bilateral Trade in Services: a Note on the Data Collected and Estimated for the Service Trade Restrictiveness Index', OECD (2008), <www.oecd.org>/.

D. Honeck, The GATS and 'Necessity', WTO March 2004 (presentation).
<www.wto.org>.

International Agreements

The Vienna Convention on the Law of Treaties, 1969, <http://untreaty.un.org>.

GATT Panel Decisions and Documents

G/2 The case of Treatment by Germany of Imported Sardines (1952), adopted on 31.10.1952, 1S/53.

G/32 Belgian Family Allowances, adopted on 7.11.52, 1S/59.

L/167 United States – Taxes on Petroleum and Certain imported Substances, adopted on 17.6.1987 34S/136.

L/334 The Working Party on 'Other Barriers to Trade', adopted on 3.3.1955, 3S/222.

L/833 Italy – Discrimination against Imported Agricultural Machinery, BIDS 7S/60, adopted on 23.10.1958.
L/5333 United States – Imports of Certain Automotive Spring Assemblies, adopted on 26.5.1983, 30S/107.
L/5504 Canada – Administration of Foreign Investment Review Act, adopted on 7.2.1984, 30S/140.
L/5623 The Panel Report on 'Japanese Measures on Imports of Leather', adopted on 15/16.5.1984, 31S/94.
L/5778 EEC – Production Aids Granted on Canned Peaches, Canned Pears, Canned Fruit Cocktail and Dried Grapes, 1985 (unadopted), <www.wto.org>.
L/5863 Canada – Measures Affecting the Sale of Gold Coins, dated 17.9.1985 (unadopted), <www.worldtradelaw.net>.
L/6053 US – Nicaragua Trade, dated 13.10.1986 (unadopted), <www.worldtradelaw.net>.
L/6175 US – Taxes on Petroleum and Certain Imported Substances, adopted on 17.6.1987, 34S/136.
L/6253 Japan – Restrictions on Imports of Certain Agricultural Products, adopted on 22.3.1988, 35S/163.
L/6309 Japan – Trade in Semiconductors, adopted on 4.5.1988, BIDS35S/116.
L/6439 United States – Section 337 of the Tariff Act of 1930, adopted on 7.11.1989, 36S/345.
L/6491 EEC- Restrictions on Imports of Dessert Apples, adopted on 22.6.1989, 36S/93.
L/6513 EEC – Restrictions on Imports of Apples, complaint by the United States, adopted on 22.6.1989, 36S/135.
L/6627 EEC – Payments and Subsidies Paid to Processors of Oilseeds and Related Animal-Feed proteins, adopted on 25.1.1990, 37S/86.
L/6631 United States – restrictions on the Importation of Sugar and Sugar-Containing Products Applied Under the 1955 Waiver and Under the Headnote to the Schedule of Tariff Concessions, adopted on 7.11.1990, 37S/228.
L/6657 EEC – Regulation on Imports of Parts and Components, adopted on 16.5.1990, 37S/132.
DS10/R Thailand – Restrictions on the Importation of and Internal Taxes on Cigarettes, adopted 7.11.1990, 37S/200.
DS17/R Canada – Import, Distribution and Sale of Alcoholic Drinks by Provincial Marketing Agencies, adopted 18.2.1992, 39S/27.
DS18/R United States – Denial of Most-Favored-Nation Treatment as to Non-Rubber Footwear from Brazil, adopted on 19.6.1992, 39S/128.
DS/21R United States – Restrictions on Imports of Tuna, dated 3.9.1991 (unadopted), 39S/155.
DS23/R United States – Measures Affecting Alcoholic and malt beverages, adopted on 19.6.1992, 39S/206.
DS/29R United States – Restrictions on the Import of Tuna, dated 16.6.1994 (unadopted), 33 I.L.M 839 (1994).

WTO Dispute Settlement Decisions and Documents

WT/DS2/R United States – Standards for Reformulated and Conventional Gasoline, adopted on 20.5.1996.

WT/DS8,10,11/R Japan – Taxes on Alcoholic Beverages, adopted on 1.11.1996.

WT/DS22/R Brazil – Measures Affecting Desiccated Coconut, adopted on 20.3.1997.

WT/DS24/R, AB/R United States – Restrictions on Imports of Cotton and Man-Made Fibre Underwear, adopted on 25.2.1997.

WT/DS26,48/R, AB/R European Communities – Measures Concerning Meat and Meat Products (Hormones), adopted on 13.2.1998.

WT/DS27/R, AB/R European Communities – Regime for the Importation, Sale and Distribution of Bananas, adopted on 25.9.1997.

WT/DS31/R, AB/R Canada – Certain Measures Concerning Periodicals, adopted on 30.7.1997.

WT/DS34/AB/R Turkey – Restrictions on Imports of Textile and Clothing Products, adopted on 19.11.1999.

WT/DS38 United States – The Cuban Liberty and Democratic Solidarity Act.

WT/DS44/R Japan – Measures Affecting Consumer Photographic Film and Paper, adopted on 22.4.1998.

WT/DS45 Japan – Measures Affecting Distribution Services.

WT/DS54,55/R Indonesia – Certain Measures Affecting the Automobile Industry, adopted on 23.7.1998.

WT/DS58/AB/R United States – Import Prohibition of certain Shrimp and Shrimp Products, adopted on 6.11.1998.

WT/DS62,67,68/AB/R European Communities – Customs Classification on Certain Computer Equipment, adopted on 22.6.1998.

WT/DS69/R, AB/R European Communities – Measures Affecting Importation of certain Poultry Products, adopted on 23.7.1998.

WT/DS70/AB/R Canada – Measures Affecting the Export of Civilian Aircraft, adopted on 20.8.2000.

WT/DS75,84/AB/R Korea – Taxes on Alcoholic Beverages, adopted on 17.2.1999.

WT/DS80 Belgium – Measures Affecting Commercial Telephone Directory Services.

WT/DS90/R India – Quantitative Restrictions on Imports of Agricultural, Textile and Industrial Products, adopted on 22.9.1999.

WT/DS105 European Communities – Regime for the Importation, Sale and Distribution of Bananas.

WT/DS108/AB/RW United States – Tax Treatment for "Foreign Sales Corporations" – Recourse to Article 21.5 of the DSU by the European Communities, adopted on 29.1.2002.

WT/DS110/R, AB/R Chile – Taxes on Alcoholic Beverages, adopted on 12.1.2000.

WT/DS117 Canada – Measures Affecting Film Distribution Services.

WT/DS121/R, AB/R Chile – Taxes on Alcoholic Beverages, adopted on 12.1.2000.

WT/DS135/R, AB/R European Communities – Measures Affecting Asbestos and Asbestos-Containing Products, adopted on 5.4.2001.

WT/DS139,142/R, AB/R Canada – Certain Measures Affecting the Automotive Industry, adopted on 19.6.2000.

WT/DS146,175/R, AB/R India – Measures Affecting Trade and Investment in the Motor Vehicle, Sector, adopted on 5.4.2002.

WT/DS155/R Argentina – Measures Affecting the Export of Bovine Hides and Import of Finished Leather, adopted on 16.2.2001.

WT/DS161,169/R, AB/R Korea – Measures Affecting the Imports of Fresh, Chilled and Frozen Beef, adopted on 10.1.2001.

WT/DS176/R, AB/R United States – Section 211 Omnibus Appropriation Act of 1998, adopted on 2.1.2002.

WT/DS184/R, AB/R United State – Anti Dumping Measures on Certain Hot-Rolled Steel Products from Japan, adopted on 23.8.2001.

WT/DS204/R Mexico – Measures Affecting Telecommunication Services, adopted on 1.6.2004.

WT/DS245/R, AB/R Japan – Measures Affecting the Importation of Apples, adopted on 10.12.2003.

WT/DS246/R, AB/R European Communities – Conditions for the Granting of Tariff Preferences to Developing Countries, adopted on 20.4.2004.

WT/DS268/R, AB/R United States – Sunset Reviews of Anti-Damping Measures on Oil Country Tubular Goods from Argentina, adopted on 17.12.2004.

WT/DS269,286/R European Communities – Customs Classification of Frozen Boneless Chicken Cuts, adopted on 27.9.2005.

WT/DS276/AB/R Canada – Measures Relating to Exports of Wheat and Treatment of Imported Grain, adopted on 27.9.2004.

WT/DS285/R, AB/R United States – Measures Affecting the Cross-Border Supply of Gambling and Betting Services, adopted on 22.5.2007.

WT/DS286/R, AB/R United States – Sunset review of Anti Dumping Measures on Oil Country Tubular Goods from Argentina, adopted on 17.12.2004.

WT/DS291,292,293/R European Communities – Measures Affecting the Approval and Marketing of Biotech Products, adopted on 21.11.2006.

WT/DS302/AB/R Dominican Republic – Measures Affecting the Importation and Internal Sale of Cigarettes, adopted on 19.5.2005.

WT/DS308/R, AB/R Mexico – Tax Measures on Soft Drinks, adopted on 24.6.2006.

WT/DS309 China – Value-Added Tax on Integrated Circuits.

WT/DS315/R,AB/R European Communities – Selected Customs Matters, adopted on 11.12.2006.

WT/DS320/R United States – Continued Suspension of Obligations in the EC-Hormones Dispute, adopted on 14.11.2008.

WT/DS332/R, AB/R Brazil – Measures Affecting Imports of Retreaded Tyres, adopted on 17.12.2007.

WT/DS333 Dominican Republic – Foreign Exchange Fee Affecting Imports from Costa Rica.

WT/DS339,340,342/R, AB/R China – Measures Affecting Imports of Automobile Parts, adopted on 12.1.2009.
WT/DS343/R, AB/R United States – Measures Relating to Shrimp from Thailand, adopted on 1.8.2008.
WT/DS345/R, AB/R United States – Customs Bond Directive for Merchandise Subject to Anti Dumping/Countervailing Duties, adopted on 1.8.2008.
WT/DS363/R, AB/R China – Measures Affecting Trading Rights and Distribution Services for Certain Publications and Audiovisual Entertainment Products, adopted on 19.1.2010.
WT/DS366/R Columbia – Indicative Prices and Restrictions on Ports of Entry, adopted on 20.5.2009.
WT/DS367/R Australia – Measures Affecting the Importation of Apples from New Zealand, published 9.8.10 (not adopted yet).
WT/DS371/R Thailand – Customs and Fiscal Measures on Cigarettes from the Philippines (complaint withdrawn).
WT/DS375, 376, 377/R EC and its Member States – Tariff Treatment of Certain IT Products, published 19.8.2010 (not adopted yet).
WT/DS378 China – Measures Affecting Financial Information Services and Foreign Financial Information Suppliers.
WT/DS45/1 Japan – Measures Affecting Distribution Services, request for consultations by the United States, 20.6.1996.
WT/DS45/1/Add.1 Japan – Measures Affecting Distribution Services, request for further consultations by the United States, 26.9.1996.

European Court of Justice Judgments

Case 266/81 *SIOT v. Ministro del Finanze,* ECR [1983] 731.

GATT Official Documents

Punta Del Este draft Declaration (1986), <http://sul-derivatives.stanford.edu>.
C/M/236, Streamline Mechanism for Reconciling the Interests of Contracting Parties in the Event of Trade Damaging Act 36S/67.
GATT/CP.4/39, the Working Group concerning 'The Australian Subsidy on Ammonium Sulfate' from 1950, adopted on 3.4.1950, 11/188.
ECPT/C.II/5 – preparatory committee meeting in London.
EPCT/A/PV 33 (1947).
ECPT/TACPV/19.
L/1235 The report of the Committee on Regional Trade Agreements examining the Treaty of Rome, 1957, adopted on 4.6.1960, S/9.
L/1923 Uruguayan Recourse to Article XXIII adopted on 16.11.1962.
L/3149 A note by the Director General, dated 29.11.1968.
L/4904 Declaration on Trade Measures Taken for Balance-of-Payment Purposes, adopted on 28.11.1979, 26S/205.

WTO Official Documents

Decision on Institutional Arrangements for the GATS, <www.wto.org>
Decision on Certain Dispute Settlement Procedures for the GATS, <www.wto.org>
Draft Model Schedule of Commitments on Basic telecommunications, Informal Note by the Secretariat, Job No. 1131, 12.4.1995.
MTN.GNS/10 Negotiation Group on Services, Note on the Meeting of 15–17 September 1987, 15.10.1987.
MTN.GNS/24 Note on the Meeting of 17–21 July 1989, 28.8.1989.
MTN.GNS/25 Note of the Meeting of 18–22 September 1989, 23.10.1989.
MTN.GNS/35 Group of Negotiations on Services, Uruguay Round, Draft, Multilateral Framework for Trade in Services, Introductory Note by the Chairman on the GNS Negotiations on a Framework Agreement, 23.7.1990.
MTN.GNS/49 Informal GNS Meeting – 10.12.93, Chairman's Statement, 11.12.1993.
MTN.GNS/W/120 Services Sectoral Classification List, 10.7.1991.
MTN.GNS/W/139 Definitions in the Draft General Agreement on Trade in Services – Note by the Secretariat, 15.10.1991.
MTN.GNS/W/164 Scheduling of initial Commitments in Trade in Services: Explanatory Note, 3.9.1993.
MTN.GNS/W/164/Add.1 Scheduling Guidelines: Background – Note by the Secretariat, 10.10.1997.
MTN.GNS/W/177/Rev.1 Uruguay Round – Group of Negotiations on Services – Issues Relating to the Scope of the General Agreement on Trade in Services – Note by the Secretariat, 4.11.1993.
MTN.GNS/W/177/Rev.1/Add.1 Uruguay Round – Group of Negotiations on Services – Issues Relating to the Scope of the General Agreement on Trade in Services – Note by the Secretariat – Addendum, 6.12.1993.
MTN.GNS/W/178 Taxation Issues Related to Article XIV(d) – Note by the Secretariat, 15.11.1993.
MTN.GNS/W/178/Add. 1 Taxation Issues Related to Article XIV(d) – Note by the Secretariat – Addendum, 30.11.1993.
MTN.TNC/W/FA General Agreement on Trade in Services, in Draft Final Act Embodying the Results of the Uruguay Round of Multilateral Trade Negotiations, 20.12.1991, Annex I.
S/C/M/1 Council for Trade in Services – Report of the Meeting Held on 1 March 1995 – Note by the Secretariat, 22.3.1995.
S/C/M/10 Council for Trade in Services : Adoption of Decision on the Notification of the Establishment of Enquiry and Contact Points, 28.5.1996.
S/C/M/30 Council for Trade in Services, Report on the Meeting Held on 14 October 1998.
S/C/M/34 Report of the Meeting Held in 22 and 23 March 1999 – Note by the Secretariat, 16.4.99.
S/C/M/44 Council for Trade in Services – Council Review of MFN Exemptions – Report of the Meeting Held on 29 May 2000 – Note by the Secretariat.

S/C/M/45 Council for Trade in Services – Council Review of MFN Exemptions – Report of the Meeting Held on 5 July 2000 – Note by the Secretariat.

S/C/M/47 Council for Trade in Services – Council Review of MFN Exemptions – Report of the Meeting Held on 5 October 2000 – Note by the Secretariat.

S/C/M/50 Council for Trade in Services, Report of the Third Session of the Review Mandated under Paragraph 5 of the Air Transport Annex, held on 9 October 2001- Note by the Secretariat.

S/C/M/76 Council for Trade in Services – Council Review of MFN Exemptions – Report of the Meeting Held on 30 November 2004 – Note by the Secretariat.

S/C/M/78 Council for Trade in Services – Council Review of MFN Exemptions – Report of the Meeting Held on 23 February 2005 – Note by the Secretariat.

S/C/M/89 Council for Trade in Services, Report of the second session of the review mandated under paragraph 5 of the Annex on Air Transport Services held on 2 October 2007 – Note by the Secretariat.

S/C/N/34 Council for Trade in Services, Notification pursuant to Article V*bis* of the General Agreement on Trade in Services, Denmark, 2.12.1996.

S/C/N/35 Council for Trade in Services, Notification pursuant to Article V*bis* of the General Agreement on Trade in Services, Iceland, 2.12.1996.

S/C/N/36 Council for Trade in Services, Notification pursuant to Article V*bis* of the General Agreement on Trade in Services, Norway , 2.12.1996.

S/C/N/37 Council for Trade in Services, Notification pursuant to Article V*bis* of the General Agreement on Trade in Services, Sweden , 2.12.1996.

S/C/N/38 Council for Trade in Services, Notification pursuant to Article V*bis* of the General Agreement on Trade in Services, Finland , 2.12.1996.

S/C/W/1 First Meeting of the Council for Trade in Services – Note by the Secretariat, 15.2.1995, 2–3.

S/C/W/5 GATS and Statistics on Trade in Services, 17.7.1995.

S/C/W/13 Interim Report on the Status of Consultations on Taxes and Subsidies at the Sub-Central Level, 30.1.1996.

S/C/W/75 Presence of Natural Persons (Mode 4) – Background Note by the Secretariat, 8.12.1998.

S/CSC/W/34 Committee on Specific Commitments, Note by the Secretariat: Additional Commitments Under Article XVIII of the GATS, 30.7.2002.

S/ENQ/78/Rev.10 Council for Trade in Services – Contact and Enquiry Points Notified to the Council for Trade in Services – Note by the Secretariat – Revision, 13.6.2008.

S/ENQ/78/Rev.11 Council for Trade in Services – Contact and Enquiry Points Notified to the Council for Trade in Services – Note by the Secretariat – Revision, 26.10.2009.

S/GBT/W/2/Rev.1 Note for Scheduling Basic telecommunications Services Commitments, Note by the Chairman, 16.1.1997.

S/L/2 Decision on Certain Dispute Settlement Procedures for GATS dated 4.4.1995.

S/L/5 Guidelines for Notifications under the General Agreement on Trade in Services – Adopted by the Council for Trade in Services on 1 March 1995, 4.4.1995.

S/L/19 Decision on Commitments in Basic Telecommunications – Adopted by the Council for Trade in Services on 30 April 1996.

S/L/20 Fourth Protocol to the General Agreement on Trade in Services, 30.4.1996.

S/L/23 Decision on the Notification of the Establishment of Enquiry and Contact Points – Adopted by the Council for Trade in Services on 28 May 1996.

S/L/24 Decision on Maritime Transport Services, adopted by the Council for Trade in Services on 28 June 1996.

S/L/28 Decision on the Acceptance of the Second and Third Protocols to the GATS (1996).

S/L/44 Trade in Services – Decision Adopting the Fifth Protocol to the General Agreement on Trade in Services – Adopted by the Committee on Trade in Financial Services on 14 November 1997.

S/L/45 Fifth Protocol to the General Agreement on Trade in Services.

S/L/64 Disciplines on Domestic regulation in the Accountancy Sector, 17.12.1998.

S/L/74 Work Programme on Electronic Commerce – Progress Report to the General Council, 27.7.1999.

S/L/80 Procedures for the Implementation of Article XXI, the General Agreement on Trade in Services (modification of Schedules), adopted by the Council for Trade in Services 19.7.1999.

S/L/84 Procedures for the Certification or Rectifications or Improvements to Schedules of Specific Commitments, adopted by the Council for Trade in Services 20.4.2000.

S/L/91 Trade in Services – Decision on the Guidelines for the Scheduling of Specific Commitments under the General Agreement on Trade in Services (GATS) adopted 23.3.2001.

S/L/92 Guidelines for the Scheduling of Specific Commitments Under the General Agreement on Trade in Services (GATS), published 28.3.2001, 35–40, adopted by the Council for Trade in Services on 23.3.2001, S/C/M/52, para. 11.

S/L/93 Guidelines and Procedures for the Negotiations on Trade in Services, adopted by the special session of the Council for Trade in Services on 28 March 2001, 29.3.2001.

S/L/106 Procedures for the Certification and Terminations, Reductions and Rectifications of Article II (MFN) Exemptions, 11.6.2002.

S/WPDR/M/18 Report on the meeting held on 22 October 2002, 3.12.2002.

S/WPDR/M/19 Report on the meeting held on 4 December 2002, 29.1.2003.

S/WPPS/W/9 Note by the Secretariat – The Relevance of the Disciplines of the Agreement on technical Barriers to Trade (TBT) and on Import Licensing procedures to Article VI:4 of the GATS, 11 September 1996.

T/N/S/6 Council for Trade in Services – Special Session – Modalities for the Treatment of Autonomous Liberalization, 10.3.2003.

TN/S/13 Council for Trade in Services – Special Session – Modalities for the Special Treatment for Least-Developed Country Members in the Negotiations on Trade in Services on 3 September 2003, 5.9.2003.

WT/L/274 Work Program on Electronic Commerce Adopted by the Council for Trade in Services in 25.9.1998.

WT/L/671 General Council, Transparency Mechanism for Regional Trade Agreements, Decision of 14 December 2006, 18.12.2006.

WT/REG/M/16 Note on the Meeting of 16–18 and 20 February 1998.

WT/REG3/Add. 1 Enlargement of the EC – Accession of Austria, Finland and Sweden – Questions and Replies, Addendum, 23.4.1997.

WT/REG3/M/5 Examination of the Enlargement of the EC: Accession of Austria, Finland and Sweden – Note of the Meeting of 14 July 1997, 12.8.1997.

WT/REG4/M/4 Examination of the North American Free Trade Agreement, Note of the Meeting of 24 February 1997, 16.4.1997.

WT/REG40/M/1 Examination of the Protocol on Trade in Services of the Australia – New Zealand Closer Economic relations Trade Agreement, 4.12.1997.

WT/REG50/2, WT/REG51/2, WT/REG52/2, Committee on Regional Trade Agreements – The European Communities-Hungary Europe Agreement, Services; the European Communities-Poland Europe Agreement, Services; The European Communities – Slovak Europe Agreement, Services, Communication from the Parties, 24.4.1998.

WT/REG50/M/1, WT/REG51/M/1, WT/REG52/M/1, Examination of the EC-Hungary, Poland, Slovak Europe Agreements – Note of the Meeting of 18 February 1998, 19.3.1998.

WT/REG50/M/2 Committee on Regional Trade Agreements – Examination of the European Communities-Hungary Europe Agreement, Services; the European Communities-Poland Europe Agreement, Services; the European Communities – Slovak Europe Agreement, Service, the Meeting of 18 February 1998, 19.3.1998.

WT/REG/W/15 Guidelines on Procedures to Improve and Facilitate the Examination Process – Note by the Chairman, 6.5.1997.

WT/REG/W/18 Committee on Regional Trade Agreements – Communication from Australia, 17.11.1997.

WT/REG/W/19 Committee on Regional Trade Agreements – Communication from Hong Kong, China, 17.11.1999.

WT/REG/W/21/Rev.1 Committee on Regional Trade Agreements, Systemic Issues Related to 'Substantially All Trade' – Background Note by the Secretariat, 5.2.1998.

WT/REG/W/37 Committee on Regional Trade Agreements – Synopsis of 'Systemic' Issues Related to Regional Trade Agreements – Note by the Secretariat, 2.3.2000.

WT/TC/NOTIF/GATS1 Technical Cooperation Handbook on Notification Requirements – GATS, 15.10.1996.

Hong Kong Ministerial Declaration <www.wto.org>.

PRESS/80 'Services in a Borderless Economy', a speech by Renato Ruggiero, Director General of the WTO, in the 2nd DEBIS conference in Berlin, 23.10.1997.

PRESS/122 The New Multilateral Trade Negotiations, the EU and its Developing Country Partners: an Agenda for Action, 19.2.1999.

Report of the chair of services negotiations issued on 26.5.08, see: <www.wto.org>.

WTO Secretariat, Trade in Services Division Papers

'Services Negotiations under the GATS: Current State of Play (Request-and-Offer Process), WTO Secretariat, Trade in Services Division, February 2006, 2.
WTO explanatory paper, WTO Secretariat, 29.3.2006 (3776.4).

UN Documents

Yearbook of the International Law Commission (1966), Vol II, A/CN.4/SER.A/1966/Add.1,219 and 220.

Data Sources

<http://unstats.un.org>.
<www.oecd.org>.

Index

S

T

U

V

W

Z

GLOBAL TRADE LAW SERIES

1. Emmanuel T. Laryea, *Paperless Trade: Opportunities, Challenges and Solutions*, 2002 (ISBN 90-411-9897-0).
2. Xiang Gao, *The Fraud Rule in the Law of Letters of Credit: A Comparative Study*, 2002 (ISBN 90-411-9898-9).
3. Yuwa Wei, *Comparative Corporate Governance: A Chinese Perspective*, 2003 (ISBN 90-411-9908-X).
4. Ross P. Buckley (ed.), *The WTO and the Doha Round: The Changing Face of World Trade*, 2003 (ISBN 90-411-9947-0).
5. Bradley J. Condon, Joyce C. Sadka, Tapen Sinha (eds), *Insurance Regulation in North America: Integrating American, Canadian and Mexican Markets*, 2003 (ISBN 90-411-2226-5).
6. Jan Hoogmartens, *EC Trade Law Following China's Accession to the WTO*, 2004 (ISBN 90-411-2301-6).
7. Yang Guohua, Bryan Mercurio, Li Yongjie, *WTO Dispute Settlement Understanding: A Detailed Interpretation*, 2005 (ISBN 90-411-2361-X).
8. Jan Job de Vries Robbé, Paul U. Ali, *Securitisation of Derivatives and Alternative Asset Classes, Yearbook*, 2005 (ISBN 90-411-2375-X).
9. Markus W. Gehring, Marie-Claire Cordonier Segger, *Sustainable Development in World Trade Law*, 2005 (ISBN 90-411-2366-0).
10. Yann Aubin, Arnaud Idiart. *Export Control Law and Regulations Handbook: A Practical Guide to Military and Dual-Use Goods Trade Restrictions and Compliance*, 2007 (ISBN 90-411-2601-5).
11. Henry Kibet Mutai, *Compliance with International Trade Obligations: The Common Market for Eastern and Southern Africa*, 2007 (ISBN 978-90-411-2664-1).
12. Yong-Shik Lee, *Economic Development through World Trade: A Developing World Perspective*, 2007 (ISBN 978-90-411-2681-8).
13. Yanning Yu, *Circumvention and Anti-Circumvention Measures: The Impact on Anti-Dumping Practice in International Trade*, 2007 (ISBN 978-90-411-2686-3).
14. Ross Buckley, Vai Io Lo, Laurence Boulle, *Challenges to Multilateral Trade: The Impact of Bilateral, Preferential and Regional Agreements*, 2008 (ISBN 978-90-411-2711-2).
15. K.D. Raju, *World Trade Organization Agreement on Anti-dumping: A GATT/WTO and Indian Jurisprudence*, 2008 (ISBN 978-90-411-2780-8).
16. Xiaochen Wu, *Anti-dumping Law and Practice in China*, 2008 (ISBN 978-90-411-2790-7).
17. Amin Alavi, *Legalization of Development in the WTO: Between Law and Politics*, 2008 (ISBN 978-90-411-2795-2).
18. Henrik Andersen, *EU Dumping Determinations and WTO Law*, 2009 (ISBN 978-90-411-2827-0).

19. Sherzod Shadikhodjaev, *Retaliation in the WTO Dispute Settlement System*, 2009 (ISBN 978-90-411-2811-9).
20. Yi Shin Tang, *The International Trade Policy for Technology Transfers: Legal and Economic Dilemmas on Multilateralism versus Bilateralism*, 2009 (ISBN 978-90-411-2825-6).
21. Reem Anwar Ahmed Raslan, *Antidumping: A Developing Country Perspective*, 2009 (ISBN 978-90-411-3128-7).
22. Pietro Poretti, *The Regulation of Subsidies within the General Agreement on Trade in Services of the WTO: Problems and Prospects*, 2009 (ISBN 978-90-411-3162-1).
23. Esther Lam, *China and the WTO: A Long March towards the Rule of Law*, 2009 (ISBN 978-90-411-3144-7).
24. Jorge Alberto Huerta Goldman, *Mexico in the WTO and NAFTA: Litigating International Trade Disputes*, 2009 (ISBN 978-90-411-3169-0).
25. Laurence Boulle, *The Law of Globalization: An Introduction*, 2009 (ISBN 978-90-411-2828-7).
26. Daniel Lovric, *Deference to the Legislature in WTO Challenges to Legislation*, 2010 (ISBN 978-90-411-3145-4).
27. Gregory W. Bowman, Nick Covelli, David A. Gantz, Ihn Ho Uhm, *Trade Remedies in North America*, 2010 (ISBN 978-90-411-2840-9).
28. Madalina Diaconu, *International Trade in Gambling Services*, 2010 (ISBN 978-90-411-3248-2).
29. Mohamed Ramadan Hassanien, *United States Bilateral Free Trade Agreements: Consistencies or Conflicts with Norms in the Middle East?*, 2010 (ISBN 978-90-411-3281-9).
30. Markus W Gehring, Marie-Claire Cordonier Segger, Andrew Newcombe, *Sustainable Development in World Investment Law*, 2010 (ISBN 978-90-411-3166-9).
31. Nellie Munin, *Legal Guide to GATS*, 2010 (ISBN 978-90-411-2824-9).